A Clinical Approach to Marital Problems

Second Edition

A Clinical Approach to Marital Problems

DIAGNOSIS, PREVENTION AND TREATMENT

By

BERNARD L. GREENE, M.D.

Emeritus Clinical Professor of Psychiatry
Abraham Lincoln School of Medicine at the Medical Center
University of Illinois, Chicago, Illinois

Emeritus Clinical Professor of Pastoral Psychology
Garrett-Evangelical Theological Seminary, Northwestern University Campus
Evanston, Illinois

Founder, Marital Department, Forest Hospital
Des Plaines, Illinois

Fellow and Approved Supervisor
American Association for Marriage and Family Therapy

With the Collaboration of

Marsha Greene Grossman, B.A., M.A. M.F.C.

California Family Study Center
Azuza Pacific College
Azuza, California

With a Foreword by

C. Ray Fowler, Ph.D.

Executive Director
American Association for Marriage and Family Therapy

CHARLES C THOMAS • PUBLISHER

Springfield • Illinois • U.S.A.

Published and Distributed Throughout the World by
CHARLES C THOMAS • PUBLISHER
Bannerstone House
301-327 East Lawrence Avenue, Springfield, Illinois, U.S.A.

© *1970, 1981, by* CHARLES C THOMAS • PUBLISHER

ISBN 0-398-04138-5

Library of Congress Catalog Card Number: 80-21215

Printed in the United States of America
V-R-1

Library of Congress Cataloging in Publication Data

Greene, Bernard L
  A clinical approach to marital problems.

  Includes bibliographical references and indexes.
  1. Marriage. I. Greene, Marsha June, joint
author. II. Title. [DNLM: 1. Marital therapy.
WM55 G799c]
HQ728.G65   1981   362.8'286   80-21215
ISBN 0-398-04138-5

To my wife
LENORE

FOREWORD

RARELY does a slim (under 200 pages) volume achieve the encyclopedic comprehension of the subject managed by *The Psychotherapies of Marital Disharmony* (1965). From the moment of its publication fifteen years ago, its editor, Bernard L. Greene, M.D., has been increasingly recognized for his outstanding ability to identify, organize, and synthesize the diverse products of the surging field of marital and family therapy. This initial volume by Doctor Greene was followed five years later by *A Clinical Approach to Marital Problems* (1970).

Now he has combined the best of both volumes into this single revised work. Retaining the best of the classic contributions to the earlier volumes, Doctor Greene has incorporated their diversity into a pragmatically unified framework of general system theory (GST). Those traditional practitioners for whom psychoanalytic theory and methodology constitutes the firm path of psychotherapy will be impressed — and hopefully reassured — that diversity is not necessarily destructive and that the newer therapies may exist side-by-side with the older therapies without threatening the integrity of any of them. So, the advocates of the nonpsychoanalytic therapies can see through Doctor Greene's comprehensive presentation a wider vision of the structure of human experience.

In such an encyclopedic enterprise as this, everyone profits from the mutual stimulation generated in the circulation of ideas through many levels of reality. From the most exalted of classical psychotherapeutic constructs of the early theorists to the vigorously pragmatic paradigm of the "two jukeboxes on a seesaw," readers will be enriched and their therapeutic skills enhanced — be they trainees, practitioners, or trainers in marital and family therapy.

C. Ray Fowler, Ph.D.

PREFACE TO THE SECOND EDITION

THIS revision reflects my ongoing professional experience and multidisciplinary coverage prior to 1980. I have included pertinent material from *The Psychotherapies of Marital Disharmony* (1965) and *A Clinical Approach to Marital Problems* (1970).

During World War II, as chief of Neuropsychiatry, 21st General Hospital (Barnes Hospital Unit of Washington University at St. Louis, MO, serving in the Mediterranean and European Theatres) and as the commanding officer, Neuropsychiatric Hospital at Columbus, IN, I initiated group therapy sections because of the tremendous number of patients. Following my service in the army, I became clinical director of the Veteran's Rehabilitation Center in Chicago, where I continued practicing psychiatry, including the combined technique of individual and group psychoanalytically-oriented therapy, and participating in psychodrama where the patient re-enacted his life's story with a supporting cast of professional actors directed by the hospital's director, Doctor Alfred P. Solomon.

In 1951, I completed my psychoanalytic training at the Chicago Institute for Psychoanalysis. In 1955, I chose to shift my career* as a classical analyst to include both psychoanalysis and concurrent psychoanalytic marital therapy. This was precipitated when two of my married female patients became divorced. Their husbands initiated the divorce proceedings because of resentment toward their wives' isolation from them during classical therapy. I realized that if these husbands could have participated in therapy or at least had the option to discuss their wives' behavioral changes, their marital relationship might have survived.

This dramatic shift in my approach to helping patients had roots in my past medical learning. As early as 1930, one of my teachers, the head of the department of psychiatry at the medical school of the University of Illinois, broadened my outlook upon the treatment of mental illness. He advocated my studying the whole family at the Institute for Juvenile Research in order to better understand each

---

*Greene, Bernard L.: Careers in marital therapy — introduction. *Career Directions*, Sandoz Pharmaceutical (D J Publications) *4*:2-10, 1974.

individual family member. Now as I viewed these four adults and their eight offsprings emotionally torn apart by divorce, I realized therapy influenced the whole family unit when treatment included *any* member of the family. It was at that time I focused upon the dyadic relationship as the core of therapy and thus included the spouse (and the children whenever indicated).

This book also reflects the rapid and ongoing sociocultural changes in the past decade, e.g. two dramatic trends are the progressive increase in nonmarital dyadic relationships and the multiple problems of "reconstituted" families. I define dyadic relationships as any pair-coupling having intimate relationships for a minimum of three to six months with the purpose of establishing a pattern of transacting personalities.

This book is for the professional who uses therapeutic skills to prevent and modify dysfunctional relationships under contractual arrangements. My theoretical framework continues to be a modified General System Theory as a *pragmatic* biopsychosocial model with its emphasis on diagnosis, prevention, and therapy.

This textbook will describe my techniques, which include crisis therapy, classical one-to-one therapy, collaborative dyadic therapy, concurrent dyadic therapy, conjoint dyadic therapy, and combined techniques. The combined techniques include: simple, conjoint family, combined-collaborative, and couples' group therapies. Two additional therapies will be explained: sexual dysfunction and the therapy used when one partner has a primary affective disorder.

Prior to any specific technique is the need for *diagnosis*. The evaluative phase consists of a biographical relationship questionnaire, initial individual interviews, and a conjoint diagnostic and disposition session. The questions in the questionnaire reflect the General System Theory view of the individual intrapersonally, interpersonally, and environmentally.

The family remains a viable social unit essential to the total development of a healthy society. My hope for this book, as in my past ones, is to offer new ideas and techniques to aid mental health professionals deal with individual, dyadic, and family problems.

Bernard L. Greene, M.D.

PREFACE TO THE FIRST EDITION

$\mathbf{K}$APLAN* has succinctly defined therapy as "a psychological treatment whereby a trained therapist develops a planned relationship with a patient or client with the expressed purpose of relieving suffering, it will include therapy carried out by a variety of individuals with differing backgrounds and training." For the purposes of this book, there is no need to differentiate the special areas of competence of the various disciplines. For simplicity, practitioners of all disciplines will be referred to as "therapist" (whether it be psychotherapy, marital counseling, multiclient interviewing, psychoanalysis, or any other). In this book therapy does not imply any particular level of treatment.

Many marriages are being lived out in a mood of quiet desperation while therapists talk about the durable incompatibility of many unions. The professional knows that there are many situations that look good on the surface but present serious hidden difficulties.

With the many serious problems in marriage, it is necessary for professionals to go outside of their regular academic training if they want to become skilled in the field of marriage therapy. Most professionals feel that their formal training in marital therapy was inadequate. Additional training has to be obtained either through study in a doctoral program or through prolonged clinical training experience in a hospital or counseling center. Academia has not yet solved the problem of giving men training that is adequate to the marital problems in the modern community.

The concepts in this book grew out of my experiences and thoughts as an active clinician (psychiatrist and psychoanalyst), as a synthesizer of the creativity of others, and finally, as a teacher. For the past ten years I have limited my clinical practice exclusively to marital disharmony. Initially, the teaching phase was limited to psychiatric residents, then to psychiatrists, psychologists and social workers. The third phase included marriage counselors and workers in the educational field. The final phase was the inclusion of the clergy. Special

---

*Alex H. Kaplan: Social work therapy and psychiatric psychotherapy, *Arch Gen Psychiat,* 9:95, 1963.

seminars for the latter were given at the Forest Hospital (a private psychiatric hospital in Des Plaines, Illinois) and at the Garrett Theological Seminary in Evanston, Illinois.

A clear distinction exists between marital therapy and individual psychotherapy. In marital therapy "the marriage is the patient," which means that the work is done with both husband and wife and that what is explored is the *relationship* which exists between them. In individual psychotherapy, the area that is explored is primarily the intrapsychic dynamics of the individual.

Throughout this book the emphasis will be on the understanding of the multiple elements influencing a marriage. The very important relationship between the therapist and the marriage partners can only be stated but has to be dealt with in face-to-face relationships between the teacher and the student.

Since childhood patterns of reactions influence our adult methods of adjustment, it may help the student to visualize a jukebox with many "records" of old modes of reaction which are stimulated by current situations. The fact that tastes in music may vary can be the beginning of areas of conflict. It is important to recognize that "records" of childhood can be inappropriate in adult life. The playing of old "records" can lead to serious problems — premarital, marital, or postmarital.

One of the goals in marital therapy is to help each individual mature to the point at which he or she is responding to present experiences and relationships in terms of the real meanings and values and not in terms of symbolic meanings from childhood.

The comprehensive approach used in this book is one of breadth as well as depth. My experience in the fields of classical psychoanalysis and psychiatry guarantees a depth approach. The choice of a general system theory as a model of analysis of marital problems guarantees breadth. The therapist should find no difficulty in discovering where he and his concerns fit into this approach.

The data to be presented in this book will be based on 750 couples with marital disharmony who were personally managed by me. Five hundred couples were taken from my private practice and 250 couples were seen at the marital department of the Forest Hospital. The data presented is not applicable for quantification. The disguised clinical vignettes to be presented do not prove anything in and by themselves. The orientation was primarily therapeutic and pragmatic.

This book has been organized in the following manner: Chapter I deals with an eclectic "organismic" model based on "general system theory," applicable to the social institution of marriage. Chapters II through XIX present a method of evaluating marriage problems and discuss the importance of the biographical marital questionnaire. Chapter XX is devoted to the conjoint diagnostic and disposition session. Finally, Chapters XXI through XXVIII discuss the prevention and management of marital problems.

BERNARD L. GREENE

ACKNOWLEDGMENTS TO
THE SECOND EDITION

To my teachers Franz Alexander, who personified the spirit of experimentation in Psychotherapy, and Thomas M. French, who personified the spirit of experimentation in Dream Interpretation.

B.L.G.

ACKNOWLEDGMENTS TO
THE FIRST EDITION

I WISH to thank my dear friends, the Reverend Carroll A. Wise and Dr. Samuel Liebman, for the help given me in preparing this manuscript and for the many corrections they have suggested, and Dr. Alfred P. Solomon, who first suggested I do marital therapy.

B.L.G.

CONTENTS

PART ONE
DIAGNOSIS

A Clinical Approach to
Marital Problems

PART ONE

DIAGNOSIS

Chapter I

INTRODUCTION
A Multioperational Approach

PSYCHOTHERAPY continues to be replete with rigidly held but widely varied doctrines.[1] "Psychotherapy, like all healing arts, has always presented two faces: one, as old as mankind, the religio-magical; the other, of more recent vintage, which may be termed scientific."[2] Thus, psychotherapy should be viewed as a multidisciplinary system consisting of a conglomeration of arts and sciences.[3] The uniqueness and complexity of each pair-coupling and/or family, the scientific immaturity in our field, the lack of an acceptable typology, and the process used in the evaluation of therapies often leads to selection of techniques based upon personal preference or vested academic interest rather than adequate research methodology.[4-11]

Progress in other disciplines, however, is often unnoted, poorly understood, or simply disparaged.[12-14] I am not referring to the popularity of some so-called "psychotherapies" that promise quick cures and are throwbacks to the magical, religious, and inspirational patterns of the faith healers of the past.[15-16] The wise words of Franz Alexander are as pertinent today as they were two decades ago: "Instead of progressive improvements of knowledge and practice, the tendency to rest on the laurels of the past appears in the form of dogmatism . . . reevaluation [of knowledge] necessarily leads to changes and requires constant revision of techniques of treatment and STEADY EXPERIMENTATION [emphasis added]. . . ."[17]

Understanding and assessing patient needs and goals is difficult because of the complexity of our society, the uniqueness of individuals, pair-couplings, families, and the variety of human relationships which vary "even within a subculture or at a particular point in time, let alone across cultures or over time . . ."[18]; however, the best therapists, e.g. Peter A. Martin,[19] use flexibility in their therapeutic approach to meet the challenge.[20-26]

Therapists are discovering the value of teamwork; so rigid, traditional lines between established professions are disappearing and thereby greater effectiveness is emerging. Engel succinctly states my

5

view:

> ... the key to optimal patient care is *collaboration, communication* and *complementarity* among all branches of the health professions ... [which is] only possible when the various disciplines share in common a basic set of assumptions and principles. Otherwise each of the different health professions is tempted to evolve its own more limited model, suitable for its own purposes, but in practice likely to *inhibit collaboration, confuse communication* and *substitute competition for complementarity* [italics added]. . . .[27]

Most therapists agree that the goal of therapy is not to save all dyadic relationships, but to assist couples to define where they are *now* in their relationship, to determine what they want to do about it, and to help them reach their goal. Therapy can promote homeostasis in the family system by sharing resources for problem-solving, strengthening the complementarity of the relationships, and encouraging more adequate controls and defenses for copying with stress underlying all changing life events. Every therapist's major goals should include the *minimum therapy for the maximum results* and to focus upon **prevention.**

Some therapists have specific goals due to their orientation and setting[28]: religious-associated facilities, family service agencies, college and university-student facilities, independent organizations, and conciliation court facilities, etc. . . . The public most frequently seeks help from members of the cloth, next from social workers, then psychologists, followed in frequency by educationally associated counselors, therapists, and educators, and finally by lawyers and psychiatrists.

Therapy begins only after an adequate diagnosis has been formulated. To aid in this goal, I have each patient, whenever possible, complete and submit my biographical relationship questionnaire (Chapter IV) prior to the first evaluative session (Chapter III). The theoretical underpinning of my questionnaire and therapeutic approach is based upon a modified, pragmatic General System Theory developed by the late Bertalanffy.[29]

My professional experience continues to support my focus upon the dyadic relationship[30-31] as the "identified patient." I believe that the couple's relationship is the cog in the family wheel and the radiating spokes can include children, grandparents, and all significant others within family networks or in the larger sociocultural matrix. Once the couple's relationship is functionally satisfying, their subsystem-related problems can then be explored, if so desired by the couple.

Deciding which technique or combination of approaches to employ at any given therapeutic moment takes intuition and experience.[32] Not every therapist can feel comfortable using all the available approaches, but knowledge of these will provide the patient the best care; if the therapist cannot use the most appropriate technique for a patient, then referrals can occur. The therapist must tailor the approach to the individual as well as the mutual needs of those involved in the total problem. Too many patients permit their lives to get encumbered with useless regrets instead of using the same energy to make living more productive.[33]

In the evolution of my therapeutic techniques, I began by focusing upon the individual in the dyadic one-to-one relationship. I investigated the patient's environment only to the extent necessary for achieving my therapeutic aim of intrapsychic changes. Treatment failures necessitated the inclusion of the relationship between husband and wife as well as their individual personalities. The triadic approaches, including concurrent, conjoint marital, and combined techniques were thus utilized. Finally, because of therapeutic impasses with certain couples, I had to move beyond the marital relationship to include children, who were contributing to the marital discord. Treatment can thus be visualized in terms of a spectrum of therapeutic settings which includes dyadic approaches of classical and collaborative techniques at one end and triadic approaches of concurrent, conjoint marital and combined therapies in the middle, and conjoint family therapy and group therapies at the other end.[34-40]

My techniques include the following:

1. *Crisis Psychotherapy:* a custom-tailored approach to the individual's, couple's, or family's needs. This orientation stresses the implications of the *current, circumscribed* issues. The focus is on a rapid, dynamic assessment of the crisis, which is followed by psychotherapy of the individual(s) based on this evaluation.

2. *Classical Psychotherapy:* a multidisciplinary dyadic approach where the patient's feelings and behavior is explicitly the focus of treatment.

3. *Collaborative Psychotherapy:* each partner is seen by a different therapist who communicates with the permission of the couple for the purpose of maintaining the marital/nonmarital relationship. An important subtype is the treatment of a couple when one partner has a primary affective disorder (this technique will be discussed separately).

4. *Concurrent Psychotherapy:* both partners are treated individually but synchronously by the same therapist — a *triadic* approach.

5. *Conjoint Couple Therapy:* both partners are seen together in the

same session by the same therapist or by cotherapists. The most common approach for the treatment of sexual dysfunctions is conjoint.

6. *Combined Psychotherapies:*
   a. *Simple:* a pragmatic combination of individual, concurrent and conjoint sessions in various purposeful combinations.
   b. *Conjoint Family Therapy:* includes one or more children and views the family's functioning as an interdependent transactional unit.
   c. *Combined-Collaborative:* each partner is seen by a different therapist with regular joint sessions in which all four persons participate.
   d. *Couples' Group Psychotherapies:*
      1. Four couples are seen in a group setting.
      2. A combined approach is used for group and individual sessions.
   e. *Special Therapies:*
      1. Sexual dysfunctions.
      2. Therapy designed to help a couple when one partner has a primary affective disorder (manic-depressive illness).

Table I shows the frequency with which I used each type of technique with the couples I have seen in the past twenty-six years.

It is encouraging that Berkeley has a program available that emphasizes interdisciplinary collaboration. Berkeley's program involves five years of training, and successful trainees receive a doctor of mental health degree (D.M.H.).[41] This program is cosponsored by the University of California at Berkeley, Mount Zion Hospital and the Langley-Porter Neuropsychiatric Institute. The program combines training elements from the disciplines of psychiatry, psychology, and social work. It was first suggested years ago by Lawrence Kubie, Holt (1971),[42] and Moulton (1975),[43] among others. In the D.M.H. program, psychiatrists back up the primary treatment system, e.g. clinics, community mental health centers. These doctors participate in the education and supervision of other professionals including consultation and treatment of the more difficult problems.[44]

In conclusion, I wish to stress that the major emphasis of every psychotherapist should be *prevention.* I believe that there can be no therapy without an adequate diagnosis and evaluation of the presenting problem.[45] in order to make the most accurate evaluation and proceed with treatment, it is essential to pursue personal and professional growth.[46] Because the methods of observing and analyzing the numerous variables with psychotherapy, research findings cannot

TABLE I

COUPLES OBSERVED IN THE PAST TWENTY-SIX YEARS

YEAR	REJECTS — refusals	CRISIS	CLASSICAL	COLLABORATIVE	CONCURRENT	CONJOINT	COMBINED
1954	0	0	1	3	0	0	0
1955	3	4	1	4	3	0	0
1956	1	4	1	4	3	0	0
1957	1	3	2	2	3	0	0
1958	1	2	6	2	8	0	0
1959	2	4	6	1	12	0	0
1960	5	4	3	1	17	0	0
1961	5	4	3	0	17	0	0
1962	6	10	2	1	12	3	2
1963	8	12	4	4	16	7	10
1964	20	29	6	5	13	18	20
1965	20	30	6	3	12	4	15

Year							
1966	16	16	10	4	11	10	11
1967	18	17	11	3	15	20	24
1968	15	23	6	2	5	12	9
1969	16	19	10	4	10	6	13
1970	14	20	5	4	2	9	9
1971	14	27	11	4	5	19	12
1972	13	26	7	2	5	8	18
1973	8	48	7	1	8	4	16
1974	15	28	10	2	17	8	10
1975	5	26	11	5	2	3	12
1976	5	3	2	0	2	3	6
1977	3	5	2	0	2	3	4
1978	4	5	1	0	2	3	4
1979	5	4	1	0	3	3	5
TOTALS	223	373	135	61	205	143	200

Total Couples: 1340

present the full scope of the issue. As Jerome Frank (1979) notes, ". . . psychotherapeutic practice [is] essentially [a] subjective experience for both patient and therapist . . . (and so) the relevance of research findings for therapeutic practice will probably remain modest."[47] Although I said it fifteen years ago[48] I still find that I cannot teach every trainee the complex skills required for the full spectrum of therapies of dyadic and family discord, but I can explore with my supervising pupils those which match their abilities and those which would be less effectively executed. Recognition of the latter is a help to future patients and referrals do not mean personal failure by any standard.[49-51] Regina Flesch succinctly summed up the novice's dilemma: "There is no royal road to marital accord,"[52] and, there is no express route to learning all the techniques that may alter marital-nonmarital and family disharmony!

REFERENCES

1. Karasu, Toksoz B.: Psychotherapies — overview. *Am J Psychiat, 134*:851-63, 1977.
2. Frank, Jerome: The two faces of psychotherapy. *J Am Acad Psychoanal, 20*:13-16, 1976.
3. Weissman, Myrna M. and Klerman, Gerald L.: Epidemiology of mental disorders. *Arch Gen Psychiat, 35*:705-12, 1978.
4. Sander, Fred: Marriage and the family in Freud's writings. *J Am Acad Psychoanal, 6*:157-74, 1978.
5. Malan, David H., Heath, E. Sheldon, Bacal, Howard A. and Balfour, Frederick H. G.: Psychodynamic changes in untreated neurotic patients. *Arch Gen Psychiat, 32*:110-26, 1975.
6. Beck, D. F.: Research findings in the outcomes of marital counseling. *Social Casework, 56*:153-81, 1975.
7. Mendel, Werner M.: Open end therapy with planned interruption. *J Operational Psychiat, 6*:116-28, 1975.
8. Gurman, Alan S.: The effects and effectiveness of marital therapy — a review of outcome research. *Family Process, 12*:145-170, 1973.
9. Kubie, Lawrence S.: The process of evaluation of therapy in psychiatry — critical influence of the timing of assessment in its outcome. *Arch Gen Psychiat, 28*:880-84, 1973.
10. Beck, Dorothy F.: Research findings on the outcome of marital counseling. *Social Casework, 56*:153, 1975.
11. Kazdin, Alan E. and Wilson, G. Terence: Criteria for evaluating psychotherapy. *Arch Gen Psychiat, 35*:407-16, 1978.
12. Marmor, Judd: Editorial — the new therapies. *J Am Acad Psychoanal, 5*:3-4, 1977.
13. Taggart, Morris: Abstracts. *J Marital & Family Therapy, 5*:97-100, 1979.
14. Paolino, Thomas J., Jr. and McCrady, Barbara (Eds.): *Marriage and*

Marital Therapy: Psychoanalytic, Behavioral and Systems Theory Perspectives. New York, Brunner-Mazel, 1978.

15. Stone, Alan A.: Jack Weinberg, M.D. — One hundred and sixth president, 1977-1978. Am J Psychiat, 135:904-905, 1978.

16. Morgan, James, Shafi, Mohammad, Shapiro, Arthur K., and Dean, Stanley R.: The task force on meditation of the Amer. Psychiatric Assn. Am J Psychiat, 134:720, 1977.

17. Alexander, Franz: The Scope of Psychoanalysis. New York, Basic Books, Inc., 1961, pp. 541-45.

18. Sheldon, Alan: Some Cybernetic Notes on Marriage: Steps Toward a Model? Presented at the 30th Annual Conference, American Group Psychotherapy Assn., Feb. 1973 (Section of Systems and Group Psychotherapy) Detroit, Michigan.

19. Martin, Peter A.: A Marital Therapy Manual. New York, Brunner-Mazel, Inc., 1976.

20. Marmor, Judd: Presidential address — psychiatry in 1976, the continuing revolution. Am J Psychiat, 133:739-45, 1976.

21. Olson, David H. L. and Sprenkle, Douglas H.: Emerging trends in treating relationships. J Marr & Family Counseling, 2:317-29, 1976.

22. Berman, Ellen M. and Lief, Harold I.: Overview of marital therapies in current use. In Usidin, Gene (Ed.): Overview of the Psychotherapies. New York, Brunner-Mazel, 1975.

23. Gurman, Alan S. and Rice, David G. (Eds.): Couples In Conflict. New York, Aronson, 1975.

24. Nichols, William C. Jr.: The field of marriage counseling — a brief overview. Family Coordinator, 22:3-13, 1973.

25. Greene, Bernard L.: Psychiatric therapy of marital problems — modern techniques. In Masserman, Jules (Ed.): Current Psychiatric Therapies, vol. 12. New York, Grune, 1972.

26. Issacharoff, Ammon: Careers in marital therapy-introduction and rationale. Career Directions, 4:11-23, 1974 (D. J. Publications, Inc).

27. Engel, George L.: Letter to editor, Psychologists and DSM-III. Psychiatric News, 13:2, 1978.

28. Redlich, Fritz and Kellert, Stephen R.: Trends in American health. Am J Psychiat, 135:22-28, 1978.

29. Friedman, Lawrence: How real is the realistic ego in psychotherapy. Arch Gen Psychiat, 28:377-83, 1973.

30. Ackerman, Nathan: Personal discussion at a winter meeting of the Academy of Psychoanalysis in New York City.

31. Beels, C. Christian and Ferber, Andrew: What family therapists do. In Ferber, Andrew, Mendolsohn, Marilyn, and Napier, Augusty (Eds.): The Book of Family Therapy. Boston, HM (Science House, Inc.), 1972.

32. Strupp, Hans H. and Hadley, Suzanne, W.: Specific vs. nonspecific factors in psychotherapy — a controlled study of outcome. Arch Gen Psychiat, 36:1125-36, 1979.

33. Naftalin, M.: Watch your language. J Am Acad Psychoanal, 3:307-19,

1975.

34. Greene, Bernard L.: Marital disharmony: Concurrent analysis of husband and wife: a preliminary report. *Dis Nerv System, 21*:73-8, 1960.
35. Greene, Bernard L.: *A Clinical Approach to Marital Problems: Evaluation and Management.* Springfield, Thomas, 1970.
36. Greene, Bernard L., et al.: Marital therapy. *Am J Psychiat, 133*:827-30, 1976.
37. Greene, Bernard L., et al.: The psychotherapies of marital disharmony with special reference to marriage counseling. *Medical Times, 9*:243-56, 1963.
38. Greene, Bernard L.: *Multi-operational Psychotherapies of Marital Disharmony.* Paper presented at the annual meeting of the American Psychiatric Assn., May 7, 1964, in Los Angeles, CA.
39. Berman, Ellen M. and Lief, Harold I.: Marital therapy from a psychiatric perspective — an overview. *Am J Psychiat, 132*:583-92, 1975.
40. Kaslow, Florence W.: Essay review — marital therapy, monogamy and menages. *J Marr & Family Counseling, 1*:281-87, 1977.
41. McDonald, Margaret C.: Doctor of mental health — nascent discipline? *Psychiatric News, 13*:3, 1978.
42. Holt, Robert R. (Ed.): *New Horizons for Psychotherapy: Autonomy as a Profession.* New York, Int Univ Press, 1971.
43. Moulton, Ruth: The future of psychoanalysis. *J Am Acad Psychoanal, 3*:349-51, 1975.
44. Sandifer, Myron G.: The education of the psychiatrist as a physician. *Am J Psychiat, 134*:51, 1977.
45. Martin, Peter A.: *A Marital Therapy Manual.*
46. Shapiro, Deane H., Jr. and Gilber, David: Meditation and psychotherapeutic effects. *Arch Gen Psychiat, 35*:294-302, 1978.
47. McDonald, M. C.: Jerome Frank looks ahead. *Psychiatric News, 19*:14, 1979.
48. Greene, Bernard L. (Ed.): *The Psychotherapies of Marital Disharmony.* New York, Free Pr, 1965.
49. Yager, Joel: Psychiatric electicism — a cognitive view. *Am J Psychiat, 134*:739, 1977.
50. Vincent, Clark E.: Isms, schisms, and the freedom for differences. *J Marr & Family Counseling, 2*:99-110, 1975.
51. Silverman, Hirsch L.: *Marital Therapy: Moral, Sociological and Psychological Factors.* Springfield, Thomas, 1972.
52. Flesch, Regina: Treatment goals and technique in marital discord. *Soc Casework, 49*:388, 1949.

Chapter II

A PRAGMATIC HYPOTHESIS OF THE GENERAL SYSTEM THEORY
— a suprasystem paradigm* —

MEETING the uniqueness of each individual and the complexity of each relationship has demanded a holistic outlook.[1-12] My framework continues to emphasize pragmatism[13-17] based on the general system theory (GST) of Bertalanffy[18-31] which has undergone modification in response to valid criticism.[32-35] No one model, whether based on considerations of intrapersonal elements, interpersonal relationships, sociocultural factors, or ideological preferences, can describe all the transactions within a dyadic relationship. All behavior has meaning, and all partners are motivated by internal activities. In addition to this *intrapersonal system*, every individual has meaningful relationships with others *(interpersonal system)* and lives in a sociocultural matrix *(environmental system)*. All three systems (see Fig. 1) have open boundaries and contain components in constant transactions of varying intensities.[36] Dyadic disharmony results from these three systems continually transacting with each other creating permutations which are dysfunctional.

In the past three decades, Bertalanffy has introduced the term *general system theory* (GST) as a symbol for a key concept and thus initiated a trend toward unified "interdisciplinary" theory. He defines a system as a complex of components in mutual interaction. He postulates complex open systems that have their own inherent lawfulness, such as feedback: "the result of a reaction is monitored back to the 'receptor' side so that the system is held stable or led toward a target or goal." Bertalanffy states that to the system theorist the totality of experience appears as a hierarchical order; the major levels are the inorganic, the living, and the symbolic world. He prefers the term *symbolic* to define those functions that separate human from animal behavior and form the sociocultural human superstructure.

---

*Whereas in earlier writings I described myself as an eclectic, I now prefer the term *pragmatic*. Pragmaticism tests the validity of concepts by evaluating its *practical* results.

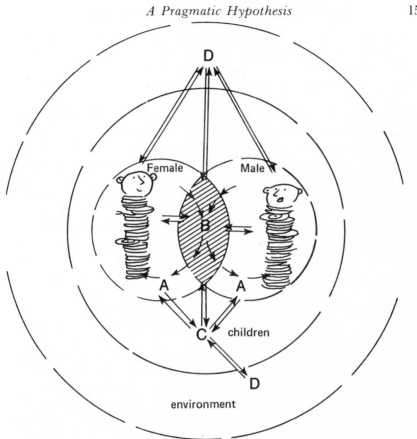

Figure 1. This shows the pair-coupling as an open system. **A,** Intrapersonal system; **B,** Interpersonal system (dyad); **C,** Interpersonal system (sibling subsystem), *note* **B** + **C** = family system; and **D,** Environmental system.

He notes that mankind does not consist of isolated individuals but is organized in a hierarchy of systems. Therefore, he suggests that the GST gives a theoretical framework for therapeutic measures such as family therapy. Since pair-coupling is a subsystem of the family, the GST is applicable to marital/nonmarital therapy.

Each system consists of transacting elements within penetrable boundaries, thus insuring "openness." Each system has a temporal and spatial existence with structure derived from its past; its present is relatively stable, and its future has possible evolutionary potential. The constancy of the system is dependent upon a continuous exchange and flow of the transacting components. Each open system maintains its organization by goal-seeking activities characterized by "equifinality," indicating that the same final state can be reached from different initial conditions and in different ways. This is in contrast to equilibria in closed systems that are determined by initial conditions. Each system may maintain itself by realignment of gradients, by partial sacrifice of structure or function or by decreasing its boundaries to permeability. Finally, each system is in active interplay with other systems in its environment that are significant for its viability. All systems are involved in encoding,[37] processing, retrieving, and transmitting information.

I view the human being as a person with symbol-making abilities as well as a reacting organism utilizing thoughts, emotions, gestures, postures, and total movement in relation to significant others. Relationships can occur at random as a product of individual inclinations or can be affected by the values, ideas, and sanctions of significant others. Thus, our focus is directed to the relationship between people enmeshed in a sociocultural matrix.

INTRAPERSONAL SYSTEM

There is an intricate relationship between the brain as a biological entity and as a determinant of human behavior.[32-39] The study of the brain as the central organ, in varying degrees of spontaneous activity (even during sleep), reveals its continuous response from internal and external stimuli.[40-43] This data is integrated by means of neuro-humoral reactions which initiate physical and behavioral changes. The complexity of the brain is reflected in biopsychosocial relationships, e.g. the importance of genetics[44-46] has been demonstrated in dyadic-family therapy when one partner has a primary affective disorder (manic-depressive illness, Chapter XXVII). Another important observation has been the demonstration of functional differences in the cerebral hemispheres.[47-52] The left hemisphere, in virtually all right-handed individuals, is specialized for an analytic, linear mode of information processing, and the right cerebral hemisphere is for holistic concepts, including musical and emotional functioning. The right hemisphere is global and intuitive and reacts rather than for analytic thinking. On the other hand the left hemisphere is analytic, critical, calm and intellectual. There are infinite interconnections among all areas of the brain which have an important influence on cognitive structures, defensive reactions, variations in states of awareness, and personality style that are closely intertwined with behavior. Previous neurosurgical operations on the brain have had an important influence on advances made in psychology and neurophysiology. Thus Eric Berne was influenced by the neurosurgeon, Wilder Penfield[53], to change the tripartite constructs of Freud's superego, ego and id to the phenomenological model of transactional analysis of parent, adult and child.

In Franz Alexander's last writings he had prophesized that learning theories would eventually achieve paramount importance. Learning theories have produced new concepts about infants including evidence that even *prenatal* infants[54] are exposed to stimuli from within the parent as well as from the environment, which result in the modification of the infant's ongoing behavior patterns — similar to what ethologists label "imprinting" in animals. To become human, the infant experiences continuous ongoing processes of growth, adaptation,[55] and social initiation into the cultural values of his/her environment. In the infant's maturation, its personality becomes a distillation along developmental life cycle periods incorporating informational inputs from the preceeding adaptational level. The child's personality progresses (unless fixation or regression occurs due to unfavorable circumstances) to more complex levels of behavior involving perceptions, cognition,[56] coping mechanisms,[57] and emotions.

The word *emotion* has many connotations including the synonyms *affect* and *mood*. I define these terms temporarily with *affect* representing current feelings while *mood* refers to a prolonged state of feelings.[58] Also, emotions are *subjective* to the individual while mood is an observable, *objective* emotional phenomena. Emotions are a complex transaction of physiological and psychological states, communicational needs,[59] and danger signals. The total phenomena of emotions results in character development and behavior, in coping attempts (including psychopathology[60]) and in rationality[61].

Dynamic psychology maintains the individual as a holistic unit able to offset fragmentation by integrating all aspects of the intrapersonal, interpersonal, and environmental elements. Dynamic psychology has had its development from various theoretical positions primarily due to the seminal concepts of Freud. Freud frequently modified his hypotheses and in his last work stated: "We look forward to their being modified, corrected, and more precisely determined as more experience is accumulated and shifted."[62-80] In spite of differing theoretical orientations, the majority of psychodynamic therapists accept four of Freud's constructs: the unconscious — forces outside immediate awareness which influence development and behavior; the personality — the result of the interplay of genetic endowment and

personal history; the role of early experiences — underpins the formation of character; and the importance of transference phenomena.[81]

As the field of psychodynamics expanded, Margaret Mahler, an
eminent child analyst and theorist worked with the preverbal development of the infant (while in England, Melanie Klein was pioneering
in the same area). Mahler's interest in autistic children led her and her
colleagues to establish general theories involving the developmental
process[82] that focus upon the *parenting process* keeping in mind the
child's genetic endowment and specific environment. Their theory
notes the *separation-individuation* process usually occurs within the
first three years. They further outlined four phases of the separation-
individuation process: differentiation in the development of the body
image; practicing leaving the mother; rapproachment; and consolida-
tion of individuality and the beginnings of emotional object constancy. This separation-individuation phase, which plays an
important role in all subsequent relationships, results in an increasing awareness of the self (intrapersonal system), of the significant
other and other object relationships (interpersonal system), and of the
reality in the outside world (environmental system). Mahler feels that
the rapproachment phase is the most important, since this subphase
leads to the latency period, followed by adolescence, and finally toward adulthood.[83]

The separation-individuation model of Mahler has been described
by a number of clinicians as a framework of development in certain
areas of the entire life cycle. Gralnick's quote is appropos when he
said that there is insufficient evidence "that between the age of three
to five months the infant forms a symbiotic relation to its mother.
Nor am I taken with the idea that any failure in separation-
individuation is a basic cause of adolescent psychopathology. There is
much more involved, as a later exploration of Arieti's (1974) recent
ideas will show. My conviction about the importance of interdependence to mental health compels me to question the value of even
conceptualizing in terms of 'separation-individuation' because of its
overtones."[84] Building upon Mahler's model, Blos[85] presents four developmental tasks needed for adolescent closure and the entrance into
adulthood: the role of a *second* separation-individuation phase; maintaining ego continuity; resolving residual traumas; and an appropriate sexual identity.[86]

Erik Erikson's[87] (1950) concept of "developmental task" based on
the "epigenetic principle" states that each individual goes through
eight stages in the life cycle. Thus everyone has a "ground plan" from
which parts arise in an unfolding spiral until "all parts have arisen to

form a functioning whole." Each stage results in specific crises which the person must solve in order to move onto the next phase. Different degrees of anxiety are associated with each stage. It is the degree of anxiety, however, that determines whether progression is smooth or pathological, i.e. regression, fixation, or progression. One stage that of midlife is currently the vogue — labeled midolescence or middlescence.[88-89] I agree with others[90-94] that the midlife crisis is a *myth* because most people cope with their problems at this stage remarkably well.

INTERPERSONAL SYSTEM

The interpersonal system will be limited to transactions with all significant others starting roughly around the age of eighteen years onward. Obviously its separation from the other systems is only for didactic reasons since no infant can exist without the formation of the first human bond — that with a mother or its surrogate that is culturally influenced. Although Freud's original formulations were interpersonal, it was other psychoanalysts, e.g. Sullivan, Erikson, Horney, who stressed all dyadic inputs in the development of personality and relationships. Finally, analytic family therapists, especially Ackerman, Grotjahn, Bowen, Lidz, Wynne, and Don Jackson pioneered in the role of family transactions in the development of the individual and his relationships. The psychodynamics of all relationships are relatively similar in principles.[95] Since there is still no formally accepted classification[96] (the one proposed by Otto Pollak in 1965[97] **by parental stages is as pragmatic as others.[98-101]**) I shall quote freely from his classic chapter as it pertains to interpersonal transactions. My modifications will be added wherever I feel it is appropriate.

> "Sociological concern with . . . (transactional) patterns, small-group analysis, and role theory provides a safeguard against concentrating on a specific individual and thereby becoming involved in the intrapsychic conflicts of one individual only . . . Every human relationship . . .(involves the three systems of the GST) in long lasting transactions that can be understood only if (all) systems are considered as having equal claim to diagnostic attention. Concentration on one individual in diagnosis or therapy is based on the assumption that solution of the . . . conflicts in one partner in a human relationship will have beneficial consequences for the solution of the . . . conflicts of the other. Although such may be the fact in certain constellations, it cannot be taken for granted. Actually, it is interesting to note that . . . the improvement of one family member sometimes results in the deterioration of another . . . these clinical

observations . . . have failed to receive the response they deserve . . . Dichotomies . . . , between the individual and his environment, the individual and his family, or a child and his parents
operate under the (sociological) perceptual principle of figure and
ground . . . Concepts like interaction, social system, small groups,
and life cycle of the family . . . enforce consideration by the . . . therapist of all human beings involved in these constellations. Sociologists work routinely with these concepts. They do so, however,
without sufficient awareness of the influence of intrapsychic conflict,
unconscious motivation, and ambivalence upon the nature of the
interaction patterns they describe, the group processes they try to
observe, and the performance of the social roles they try to classify
and put into the perspective of social change.

Integrating these (various) points of view and the concepts to
which they have led unfortunately produces a high degree of complexity. It vastly increases the number of phenomena to be considered and demands decisions about . . . therapeutic planning. . . .

In family diagnosis, it is convenient to classify the multiplicity of
relationships into three subsystems: the marital (dyadic) system, the
parents-and-children system, and the siblings system. Each of these
three subsystems is composed of a plurality of . . . (transactional)
patterns: between husband and wife, between parents and children,
and among siblings.

Another and very important sociological point of view in diagnosing a family is based on the conception of the family as a small
social organization that goes through various phases of development
(as they form, expand, and contract[102-103]). Sociologists speak of the
life cycle of the family, and . . . mention the differences in life tasks
that confront families at different stages of their development. Again,
it is convenient to distinguish a number of phases. First, there is that
phase of the family life cycle reflecting the effort of husband and
wife (pair-coupling) to form the basis of a new family system distinct
from their background families. The next phase is usually that of
child bearing and child rearing. The third is the one in which the
children leave the home; it comes to an end when the last child has
established himself independently ("empty nest syndrome"[104]). There
follows a phase in which . . . partners again present a two-person
family and ultimately one in which only . . . (one) partner is the
survivor.

Within every subsystem and at every stage of the life cycle, there
exist various dimensions of complementary need that serve two purposes: satisfaction in the present and preparation for the future. . . . In all phases of the family's life cycle, the dimensions of
need complementarity in the (dyadic) relationship can be classified
as interpersonal reorientation, sexual and economic spheres, and ego
strengthening, although they may differ in weight and content as the
family passes from one developmental phase to another. Table II is

an attempt to show (transactional) patterns in these various dimensions and their changes from stage to stage of the life cycle. It will be noted that every phase is separated from another by a crisis of transition, in which the function of the partners is visualized as mutual assistance.... The (transactional) patterns of healthy dyadic relationships in the various phases of family development are based on the assumption of satisfactory exchange relationships in which partners function at the same time as resources and recipients of need satisfaction....

The (transactional) patterns* can be violated in various ways and partners may suffer a condition of mutual starvation. In any one dimension of need complementarity, they may fail to give each other the satisfaction compatible with conditions of health. They may fail to provide each other with new anchors of intimate association and may thus fail to help each other in psychological separation from their respective parents. They may fail to give each other sexual gratification. They may fail each other in accepting the division of labor between earner and homemaker in family life. They may destroy each other's socially adaptive defenses. Such failures usually represent the contents of the presenting symptoms. In any one of the forms of therapy in which both ... partners are being treated, there comes a point, however, at which an obstacle to improvement on a deeper level is encountered. This obstacle frequently reveals itself as an operation of the exchange principle on a more regressive or arrested level.

Failure to furnish each other with new and age appropriate anchors of intimate association may permit maintenance of unresolved oedipal ties to the parents of the partners. Failure in the sexual sphere may permit regressive gratification like masturbation or acting out, as in adultery. On the other end of the developmental spectrum, denial of permissiveness with nonpathological regression may permit (the partners) ... to aid each other in refusal to acknowledge their physical and psychological aging and may thus aid them in an unrealistic attempt at permanence in interpersonal and intrapersonal maturity. This point suggests that an integrated approach to diagnosis of ... (relationship transactions) will have to cover overt dysfunction as well as covert function of the exchange principle. Such failures of the partners to perform age appropriately and phase appropriately during the life cycle of the ... (relationship) furnish a measure of psychological justification for arrested or regressive interaction. They thus present a 'double bind'[105] situation, not only in terms of communication as explored by the (late) Don Jackson group (Palo Alto, CA) but also in terms of cooperation.

The obstacle to the improvement of marital (nonmarital) interaction can also, however, lie in a disharmony between the ego ideals of

---

*Pollak wisely prophesized the central core of dyadic disharmony to be the relationship between the partners.

TABLE II

TRANSACTIONAL PATTERNS AT DIFFERENT STAGES IN THE PAIR-COUPLING LIFE CYCLE

Dimension of need complementarity	Function in pair-coupling before arrival of children	Function in pair-coupling and child rearing
Interpersonal reorientation	1. Providing a new and age appropriate anchor of intimate association in place of parental anchor 2. Acceptance of nonpathological regression in partner 3. Security of receiving consideration and care 4. Security of sharing a spectrum of common interests	1. Permitting the other to find additional anchors of intimate association in children 2. Supporting each other in accepting restriction of freedom to accept nonpathological regression, because of presence of children and protecting other against stimulation of regression through interaction with children 3. Security of receiving consideration and care 4. Security of sharing an increased spectrum of common interests through concern with children in daily living
Sexual sphere	1. Proceeding toward harmony in biological completion 2. Social permissibility of the experience 3. Coupling effect of 2 4. Promise of realization of self through reproduction	1. Greater harmony in biological completion 2. Social permissibility of the experience 3. Coupling effect of 2 4. Realization of self through reproduction
Economic sphere	1. Division of labor between earner and homemaker, with possible modification due to entrance of women in labor market 2. Provision of experience of tangible property through home 3. Promise of economic security through earning power of women	1. Division of labor more pronounced due to the demands of child rearing 2. Provision of experience with tangible property through home 3. Helping one another in coping with decreased economic security resulting from expense of child rearing
Ego strengthening	1. Help in learning spouse roles 2. According one another freedom to express individuality and help in maintenance of identity feelings 3. Support in maintenance of socially adaptive defenses	1. Help in learning roles and changed parenting roles 2. According one another freedom to express individuality and help in maintenance of identity feelings plus protecting each other against using children for wish fulfillment and identity 3. Continuation of support in maintenance of socially adaptive defenses.

ASSISTANCE IN CRISIS OF TRANSITION

TABLE II (continued)

TRANSACTIONAL PATTERNS AT DIFFERENT STAGES
IN THE PAIR-COUPLING LIFE CYCLE

Function in pair-coupling and child leaving	Function in pair-coupling after children have left

ASSISTANCE IN CRISIS OF TRANSITION

1. Permitting the other feelings of loss over departure of children and furnishing stimuli for reorientation (redistribution libido-energy)
2. Renewed acceptance of nonpathological regression in partner and protecting one another against climacteric reactions to leaving of children
3. Security of receiving consideration and care
4. Security of sharing a spectrum of common interests through compensation for disappearance of children from contacts of daily living

1. Supporting other in continued search for new stimuli of reorientation, including coping capacity with loss of partner
2. Increased permissiveness with nonpathological regression
3. Changes in security of receiving consideration and care
4. Permitting one another a decrease in spectrum of common interests because preparation for loss of partner requires divergent interests

---

1. Support in the disturbance of oedipal repressions in the partner due to sexual maturation of children of opposite sex
2. Social permissibility of the experience
3. Coupling effect of 2.
4. Promise of grandchildren

1. Support in decline because of psychological aging
2. Social permissibility of the experience
3. Coupling effect of 2.
4. Realization of reproduction beyond own children

---

1. Experimenting with modification in patterns of division of labor
2. Provision of experience with tangible property through home
3. Increase of economic security through wife's renewed availability for gainful employment because of freedom from demands of child care

1. Further experimentation in division of labor and employment in preparation for retirement
2. Acceptance of reduction of home scale
3. Helping one another to accept decrease of economic security because of difficulty in finding new employment or because of reaching retirement age

---

1. Help in learning changed roles in both spheres
2. According one another freedom to express individuality and help in maintenance of feeling of identity
3. Support in maintenance of socially adaptive defenses plus tolerance for loss of socially adaptive defenses and guilt feeling over death wishes

1. Help in learning changed partner roles and becoming ready for bereavement roles*
2. According one another freedom to express individuality and help in maintenance of identity
3. Increased support in maintenance of socially adaptive defenses plus tolerance for loss of socially adaptive defenses and guilt feeling over death wishes

*Usually not practical because of repression of death thoughts.

the partners and the social-role demands they are asked to meet due to cultural change. The marital (nonmarital) dysfunction may not be compensated for by secondary gratification catering to the needs generated at early levels of development. It is possible that the four basis forms of dysfunction in . . . (transactional) patterns are the result of failure in establishing harmony between residual self-demands to live up to the requirements of obsolete self-images and new role patterns.

Our times are characterized by a distinctive trend toward exchangeability of men and women in the performance of social roles formerly exclusively assigned to one or the other sex. Fathers are taught to feed and bathe infants, wives are taught to equal men as wage-earners in the same lines of work, and both husband and wife are taught to share to burden of social-role performance rather than to divide it in terms of sex-specific role allocation. In consequence, sexual identification is reduced to the biological sphere. Women who are aware of their power to support the family and of their enforced authority in the home due to the fathers' absence often try to dress as if they were sex objects forced to attract men by the symbols of their sexuality rather than by the resource capacity in human relations that they represent. Men wash dishes but refuse to wear aprons. They can accept the higher living standard and retirement security provided by the earning power of their wives but find maintenance of their self-images in the fact that their take-home pay is higher than that of their wives. They may be tempted to try to prove their virility by acting out sexually rather than by trying to elicit and stimulate sexual responses in their wives. When faced with the problem of sharing home maintenance, women may be tempted to maintain their feminine self-images by combining the burdens of earning adequate incomes and keeping up adequate standards of home care. Males try to keep up their self-images by refusing to carry out tasks of home maintenance or child discipline that their wives would like to see them perform. And basically there is interpersonal conflict because, when the principle of sharing role performances replaces the principle of the division of labor, the attitudes of accounting and balance are introduced into a social system. Again, covert and overt need satisfaction and frustrations create 'double bind' situations. A male may refuse to let his partner share the economic burden of supporting the family and may thus introduce dysfunction into the economic dimension of the relationship on the manifest level. Covertly, he may fight for the maintenance of his masculine self-image.

In the area of conflict between ego ideal and role demand, identification with one's own sex and the nature of involvement in performance of life tasks are greatly handicapped by the failure of the helping professions to rethink the concepts of masculinity and femininity for themselves as well as for their patients. It has become a ritual to accuse wives of being dominant, aggressive, and frigid and husbands of being submissive, passive, and sexually either unresponsive or acting out. Therapeutic goal setting is also ritualized in the recommendation that the husband should be strengthened and that the partner should be helped to accept her own sex. These two rituals imply failure to provide the helper himself as well as the patients with socially feasible and morally acceptable goals. Here the task of the therapist will not be to present a model of age- and phase-appropriate conquest of ambivalence but to formulate new models of masculinity and femininity with which people can live in our time without being exposed to the 'double bind' between modern ego demands and antiquated ego ideals. This task, however, is one for which the helping professions are poorly prepared. It requires creativity instead of liberation, fashioning of civilization rather than helping people to cope with its discontents.

ENVIRONMENTAL SYSTEM

The environmental system involves all systems of the GST.[106-107] As we begin the 1980s, this system may be most influential since the future is so unpredictable due to ecosystem problems, atomic concerns, etc. . . . In addition, cultural barriers are rapidly disappearing due to travel (supersonic transport) and communication (instant TV reporting by satellite) revealing basic similarity among men and women as opposed to their differences.[108] For professional growth, the therapist should acquire cultural concepts,[109] anthropology,[110] sociology and social psychology,[111-114] cultural psychiatry,[115] etc.

The rubric of culture consists of behavioral patterns (specific and implicit) acquired and transmitted by various symbols of a group of individuals in a specific territory. Except for isolated areas in the world, the traditional values and their artifacts are subject to the relentless ongoing changes from the interlock of all systems of the GST. Culture includes social institutions, social networks, changing social class stratification, changing sex roles,[116-120] changing life styles,[121-126] changing child rearing practices and their impact on personality, and the blight and flight of individuals, e.g. religious cults.[127]

In the past decade, the feminist movement continues to offer new opportunities for self-fullfillment involving all three systems of the GST: intrapersonally in sexuality; interpersonally in changes in family and mating patterns; and environmentally in work opportunities outside the home. Rapoports'[128] propose the concepts of *equity* as having advantages over that of equality. By equity they mean equal opportunity plus the feeling of fairness, i.e. the fair allocation of opportunity and of *constraints.* Unfortunately, the feminist movement has resulted in too many one parent families — the divorce rate has increased.[129] It is the children who suffer the most because they do not have adequate parenting.[130] In many situations, it is the men who have been liberated — from their responsibilities, both financial and parental. For the majority of women, self-awareness and new opportunities for self-fulfillment has become an illusion[131] ending in depression, despair, alienation, anxiety, physical depletion, and anger.

Ruth Moulton[132] has described four major syndromes she has observed in her female patients comparing women she treated in the fifties to those seen in the seventies, a span of two decades. Although occasionally there is an overlap, the four major syndromes are as follows: *reentry anxiety* — when a long-homebound woman returns to work in the outer world; *performance anxiety* — difficulty in asserting herself or her fear of success; the *"good girl's"* difficulty when faced with hostility; and *identity conflict* between personal and professional roles in which marriage is often seen as a threat to autonomy. She concludes her article by stating: "The new feminism, while opening up new paths for both sexes and loosening sex-role stereotypes, has also unleashed new anxieties." I am in accord with Doctor Moulton that "a stable equilibrium will be achieved only after the effects of rapid cultural change have been dealt with individually and socially." The new feminism and other sociocultural changes will not destroy the institution of marriage nor the family despite negative predictions over the past century. Finally, any dyadic relationship is a growth process, *not role playing.* Partners are best served when tasks and functions are divided according to wishes, capacities, interests, abilities, and needs. This requires maturity, morals, and effort.

The family systems have been changing during each century of modern history and maintaining its viability, despite dire predictions[133] for the following reasons: its rooted in morality;[134] the continuity of society; its resourcefulness; and transmitting its ongoing history. Hence, the family " . . . is the substance of the past, the wellspring of the present, and the foundation of the future."[135] A grave concern to many professionals in the field of mental health is the pervasive hedonism in our society.[136] The "living together" arrangement[137-138] lacks adherence in institutional forms. Cohabitation without commitment may be fun, but rarely leads to growth. At the core of the family there must be an ethical imperative. Marriage without children is not a family, it is a couple who are married. If a society is to survive there must be children. Above all, there must be a system of values — the social glue that holds a family together. Morality is best viewed from a developmental approach beginning in infancy and continuing through the entire life cycle. Implicit in this approach is the transactional interplay of cognition, emotions, and the sociocultural milieu underlying moral experience, religion, and ethics.[139-140] All institutions are in the process of change, but that does not necessarily mean decline![141]

THE TWO "JUKEBOXES" AND THE SEESAW"

The open-ended inclusive paradigm of pair-coupling based on the GST has led empirically to a simple pragmatic model, readily utilizable both for teaching and therapeutic purposes. The dyadic relationship is presented as consisting of two partners (two jukeboxes with "records" — intrapersonal system), each unique in personality and seated at opposite ends of a seesaw (interpersonal system). The transactions represented by the ongoing reciprocal swings of the seesaw may be pleasant or painful. Further, the playground on which the

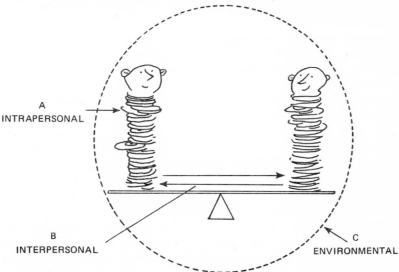

Figure 2. The suprasystem. **A,** Jukebox (intrapersonal system); **B,** Seesaw (interpersonal system); **C,** Sociocultural system of environmental forces (kinship networks, cultural values, and so on).

seesaw is found constitutes a complex social field of divergent environmental forces (environmental system) (see Fig. 2, courtesy of Reverend Bruce Mase).

The environmental forces include a number of subsystems that have varying effects upon each relationship. The family boundaries are not the same at all times or for all members as the result of the life pattern of each individual and of each relationship. In our culture, a newborn is considered a member of the family, but his membership is less clear when he leaves. This kinship network plays an important role in every relationship. As comparative studies of the various social classes of our society reveal different definitions regarding the composition of the nuclear family, sociocultural influences will be explored. Although each family's boundaries are spatially definable, these boundaries are permeable. Interchanges between the family and the subsystems, e.g. economic, occupational, religious, political, recreational, are constantly occurring. The complexity of our society with its progressive specialization forces the family to become structurally dependent on the multiple subsystems in its social matrix. In the treatment of dyadic and/or family problems, this structural dependence of the family makes it mandatory for the therapist to fully understand the interchanges between the nuclear family and its environment.

An individual may be compared to a jukebox containing a library of permanent stereophonic "records" (encoded information introjects stored in the brain of a neurophysiological nature whose structure awaits further scientific clarification, e.g. nucleic acids as repositories of information) capable of not only playing any past record but also capable of encoding (learning) new records. A record can be considered to be a real phenomenon and not an abstraction and is the blend of the three main voices (*inner child*, parental, and *pia*, i.e. *p*erceptive-*i*ntegrative-*a*daptive functions of the brain) reflecting the reality of either a past or present encoding. It is very common for a partner to emphatically comment: "He sounds exactly like his mother and his mannerisms are just like hers too."

The voice of the inner child is present from birth and remains with the individual forever. The main attributes of the inner child include curiosity, creative play, creativity, and sensuality. The voice of pia is nonemotional and is a data-processing mechanism with both an internal (intrapersonal system) and external (interpersonal and environmental systems) input. At birth the voices of the pia and the inner child are indistinguishable.

With the development of object relationships and influenced by separation anxiety, the sound of the third important voice is heard. It is that of sociocultural values and attitudes that I refer to as the *parental*, after Berne.[142]

The jukebox contains an internal mechanism that plays the records. The internal mechanism can be equated to the executive function of the brain.[143] The jukebox undergoes slow but progressive deterioration due to the inevitable aging process and to unavoidable trauma, e.g. illnesses or accidents. The deterioration is extremely variable, from imperceptible to gross changes, unique for each individual during his life cycle. This designation of the individual as a jukebox is mechanistic only for purposes of explanation.

The formation of character is the result of multiple systems of transactions in circularity (feedback loops), of which biology is only one factor, along with interpersonal and cultural determinants. The various possible determinants of the personality in action are explored in the presentation of the twenty-three items of the biographical relationship questionnaire (Chapter III).

Conclusion

The GST paradigm will be further modified in the future because of the multiple, unclear factors that reciprocally but clearly shape individuals in their relationships. To separate the components of a person is to lose track of the whole person who exists in his ever-changing environment. My use of the GST is an effort to put the three systems and their subsystems into a holistic theory for purposes of diagnosis, prevention, and the treatment of individuals in their transactions. The GST is helpful for many therapists to understand the interface between different levels of coping and the vicissitudes of open transactional feedback systems. It also aids visualization of the longitudinal effects and phases from prenatal to death. As Luria states, "To cope with the stresses and pressures that our own species will have to face in the next couple of centuries and to create a world fit for the new billions of human beings to live in, we shall have to understand as precisely as possible all interactions within our own body. We shall need to acquire a molecular understanding of the unique human brain, of human language, of human cognition . . . science may be regarded as a means used by the human species to adapt itself to the environment."[144]

A pragmatic viewpoint of the various systems of the GST, where problems within anyone of these areas may produce ripple effects within the other systems, will be presented in the twenty-three items of the biographical relationship questionnaire (BRQ). The open-ended BRQ (Chapters IV through XVIII) includes clues or data that are helpful in the resolution of the problems of the individual in pain. When one launches into the many uncharted areas of psychotherapy, the material just presented indicates that the road to competency involves ongoing commitment to personal and professional growth — a most difficult and time consuming process. **There are no short cuts.** The next chapter will discuss the initial interviews.

REFERENCES

1. Bursten, Ben: Psychiatry and the rhetoric of models. *Am J Psychiat, 136:* 662-66, 1979.
2. Lipton, Morris A.: Editorial — diverse research strategies for depression and alcoholism, *Am J Psychiat, 136:* 497-501, 1979.
3. Unger, William L.: Applying complementarity to psychiatry. *Southern Calif. Psychiatric Society News, 24:* 1 & 3, 1977.
4. Westermeyer, Joseph, Bush, Janet, and Wintrob, Ronald: A review of the relationship between dysphoria, pleasure, and human bonding, *J Clin Psychiat, 39:* 415-19, 423-24, 1978.
5. Lifton, R. J.: From analysis to formation — towards a shift in psychological paradigm. *J Am Acad Psychoanal 4:* 63-94, 1976.
6. Marmor, Judd: Presidential address — psychiatry 1976, the continuing revolution. *Am J Psychiat, 133:* 739-45, 1976.
7. Laner, Mary R.: The medical model, mental illness, and metaphoric mystification among marriage and family counselors, *Family Coordinator, 25:* 175-81, 1976.
8. Roth, Nathan: Free association and creativity. *J Am Acad Psychoanal, 3:* 373-81, 1975.
9. Alger, Ian: Psychoanalysis and family systems. *J Am Acad Psychoanal, 3:* 235-38, 1975.
10. Blaney, Paul H.: Implications of the medical model and its alternatives. *Am J Psychiat, 132:* 911-14, 1975.
11. Pinderhughes, Charles: Ego development and cultural differences. *Am J Psychiat, 131:* 171-76, 1974.
12. Neubeck, Gerhard: Toward a theory of marriage counseling — a humanistic model. *Family Coordinator, 22:* 117-22, 1973.
13. von Bertalanffy, Ludwig: General system theory and psychiatry. In Arieti, Silvano (Ed.): *American Handbook of Psychiatry*, Vol. III. New York, Basic Books, 1966, pp. 705-721.
14. von Bertalanffy: General system theory — a critical review. In Buckley, Walter (Ed.): *Modern Systems Research for the Behavioral Scientist.* Chicago, Aldine, 1968, pp. 11-30.
15. von Bertalanffy, Ludwig: *Robots, Men and Minds.* New York, Braziller, 1967.

16. von Bertalanffy, Ludwig: *General System Theory: Foundations, Development, Applications.* New York, Braziller, 1968.
17. Lederer, William J. and Jackson, Don D.: *The Mirages of Marriage.* New York, Norton, 1968, pp. 87-97.
18. Halpern, Howard A., Canale, Joseph R., Gant, Bobby L. and Bellamy, Cheryl: A systems-crisis approach to family treatment, *J Marital and Family Therapy,* 5: 87-94, 1979.
19. Phillips, Clinton E.: Toward a theory of marriage and family counseling systems eclicticism. Students handouts available from the author, Director of California Family Study Center, 4400 Riverside Drive, Burbank, CA 91505.
20. Phillips, Clinton E.: Notes on system theory. Students handouts available from the author, Director of California Family Study Center, 4400 Riverside Drive, Burbank, CA 91505.
21. Seagraves, Robert T.: Conjoint marital therapy. *Arch Gen Psychiat, 35:* 454, 1978.
22. Fleck, Stephen: A general systems approach to severe family pathology. *Am J Psychiat, 133:* 669-73, 1976.
23. Grinker Sr., Roy R.: *Psychiatry in Broad Perspective.* New York Behavioral Pubns, 1975.
24. Marmor, Judd: The future of psychoanalytic therapy, *Am J Psychiat, 130:* 1197-1202, 1973.
25. Berman, Ellen M. and Lief, Harold I.: Marital therapy from a psychiatric perspective: an overview. *Am J Psychiat, 132:* 585, 1975.
26. Bonstedt, Theodor: Development of new identity during psychiatric training. *Psychiatric Opinion 12:* 32-36, 1975.
27. Boerop, Bate J.L.D : General systems theory and family therapy in practice. *Family Therapy, 2:* 69-77, 1975.
28. Holder, Harold D. and Stratas, Nicholas E.: A systems approach to alcholism programming. *Am J Psychiat, 129:* 64-69, 1972.
29. Broderick, Carlfred B : Beyond the five conceptual frameworks — a decade of development in family theory, *J Marr & Family, 33:* 139-59, 1971.
30. Steinglass, Peter, Weiner, Sheldon, and Mendelson, Jack H.: A systems approach to alcoholism — a model and its clinical application. *Arch Gen Psychiat, 24:* 401, 1971.
31. Witenberg, Earl G. (Ed.): *Interpersonal Psychoanalysis — New Directions.* New York, Wm. A. White Institute, Gardner Press, 1978.
32. Gray, William: Emotional cognitive structures — a general systems theory of personality. General Systems 18: 240, 1973.
33. Duhl, Bunny S. and Duhl, Frederick J.: Cognitive styles and marital process. Presented at American Psychiatric Association annual meeting, Anaheim CA, May 9, 1975.
34. Martin, Peter A.: *A Marital Therapy Manual.* New York Brunner/Mazel, 1976.
35. Simon, Robert M : On eclecticism. *Am J Psychiat, 131:* 135-39, 1974.

36. Betz, Barbara J.: Some neurophysiologic aspects of individual behavior. *Am J Psychiat, 136:* 1251-56, 1979.
37. Masserman, Jules H.: Presidential address — the future of psychiatry as a scientific and humanitarian discipline in a changing world. *Am J Psychiat, 136:* 1013-19, 1979.
38. Beach, Frank A. (Ed.): *Human Sexuality in Four Perspectives.* Baltimore, Md., John Hopkins Univ Press, 1977.
39. Frazer, Alan and Winokur, Andrew (Eds.): *Biological Bases of Psychiatric Disorders.* Jamaica, New York: Spectrum Pub, 1977.
40. Globus, Gordon G.: Consciousness and brain — I, The identity thesis. *Arch Gen Psychiat, 29:* 153-160, 1973.
41. Globus, Gordon G.: Consciousness and brain — II. Introspection, the qualia of experience, and the unconscious. *Arch Gen Psychiat, 29:* 167-176, 1973.
42. Serban, George (Ed.): *Psychopathology of Human Adaptation.* New York, Plenum Press, 1976.
43. Heath, Robert G: Applications of Sandor Rado's adaptational psychodynamic formulations to brain physiology. *J Am Acad Psychoanal, 2:* 19-25, 1974.
44. Bohman, Michael: Some genetic aspects of alcoholism and criminality, *Arch Gen Psychiat, 35:* 269-76, 1978.
45. Cohen, Donald J., Dibble, Eleanor, and Grawe, Jane M.: Parental style-mothers' and fathers' perceptions of their relations with twin children. *Arch Gen Psychiat, 34:* 445-51, 1977.
46. Wener, Paul H., Rosenthal, David, Rainer, John D., Greenhill, Laurence and Sarlin, M. Bruce: Schizophrenics' adopting parents psychiatric status. *Arch Gen Psychiat, 34:* 778-84, 1977.
47. Smokler, A. and Shevrin, Howard: Cerebral lateralization and personality style. *Arch Gen Psychiat, 36:* 949-54, 1979.
48. Hoppe, Klaus D.: Split-brain — psychoanalytic findings and hypotheses, *J Am Acad Psychoanal, 6:* 193-213, 1978.
49. Kinsbourne, Marcel (Ed.): *Asymmetrical Function of the Brain.* New York: Cambridge Univ Pr, 1978.
50. Jaynes, Julian: The Origin of Consciousness in the Breakdown of the Bicameral Mind. Boston, HM, 1977.
51. Galin, David: Implications for psychiatry of left and right cerebral specialization — a neurophysiological context for the unconscious processes. *Arch Gen Psychiat, 31:* 572-83, 1974.
52. McKee, G. Humphrey, B., and McAdam, D.: Scaled lateralization of alpha activity during linguistic and musical tasks. *Psychophysiology, 10:* 441-43, 1973.
53. Penfield, Wilder: Neurophysiological basis of the higher functions of the nervous system, In Field, J. (Ed.): *Handbook of Physiology: Section 1. Neurophysiology.* Washington, DC, American Physiological Society, 1959-1960.
54. Lourie, Reginald S: The first three years of life — an overview of a new frontier. *Am J Psychiat, 127:* 1457-63, 1971.

55. Serban, *Psychopathology of Human Adaption.*

56. The academy forum, *Am Acad Psychoanal, 23:* 2, 4-10, 16, 1979.

57. Vaillant, George E : Theoretical hierarchy of adaptive ego mechanisms — a 30 year follow-up of 30 men selected for psychological health. *Arch Gen Psychiat, 24:* 107-118, 1971.

58. Owens, Howard and Maxmen, Jerrold S.: Mood and affect — A semantic confusion. *Am J Psychiat, 136:* 97-99, 1979.

59. Ketai, Richard: Affect, mood, emotion, and feeling — semantic considerations, *Am J Psychiat, 132:* 1215-17, 1975.

60. Socarides, Charles W. (Ed.): *The World of Emotions: Clinical Studies of Affects and Their Expression.* New York: Int Univ Pr, 1977.

61. Gaylin, Willard. *Feelings: Our Vital Signs.* New York: Harper and Row, 1979.

62. Freud, Sigmund. *An Outline of Psychoanalysis.* New York: Norton, 1949, p. 36.

63. Chrzanowski, Gerard: Some present day psychoanalytic currents on the European continent. *J Am Acad Psychoanal, 5:* 175-85, 1977.

64. Strean, Herbert S.: *Crucial Issues in Psychotherapy.* Metuchen, New Jersey, The Scarecrow Press, Inc., 1976.

65. Klein, George S.: *Psychoanalytic Theory: An Exploration of Essentials.* New York, Int Univ Pr, 1976.

66. Engel, George L.: Psychoanalysis — alive and well at 80. *JAMA 231:* 579-82, 1975.

67. Eckardt, Marianne Horney: Psychoanalysis today — some philosophical issues. *J Am Acad Psychoanal, 2:* 41-54, 1974.

68. Risenblatt, Alan D. and Thickstun, James T.: *Modern Psychoanalytic Concepts in General Psychology.* Part One — General Concepts and Principles; Part Two — Motivation, Psychological Issues Monographs 42 & 43. New York, Int Univ Press, 1978.

69. Kohut, Heinz: The psychology of the self. With Goldberg, Arnold I. (Ed.): A Casebook of Narcissistic Personality Disorders. New York, Intl Univ Press, 1977.

70. Piaget, Jean: *Structuralism,* translated by C. Maschler, New York, Basic Books, 1970.

71. Piaget, Jean and Inhelder, B.: *The Psychology of the Child,* translated by H. Weaver. New York, Basic Books, 1969.

72. Friedman, Lawrence: Piaget and psychotherapy. *J Am Acad Psychoanal, 6:* 175-92, 1978.

73. Pattison, E. Mansell: The behavioral sciences in medical education. *J Operational Psychiat 6:* 113-22, 1975.

74. Aring, Charles D : The Freudian influence. *J Am Med Assn, 237:* 651, 1977.

75. Wittenberg, Earl G. To believe or not to believe. *J Am Acad Psychoanal, 4:* 433-45, 1976.

76. Erikson, Erik: Erikson on growth. *Psychiatric News, 19:* 1, 14, 33, 1979.

77. Bieber, Irving: The psychoanalytic treatment of sexual disorders, *J Sex &*

Marital Therapy, 1: 5-15, 1974.

78. Brody, Sylvia and Axelrad, Sidney with Horn, Ethel, Moroh, Marsha, and Taylor, Marvin: *Mothers, Fathers, and Children: Explorations in the Formation of Character in the First Seven Years.* New York, Int Univ Press, 1978.

79. Bowlby, John: *Separation-Anxiety and Anger,* — Vol II Attachment and Loss, New York, Basic Books, 1973.

80. Anthony, E. James: Panel on child analysis at different developmental stages. *J Am Psychoanal Assn, 12:* 1, 1964.

81. Salzman, Leon: Modern psychoanalytic theory and practice in the neuroses — a review. *J Am Acad Psychoanal, 2:* 261-8, 1974.

82. Mahler, Margaret S., Pine, Fred, and Bergman, Anni: *The Psychological Birth of the Human Infant.* New York, Basic Books, 1975.

83. Kaplan, Louise J.: *Oneness and Separateness: From Infant to Individual.* New York, Simon & Shuster, 1978.

84. Gralnick, Alexander: In-patient psychoanalytic psychotherapy of adolescents. *J Am Acad Psychoanal, 7:* 437-45, 1979.

85. Blos, Peter: In Feinstein, Sherman C. and Giovacchini, Peter (Eds.): Adolescent Psychiatry, Vol. V. New York, Aronson, 1977.

86. Kaplan, Eugene A. and Johnson, Frank A.: The adolescent "crush." *Med Aspects Hum Sexuality, 12:* 57-70, 1978.

87. Erikson, Erik E.: *Identity: Youth and Crisis.* New York, Norton, 1968.

88. McMorrow, F.: *Midolescence: The Dangerous Years.* New York, Strawberry Hill Publishing Company, Inc., 1974.

89. Shecter, David E: Notes on some basic human developmental tasks. *J Am Acad Psychoanal, 3:* 267-76, 1975.

90. McHugh, Paul: Henry Phipps professor of psychiatry and psychiatrist-in-chief, The John Hopkins Univ Hospital.

91. Stein, Stefan, P., Holzman, Stephen, Karasu, T. Byram, and Charles, Edward S.: Mid-adult development and psychopathology. *Am J Psychiat, 135:* 676-81, 1978.

92. Targ, Dena B.: Toward a reassessment of women's experience at middle age. *Family Coordinator, 28:* 377-82, 1979.

93. Neugarten, Bernice L.: Time, age, and life cycle. *Am J Psychiat, 136:* 887-93, 1979.

94. Neugarten, B. L. and Datan, N.: Sociological perspectives on the life cycle. In Baltes, P.B. and Schaie, K.W. (Eds.): Lifespan Developmental Psychology: Personality and Socialization. New York, Acad Pr, 1973.

95. Coleman, Sandra B.: A developmental stage hypothesis for nonmarital dyadic relationships. *J Marr & Family Counseling, 3:* 71-76, 1977.

96. Lewis, Jerry M., Beavers, W. Robert, Gossett, John T., and Phillips, Virginia A.: *No Single Thread, Psychosocial Health in Family Systems.* New York, Brunner-Mazel, 1976.

97. Pollak, Otto: Sociological and psychoanalytic concepts in family diagnosis. In Greene, B.L. (Ed.): The Psychotherapies of Marital Disharmony. New York, Free Press, 1965, pp. 15-26.

98. Sprey, Jetse: Family power structure — a critical comment. *J Marr & Family, 34:* 235-38, 1972.
99. Berman, Ellen and Lief, Harold I., Marital therapy from a psychiatric perspective.
100. Sager, Clifford J.: A typology of intimate relationships. *J Marr & Family Counseling, 3:* 83-112, 1977.
101. Sprenkle, Douglas H. and Olson, David H.L.: Circumflex model of marital systems — an empirical study of clinic and nonclinic couples. *J Marr and Family Counseling, 4:* 59-74, 1978.
102. Berman, Ellen and Miller, William: Interview — transition periods in sexual-marital life — an adult developmental perspective. *Med Aspects Hum Sexuality, 12:* 124-36, 1978.
103. Russell, Axel and Russel, Lila: Exorcising the ghosts in the marital system. *J Marr & Family Counseling, 4:* 71-78, 1978.
104. Spence, Donald and Lonner, Thomas: The "Empty Nest" — a transition within motherhood. *Family Coordinator, 20:* 369-75, 1971.
105. Berger, Milton M.: *Beyond the Double Bind.* New York: BrunnerMazel, 1978.
106. Rumbaut, Ruben D.: Life events, change, migration, and depression. In Fann, William E., Karacan, Ismet, Pokorny, Alex D., and Williams, Robert L. (Eds.): *Phenomenology and Treatment.* New York, Spectrum, 1977, pp. 115-26.
107. Modell, John, Furstenberg, Frank F., Jr., and Hershber, Theodore: Social change and transitions to adulthood in historical perspective. *J Family History, 1:* 7-32, 1976.
108. Dunham, H. Warren: Society, culture, and mental disorder. *Arch Gen Psychiatry, 33:* 147-56, 1976.
109. Schram, Rosalyn W: Marital satisfactions and the family life cycle — a critique and proposal. *J Marr & Family, 41:* 7-12, 1979.
110. Kleinman, Arthur: Clinical relevance of anthropological and cross-cultural research — concepts and strategies, *Am J Psychiat, 135:* 427-31, 1978.
111. Srole, Leo, Langner, Thomas S., Michael, Stanley T., Kirkpatrick, Price, Opler, Marvin L., and Rennie, Thomas A.C.: In Srole, Leo and Fischer, Anita Kassen (Eds.): *Mental Health in the Metropolis: The Midtown Manhattan Study,* Book Two, revised. New York: Harper Torchbooks (Harper & Row), 1977.
112. Mogey, John: Review essay — residence, family kinship: some recent research. *J Family History, 1:* 95-105, 1976.
113. Otto, Luther B.: Class and status in family research, *J Marr & Family, 37:* 315-22, 1975.
114. Edwards, John N. and Brauburger, Mary B.: Exchange and parent-youth conflict, *J Marr & Family, 35:* 101-107, 1973.
115. Favazza, Armando R, and Oman, Mary: Overview — Foundations of cultural psychiatry, *Am J Psychiat, 135:* 293-303, 1978.
116. Lewis, Robert and Pleck, Joseph H (Guest Eds.): Men's roles in the

family. *Family Coordinator, 28:* 429-32, 1979.

117. Humphrey, Frederick G.: Changing roles for women — Implications for marriage counselors. *J Marr & Family Counselors, 1:* 219-27, 1975.

118. Benedek, Therese: The polarity of the sexes and its decline. *J Am Acad Psychoanal, 5:* 31-41, 1977.

119. Auerswald, Edgar H.: Family, Change and ecological perspective. In Farber, Andrew, Mendelsohn, Marilyn, and Napier, Augustus (Eds.):*The Book of Family Therapy.* Boston, HM, 1972.

120. Kirkendall, Lester A. and Whitehurst, Robert N. (Eds.). The New Sexual Revolution. New York, D W Brown, 1971.

121. Kaslow, Florence W. and Gingrich, Gerald: The clergyman and the psychologist as marriage counselors: differences in philosophy, referral patterns and treatment approaches to non-marital relationships. *J Marr & Family Counseling, 3:* 13-21, 1977.

122. Leslie, Gerald R. and Elizabeth M.: *Marriage in a Changing World.* New York, Wiley, 1977.

123. Libby, Roger W. and Whitehurst, Robert N. (Eds.): *Marriage and its Alternatives: Exploring Intimate Relationships.* Illinois, Scott F, 1977.

124. Sussman, Marvin B: The four F's of variant family forms and marriage styles. *Family Coordinator, 24:* 563-76, 1975.

125. Smith, James R. and Smith, Lynn G.: *Beyond Monogamy.* Baltimore: The John Hopkins Univ Press, 1974.

126. Cogswell, Betty E.: Variant family forms and life styles — rejection of the traditional nuclear family. *Family Coordinator, 24:* 391-406, 1975.

127. Schwartz, Lita L. and Kaslow, Florence W.: Religious cults, the individual and the family. *J Marital & Family Therapy, 5:* 15-26, 1979.

128. Rapoport, Rhona and Rapoport, Robert N.: Men, women, and equity. *Family Coordinator, 24:* 421-32, 1975.

129. National Center for Mental Health Statistics. Summary report. Final divorce statistics, 1978 (Monthly Vital Statistics Report, 27 — Aug 8, 1978). Washington, D.C. U.S. Govt Print Office, 1978.

130. Zimmerman, Carle C.: The future of the family in America. *J Marr & Family, 33:* 323-33, 1972.

131. Rossi, Alice S: Family development in a changing world. *Am J Psychiat, 128:* 1057-66, 1972.

132. Moulton, Ruth: Some effects of the new feminism. *Am J Psychiat, 134:* 1-6, 1977.

133. Reiss, Ira L.: *The Family Systems in America.* New York, HR&W, 1975 p. 317.

134. Kardiner, Abram: The social distress syndrome of our time, Parts I & II. *J Am Acad Psychoanal, 6:* 89-101, 215-230, 1978.

135. Setleis, Lloyd: An inquiry into the moral basis of the family. *Social Casework, 59:* 203-10, 1978.

136. Wyschogrod, Edith: Sons without fathers — a study in identity and culture. *J Am Acad Psychoanal, 6:* 242-269, 1978.

137. Kempler, Hyman L: Extended kinship ties and some modern

alternatives, *Family Coordinator, 25:* 143-49, 1976.

138. Foster, Henry H. and Freed, Doris J: Nonmarital partners — sex and serenity. *J Divorce, 1:* 195-211, 1978.

139. Maddock, James W: Morality and individual development — a basis for education. *Family Coordinator, 21:* 291-302, 1972.

140. Leslie, Gerald R: In my opinion — personal values, professional ideologies, and family specialists; a new look. *Family Coordinator, 28:* 157-62, 1979.

141. Trost, Jan: Married and unmarried cohabitation — the case of Sweden, with some comparisons. *J Marr & Family, 37:* 677-82, 1975.

142. Berne, Eric: Recent advances in transactional analysis, in *Current Psychiatric Therapies,* Vol. VI. New York, Grune, 1966, pp. 114-124.

143. Dyrud, Jarl E. and Donnelly, Charles: Executive functions of the ego, *Arch Gen Psychiat, 20:* 257, 1969.

144. Luria, S. E: Goals of science, *Bulletin of the Atomic Scientists, 33:* 33, 1977.

Chapter III

THE INITIAL INTERVIEWS

AT the outset I will refer to individuals coming for therapeutic help as patients. I agree with Jack Weinberg's[1] statement in his American Psychiatric Association's address (1977) that the term client be dropped: "There is nothing inappropriate in the term 'patient' for its root derivation means to suffer, and who else indeed should be entitled to help in the health delivery system than sufferers."

The techniques of therapy are undergoing profound changes toward spontaneous transactions occurring between patient and therapist. During the initial interview the patient sizes up the therapist[2-5] as an individual who is "impartial" and as a person capable of making some recommendations that will be helpful in the present crisis. He begins to develop conscious and unconscious attitudes toward the therapist. Simultaneously, the therapist gains diagnostic information, also observing the kind of transactions going on and is in a position to act upon it. In my clinical experience, the first ten minutes of the interview is extremely important to alleviate anxiety and/or hostility (which is often a defense against severe apprehension) and create a "working alliance"[6] so that the patient feels comfortable and will return for treatment.

The request for help with a dyadic problem may be unilateral or bilateral. An early appointment is advisable, as crises respond best when dealt with at the height of tension. At one extreme are those who are adamant that they are not in need of help and that the problem is entirely due to their mate.

> Doctor, there is nothing wrong with me, and the only reason I agreed to come was that our minister strongly suggested I see you. We argue constantly. She blames me, but who can stand fifteen or thirty minutes of constant criticism without a retort and finally a heated argument. Why does she have to blow up over the smallest things and exaggerate its importance? Why does she have to build herself up into a screaming woman who can't be talked to? Why does she come back from visits with neighbors and give me an exaggerated version of what made her mad? Why are the events which trigger these outbursts and tantrums so accumulative? She gets mad over small items — I dropped in for a beer at the tavern and started

talking with the guys and before I knew it I was two hours late for dinner; she builds it into a huge argument. She then starts bringing up all the old fights and changing previous events to make more to fight over. I once told her mother off about a Christmas gift and she has never let me forget that one.

At the other end are those couples who are willing to do anything to alleviate the discord and who are eager for therapy. One such case involved Mr. and Mrs. B.:

> Mr. B: We want to save our marriage because we really like each other a lot. We have come to realize our individual problems, which do not effect our functioning in the world outside marriage, but which seem to be causing our relationship a great deal of trouble. I'm self-centered. I procrastinate: I have to force myself to keep clean; and, I can't change most habits as easily as I should — there is a terrible gap between my intellectual under-standing of a problem and my visceral understanding of it. If you could only help us . . .
>
> Mrs. B: Obviously we feel the marriage is worth saving or we would not be here. I feel it could be very good if our personal problems were straightened out. We have much to give each other and we had an awful lot of fun together. We want to continue to have each other's companionship as best friends.

Very often a partner will be uncooperative, either refusing to be inter-viewed or coming under coercion. If a partner refuses to call for an appointment when requested by the patient, the therapist should take the initiative and telephone the reluctant partner. At that time, the therapist explains to the partner that his information would be most valuable in dealing with the overall problem. Rarely in my experience (approximately 5% of those telephoned) will a partner refuse to be interviewed, especially when the therapist employs tact.[7] Coercion may result from an actual threat by the partner ("either we see a marriage counselor or we see a lawyer") or by an act where one spouse has consulted a lawyer and started divorce proceedings. If the couple is not married, the threat of separation or legal procedures could have been used as well. The hostility and/or anxiety is best handled by "neutralization." The therapist responds to the overt or covert hos-tility by stating "You are very angry at having been forced into coming here. No one likes to be coerced into doing anything. If you say you are not angry, you would be trying to kid yourself. However, I'm here to explore the situation with you, and it is your prerogative to continue or to not." Usually this empathic statement breaks the ice and facilitates communication for a more cooperative atmosphere. Anger is a normal reaction to the invasion of one's privacy — the home is one's castle. Hostility can be a defense against the anxiety of a family secret such as homosexuality or infidelity. Occasionally, anger may be due to past unfortunate experiences with therapy.

A transactional basis for therapy begins at the time of the first request for an appointment.[8] By holding the expectation that both partners will participate in the initial evaluations, they usually do. At times one partner may appear to be very cooperative, but it is soon observed that this cooperation is only lip service.[9] This could be the Bernean "game*" of malingering, "Look How Hard I've Tried." Focusing on the relationship as the designated patient, the therapist can strongly influence the expectations and behavior of the partners.

My concept of pair-coupling is a *meaningful relationship* between two individuals based upon *mutual respect,* which in turn is based upon *self-respect.*[10] I point out that it is the relationship that is under observation and not the partners (seated at either end of the seesaw). They are advised that when their relationship stabilizes, it is their prerogative to revise their commitment or contract to meet changing needs and circumstances. Don Jackson's[11] contract of marriage (relationships) consists of two facets, sexual and collaborative. It also stresses the collaborative factor to be more important and to consist of four characteristics: voluntary, permanent, exclusive (no other liasons), and goal-oriented. For further reading, Sager[12] has written a lucid account of dyadic contracts.

I believe that every relationship is a partnership. No problem can exist that does not affect each partner; and, the solutions will come from both — it takes two to tango. Thus an individual partner is released from sole responsibility.

The stage (clinical setting) is set for both partners to view the transactions between them; both have a chance to experience what help might come from therapy without committing themselves beyond the initial evaluation. It is explained that the evaluation consists of one to three individual sessions (usually two), plus a final conjoint diagnostic and disposition session. In the latter session, transactions between the partners can be observed firsthand. They are told that I will make a statement at the last evaluative session as to my impressions and recommendations.

At this point I describe to my patients my frame of reference (usually expressing myself in the simplest language possible) and draw the seesaw, the jukeboxes, and the base anchored in the sociocultural milieu (see Chapter II, Fig. 2). This conceptual frame is easily grasped

---

*Eric Berne uses the term *game* to refer to sequences of behavior that are governed by rules. It has no playful connotations.

by the couple. I stress how learning theories help explain how an individual can encode new "records" in one's jukebox. My purpose is to divert responsibility from the partners as individuals and as guilty parties, while focusing upon the relationship as the problem. If I am successful, each partner will be less accusative or defensive, and each will have a better understanding of how their current responses are rooted in learned behavior from the past, i.e. one is playing "records" of the past no longer valid for current relationships.

If one partner is unduly *suspicious*, I continue the evaluation *conjointly from then on*. This inclusion prevents the patient from being subjected to a barrage of questioning as to what was discussed in the preceding sessions. Flexibility in treatment is mandatory at all times.

The individual diagnostic phase permits each partner to fully relate his/her presenting complaints. Being seen individually permits the revelation of secrets, which in my experience are known by the partners either consciously or *unconsciously;*[13] also, either party may vent his feelings without fear of retaliation.

Conjoint interviews are indicated when the therapist senses that individual sessions may produce distortion by a patient. Continuing conjoint sessions should be permitted until a clear picture of the problem is obtained or until a working alliance is established with the suspicious mate. Then the therapist may use individual sessions if necessary.

SILENCE

At this point, an understanding of the implications of silence, on the part of the patient, is important for communication.[14] Watzlawick and associates[15-16] hypothesize that it is impossible *not* to communicate in the presence of others. (A passenger in an airplane who closes his eyes is communicating that he does not wish to talk. Others "get the message" to leave him alone.) In keeping with my conceptual frame of multicausality, the phenomena of silence can be viewed from at least three GST systems: intrapersonal, interpersonal, and environmental. Symptoms, so-called ego defenses (such as projection, denial, and rationalization), and personality are not merely intrapersonal (intrapsychic) entities, but the endpoint of the intertwining of all elements of the GST. For example, an infant is not born with a phobia; it is a learned reaction to someone or something in its environment.

In my clinical experience, the intrapersonal system triggers silence for eight reasons:

1. A pervasive anxiety about entering therapy.
2. A fear that furious internal anger will become manifest and/or uncontrollable.
3. An intense introspection on the current crisis.
4. A symptom of depression.
5. A manifestation of a schizoid personality (with an unawareness and often inaccessibility of inner emotions).
6. A psychotic flight from reality.
7. A low intelligence or poor verbal facility.
8. An inadequate or poor self-image.

The most common reason for interpersonal impediments to communication is the presence of a secret. This may be due to either the content of the secret or the relationship with the interviewer. The four most frequent secrets include extramarital affairs, homosexuality, incestuous experiences, or prejudices of racial or religious nature that cause one partner to anticipate rejection by the therapist.

In the environmental system, silence may be a manifestation of an identification with silent parents, or it may be where outsiders (strangers) are viewed as potential hostile persons. Silence in the interview may complement a reaction to an incomplete questionnaire.

THE BIOGRAPHICAL RELATIONSHIP QUESTIONNAIRE (BRQ)

If the BRQ's are not obtained prior to the first interview, each patient is given a questionnaire at the end of the first session. Patients are instructed to fill out their forms *in private* so that each present an honest history without fear of retaliation by the other. It is also suggested that they add as many extra pages of information to the BRQ as is necessary. I inform the couple that the BRQ's accelerate the evaluation; therefore, if completed and returned before their next session, I will read them at my leisure without charge. Data from the BRQ's have proven useful in obtaining background information of the partners, more often than in the initial diagnostic interviews. The BRQ has undergone continuous modification with clinical usage and modification in the GST. This questionnaire is *specifically* designed to encompass all elements of the GST.

Procrastination in returning the BRQ, minimum statements, or refusal to fill out the form are informative. A suspicious spouse may be very reluctant to put his thoughts or complaints in writing. Occasionally, meagerness of data reflects limited schooling or intelligence, and the therapist can complete or complement the form. Psychotic preoccupation may prevent or distract the individual and reveal itself in both content and/or spareness of information. Procrastination may suggest an obsessive-compulsive personality or neurosis, since doubt is characteristic of these individuals, resulting in inability to commit themselves to definitive statements.

Refusal to fill out the BRQ may indicate hostility by a patient to an outsider's invasion of his privacy. Rejection of the BRQ may indicate anger at the partner for involving another person in the solution of their strife, since one's narcissism is threatened by the suggestion that he cannot solve the problems alone. Finally, refusal to fill out the BRQ may indicate lack of motivation in regard to maintaining the relationship and should alert the therapist to the possibility of the Bernean game, "Look How Hard I've Tried."

The completed BRQ can also be valuable in the later sessions as points of departure for further exploration of unsettled areas in the relationship. The patient coming for help is deeply involved with himself and is often caught in a mass of undifferentiated feelings toward his partner. Questions on the BRQ are designed to reveal feelings of the self and the partner about the affectional aspects of the marriage, feelings about kinship networks, division of responsibility in the home, and what each partner views as the major areas of difficulty. It is important to know that statements written or oral cannot be taken at face value — people frequently write or say one thing and mean something else. In the following chapters (IV through XIX) each subheading of the BRQ will be explored, and reasons for ascertaining specific data and illustrative clinical vignettes will be presented.

REFERENCES

1. Weinberg, Jack: Response to the presidential address. *Am J Psychiat, 134:* 739, 1977.
2. Kaplan, Alex H: Social work therapy and psychiatric psychotherapy. *Arch Gen Psychiat, 9:* 95, 1963.
3. Goldstein, Arnold P: Maximizing the initial psychotherapeutic relationship. *Am J Psychotherapy, 23:* 430, 1969.
4. Sandifer, Myron G., Jr., Hordern, Anthony, and Green, Linda M: The psychiatric interview — the impact of the first three minutes. *Am J Psychiat, 126:* 968, 1970.
5. Console, William A., Simons, Richard C., and Rubenstein, Mark: *The First Encounter: The Beginnings in Psychotherapy.* New York, Aronson, 1976.
6. Greenson, Ralph R.: *Explorations in Psychoanalysis.* New York, Intl

Univ Pr, 1978.

7. Berger, Miriam E: A note on luring a resistant spouse into marital therapy. *J Marr & Family Counseling, 1:* 387-88, 1975.
8. Brodey, Warren M.: *Changing the Family.* New York, Potter, 1968, pp. 17-24.
9. Napier, Augustus Y: The rejection-intrusion pattern — a central family dynamic, *J Marr & Family Counseling, 4:* 1978.
10. Stapleton, Jean and Bright, Richard: *Equal Marriage.* Nashville, Abingdon, 1976.
11. Jackson, Don D.: Family rules — the marital quid pro quo. *Arch Gen Psychiat, 12:* 589, 1965.
12. Sager, Clifford J.: *Marriage Contracts and Couple Therapy.* New York, Brunner-Mazel, 1976.
13. Seidenberg, Robert: Fidelity and jealousy — sociocultural considerations, *Med Aspects Hum Sexuality, 3:* 8, 1969.
14. Zuk, Gerald H.: On the pathology of silencing strategies. *Family Process, 4:* 32, 1965.
15. Watzlawick, Paul, Beavin, Janet, and Jackson, Don D.: *Pragmatics of Human Communication.* New York, Norton, 1967.
16. Watzlawick, Paul, Weakland, John, and Fisch, Richard: *Change — Principles of Problem Formation and Problem Resolution.* New York, Norton, 1974.

Chapter IV

THE BIOGRAPHICAL
RELATIONSHIP QUESTIONNAIRE

THE diagnostic process is continuous throughout a patient's treatment. The collection of verbal and nonverbal data is important to cover the broadest scope of the patient's personal history, current problem, and ongoing goals. The biographical relationship questionnaire (BRQ) has been my diagnostic tool for many years, because it helps evaluate individuals and relationships by gathering essential data from all three GST perspectives. I began refining and modifying Maholick's and Shapiro's[1] questionnaire many years ago.[2] The BRQ's six revisions reflect my clinical experience, the growing frequency of nonmarital dyads, and scientific knowledge gathered from reviewing multidisciplinary research and literature, which seems to make major shifts every six to ten years.

The BRQ has many purposes. It supplements data given in therapy sessions. It is filled out in confidence so that an unabridged version of the problem is more easily revealed. Its thought provoking questions often produce reflective thinking, startling new observations, memories or fantasies, and often a clearer view of the conflicts, feelings, thoughts, behavior, goals, etc. By comparing the dyad's answers, often contrasting or more complete dovetailing information is revealed which may help identify the source of the conflict or overt symptom. The BRQ helps me view the process of the relationship beyond the content (complaints). It permits the broadest coverage of potentially significant factors. It allows patients to reveal facts, opinions, and feelings about the self, the partner, significant others, kinship networks, the division of roles and responsibilities, etc.

One major change in the BRQ is the inclusion of item #22 which collects comprehensive data about sexuality.* The taking of a *verbal* sexual history is often a touchy subject requiring tact and timing. A written sexual history is often less threatening and an informative tool for any therapist. Also, while many patients rarely give honest responses to direct questioning of their intimate sex life and sexual problems, their BRQ answers are frequently more straightforward.

---

*Domeena C. Renshaw developed this section of the questionnaire and has given her permission to use it.

The BRQ format permits patients to feel protected against criticism, censure, disapproval, or anticipated ridicule, since their answers are confidential. Patients having had experiences of incest or rape are more apt to reveal this information on the BRQ form. My experience has demonstrated that intensive therapy will eventually reveal the same information, but this process can frequently be hastened through the BRQ.

Although all information is revealing as to structure, content, and lacunae, questionnaires seldom bring one to the core of the problem.[3] However, my experience has substantiated the use of the BRQ in the diagnostic sessions to facilitate transactions on a verbal and non-verbal level; to help focus on the foremost issues; and to help prompt the recall of the patient's past life events due to conscious or unconscious memory loss[4] and distortion.[5-6] Just as it is essential in the practice of medicine to have a wide knowledge of many areas of possible significance in an illness, the therapist should be exposed to a conceptual frame that permits a broad coverage of many potentially significant factors. In any couple only some of these factors may be of immediate concern, and I therefore suggest the omission of some of the BRQ questions when they are not relevant (#22 is one example). Unless the conceptual scheme is broad enough to encompass most of the factors that are likely to influence the relationship, critical conditions may be overlooked. The highly respected pioneer marital therapist David Mace[7] among many others, share the same position that a profile of each patient's personal history and current relationships is *absolutely essential* for effective therapy and he would never proceed without it.

The completed BRQ can also be valuable in the later interviews as points of departure for further exploration of unsettled areas in the relationship. The individual coming for help is deeply involved with himself and is often caught in a mass of undifferentiated feelings toward his partner.

The remainder of this chapter will discuss each question/item on my BRQ from two different perspectives: why the question was included and the therapeutic value of the answers. The sixteen page BRQ contains twenty-three items (see appendix for continuous form). *Item # 1 is Age.*

All individuals are influenced by time, timing of event, and their age. As a result, the chronological ages of my patients have an influence upon my observations and treatment. Of the 1340 couples seen privately, 5 percent were younger than twenty years of age and 5 percent were older than 60. Fifteen percent were in their twenties;

24 percent were in their thirties; and, half were either in their forties or fifties. Except for those patients under twenty-five, there were twice as many women as men younger than their partners. From age sixty on, the men were younger than their partners.

National statistics indicate most men who marry do so between twenty and twenty-six and most women are between the ages of nineteen and twenty-three,[8] usually following graduation from high school or college. The developmental tasks and crises have previously been described in Chapter II, pp. 20-21. Farnsworth, who has spent his entire professional life dealing with young people, has published his concern for the young adult who is characterized by hedonism and loss of integrity.[9] Professionals should be concerned by the attitude of many young adults who do not acknowledge a deep commitment at the time of marriage; such people often think: "If it doesn't work, we can get divorced." Such a statement implies that the final responsibility for divorced people and their offspring is their kinfolk or society. Based upon such thinking as well as the unhealthy environment in which many children from broken homes are forced to live, society (for its own preservation) may have to assume the moral responsibility of birth limitation.[10]

When evaluating the BRQ item on age, the ages of the partners are influenced by sociocultural forces. American society still promotes marriage: marriages are termed early if teenagers under eighteen, *traditional* (on time) if couples are between nineteen and twenty-two, and late when couples are older than twenty-two.[11] These definitions may vanish, as Vincent[12] points out, because age differentials in pair-couplings are occuring with many couples opting for the living together arrangement — marrying later in life. Girls are indoctrinated to attract men who have sophistication, higher social class, maturity, and financial security. These characteristics are more likely to be found in men over forty. Likewise, some young men may look to women their senior for refinement, understanding, social finesse, and worldly wisdom. I have observed many relationships with a marked age differential reflect hedonistic underpinnings of a "live for the moment doctrine." Marked age differentials in dyad partners are increasing in number for many reasons, such as divorce, desertion, death, and the influence of mass media which emphasizes youth, beauty, and money and devalues all else.

When a troubled couple come for help and there is a great age difference, I look for the process or purpose that attracted them in the first place. This type of relationship may be an attempt by the older partner to mold the younger individual into an "idealized" person

("Pygmalion"). Also, it may be for financial consideration. Or, it may reflect the younger partner's search for a parental figure. I am alert to the motivation behind this type of union because symptoms often reflect a shift in the transactional base by one partner which produces anger, anxiety, or confusion in the other.

Chronological age is an element in evaluating a relationship, but not always a significant problem. For example:

> Mr. A, age sixty-seven, had been married twice and both ended in divorce. The first marriage lasted twenty years and ended because of his hedonistic behavior. The second marriage of two year duration ended because of strong, clashing personalities. He sought remarital therapy before his third marriage attempt. Miss L, age thirty-two, was looking forward to her first marriage. Both stated their deep love for one another. Their relationship was constructive except that Mr. A's BRQ revealed a hospitalization for an acute heart attack and coronary by-pass surgery. During the two months of remarital therapy, some potential areas of conflict were resolved. Miss L was made fully aware of Mr. A's health prognosis, but that did not alter her feelings. They were married. The *routine yearly marital checkups* showed them happily wed.

When one partner verbally expresses concern over the youthfulness of the mate, the BRQ is very informative and can help evaluate the issue from the perspective of both. For example:

> Mrs. B, age forty-seven, began her second interview by stating that her husband is twenty-three years old. She thinks that he is staying in the marriage for her money and not out of love for her. This marriage was based on a practical agreement: she being pregnant out of wedlock, he would marry her, and she would pay his college expenses. The infant died after premature birth, but their marriage continued. She suspected his love. Mr. B firmly stated his love for her. The focal point of the session then shifted: she did not like his criticism and solicitous behavior. Surprisingly, her final statement of her resentment was that ". . . he is treating me like a father would treat his child."

It was apparent from the diagnostic phase with this couple that the important issue in the marriage was not one of age nor one of finances. Knowing that information permitted me to observe more salient aspects of their relationship from the beginning of the interview.

When the woman is half the age of her partner, the selection process may be due to a woman's unresolved relationship with her father. The partner will establish symbolically the father-daughter relationship she seeks. This does not necessarily lead to discord. On the other hand, this can lead to severe disharmony when the man wants a mature peer and not a daughter. For example, in one clinical case, the man was very pleased with his sweetheart's "cute" behavior, but after they were married several years he felt confused as he was greeted at his front door, after work, by his wife and little daughter, both vying for hugs and kisses. The females were in a competitive relationship that finally brought the man into therapy. The wife came into therapy sessions and competed with her husband for my sole attention. I disrupted her transactional process by referring her to another therapist for collaborative therapy. This type of relationship frequently reflects an unresolved oedipal conflict between daughter and father.

Age is an indicator of developmental stages, some of which are factually observed, but some are speculated upon as those called the "seven year itch" at age thirty,[13] the "twenty year itch" at age fifty, and the midlife crisis stage at ages forty through sixty.[14,15] As stated in Chapter II, I now feel as others do, including Notman[16] and Kerckhoff[17] that many of these speculations are myths. Neugarten (1979) succinctly expresses my views: "Whatever the social and social-psychological changes of adulthood, internal personality changes occur slowly. They reflect the accumulations of life events and the continuities and discontinuities in conscious preoccupations, and they are influenced by the perceptions of change in the significant people with whom we interact. . . . The inner life becomes altered over the life span, but it is doubtful that people change internally at, for example, regular 10-year intervals. This is because at both the aware and unaware levels of the mind, the present has always the elements of the past contained within it."[18]

In the past decade, there has been a gradual increase in social approval[19] for senior citizens to develop marital or nonmarital relationships. Some of this acceptance is due to increase in their own self-worth and longer life expectancy.[20] The increasing divorce rate among senior citizens disrupts financial and emotional security and fragments kinship networks; a shortage of low cost and adequate housing forces older individuals to fend for themselves. There can be no doubt that the offsprings of these senior citizens are moving away from those traditional values which stress obligations to parents. In addition, there is no substitute for a dyadic relationship that fosters need complementarity of interpersonal reorientation, sexuality, economics, and ego strengthening.

Question #2 inquires about the dyadic status: *First relationship or marriage? yes — no — How long* ——— *?* This area is dealt with in complete depth in item #13.

In my clinical practice, 5 percent of my patients had relationships less than one year duration. About 20 percent of the relationships ranged from one to five years in duration. About 25 percent of the couples had a relationship between five to ten years. About 20 percent were together for about ten to fifteen years. About 15 percent were married fifteen to twenty years. 10 percent more were married twenty to twenty-five years; and 5 percent were married longer than twenty-five years.

Current national studies record 15 percent of the dyadic pairs who seek psychotherapy are living together without a legal marital contract — the so-called LTA (living together arrangement). Growing social acceptance and increasing inflation are contributing to the rise in LTA (something already common in many European societies). Davidoff cites 286,000 as the census figure between 1960 to 1970 in America who have LTA situations and adds: " . . . obviously these are not true figures (many deny or avoid stating their life-style) and the number by 1980 will be far greater since such 'arrangements' are being accepted by more segments of the population."[21] She estimates that one-third are under age twenty-five, about one-sixth are over sixty, and the remainder are between twenty-five and sixty. Both Davidoff[22] and Coleman[23] view LTA as part of a new developmental phase. Davidoff has anticipated this new phenomenon's effect upon all GST systems and feels that eventually LTA will prove to be constructive. The opposite view is held by Voth, myself, and many others. We feel that " . . . all life springs from the family, the fundamental unit of a society, and mothering is probably the most important function on earth . . . (The) 1.3 million unmarried couples living together . . . have answered nature's mating call, but lack the psychological wherewithal to make the commitment stick."[24]

Question #3 on the BRQ asks " . . . *is your religion the same as that of your partner and/or his family?*" This question is not explored at the beginning interview unless the couple indicates that it is a conflictual area. It does alert the therapist to possible differences in attitudes, values, and rituals which may need to be reviewed by the couple. My experience is mainly with married couples and for the most part have had the same religious beliefs (only 20 percent involved mixed religions).

Question #4 asks the occupation of both partners. Further inquiry occurs on #20. The intention is to understand the life-style of the couple. Also the type of speech patterns common to their professions. The therapist can use this knowledge to neutralize any anxiety and/or hostility that an initial interview often generates. The type of occupation may reveal clues about their personalities, e.g. an accountant may be more comfortable with mathematical figures than with the human figure and/or have more tendencies toward obsessive-compulsiveness; a salesperson, however might tend to be gregarious and possibly geared to excessive drinking. One's occupation may show a "workaholic" who seeks therapy to reduce or avoid marital-/nonmarital, career, and/or financial responsibilities. Other times, this question may reveal intrapersonal, interpersonal, and environmental stresses, e.g. the transfer to new locality. Although the transferred worker does not lose his identity, it is the spouse who may find the uprooting process difficult, especially if children are involved.

Question #5 (and later #17) *reveals the educational level completed by each patient.* I have found that people with less education seek more active and directive therapeutic interventions: this person wants direct answers and/or medication. People I have seen who have college degrees (85% of my male patients are college graduates) usually seek psychological or intellectual answers. (I am stating for the readers' benefit that I have not had much experience with problem couples who did not complete grammar school.) Of my patients, 15 percent male and 30 percent female were high school graduates, approximately 20 percent had some college education, approximately 34 percent were college graduates, and 29 percent of the men and 9 percent of the women had postgraduate degrees.

Question #6 asks for the ages and names of offspring. When dyadic discord occurs, the children are frequently recipients of parental scapegoating and/or dysfunctional alliances. This information is of special concern when evaluating "reconstituted marriages." Another type of information ascertained is the presence or absence of children. One American study published statistics in 1976 that stated that of "...all the ever-married women aged 30 to 40, only 10.5 percent were childless. Of all wives, the current incidence of permanent, deliberate childlessness is about 5 percent."[25] Many dyads are formed with the original agreement to remain childless. Later, if one person changes in attitude, a conflict may ensue. The therapist may then choose to explore the couple's philosophy as to hedonistic costs and rewards,[26-27] as to a fear of increased financial and/or emotional responsibility, as to a desire for self-actualization, as to a wish to preserve their special intimacy of being a couple, and as to the loss of a dual earning capacity and/or increased responsibility if both must continue to work. Although voluntarily childless dyads perceive a variety of disapprovals from society (kinship networks included), recent literature implies that these couples remain impervious to this pressure.[28-29] Many rationalizatons are based upon the following variant world view: "... the selection perception of the consequences of parenthood; differential associations resulting in physical and psychological isolation from conflicting world view; structuring trial parenthood so as to reaffirm existing biases; and capitalizing upon social ambivalence towards parenthood. . . ."[30] In my clinical practice, 19 percent of the couples had *no* children; 11 percent had only one child;[31] 34 percent had two children; 26 percent had three children; and 10 percent had four or more children.

Question #7 asks for the source of referral and whether there is pressure from just one partner to seek therapy. The source of referral may be valuable as a means to reveal any previous help obtained, because there are situations where it is wise to refer the couple or one member back to the original referring agency or individual therapist. Knowledge about the type of pressure placed upon one partner by the other can aid the therapist in deciding which approach to use with the couple. Such knowledge also can help in establishing rapport and therapeutic trust.

Question #8 is placed on the first page because of its value for the therapist and the patient. The question *"Why are you now seeking help?"* stimulates a review of the problem and may crystalize the patient's thinking and emotions about the situation and the people involved. For the therapist, it focuses on the here and why of the precipitating crisis or problem. Over the last ten-year period, I have noticed a change in response to this question. My patients now state the following: 50 percent are in the divorce process, actually separated, or under the ultimatum to "get help or else"; 20 percent want to improve their relationship; 10 percent seek relief from constant bickering or violence; and 10 percent have a partner who threatens suicide or has attempted suicide (see item #11 for further discussion). Infidelity, an acute crisis involving a child, alcoholism, and a suspicious partner are a few of the less frequent answers (approximately 10% of those responding on the BRQ).

Crises are *realities and not categories,* although frequently dyadic disharmony centers around content when it should be the relationship. It is the therapist's job to focus upon the relationship. Crises are realities when the therapist is confronted with a serious dyadic or individual problem which involves the interplay of the three GST systems and their numerous subsystems and feedback loops. (see Chapter XXII for further discussion)

The purpose of question #9 is to obtain each partner's specific complaints. The question states: *"What are your complaints and when did trouble first begin in your relationship?"*

a. Lack of communication
b. Constant arguments and/or physical abuse
c. Unfulfilled emotional needs
d. Sexual dissatisfaction (Turn to item #22 for further analysis)
e. Financial disagreements
f. Conflicts about children
g. Infidelity
h. Problems with parents or in-laws
i. Alcoholism
j. Domineering partner
k. Suspicious partner
l. Other_____

The frequency of complaints has changed since 1962 when I did a survey of my patients' responses. In 1962, the most frequent response was "Spouse does not fulfill emotional needs." The following list reflects the remaining complaints in diminishing frequency: constant arguments, sexual dissatisfaction, financial disagreements, infidelity, in-law trouble, lack of communication, alcoholism, conflicts about the children, and suspicious spouse. In 1970, I did a new survey which included 750 couples and found a new order of complaints. Again, these are listed in order of the highest frequency:

1. Lack of Communication[32]
2. Constant arguments
3. Unfulfilled emotional needs
4. Sexual dissatisfaction
5. Financial disagreements
6. In-law trouble
7. Infidelity
8. Conflicts about children
9. Domineering spouse
10. Suspicious spouse
11. Alcoholism
12. Physical attack

In the last ten year period only slight changes have occurred in frequency. The first five complaints (see 1970 list) have remained the same. The sixth most frequent complaint has shifted to conflicts about children. The seventh is infidelity. The eighth is problems with parents or in-laws. The ninth is alcoholism. The tenth is domineering partner. The eleventh is suspicious partner.

Many couples have one major complaint, but often it does not accurately state their problem. The diagnostic interviews frequently reveal even more significant ones. The following clinical vignette describes a couple whose referral states the overt problem as their continuous quarreling about their son. (This couple was referred because their son's therapist observed a marital problem in this family. It was fortunate for this couple that someone initiated and attempted to get help for them.)

Mr. and Mrs. B are professional people. They had been married twenty-five years (the first marriage for each). Mrs. B verbally attacks and depreciates her husband, while he makes only half-hearted defensive attempts. Only toward the end of their CDD session does she display some support and concern for him. The following material describes the course of the initial interview with Mr. and Mrs. B:

> Mrs. B initiated the interview. She said that they were here because of their son, who has an underachiever record at school. They came because the high school counselor said they needed marital counseling for their son's sake.
>
> Mr. B stated that for a long time he and his wife felt they could work out the problem between them. Unfortunately, the family difficulties were increasing in so many ways that they were now willing to accept outside help.
>
> Mrs. B indicated that she would go along, but expressed reservations about the efficacy of treatment and feared it might upset her. She suggested that her husband speak now.
>
> Mr. B then commented that his wife thought that he drank too much. He immediately defended his position by stating that he only had two martinis each noon (with his associates) and several highballs after or during dinner.
>
> Mrs. B interrupted him to ask about the two *screwballs* (an important slip of the tongue), "I mean the two screwdrivers." He countered that if she was referring to this morning, it was only because of what had happened last night.
>
> Mrs. B replied that she was tired of having the wool pulled over her eyes. She knew he had been running around with another woman for a year now! Bitterly, she said that she was tired of listening to his lies and of having to check up on him.
>
> Mr. B denied the affair and stated it was just an employer-employee relationship with his secretary; he was fed up with her constant accusations and suspicions.

The transactional, dysfunctional process of accusation, counteraccusation, denial, and attack continued until I intervened (see Chapter XXI for therapeutic principles). After listening and observing this couple, the overt problem they labeled as their trouble with their son was only the backdrop to their relationship turmoil. Even this couple became aware of the multiple levels of their conflict, because they circled every complaint listed under item #9. For this couple as with all my patients, I stressed the *relationship* between the partners as the "identified patient" and encouraged their self-respect and consequently mutual respect between them.

REFERENCES

1. Maholick, Leonard T., and Shapiro, David S.: Changing concepts of psychiatric evaluation. *Am J Psychiat, 119:* 233, 1962.
2. Greene, Bernard L.: Training clergymen in marriage counseling. *Pastoral Counselor, 5:* 42, 1967.
3. Schor, Stanley: Editorial — questionnaire studies. *JAMA, 223:* 1497, 1973.
4. Kaslow, Florence: What personal photos reveal about marital sex conflicts, *J Sex & Marital Therapy, 5:* 134-41, 1979.
5. Jenkins, David C., Hurst, Michael W., and Rose, Robert M.: Life changes — do people really remember? *Arch Gen Psychiat, 36:* 379-84, 1979.
6. Uhlenhuth, E.H., Balter, M.B., Lipman, R.S., et al.: Remembering life events. In Strauss J.S., Babigian, H.M., and Roff, M. (Eds.): *The Origins and Course of Psychopathology: Methods of Longitudinal Research.* New York, Plenum Press, 1977, pp. 117-132.
7. Mace, David R.: Some experiments with marriage counseling procedures. *Family Coordinator, 22:* 23-30, 1973.
8. Lasswell, Marcia E.: Is there a best age to marry? — an interpretation. *Family Coordinator, 23:* 237-42, 1974.
9. Farnsworth, Dana L.: The young adult: an overview. *Am J Psychiat, 131:* 845-51, 1974.
10. Fengler, Alfred P.: The affects of age and education on marital ideology. *J Marr & Family, 35:* 264-70, 1973.
11. Elder, Glen H. Jr. and Rockwell, Richard C.: Marital timing in women's life patterns. *J Family History, 1:* 34-53, 1976.
12. Vincent, Clark E.: Sexual interest in someone older or younger, *Med Aspects Hum Sexuality, 2:* 6, 1968.
13. Berman, Ellen M., Miller, William R., Vines, Neville, and Lief, Harold I.: The age 30 crisis and the 7-year-itch. *J Sex and Marital Therapy, 3:* 197-204, 1977.
14. Stein, Stefan P., Holzman, Stephen, Karasu, Byram T., and Charles, Edward S.: Mid-adult development and psychopathology. *Am J Psychiat, 135:* 676-681, 1978.
15. Vaillant, George E.: *Adaptation to Life.* New York, Little, 1977.
16. Notman, Malkah: Midlife concerns of women: implications of the menopause. *Am J Psychiat, 136:* 1270-74, 1979.
17. Kerckhoff, Richard K.: Marriage and middle age. *Family Coordinator, 25:* 5-11, 1976.
18. Neugarten, Bernice L.: Time, age, and life cycle. *Am J Psychiat, 136:* 887-

93, 1979.
19. McKain, Walter C.: A new look at older marriages. *Family Coordinator, 21:* 61-69, 1972.
20. Kent, Donald P. and Matson, Margaret B.: The impact of health on the aged family. *Family Coordinator, 21:* 29-36, 1972.
21. Davidoff, Ida F.: "Living Together" as a developmental phase: a holistic view. *J Marr & Family Counseling, 3:* 67-76, 1977.
22. Davidoff, "Living Together" as a developmental phase.
23. Coleman, Sandra B.: A developmental stage hypothesis for non-marital dyadic relationships, *J Marr & Family, 3:* 71-76, 1977.
24. Voth, Harold: *Am Med News,* Oct. 20, 1978, p. 18.
25. Veerers, J. E: Incidence of voluntary childlessness. *Med Aspects Hum Sexuality, 13:* 102, 1979.
26. Houseknecht, Sharon K.: Childlessness and marital adjustment. *J Marr & Family, 41:* 259-65, 1979.
27. Scanzoni, John H.: *Sex Roles, Life Styles, and Childbearing.* New York, Free Press, 1975.
28. Kaltreider, Nancy B. and Margolis, Alan G.: Childless by choice. *Am J Psychiat, 134:* 179-82, 1977.
29. Bernard, Jesse: *The Future of Motherhood.* New York, Penguin Books, 1974.
30. Veerers, Incidence of voluntary childlessness.
31. Hawkes, Sharryl and Knox, David: *One Child by Choice.* Englewood Cliffs, NJ: P.H., 1977.
32. Rottenberg, A.: On anger, *Am J Psychiat, 128:* 454-60, 1971.

Chapter V

PATHOLOGICAL COMMUNICATION

PATHOLOGICAL communication is the foremost complaint in dyadic therapy.[1-2] There is still no generally acceptable and complete theory about human communication,[3][4] but anyone involved in pathological communication (lack of talking, constant arguments, and/or violence) can describe its results. It is not surprising that women now list such a complaint more frequently than men. Women who do not work outside the home have more opportunity to attend educational classes[5] and they are finding out that it is socially acceptable to voice their complaints — when the household chores are completed they would like more companionship with their husbands.

Three decades ago Jurgen Ruesch, influenced by the GST, was the first psychiatrist to write extensively on the pragmatic and theoretical exploration of communication. He stated: "Properties or functions described are no longer bound to a structure of a given magnitude, as is the case with the abstractions of the behavioral or social scientists, in as much as input, output, and central processes are characteristic of cell, organ, organism, group, society, or automaton."[6-8] Most communication theories have the transactional characteristics of the GST which incorporates properties or functions of communications, whether verbal[9] or nonverbal. There are many acceptable ways of communicating and relating in a relationship that are unique to the partners and understood only by them.

In order to communicate and relate to each other, the couple must share a code or language. Ruesch[10] also points out that matters get more complicated when one considers actions as messages since involuntary messages[11] may cause as much reaction as intentional ones. Nonverbal communication includes gestures, such as facial expressions,[12-13] posture, voice inflection, the pace and sequence of words, etc. . . . Bodily movements, for example, are an integral part of the self and by observing what the body is doing, the therapist can determine what the self is doing. Scheflen and his colleague Birdwhistell were pioneers in the value of body language and communicational structure. They developed methods of making more exact descriptive accounts of the postural-gestural background of communication ("kinesic").[14-15] They have demonstrated that in ordinary social inter-

57

change between people, signals are picked up unconsciously. A complex transactional exchange occurs since the messages received are continuously being altered through the attitudes of both receiver and sender.

The book by Watzlawick and associates[16-17] on pragmatic communication maintains its value for therapists. They present some attributes of communication that fundamentally influence interpersonal relationships. They discuss these attributes in the nature of tentative axioms. The first axiom is that it is *impossible not to communicate in the presence of others.*

Another axiom differentiates between content and relationship. Frequently arguments are focused on content when the real source of conflict is the disturbed relationship between the couple.

> If a husband brings home flowers for his wife, the content will be the flowers but the relationship will determine the transaction between them. She may comment that it was very thoughtful of him to bring the flowers, give him a kiss and state that they will make a lovely center piece on the dinner table. Or, she may angrily state that if he is trying to buy peace for his rudeness at the breakfast table, he has another guess coming. On the other hand, she may coyly state that although the flowers will make a lovely center piece, does he have ideas in mind for later in the evening — another sort of "piece"?

Another axiom is that the relationship between individuals is influenced by the *dynamic punctuation of the messages between the persons.* A common example is in the game described by Eric Berne,[18] "If It Weren't For Him," where the husband complains that the reason he does not cut the grass is because his wife is always nagging him to do so, whereas the wife retorts that unless she nags him he never does anything around the house.

Still another axiom describes how individuals *"communicate both digitally and analogically,"* with the content feature of communication transmitted as digital and the relationship aspect conveyed as analogical. The digital mode of communication is an arbitrary code of using a word to establish a relation between a name and thing. Analogical communication in nonverbal and includes facial expressions, gestures, body positions, voice modifications and similar phenomena.

The last axiom advanced is that all communicational transactions are either *symmetrical* or *complementary.* In the complementary relationship, one spouse's behavior complements that of his partner's leading to dovetailing and closure, whereas in the symmetrical type the partners tend to mirror each other's behavior, resulting in escalation and the second most common dyadic game, "Uproar."

Clinically, these axioms have been found to be extremely useful in the management of dyadic problems. For example, the impossibility of not communicating makes all relationships interpersonal and communicative and helps explain a technical maneuver, to be presented as Transient Structured Distance in Chapter XXI.

In my clinical cases, I have found the following list of complaints about lack of communicating presented by the couples:

1. Narcissistic partner — whose orientation is self-centered and not on the relationship.
2. Indifference — an actual negative approach toward the partner's feelings, needs, and wishes or even a lack of respect leading to a lack of concern.
3. Inability — an incapability to reinforce and support the partner; what Berne refers to as "stroking."
4. Inflexibility — a rigid set of attitudes and values which do not permit the individual to deviate from a fixed pattern or code.
5. Inexperience — a lack of experience in positive, meaningful relationships.
6. Crossed transactions — digital and analogic modes of communicating in which areas of verbal and nonverbal communications have little in common.
7. Avoidance maneuvers — where one partner avoids communication by withdrawing (however, since in a relationship one cannot not communicate, the partner clearly gets the message of rejection).
8. Distortion — messages are received, but not as sent.

The following extracts from clinical cases illustrate the above:

NARCISSISTIC PARTNER (1), the most common complaint.

Mrs. A bitterly stated: "He seems more of an observer to life than a participant and is wrapped up in his own private world."

Mr. A calmly commented: "She is impatient in discussing anything. She is highly emotional and can easily get upset. She insists on having things her way." (Symmetrical escalation in this couple.) "At the height of her temper she is very insulting. Her words are very sharp and hurting." (Each accuses the other of being self-centered.)

The conjoint diagnostic and disposition session highlighted their narcissistic orientation. He was very polite, talked about their problems in an intellectual manner, and seemed embarrassed at seeking therapy. She gave the impression of being a somewhat angry individual. She was also very courteous, handled the conversation about their difficulties in an intellectual manner, and gave the impression that there was little hope for change in the marriage but was willing to seek therapy because her husband wished this. Both spouses seemed reluctant to state their conflicts in any manner which might reflect discredit on the other. They said that their marriage seemed to have developed down to a practical situation rather than a marriage; also, they went their own way and both were strong-willed (lack of complementary closure). Both complained of lack of communication, that they do not or cannot talk things through, accusing each other of not comprehending their communications (although both are college graduates). The major difficulties and arguments seemed to evolve around finances because they argue over what to buy, how to save, and what to do with their money. (The symmetrical escalation in this couple is a good example of a disturbance of communication due to confusion between content and relationship, based on the question of who was right in regard to some minor content matter, each accusing the other of being self-centered.)

2. *Indifference* was the next in frequency of complaint:

> Mrs. B began the conjoint session by bitterly complaining about her husband, "After we were married, Jim started going to school, and this was my first experience away from home, pregnant, and in a strange locale knowing no one. There was no time spent together because he always had to study. The only conversation I had to offer was neighborhood gossip, which he made clear to me that he wasn't interested in hearing. My rules around the home were never backed up by him and only when his things were disturbed did he correct the children. The further apart we grew in communication the further apart we grew sexually, and gradually I was not anxious for his advances. Most of the time I was too tired physically and mentally and furious at his indifference to my feelings and needs. He'd demand sex or start an argument. To avoid trouble I would submit. Now I don't care at all. I've gotten to the point where reading, painting or knitting satisfy the need I once had for his companionship."
>
> Mr. B replied: "I admit that when I was at school I was too wrapped up in myself and my studies. But now she avoids me and seldom tells me about the children's problems as they develop. She must be left alone, shut-up in her bedroom, she reads for hours until midnight or later. No show of affection is normal among man and wife, she claims. When I try to communicate with her, she withdraws and then blames me for being indifferent."

Indifference, which is a deadly form of rejection, implies, the partner no longer exists.[19] As one individual aptly stated: "I may as well be talking to the wall in most instances as to talk to her."

3. *Inability,* the third most common complaint.

> Mr. C began the interview by stating that probably their basic problem was total lack of communication and their sex life was not satisfactory to his wife.
>
> Mrs. C interrupted, with controlled anger she added: "What little sex we have (note the needle) has been quite satisfactory, but there is a financial problem and basic religious differences. Since the very start of our marriage he tends to stay in bed till late in the mornings and is always late for work. We are different in makeup. I have a lot of get up and go, he is the opposite. When he was courting I misinterpreted his inability to give of himself as the mark of a gentleman and respect for me as a woman."
>
> Mr. C comments that in his childhood there was little display of affection between his parents and very little communication: "Our family was like that painting of the New England farmer, his wife, and the pitchfork. I would like to talk to my wife, but it doesn't come easy. On the other hand, I've been raked over the coals for the last ten years and receive nothing but constant criticism from her. I have to do everything on schedule, and this irritates me no end. I do not want to eat as soon as I get home from work. I would like to relax with a drink."
>
> Mrs. C at this point, started to cry, stating that she does not know why he hates her so. She is, she supposes, very critical, but she doesn't like to see him go off to work unshaven, with holes in his shoes, and she supposes that instead of bringing him up to her normal standards, she has slipped down to his (another needle).
>
> He retorts: that the lack of sex is probably due to his anger, as they argue all day long and she expects to have sex that night.

This inability to support and reinforce the partner is primarily the replaying of a past faulty parental model of identification. One partner succinctly put it: "We are not in close communication with each other and never have been. It is a definite lack in both of us to give to each other. I feel we cannot nourish it now."

4. *Inflexibility,* fourth in frequency.

> Mr. and Mrs. D were referred by their respective divorce lawyers. Mrs. D related the following: "Lack of communication has always been a problem between us. He's a schemer and I'm a dreamer. Our minds start working on opposite poles and sometimes it takes forever for them to meet. I hurt his feelings by what I say; and he hurts mine by what he says, with or without any intention of doing so. Until recently I practically had to make an appointment with him to talk anything over. It is difficult for him to even discuss serious matters with me, and invariably it goes through an argument before a solution can be reached. The argument part for years produced a ha-

rangue in him and tears in me. Finally, a year ago, I realized I was
not that bad and began to talk back. I was confident enough to be
able to defend myself rationally. I was not able to do this before
because I know that most of the things he complains of in me have
plenty of truth in them, and for this I have no defense and can only
try to improve. I can tell him why, but that does not seem to help. I
had not known specifically what was wrong with him until last year
when I read some psychology books. When it comes right down to it,
I still can't understand what he says to me. He often tells me how
stupid I am, but it must be because I can't see his viewpoint. When I
believe he is wrong and point this out and tell him why, he can be
expected to fly into a rage. So the pattern of his anger and my tears,
which lasted for fifteen years, has now changed to his anger and my
calmness. I get very upset, but I am outwardly calm, and he is angry
and violent. It's almost as if I have to lie to satisfy him, that is, in
order to resolve an argument. Everything has to be his way about the
management of finances, the rearing of children, the appearance of
the home, and so on."

Inexperience (5), *crossed transactions* (6), *avoidance maneuvers* (7),
and *distortion* (8) occurred in the remaining 20 percent of the couples.
An example of inexperience is the following: "He seems to lack a
basic understanding of women and their variable moods. I'd like a
more outward show of affection and conversation! He just doesn't
have the experience. Marriage should be the beginning of life, not the
end."

In crossed transactions, frequently the problem is in content and
relationship communication. Digital messages (content) are concise,
but analogic communication (relationship) is antithetical, frequently
resulting in incompatible interpretations. As one husband complained:

> We are on different wavelengths. We have a constant communica-
> tion problem and misinterpret each other. She takes everything I say
> literally. She says she can't tell when I am jesting and when I am
> serious. When I bring her a box of candy, I don't know whether she
> will react with pleasure, suspicion, or anger. Intellectually we com-
> municate well, emotionally we do not. I write poetry which she
> judges by mechanical standards and fails to recognize the spiritual
> and emotional content to any significant degree. She does not appear
> to appreciate my expression of love, beauty or compassion."

Avoidance maneuvers, illustrated below, where one partner avoids
communicating by withdrawing: "I don't communicate with her because I am always afraid of discussing most problems for fear of an
argument. My wife is quick tempered and usually takes things the

wrong way so I keep my distance."

Another partner related: "Whenever we have an argument, there is one of two methods used: "cold war" — sometimes lasting as long as ten days, and I would always be the one to break the ice even though the disagreement was started by him — or he would lose his temper and hit me. So I avoid him as much as possible."

Another woman bitterly complained: "He is noncommunicative. I can't talk to him. He won't admit that I am right. I am right 98 percent of the time. He has taken all the fun out of life. He tolerates all my abuse and doesn't defend himself. I am talkative and he is closemouthed. He says he avoids talking to me in order to avoid arguments. I scream to get a rise out of him but can't get it."

Distortion: "She interprets things I say in her own way, which tends to distort and create tension and arguments."

My clinical experience coincides with the observation of David Mace who states: " . . . that the fundamental cause of marital (dyadic) failure . . . is the inability resolve the *anger* (italics added) which is inevitably generated in an intimate relationship."[20-27] Although we all have experienced the emotion of anger, the definition of anger is subsumed under terms as hostility, aggression, violence, and so on. If anger is not expressed overtly, it can manifest itself in depression (obvious or "masked"), destructive acts, and interpersonal problems, all of which involve the three systems of the GST. Anger is a normal reaction that enables the individual to cope with crises, whether frustration or threats to one's survival. The physiological responses to anger, whether due to fear or frustration, were inherited from the beginnings of man as life was a constant struggle for survival. Civilization has decreased danger, but increased frustration, especially in interpersonal relationships. Mace[22] delineates four forms of anger: initial anger, an entirely healthy reaction; sustained anger; suppressed anger; and vented anger. Every relationship involves ambivalence — love as well as anger. Freud* stressed the phenomena of ambivalence in his writings. A relationship does not exist when emotions are not present, either bilaterally or *unilaterally*. It is important to remember

---

*Freud broke many of the idols of traditional psychology when he introduced his psychodynamic theory of behavior. His seminal ideas require no emphasis here. Psychoanalysis postulates that behavior is primarily the outcome of a hypothesized interplay of intrapsychic vectors which follow closely the thermodynamic laws of energy in physics. The interdependence between man and his environmental matrix remain a neglected field of orthodox psychoanalytic study. Certain basic psychoanalytic concepts remain important for understanding human behavior: the unconscious, transference, *ambivalence*, conflict and repression.

that anger often results in violence (regardless of the educational, occupation, or social status[23]). Therefore, I was not surprised when my data revealed that constant arguments, many ending in physical abuse,[24-25] was the second most frequent relationship complaint. This complaint in my data was equally distributed between the sexes, about 50 percent.[26-27]

Domestic violence is a serious problem for women ("the battered women syndrome") [28-29] and even men. In my experience this complaint occurred in about 5 percent of the couples. Various elements of the GST framework can spur domestic violence: alcoholism[30] (intrapersonal system); incessant questioning about alleged infidelity ("district attorney syndrome") . . . interpersonal system; excessive irritability from within or external to the home environment; the request for divorce or termination of a relationship; and at times, sadomasochistic relationships. In 1971, an entire volume of the Journal of Marriage and the Family was devoted to violence and the family, and in March 1978, the Senate and House subcommittes listened to the outcry from the American Public. It is important to distinguish assertiveness from aggression which helps define the issue and problem. In assertiveness there is a direct assertion of an individual's need or wish, whereas in "aggression" there is a threat of punishment upon the partner to perform the desired act.[31] As the public demands solutions and attention to domestic violence, the therapist may be able to make a significant contribution within his office as well as through research and published material.

REFERENCES

1. Rausch, Harold, Barry, William A., Hertel, Richard E., and Swain, Mary Ann: *Communication, Conflict, and Marriage.* San Francisco, CA, Jossey-Bass, 1974.
2. Ferreira, Antonio J. and Winter, William D.: Information exchange and silence in normal and abnormal families. *Family Process, 7:* 251, 1968.
3. Ackerman, Brian L.: Relational paradox — toward a language of interactional sequences, *J Marital & Family Therapy, 5:* 29-38, 1979.
4. Hammond, Corydon D., Hepworth, Dean H., and Smith, Veon G.: *Improving Therapeutic Communication.* San Francisco, CA, Jossey-Bass, 1977.
5. Wells, Richard A. and Figurel, Jeanne A.: Techniques of structured communication training. *Family Coordinator, 28:* 275-81, 1979.
6. Ruesch, Jurgen and Bateson, Gregory: *Communications: The Social Matrix of Psychiatry.* New York, Norton, 1951.
7. Berger, Milton M. (Ed.): *Beyond the Double Bind.* New York: Brunner-

Mazel, 1978.

8. Ruesch, Jurgen: Social process, *Arch Gen Psychiat, 15:* 577, 1967.

9. Rosen, Victor H.: In Atkin, Samuel and Jucovy, Milton E. *Style, Character and Language.* New York: Aronson, 1977.

10. Ruesch, Jurgen: *Knowledge in Action: Communication, Social Operations, and Management.* New York, Aronson, 1975.

11. Spiegel, John P. and Machotka, Pavel: *Messages of the Body.* New York, Free Press, 1974.

12. Ekman, Paul and Friesen, Wallace V.: *Unmasking the Face: A Guide to Recognizing Emotions from Facial Clues.* Englewood Cliffs, NJ, P-H, 1975.

13. Scheflen, Albert E.: Susan smiled — an explanation in family therapy. *Family Process, 17:* 59-68, 1978.

14. Scheflen, Albert E.: *Body Language and Social Order: Communication as Behavior Control.* Englewood Cliffs, NJ, P-H, 1972.

15. Scheflen, Albert E.: *Communicational Structure: Analysis of a Psychotherapy Transaction.* Bloomington, Ind U Pr, 1973.

16. Watzlawick, Paul, Beavin, Janet H., and Jackson, Don D.: *Pragmatics of Human Communication, A Study of Interactional Patterns, Pathologies, and Paradoxes.* New York, Norton, 1967.

17. Jackson, Don D. and Bodin, Arthur M.: Paradoxical communication and the marital paradox. In Rosenbaum, Salo and Alger, Ian (Eds.): *The Marriage Relationship.* New York, Basic Books, 1968, pp. 3-20.

18. Berne, Eric: *Games People Play.* New York, Grove Press, 1964.

19. Watzlawick et al., Pragmatics of Human Communication.

20. Mace, David R.: Marital intimacy and the deadly love-anger cycle. *J Marriage & Family Counseling, 3:* 131-137, 1976.

21. Charny, Israel W.: Marital love and hate. *Family Process, 8:* 1, 1969.

22. Mace, D.R., Marital intimacy and the deadly love-anger cycle.

23. Bailey, Kent G.: The concept of phylogenetic regression. *J Am Acad Psychoanal, 6:* 5-35, 1978.

24. Chapman, Jane R. and Gates, Margaret: *The Victimization of Women.* Beverly Hills, CA, Sage Publications, 1978.

25. Trainor, Dorothy: Wives also seen as instigators of spouse abuse. *Psychiatric News, 12:* 30-31, 1977.

26. Gelles, Richard J.: *The Violent home: A Study of Physical Aggression Between Husbands and Wives.* Beverly Hills, CA, Sage Publications, 1974.

27. Seiden, Anne M.: Aggression: Toward women and by women. *Psychiatric News, 13:* 20-21, 1978.

28. Benedek, Elissa P. and Symonds, Martin: Incidents of battered wives said under-reported. *Psychiatric News, 13:* 25-31, 1978.

29. Roy, Maria (Ed.): *Battered Women: A Psychosociological Study of Domestic Violence.* New York, Van Nostrand Reinhold Co. (Litton Educational Pub.), 1977.

30. Hanks, S.E. and Rosenbaum, C.P.: Battered women: A study of women who live with violent alcohol-abusing men. *Am J Orthopsychiat, 47:* 291-306, 1977.
31. Alberti, Robert E. and Emmons, Michael L.: Assertion training in marital counseling. *J Marr & Family Counseling, 2:* 49-54, 1976.

Chapter VI

UNFULFILLED EMOTIONAL NEEDS
AND THE INNER CHILD

WHEN my questionnaire was formulated, two decades ago, the most frequent marital complaint was unfulfilled emotional needs. Currently this complaint is third in frequency and is occurring in 50 percent of the dyads I treat. Women complain more frequently about unfulfilled emotional needs than do men, in a ratio of 3 to 2. The frustration from unmet emotional needs centers within each person's "inner child" (a concept developed by Missildine[1]). Dyadic discord can result when the inner child feels that the dyadic partner is overly critical[2] or abusive ("nonstroking" behavior), or when a partner feels he/she is unlovable. Because it is the voice of the inner child which is the complainer in unfulfilled emotional needs, therapists need to evaluate what portion of the dyad's discord is due to the intrapersonal inner child's voice and what steps can be taken to relieve or fulfill the needs of the inner child. Without understanding the conceptual model of the inner child, it would be difficult to analyze its needs or to fulfill them.

In the early 1960s, Missildine observed that somewhere and at some time everyone was a child; at the same time, he noted that adult distress, unhappiness, and much dyadic discord often stems from ignoring our lives as children, discounting our childhood, or omitting it in our adult considerations about ourselves and others. The ongoing voice of the inner child influences, often determines, and frequently dominates the individual's relationships. The degree of impact depends upon the intensity of resonance or dissonance with the other two intrapersonal voices: the parental voice and the pia voice (*p*erceptive, *i*ntegrative, and *a*daptive processes/functions).

The inner child develops when the earliest emotional needs occur — in the early relationship between the infant and mother. Thus closeness, warmth, tenderness, fondling, and kissing are basic to the normal emotional maturation of each person. The term *libidinal* (coined by Freud) covers a wide spectrum of feelings and behavior; this spectrum's range includes warmth to sexual intimacy and depends upon the biopsychosocial functioning level of the individual. The inner child is involved in *play* and *creativity*. In the second year of life, the stimulating world of *curiosity* emerges, which is the fourth voice of the inner child. With progressive maturation, the libidinal needs surface and seek fulfillment. Sexual dissatisfaction is the fourth most common dyadic complaint (see BRQ #22). Recently, Heinz Kohut's[3] concepts on narcissism add another dimension to the attributes of the inner child.

When people disown, ignore or dismiss their inner child's emotional needs, or when they try to overcome these by scolding and belittling themselves (often through a silent and internal dialogue), discord and emotional frustration often results. The very nature of humanity's emotional development makes it impossible to avoid the inner child's needs.

The inner child functions by utilizing energy. This energy can be conceptualized by Franz Alexander's "surplus energy" postulate.[4] He describes the individual as having a daily specified amount of energy that is primarily used for utilitarian functions such as eating, breathing, and so on. Excess energy is discharged in either play or sex with such factors as age, maturation, inclination, external circumstances, and personal preference having a decisive input.

The voice of the inner child remains about the same throughout life, while the parental and pia voices are subject to aging and environmental stress. The parental voice expresses the sociocultural values and attitudes proposed or modeled by significant others. At all times the parental voice expresses value orientations and/or stroking attitudes.

In reviewing the complaints of unfulfilled emotional needs, the six main complaints are listed below in order of frequency.

1. Frustration of dependency needs.
2. Making the inner child feel inadequate.
3. Making the inner child feel unloveable.
4. Avoidance of household repsonsibilities.
5. Seeing partner as "another child in the household."
6. Differences in recreational needs.

Clinical vignettes illustrating the above will follow. A example of frustration of dependency needs: "He is not happy about the things that make me happy, such as, the Christmas season, birthdays, some aspects of vacations. If I am ill or have any physical problem, he ignores me. When I burned my hand, he never asked how it was or if it was healing. He never offers to help around the house or with the children if I am ill in bed. Each time one of our children were born, he has gone to bed ill, leaving me to tend the baby and him!" The second category of unfulfilled emotional needs: a variation of the marital games described by Berne as "Yes But," consists of making the inner child feel inadequate. For example:

> Mr. and Mrs. C were referred for marital therapy. His main com-
> plaint was that she was drinking too much: "She does not get drunk,
> but three highballs when we go out socially is too much. When she
> has a few drinks she tells me off. We have been married fifteen years
> and this has never happened before. I saw my father's health deterio-
> rate from drinking too much. He was a hard worker, a kind and soft
> person. Occasionally he would stop after work for a few beers with
> his friends. He would catch hell from mother when he got home.
> Mother was the strong person in our family, relatively good-natured,
> domineering, immaculate housekeeper and a good cook. She criti-
> cized my father in everything he did around the house."

> Mrs. C, a petite, pleasant, cooperative woman in her midthirties.
> She worked in the same office since her marriage as a private secre-
> tary: "We have never quarreled until recently when I have had a few
> drinks I tell him off. We have no children because he does not want
> any. Everything has to be his way. He wants everything I do to be
> perfect. When I am in the kitchen he will watch me and count my
> steps to correct me if I'm not logical and precise. He can't stand
> doors left ajar. He watches me prepare food, what pans or pots I
> should use, what condiments to add, etc . . . This makes me nervous.
> He is a good cook, in fact everything he does is perfect. At times he
> will come home with clothes he purchased for me. He has good taste
> but I would prefer to buy my own clothes. Now more and more I feel
> like a half-wit and stupid, yet, I have a lot of responsibility at work.
> My boss thinks highly of me, but my husband will first praise me
> then criticize me."

This is a good example of the "Pygmalion" syndrome. Mr. C is
playing the "records" of his mother in his "parental" voice. The
following is a vignette of the third category: Making the inner child
feel unlovable:

> Mr. and Mrs. D came for therapy at the request of their respective
> divorce lawyers. Mr. D, a contented bachelor at thirty, had been
> pressured into marriage after three years of steady dating by his wife.
> Both are intelligent, have mutual interests and happy in their respec-
> tive careers. Mr. D admitted that after marriage he began to with-
> draw emotionally from his wife when she became more possessive
> of him; and that he felt with marriage she was showing her true
> self.

> Mrs. D denied being possessive, but complained that her husband
> was too wrapped up in his work and too exhausted when he came
> home to care about her needs: "I've gotten to the point where I feel
> that I should leave him, yet, I am afraid of being alone. I hate to lose
> what I have, modest though it is. He is so exhausted when he comes
> home. It just occurred to me that when he wants sex he has to get

half gassed. I must be a lousy love object that he has to be intoxicated to make love . . . I try to meet his needs, but get no feedback. I don't sense any particular respect for me, and many times, down right antagonism. He never apologizes when he is wrong. To be treated like you don't exist is the worst thing in the world. I try to please him my making special gourmet meals, things he likes, but not a word of praise or thanks. At times I get the feeling that I am repulsive to him."

The following abstracts are typical of the fourth category, avoidance of household responsibilities:

"I am furious at my wife. She is lazy and ungiving to me and the children. I can't count on her for anything. I have the feeling that any man who treated her nicely could have been her husband. She gives no affection and apparently expects none. I have to make my own breakfast. She usually gets up about ten in the morning. It's a good thing that we have a cook or the children would not be fed either. She wants to be a 'free agent' with all the benefits of a wife but none or few of the responsibilities."

Another example of #4 where an aggressive woman married to a passive, effeminate man, gives this complaint: "The masculine duties around our house are done by me; such as cut, rake and fertilize the grass; wash halls and paint, refinish furniture; tile the floors; etc . . . These are not a woman's responsibility. Whenever I ask him to do something around the house, he always says, tomorrow. Yet tomorrow never comes around so I end up doing it."

The complaint of unfulfilled emotional needs, #5 on the list, as that of seeing a partner as "another child in the household" example follows:

"He does not fill my emotional needs in that I do not feel protected by him, except our financial needs. His instinctive response to anything I say is, "No!" He is more of an observer to life than a participant. He is wrapped up in his own private world to an extreme degree. I feel like his mother, always pushing him to things. I am the boss of the family which I definitely do not want to be. If we go out for an evening, it is at my suggestion. I have to decide where to go and what to do. I consider myself mother of three children, he being the third child. I need someone to lean on and to look up to."

Finally, #6, differences in recreational needs of the inner child complaint (BRQ item #19 gives significant information on the creativity, curiosity and play of the inner child). Typical of this complaint is the following: "My husband and I share little in common; he likes Westerns and I like Puccini."

Question #10 deals with any prior individual, group, or relationship therapy: *"If you have ever received any help with respect to yourself, your marriage or relationship, circle the following: psychiatrist, physician, psychologist, counselor, clergy, social worker, agency, or other. Give names(s) of person, address, and your opinion of the results.*

Past and current information helps evaluate the individual's situation, clues about motivation for therapy and when the problem began. Often it is the woman who seeks help which may be a culturally induced role. Also, the therapist learns the type of treatment the patients had received in the past (directive, nondirective, or explorative) that may influence the overall course of therapy. Finally, with written permission from the patient(s), the therapist can request clinical information from a previous therapist, agency; or hospital.

REFERENCES

1. Missildine, Hugh W.: *Your Inner Child of the Past.* New York, Simon and Schuster. 1963.
2. Berne, Eric: *Transactional Analysis in Psychotherapy.* New York, Grove Press, 1961.
3. Kohut, Heinz: *The Analysis of Self.* New York: Intl Univ Pr, 1971.
4. Alexander, Franz: Lecture at the Chicago Institute for Psychoanalysis, 1948.

Chapter VII

SUICIDE

SUICIDE is a multidisciplinary problem.*,[1] My
experience parallels that of Ross: "... often leading questions about
suicidal thoughts are necessary, for direct questioning will often reveal otherwise concealed suicidal intentions. There is no evidence that
such questions asked in a proper way have any aggravating effect
upon the patient. The reverse is usually true...."[2] Question #11 asks:
*Have you or your partner ever attempted suicide? yes — no — If so,
give dates and details.*

Heriditary research, particularly in the 1970s, has validated the view
that family history is as important to a therapist as obtaining a personal history. This question also includes some family history: *Has
anyone in your or your partner's family (including close relatives)
ever attempted suicide? yes — no — If yes, give details.* Answers to
this question may reveal primary affective disorders (manic-depressive
illness) that have some hereditary base[3] and can alert the therapist to
suicidal tendencies. My theory is to always trace the multigenerational
course of each individual with a personal or family history of suicide,
this can include thoughts, attempts, and fatalities. I share the responsibility for suicidal information with significant others and raise the
issue in the diagnostic, individual, and conjoint sessions.

When the BRQ alerts me to suicidal tendencies, I then proceed with
individual and/or conjoint diagnostic sessions. This may include
significant others and focuses on the suicidal issue. Since effective
denial mechanisms are extremely likely in both the family and the
person who has attempted suicide, I spend whatever time is necessary
to permit those involved to understand the psychological dynamics of
the suicidal act.[4] Often the nonsuicidal partner does not relate the
suicide attempt (either on the BRQ or in a therapy session) because of
conscious or unconscious wishes that the partner would in effect
"drop dead" and his guilt about these wishes. Influences contributing
to emotional instability include *experience of loss,* as friends and
family geographically move away; *fragmentation of family networks;*

---

*The Suicide Prevention Center in Los Angeles, under the direction of Edwin S.,
Schneidman, Norman L. Faberow, and Robert E. Litman, has been in the forefront in
furthering basic understanding about the phenomenon of suicide.

degenerative and cancerous conditions; singleness, due to separation, divorce, or death, *loss of work opportunities; destructiveness of drug addictions;* etc . . .

The myth that people who verbalize their intent or have made unsuccessful attempts at suicide will never commit a successful suicide is obviously *untrue!*[5] Therapists maintaining a high *index of suspicion* can frequently prevent the loss of life.[6-8] There is a definite relationship between depression and suicide. A *depressive diagnosis* is often as good a predictor of suicidal behavior as is a history of attempted suicide — about 3 percent will attempt suicide one year later and 6 percent in subsequent years.[9] One-fifth of those who have made *serious* suicide attempts, commit a successful suicide within the next five year period.[10]

It is very important, in the prevention of suicide, that the therapist reassures the patient that he is available at all times. In addition to being available, the therapist should impress upon the nonsuicidal partner or significant others the seriousness of the situation and the importance of *close surveillance.* Clinical experience indicates continuous surveillance for high risk suicidal persons during the first three to six months after the initial therapeutic contact.

Depression is the most common psychiatric diagnosis made. The word *depression* covers a bell-shaped curve spectrum of moods and behavior. In this clinical syndrome there is a cluster of symptoms of severity and persistence: *dysphoric mood,* accompanied by anergia, sleep and appetite disturbances, loss of pleasure, feelings of self-reproach and guilt, *suicidal thoughts,* etc. At times, it seems, we know very little, as Shakespeare[11] (at the turn of the seventeenth century) in *The Merchant of Venice,* Antonio's soliloquy so aptly tells us:

"In sooth I know not why I am so sad.
It wearies me; you say it wearies you;
But how I caught it, found it, or came by it,
What stuff 'tis made of, whereof it is born,
I am to learn."

Although we do not know what causes cyclothymic reactions or how to adequately classify the various types of depression, I have conceptualized these reactions[12] along a continuum that may be divided into three categories:

1. *Cyclothymic tendencies, mild* mood swings that pass reasonably rapidly and consist of sadness, depression, or feeling blue and that are present in everyone.
2. A *cyclothymic personality* is characterized by *moderate* highs and lows in mood. This type of an individual frequently relates,

if questioned, a past history of several depressive episodes of increasing frequency, intensity and duration. Caution is indicated in advising marriage to an individual with this type of personality.

3. *Cyclothymic psychosis* (primary affective disorder or manic-depressive illness) is characterized by *severe* mood swings.

Often the cyclothymic personality develops a primary affective disorder that contributes to turbulent dyadic relationships, with devastating effects, not only on the partner but also on the children. The following clinical vignette is an example:

> A male, twenty-five years of age, handsome, well built, was seen in an emergency consultation. He was in a severe, (but not psychotic) anxious depression. He was extremely worried about his impending wedding. He was completing his graduate course in two weeks and his wedding was the day after graduation. His medical history revealed two depressive episodes — one occurred in his senior year in high school, lasting a week; the other occurred in his last year of college, lasting three weeks. He had been symptom-free up until this time, but then he became restless and irritable. He couldn't sleep, would awake at four each morning. He had trouble concentrating, felt worthless, and was concerned about his impending marriage. The courtship was smooth, uneventful, and happy. His fiancée was attractive, intelligent, and a college graduate. She was happily looking forward to their marriage.
>
> His depression began to lift when I suggested he postpone his wedding and get intensive psychotherapy. Treatment was continued under another therapist who advised him not to get married. However, he went against this advice and did get married. His depression returned; he made a serious suicidal attempt and he was hospitalized. At that time his wife was caring for their six-month old baby.

Time is the important factor in reversing a depression, usually this occurs spontaneously. The reactive depressions account for about 90 percent of the depressives seeking help. The following vignette is typical of the reactive depressive reaction to a threatened divorce:

> Mrs. A, a slim, short, brunette, was referred by her minister for marital therapy and treatment for her depression. Initially she maintained a firm control over both her feelings and her verbalizations by pursing her lips and by a precise, clipped manner of speech. As the sessions progressed, she appeared to relax her controls and express deep feelings of depression and a longing for resolving her marital difficulties. Aside from a prolonged period of inadequate sexual adjustment and an inability to communicate her feelings to her husband, she bemoaned her husband's abrupt announcement that he

wanted a divorce.

At this point her husband was invited to join her therapy sessions. He complained that she was frigid since the time of their honeymoon, but she disagreed. She stated that by the end of their honeymoon: "he no longer was romantic; no foreplay and acted like a brute. I tried to tell him, but he didn't say anything or answer. I resented him more and more, and our sex relations deteriorated, we had sex twice a year. I also resented his traveling and being home only on weekends. But when he asked for a divorce, I went to pieces. I couldn't stop crying. I was so lonely. I don't want a divorce. I am so remorseful about what I have done." At this point Mrs. A cried uncontrollably. She stated that the only solution was to kill herself and her child. She was given considerable reassurance, told that there was hope since her husband was cooperating in the therapy. She was told that she could call me at any time, day or night, if she felt the need.

Mr. A was pleasant and cooperative. While complaining about his wife's frigidity, he seemed genuinely concerned about hurting her through a divorce action. He had no feelings of love but just "admiration" for his wife. Besides, he revealed, there was another woman who met all his needs, both emotional and sexual. He did agree to therapy, particularly when it was pointed out to him that she could commit suicide and also take the life of their child.

This couple illustrates a reactive depression on the part of the spouse to the request for a divorce, with the depression resulting from a turning in of hostility. Unable to attack her husband outwardly, she thinks of destroying the internal mental representation of him, but in so doing she destroys herself.

In another somewhat similar situation where I was treating the husband, and another therapist was treating the wife, the man was not willing to cooperate by waiting until his wife was anchored in treatment. When she found out that he wanted a divorce, she killed her three children and herself.[13]

In conclusion, although all three systems of the GST are involved in precipitating suicide thoughts, feelings and/or acts, I continue to classify depressive disorders into two categories: primary affective disorder (endogenous) is mainly a biological illness involving all subsystems of the *intrapersonal* with secondary interlocking of the interpersonal and environmental forces; the second category includes secondary or reactive depressions where a specific event or group of life events have precipitated an illness.[14] In this category, all three systems of the GST are involved, but primarily the interpersonal and environmental.

Psychological tests have little value in assessing suicidal risks.[15]

Motto's[16] research suggests that a clinical model approach of specific predictor variables may be a better indicator of the likelihood of suicide.

REFERENCES

1. Fawcett, Jan, Leff, Melitta, and Bunney, William E.: Suicide. *Arch Gen Psychiat, 21:* 129, 1969.
2. Ross, Mathew: Suicide among college students. *Am J Psychiat, 16:* 220, 1969.
3. Greene, B. L. et al.: Marital therapy when one spouse has a primary affective disorder. *Am J Psychiat, 133:* 827-30, 1976.
4. Cantor, Pamela C.: The effects of youthful suicide on the family. *Psychiatric Opinion, 12:* 6-11, 1975.
5. Kovacs, Maria, Beck, Aaron T., and Weissman, Arlene: The communication of suicidal attempt — a reexamination. *Arch Gen Psychiat, 33:* 198-201, 1976.
6. Wetzel, Richard D.: Hopelessness, depression, and suicidal a intent. *Arch Gen Psychiat, 33:* 1069-73, 1976.
7. Beck, Aaron T., Resnick, Harvey L.P., and Lettieri, Dan J. *The Prevention of Suicide.* Bowie, Md., Charles Press, 1974.
8. Yamamoto, Joe, Roath, Michael, and Litman, Robert: Suicides in the "New" community hospital. *Arch Gen Psychiat, 28:* 101-2, 1973.
9. Avery, David and Winokur, George: Suicide, attempted suicide, and relapse rates in depression, *Arch Gen Psychiat, 35:* 749-53, 1978.
10. Rosen, David H.: The serious suicide attempt. *JAMA, 235;* 2105-10, 1976.
11. Shakespeare, William: The Merchant of Venice. In Wright, William Aldis (Ed.): The Complete Works of William Shakespeare. Philadelphia, Blakiston, 1936, pp. 447-476.
12. Greene, Bernard L., Contraindications to marriage. *Med Aspects Hum Sexuality, 2:* 4, 1968.
13. Kiev, Ari: Cluster analysis profiles of suicidal attempts. *Am J Psychiat, 133:* 150, 1976.
14. Weissman, Mryna M. et al.: Symptom patterns in primary and secondary depression. *Arch Gen Psychiat, 34:* 854-62, 1977.
15. Neuringer, Charles (Ed.): *Psychological Assessment of Suicidal Risk.* Springfield, IL, Thomas, 1974.
16. Motto, Jerome A.: The psychopathology of suicide — a clinical model approach. *Am J Psychiat, 136:* 516-20, 1979.

Chapter VIII

THE RELATIONSHIP PHASES

love is not blind,
it is deaf.

QUESTION #12 involves information about dyadic relationships. There are three sections: (a) *How did you meet your partner?* (b) *Describe your courtship (relationship), giving duration and whether smooth, stormy, etc. (c) If married, did you have a honeymoon? yes — no — Describe your reactions, partner's behavior, etc.*

PARTNER SELECTION

A dyadic relationship occurs between two individuals who are unique in their existence and may have met without strategy of intelligence nor magic of romance, but through sheer chance. In spite of many longitudinal studies on pair selection and development and the verification of research data/theoretical formulations, conclusions have not confirmed any one concept.[1] Efforts at developing typologies or theories of relationship patterns are of questionable value, even for couples in specific localities (individuals are too unique to make valid broad generalizations). There are so many diverse elements involved in the selection of a partner that an understanding of all inputs from the three GST systems contributes the best current framework in understanding the elements and processes involved.

My collective clinical data of 2400 couples shows that 60 percent met through pure chance, 35 percent met through friends and relatives,[2] and that 5 percent met by using an intellectually planned strategy.

In reviewing relationships occurring by chance, the literature indicates that meaningful pair-couplings occur by phases.[3-8] The first stage is being "attracted to" the other, consciously or unconsciously.[9-10] The couple's response to each other may be that of pleasantness or a sense of comfort. The next step in the process was a search for mutuality of things, thoughts, people, professions, activities, and/or interests, etc. which they could share. Frequently, each person projects on the other his unconscious gestalts (those projective identifications which may or may not be valid for their relevancy to the current relationship!). When projections are occurring in their transactions, these may work constructively or destructively. The latter frequently cause disappointment, startling surprises, and/or painful confrontations. Sharing is a basis for continuing the relationship. During this phase, frequently without the full awareness of either person, projections occur. Such occurrences include projective identifications both conscious and unconscious[11-12] which may or may not be valid for the two people. If the couple seeks therapy before they consummate their relationship with marriage, they may be able to explore the underlying dynamics and processes and make any unconscious elements conscious.

Another phase in a couple's ongoing development involves the acceptance of mutually assigned roles. During premarital therapy, this area is a significant one to assess. The therapist should note if the couple has a good "fit." The partners need not be identical in their manner of behavior or in their personality configurations (intrapersonal system input), but they should be able to communicate, to compromise, and participate in a mutual give and take (sensitivity, caring, self-respect, and mutual respect are only some factors included in this area). The couple should have a commitment that is not hedonistic. Such good relationships reflect a sense of constant "*work*." Work in this sense does not mean unpleasant exhaustion, but rather continual interest and sensitivity in the needs of one's partner. At times these people should display a "helping out" in physical and nonphysicial areas, i.e. roles, responsibilities, chores. The therapist should not assume that dissonant orientations indicate a poor "fit." Rather, the therapist should view all behavior in terms of the acceptability between the couple. Pollak's four dimensions of need complementarity is a great help to evaluate the core relationship in a pair-coupling (see Chapter II).

Another important aspect to relationship evaluation includes the frequency and form of quarreling and the way in which conflict is resolved.[13] In the therapeutic setting, a new perspective can be introduced: an emphasis upon their process of transacting rather than the content of their conflict. The couple's process will include an analysis of their strengths, their regressions, their fixations, and progressions. This is important because in my clinical experience, 60 percent of conflictual areas appeared before marriage.

For individuals to develop meaningful, age-appropriate dyadic relationships, they must replace their previous parental anchors. Disengagement involves separation from all relationships, both kinship and social, that interfere with a commitment to the relationship. At this point it is important to differentiate between kinship bonds and the concept of role. The concept of role deals with the expectations, obligations, and rights of the person in a particular status and encompasses more than the concept of bond. Furthermore, each role includes reciprocal positions related to it, e.g. father-son, father-daughter relationships and so on. On the other hand, the concept of bond implies a hierarchy of ties, of obligations and feelings between those in a reciprocal kinship status. These bonds produce a pattern of organization within a kinship network, i.e. the bond between mother and son is stronger than the bond between siblings. Thus disengagement on the part of the engaged couple from their respective kin is often difficult.[14] This disengagement from respective kinship networks must be resolved either before an engagement or during the engagement period for the couple to proceed with their new social unit.

Exclusivity should not be confused with the disengagement process from parental anchors or kinship bonds. The disengagement type of exclusiveness I refer to is the development of a functionally dyadic unit that can determine their goals, transactional patterns, rituals, and friendships, etc. along mutually acceptable paths; not a total severing of all previous friendships or relatives. However, a previous "romantic affair" friend, now seen casually, e.g. lunch, may be destructive to pair-coupling. At times, some relationships encroach on the leisure time a couple has for themselves. The allocations for such relationships should be worked out, otherwise complaints, conflicts, arguments, anger and bitterness will develop. Following are two examples: "You are always going out with the 'boys' and "You sure are considerate and empathetic to *your* friends, spending hours on the phone, but when it comes to me . . . "

The following clinical extract illustrates the marital conflict produced when parental anchors have not been altered and marital exclusiveness has not occurred:

> Mr. and Mrs. V married three months, came into therapy complaining about continuous quarreling over their in-law relationship. Mrs. V stated bitterly that their arguments have destroyed all mutual interest and compatible areas. Also, her husband seemed to believe that since he "gave in" or accepted her relationship with her family prior to marriage that now, he expected her to "give up" those ties.
>
> Mr. V interrupted his wife and admitted that much of what she said was true, but his intention was to avoid arguments. Whenever he disagreed with her, she would react with furious anger and accuse him of calling her "stupid and a dumb blond." He felt that she knew he appreciated her intellect but that he could not have a discussion

without her feeling challenged as a person. He said that he was probably too agreeable before marriage, but now he is more outspoken about his feelings. He could not tolerate the amount of time she was spending with her mother. She phones her mother every night and they talk for hours, unless her mother spends the evening with us (which happens almost every other night)! In addition, his mother-in-law buys gifts for his wife that should be bought by him. The list became endless. His last comment: "Two is a marriage, but three is a crowd. I can't see why she has to call her mother about everything that happens between us."

Discussing self-disclosure can cause harm and conflict. There is nothing gained by probing into the past.[15-16] Freud's dictum that "let sleeping dogs lie" (although it referred to the termination of analysis originally) is equally applicable to this situation.

Another important area in the development of a meaningful relationship is a mutual satisfactory sexual adjustment (contingent on each individual's norms for sexuality). For many, the liberalized sexual freedom of recent years has primarily affected *attitudes* more than behavior.[17-18] Sociologists have found that it takes a long time to incorporate new moral or social values that differ with the family of origins'. Influences from the interpersonal and environmental systems that are speeding up such value changes include peer groups, political ideologies, drug usage, shifting dormitory regulations at colleges, availability of contraceptive information, devices and medical procedures, low cost abortions, the morning-after pill, etc.

In spite of ways to avoid or end an unplanned pregnancy, statistics show an increase from 10 percent to 15 percent.[19-21] While some couples who get married because of pregnancy can and do have a successful relationship, for many this creates a crisis of considerable magnitude.[22-23] The following clinical vignette illustrates the latter:

Mr. and Mrs. J were referred for therapy because of the husband's compulsive ruminating that his wife would become unfaithful. He stated: "That for the past two years she seemed disinterested in sex with him and he was suspecting another man."

Mrs. J began her first session as follows: "I guess I always wanted and tried to have a perfect marriage, but after two years I began to have doubts about whether or not I married the right person. I knew I cared and respected him , but I never felt that I had chosen him. We had to get married as I was pregnant. I began to wonder whether I really loved him. Slowly, I guess, I became unsure of making love, that is, I didn't feel excited anymore. I didn't enjoy going to bed, in fact, at times I disliked it, but tried not to let him know this . . . I knew I cared very much in every other way for him, but, when it came to sex, it didn't excite me. Up until this time I enjoyed sex with him fully, but now I began to fantasy about other men. I was a freshman in college when I got pregnant and married. I really enjoyed school and all the social activities and I resented it when I got pregnant. I didn't want to get married but my father insisted when he found out. I've always resented that I was unable to finish college."

Mr. J "Sexual dissatisfaction is probably the best topic to describe our trouble, although I don't believe it's dissatisfaction, but rather a lack of one or both to work for satisfaction. My wife is very attractive and excites me easily. The problem is that in the last two years of our marriage I have failed to help her reach a climax. For the first two years she was very satisfied, then this lonely unsatisfied feeling developed, now she has built this thing up to something like she has and I don't understand what has happened."

In this first conjoint session, Mrs. J relates her feelings of anger at her father for forcing her to get married, and at her husband who told her he planned the pregnancy because he was afraid she was going to marry someone else. Mr. J insists that they were in love but he was angry at her when she refused to marry him.

In the fourth conjoint session, Mrs. J related the following dream: "We are at a party. We were switching partners. It was okay with me. But I got upset when my husband went over and asked a girl to dance before I was asked. He held her close while they danced. I was angry and said, 'You always do more than you are supposed to!'"

The associations revealed that her impregnation occurred when she accepted his invitation to meet him at his friend's apartment to discuss their relationship during college days. When asked why she had gone to the apartment, she replied, smilingly: "I didn't expect anything to happen." The remaining conjoint session dealt with their respective guilt and anger.

Mrs. J related another dream: "We are back in college driving in his car. We need gasoline. He stopped at the self serve pump. Later, when he got in the car, I said, *You forgot to put the cap back* on the gasoline tank."

In this dream she reveals a joint occupancy in the car, and a joint *need* for gasoline (or, as I interpreted, for sex). At the same time she places the sole blame for their sexual act and her impregnation on her spouse — he got out to fill his tank and left the gas cap off (symbolically, his condom). In Freudian terminology, projection: In Bernean phraseology, "If It Weren't for Him." This dream was a turning point in their therapy. The interpretation of the dream gave her a new view of her unwanted pregnancy — it takes two to do it!

This couple demonstrates the unconscious collusion between the mates. Her material revealed her feeling of being trapped into marriage, yet she willingly met him at his friend's apartment.

Another area in the evaluation of the relationship includes transactions dealing with the division of labor between earner and homemaker and the clarification of roles. The couple may agree to have one partner work to enable mate to complete education (academic or vocational); or both work toward a down payment on a house, boat or whatever. The role expectations of the two individuals can be categorized under two main activities: to provide for the material things; and, to provide nurturance-succorance, whether it be woman's or man's work. Regardless of which individual assumes primarily the instrumental role, there has to be a realistic conception of the economic problems. The task accepted must not only be intrapersonal in terms of the individual's capacity to contribute to the economic needs of the relationship, but also each must work out an arrangement ego-syntonic to their own self-images. Usually it is the male who is expected to take on the instrumental role and the female the nurturant-affectional role. However, with younger individuals entering marital/nonmarital relationships, partners or couples opting for no children, and dual work or career situations, this financial sphere is resulting in more dyadic conflicts.(See question #20, Chapter XV).

Finally, in the ego-strengthening sphere, communication, maturity and chronological age play important roles in the process of changing casual dating into a serious relationship. Communication, however, is the most salient factor in establishing relationships because of its transactional nature. Krain[24] has studied the communication among couples during three stages of dating; these studies suggest a linear developmental communication process rather than a curvilinear. His sample reveals developmental process, as well as filtering or selective process.

The ego-strengthening sphere involves transactions in which each person helps the other learn future dyadic roles. Ideally, each one accords the other the freedom to express individuality and encourage the maintenance of a healthy self-image and feelings of self-esteem. In addition, both help establish a couple identity, learn how to communicate and develop transactional patterns to support each other in decision-making and problem-solving. Mutual, instead of narcissistic, adaptive coping measures become important.

HONEYMOON

For many couples, the traditional honeymoon resulted in the first manifestation of a psychosocial crisis, instead of pleasant expectation. My data showed that in one-third of the couples the first emotional stress manifested itself at this time. A common complaint among these couples was that of the Bernean game of "Uproar," a good example was where the man wanted to take his dog along on their honeymoon. His wife agreed, but arguments ensued when he insisted that his dog sleep in bed with them.

A frequent cause of argument revolves around the topic of residence. Residence is an area dealing with interpersonal reorientation. Some individuals may assume that this is not an important issue to discuss during courtship. Residence is patterned and related to social values and expectations and is a basic concept of kinship networks. Marriage inevitably involves a dislocation for one or both partners. Frequently there is great emotional investment connected to where one lives in relation to relatives. The following couple illustrates the importance of residence:

> Mr. and Mrs. X were born and raised in San Diego. A job change caused them to move to Chicago. Mrs. X feels that this is the crux of their problem. She is very unhappy and wants to return to San Diego, but her husband wants to stay. He accepted this offer as it involved a promotion and a substantial increase in salary, although she was bitterly opposed to moving. Mrs. X missed her family and friends. Also, when they were on their honeymoon, they had argued about where they would live. At that time she specifically said that she did not intend to leave San Diego where her parents live, regardless of circumstances; and he promised to stay "put."
>
> Mr. X interrupted by stating: that he had expected her to change her views later in their marriage.

This woman did not disengage from her parental anchor and it manifested itself in overdependency upon her parents. A similar overdependence, in other couples, disrupted the honeymoon by daily telephone calls to parents by *either spouse*.

Intimacy becomes a real challenge to the couple especially if there has not been premarital sex. The bride who had been impressed with her husband's gentlemanly behavior, in contrast to her previous boyfriends, is suddenly aware that her "inexpressive"[24] husband is too much of a *gentle man*. Not only the challenge of aloneness to intimacy, but the entire area of sexuality comes to the forefront.

Though premarital sexual relationships were satisfactory, sexual histories showed that many individuals complained about their sexual dissatisfaction on their honeymoon. Wheareas 60 percent of the male patients related their sexual relationships as satisfactory, only 50 percent of the women agreed with their partners. In the ratio of 4 to 3, women felt that sex could have been better as to meeting their needs. It is rare that one hears of nonconsummation of the sexual act, but it does occur.[26-27] Mr. and Mrs. Z, married six years, were referred because Mrs. Z wanted a divorce; also, they had sexual problems. Mr. Z prematurely ejaculated on contact with wife's vaginal orifice. They had never consummated their marriage. Mrs. Z had gone to motels with other men who could not penetrate her vaginal opening. She consulted a gynecologist who was unable to insert the vaginal speculum because of vaginal spasms. He suggested therapy, but she refused. Other physical conditions that may cause sexual problems on a honeymoon include imperforate or rigid hymen, honeymoon cystitis,[28] etc. Male sexual dysfunctions may also surface on the honeymoon. Premature ejaculation, although this may not cause conflict, can be interpretated as a sign of marked sexual excitement; however, premature ejaculation, if it persists, will eventually cause dyadic problems. On the other hand, if a male with erectile dysfuntion is matched with a disinterested or nonorgastic female, this will not be a problem. Impotence (nonerectile dysfunction) was rarely noted on the BRQ.

In couples who had been in a living-together-arrangement, who later chose marriage, a honeymoon was a special vacation rather than the first attempt at total intimacy and unity.

REFERENCES

1. Reiss, Ira L.: *The Family System in America.* New York, HR&W, 1971, p. 105.
2. Ryder, Robert G., Kafka, John S., and Olson, David H.: "Separating" and "Joining" influences in courtship and early marriage. *Med Aspects Hum Sexuality, 6:* 13-35, 1972.
3. Peck, Bruce B. and Swarts, Edward: The premarital impasse. *Family Therapy* (J Family Therapy Institute of Marin), *11:* 1-19, 1975.
4. Murstein, Bernard I.: Stimulus-value-role: a theory of marital choice. *J Marriage & Family, 32:* 465-81, 1970.
5. Murstein, Bernard I.: *Who Will Marry Whom?* New York: Springer, 1976.
6. Levinger, George and Rausch, Harold L. (Eds): *Close Relationships: Perspectives on the Meaning of Intimacy.* Amherst, Mass: Univ Mass Press, 1977.
7. Rubin, Zick and Levinger, George: Letter to the Editor — theory and data badly mated: a critique of Murstein's SVR and Lewis's PDF models of mate selection. *J Marr & Family, 36:* 226-30, 1974.
8. Lewis, Robert A: A longitudinal test of a developmental framework for premarital dyadic formation. *J Marr & Family, 35:* 1625, 1973.
9. Greene, Bernard L: Viewpoints — How valid is sex attraction in selection of a mate. *Med Aspects Hum Sexuality, 4:* 23, 1970.
10. Wahl, Charles W., Berscheid, Ellen, Roth, Nathan, Ottenheimer, Lilly &

Murstein, Bernard I.: Viewpoints — what accounts for preferences regarding sexual attractiveness. *Med Aspects Hum Sexuality, 12:* 39-50, 1978.

11. Kephart, William M.: Evaluation of romantic love. *Med Aspects Hum Sexuality, 7:* 92-112, 1973.

12. Raths, Otto N., Bellville, Titus P., Bellville, Carol J. and Garetz, Floyd K.: The counterphobic mechanism as a force in mate selection and marital stability. *Family Coordinator, 23:* 295-301, 1974.

13. Landis, Judson T.: Danger signals in courtship. *Med Aspects Hum Sexuality, 4:* 35-46, 1970.

14. Leichter, Hope J. and Mitchell, William E. (with collaboration of Candace Rogers and Judith Lieb): *Kinship and Casework.* New York, Russell Sage Foundation, 1967.

15. Mathis, James L.: Men's ambivalence toward wives' sex experiences. *Med Aspects Hum Sexuality, 12:* 27, 1978.

16. Davidson, Kenneth J: Attitudes toward first coitus. *Med Aspects Hum Sexuality, 11:* 108-109, 1977.

17. Halleck, Seymour L.: Sexual problems of college students. *Med Aspects Hum Sexuality, 2:* 14, 1968.

18. Gagnon, John H. and Simon, William: Prospects for change in American sexual patterns. *Med Aspects Hum Sexuality, 4:* 100, 1970.

19. Maxwell, Joseph W., Sack, Allan R., Frary, Robert B. and Keller, James F.: Factors influencing contraceptive behavior of single college students. *J Sex & Marital Therapy, 3:* 265-73, 1977.

20. Reiss, Ira L., Banwart, Albert, and Foreman, Harry: Premarital contraceptive usage: a study and some theoretical explorations, *J Marr & Family, 37:* 619-30, 1975.

21. Peterman, Dan J., Ridley, Carl A., and Anderson, Scott M.: A comparison of cohabiting and noncohabiting college students, *J Marr & Family, 36:* 344-54, 1974.

22. Vincent, Clark E.: The physician as counselor in nonmarital and premarital pregnancies. *Med Aspects Hum Sexuality, 1:* 28, 1967.

23. Fisher, Esther O.: *Help For Today's Troubled Marriages.* New York, Hawthorn Books, 1968, p. 199.

24. Krain, Mark: Communication among premarital couples at three stages of dating, *J Marr & Family, 37:* 609-18, 1975.

25. Balswick, Jack: The inexpressive male — functional-conflict and role theory as contrasting explanations. *Family Coordinator, 28:* 331-36, 1979.

26. Rapoport, Rhona and Rapoport, Robert N.: New light on the honeymoon, *Hum Relations, 17:* 33, 1964.

27. Friedman, Leonard J.: *Virgin Wives: A Study of Unconsummated Marriages.* London, Tavistock Pub., 1962.

28. O'Donnell, R.P.O.: Chronic honeymoon cystitis — correction by surgery, *Brit J Sexual Medicine, 3:* 20-23, 1978.

Chapter IX

PREVIOUS RELATIONSHIPS

QUESTION #13 on the BRQ states: *Any previous relationships or marriages? yes — no — If yes, did the relationships or marriages end by divorce, death, or desertion? Give details:*

Information about a former dyadic relationship may provide insight into object choices and object relationships.[1-2] Knowledge of previous relationships is also helpful in evaluating the current conflicts of the couple. However, the family myths, the paucity of scientific studies, and the many variables make generalizations mandatory. The three main variables include the following:

1. The many contradictions in the literature about the outcome of remarriage.
2. The unreliability of retrospective data.
3. The heterogeneous composition of the remarried population — the three marital types (single, divorced, and widowed) intermarry, and each party is unique as to marital background (once divorced, twice divorced, and so on).

A progressive increase in variant and experimental dyad relationships[3] has occurred in the past decade — the most frequent being the living-together-arrangement (LTA). Therefore, the variables listed above also apply to these life-styles. Complicating the picture is the explosion in divorce rates with the largest remarriage statistics[4] as of 1975.

Since "man is not an island unto himself," the need for dyadic relationships will continue; individuals reestablish pair-couplings after the previous one ended. The remarriage and LTA rate varies from state to state. As one would expect, remarriages were highest at the younger ages. Remarriage rates were higher for men then for women. The remarriage rates for the divorced females were higher than that for the widowed. Also noted, if both have had previous marriages, males chose much younger partners. An important finding from research data indicated that most divorced individuals choose to remarry in a relatively short period after their divorce. My data shows that whereas 21 percent of the married couples have been previously married before 1970, the past decade shows an increase to 30 percent. The literature on the outcome of a remarriage is still equivocal: there are some studies that suggest remarriages are as successful as other marriages, and others suggest that remarriages are a repetitive phenomenon — only the partner has changed.

Information of previous relationships is of importance in assessing the current conflictual pair-coupling as to prognosis and treatment. In keeping with the theoretical position of GST, all levels of information become valuable for the conjoint diagnostic and disposition session. In focusing on the environmental system, it is important to keep in mind that many previous dysfunctional relationships have a deficiency of relationship boundaries. This often leads them to involve extended kin in their conflicts, and/or are influenced by them. Finding out if these same forces are still producing conflict is important.[5] As many new relationships occur later in life, the kin-ship networks, particularly in-laws, may now accept the pair-coupling, or, may be distant with little or no influence. Difficulties with children were observed in more than 50 percent of the conflicted couples anticipating or following remarriage.[6] The following couple came for remarital therapy presented this type of problem:

> She: "If I were to marry him, he would like to have his children live with us. They are now living with his former wife who has custody of them. I like his children but I am concerned that his primary relationships are with his children instead of me. He has great guilt feelings about being away from them. A parent does not immerse himself in his children as he does. He mentioned to me at one time that some of the women he had gone out with had actually been jealous of his children. I said, it wasn't the children but he who makes them jealous. I also told him that I didn't want to be involved in a situation where the children call the shots. Basically, his children have a way of winding him around their fingers. I think it is hard for him to believe I do love his children. They have been at my house off and on all summer. I do have a good relationship with them. To me, they are kids, like mine."

In this situation, the solicitude of the father for his children of an earlier marriage resulted in frequent quarreling during the courtship, led to remarital therapy where the relationship to his children were clarified, ground rules established about their behavior, and a good relationship ensued.

Other environmental forces influencing the current relationship may include direct or indirect intervention by a former spouse through the children. Finally, adverse reactions of friends to the new partner can precipitate disharmony.

The intrapersonal and interpersonal forces play a significant role in dyadic discord. The intrapersonal forces include such psychodynamic factors as guilt feelings. When one partner feels guilty, unconscious provocation of his mate may provoke painful retaliation. "The currency of guilt is punishment." The guilt may be due to conscious or unconscious death wishes toward the former partner. There may be conscious guilt at having forced a divorce on a partner who is now unhappily married or not married at all. Another force is the repetition of mate choices based on conscious or unconscious homosexual feelings or behavior defended against by marriage. Some men select beautiful seductive women to conceal their inadequate sexual performance. These and many other unconscious forces may be at the root of the discord, therefore, knowledge of previous relationships is valuable. In several couples involving remarriage by widow or widower, the deceased spouse was so idealized and the new partner so continuously and unfavorably compared that constant and bitter quarreling occurred.

Object relationships and choices reflect their historical development as phenomenological voices in the records of the individual (see Chapter II). These sequential object relationships operate in all current pair-couplings. Painful records are often reacted to internally as well as projected onto the partner (via the phenomena of projective identification) who is then attacked, thus setting off a series of bitter arguments and/or complaints.

Thirty-five years ago, Mittlemann suggested that the neuroses of marital partners complement each other with dovetailing of conflictual and defensive patterns on early developmental levels.[7] Giovacchini extends these conclusions and emphasizes the mutually adaptive qualities of the marital relationship (see Chapter XXIII). He describes two types of dyadic relationships, which are helpful in understanding pair-coupling discord and sequential relationships. First, a *character object relationship,* typified by a total characterological involvement between the couple requiring total personality, including the specific character defenses of the significant other in order to maintain intrapsychic equilibrium. Second, a *symptom object relationship,* transitory in nature and not requiring the total personality of the partner, only a particular trait or symptom and the depth of involvement is only a partial one, e.g. underachiever. The circumscribed meaning of the dyadic relationship leads to repetitive marriages or pair-couplings. In addition to potential and realized conflicts, Messinger points out that dyadic partners who have previously been married can anticipate even broader areas of conflict: "The complexities arise primarily from the ties each partner has to the previous marriage, through children, through financial and custodial settlement, through ex-spouse and ex-spouse's family, and through former social life. Added to these are the complexities involved in the present marital and family situation, which is frequently taxed with 'doubling' of parental roles and responsibilities of the new spouse to the partner's children from the previous marriage, as well as the ambiguous roles and relationships of the partner's children to parent's new spouse."[8]

The topic of "reconstituted" families will be discussed in detail in Chapter XX.

REFERENCES

1. Greene, Bernard L.: Sequential marriage: repetition of the change? In *The Marriage Relationship*. Rosenbaum, Salo and Alger, Ian (Eds.): New York, Basic Books, 1968, pp. 293-306.
2. White, Lynn K. Sex differentials in the effect of remarriage on global happiness. *J Marr & Family, 41:* 869-76, 1979.
3. Weitzman, Lenore J.: To love, honor, and obey? Traditional legal marriage and alternative family forms. *Family Coordinator, 24:* 531-48, 1975.
4. "Remarriages, United States" VITAL AND HEALTH STATISTICS, Series 21, No. 25, DHEW Publication No. (HRA) 74-1903, 27 pp. U.S. Government Printing Office, Washington, D.C. 20402.
5. Anspach, Donald F.: Kinship and divorce, *J Marr & Family 38:* 323-30, 1976.
6. Greene, Bernard L.: Remarriage and the physician. *Med Aspects Hum Sexuality, 4:* 12-17, 1970.
7. Mittlemann, Bela: Complementary neurotic reactions in intimate relationships, *Psychoanal Quart, 13;* 479, 1944.
8. Messinger, Lillian: Remarriage between divorced people with children from previous marriages — a proposal for preparation for remarriage. *J Marr & Family Counseling, 32:* 193-200, 1976.

Chapter X

ORIGINAL FAMILY
Childhood Environment

THE family members (parents, siblings and significant others) exert an important influence upon every pair-coupling by their relationships, attitudes, values, rituals, myths, etc. Question #14 explores this area by the following questions:

a. Father: first name only   Retired?   Yes   No
                                    Occupation
   age at marriage and currently   age at death   Cause
                                    Retired?   Yes   No
b. Mother First name only   Occupation
   age at marriage and currently   age at death   Cause
c. Brothers and sisters: First name only   age   sex

(There is space on the form to permit a fast visual illustration of the sibling position by use of stick figures, e.g. male= ♂ and female= ♀.)

Human functioning starts from the original interpersonal one of the family of origin. From the original infant-parental bonding, as Zwerling points out, the endpoint is the group formation of society.[1] Man differs from other primates in the capacity for abstraction which allows the relationship with others to be real, distorted, fancied, symbolic, and recalled. Not only is the original bonding important, but also the acquisition of the cognitive system[2] of his original group: "The normal socialization process moves the individual in his relationship with the group's system from compliance through identification, to internalization, and finally promulgation. The parent who teaches the way through the maze to his child has completed the cycle."[3]

A growing sociocultural problem is the increasing alienation by American youth from their families of origin, largely due to being "given the leftovers of adult time and energy."[4] The initial parental reaction to the addition of each child into their dyad may be influenced by many elements in the GST systems. The age of the partners at the time of their dyadic relationship or at the time of pregnancy may be one influence. Marital age has been the object of previous studies, but rarely within a life-course framework. An exception is the scholarly article by Elder, Jr. and Rockwell: "The timing of first marriage is a watershed event for individuals. Its occurence, whether 'early,,' 'on time,' or 'late' (in accordance with social norms) has well established consequences for the subsequent life course and family relationships. These consequences are expressed in: (1) the marriage market, mating options, and their resulting patterns — women who marry relatively late encounter a more restricted field of age-eligible men than do those who marry at the usual time; (2) the asynchrony of events across career lines (marital, parental, and socioeconomic) as expressed in the economic squeeze of early marriage and the advantage of late marriage; and (3) the interpretation of experienced events — timing variations have consequences that shape the meaning of events."[5] Many couples who marry at age thirty-five or older do not want children, and children that result from these couples are usually not planned nor wanted. Couples under ages twenty-five, who have children, planned/unplanned, accept them with less difficulty.

Until recently little attention has been given in the literature to father-child relations and the role played by these relations in character development.[6-7] The role of the individual's father is important, e.g. is he charismatic[8] or was he absent during the individual's growing up? We are interested as to the father's age, occupation, and whether or not he is living. The father's occupation gives a clue as to the sociocultural background of the patient. The working mother, whether married or single[9] also has an effect upon the children. For example, was mother depressed, tired, degree of supervision, etc.

The personality of all individuals is a crystallization of cognitive development involving both the pia and inner child voices, value orientations creating the parental voice in the records, and the effects of the structural arrangements in the family-parental and especially the ordinal position of the person. In this chapter the role of the father's and mother's influence upon an individual will be presented as it pertains to encoding of value orientations, the importance of the ordinal position of each individual as it can affect a relationship, and, lastly, the impact of the parental transactions upon each partner during their residence at their original home.

The formation of values,[10] as heard faintly or loudly coming from the parental voice of each record, results from those values we had as children and adolescents. These values come from the interpersonal and environmental systems the individual is transacting with.

The influence of the parental voice, as seen in Figure 3, is both

A Clinical Approach to Marital Problems

direct and indirect where it contributes to the formation of the records.

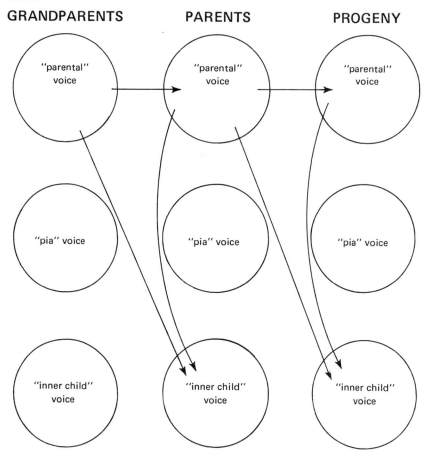

Figure 3. Transmission of values between generations.

Parents exert direct influence by guidance, reassurance, praise, and
criticism — either overtly or covertly — and indirect influence by
their parental voices encoded in their children's records. What a child
feels and how he reacts are the reactions of his parents to him.
Children have parents (or parental surrogates) who provide positive
or negative guidance, whereas adults act as parents to themselves by
means of their parental voices. Thus, adults continue the parental
values and attitudes that were imposed on them during childhood and

adult life and impose them on their own children. Berne[11] delineates four ways in which a parental figure can influence a child: demeanor, gestures, voice, and vocabulary. Clinically, I use his expression of stroking to express a positive attitude or action by a partner and critical for an opposite attitude toward another individual. Cappon defines values as: " . . . abstract standards which become imbedded in habitual judgements, attitudes, systems and ways of life. Thus values transcend the temporal impulse and even the psychological impetus or motivation which initiated an interest and prompted its attachment to an object, to form a value."[12] He divides the determinants of values into four categories: biological, social, psychological, and ecological. The biological determinant of one's values involves the intrapersonal system and is an innate quality of the inner child. The social determinants involve both the interpersonal and environmental systems, in which parental values play an important role. The psychological determinants of values involve primarily the intrapersonal system in circular causality with components from both the interpersonal and environmental systems and are heard from the parental voices of the records. The ecological determinants of values results from transactions with the environmental system, e.g. conflict arising from rural upbringing and values clashing with those of the city which supplies the monies for existence.

The encoding of values[13-15] goes on in an inflexible manner, whether the parents or any element in the interpersonal and environmental systems will it or not. Values are always in relation to other people (interpersonal system) in a given sociocultural milieu in time or space (environmental system). The axiological code of the nature of values and the types of values, whether secular or religious, is in relationships between individuals. The earlier the encoding of parental voices, the more forceful their replay in courtship and dyadic relationships as a result of projective identification and unconscious collusion.

The transactions between siblings, which is next in important to the parental relationship, plays an important role in all pair-couplings. In addition to the ordinal position between the siblings, other intersibling psychological variables include age, sex, sibling rivalry, and the pleasure-pain level of the child due to space, time, types of activities, and degrees of emotions involved. Females feel closes to sisters than males to brothers.[16] Also, the more children in the family, the less satisfaction between the parents because of possible coalitions between parent and one or more siblings.[17] The triadic arrangements may produce conflicts of interest, opinions, pleasure-pain affects that result, not only between the siblings, but also the core adult relationship and the entire adaptation of the family. With the presence of children, a "house" is more a "home" because children instigate socialization functions with special activities and the setting of values. A role parents tend to resent is that of referee to offset inter-sibling conflict. Parental discipline influences the off-spring's norms of distributive justice and disciplinary techniques, which carry over into adulthood.[18]

Ordinal position among siblings frequently gives the therapist an understanding of the current dyadic disharmony. Altus[19] reviewed some of the literature for the past one hundred years and noted that ordinal position among siblings related to potential eminence and educational learning. He states: " . . . it seems a fairly safe assumption that there is a kind of academic primogeniture operating at the college level." Walter Toman[20-21] author of a book on family constellation should be required reading, I believe, for all therapists.

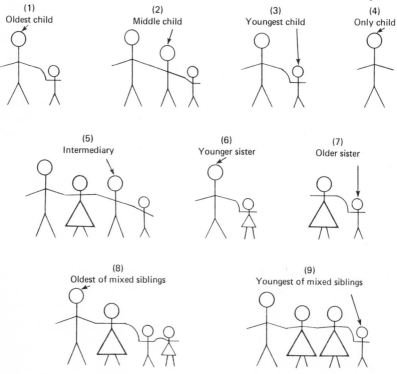

Figure 4. Male ordinal positions.

He presents ten basic sibling positions, and he does this in extensive character portraits. I have followed his classification in analyzing couples, using five categories: oldest, youngest, intermediate, singleton, and middle child. In my cases, 35 percent were the oldest; 27 percent were the youngest; 18 percent were intermediate; 15 percent were singletons; and 5 percent were the middle child. The intermediate refers to a family having more than three children. I use the following figures to represent the ordinal position and place them in the special indentation on the BRQ form. Figure 4 shows the possible positions for the male partner.

Toman's studies were based on clinical psychological work and described enduring relationships. The ordinal position may help in understanding how some of the "records" can be projected into one's partner or child to produce dyadic discord. Not infrequently, dyadic disharmony occurs during pregnancy or birth of the first child. The record activated or played will be determined, at times, in the selection of the partner and codetermined by the kinds of individuals one has been living with the longest and most intimately. The relationship can duplicate the earliest interpersonal relationships in degrees varying from complete duplication to none at all. Toman hypothecates that the closer the new relationships resemble the earlier ones, the more successful will be the new ones. For example, if an older brother of a sister relates to the younger sister of a brother (see Fig. 5), they are duplicating their childhood relationships regarding seniority rights. In addition, both are used to relating to the other sex and should have no dyadic conflicts in that area. In the last one hundred couples having this reduplication of the family constellation, the relationship complaints were minimal and had the best prognosis in therapy.

Figure 5. Marriage duplicating earlier relationship.

The younger members in a dyadic relationship, with older siblings of the same sex, seemed to have the greatest problems (see fig. 6).

Younger brother of a brother   **Younger sister of a sister**

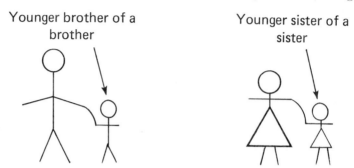

Figure 6. Most conflictual in dyadic combinations.

With this combination of pair-coupling, sexual dysfuntional problems and conflicts occurred from the unconscious wish to be dependent. Parenthood also interfered with their dependency needs. For example, the following couple demonstrates the typical complaints and transactional process which occurs:

> Mrs. A: "I feel my marriage is not a marriage and never has been. I have been living with a very complicated husband. I do not understand him. It seems he doesn't want to be understood. He's indifferent. I do not care for him. My only concern is the effect of a separation on my daughter. I feel very guilty about her. Neither he nor I wanted children. Her conception was unplanned. Now that she is in high school I don't think a divorce would upset her. I believe my husband and I would be better off separated. My husband does not fulfill my emotional needs. I want someone to love me, and at times I feel he wants to be mothered or taken care of. As to sexual satisfaction, I have had to submit to sexual acts that I hated, but submitted to to avoid arguments. At one time, when we were married five years, I was quite taken with a friend of ours. I was lonely, my husband was working almost every night and although we did not have any intimate relations, our mutual feelings toward each other was discovered; and, of course, never forgotten by my husband. I wish we would have divorced then. I have been faithful ever since, but my husband cannot forget or forgive."
>
> Mr. A: "We are constantly arguing, one sided, more in the form of her nagging. I am dissatisfied sexually. Her way or nothing and her choosing the time. She is always rough on me and amorous with male partners when she has a number of drinks. If I scold her, she gets insulting in and out of public."

When an older brother of a sister marries the older sister of a sister (see fig. 7), conflict frequently develops.

Older brother of a
sister

Older sister of a
sister

Figure 7. Marital combination that can lead to disharmony.

Most often, the complaints are decision making and power struggles.[22] An example is illustrated in the following extract:

Mr. B: "There is little, if any, emotional show in a positive manner on her part. We cannot reach agreement on anything! She is very indifferent to sexual relations, almost none and then only when she wants sex. We disagree on financial disbursements."

Mrs. B: "We can't understand each other's emotional needs. If I even try to indicate feelings of unrest, he turns away. We have constant arguments. I don't feel he is a friend, so I turn away from sexual activity. My husband does not pursue me. We have basically different philosophies about money. He feels, if you want something badly, the heck with whether you have the money or not; he has confidence that he'll get the money somehow. We seem to be on different wavelengths and in different worlds. What he enjoys, I don't and vice versa."

Another type of dyadic combination leading to discord occurs when the older brother of a brother bonds with the older sister of a sister (see fig. 8).

Typical of this pair-coupling combination is sexual and seniority conflicts. An example is the following extract:

Mr. C: "Constant arguments. We have considerable trouble agreeing on many subjects. This is the result of differences on ideas and goals. Sexual dissatisfaction is the result of no activity. My wife has become very passive in this regard and apparently could care less. We seem to have trouble understanding each other. We don't communicate."

Mrs. C: "Our real problem is lack of communication. Emotional needs are something that must never be acknowledged — feeling

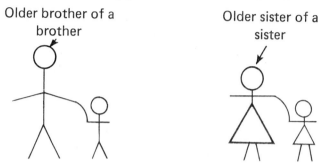

Figure 8. Another combination that can lead to disharmony.

deeply, getting excited, or enthused about something, being sad and crying are things you must never do. Unfortunately, I do all these things so we have problems, so no sex."

Another ordinal combination is where the older brother of a sister is paired with the younger sister of a sister with no problem over seniority rights, but the female partner, because she is unaccustomed to having a man around, may present problems. Reversal of learned ordinal role does occur, and does not necessarily relate to a therapeutically conceived "ideal" partner. Human creativity can often match the pressing needs of any conflictual or unfamiliar situation.

In families with more than one child, the children have each other to relate to, as well as their parents. Siblings are forced, not only to compete with each other, but also to share. Being an only child usually makes that child extremely important and valuable to his parents, more so if impregnation took a long time. In other families, a single child of parents who are unhappily married, may become the focus of emotional (or even sexual) gratification of the discontented mother or father. Disharmony may be present where a singleton looks for a parent in his/her partner, rather that a partner. Frequently, the singletons wish to remain children in their dyadic relationship and may be content without offsprings — often marrying late in life to avoid having children. (Occasionally, a singleton may react in marriage by having many children: "I know what it's like to be an only child, that is why we have four.") The following extract illustrates where a singleton, in a dyadic relationship, remains a child into adulthood, expecting their parents to provide for their emotional and material needs:

Mr. and Mrs. D came for help because of constant arguments following his job transfer to another state. Mrs. D resented the move since she was very close to her mother. Since their move, she phoned her mother every evening. Before their move, she spent a great deal of time with her mother. Mr. D rented a house thinking this would make his wife happier in adjusting to the move, as it would keep her busy since she no longer wanted to work. This only made matters worse. Her constant nagging him to keep up the maintenance of the house often led to quarreling, but the main area of arguments centered about the long distance from her mother.

Mr. D related that their courtship had been very smooth and had been over a long period of time. He was ten years her senior. There had been pressure from mutual friends that they marry and settle down and have a family now that she turned thirty. They had premarital sex. After marriage Mrs. D continued to use contraception without objection on her husband's part. Both agreed to begin a family later.

Mrs. D related an incident which happened two years ago, which she can neither forget nor forgive. He had sold stock, the accumulation of both their savings and gifts from respective families, and bought an expensive sports car against her wishes. Also, they do not have a practical budget to follow. This is a problem for both as she dribbles money away, too, on little things, whereas he is more willing to go into debt for big things.

Mr. D stated that his wife associated security with living near her parents, but her total rejection of him was unexpected. He admitted he was not the easiest person to live with and increasingly found himself getting bored with his work. Making matters worse, since his transfer, his wife rejected him sexually. When questioned about their sexual relations, Mrs. D angrily defended herself: "I told him not to move here, and he knew my feelings about it. But he was too lazy to look for another job. I don't feel I'm consciously using sexual relations as a bribe. I don't feel toward him as I once did."

There are additional factors to consider that may alter the therapist's perspective toward ordinal position of the spouses: the age differential between siblings will influence how they relate to each other; siblings with an age differential of more than seven years may encourage the older child to regress and act like the younger one; gender role is assigned by parents or physicians[23, 24] and if the physical gender does not match what the parent wanted in the baby, the child's personality development will respond to adult training; and the physical surroundings will affect the child's development (boarding school, single parent home, living in an adult community, etc.). Emotional trauma from divorce, desertion, or death[25] will also effect the growing child. Another factor is personality configuration related to ordinal position, e.g. oldest brother of brother(s) is frequently accustomed to being in charge of others while the youngest brother in the same situation may be capricious, willful, and ambivalent in his relationships to his elders.

Question 14d asks: *Describe your parents, what they were like as people, and how they got along in their marriage. How did you get along with them? Describe your family's circumstances as you were growing up. Include anything else that would give a clearer picture of your family experiences and relationships.*

In the couples I have treated, 40 percent of the males described their parents' marriage as unhappy, 35 percent as average, 10 percent as very happy, and 15 percent stated that they were raised by a single parent[26, 27] (often from a divorce situation). The statistical figures were much higher for my female patients: 55 percent felt their parents were unhappily married; 25 percent said average, 5 percent said very happy, and 15 percent were raised by only one parent. Memories of childhood experiences varied from 50 percent recalling unhappy ones, 35 percent stating fairly happy ones, and 15 percent remembering very happy ones.

Important for the evaluation of dyadic disharmony of the couple is the understanding of both the past and the current relationships with their respective parents. Kinship ties often offer many supports for the couple seeking help, financial and otherwise. The many diverse forces influencing a relationship include (1) the model of marriage each patient was exposed to during his childhood and adolescence in observing the marital relationships of his parents, (2) the personalities of individual family members, parents, siblings as well as other kin living with or influencing the family, and (3) the social and cultural values of the family. Also important in evaluating dyadic discord is how retrospective data can be distorted over time, not a new observation since this same type of distortion was recognized by Freud and led to the revision of his theory about sexual exploitation during childhood. Freud realized that what was remembered may be mere fantasy rather than fact, or the reverse.

The family of origin's significant adult figures have a definite psychological effect on the offspring. Patterns of communication (whether clear or those of "double bind" messages) become the model for the children and will contribute to what is labeled as "normal." The type of power structure within the family of origin influences the offspring. The power can be of an egalitarian type, an authoritarian type where there is a single dominant member with all others submissive, and lastly a parental pattern of chaos. Children are keen observers and efficient imitators of any power system they experience. A child's tendency to compromise, negotiate, remain stubborn, or passively submit to another's requests/demands will be distinctly influenced by the models observed in the childhood family system. The significant adult figures during early childhood will either provide or deprive the children of individuation/separation experiences, peer relationships experiences, and behavior which substantiates mutual self-respect and self-esteem. In this process, the expression of emotions will either be approved of, avoided, or punished. Fortunately (or unfortunately) there are other influences upon the growing child beyond the family system: relatives, peers, teachers, mass media personalities, etc.

There are many ways to view the effect of the past upon the growing child and the adult. Lewis and colleagues present a multidimensional picture of family life styles not based on cause and effect: there is "no single thread (in the) psychological health in family systems."[28] Romano and Geerstma[29] note the influence of a parent's illness upon the children. Miller and Gerard[30] recently presented an integrative review of the family influences which included the development of creativity in children. The environment of the family of origin often is the model for the future, and the extent of the influence of parents and all significant others is great.

The BRQ questions and/or diagnostic interviews attempt to reveal when the inner child feels most comfortable (*the at-home feeling*). This perspective of the adult personality is important in understanding how idiosyncratic problems in adults arise and contribute to dyadic disharmony. I am indebted to Michael Daly's article,[31] which brought to my attention a book by Levy and Monroe (1938) that states that people have a tendency "to create a home similar to the one we grew up in. We feel most comfortable in a familiar environment. It makes little difference whether this environment is a healthy one."[32] In a similar vein, Missildine[33] speaks of the child in every adult which seeks the feeling of being at-home regardless of the peculiarities of the original family. Not infrequently, dyadic discord results from the clashes of the inner children of a couple with different family backgrounds. The following extract is typical in a case history:

> Mr. E was a gregarious, successful business man. He was raised in a home where friends, neighbors, and relatives were coming and going. He married a reserved, quiet woman.
>
> Mrs. E remembered her childhood as an average one. Her parents rarely invited guests over. Her parents always spoke to each other in a reserved and dignified manner. She was not able to invite any playmates to visit without her mother's permission. No one, not even relatives ever thought of dropping in without an invitation. Being a meticulous housekeeper, she only felt comfortable when her home was neat and orderly.

Mr. E recounted the following excerpt from a recent quarrel with his wife: "I had, on the spur of the moment, invited a business acquaintenance to our home for a drink without telling my wife. I don't have a home, but a museum. In fact, at times it feels like a mausoleum. At first she said I couldn't have company over until the house was completely finished. It's now two years and I've yet to have a dinner party. . . . "

When confronted with this complaint, Mrs. E at first denied his accusations and then admitted she couldn't run a house like his mother did: "His relatives called his home 'Grand Central Station.' People were always eating there, sleeping there, and partying there. I'm just not that type!"

I explain how normal it is for anyone's inner child to seek the same type of experiences that had occurred in their childhood home. Such patterns represent security or an at-home feeling. As the couple began to understand the influence of their youth, they could view their current behavior as a replay of past records where the parental voices had different values and attitudes. This type of understanding is most productive therapeutically.

A number of my patients were raised in families where there were sexual problems between their parents, also incestuous parent-child relationships or inter-sibling sexuality (to be discussed under item #22). Parental problems manifest themselves in many ways (from domestic abuse to varying stages of withdrawal — separate bedrooms, non-expression of emotions, "emotional divorce" etc.). In my clinical experience I have noted that there are *no* "family secrets." Consequently, if a parent is having affairs or is homosexual or actively bisexual, the offspring(s) will often feel confused about his own sexual identity and/or behavior. Also upsetting to a child, and more so to an adolescent, is the lack of intergenerational boundaries. For the adolescent, multiplicity of *reciprocal* behavioral reactions can be precipitated by the lack of boundaries. Sexual sibling experiences between opposite sex and/or same sex may influence both current and future sexual attitudes and relationships in general. Another area involves that of privacy. Many parents should consider the impact of nudity or even their sex act[34,35] on their children's emerging sexual feelings and thoughts. Parents overestimate the ability of children to cope with sexual stimulation, e.g. seductive apparel, exposed genitalia, breasts.

Parenting is influenced by experiences within all three systems of the GST.[36] In addition to direct contacts by a parent toward an offspring are the effects of parental absences, e.g. long-term loss of a father,[37-40] etc. Variables include the length of absence, ages of the child and parents[41] and the quality of the parent-child relationship.

The network concept has gained increasing attention in this decade.[42,43] The findings in most studies reveal variations by patient's age in terms of the life cycle phase in the relationship. Once parental anchors are replaced by meaningful pair-couplings, a reestablishment of ties occur with the family of origin, kin,[44] and significant others. As couples grow older, they move away from family ties to relate more to their friends who are geared to their needs and concerns.[45] Diagnostic evaluations and therapy should include this aspect when pertinent.

The homeostatic transactions in a dysfunctional family may be based on conscious or unconscious scapegoating and/or collusion with a child(ren). Different life events can effect such transactions, e.g. the death or birth of a child or significant other, onset of adolescence, etc. Not uncommon is the need of a parent(s) to have his child act out the unconscious wish for antisocial behavior, e.g. sexual or delinquent. Scapegoating can maintain the emotional stability of a parent or even of the family. Its function is to displace unacceptable behavior or emotions onto another, for example, accusing an adolescent of "acting like a slut," may cause the child to decide that "as long as I am called the name, I will play the game." Thus, each successive generation contributes to sociocultural changes as well as specific sociohistorical events.[46,47] It is the young rather than the old who carry the torch for change.

Parenting is not an easy task nor are there clear guidelines formally taught. In my clinical experience I have found several common pathogenic patterns that produce havoc with children: parental overcontrol, strict demands for perfection, parental submission to the demands of one's offspring, and overindulgence. In addition there can be disasterous results when parents are overly domineering, demand their children to parent them, exhibit long periods of depression, overanxiousness, hypochondria, passive-submissiveness, and inadequacy, etc.[48-50]

Overcontrolling Parent

A parent who continually supervises, coerces, constrains, and directs the child is overcontrolling. The child may react with compliance or rebel overtly or covertly, e.g. procrastination, dawdling, and so on. Just as the real child may react with compliance or rebellion, so may the "inner child" of the parent. Not only do we demand of others what we frequently demand of ourselves, but also our inner child responds like our real children. Dyadic disharmony can occur when one person attempts to coerce the inner child of his partner or, in the case of projective identification, one adult reacts to the coercion of his own parental voice as if it were coming from his mate. The following clinical example is illustrative of such a transactional pattern:

> Mr. F began the first interview by stating that he and his wife had been separated for approximately two months and that both would like to get back together. However, Mrs. F refuses reconciliation until some of their problems are worked out. The problem is stated that they do not agree about how to discipline their older teenage son who is a child from her first marriage. Mrs. F states that her husband harps at the kids all the time, whereas he claims she sticks up for them all the time. Finally, last Christmas, he got fed up and left. When he wanted to return, she wouldn't have anything to do with him.
>
> Mr. F stated that " . . . it seems that everything I say to my older son is interpreted by my wife to be picking on him or belittling him. The older one will stand and argue with me over anything I tell him to do. I hate when he says, I'll do it in a minute, as soon as I finish reading.' If his mother hears me arguing with him, she'll tell him to do whatever he wants and to ignore me. He was not that way before he entered high school. He used to be a good student, and we got along fine. Now he doesn't get his homework in on time, and for the last two years all we do is argue." Mr. F could only find problems with his son and now felt that the boy didn't want to have anything to do with him.

In order to find out Mr. F's "at home feeling" (part of his inner child), I asked him to describe his family of origin. An excerpt follows:

> "I come from a Lutheran background, Missouri Synod, and my mother is a very set person, decidedly so; she never changes her mind about anything. She is very old-fashioned which includes even the plumbing in her house. Religion meant everything to her, and she was furious when I married a Catholic. My father is the boss in the family and a firm disciplinarian with a violent temper. As a youngster I couldn't make a move without his permission. (Mother was a firm disciplinarian too.)"
>
> Mr. F spoke of his love for his wife and children and about his confusion at how the kids seem to be "steering" them apart. He wants to resolve the conflict over how to discipline their children.
>
> During this same session Mrs. F began angrily: "My husband and I seem to disagree on everything that concerns our two children. He does not leave them alone. He is a constant complainer. He ridicules them. They have never done anything that could be considered se-

riously wrong. At the dinner table they are told they don't chew right, drink right, sit right, and so on. They are constantly told they are wrong. He never says anything decent to them. He even reprimands me! He tells me how my housekeeping irritates him (I do admit that I am not the best cleaner). Our marriage is now one constant argument . . . and I cannot take it anymore."

Mr. F is replaying his parental voices of his strict parents within his marriage. As his frustration mounts toward his wife's opposition to him (afterall, the man should be the boss as was his father), he expresses these feelings for her via his son (scapegoating).

Perfectionistic Parent

This parent demands perfection from his child and gets it by withholding acceptance. In contrast to the controlling parent who is apt to be tempermental in behavior, the perfectionistic parent is outwardly calm and typically manifests an obsessive-compulsive personality.[51] A good illustration of this parental type appeared in a cartoon in the *New Yorker* magazine. As a father looks at his son's report card, the caption reads: "A Zimmerman does not get a B.'"

The demand for performance creates in many children a rebellion characterized by underachievement. The inner child rebels because he feels he is not loved for what he is but only for what he can do. On the other hand, the withholding of full acceptance by the parent can lead to overachievement by the child in various areas, such as sports, scholarship, or music, but with loss of pleasure in any accomplishment. Such children drive themselves with progressive demands for perfection as they internalize their parents' voices/demands. Later these parental voices for perfection will affect a future spouse and offspring. The following clinical case reflects dyadic discord from similar parental voices:

Mr. and Mrs. G were referred for therapy by her gynecologist whom Mrs. G had consulted at her husband's insistence that she do something about her frigidity. At her initial interview she mentioned the difficulty with their only child, an underachiever.

Mr. G, a professional man, was brilliant, and had the look of a polished, successful professional. His wife had a similar appearance. Mr. G calmly stated that he was disappointed in his marriage. "I believe that we have consistently failed to develop a feeling of mutual understanding. My wife is quite reserved, and, while she may feel emotion, she does not show it overtly. Her reserve extends to our lovemaking, where she has never been able to completely abandon herself to the sex act. We have consulted numerous marriage art manuals that I have brought home, but without success in changing our lovemaking. Undoubtedly I have placed too much stress on our sexual relations. . . . I believe that generally I am an easy-going kind of person . . . I try not to be too critical of others, since this was an early failing. Now I try to be forgiving of faults in others — ironically, except with reference to my wife and son. . . . "

Mr. G revealed that his father was a very capable person and always demanded he do everything to the best of his ability; however, he never did achieve enough to please his father. "I graduated with honors from high school, second in my class, but all my father said was, 'why wasn't I valedictorian'" As for being disciplined by his father, Mr. G could not recall being physically punished, but just one look from his father was sufficient to do whatever was expected.

Mrs. G also spoke in an even-tempered manner: 'We lack communication, which I guess has produced my husband's sexual dissatisfaction with me . . . so that now we don't adequately fulfill one another's emotional needs. The lines of communication are one-way: I try to convey my feeling verbally while he keeps pretty much to himself. I resent his tendency to disparage everything I do. He constantly gives me a look which says "It could have been done better!" From the beginning of our marriage I have resented his mechanical approach to sex. His idea of great sex is to follow a manual which says, '. . . rub the clitoris six times, press each nipple twice and presto — the grand orgasm.' For me, his approach has lead to a mechanical ritual devoid of intimacy and caring. . . . Perfection and coldness is his way with our son too. Nothing he does is good enough."

Mr. G may complain bitterly about his own perfectionistic parents, but he continues to repeat the same pattern with his wife and son. In addition, the internalized, critical parental voices cause self-belittling and an ever-increasing level of perfection. Missildine notes that perfectionists are usually very intelligent, well educated, and economically better off than most people;[52] however, such people often cannot enjoy their success since their internalized parental voices endlessly demand them to do "still better." Mr. G is typical of many perfectionists who have geat difficulty in developing intimate relationships with significant others. In his case as with many other perfectionists, the sex act is a performance task instead of an intimate emotional exchange of deep feelings. Many spouses or partners who dislike such a relationship will retaliate by faking or unconsciously exhibiting frigidity. In this way, the perfectionist is left with a cold fish for a partner and a sex manual in his hand. As one wife of such a person said, "He has a solid gold fountain pen, but for me it doesn't work."

Perfectionists are not only demanding of themselves, but expect high levels of performance from others. Mr. G's son is typical of the rebellious child raised by such parents.

A perfectionist can be a man or woman. For a housewife and mother, her perfectionistic demands may produce a continuously exhausted homemaker and an overconscientious mother. In Bernean terms, she plays the marital game of "Harried."[53]

Submissive Parent

This parent reverses his parental role, and instead of setting limits to his child's immature demands and behavior, he sacrifices his own prerogatives. He creates a selfish, self-centered child who as an adult is indifferent to the feelings and rights of others. The parental voice is so faint that at times it seems to be entirely missing. Usually the voice of the inner child sings out as though it was playing an unaccompanied sonata: creative, extremely curious, full of fun and play, and sexual. Without the inhibiting and restraining parental voice, these children as adults are attractive, warm people who make friends easily, are impulsive and apt to overindulge in food, alcohol, and women/men. Their physical attractiveness, spontaneity, creativity, unbounding confidence and charm often attract a partner who is inhibited, compulsive, controlled, and extremely conscientious. The following clinical vignette is typical of such a couple:

Mr. and Mrs. H were referred by their family physician because Mr. H had recently been unable to function as an account executive for an advertising agency due to his excessive drinking. Mr. H was an attractive, warm, gracious, impeccably dressed man, whose corporation was anxious for his recovery. Mrs. H had a resigned look on her face. She sat rigidly, quietly, and shyly.

Mr. H related his personal history. Some of the salient features he described included his being the only child of doting parents. His parents catered to his every wish and whim, even though they had financial problems. He talked about how envious his high school peers were when he persuaded his parents to give him a sports car on his sixteenth birthday (and he did not care that they had to borrow money for it). When he met Gloria, Mrs. H, in his sophomore year at college, he never remembered her complaining about his life-style or behavior. When he began to drink too much, his fraternity brothers always covered up for him. Called to the dean's office because of driving too fast while under the influence of alcohol, he impulsively quit college (this was at the end of his sophomore year). A family friend owned an advertising agency, and he went to work for him. He was soon very successful because of his creativity, confidence, and physical attractiveness. He was a natural account executive because of his ability to relate quickly and spontaneously with his clients.

Mrs. H had again met her husband when she went to work for her father. She became Mr. H's secretary and idolized him from the start. Although she had seen him drunk prior to their marriage, she found excuses for his excess and any oversights he made at work. When her parents discouraged her plans to marry Mr. H, she only became more adamant. She believed she could settle him down once they were married (he was known as a lady's man as well as one to get smashed). Now married to him for many years, his drinking has only increased, she suspects him of having affairs, and his manner in disciplining their five year-old son infuriates her. Her husband was inconsistant and a pushover with their son! If she tries to insist on rules, Mr. H will yell at her and blame her for not being a better mother. Just the other day when their son broke an expensive lamp, her husband became furious with her for punishing him and blamed her for not watching the boy more carefully.

Mr. H is repeating the patterns he learned as a child. He is overly submissive and cannot foster responsible behavior in his son.

Overindulgent Parent

This parent waits upon the child unceasingly — a cornucopia of presents and attention. Since all the child's needs are anticipated, the inner child's creativity, curiosity, creative play, and even sensuality may become blunted Without any incentive to become involved interpersonally or environmentally, the child may display a bored and blasé manner — *enfant gâté*. As an adult, the parental voice influences the inner child to be bored, passive, disinterested, discontented and unable to establish meaningful relationships, since this type of offspring always expects others to take care of him. There is a lack of initiative and an inability at persistent effort. Whereas the inner child of an adult with a submissive parent is *active* and *demanding*, the inner child of the overindulged adult is *passive* and *bored*. A dyadic relationship with this type of individual is frustrating, since the partner has originally mistaken the partner's boredom and blasé manner for sophistication. Typical of the overindulged adult is the following vignette:

> Mr. S was a tall, immaculately dressed man. He spoke in a somewhat affected manner and nervously puffed on a thin pipe. He appeared bored and indifferent during the initial interview: "I have some pretty definite ideas on how I want to live. I compromised to some extent when I got married. I had to give up living in a mansion and settle for a townhouse. With her, I've got courage to do many things.

Basically she is unable to go along with my ideas. She has strong ideas, and when she does not get her way, she throws a fuss. She is not a wife the way I think of a wife. When I was in Europe studying, the women were different, grateful when the man was at home."

Mr. S was a product of his home life. He related that his parents gave him cars, trips to Europe and England, and anything and everything he wanted. He never remembered having to wait for anything he asked for . . . and that, hesitantly mentioned, might have made him a little "spoilt" by some people's standards. He then turned to his wife and said, "When I suggested that we live in a cheaper way so that I wouldn't have to keep running to my parents for money, you suggested that I go to work. I am the creative and inventive type, but just haven't gotten around to it yet."

Mrs. S was a very attractive blond. She wore a tight-fitting sweater to help reveal her full figure. She appeared depressed, showed very little spontaneous affect and at times appeared on the verge of tears: "I just don't understand it all. Here I marry the bachelor of the year, and he turns out to be a bust. I thought he would settle down when we married, go to work and want a family. Instead, he still is a playboy. Occasionally he will want to go away by himself. His folks have been supporting us. My father says he is a spoiled brat. When we are skiing everything is fine. But when we get home, his complaint is that he is bored and that I should anticipate his wants. He had quite a reputation as a lover, but I was disappointed in that I had to be the aggressor. He is a wonderful lover, but I don't get it. I've never met anyone like him before."

In this chapter, I have presented some observations about the role of parental influences as it affects not only the personalities of each patient, but also the dyadic relationship and even offspring. The importance of the ordinal position and family constellation of each partner was also touched upon. An interesting finding was that almost one-half of the patients reported that their parents' marriages were unhappy. Further one-half of the partners stated that their own childhood experiences were unhappy. Perhaps a poor marriage between parents will then be the model for a relationship as the youngsters mature. There are countless ways in which a family exerts its influence on a child(ren) to make the child an extension of itself, its myths and rituals. A "normal" family environment is dependent upon the adults working as a healthy unit, with maintenance of appropriate intergenerational boundaries[54] and adhering to their appropriate sex-linked roles. Since everyone is unique in their existence, all members of a family transact in their own uniqueness — everyone and every social unit is different.

REFERENCES

1. Zwerling, Israel: Role variations in normal and pathological families. Paper presented at the annual meeting of the Amer. Psychiat Assn., May 5, 1971, Washington, D.C.

2. Anthony, E. James, Koupernik, C., and Childand, C.: *The Child in His Family: Vulnerable Children.* New York, Wiley, 1978.

3. Adler, Herbert M. and Hammett, Van Buren O.: Crisis, conversion, and cult formation — an examination of a common psycho-social sequence. *Am J Psychiat, 130:* 861-64, 1973.

4. Bronfenbrenner, Urie: Raising your children. *Today's Health, 50:* 36-39, 1972.

5. Elder, Glen H., Jr. and Rockwell, Richard C.: Marital timing in women's patterns. *J Marital & Family Therapy, 1:* 34-53, 1976.

6. Walters, James and Stinnett, Nick: Parent-child relationships, a decade review of research. *J Marr & Family, 33:* 70-111, 1971.

7. Men's roles in the family: Special issue of the *Family Coordinator, 28 (4),* Oct. 1979.

8. Miller, Milton H. and Roberts, Leigh M: Psychotherapy with the children or disciples of charismatic individuals. *Am J Psychiat, 123:* 1049, 1967.

9. Starr, J. and Garns, D.: Singles in the city. *Society, 9:* 43-8, 1972.

10. Thurnher, Majda, Spence, Donald, and Lowenthal, Marjorie F.: Value confluence and behavioral conflict in intergenerational relations. *J Marr & Family, 36:* 308-19, 1974.

11. Berne, Eric: *Transactional Analysis in Psychotherapy.* New York, Grove Press, 1961, pp. 72-74.

12. Cappon, Daniel: Values and value judgement in psychiatry. *Psychiat Quart, 1,* July, 1966.

13. West, Louis Jolyon: Ethical psychiatry and biosocial humanism. *Am J Psychiat, 126:* 226, 1969.

14. Arlow, Jacob A.: Reaches of intrapsychic conflict. *Am J Psychiat, 121:* 425, 1965.

15. Greenbaum, Henry: Imitation and identification in learning behavior. In Merin, Joseph H. (Ed.): *The Ethiology of the Neuroses.* Palo Alto, Science & Behavior Books, 1966, pp. 69-79.

16. Bowerman, Charles and Dobash, Rebecca M.: Structural variations in inter-sibling affect. *J Marr & Family, 36:* 48-54, 1974.

17. Miller, Brent C.: Child density, marital satisfaction, and conventionalizaton — a research note. *J Marr & Family, 37:* 345-47, 1975.

18. Ihinger, Marilyn: The referee role and norms of equity — a contribution toward a theory of sibling conflict. *J Marr & Family, 37:* 515-47, 1975.

19. Altus, William D: Birth order and its sequelae. *Science, 151:* 44, 1966.

20. Toman, Walter: *Family Constellations: Its Effects on Personality,* 3rd ed. New York, Springer, 1975.

21. Bowen, Murray: The use of family theory in clinical practice. *Compr Psychiat, 7:* 345, 1966.

22. Kolb, Trudy M. and Straus, Murray A: Marital Power and marital happiness in relation to problem-solving ability. *J Marr & Family, 37:* 756-66, 1974.

23. Green, Richard: Sexual Identity of 37 children raised by homosexual or transsexual parents. *Am J Psychiat, 135;* 692-97, 1978.

24. Miller, Brian: Gay fathers and their children. *Family Coordinator, 28:* 544-52, 1979.

25. Lamb, Michael E.: The effects of divorce on children's personality development. *J Divorce, 1:* 163-74, 1977.

26. Jacobson, Gary and Ryder, Robert G.: Parental loss and some characteristics of the early marriage relationship. *Am J Orthopsychiat, 39:* 779, 1969.

27. Williamson, Donald S.: New life at the graveyard: a method of therapy for individuation from a dead former parent. *J Marr & Family Counseling, 4:* 93-101, 1978.

28. Lewis, Jerry M., Beavers, Robert W., Gossett, John T., and Phillips, Virginia A.: *No Single Thread, Psychological Health in Family Systems.* New York, Brunner-Mazel, 1976.

29. Romano, John and Geerstma, Robert H.: Parent assessment in research on the vulnerability of children and families to mental disorder. *Am J Psychiat, 135:* 813-15, 1978.

30. Miller, Brent C. and Gerard, Diana: Family influences on the development of creativity in children — an integrative review. *Family Coordinator, 28:* 295-312, 1979.

31. Daly, Michael J: Sexual attitudes in menopausal and postmenopausal women. *Med Aspects Hum Sexuality, 2:* 48, 1968.

32. Levy, John and Munroe, Ruth: *The Happy Family.* New York, Knopf, 1938.

33. Missildine, W. Hugh: *Your Inner Child of the Past.* New York, Simon and Schuster, 1963.

34. Myers, Wayne A.: The primal scene — exposure to parental intercourse. *Med Aspects Hum Sexuality, 8:* 156-165, 1974.

35. Laury, Gabriel V.: Effect of faulty sleeping arrangements on children's sexuality. *Med Aspects Hum Sexuality, 10:* 16-17, 1976.

36. Vincent, Clark E: An open letter to the "caught generation." *Family Coordinator, 21:* 143-50, 1972.

37. Anderson, Robert E.: Where's dad?, *Arch Gen Psychiat, 18:* 641, 1968.

38. Kestenbaum, Clarice J. and Stone, Michael H.: The effects of fatherless homes upon daughters — clinical impressions regarding paternal deprivation. *J Am Acad Psychoanal, 4:* 171-90, 1976.

39. Crumley, Frank E. and Blumenthal, Ronald S.: Children's reactions to temporary loss of the father. *Am J Psychiat, 130:* 778-82, 1973.

40. Sauer, Raymond: Absentee father syndrome. *Family Coordinator, 28:* 245-49, 1979.

41. Seligman, Roslyn, Glesser, Goldine, Rauh, Joseph, and Harris, Leonard: The effect of earlier parental loss on adolescence. *Arch Gen Psychiat, 31:* 475-79, 1974.
42. Firth, R., Hubert, J. and Forge, A.: *Familes and Their Relatives.* London, Routledge and Kegan Paul, 1970.
43. Botts, E.: *Family and Social Networks* (2nd ed.). London, Tavistock Pub., 1971.
44. Frank, Helen: Antistereotypical reflections on today's grandmother. *J Family Counseling, 1:* 40-46, 1973.
45. Shulman, Norman: Life-cycle variations in patterns of close relationships. *J Marr & Family, 37:* 813-21, 1975.
46. Roth, Martin: Human violence as viewed from the psychiatric clinic. *Am J Psychiat, 128:* 1043-56, 1972.
47. Nye, Ivan F: Ambivalence in the family — rewards and costs in group membership. *Family Coordinator, 25:* 21-31, 1976.
48. Spiegel, John P. and Bell, Norman W.: The Family. In Arieti, S. (Ed.): American Handbook of Psychiatry, Vol. I. New York, Basic Books, 1959, p.114.
49. Jenkins, Richard L; Classification of behavior problems of children. *Am J Psychait, 21:* 1032, 1969.
50. Meninger, Roy W.: What values are we giving our children. *Menninger Quart, 20:* 1, 1966-67.
51. Adams, Paul L.: Family characteristics of obsessive children. *Am J Psychiat, 128:* 1414-17, 1972.
52. Missildine, W. H., *Your Inner Child of the Past.*
53. Berne, Eric. *Games People Play.* New York, Grove Press, 1966.
54. Harbin, Henry T. and Madden, Dennis J. Battered parents — a new syndrome. *Am J Psychiat, 136:* 1288-91, 1979.

Chapter XI

RELATIONSHIP WITH CHILDREN

Question #15 states: *Describe your children and your relationship with them. What are the problems and conflicts that arise and how do you deal with them? How do you feel about being a parent? a step-parent? a parental surrogate?*

In the past decade there has been a large number of living-together-arrangements[1] (nonmarital couples) and an increasing number of remarriages (reconstituted marriages). In addition, the latest statistics now reveal that about one-fourth of all households have a single parent, and many singles have a live-in partner. Answers to this item reveal additional information about the partners' parental voices, and further information about their inner child as well. In addition, the answers may reveal each partner's response to the inner child of his mate and child(ren) present.

Information is obtained as to values, attitudes, feelings, and behavior of the respective partners in the following areas:

1. Discloses the cultural transmission of values between the generations as heard coming from the parental voices.
2. Offers some correlation about the information obtained under item 14d (discussed in Chapter X where each spouse is asked to describe his childhood).
3. Reveals further information about item 9f (see Chapter IV which deals with the specific dyadic complaint of conflicts about children).
4. Divulges the possible scapegoating of a child.
5. Discloses conscious or unconscious relationships with children, e.g. unconscious collusion between parent and child: emotional, incestuous, and so on.

To have children or not is a significant decision for any couple.[2] If one partner reverses the decision against offspring, a conflict frequently develops. Should a pregnancy occur under such circumstances, the ensuing hostility may even be projected onto the newborn. Bernard[3] regards childbearing not as a biological imperative, but as a function of social pressures.

The inclusion of a child(ren) on a previous one-to-one relationship will influence the dyadic transactions, especially the impact of the firstborn.[4-8] (Frequently the firstborn may trigger a reaction of infidelity and even alcoholism.) The introduction of a child into the dyadic relationship necessitates changes in the respective roles of the partners, especially the need to share. Other changes include adjusting to differences in space and time available for each family member, adjusting to possible sibling-rivalry problems in one's past, and childrearing practices, etc. There is no doubt that the entrance of the first child permanently alters the life cycle of the couple.[9] Whereas the focus in the past literature has been on parenthood as a crisis and/or a growth experience involving adaptive coping mechanisms, current research has focused on the transition as a *process.* Barnhill and his colleagues differentiate six tasks if the transition is to be rewarding: "decision-making, mourning, empathic responding, integrating, differentiating from the extended family and establishing family boundaries, and synergizing."[10] Figley points out that research has suggested five variable influencing the impact of a child(ren) on the marital (dyadic) transactions:

1. The child as an initiator of change in the familial unit.
2. The number of children in the family.
3. The timing of the birth of the first child.
4. Child spacing, the interval between marriage and the birth of the first child and subsequent children.
5. Child density, the concetration of children in the family, a ratio computed by dividing the number of children by the number of years married.[11]

The literature in the seventies has reflected a more comprehensive view of parent-child relationships. Instead of discussing pathogenicity in mothering and mother-child relationships (momism), there is a shift to valuing the role of fathering upon the psychosocial development of the child(ren); however, the role of a father (or surrogate) is in flux. Current trends indicate that this role is getting so diffuse in meaning that parental dysfunction has increased. In the past historical crises, the individual father might be discredited or rejected, but not the whole role of *fatherhood.* If such trends continue, the transmission of values and stability will deteriorate. This "parental deprivation"[12] has enormously increased asocial, ineffective, and insecure people. The skills necessary to develop intimate transactions are dependent on learning social behaviors taught within the home, which means society must restore the balance in parental roles.

The mother's role can greatly influence the child in emotional expressiveness if she is active in the child's growing-up years. Women who ignore, avoid, or work outside the home will have a different impact upon their children. The father's role can provide more than a model for coping with a task-oriented environment if he is actively involved in the rearing of his children.

Parents can either overtly or covertly influence a child by their vocabulary, demeanor, voice, and gestures, e.g. unconsciously encouraging confidence, low self-esteem, antisocial behavior, etc.[13,14] What a child feels and how he reacts depend upon the behavior his parents use toward him. These reactions can produce a positive or negative self-image. Because of his dependency upon his parents, the greatest anxiety is due to fear of rejection. Obviously, proper guidance, praise, reassurance and above all warmth, tenderness, care, and love are constructive for the child and influences the quality of the child's current and later interpersonal relationships with other individuals.[15] If there is parental preference[16] of one child over another, pathogenic repercussions may occur for *each* family member. Favoritism can be expressed either covertly or openly by preferential admiration, interest, affection, etc. Preferred children usually feel superior to others, not only their siblings, but even the other parent (which for the child may then unconsciously trigger guilt). The latter may result in underachievement. The nonpreferred child who develops feelings of inferiority may also develop hostility toward the parent(s). The dual edge to hostility is guilt over those conscious or unconscious "evil" thoughts. The personality undergoing dysfunctional development is then likely to produce trauma and future unhappiness. On the other hand, the nonpreferred may strive for achievement in areas not developed in the preferred child. All types of reactions may occur in all members of the family.

In the past decade, reconstituted families have increased in numbers.[17] If the trend continues, about one-sixth of all children will live in families where their role is a stepchild. New challenges and conflicts[18] have occurred in the reconstituted nuclear and extended families. Also, the social impact has been felt by the larger community.[19] Obviously, the children are the innocent sufferers, as Gardner points out.[20] For this type of child, the new family setting, the extra-parental figures, and the new family systems to develop and decipher contribute to insecurity and frequent acting out behaviors. These in turn add stress to the household, whether that of the single parent or that of a new marriage and family structure. New roles and expectations occur because new tasks are involved, e.g. assuming roles of stepchildren, of stepmother, and stepfather.[21,22] Many women feel very vulnerable in attempting the role of stepmother.[23] With younger stepchildren the bonding is easier to establish and maintain, because youngsters are dependent and around the house more which makes helping them and knowing them easier. With adolescent stepchildren, a new mothering figure increases the stress for all concerned. Whiteside and Auerbach[24] raise the issue of the multiplicity of role responsibilities by listing the varying new and possible family structural relationships a child might experience after a divorce. Some of these relationships include natural parents with new spouses, natural siblings with stepsiblings and/or halfbrothers and halfsisters, and the assortment of biological grandparents and relatives and stepgrandparents and relatives, etc. Whiteside and Auerbach also raise the issue of incestuous feelings and/or actions on the part of some teenage stepchildren toward one another.[25] In effect, the reconstituted family is confronted with a more complex environment to cope with than the first marriage-family one; the challenge can be successfully met by those with flexible attitudes and a strong commitment and unsuccessfully for those who expected a storybook situation without effort on their part.

In conclusion, from a socio-historical perspective of the evolution of the family over thousands of years there have been shifts in the family structure and relationships. I believe that all parents or surrogate parents try to do their best in raising their children. What Schmiel wrote a decade and one-half ago is still pertinent: " . . . parents have come under increasingly severe criticism. Poor parents are accused of neglect and affluent ones of indulgence. Blaming and punishing parents tend to undermine their constructive influence and hence to aggravate the situation . . . producing a generation of guilt-ridden parents which is not the answer."[26]

The recent Supreme Court decision (1979) has again given responsibility back to the parents as far as being able to commit offspring to mental hospitals; the court's reasoning was based upon their qualified judgement that the *great majority of parents* have the best interest of their children at heart, and this applies to all areas of parenting.

REFERENCES

1. Ridley, C.A., Peterman, D.J, and Avery, A.W.: Cohabitation — does it make for a better marriage? *Family Coordinator, 27:* 129-36, 1978.
2. Grunebaum, Henry and Abernethy, Virginia: Maritial decision making as applied to family planning, *J Sex & Marital Therapy, 1:* 63-74, 1974.
3. Bernard, Jessie: *The Future of Motherhood.* New York, Penguin Books, Inc., 1974.
4. LaRossa, Ralph: *Conflict and Power in Marriage: Expecting the First*

Child. Los Angeles, Sage, 1977.

5. Kardner, Sheldon H. and Fuller, Marielle: The firstborn phenomenon among psychiatric residents. *Am J Psychiat, 129:* 350-402, 1972.
6. Belsky, Jay: The interrelation of parental and spousal behavior during infancy in traditional families — an exploratory analysis. *J Marr & Family, 41:* 749-755, 1979.
7. Esman, Aaron H: Marital psychopathology: its effects on children and their management. In Rosenbaum, Salo and Alger, Ian (Eds.): The Marriage Relationship. New York, Basic Books, 1968, pp. 133-143.
8. Greenberg, Martin and Brenner, Paul: The newborn's impact on parent's marital and sexual relationship. *Med Aspects Hum Sexuality, 11:* 16-29, 1977.
9. Russell, Candyce S: Transition to parenthood — problems and gratifications. *J Marr & Family, 36:* 294-302, 1974.
10. Barhnhill, Laurence, Rubenstein, Gerard, and Rocklin, Neil: From generation to generation — fathers-to-be in transition. *Family Coordinator, 28:* 229-35, 1979.
11. Figley, Charles R.: Child density and the marital relationship. *J Marr & Family, 35:* 272-82, 1973.
12. Galdston, Iago: The rise and decline of fatherhood — toward an understanding of our time. *Psychiatric Annals, 2:* 10-17, 1972.
13. Singer, Melvin: Delinquency and family disciplinary- configurations. *Arch Gen Psychiat, 31:* 795-98, 1974.
14. Foster, Randall M.: Parental communication as a determinant of child behavior. *Am J Psychotherapy, 25:* 579-90, 1971.
15. Swanson, Bernice M. and Parker, Harry J.: Parent-child relations: a child's acceptance by others, of others, and of self. *Child Psychiatry Hum Dev, 1:* 243-54, 1971.
16. Bieber, Irving: Pathogenicity of parental preference, *J Am Acad Psychoanal, 5:* 291-98, 1977.
17. Kleinman, Judith, Rosenberg, Elinor, and Whiteside, Mary: Common developmental tasks in forming reconstituted families. *J Marital & Family Therapy, 5:* 79-86, 1979.
18. Wilson, Kenneth, Zurcher, Louis A., McAdams, Diana Claire, and Curtis, Russel L: Stepfathers and stepchildren — an exploratory analysis from two national surveys. *J Marr & Family, 37:* 526-36, 1975.
19. Kalter, N.: Children of divorce in an outpatient psychiatric population. *Am J Orthopsychiat, 47:* 40-51, 1977.
20. Gardner, Richard A.: *Psychotherapy with Children of Divorce.* New York: Jason Aronson, 1976.
21. Duberman, Lucille: Step-kin relationships. *J Marr & Family, 35:* 283-92, 1973.
22. Gardner, Richard A.: Intergenerational sexual tensions in second marriages. *Med Aspects Hum Sexuality, 13:* 83-92, 1979.
23. Walker, K.N., Rogers, J., and Messinger, L.: Remarriage after divorce — a review. *Social Casework, 58:* 276-85, 1977.

24. Whiteside, Mary F. and Auerbach, Lynn S.: Can the daughter of my father's new wife be my sister. *J Divorce, 1:* 271-283, 1978.
25. Whiteside, M.F. and Auerbach, L.S., Can the daughter of my father's new wife be my sister?
26. Schmiel, John L.: How to help parents of adolescents. *Physician's Panorama, 5:* 4, 1967.

Chapter XII

PERSONALITY AND
SCHOOL ADJUSTMENT

PERSONALITY

Question #16 asks each patient the following question: *Describe the kind of person you are: feelings of inferiority, sensibility, sensitivity, anxiety, etc.*

The term *personality,* which at best is a hypothetical concept, includes many aspects of human psychology and functioning. It includes genetic endownment which establishes the uniqueness at birth, interpersonal, experiential and environmental transactions and psychopathological vectors. These in turn idiosyncratically affect each individual who weaves his fate, his personality and his world. Thus, personality dynamics are more accurately perceived within the open GST frame of reference. Removal of an ego-syntonic symptom may result in negative reverberations in one or all subsystems. The three main clinical findings in my data are:

1. Concepts about self-image
2. Elicitation of feelings, behavior, and psychiatric symptoms
3. Thumbnail sketches of personality configurations

In my experience, almost 40 percent of the women and 30 percent of the men complained of a poor self-image. Typical are the following statements:

1. I am supersensitive to criticism. I have an inferiority complex. I feel as if I always have to go one better to prove my worth. I feel as if nobody could really want the real me.
2. I have feelings of inferiority, feel insecure socially, and am immature.
3. I am rather primitive in that I am not city bred.

My bias about a relationship is clearly stated to the couple in the evaluative phase, namely, that a pair-bonding must be *meaningful* and based on *mutual respect,* which in turn hinges on *self-respect.* Thus the concepts about self-image become very important![1] (What one feels about one's self in terms of the jukebox can be read in

Chapter II.)

The answer to what is "normal behavior" and a "healthy self-image" (synonyms: self-worth and self-respect) is continually being revised. Sabshin lists four functional perspectives for normalcy[2] based upon the medical model. The first perspective views health as a reasonable rather than an optimal state, with normality the major portion of a continuum. The second perspective of normalcy is utopia, which holds normality as the optimal organization of the psychic apparatus and its mental characteristics " . . . that culminates in optimal functioning." Clinically, I use O. Spurgeon English's utopian philosphy, which is to enterain one's self, to entertain others — meaningful relationships with significant others — to entertain a new idea, and to work effectively.[3] This orientation is illustrated in Figure 9.

Sabshin's third perspective, normality as average, is based on the mathematical principle of the bell-shaped curve. Whereas the perspectives just described visualize normality and abnormality as a straight line continuum, the bell curve view conceives the middle range as normal and both extremes as abnormal. The fourth concept conceptualizes normality as a process with behavior the end result of transacting systems that change over time.[4,5] GST offers a broad perspectus: relationships continually change over time — a process viewpoint.

PERSONALITY CONFIGURATIONS

Selecting a partner and forming a pair does not prevent intra- or interpersonal dysfunctions. Current classifications of psychiatric disorders are based upon clinical experience; their significance is mostly pragmatic rather than scientific. Individuals and their transactional behavioral patterns are infinitely complex and capable of being classified in a variety of ways. The new diagnostic labeling system — DSM-III[6] — proposed by the American Psychiatric Association reflects enormous effort on the part of a task force and is complicated[7] and esoteric. DSM-III lists twelve personality disorders.* Neuroses and psychotic reactions are diagnosed mainly on the basis of intuition and specific symptoms; personality disorders are diagnosed according to patterns of behavior. Neurotic or psychotic reactions do not change the individual's basic personality configuration. The "borderline pa-

---

*The personality disorders listed are as follows: paranoid, schizoid, schizotypal, histrionic, narcissistic, antisocial, borderline, avoidant, dependent, compulsive, passive-aggressive, and atypical.

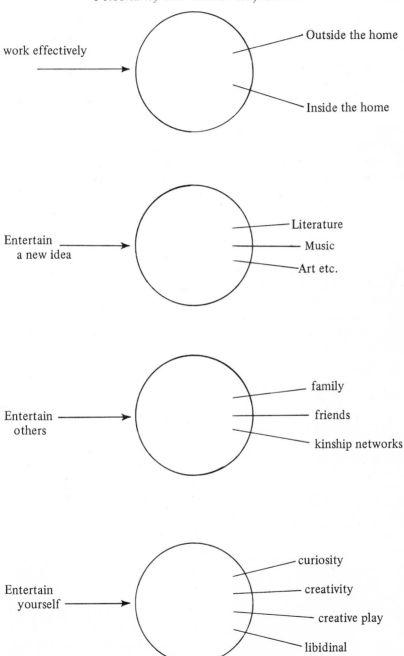

Figure 9. Normality as utopia and process.

tient" (suggested first by Stern more than forty years ago[8]), finally, is the object of considerable study. This type of patient displays behavior which falls between "neurotic" and "psychotic."[9-16] Since the schizophrenic syndrome has interested people for approximately eighty years, further knowledge has increased slowly.[17, 18] In my experience, the spectrum concept of schizophrenia offers the most careful approach for the patient.[19]

Each therapist, regardless of orientation, should read one of the current textbooks on psychiatry so that the many ways psychiatric disorders manifest themselves can be recognized. In addition, it is important to be aware of the symptoms and manifestations of organic cerebral disease[20, 21] Organic and nonorganic disorders exist, and both must be carefully considered before making a diagnosis and determining any therapeutic treatment.[22-24]

The most common personality configuration in my clinical data involves one partner in the dyad who has obsessive-compulsive manifestations (either moderate to severe in intensity . . . approximately 12% of the dyads in my practice). Although written more than a decade ago, Salzman's classic book[25] describes obsessive-compulsives' traits, attitudes, and defenses. He uses an adaptive point of view, which incorporates a spectrum of severity. He classifies personality configurations by delineating three levels:

1. Obsessive tendencies are present in all persons, e.g. the nightly rituals most people use at bedtime.
2. The obsessive personality has a more congealed set of defenses, but it may produce no noticeable failure in living and may even bring about marked success:

    In one of my couples with constant discord, the husband was very successful as a principal. When asked to describe what kind of a person he was, he replied in a staccato manner: "I'm opinionated, take charge of any situation, precise, meticulous, methodical, possessive, keep my emotions fairly bottled up, and patience is not my virtue. I like things done my way if no good reason is advanced for doing it any other way."
3. The behavior patterns of the obsessive-compulsive neurosis often impair the individual's effectiveness and may produce bizarre symptoms.

The obsessive individual is one whose inner parental voices demand perfection — the end result of living in an environment where the major emphasis for approval would be the attainment of perfection. As Salzman notes, if one is to be absolutely safe and certain, he has to know everything to predict and prepare for the future. This illusion of perfection for security results in personality compulsivity and rigidity: "one must never make an error or admit a deficiency." Thus, any threat internally from the parental voice or externally from a partner would result in varying degrees of anxiety. My clinical experience confirms the study of Hays[26] who found that the obsessional personality is the end result of all three systems of the GST.

For clinical effectiveness, it is important to differentiate compulsiveness from perfectionism (although the two may coexist). Hollender's description is most clear: "Compulsiveness refers to a pattern of behavior that serves to fend off unacceptable feelings or impulses, perfectionism to a performance designed to evoke commendation. Compulsiveness *protects* against disapproval; perfectionism *reaches* for approval."[27] The compulsive repeats his inappropriate behavior with inability to inhibit it and which he admits is irrational. The perfectionist does not look at his behavior as inappropriate but always looks for defects or flaws. In the "Pygmalion syndrome" the partner demands of the other what he demands of himself. This is often manifested, as one partner acts in a domineering, depreciating, and controlling manner. The complaint of a "domineering partner" (the BRQ item #9) is circled tenth in frequency. The domineering individual always feels in the right; black is black and white is white with no shades in between. Consequently these people refuse to compromise and are difficult to live with. The dyadic relationship is usually stormy unless the other partner obeys and never complains. The price paid for not complaining, however, is high — depression. The depressions develops as the partner turns anger inward. Other equally destructive ways the partner may react with include alcoholism, "romancing" the charge account card, infidelity, etc. Frequently the courtship reveals the Pygmalion syndrome; so, premarital counseling may be most helpful.

The following couple did not seek preventive therapy, however, their case illustrates the reaction of a spouse to her Pygmalion acting husband. She could not express her resentment openly so she chose to take the escape of alcohol. Alcohol helped her contain her hostility and neutralize her anxiety over his demands.

Mr. and Mrs. B were married for fifteen years and were childless. Mr. B complained that " . . . we are raising hell with each others nerves. I recently blew up when she had too much to drink at a dinner party."

Mr. B was a tall, well-built man with a goatee. He spoke deliberately and thus slowly, often pausing as he searched for the precise word he wanted. He kept searching for answers to what may be causing their problems.

As he sought his own answers, he casually expressed the belief that he might be in error toward his wife. He spontaneously excluded sex or extramarital interest as possible elements to their problem. He preferred to label the discontent as related to apparent resentment which could be traced to episodes with his wife drunk. Mr. B said, "I have been accused of being a perfectionist. In my own mind, no! But everything has to be just right. I have to be immaculately dressed and like my wife the same way. A straight line has to be straight. When I was a kid, I was taught to cook. I enjoy cooking and resent that she has no desire to cook or keep house."

Mrs. B was a small, slender woman with an intensely businesslike demeanor. She spoke with concern of their difficulties which had arisen between them over the past two years. Her chief complaint was that he tended to criticize her household operations like an efficiency expert. He feels everything I do should be perfect. He'll correct me if I'm not logical and precise. He watches me so carefully until I could go crazy! He makes me feel so nervous that I have started to drink too much. I do drink at home, but never at work. I've been a private secretary for the past ten years for the same vice-president and receive only praise there! When I do drink, *I can tell Jim things* that normally I couldn't because at that time he won't say anything . . . he'll just listen.

Another example of Pygmalion transactions was apparent in a couple seeking premarital therapy:

"I don't know why Tim is so angry at me and wanting to call off the wedding. All my suggestions have been for his benefit. Early in our courtship he would visit me twice a week but on other nights if I chanced to call after supper I would find that he had already gone to bed at 7 o'clock. He seemed perennially tired. In fact, I gave him a copy of *How Never to Be Tired*. He seems to resent my correcting his table manners which are very poor. I told him to chew with his mouth closed and not to place his napkin under his chin, but he ignores my suggestions. I have encouraged him to start college in the evenings, and he has done that, but with constant complaints. I just can't figure out why he gets so mad when all I am trying to do is help him improve!"

After a few sessions, I suggested that they try to resolve some of the tension over constant "helpfulness" *before* they go ahead with wedding plans. Unfortunately they ignored my advice and returned a year later with the same complaints as a married couple. In 100 couples complaining of a critical partner, the content of their complaints varied, but the discordant relationship was the same type and had been apparent during their courtships.

The next most common configuration which occurred in 15 percent of my patients was that of depressive reactions.[28] This topic was previously discussed under item #11, Chapter VI, on suicide. Frequently, the incidence of this disorder depended on the clinical setting. Thus Weissman and her colleagues[29] found depressive disorders the most common diagnosis with depressive personality the most frequent (4.5%).

Anthony and Benedek present a comprehensive review of depression with emphasis on the experience of depression as part of a universal human vulnerability. They suggest that depression itself may be an existential human experience closely related to human survival due to certain type of stress.[30] Important to point out to the patients is that the *depressive withdrawal*, e.g. loss of libido in partner, disinterest in general, may be misinterpretated as *rejection* instead of as a symptom of mental illness. The following vignette is a good example:

Mr. A, referred by his minister, requested therapy because his wife was having an affair with the next door neighbor. Mrs. A was brought into therapy and admitted the relationship, but defended herself by stating that the past six months has driven her to have an affair. She complained how her husband had lost interest in the activities of their business, and left the entire burden on her shoulders. That alone would not have made other men attractive to her, but their married life had been very active sexually up until 6 months ago and then *ended*. He made no advances toward her and rejected any of her approaches. Recently she talked to her next door neighbor about her predicament. He was very sympathetic and understanding. When his wife went out of town, the inevitable occurred — they became sexually involved. It was only after the neighbor's wife returned, and the affair ended, that she exploded with anger. This precipitated the blow-up and the conference with their minister.

Mr. A appeared depressed throughout the session. When the clinical diagnosis of depression was made, I explained the change of mood and behavior was due to an emotional illness, and what Mrs. A mistook for *rejection* and disinterest was a man withdrawn in depression. With medication, his depression lifted. They continued conjoint therapy until their marital discord was thoroughly understood, and they were able to overlook each other's upsetting responses. This took a total of two months.

In spite of the numerous studies at various research centers,[31-35] it is pragmatically valid and certainly advisable to distinguish between primary affective disorder (endogenous) and reactive depression. Endogenous depression, as examplified in the above vignette, is precipitated primarily from the intrapersonal system vis-à-vis stressful situational life events. (For a comprehensive discussion of primary affective disorder see Chapter XXVII.) I recommend highly Chodoff's critical review[36] for anyone unfamiliar with the depressive personality. In conclusion, I take a careful history from *both partners* and relatives if possible to differentiate the two conditions, since a genetic factor is present in the great majority of primary affective disorders (manic-depressive or endogenous illnesses). This is most important in the different treatments used in this type of dyadic disharmony.

The third frequent type of configuration listed under question #16 is that of projective defense reactions. I view the paranoid process as the core to normal and pathological experiences.[37,38] There is a spectrum of severity that begins with *projection*, the most common of all defense mechanisms. Projection is a form of mild paranoia and can be part of normal adaptive processes. For example, we all use projection to deal with painful experiences, whether we are a child, adolescent or an adult! Such projective statements might include the following: "I'm not to blame, he or she did it." The most common game using Bernean terminology is "If it weren't for him/her." Such thinking can be seen in the following couple whose bitter quarreling about the children propelled them into therapy:

> Mr. and Mrs. B were referred by her lawyer whom she had consulted about a divorce: "I'm unable to take any more of these bitter and silly quarrels about how to raise the children, his inconsistency regarding their discipline, his anger and pouting about how to raise them religiously and, to add salt to the wound, the influence of my mother-in-law. She considers my family, my husband and children, as much hers as they are mine. She is not malicious about this, but when she visits, and this is too often, she takes over my house and much more. I have the feeling that it is not my home or creation. When I discuss these things with my husband, he explodes."
>
> Mr. B, a well-dressed, well-controlled, and quiet mannered, professional man, stated that "he wanted to save the marriage, although their last quarrel about the children was just too much. When she threw the casserole of creamed lobster at me, I yelled back and should have clobbered her, but instead I cleaned up the mess. Our children have been the primary force keeping our marriage together, although I was not prepared for their arrival. The timing of their conceptions was largely a matter of their mother's choice. She started haranguing me about having a baby during our honeymoon. I resisted on the basis that we were not financially ready and had plenty of time to start a family. She had no religious objection to using contraceptive measures, I wanted to put aside money for a house, furniture, travel, and getting to know each other in the context of the marriage setting. After we spent most of our savings on

furniture and moved into a rented house, her requests for a baby became more frequent. After a year of repeated requests, 'all her college friends had babies,' and since our sexual relations had decreased to once or twice a week, I agreed partly on the basis of having the prospect of increasing the frequency and partly because it made me feel badly to continue refusing her. She has never let me forget that she had to wait a year to get pregnant, at the ripe old age of twenty-two. At no time did I have or express the desire to have the baby. This has always infuriated Nancy. The three other children happened accidently on purpose, as a result of improper contraceptive measures on her part (note how he is playing the game of projection: "If It Weren't For Her"). Although I held the financial purse strings, she held the sexual purse strings, and during pregnancies I could have sex whenever I wanted to. Her response was that she was sorry that I did not want to have the children; but, that she did and would not go along with waiting. As a result, I have been less than an ideal father as the children came along. I felt that they were forced on me; also, I felt some initial resentment in each case. Nancy was interested in having babies but not in taking care of them, according to my standards. With each child, I end up bathing them at night, feeding them, playing with them, and setting limits in their behavior. This has led to innumerable quarrels."

This couple represents a combination of the domineering partner and the projective mechanism of the Bernean game: "If It Weren't For her/him."

The paranoid personality is a deeper disorder and more serious. This condition can produce, what I have described, as the "District Attorney Syndrome."[39] The eleventh in frequency among the BRQ relationship complaints involves an unjust accusation of infidelity by a suspicious partner. The following vignette is illustrative:

Mr. S angrily stated: "For the past year our relationship has been somewhat rocky. My work requires considerable travel. Before, during and after each trip, Jane makes constant references to infidelity, potential infidelity, how my time is spent, how the money is spent and on whom, whether the time and money were necessary, what time I leave to make my calls, what time I return and why, where I eat and with whom, etc. I am facing a problem that to me is utterly fantastic and one I never had to face before. It is destroying what by all odds should be a very happy relationship. Now it seems I must spend most of my time proving that I have done nothing wrong when I am not with her."

Mrs. S, in a resigned attitude, stated: "I would like to have an understanding with John that our love is strong enough not to waver, and that we won't ever be unfaithful to each other. The first year of our courtship was very smooth. He was fun to talk to; we liked doing the same things and got along well. But in the past year, since he began traveling, he is not confiding in me about past or present family affairs or about his business trips — where he went for dinner, his time schedules, who he saw while he was out of town or here in town, no communication. My questions about other women set him off violently. He often strikes at me viciously, then says he is sorry. I have found lipstick on his shirts and handker-chiefs, and blonde hair on his jacket. He claims they are mine. He gets angry when I question him and he refuses to discuss it."

This couple and many couples with the same type of complaint usually have been quarreling over suspected infidelity for years. Very often a partner will state that the repeated questioning is driving him/her insane and is like a "district attoney." This type of complaint is related to the condition of pathological jealousy.

Completing the projective spectrum is the *paranoid psychotic reaction* with severe distortion of reality and bizarre complaints. The therapist should be alerted to comments, made in question 16, such as, "I'm very jealous,"[40] "I feel people try to take advantage of me," "At times I feel my partner may be trying to poison me," etc. It is important to keep in mind that the suspicious and paranoid individual is *hypervigilant*, and often times there is some truth to their suspicions.

In conclusion, paranoid ideas can be perceived along a continuum of mild, where suspiciousness is primary; moderate, where projection is manifested by fluid delusions; and severe, characterized by severe delusions.[41]

The fourth personality configuration, in terms of frequency, were patients whose behavior may be classified under a spectrum of mild to severe "hysteria."[42-48] These patients range from normality to hysterical psychotic reaction.[49] The first type on the spectrum is beautifully described by Grinstein[50] as the "doll" (in current slang, as "plastic") whose narcissistic self-preoccupation allows her to look sexually feminine, but prevents her from following through and is sexually anorgastic. These women dress in the height of fashion, are impeccably groomed, have their hair styled in the latest vogue, and are conspicuous by their excessive makeup. The new DSM-III classification of hysteria has been radically changed into two main categories: hysteria as a subtype under neurotic disorders and hysterical under personality disorder.[51] The hysterical personality usually refers to female patients, but can also be seen in men[52] with the following characteristics: seductiveness, histrionic behavior, excitability, marked emotional lability, often taking the form of emotional storms, and extreme forms of dependency, which are manifested in clinging and demanding interpersonal relationships (especially characteristic in their patient-therapist relationship). Hyler and Spitzer[53] point out that when using the DSM-III's "inclusion and exclusion criteria" (where the physical mechanism explains the symptom and the linkage of symptoms to psychological forces) the symptom initiation is under voluntary control. Also, when using the DSM-III as a guide, the patient's obvious environmental goals, the differential diagnosis of somatoform disorder, the factitious disorder, the malingering, the psychological factors affecting physical conditions, and the undiagnosed physical illness can be differentiated.

The fifth type of personality configuration has been described under the rubric of character disorders that include psychopath, sociopath, dyssocial, etc. Character or personality is made up of the repetitive patterns of behavior that an individual has adapted to his inner beliefs and values and to those of the prevailing cultural milieu. The "normal" person's behavior is in harmony with his value system. In character disorders, behavior is "abnormal" primarily as judged by the value system of others. Since the individual is unaware of this, he does not experience anxiety or guilt. The diagnosis of character disorder is based on antisocial behavior — his psychopathic actions are inappropriate to his educational background and to the values and behavior of his parents or authorities. He is usually indifferent to the impact of his behavior on others since he lacks shame or remorse. On occasion he may suddenly react violently. He is a great rationalizer and convincing in his excuses because of his good intelligence and charm. He is often unable to form lasting relationships because of his excessive narcissism and incapacity for object love. Frequently there is a long history of dyssocial behavior. Many of these individuals describe themselves as "impulsive" with an inability to endure delays in need satisfaction. Others describe themselves as "loners" or "on the outside looking in," in describing their sense of isolation. Still other types of character disorders, in addition to the borderline states[54] just mentioned, include the addictions — alcohol or drugs.

Psychopathy consists of a variety of dyssocial behavior and, thus, cuts across diagnostic classifications.[55,56] It is important to differentiate antisocial behavior from character psychopathology. Bursten describes a "new" type of psychopath labeled "manipulative."[57] The psychopathic "manipulator" affects all sociocultural classes and his behavior will command increasing attention from all mental health professionals and related disciplines.

In conclusion, the concepts of one's self-image and the clusters of personality traits (into types of personality configurations) influence all dyadic relationships. Therapists have to consider the intrapersonal system with any dysfunctional relationship, because a personality disorder may be present in one or both partners.

SCHOOL ADJUSTMENT

Number seventeen, on the BRQ, asks each patient about his/her school adjustment: *How well did you do as far as grades were concerned? What extracurricular activities did you participate in? What problems did you have in school?*

The records encoded during an individual's schooling may at times be valuable in estimating the intensity of the three different voices, especially an approximation of the innate intellectual capacity of the individual. When one begins schooling, two main variables appear: the demands of school authorities in terms of performance academically and behaviorally and the relationships with peers. Frequently some individuals focus on intellectual pursuits in order to escape their anxiety about their object relationships to their peers. On the other hand, since each person matures at different rates, and since the environmental influences change, various modes of adjustment manifest themselves. The following clinical excerpt shows adjustments at different time intervals:

Mrs. E answered, "I learned to read at age five, before I entered first grade. Though bright, I was not mature enough for first grade and was tense. I often wet my pants, for example, because I was afraid to ask to be excused. My first two years of schooling was at a parochial school, run by rather formidable nuns who rewarded me with a gold star or disciplined me with a ruler across the knuckles. Later I went to the public school and was more relaxed. I liked school and have been an avid reader since the age of four. I read everything in sight. I had a few good friends as I grew up. I had what I felt to be an extremely large and ugly nose. Of course, my 'enemies' soon found this tender spot and would tease me about it. In general, I had enough friends and was respected even by those who didn't like me because I was smart.

After grade school I attended a large high school with excellent facilities for its 5000 students. I went right into honor classes because of my high IQ. I did not maintain my potential. The school was enormous and at times overcrowded. My parents were not sophisticated in the ways of getting the best out of a school for their children, and I did not know how either. So, I became lost in the shuffle, maintaining a barely adequate average to enter college. Socially, I had my own group of friends and I was very interested in boys. For some reason I chose to alienate any boys who were even vaguely interested in me. I had very few dates but my friends and I had parties with boys, and we did things together like going horseback riding, to the beach, and such.

After high school I announced that I wanted to go away to college. I felt superior to the city's public colleges to consider them, and my grades were shaky. My parents said, 'with what?' So I got a job for a year. I saved all my money and went away to college. It was perfect as my talents were appreciated. I was the editor of everything. I maintained highest honors though my time to study was at times limited. I was sailing high. All that I read seemed to fall happily together, and I developed a good, thirsty approach to knowledge which I have never lost. It was a fruitful time of my life and I was thoroughly happy."

This woman illustrates how at different stages in her life she made various social and scholastic adjustments. She made a better scholastic-peer adjustment during college, both toward females and males. It was the latter, a marital disharmony, which brought her in for therapy.

The following individual is typical of a different type of adjustment:

"I had good grades in grammar school, but I was very shy and always felt inferior. I feared and sometimes detested my teachers. In high school I was an honor student for the first two years, but in the last two years I barely passed. I was shy and had a stong inferiority complex. As a result I participated in no extracurricular activities and never dated. Part of this was due to financial problems; I had a part-time job after school. In addition, I had started to study music just before entering high school, and this kepy me busy. My parents were very strict, and I was never allowed to have friends at home."

This girl's poor peer adjustment interfered with her scholastic achievement. As a result she rationalized her situation and withdrew into music to avoid further emotional trauma.

The next two individuals describe good adjustment in all developmental areas during their school years:

"I always loved school. I was the teacher's favorite in grammar school. In high school I was coeditior of the school magazine and in the upper 3 percent of my class. I was on the honor roll. In college I made National Honor Society. I studied hard during the week and dated like mad on weekends. I was selected campus beauty queen and was active in my sorority, president in my senior year."

"I was always a very good student. I was valedictorian of my high school class. My college career was full of fun. I did well academically, participated in all sports and lead an active social life."

When I tabulated school and peer adjustment for those couples with complaints of disharmony, the men had an average social adjustment, an excellent academic adjustment, an average extracurricular activities adjustment, and a better than average self-image. In the majority of these couples, the male was the sole wage earner and in the upper socioeconomic classes. The women, however, felt less good about their overall adjustment.

A woman's self-image is influenced by the culture as much as by her personal self-assessment. For many women in America, a woman tries to "go steady"[58] and "catch a man". Many college-age women are unhappy if this does not occur. A poor self-image prevents many women from finding a mate. Those that do marry and have not developed a good self-image are often distraught when their spouses do not treat them with respect. I firmly believe than in order to have a constructive dyadic relationship, there must be mutual respect, and mutual respect is built upon each partner having self-respect. When there is an extreme imbalance in educational achievement between partners, negative effects may manifest themselves upon their relationship.[59] Item #17 on the BRQ will often reveal such a problem area.

REFERENCES

1. Jones, Warren L.: Marriage — growth or disaster. *Am J Psychiat, 125:* 1115, 1969.
2. Sabshin, Melvin: Psychiatric perspectives on normality. *Arch Gen Psychiat, 17:* 258, 1967.
3. English, O. Spurgeon: Changing techniques of psychotherapy. *Voices, 2:* 91, 1966.
4. Vaillant, George E.: Theoretical hierarchy of adaptive ego mechanism — a 30 year follow-up of 30 men selected for psychological health. *Arch Gen Psychiat, 24:* 107-18, 1971.
5. Rioch, David McK: Personality — an overview. *Arch Gen Psychiat, 27:* 575-80, 1978.
6. Diagnostic Statistical Manual (DSM-III) preliminary outline. *Psychiatric News, 13:* 14-24, 1978 (Dec 15th).
7. Akiskal, Hagop S and Webb, William L.: *Psychiatric Diagnosis: Exploration of Biological Predictors.* New York, Spectrum, 1978.
8. Stern, A.: Psychoanalytic investigation of and therapy in the borderline group of neuroses. *Psychoanal Quart, 7:* 467-489, 1938.
9. Brinkley, John R., Beitman, Bernard D., and Friedel, Robert O.: Low-dose neuroleptic regimes in the treatment of borderline patients. *Arch Gen Psychiat, 36:* 319-26, 1979.
10. Domash, Leanne and Shapiro, Roy: Dysfunctional patterns of thinking

in the borderline personality. *J Am Acad Psychoanal, 7:* 453-52, 1979.

11. Rich, C. L.: Borderline diagnoses. *Am J Psychiat, 135:* 1399, 1978.

12. Shapiro, Edward R.: The psychodynamics and developmental psychology of the borderline patient — a review of the literature. *Am J Psychiat, 135:* 1305-15, 1978.

13. Perry, J. C. and Klerman, G. L.: The borderline patient — a comparative analysis of four sets of diagnostic criteria. *Arch Gen Psychiat, 35:* 141-50, 1978.

14. Gunderson, J. G. and Kolb, J. E.: Discriminating features of borderline patients. *Am J Psychiat, 35:* 792-96, 1978.

15. Grinker, Roy, Sr., and Werble, Beatrice: *The Borderline Patient.* New York, Aronson, 1977.

16. Mack, John E.: Borderline states in psychiatry. In Greenblatt, Milton and Mack, John E. (Eds.): Seminars in Psychiatry. New York, Grune, 1975.

17. Wyatt, R. J.: Introduction: special section — current concepts of schizophrenia. *Am J Psychiat, 133:* 171-72, 1976.

18. Strauss, J. S. and Gift, T. E.: Choosing an approach for diagnosing schizophrenia. *Arch Gen Psychiat, 34:* 1248-53, 1977.

19. Reich, W.: The spectrum concept of schizophrenia. *Arch Gen Psychiat, 32:* 489-98, 1975.

20. Wells, C. E.: Chronic brain disease: an overview. *Am J Psychiat, 135:* 1-12, 1978.

21. Seltzer, B. and Sherwin, I.: Organic brain syndromes: an empirical study and critical review. *Am J Psychiat, 135:* 13-17, 1978.

22. Arieti, Silvano (Ed.). *American Handbooks of Psychiatry,* 6 Vols. New York, Basic Books, 1979.

23. Cooper, J. E., Kendell, R. E., Gurland, B. J., et al.: *Psychiatric Diagnosis in New York and London.* London, Oxford Univ Press, 1976.

24. Freedman, A. M., Kaplan, H. I., and Sadock, B. J. (Eds.): *Comprehensive Textbook of Psychiatry,* 2nd ed. Baltimore, Williams & Wilkins, 1975.

25. Salzman, Leon: *The Obsessive Personality.* New York, Science House, 1968.

26. Hays, Peter: Determination of the obsessional personality. *Am J Psychiat, 129:* 131-33, 1972.

27. Hollender, Marc H.: Perfectionism, a neglected personality trait. *J Clin Psychiat, 39:* 384, 1978.

28. Schatzberg, Alan F: Classification of depressive disorders. In Cole, Jonathan, Schatzberg, Alan F., and Frazier, Shervet H. (Eds.): *Depression — Biology, Psychodynamics, and Treatment.,* New York, Plenum Press, 1978, pp. 13-40.

29. Weissman, Myrna M., Myers, Jerome K., and Harding, Pamela, S: Psychiatric disorders in a U. S. urban community — 1975-76. *Am J Psychiat, 135:* 459-62, 1978.

30. Anthony, James E. and Benedek, Therese (Eds.): *Depression and Human Existence.* Boston, Little, 1975.

31. Hirschfeld, R. M. A. and Klerman, G. L.: Personality attributes and

134   *A Clinical Approach to Marital Problems*

affective disorders. *Am J Psychiat, 136:* 67-70, 1979.

32. Klerman, Gerald L., Endicott, Jean, Spitzer, Robert L., and Hirschfeld, Robert: Neurotic depressions — a systematic analysis of multiple criteria and meanings. *Am J Psychiat, 136:* 57-61, 1979.

33. Endicott, Jean and Spitzer, Robert L.: Use of research diagnostic criteria and the schedule for affective disorders and schizophrenia to study affective disorders. *Am J Psychiat, 136:* 52-56, 1979.

34. Wolpert, Edward A., (Ed.): *Manic-Depressive Illness: History of a syndrome.* New York, Int Univ Pr, 1977.

35. Hirschfeld, R. M. A., Klerman, Gerald L., Chodoff, Paul, et al.: Dependency — self esteem — clinical depression, *J Am Acad Psychoanal, 4:* 373-88, 1976.

36. Chodoff, Paul: The depressive personality: a critical review. *Arch Gen Psychiat, 73:* 666-673, 1972.

37. Meissner, W. W.:*The Paranoid Process.* New York, Aronson, 1978.

38. DiBella, Williston G. A.: Educating staff to manage paranoid patients. *Am J Psychiat, 136:* 333-35, 1979.

39. Greene, Bernard L.: Contraindications to marriage. *Med Aspects Hum Sexuality, 2:* 4, 1968.

40. Mazur, Ronald: *The New Intimacy: Open-ended Marriage and Alternative Lifestyles.* Boston, Beacon, 1973.

41. Abroms, Gene M., Taintor, Zebulon, C., and Lhamon, William T.: Percept assimilation and paranoid severity. *Arch Gen Psychiat, 14:* 491, 1966.

42. Merskey, Harold and Trimble, Michael: Personality, sexual adjustment, and brain lesions in patients with conversion symptoms. *Am J Psychiat, 136:* 179-182, 1979.

43. Chodoff, Paul: Psychotherapy of the hysterical personality disorder. *J Am Acad Psychoanal, 6:* 497-510, 1978.

44. Chodoff, Paul: The diagnosis of hysteria — an overview. *Am J Psychiat, 131:* 1073-78, 1974.

45. Celani, David: An interpersonal approach to hysteria. *Am J Psychiat, 133:* 1414-18, 1976.

46. Kimble, Ray, Williams, James G., and Argras, Stewart: A comparison of two methods of diagnosing hysteria. *Am J Psychiat, 132:* 1197-1200, 1975.

47. Compton, Ariel S.: Who's hysterical. *J Sex & Marital Therapy, 1:* 158-174, 1974.

48. Hollender, Marc H.: Conversion hysteria. *Arch Gen Psychiat, 26:* 311-25, 1972.

49. Cavenar, Jesse O., Jr., Sullivan, John L., and Maltbie, Allan A.: A clinical note on hysterical psychosis. *Am J Psychiat, 136:* 830-32, 1979.

50. Grinstein, Alexander: Profile of a doll — a female character type. *Psychoanaly Rev, 50:* 162, 1963.

51. Hyler, Steven E. and Spitzer, Robert L.: Hysteria split asunder. *Am J Psychait, 135:* 1500-04, 1978.

52. Luisada, P., Peele, R., and Pittard, E.: The hysterical personality in men. *Am J Psychiat, 131:* 518-522, 1974.
53. Hyler, S. E. and Spizter, R. L., Hysteria split asunder.
54. Litowitz, Norman S. and Newman, Kenneth, M: Borderline personality and the theatre of the absurd. *Arch Gen Psychiat, 16:* 268, 1967.
55. Reid, William H. (Ed.): *The Psychopath: A Comprehensive Study of Antisocial Disorders and Behaviors.* New York, Brunner-Mazel, 1978.
56. Smith, Robert J.: *The Psychopath in Society.* New York, Acad Pr, 1978.
57. Bursten, Ben: Manipulative men — their sexual attitudes. *Med Aspects Hum Sexuality, 7:* 168-96, 1973.
58. Macklin, Eleanor D.: Heterosexual cohabitation among unmarried college students. *Family Coordinator, 21:* 463-72, 1972.
59. Ferber, Marianne and Huber, Joan: Husbands, wives, and careers. *J Marr & Family, 41:* 315-25, 1979.

Chapter XIII

MEDICAL HISTORY

THE 18th question on the BRQ asks each patient seven questions pertaining to his/her past and current medical history:

a. *Family physician: Name, street, city, zip code, phone*
b. *What is your present state of health?*
c. *When did you have your last medical checkup?*
d. *What serious injuries or medical illnesses have you or any family member had, and when?*
e. *Surgical operations?*
f. *Current medications:*
g. *Habits:*
   1. *What drugs or "street drugs, e.g. coke, angel dust etc." are you presently taking:*
   2. *How much do you smoke?*
   3. *How much do you drink and how often?*
   4. *Do you think you or your partner drink too much?*

This brief medical history is especially important for the nonmedical therapist. The first question asks for the family physician so that the therapist is prepared in case of an emergency or in requesting medical data pertinent for therapy. (In emergencies, the therapist should also contact significant others.) Suicide now ranks third among the causes of death in people aged fifteen to twenty-four. The second question asks for the patient's current state of health. Some replies are short and curt but still informative:

"I'm healthy as an ox but plagued by beastly headaches." In my data one-fourth of the men said excellent while only one-eighth of the women said the same. Those replying "good" included two-thirds of the male patients and one-half of the females. Poor health was listed by 5 percent of the men and 15 percent of the women. Nervousness was stated by 10 percent of the men and 20 percent of the women. (My data shows that men have stated nervousness more frequently over the years.)

The third question notes any recent medical evaluation that is valuable when assessing a relationship problem.[1-6] This is also the first attempt by the therapist to practive prevention. As Ford has observed, patients often use hypoglycemic symptoms (low blood sugar levels) to rationalize sexual complaints. On the other hand, he notes that " . . . a surprisingly large number of these hypoglycemic patients had histories of significant sexual dysfuntions such as partial impotence in men, dyspareunia and/or inhibited responsiveness in women, and lowered libido or avoidance of sexual activity in both sexes."[7] Kaplan adds that " . . . it is unconscionable to treat a patient for an alleged psychogenic disorder (relationship) in the presence of physical pathology."[8,9]*

Any pregnant patient is asked if the pregnancy is interfering with her sexual desire and responsiveness toward intercourse.[10] I encourage such females to describe problems related to their condition.[11-14] Masters and Johnson[15] reported a decrease in sexual frequency during the first three months of pregnancy, which was followed by an increase during the next three months and then a decrease in the last trimester. Additional factors influencing sexual desire and responsiveness include physiological changes, concepts of self-image, conflicts about roles, and partners' attitudes, etc. After delivery, many women experience "Baby Blues."[16,17] Postpartum reactions are normal in men as well as women.[18,19] For most women, any mild depression at that time resolves itself without formal treatment. In my experience, when persistent moderate to severe degrees of depression (along with any other psychiatric condition) are triggered within the three months following delivery, these nondiminishing emotional upheavals should be treated by a psychiatrist.

Every pregnant patient should be advised that recent research reveals that alcohol intake increases the likelihood of birth defects — fetal alcohol syndrome.[20,21]

The termination of the childbearing phase (postmenopausal) may also precipitate an emotional crisis in some women, e.g. promiscuity may reflect a shattered identity and a desire to regain youth.[22]

The fourth question on #18 asks about any injuries,[23,24] or serious medical illnesses[25] the patient, his/her partner, or children have, or have had. The purpose of this is to double check if one or the other omitted any medical or surgical condition or injury. To illustrate: a

---

*For the nonmedical therapist, the following one page illustrations in the journal, Medical Aspects of Human Sexuality, will point out the perplexity of the problems and the need for requesting a recent, complete medical evaluation.

   a. *Vol. 11*, page 51, Oct. 1977 — Some urologic causes of dyspareunia;
   b. *Vol. 11*, page 83, July 1977 — Possible sexual effects of some female endocrine disorders;
   c. *Vol. 12*, page 103, June 1978; and,
   d. *Vol. 12*, page 51, July 1978.

male patient who had poliomyelitis as a child, with moderate atrophy of one leg, did not report this condition on his BRQ, whereas his partner reported it. Although this condition was not readily visible, the knowledge helped me understand this man's violent reaction to his wife's request for divorce and was valuable in his therapy.

Depending on the age of the patient, this question becomes more important because, as one gets older, illnesses increase. All types of illness were reported on the BRQ form and usually correspond with the general population. When the therapist feels there is something unusual about the patient's behavior, he should rule out a medical illness. For example, in this couple the wife's main complaint was sexual dissatisfaction following her partner's return from Japan. A liver profile on the husband's blood revealed a chronic hepatitis.[26] Three very important medical conditions require further discussion: coronary disease, hypertension (where medication can produce changes in sexual behavior), and diabetes.

Cardiovascular diseases add stress to dyadic relationships in many ways, e.g. sexual dysfunctions as a result of medication, anxiety about physical exertion. Hypertension[27] is an extremely common condition which frequently causes heart diseases, "strokes" etc. A common complication of heart disease is coronary infarct ("heart attacks"). The increasing coronary by-pass operations, perhaps as many as 2,000 per week, frequently lead to many relationship problems due to the likelihood of overt or masked depression, anxieties about sexual relations, to name a few.[28]

Diabetes, an oftentimes undiagnosed medical condition, is overlooked in either sex. This medical condition frequently is a cause of dyadic disharmony as it can result in depression and/or sexual dysfunction. In males who have had diabetes for six years or more, about 50 percent may have difficulties with penile erection.[29-31] In fact, impotence can preceed the diagnosis of diabetes by a year or more. The time lag depends on when the patient sought help, and on the awareness of the physician.[32] At times, however, the impotence in a diabetic may have a psychogenic basis,[33-35] or have a combination of both organic and psychogenic factors, and may respond to sex therapy. Objective tests are now available either by electroencephalography (REM — rapid eye movements — four to seven per night in normal males are correlated with nocturnal penile tumescences (NPT) or penile strip charts attached to the penis, which measure tumescences either in a dream laboratory or at the patient's home ("peter meters"). The findings in diabetic women as regarding orgasm are equivocal.[36, 37]

Surgical procedures can greatly influence any relationship. In my experience, females underwent three times as many operations as males. Hysterectomies, often done for sterilization,[38] and mastectomies (one out of fourteen women will experience this procedure during her lifetime)[39-41] are most common. Lief[42] regrets that only 10 percent of the surgeons discuss the anxieties with their patients following a mastectomy. In addition, very few surgeons tell their patients how breast surgery may affect sexual and marital relationships. Lief quotes from a study by Dornbush and her colleagues that two out of three women would have welcomed this discussion. Most postoperative women had a temporary decrease in orgastic frequency; one-fifth had no sex in the first three months after surgery; erotic breast stimulation declined in about one-half the women, and there was a marked decrease in those who could undress in front of their partners and have sex without being partially clothed. The following articles[43-48] indicate strong psychological suffering, e.g. suicidal ideation, increased use of tranquilizers and alcohol. Schoenberg[49] in an article (1979) states the importance of a partner to be involved in the therapeutic process.[50] This also applies to the psychosexual impact of treatment in female genital cancer[51] where radiotherapy often causes painful intercourse due to vaginitis, stenosis, or even atrophy.

In my clinical experience, some women use surgery for psychological purposes, either consciously or unconsciously: to alleviate unconscious *guilt* based on murderous and/or sexual impulses; as an attention maneuver directed toward the partner; and, as a manifestation of the hysterical personality where multiple operations on the abdomen result in a "gridiron abdomen." The chronicity of their medical complaints produce unnecessary operations. I would suspect that a number of women who have repeated cosmetic surgeries would fall into this category. The majority of today's surgeons know this type of woman and refuse to operate without psychiatric clearance. A clinical example of this type of personality is illustrated in the following:

> Mr. and Mrs. A, referred by their respective lawyers for counseling. Mr. A was angry at his wife for their financial difficulties due to excessive medical expenditures and splurges on clothes-buying. Mrs. A was annoyed with her spouse for being unfaithful, and more so because it was with her best friend during her convalescence from her last operation. She related the following surgical history on the BRQ: (1) appendectomy two years after marriage when she was twenty-one, for a chronic appendicitis of one-year duration, (2) exploratory laparotomy at twenty-three where adhesions (?) were found — a laparotomy is an abdominal operation for an undiagnosed

medical condition — (3) suspension of the uterus — abdominal operation — for chronic low back pain at age thirty, (4) gallbladder removed at thirty-five because of upper abdominal pains, and (5) hysterectomy at thirty-eight. It was during this last operation that her spouse was unfaithful.

In my clinical experience, the most common surgery in men that can lead to dyadic dysharmony is the vasectomy. Vasectomy can prove to be the "unkindest cut of all" in some relationships, e.g. charges of infidelity, emotional reaction to the process as a demasculating effect, unreasonable sexual demands by the male creating anxiety and/or anger in the female, etc. On the other hand, vasectomy can have a favorable affect on sexual behavior by eliminating the fear of impregnation. A vasectomy, however, is not a magic solution for relationship disharmony. A careful psychological evaluation of each couple contemplating vasection is an excellent preventive measure. Vaughn (1979) has reviewed the literature concerning the behavior and psychological responses of couples when the vasectomy was used as a contraceptive technique.[52] Cole and Byron[53] have also summarized the literature on vasectomy relevant to therapists in a single convenient format, giving a brief description of the operation and complications. Since the incidence of psychosexual problems postoperatively may run as high as 3 percent and the failure rate about one in 500 procedures, a decision should not be made without an interview(s) in-depth with both partners. The same warning about vasectomies should also be used in women before tubal ligation for sterilization. Di Musto points out the importance of educating and counseling the couple before surgery. "It has been demonstrated by multiple studies that better psychological results are obtained in those women who are sterilized for socio-economic reasons than those who undergo the operation for medical conditions."[54] His rule of thumb is to be very cautious with the couple who expect improvement of their sexual lives from tubal ligation.

Of importance is the increasing number of men undergoing penile prosthetic implants for erectile problems.[55-57] Two major prosthesis manufacturers recently reported that more than 15,000 penile prostheses have been ordered by physicians for their patients.[58] Given these statistics, it appears that the age of prosthetic treatment has arrived. I would suggest that each couple have a psychological evaluation and/or therapy before and after surgery.[59, 60]

Since sex is a reverberation of the total relationship, the couple should be made to understand that the penis is only a part of the male's sexual functioning. The penile implant does not enable the male to ejaculate or have a climax. His pleasure comes from making his partner happy or his narcissistic reasons. Unless the couple is made aware of this, anger, blame, and disappointment may result. Explicit suggestions for adequate sexual play and necessary modifications of coital positions and other interventions are helpful.

Finally, with the increasing numbers of individuals seeking *cosmetic* surgery, every therapist should know that in a recent study (1979),[61] 10 percent of these individuals, who gave no indication of an impending divorce before surgery, obtained a legal separation or divorce three to six months after surgery.

The sixth question on #18 (f) inquires about the current medication the individual is or has taken, as some medicines may effect emotions, feelings, thoughts, and behavior. Also, certain medication may give clues as to an underlying psychiatric illness, e.g. tranquilizers in anxiety states, antidepressants in depression, and the major tranquilizers in psychotic or borderline disorders. Further, the therapist can learn whether a patient has been taking medication without having seen a physician for the renewal of any prescription. Weight control pills, especially the amphetamines and thyroid medications, can not only be *addicting* but can interfere with dyadic transactions by producing irritability, low pain thresholds, and insomnia in the patient. All therapists, regardless of discipline, should own or have access to a copy of the *Physicians Desk Reference (PDR)* which lists and illustrates all drugs and describes dosage, warnings, adverse reactions and contraindications. Certain drugs, e.g. those drugs ued to control hypertension (elevated blood pressure) can cause sexual dysfunctions such as retarded ejaculation, erectile difficulties, anorgasmia in the female, and loss of sexual interest, etc.[62,63]

The seventh question on item 18 lists four subheadings with the first query about current habits: "street drugs," smoking, and alcoholic intake. Not infrequently, one partner will understate his addiction, while the other partner will reveal the problem. Occasionally, one partner will admit being an alcoholic to the surprise of the mate.[64] It is best to ask specifically the amount of alcohol the patient consumes, e.g. one man, when asked, stated he only drank two bottles of beer each night. This did not seem unreasonable to the interviewer, and it was not discussed further. When this was related to his wife, she bitterly asked: "Did you ask what size bottle?" Since I did not, she informed me that they were half-gallon bottles. With alcoholic beverages, one drink may contain an ounce or may be a double or more.

There seems to be a correlation between relaxed life-styles, more liberal sexual attitudes, and drug intake. There is a switch from the "big bottle of alcoholic beverges" to the "little bottle of pills" or a combination of both. "Quads" (methaqualone) are sold as "street drugs" and are supposed to increase sexual performance. Originally introduced as a relatively new nonbarbiturate drug for insomnia and nonaddicting, it is now recognized as a significant problem in drug abuse.[65]

"Popping" and "snorting" volatile nitrites are used prior to sexual climax to prolong the sensory effects.[66][67] The use of volatile nitrites is used extensively among homosexual men, but professionals are now seeing couples in their thirties and forties using these drugs. Patients should be warned of potential unpleasant effects as headaches, weakness, and malaise. The "speed freak" develops from a dependence on amphetamines.[68]

Mind-altering drugs, such as LSD,[69] STP, and PCP ("angel dust"),[70-72] can produce hallucinations and delusions. These dangerous drugs can induce violence. Other drugs are potentially dangerous because of their potential addictive and toxic qualities.[73,74] Concern for the young patient as well as adult patients in the use of drugs can be a help to constructive progress in therapy; the public remains uninformed about medical findings that clearly indicate definite health hazards from marijuana[75] and other drugs.

One should be suspicious when a patient does a great deal of "sniffing" (from dryness of the nostrils) during a therapy session. In several of my clinical cases, the use of cocaine was denied until one of the partners had an acute psychotic break. Bad "trips" (especially due to LSD) can be a frightening experience for any spectator. Since medical knowledge is limited as to the short and long range effects from drug usage, the therapist should discourage experimentation with drugs and limit those prescribed in therapy.

Item #18 includes a question about smoking habits. This information can be helpful as a discussion about smoking may lead into a discussion about alcoholism. Currently, I found alcoholism listed tenth in frequency as a dyadic complaint on the BRQ and 7 percent of the dyads had a member who was an alcoholic. In comparison, 8 percent to 10 percent of the general population in America has an alcohol problem. I have noticed, along with others,[76,77] that the gap is closing between the number of women and men who can be classified as alcoholics. I note a trend for more women finding themselves with a drinking problem, and in my current practice I treat two women for every three men (which was not the case ten years ago).

Alcoholism is a biopsychosocial disease involving all systems of the GST.[78-81] Current research indicates that chronic drinkers undergo physiological changes (intrapersonal system) which includes negative effects on some sexual hormones and their organs, e.g. lowered testosterone levels due to testicular atrophy and liver damage increasing the leutinizing hormone levels.[82] Decreased sexual desire and sexual dysfunctions are frequent complaints in both sexes (intra- and interpersonal systems),[83-85] as is a decrease in meeting responsibilities (environmental system — as a parent, an employer, an employee, a person behind the wheel of a car, etc.). An alcoholic is unable to control his drinking, and often he will not identify his problem. Alcoholism can be viewed as multiple diseases, with multiple causes and numerous patterns and personality configurations.[86-88]

Knowledge of the many diverse affects alcohol can have upon the whole person will make the therapist alert to its many influences upon the other GST systems. In men as young as forty, impotence is associated more often with the excessive use of alcohol than any other factor.[89,90] Alcoholism is not a specific syndrome, but an ongoing experience within relationships where one partner is an alcoholic.[91,92] There are numerous sources[93,94] as well as the National Council on Alcoholism[95] that can help therapists comprehend the full scope of the problem and possible avenues to use with alcoholics.

The CAGE questionnaire is a rapid and sensitively designed tool that indicates covert, problem drinking. This questionnaire asks whether one has ever felt you should . . .

"*C*ut down on your drinking; have people
*A*nnoyed you by criticizing your drinking; have you ever felt
*G*uilty about your drinking; and, have you ever had an
*E*ye-opener (drink) the first thing in the morning to steady your
nerves or get rid of a hang-over?[96]

It is important when treating the alcoholic to include the family, especially the spouse. Three years after therapy had ended a former patient wrote a letter of thanks for bringing his wife into therapy and into the overall approach to his problem. Because of the fact that alcoholism is not a specific syndrome, but an ongoing experience within relationships where one partner is alcoholic, I no longer support the concept of specificity in interpersonal patterns, e.g. the alcoholic game by Berne, or any other conceptualization.

In this chapter I have attempted to stress the value of the seven questions in taking a medical history by the therapist.

REFERENCES

1. Koranyi, Erwin K.: Morbidity and rate of undiagnosed physical illnesses

in a psychiatric clinic population. *Arch Gen Psychiat, 36:* 414-19, 1979.

2. Hall, Richard C W., Popkin, Michael K., Devaul, Richard A., Faillace, Louis A., and Stickney, Sondra K.: Physical illness presenting as psychiatric disease, *Arch Gen Psychiat, 35:* 1315-20, 1978.

3. Abse, D. Wilford, Nash, Ethel M., and Louden, Lois M. R.: *Marital & Sexual Counseling in Medical Practice.* New York, Harrow, 1974.

4. Wabrek, Alan J. and Wabrek, Carolyn J.: *Dyspareunia. J Sex & Marital Therapy, 1:* 234-41, 1975.

5. Wise, Thomas N: Sexual problems resulting from interactions between medical and psychological conditions. *Med Aspects Hum Sexuality, 12:* 71-89, 1978.

6. Pinderhughes, Charles A., Barrabee, Grace, E., and Reyna, L. J.: Interrelationships between sexual functioning and medical conditions. *Med Aspects Hum Sexuality, 6:* 52-76, 1972.

7. Ford, Charles V: Hypoglycemia, hysteria, and sexual function. *Med Aspects Hum Sexuality, 11:* 63-74, 1977.

8. Kaplan, Helen S.: Editorial: Sex is psychosomatic. *J Sex & Marital Therapy, 1:* 275-76, 1975.

9. Small, Michael P.: Differential diagnosis of impotence. *Med Aspects Hum Sexuality, 12:* 55-56, 1978.

10. LaRossa, Ralph: *Conflict and Power in Marriage.* Beverly Hills, CA, Sage, 1977.

11. Westbrook, M. T.: The reactions to child-bearing and early maternal experience of women with differing marital relationships. *Brit J Med Psychology, 51:* 191-99, 1978.

12. Lief, Harold I: What's new in sex research. *Med Aspects Hum Sexuality, 11:* 56-57, 1977.

13. Green, Richard (Ed.): *Human Sexuality: A Health Practitioner's Text.* Baltimore, Md., Williams & Wilkins Co., 1975.

14. Hollender, Marc H. and McGehee, James B.: The wish to be held during pregnancy. *J Psychosomatic Research, 18:* 193-97, 1974.

15. Masters, William T. & Johnson, Virginia E.: *Human Sexual Response.* Boston, Little, 1966.

16. Friedman, Morton: Obsession with mate's sexual experiences. *Med Aspects Hum Sexuality, 13:* 54-59, 1979.

17. Weissman, Myrna M: Sex-related factors in female depression. *Med Aspects Hum Sexuality, 12:* 59-60, 1978.

18. Bieber, Irving and Bieber, Toby B: Post-partum reactions in men and women. *J Am Acad Psychoanal, 6:* 511-19, 1978.

19. Youngs, David D.: Postpartum sexual problems. *Med Aspects Hum Sexuality, 13:* 94-98, 1979.

20. Cohen, Sidney: The fetal alcohol syndrome-alcohol as a tetratogen. *Drug abuse and alcoholism.* Newsletter: Vista Hill Foundation, (7798 Starling Dr., San Diego, CA 92123) 7: 1-3, 1978.

21. Greenblatt, Milton and Schuckit, Marc A. (Eds.): *Alcoholism Problems in Women and Children.* New York, Grune, 1976.

22. Prosen, Harry and Martin, Robert: Postmenopausal promiscuity. *Med*

Aspects Hum Sexuaity, 13: 26-34, 1979.

23. Heslinga, K., Schelten, A. M. C. M., and Verkuyl, A.: *Not Made of Stone: The Sexual Problems of Handicapped People.* Springfield, Ill.: C C Thomas, 1974.

24. Barton, David: Sexually deprived individuals. *Med Aspects Hum Sexuality, 6:* 88-97, 1972.

25. Scheingold, Lee D. and Wagner, Nathaniel, N.: *Sound Sex and the Aging Heart.* New York: Human Sciences Press, 1974.

26. Scheig, Robert: Changes in sexual performance due to liver disease. *Med Aspects Human Sexuality, 9:* 67-79, 1975.

27. Howard, Elliott: Sexual expenditure in patients with hypertensive disease. *Med Aspects Hum Sexuality, 7:* 82-92, 1973.

28. Abbott, Marcia A. nd McWhirter, David P.: Resuming sexual activity after myocardial infarction. *Med Aspects Hum Sexuality, 12:* 18-29, 1978.

29. Davis, Harry K: Sexual dysfunction in diabetes — psychogenic and physiologic factors (In questions and answers). *Med Aspects Hum Sexuality, 12:* 48-65, 1978.

30. Renshaw, Domeena C.: Impotence in diabetes. *Dis Nerv System, 36:* 69-71, 1975.

31. Ellenberg, Max: Impotence in diabetics — the neurological factor. *Guidelines to Metabolic Therapy, 3:* 1-2, 1974.

32. Ellenberg, Max: Impotence preceding diagnosis of diabetes. *Med Aspects Hum Sexuality, 7:* 199, 1973.

33. Renshaw, Domeena C.: Diabetic impotence: a need for further evaluation. *Med Aspects Hum Sexuality, 12:* 19-25, 1978.

34. Karacan, Ismet: Advances in treatment of impotence. *Med Aspects Hum Sexuality, 12:* 85-97, 1978.

35. Karacan, Ismet, et al.: Nocturnal penile tumescence and diagnosis in diabetic impotence. *Am J Psychiat, 135:* 191-197, 1978.

36. Ellenberg, Max: Sex and the female diabetic. *Med Aspects Hum Sexuality, 11:* 30-35, 1977.

37. Kolodny, Robert C: Sexual dysfunction in diabetic females. *Med Aspects Hum Sexuality, 6:* 98-106, 1972.

38. Lubell, Ira: Male vs. female sterilization, (In questions and answers). *Med Aspects Hum Sexuality, 13:* 135, 1979.

39. Pasnau, Robert O.: Psychological impact of mastectomy. *Med Aspects Hum Sexuality, 12:* 108-9, 1978.

40. Jamison, Kay R., Wellisch, David K., and Pasnau, Robert O.: Psychosocial aspects of mastectomy: I. The woman's perspective. *Am J Psychiat, 135:* 432-5, 1978.

41. Wellisch, David K., Jamison, Kay R. and Pasnau, Robert O.: Psychosocial aspects of mastectomy: II. The man's perspective. *Am J Psychiat, 135:* 543-546, 1978.

42. Lief, Harold I: Sexual concerns of mastectomy patients. *Med Aspects Hum Sexuality, 12:* 57-8, 1978.

43. Wise, Thomas N: Sexual functioning in neoplastic disease. *Med Aspects*

Hum Sexuality, 12: 16-31, 1978.

44. Oliver, Herman: Sexual counseling following disfiguring surgery. *Med Aspects Hum Sexuality, 11:* 55-56, 1977.

45. Leiber, Lillian, Plumb, M. M., et al.: The communication of affection between cancer patients and their spouses. *Psychosom Med, 38:* 379, 1976.

46. Witkin, Mildred H.: Sex therapy and mastectomy. *J Sex & Marital Therapy, 1:* 290-304, 1975.

47. Tyler, Edward A: Disfigurement and sexual behavior. *Med Aspects Hum Sexuality, 9:* 77-8, 1975.

48. Ervin, Clinton V: Psychologic adjustment to mastectomy. *Med Aspects Hum Sexuality, 7:* 42-65, 1973.

49. Schoenberg, Bernard: Sex after mastectomy — counseling husband and wife. *Med Aspects Hum Sexuality, 13:* 88-103, 1979.

50. Witkin, Mildred H: Helping husbands adjust to their wives' mastectomies. *Med Aspects Hum Sexuality, 12:* 93-94, 1978.

51. Weinberg, Paul C.: Psychosexual impact of treatment in female genital cancer. *J Sex & Marital Therapy, 1:* 155-157, 1974.

52. Vaughn, Richard L.: Behavioral response to vasectomy. *Arch Gen Psychiat, 36:* 815-21, 1979.

53. Cole, Steven C. and Byron, David: A review of information to vasectomy counselors. *Family Coordinator, 22:* 215-21, 1973.

54. Di Musto, Juan C: Sexual activity after tubal ligation. *Med Aspects Hum Sexuality, 7:* 174-81, 1973.

55. Sotile, Wayne M: The penile prosthesis — a review. *J Sex & Marital Therapy, 5:* 90-102, 1979.

56. Levine, Stephen B. and Lief, Harold I.: Prostheses for psychogenic impotence (in Questions and Answers). *Med Aspects Hum Sexuality, 13:* 7-8, 1979.

57. Levine, Stephen B.: Current problems in the diagnosis and treatment of psychological impotence. *J Sex & Marital Therapy, 3:* 181-182, 1977.

58. Leff, Richard: *History and Treatment of Male Impotence.* Medical Education Conferences, Medical Center of Tarzana, August 17, 1979.

59. Bullard, David: Male sexual experience with penile prosthesis (Questions & Answers). *Med Aspects Hum Sexuality, 13:* 85-86, 1979.

60. Shrom, Stan: Clinical conference — evaluation and treatment of impotence. *Med Aspects Hum Sexuality, 13:* 89-104, 1979.

61. Belfer, Myron L., Mulliken, John B. and Cochran, Thomas C., Jr.: Cosmetic surgery as an antecedent of life change. *Am J Psychiat, 136:* 199-201, 1979.

62. Seagraves, R. Taylor: Pharmacological agents causing sexual dysfunction. *J Sex & Marital Therapy, 3:* 157-76, 1977.

63. Comfort, Alex: Effects of psychoactive drugs on ejaculation, (in Letters to the Editor). *Am J Psychiat, 136:* 124-25, 1979.

64. Paolino, Thomas J., Jr. and McCrady, Barbara S.: *The Alcoholic marriage — Alternative Perspectives.* New York, Grune, 1977.

65. Kochansky, Gerald E., Hemenway, Thomas S., III, Salzman, Carl, and Shader, Richard I.: Methaqualone abusers: a preliminary survey of college students. *Dis Nerv System, 36:* 348-51, 1975.

66. Sigell, Leonard T., Kapp, Frederic T., Fusaro, Gregg A., Nelson, E. Don, and Falck, Russell S: Popping and snorting volatile nitrites — a current fad for getting high. *Am J Psychiat, 135:* 1216-18, 1978.

67. Everett, G. M.: Amyl nitrite ("Poppers") as an aphrodisiac. In Sandler, M. (Ed.): *Sexual Behavior: Pharmacology and Biochemistry.* New York, Raven Press, 1975.

68. Grinspoon, Lester and Hedblom, Peter: *The Speed Culture.* Cambridge, Mass, Harvard U Pr. 1975.

69. Bowers, Malcolm B.: Psychoses precipitated by psychotomimetic drugs. *Arch Gen Psychiat, 34:* 832, 1977.

70. Schuckit, Marc A. and Morrissey, Elizabeth R.: Propoxyphene (Darvon) and phencyclidine (PCP) use in adolescents. *J Clin Psychiat, 39:* 7-13, 1978.

71. Showalter, Craig V. and Thornton, William E: Clinical pharmacology of phencyclidine toxicity. *Am J Psychiat, 134:* 1234-38, 1977.

72. Tong, Theodore G., Benowitz, Neal L., et al.: Phencyclidine poisoning. *JAMA, 234:* 512-13, 1975.

73. Siegel, Ronald K.: Cocaine hallucinations. *Am J Psychiat, 135:* 309-314, 1978.

74. Post, Robert M: Cocaine psychoses: a continuum model. *Am J Psychiat, 132:* 225-31, 1975.

75. Janowsky, David S., Clopton, Paul L., Leichner, Pierre P., Abrams, Alan A., Judd, Lewis L., and Pechnick, Robert: Interpersonal effects of marijuana — a model for the study of interpersonal psychopharmacology. *Arch Gen Psychiat, 36:* 781-85, 1979.

76. Paolino, T. J., Jr. and McCrady, B. S., *The Alcoholic Marriage.*

77. Cohen, Sidney: *Trends in substance abuse.* Newsletter, Vista Hill Foundation, 7: 1, 1978.

78. Paolina Jr., T. J. and McCrady, B. S., *The Alcoholic Marriage.*

79. Ewing, John A.: Ewing says alcoholism is a biopsychosocial disease. *Psychiatric News, 14:* 37, 40, 1979.

80. Goodwin, Donald W., Schulsinger, Fini, Knop, Joachim, et al.: Alcoholism and depression in adopted-out daughters of alcoholics. *Arch Gen Psychiat, 34:* 751-55, 1977.

81. Nieder, Samuel and Parihar, B.: Alcoholism treatment: a comprehensive approach. *Chicago Medicine, 77:* 929-33, 1974.

82. Persky, Harold, O'Brien, Charles P., Fine, Eric, et al.: The effect of alcohol and smoking on testosterone function and aggression in chronic alcoholics. *Am J Psychiat, 134:* 621-25, 1977.

83. Lemere, Frederick and Smith, James W.: Alcohol-induced sexual impotence. *Am J Psychiat, 130:* 212, 1973.

84. Schuckit, Marc A.: Sexual disturbance in the woman alcoholic. *Med Aspects of Hum Sexuality, 6:* 44-65, 1972.

85. Renshaw, Domeena C: Sexual problems of alcoholics, *Chicago Medicine,*

78: 433-36, 1975.

86. Reich, Theodore, Robins, Lee N., Woodruff, Robert A., et al.: Computer-assisted derivation of a screening interview for alcoholism. *Arch Gen Psychiat, 32:* 847-52, 1975.

87. Straus, Robert: Alcohol and society. *Psychiatric Annals, 3:* 9-98, 1973.

88. Evenson, Richard C., Altman, Harold, Sletten, Ivan W., and Knowles, Raymond R.: Factors in description and grouping of alcoholics. *Am J Psychiat, 130;* 49-54, 1973.

89. Paredes, Alfonso: Marital-sexual factors in alcoholism. *Med Aspects Hum Sexuality, 7:* 98-115, 1973.

90. Pursch, Joseph A. Navy's famed alcoholism clinic shaped by physicians' efforts. *Am Med News* (AMA), June 8, pp. 1-8, 1979.

91. *Am J Psychiatry, 136:* 4b, April 1979.

92. Rae, J. B. and Drewery, J.: Interpersonal patterns in alcoholic marriages. *Brit J Psychiat, 120:* 615-21, 1972.

93. Schuckit, Marc A. and Morrissey, Elizabeth, R: Drug abuse among alcoholic women. *Am J Psychiat, 136:* 607-11, 1979.

94. Spalt, Lee: Screening for alcoholism, *Ill Med J, 154:* 348-51, 1978.

95. Criteria for the diagnosis of alcoholism, Criteria committee, National Council on Alcoholism. *Am J Psychiat,* 127-135, 1972.

96. Mayfield, Demmie, McLeod, Gail, and Hall, Patricia: The CAGE questionnaire: validation of a new alcoholism screening instrument. *Am J Psychiat, 131:* 1121, 1974.

Chapter XIV

SOCIAL AND CIVIC ACTIVITIES

THE 19th question on the BRQ asks each patient: *Describe your participation in social and civic activities. What are your personal hobbies and interests? How much satisfaction do you get from these activities? What problems do you have in this area?*

This item gives added insights into the voices of the "inner child" — curiosity, creativity, play, and libidinal feelings. In keeping with the GST, the alteration of any component in any system will cause changes in the other systems. For example, a partner (intrapersonal system) who changes his/her relationships with her/her friends, e. g. giving up the weekly card or golf game in order to spend more time with the new partner (interpersonal system) will alter the friendship ties of others as well (environmental and interpersonal systems). As a result of this change, friends may react with anger at disrupting a long-established foursome golf game, bridge game, Mah-Jongg® game, etc.

The concept of "togetherness" in a dyadic relationship can lead to what Cox[1] calls the "loner" coupling. He comments that statistics show that couples with many social contacts tend to have a better and more stable relationship. "When an argument occurs in the 'loner' marriage, the spouse tends to react to it in light of his prior limited heterosexual experiences. . . . If these are not appropriate to the new reality, he then has no place to turn to correct this reaction because of the private quality of his marriage (it is no one else's business)."

In the past decade, I have found Rapoports' book[2] on the subject of leisure most relevant and thought-provoking. Clinical experience indicates that couples that play together, stay together. However, leisure activities vary during the couple's life cycle and are influenced by the various institutional spheres of our industrial society.[3] Both sexes tend to participate equally in religious organizations as a form of shared leisure social life. In my data, men continue to be twice as active as women in professional, fraternal, and political organizations; and, women continue to be about four times as active in parent-teacher associations as compared to their partners. Couples without children may have significantly different patterns than the couples I have just described.

149

The increase in couples where both work full-time will influence modification of male-female roles. This often means that *both* have two demanding jobs: one outside the home and one within. Rapoport el al.[4] have observed that this trend toward symmetry between the sexes is related to the couples' enjoyment patterns, although the male's orientation is more pivotal than his partner's. More activities are enjoyed by both if the male is family oriented when offspring are present in their relationship. Another important factor in dyad durability and compatibility is how the female views the issue of women who marry and maintain their career. Those with a positive attitude toward careers for women were happier than those women with the traditional attitude of "homemaker" (which often leads to the "captive housewife" syndrome).

The voice of the inner child plays an important role in recreation and shared leisure activities. A part of the at home feeling of the inner child will determine whether performance, rather than relaxation, is essential to the leisure activity. When partner's attitudes include performance into their shared activities, the competition can add tension and conflict in their future, whether it is in leisure activities or in other areas!

There are sharp background differences among individuals with dissimilar socioeconomic upbringings and introduces a wide range of interest, attitudes, and social networks.[5] The various backgrounds individuals come from add new vitality to a dyadic relationship; while in other dyadic relationships, some differences may create feelings of stress in the inner child. A major variable in a couples' selection of leisurely shared activities is their maturity — more autonomous people have greater flexibility in attitudes and interests, which generates compatible leisure experiences. The couple's likes and dislikes become more similar the longer they live together.[6]

In conclusion, the voice of the inner child frequently overshadows the other two voices when a record involving recreation is played. Recreation in many ways resembles the happy days of childhood. Because every individual goes through different childhood experiences, recreation can be an area of bitter conflict in pair-coupling, e.g. arguments where one partner is pressured into fishing trips, or the theatre, or ballet programs, etc. Dyadic conflicts can arise over being a "golf widow" or the male resents being a baby-sitter while his partner is away with her girlfriends playing bridge. Also, dyadic discord can spiral when the partners compete strongly in tennis, golf, or bowling. Instead of the inner children playing for fun, parental voices stress performance.

REFERENCES

1. Cox, Frank D.: The honeymoon is over. *Voices, 2:* 86, 1966.
2. Rapoport, Rhona and Rapoport, Robert N. *Leisure and the Family Life Cycle.* London: Routledge & Kegan Paul Ltd., 1975.
3. Harry, Joseph; Evolving sources of happiness for men over the life cycle — a structural analysis. *J Marr & Family, 38:* 289-96, 1976.
4. Rapoport, Rhona, Rapoport, Robert, and Thiessen, Victor: Couple symmetry and enjoyment. *J Marr & Family, 36:* 588-91, 1974.
5. Ginsberg, Yona: Joint leisure activities and social networks in two neighborhoods in Tel Aviv. *J Marr & Family, 37:* 688-676, 1975.
6. Ferriera, Antonio J. and Winter, William D.: On the nature of marital relationships — measurable difference in spontaneous agreement. *Family Process, 13:* 355-68, 1974.

Chapter XV

OCCUPATION

THE 20th query in the BRQ has the following:
Describe your job or occupation. Describe your feelings about your work. How do you get along with your co-workers and employer? Have you changed jobs frequently and if so give details.

The answers to these questions are important because they give information about the individual (intrapersonal system) and some work-related relationships (interpersonal and environmental system), more so if kinship networks are involved. Just as industrial medicine has long recognized that many of their patients have overt emotional problems or covertly disguised psychosomatic reactions due to work problems, so must the therapist be aware of the role of his patient's occupation in the current dyadic crisis.[1,2] Some of the factors to be considered include fulfillment of the patient in his work setting, identification with the organization — the man in the grey flannel suit — identification with his labors, the "accident prone" person with severe emotional or dyadic problmes, the reaction to authoritative figures, the impact of working mothers, the feminist movement,[3] etc.

Work stresses are present in every job or occupation but vary in degree.[4-14] Dy and Kay observed that two-thirds of work stresses are due to interpersonal problems, the one-third arises from time pressures. They observed four "realizations": political factors existing in every organization, coping with stress by "fight, flight, or taking things in stride," the need to hear, in the same organization, that others are having similar stresses, and the need to respect one's co-workers regardless of one's feelings or responsibilities.[15] Occasionally an important complaint is a poor work record due to inefficiency and lack of creativity and it is often present in sexually inhibited men.[16] L'Abate presents an interesting thesis that a great deal of dysfunctional family patterns in children may be due to the inability of the father to shift from instrumental to expressive roles.[17] Interestingly, Mortimer's sociological analysis suggests that "the combination of a prestigious paternal role model and a close father-son relationship engenders the most occupationally vocational socialization."[18] Third party payments covered by the employer's insurance can help provide money for individual, dyadic and/or family therapy. The dollar loss is in the billions annually for businesses and industry because of personal and family problems, which result in lowered productivity, absenteeism, alcoholism, etc.

Financial problems continue to be the fifth most common complaint in my private practice and also a significant complaint noted by other therapists.[19][20] Financial problems play an important role in relationship disharmony regardless of the economic status of the couple. The entire subject involving work and money involve all three systems of the GST model.

Money is a symbolic and universally accepted means used to facilitate the movement of services and materials between people and nations. The pioneer psychoanalyst Ferenczi in 1914 alluded to the universality of money and its significance — all persons like to possess money or its equivalent. For a great many individuals and governments, money is more than the means of procuring necessities; it suggests or facilitates social status, power, and wisdom. In some instances, people choose consciously or unconsciously to be driven to "workaholism" in order to move upward socially, to compensate for feelings of insecurity or inferiority, to neutralize the anxiety of unconscious obsessive-compulsive forces, etc.

When a therapist does not take into account how widespread the feelings are from job discontent, the therapist might assume, and wrongly, that a dissatisfied dyadic relationship may not be related in some way to the tensions and lack of pride involved at work. Modern man is often denied the pleasure and self-satisfaction of a job well done because the final product may be done by other hands (an assembly line type production). When the finished product is done by the composite work of many people who do not associate with each other for spatially related reasons or for other similar reasons, there is a disappearance in pride from workmanship.[21] The therapist cannot alter such feelings in his patients, but he can help patients to find equally rewarding endeavors from other labors (see fig. 9, Chapter XII).

The career and job one selects is a decision that mingles the intrapersonal system with the interpersonal system. People choose their occupation to fit with monetary needs, with talents, and whenever possible, with personality preferences. Gregarious people usually find themselves in positions where they can socialize with others (salesman, public relations expert, etc.) while introverts may try to avoid jobs that demand constant social interchange, especially where intimacy would be significant to success on that job (researcher, pathologist, mortician, statistician, etc.). Awareness by the therapist of these psychodynamics may help in the understanding of the dyadic conflict. An accountant who is more comfortable handling a mathematical figure than a human one, might unconsciously select for a partner an individual who is outgoing and emotional, both unconsciously hoping for complementarity — his inner child hoping for *emotionality* in his behavior and her inner child hoping for more *control* of her emotions. When this does not occur, dyadic problems may ensue. The following clinical case illustrates how the personality befitting a particular profession is the same personality that leaves the office and fills the home as well:

> Mrs. D described her husband as a cool, methodical, and completely logical man who was an accountant by profession. On the BRQ, she stated that her husband was dull, staid, uncreative, and "resents my friends and activities." Elaborating at her first interview, she mentioned that "he was very logical and unemotional; when he comes home from work he first reads his mail and then the whole family lines up and reports their day's activities (just like he has his subordinates do at work). He was nonargumentative and provided me with no strength . . . I do not feel I can lean on him in a crisis or most of the time."
>
> When I met Mr. D for the first time, he behaved methodically; he took out his completed BRQ from his attaché case and immediately began to talk of his marital problems by reading off his answers. He took particular pains to leave off no details. He took out of his case several love letters as evidence of his wife's unfaithfulness (these were written by a male friend of his wife's). Succinctly he stated that he would overlook her infidelity if she would immediately stop having affairs.

Mr. D's whole manner was cool, precise, and logical. The only evidence of emotionality was the simple statement that he would overlook Mrs. D's indiscretion if she would cease having affairs. He seemed in total control of his affect and yet his last words indicated that he was upset. I told him that it would take both he and his wife coming in for therapy in order to produce the type of home environment she would want to make affairs uninviting. Marriage, afterall, involves two adults in an intimate relationship based on mutual respect, and *both* would need to change to make their relationship meaningful and satisfying.

Some people choose jobs to extend their sexual experiences. Frequently the "workaholic" who strives for power may transfer that same drive into a need to make numerous sexual conquests. A recent seven year study of some politicians concludes these professionals to be more sexually active than the average male. This study found politicians pursuing prostitutes more frequently than most males. These politicians had a tendency to find sadomasochistic sexual relationships. The study concluded that these professional men spent more money to satisfy their sexual needs than men in other professions.[22] In general, assertiveness (aggressiveness) and sexual satisfaction are significantly correlated.[23]

The impact of the environmental system upon the individual and /or the pair-coupling is revealed through some responses to question #20. An example would be an overlap of occupational and kinship roles, e.g. working for one's in-laws. About one-third of my male patients indicated that they were presently or had at some time been involved in a business with relatives. In most of these couples, the husbands were no longer associated with the business, because it lead to serious marital discord as the following clinical excerpts illustrate:

Mrs. A came for therapy following her husband's request for divorce. Married fifteen years and having fathered three children with her, he had suddenly confronted her with his request for a separation. Mr. A, who came to the initial interviews, stated how he had met his wife — while working for her father. After marriage she never let him forget that he married the boss's daughter. He disliked his father-in-law and had tolerated his wife's depreciating, belittling, and "castrating" behavior until he became financially independent in other business ventures.

On the other hand, the next couple, Mr. and Mrs. B, came for therapy following Mrs. B's request for a divorce: Mr. and Mrs. B had met at college. Mrs. B fell madly in love with the campus athletic star and after six months of a romantic courtship was pinned. A year later they were engaged against the furious anger of her father who wanted his only daughter to enter his successful business. Mr. B was amazed at his future father-in-law's behavior. President of his fraternity, an outstanding athlete and popular with his classmates, this was his first rebuff in life. The two continued to remain pinned.

The engaged couple were happy, enjoyed sexual intercourse, and, in spite of her father, married after graduation from college. Her father grudingly accepted the marriage (they eloped) and in an abrupt turnabout in his previous position, offered his son-in-law a position in his firm. After the first month of employment, a drastic change occurred between the two men; the father-in-law began to belittle the son-in-law in front of other employees. He assigned him the most menial tasks and, in general, made life miserable for him.

Mr. B reacted with severe headaches. He was irritable at home. He was furious at his wife whenever she defended her father — she could not believe her father would act as her husband described. It was at this point that a change occurred in the couple's sexual relations.

Mr. B began to have premature ejaculations. Things were brought to a furious eruption when Mrs. B went with a girlfriend to Las Vegas and returned telling her husband that she had fallen in love with another man and wanted a divorce.

Other sources of kinship difficulties between couples occur when external circumstances create a need to go out of business but emotional problems prevent putting a stop to the business.

The C's had frequent bitter arguments about his father. The elder Mr. C had been in business at the same location for many years. When the younger Mr. C got out of service, he reentered his father's business. Gradually the neighborhood deteriorated, the old customers moved away and the new ones had different tastes. The income of the firm was insufficient for two families. The young Mrs. C harassed her husband to liquidate the business, that it was time the other children participated in some arrangements for their father.

Mr. C endlessly repeated: "What was Father going to do at his age? It would kill him to give up his business."

Another aspect of the environmental system's effect upon dyads is the changing socioeconomic forces. The increasing mobility of families,[24,26] especially in the military services,[27,28] create upheaval, both physical and emotional. Outside sexual affairs may develop during the transition period, either from the stresses at the new location or the stresses severing all bonds at the old location.[29] If affairs do not occur, but one party was against the relocation, a reactive depression[30] or overt hostility can manifest itself. Dyadic crisis and/or disharmony *does not* occur with everyone; some people flow with change rather than resist it. (For further discussion of the environmental system, see Chapter II).

An important stress for the male is a promotion to an executive position. The executive should be in good health with a capacity for rapid adaptive and coping flexibility in dealing with frustrations. "No one who is anxious, easily upset, easily irritated, or inclined to be depressed if things go wrong should accept management responsibilities. The management role may also be expected to take a toll on family life."[31] Any environment in the working arena where there is constant competition to maintain employment can generate tension and anxiety, which is likely to carry over into the home environment creating dyadic and/or family disharmony.[32] It is difficult for family members not to overact to a tart answer if the family is not fully aware of the extent of the job's pressure. The situation is never simple since the wife who may hear the tart response to a greeting of "Hello" may be harboring a full day of upsets as well. In such cases where both people overact (due to a separate set of tensions and not the immediacy of the moment) they are confounded if a tape recorder recaptures their conversation. For this precise reason, I frequently ask patients to tape record any heated discussion.

World War II dramatically increased the trend for women of all ages to join the labor force. The current rate of working women increased four times that of men.[33, 34] When women began to pursue careers, the impact from that choice was felt within their lives, the three GST systems, but also in all those lives which were intertwined with those women.

Previously, the woman had tradition to follow which provided specific role expectations (dependent homemaker, wife, and mother). When the woman moved out of the domestic role, she had to develop a new philosophy and redefine her role in society. Transition stages are expected to be stressful and perplexing. Young women going through these new role definitions face less trauma if they have not married, because they have only to answer to themselves. The situation is not totally free of any obstacles, however, since many businessman do not share the "liberal" views of many women[35] who want equal pay for equal work, who want a chance to attempt complex and executive positions, and who challenge job discrimination because no job can be fit only for a man (plumbers, electricians, mailcarriers, car mechanics, etc.). Galenson observes that no rapid movement toward job equality will occur until equality in the home is established. It is in the home where sex-role stereotyping is first learned.[36]

The development of new role expectations often occurs early in childhood when the little girl identifies with her mother's behavior patterns or rejects them. Since homes today include some women who follow the traditional role of dependent homemaker and mother, in other homes where women have children and stay in the home until the youngest starts kindergarten, in other homes where the woman never stopped her job other than for a six-week pregnancy leave, and in other homes where part-time work forms a part of the woman's life-style, the patterns for youngsters are varied and will produce an inconsistent societal role model for an average girl to follow. The variables exist and each child, girl or boy, has their unique choice to accept the mother's behavior patterns or reject them.

There are arguments put forth that indicates that females are enriched when they seek professions. These advocates state that careers that are stimulating and mentally challenging will make the working woman more appealing and stimulating as a spouse and parent. These same advocates feel that females can cope with the stress from a dual life-style, work and marriage, and that women can satisfactorily resolve role differentiation and time allocation between work and a family life.[37] Men who have working spouses, however, may disagree with the ease that such life details can be mutually worked out. Husbands often feel that they have to make sacrifices for the sake of their spouses. Some men do so without resentment and bitterness while others do not. I have found in my medical practice that the female dual career produces more conflict and marital disharmony than it diminishes. Obviously more studies are needed upon the subject of two career families with special attention given for proper research methodology.[38]

Working mothers face another set of complex adjustments. These courageous individuals, especially if they are married, must juggle their time and energy in three realms: work, wife, and mother. To expect that one individual can do all three jobs with equal quality, energy, time, tolerance, and many more aspects, is a myth. That is not to say it cannot be done nor that it cannot be accepted by all parties; my statement is that the human's resources will be stretched so thin that someone or something will suffer periodically if not frequently.

Two career families are faced with major structural difficulties that necessitate individual solution since our culture currently offers no institutionalized ones.[39-44] It makes a large difference whether the woman accepts the "tolerance of domestication" thesis or traditional biblical role model, whether she expects egalitarian marital power structure, whether she is career orientated, whether she perceives discrimination in the response from husband and/or businessmen, whether she is guided by a "masculine" ethic, and whether she seeks marriage and/or offspring,[45] or whether she wants a living-together-arrangement life-style with a career her main direction in life.

Therapists who treat two-career families with relationship discord will have to sift through all the various ramifications of role expectations, attitudes toward careers, values about the quality of the home life style,[46-48] and the core of their relationship: is there mutual respect based upon self-respect?

In conclusion, a therapist should not overlook the possibility that the many roles one or both individuals are playing in a meaningful dyadic pair-coupling can deplete their resources for one another with obvious results. Hence, the importance of careful exploration of all parameters involved in work or occupation should be carefully explored,[49-56] although studies now show that men in the late 1970s are increasing their family work when their partners are employed and show no more signs of marital disharmony than spouses of housewives.[57, 58]

REFERENCES

1. Rapoport, Robert and Rapoport, Rhona: Work and family in contemporary society. *Am Sociol Rev, 30:* 381, 1965.
2. Pittman, Frank S., Langsley, Donald G. and DeYoung, Carol D: Work and School Phobias — a family approach to treatment. *Am J Psychiat, 124:* 1535, 1968.
3. Moulton, Ruth: Some effects of the new feminism. *Am J Psychiat, 134:* 1-6, 1977.
4. Figley, Charles R., Sprenkle, Douglas H., and Denton, Wallace: Training marriage and family counselors in an industrial setting. *J Marr & Family Counseling, 2:* 167-77, 1976.
5. Malen, Richard and Cornfield, Richard B: The ambitious husband and the wrecked marital relationship. *Med Aspects Hum Sexuality, 13:* 59-65, 1979.
6. Rosenthal, Stuart: Commentary on reference 5.
7. Nadelson, Carol C., Notman, Malkah, and Bennett, Mona B.: Success or failure — psychotherapeutic considerations for women in conflict. *Am J Psychiat, 135:* 1092-96, 1978.
8. Symonds, Alexandra: Stresses ahead for 'Career Women.' *Psychiatric News, 13:* 22-24, 1978.
9. Johnson, F. and Johnson C. L.: Role strain in high commitment career women. *J Am Acad Psychoanal, 4:* 13-36, 1976.
10. Rahe, R. H., Bennett, L., Romo, M., et al.: Subjects' recent life changes and coronary heart disease in Finland. *Am J Psychiat, 130:* 1222-26, 1973.
11. Rosenbaum, Salo: Work inhibition in a doctoral student. In Masserman, Jules H. (Ed.): *The Dynamics of Work and Marriage, Science and Pychoanalysis,* Vol. XVI., New York, Grune, 1970, pp 63-74.
12. Greenbaum, Esther and Greenbaum, Henry: Achievers, losers and victims. In *The Dynamics of Work and Marriage, Science and Psychoanalysis,* Vol XVI. New York, Grune 1970, pp 75-91.
13. Bieber, Irving: Disorders of the work function — an overview. In Masserman, Jules H. (Ed.): *The Dynamics of Work and Marriage, Science and Psychoanalysis,* Vol XVI. New York, Grune, 1970, pp 92-98.
14. Kantor, Rosabeth K.: *Work and Family in the United States: A Critical Review and Agenda for Research and Policy.* New York, Russell Sage Foundation, 1977.
15. Dy, A. J. and Kay, Kathleen E.: Letters to the editor: Work Stresses. *Am J Psychiat, 135:* 865-66, 1978.
16. Roth, Nathan: Occupational difficulties arising from sexual inhibitions in men. *Med Aspects Hum Sexuality, 9:* 100-109, 1975.
17. L'Abate, Luciano: Pathogenic role rigidity in fathers: some observations. *J Marr & Family, 37:* 69-79, 1975.
18. Mortimer, Jeylan T.: Social class, work and the family — some implications of the father's occupation for familial relationships and

sons' career decisions. *J Marr & Family, 38:* 241-256, 1976.

19. Rolfe, David J.: The financial priorities inventory. *Family Coordinator, 23:* 139-44, 1974.

20. Knight, James A.: Money and marital discord. *Med Aspects Human Sexuality, 6:* 8-23, 1970.

21. Kreps, Juanita M.: Modern man and his instinct of workmanship. *Am J Psychiat, 130:* 179-83, 1973.

22. Janus, Sam and Saltus, Carol: *A Sexual Profile of Men in Power.* Englewood Cliffs, N. J., P-H, 1977.

23. Whitley, Marilyn P. and Poulsen, Susan B.: Assertiveness and sexual satisfaction in employed professional women. *J Marr & Family, 37:* 573-92, 1975.

24. Kantor, Rosabeth Moss: *Men and Women of the Corporation.* New York, Basic Books Pub., 1977.

25. Seidenberg, Robert: *Corporate Wives — Corporate Casualities?* New York, Amer Management Assn., 1973.

26. Packard, Vance: *A Nation of Strangers.* New York, David McKay Co., 1972.

27. Marsh, Raymond M.: Mobility in the military — its effect upon the family system (Chap 4). In McCubbin, Hamilton I., Dahl, Barbara B., and Hunter, Edna J. (Eds.): *Families in the Military System.* Beverly Hills, CA, Sage Series on Armed Forces and Society, Vol 9, 1976.

28. Lagrone, Don M: The military family syndrome. *Am J Psychiat, 135:* 1040-43, 1978.

29. Thomas, Claudewell S., Layman, William A., Lindenthal, Jacob J., Rogers, Kenn, and Thomas, Carolyn R.: Roundtable: Sex-related problems in business. *Med Aspects Hum Sexuality, 12:* 60-71, 1978.

30. Butler, Edgar W., McAllister, Ronald J., and Kaiser, Edward J.: The effects of voluntary and involuntary residential mobility on females and males. *J Marr & Family, 35:* 219-226, 1973.

31. Greenblatt, Milton: Administrative psychiatry. *Am J Psychiat, 129:* 384, 1972.

32. Heath, Douglas H.: Marital sexuality and the psychological health of professional men. *J Sex & Marital Therapy, 5:* 103-16, 1979.

33. Hoffman, L. W. and Nye, Ivan F.: *Working Mothers.* San Francisco: Jossey-Bass, 1974.

34. Schultz, Theodore W.: Women's new economic commandments. *Bull Atomic Scientists, 28:* 29-33, 1972.

35. Rosen, Benson, Jerdee, Thomas H. and Prestwich, Thomas L.: Dual-career marital adjustment: potential effects of discriminatory managerial attitudes. *J Marr & Family, 37:* 565-72, 1975.

36. Kacerguis, Mary Ann and Adams, Gerald R.: Implications of sex typed child rearing practices, toys, and mass media materials in restricting occupational choices of women. *Family Coordinator, 28:* 369-75, 1979.

37. Nadelson, Theodore and Eisenberg, Leon: The successful professional

woman: on being married to one. *Am J Psychiat, 134:* 1071-76, 1977.
38. Rapoport, Rhona and Rapoport, Robert N.: *Dual Career Families.* New York, Penguin Books, 1971.
39. Holmstrom, Lynda L.: *The Two-Career Family.* Cambridge, Mass, Schenkman, 1972.
40. Burke, Ronald J. and Weir, Tamara: Relationship of wives' employment status to husband, wife and pair satisfaction and performance. *J Marr & Family, 38:* 279-87, 1976.
41. Berman, Ellen, Sachs, Sylvia, and Lief, Harold: The two-professional marriage: a new conflict syndrome. *J Sex & Marital Therapy, 1:* 242-53, 1975.
42. Johnson, C. L. and Johnson, F. A.: Attitudes toward parenting in dual-career familes. *Am J Psychiat, 134:* 391-5, 1977.
43. Johnson, Frank A., Kaplan, Eugene A. and Tusel, Donald J.: Sexual dysfunction in the "two-career" family. *Med Aspects Hum Sexuality, 13:* 7-16, 1979.
44. Zemon-Gass, Gertrude and Nichols, William C., Jr.: "Take me along" — a marital syndrome. *J Marr & Family, 37:* 209-17, 1975.
45. Movius, Margaret: Voluntary childlessness — the ultimate liberation. *Family Coordinator, 26:* 57-63, 1976.
46. Rapoport, Robert, Rapoport, Rhona, and Bumstead, Janice (Eds.): *Working Couples.* New York, Harrow, 1978.
47. Mogul, Kathleen M.: Women in midlife — decisions, rewards, and conflicts related to work and careers. *Am J Psychiat, 136:* 1139-43, 1979.
48. Poloma, Margaret M. and Garland, T. Neal: The married professional woman — a study in the tolerance of domestication. *J Marr & Family, 33:* 531-40, 1971.
49. Ericksen, Julia A., Yancey, William L., and Ericksen, Eugene P.: The division of family roles. *J Marr & Family, 41:* 301-13, 1979.
50. Scanzoni, John H.: *The Black Family in Modern Society.* Boston, Allyn and Bacon, 1971.
51. Galenson, Marjorie: *Women and Work: An International Comparison.* Ithaca, New York State School of Industrial and Labor Relations, 1976.
52. Seiden, Anne M.: Overview — Research on the psychology of women — II. Women in families, work, and psychotherapy. *Am J Psychiat, 133:* 1111-1123, 1976.
53. Burke, Ronald J. and Weir, Tamara: Relationship of wives' employment status to husband, wife and pair satisfaction and performance. *J Marr & Family, 38:* 279-87, 1976.
54. Hudis, Paula M.: Commitment to work and to family — marital-status differences in women's earnings. *J Marr & Family, 38:* 267-78, 1976.
55. Safilios-Rothschild, Constantina: Family and stratification: some macrosociological observations and hypotheses. *J Marr & Family 37:* 855-60, 1975.

56. Arnott, Catherine C.: Husbands' attitude and wives commitment to employment. *J Marr & Family, 34:* 673-84, 1972.
57. Pleck, Joseph H.: Men's family work — three perspectives and some new data. *Family Coordinator, 28:* 481-88, 1979.
58. Booth, Alan: Does wives' employment cause stress for husbands? *Family Coordinator, 28:* 445-48, 1979.

Chapter XVI

RELIGION

QUESTION #21 on the BRQ form raises the issue of religion: *What is your religious preference? What religious and other church-sponsored activities do you participate in? How often is your participation? How have the teachings and values of your church and your faith influenced your marriage?*

The stereotype conflict of couples seeking therapy because they have different religious beliefs is still valid, although not as frequent as one might expect. Couples do find the concrete and imminent arrival of their firstborn precipitous of religious reawakening. For anyone with religious beliefs, there are religious traditions surrounding the birth of an offspring and later the inclusion of such children into the ideology of the religious group. If couples were not married, but find that they have produced a fetus, they now become embroiled in discussions their religious backgrounds will help control. They will decide unilaterally or bilaterally to end the pregnancy or permit the baby's birth, and legal marriage between them may not become an issue. In spite of "liberal" views which accept living-together-arrangements, Bell found that the lawful monogamous marriage is still seen as the only acceptable setting for sexual pleasure and procreation.[1] For the therapist who may or may not have liberal views about LTA the evaluation of a couple participating in LTA will have the same level of anxiety as a married couple (if not more) should pregnancy trigger religious reawakening.

One couple I had can illustrate concisely the problem the first pregnancy sparked:

> Mr. A phoned for an appointment. His tone and speech pattern reflected his intense level of anxiety. I saw him immediately and he related the following information: "I have been married just seven months. My wife is now six weeks pregnant and I have packed my bags to leave her. She was the one who wanted the baby; I did not! We had arguments and she stopped taking her birth control pills. All along she resented taking them because of her religious beliefs. I knew she had stopped the 'pill' but I thought she was in her safe period. Religion is the biggest thing, inseparable from our problem. My own identity is at stake. I'm reacting without being able to understand why I'm reacting. I keep emphasizing my Jewish identity

163

to her, my wanting to go to Temple now on Friday nights and also wanting to take Hebrew classes on Monday nights. I was never religious before, had frequently accompanied her to Catholic Mass during our courtship and really didn't think it was so bad then. Now I am reluctant to accompany her to mass and am rethinking my statement that she could raise our children Catholic. The only way out of this mess seems like the door, but I called you because I know she is the most fascinating person I have even known. I really love her, but don't know what has come over me. This religious obsession has taken control and we are equally bewildered and confused."

Intermarriages occur and some meet with family acceptance while others do not. Some churches and temples have relaxed their rules regarding intermarriages, which helps reduce the initial adjustment to marriage by the parties; however, as the clinical example of Mr. A revealed, the religious differences can be reopened with the first pregnancy.

The questions under item #21 attempt to record the individual's religious commitment and the ways such commitments influence the dyadic relationship. The range of religious commitment follows a bell-shaped curve with the majority having moderate religious commitment and the outer ends of the continuum revealing agnostic or fanatical beliefs. The attitude of one's parent (parental voices) is often crucial in determining an individual's adult attitude toward religion. The person's attitude ranges along a linear continuum from compliance at one end to rebellion at the other end. These attitudes are clearly stated in the biblical story where the first parental voice was God's, telling Adam and Eve not to eat the fruit of the tree of knowledge. At first Adam and Eve complied, but then they rebelled, and the apple was consumed.

My clinical observations indicate a positive influence of shared religious beliefs upon harmony in dyadic relationships. When such couples opt for legal marriage, they benefit from the religious approval of their congregation and /or family. Attending religious activities usually reinforces the cohesion of the couple. An interesting aspect of this occurs with former priests who marry former nuns. The congregation may or may not accept such couples, but the couple's religious beliefs form a strong marital bond for them. In those unique couples I have treated, the complaint was never religious, but the more frequent and typical complaint of any couple: lack of communication and/or unfullfilled emotional needs.[2]

Just as it is obvious that couples can have genuinely distressing tensions over religious ideology and religious traditions and family reactions to intermarriages, some couples can list religious differences as the sole precipitator of their marital strife when it is only a cloak for more complex problems. The following excerpt is such an example:

Mr. B, age fifty-five, was referred by the industrial surgeon at his work. His work record showed his stability; he had never missed a day in fifteen years and had constantly increased the level of his skills. The presenting problem was religious in nature: Mr. A did not believe in contraceptives and since his wife would not abide his unilateral decision, she refused intercourse. The situation was chronic; they had no intercourse in two years.

I looked over the information given on his BRQ. It revealed that he had joined different small churches during the past ten years. He changed churches, however, because he would have some nonspecified disagreement with the preacher. The last church he had joined, just two years previously, had been a very fundamentalistic one. The preacher insisted that sex was only for procreation and should not be initiated unless that was the intent. The marital problem occurred when he told his wife of six years that she was to stop using contraceptives.

During the initial interview, I became aware of his severe paranoid thinking process. By the end of the second session, I heard him discuss current auditory hallucinations and made a diagnosis of severe paranoid psychosis. I felt his condition had been chronic but not manifesting himself in such a way to draw comment from anyone but his wife. He had a job that was solo in nature and nocturnal so that none of the company's employees were aware of the voices he heard while at his job. His religious confrontations with various preachers were part of his reaction to his psychiatric condition which I did not feel should be tampered with. Her choice would be to accept his ego-syntonic behavior and remain married or dissolve the relationship.

She told me that she had already seen her gynecologist who recommended a hysterectomy for her pain and bleeding (due to endometriosis). She was thirty-nine years old and not adverse to this surgery. She was relieved to understand what was causing her husband's behavior toward sex. She had no complaints otherwise.

The last area of religious differences which influence dyadic harmony is caused when couples have a child who joins a cult. Many have a child who "disappears" and the tensions about the missing offspring can shift the marriage focus to that loss. The dyad's intimacy and pleasurable sharing gets little attention while the deeper and more pressing issue of their offspring is present. Even after hearing from the child and knowing that the cult is looking after their offspring does not reduce all of the parents' anxiety. Mass media has conveyed that many cults are using drugs and encouraging sexual experiences for their members. Most parents want their offspring to return and not to be under the influence of strangers, especially those with fanatical leanings and personality disorders. Nicholl II found that "religious conversion" by college students can be a positive experience. He interviewed a small group of college undergraduates who experienced what they labeled as a "religious conversion." Nicholl II said that "most had experienced untoward effects from past involvement with drugs, (but) their religious experience produced the opposite — a marked improvement in ego functioning."[3] Although such research is optimistic, the Manson cult did not encourage such development in its members. Parental worries will not be easily relieved by one encouraging study. In addition, these worries can interfere with marital relationships.

In reviewing the answers to question #21, I found it difficult to trace definite lines of acculturation and change. There was an extreme diversification in the religious beliefs and practices of dyads. This diversification was so complex that I found it impossible to compare relationships.[4] However, there was a definite trend away from orthodoxy between the older and younger generations. Occasionally, there was a reversal, with the younger generation being more religious than the preceeding one.

I am glad that there is no conflict between religion and the foundation of psychiatry.[5] I certainly found none during the decade I taught at the Garrett-Evangelical Theological Seminary in Evanston, Illinois. Religion offers humanitarian values and supports family cohesiveness. Society depends upon enough individuals following the tenets of religion. Psychiatry as well as other mental health professionals offer people in pain or under emotional stress another avenue to explore new coping skills or modify old ones so that their problems can be alleviated. In fact, 91 percent of the religious institutions surveyed were satisfied with the results from the therapy their parishioners received.[6,7]

REFERENCES

1. Bell, Robert E: Religious involvement and marital sex in Australia and the United States. *J Comparative Family Studies, 2:* 102-9, 1974.
2. Araoz, Daniel L.: Marital therapy with former priests. *Psychotherapy — Theory, Research & Practice, 9:* 337-39, 1972.
3. Nichol II, Armand N.: A new dimension of the youth culture. *Am J Psychiat, 131:* 396-401, 1974.

4. Besanceney, Paul H.: *Interfaith Marriage: Who and Why*. New Haven, Conn., College and Univ Press, 1971.
5. Franzblau, Abraham N. et al.: Report of the task force on religion and psychiatry: Phase III. *Am J Psychiat, 135:* 775-78, 1978.
6. Franzblau, A. N. et al.: Report of the task force on religion and psychiatry.
7. Davidson, Leah: Catholic patients — modifications of technique for a subculture based on sublimation. *J Am Acad Psychoanal, 7:* 601-10, 1979.

Chapter XVII

SEXUAL HISTORY

THE question #22, on sexual history,[1-3] is a *new* topic to the BRQ (see appendix) because of the voluminous literature and advances made in the past decade.[4-8] Recently, many educators of all disciplines are including courses on sexology in an effort to present an approach to this fundamental aspect of human life.

There are six main questions on this item and forty-four subheadings as follows:

Sexual history (with permission of Professor Domeena C. Renshaw, M.D., Director, Loyola University Hospital Sex Dysfunction Clinic, Stritch School of Medicine, Maywood, Illinois) (minor modifications).

  a. *Miscarriages?   Abortion(s)?   Details:*
  b. *Extramarital or relationship activity?*
     Does partner know?   Partner swapping or swinging?
  c. *Sexual problems/satisfaction: What do you consider your partner's most significant sexual problem?*
     How does this affect your sexual function?
     What do you consider your most significant sexual problem?
     How does this affect your partner's sexual function?
     How does he/she view your sexual problem?
     How have you as a couple tried to handle the sexual problems so far?
     What is your concept of optimum sexual function for a woman?   For a man?
     Own sexual satisfaction?   yes   no   What are your feelings after sex?
     Frequency of affectionate expression per week?
     Frequency of intercourse per week?
     Difficulties:
       Female
         infrequent climax   No climax
         Repulsion: Why?
         Pain: Where?
       Male
         Erection/difficulty: Yes   No

168

Morning erections?   *Frequency per week*
With masturbation?   *With specific partner?*
Ejaculation: premature: *Delayed:*
Kissing: yes/no   *Who initiates?*   *Preference*   *Aversion*   *Conflict*

Foreplay: yes/no   *Who initiates?*   *Preference*   *Aversion*   *Conflict*
Afterplay: yes no
d. *Masturbation:*
Age first masturbated: *Frequency premarriage:*
Frequency per week now: *Does partner know?*
Feelings: *Masturbatory fantasies:*
e. *Sexual Variations:*
Fellation: yes/no   *Who initiates?*   *Preference*   *Aversion*   *Conflict*
Cunnilingus: yes/no   *Who initiates?*   *Preference*   *Aversion*   *Conflict*
Anal intercourse: yes/no   *Who initiates?*   *Preference*   *Aversion*   *Conflict*

f. *Additional sexual history/experience:*
Reading sexual material: yes/no   *Who initiates?*
   Preference   *Aversion*   *Conflict*
Venereal disease: yes no   *Type*
Method of contraception:
B.C. pill   *Duration*   *Feelings*
brand   *Symptoms*
intrauterine device   *Vaginal cap*
foam   *jelly*   *rhythm*   *condom*
Conflict in this area:

Rape (real):
Rape (fantasies):
Specific fears about sex:

Specific guilts about sex:

Specific hang-ups about sex:
Unconsummated sexual relationship
Incest: (details — touch/full coitus. How much alcohol involved?)

Specific sexual enjoyment: (specific clothing, cross-dressing etc.)

Homosexual fears:
Homosexual episode/s:

Can you have sexual discussion with partner?

Any special comments (in detail):

In our most recent writing (1979), we stated: "In our pluralistic society there are as many responses as there are couples as to what is meant by a 'sexual problem'. . . . Most surveys indicate that sexual dissatisfaction plays less of a role than is generally believed . . . sexual difficulties are a *consequence* rather than a *cause* of marital conflict (divorce). . . . In our last study . . . sexual problems were fourth in frequency of dyadic complaints although stated in 80 percent of the couples by either one or both partners. . . . (In therapy) couples usually failed due to other unsolved dyadic problems."[9]

My therapy is focused upon the belief that it is the relationship that is the core of pair-coupling disharmony. Nevertheless, the BRQ provides each patient an opportunity to reveal areas that are stressful and possibly is increasing the tension level in the relationship. Stress, tension, anxiety, guilt, and worry in the sexual subsystem of the intrapersonal and interpersonal systems will have implications upon the couple's sensitivity to each other; their type of response to each other, and their feelings of self-respect and mutual respect, to mention but a few aspects of the total situation. I assess the answers revealed by both partners carefully. The answers that have a great impact on the couple's relationship will be explored while those that have little ramifications will be left for a later time.

Many professionals have accepted as a truism the *myth* that the sexual relationship of a couple may be regarded as a microcosm of the dyadic relationship. In an article (1976), I described sex as a reverberation of the total relationship that may mirror the same power struggles, defense mechanisms, ability to be close or distant, spoiling of a partner's or one's own pleasure at the moment of fulfillment, masochistic or sadistic stance, dependency, or parental attitudes that may prevail during sex.[10] Moulton (1977) feels that the core problem in many sexual dysfunctions is " . . . that of the man who has a great stake in the mastery of the woman because of his fears of her domination over him."[11]

When Kinsey and his colleagues (1948 and 1953) reported their monumental study on sexual behavior,* many myths of sexuality were exposed and individuals began to be more candid. Kinsey's work was followed by Masters' and Johnson's seminal research, speeches, articles, and books about sexual behavior and sex therapies.[12-15] As sex became a respectable topic for discussion, cultural attitudes and values had a chance to be viewed and evaluated openly.[16-19] American culture felt the impact from three wars (World War II, Korean, and Vietnam), which encouraged sexual attitude changes by women who assessed their abilities and potentials in the labor market. The feminist movement took hold and behavior patterns were challenged.

What changes have occurred since the Kinsey's first report? Some studies indicate that premarital sex became more frequent, and college women began to take a more aggressive role with men.[20,21] For some women, as for men, sexual freedom reduces the immediacy of seeking marriage and may help reduce the divorce rate.[22] Only time will help determine the gains from sexual freedom. Moulton is aware that " . . . the unconscious lags far behind; in spite of individuals subscribing to new sexual ethics or new sexual roles, they are apt to find the haunting past (a problem)."[23]

Sociological research indicates that the changes in the so-called sexual revolution are more evolutionary than revolutionary.[24] Although there are many books to help both sexes understand what might make sex more enjoyable, " . . . women still complain about male ignorance in satisfying them and men express mystification about female sexuality."[25-27] It is possible that some women are sexually dissatisfied as a result of their culturally inferior status as women.[28] One significant issue to consider is the impact of a couple's total relationship upon their sexual intimacy. Sexual dysfunction can be a reflection of emotional problems.[29]

In 1975, a new journal on sex and marital therapy was published.† In that journal I discussed my clinical observations about sex.[30] I found that sex was a reverberation of a couple's total relationship. Even if sexual dysfunction originated from intrapsychic conflicts or from environmental factors, problems in the total relationship has a reverberating quality which fostered deteriorating cycles for the dyad.

---

*The studies of Kinsey and his associates (A. C. Kinsey, W. B. Pomeroy, and C. E. Martin: *Sexual Behavior in the Human Male,* and A. C. Kinsey, W. B. Pomeroy, C. E. Martin, and P. H. Gebhard: *Sexual Behavior in the Human Female.* Philadelphia, Saunders, 1948 and 1953, respectively) suggest that one half of all married men and more than one-quarter of all married women have committed adultery during the course of their married life.

†*Journal of Sex and Marital Therapy,* Clifford Sager and Helen S. Kaplan, editors.

Such cycles occurred whether couples were married or *not* married.[31] The bonds between people, married or not, appeared the same. Couples stayed together because of many conscious and unconscious forces: fear of loneliness, phobic fear of being alone, addiction to a masochistic life-style,[32] as well as all the positive reasons. It is a myth that couples stay together because of sex.

Item *a* asks about miscarriage and/or abortion. The issue of progeny may lead to dyadic disharmony when the female, most frequently, makes incessant demands upon the partner to increase their success at impregnation (visit clinics, etc.). In the past five years, articles have been appearing on the reactions of *males* when a near-fatherhood experience ends in a legal abortion.[33]

Item *b* asks about extramarital or relationship activity, partner swapping or swinging, etc. The definition of infidelity is a lack of faith, trust, or loyalty. The types of sexual conduct that partners will tolerate is diverse. While some will make a big case out of a furtive glance, others will overlook even blatant sexual behavior with a "third party." A recent couple complained about the woman's anger over the least look of her partner toward any female. She calmed down after being told that she overreacted to his innate curiosity (an attribute of the inner child is curiosity). Another way to calm this woman would be to use humor, to give her another perspective about the situation; for example, the therapist could relate a humorous story. One I have used with success describes two couples, one is French and the other is American. As they walk along a Parisian street a beautiful woman walks past and the two men notice her, but the Frenchman turns and stares. The American wife turns to her female companion and indignantly asks, "Aren't you furious at your husband?" The woman replies, "When he *stops* looking, then I will really be upset."

There have been categories and types of extramarital involvement proposed by different individuals. Broderick suggest four types.[31] Kaslow and Gingrich[35] discuss ten general patterns of nonmarital couples and group sex; the following are four out of the ten they list.

1. Unmarried heterosexual couples living together or sleeping together frequently.
2. Unmarried homosexual couples living together in sexual intimacy.
3. Extramarital affairs conducted in secrecy: (a) both married to someone else and (b) one married, one single.
4. Comarital relationships: extramarital involvements about which

the spouse knows and that are not considered competitive with the marriage.

At one time, the O'Neills' advocated "open marriage"[36] as a healthy option for couples, however, they have since retreated from advocating such a life-style. Some couples have tried a variety of group sex experiences with varying degrees of lasting pleasure, e.g. swinging.[37-40] Others have experienced consensual adultery, which is viewed as an adjunct to marriage: menáge a trois — simultaneous sexual activity involving three individuals — orgies, weekend groups, etc.

Although more women today are less patient about a partner's extra-dyadic relationships and more men are determined to make the relationship work after discovering their partner's unfaithfulness,[41] infidelity remains the seventh most common dyadic complaint as it was a decade ago. The major change in the last decade as reflected on my BRQ[42] is that one out of five (instead of one out of six) complain about unfaithfulness. Even this figure is not totally indicative of what couples are experiencing, because intensive therapy often reveals another third who will state that unfaithfulness has occurred in their relationship.[43] Some individuals are surprised at the admission of extramarital unfaithfulness, but in my experience, there are very few family secrets. It is important for the therapist to keep in mind that occasionally a patient will misrepresent the patient's partner; deeply disturbed patients who have a paranoid reaction can "believe" their spouse unfaithful.

The environmental system, with its sociocultural forces, can influence the development of extramarital affairs.[44-46] Women who are in the job market, as well as men, have an "occupational propinquity" influence upon their behavior. Vincent states that "eyebrows would quickly rise if a husband were to have coffee or lunch with the wife of his neighbor several times a week, but, in a work situation, equally close male-female relationships can develop during coffee breaks, lunch periods, and shared 'business projects' without raising any eyebrows."[47]

In some instances of infidelity, an annual Christmas party might change a nonsexual employer-employee relationship into a more intimate one. It is often the availability of alcohol and the relaxed atmosphere that contributes heavily to altering behavior between an "idealized boss" and his secretary or any other work relationship. In one of my couples, such a party brought about a sexual affair between the boss and his secretary. When the boss decided to remain loyal to his wife and not discuss obtaining a divorce, the secretary became very emotional. The boss recommended she come to me for therapy; and for this woman, it was most useful. Although she decided early in the initial interview to resign from her job and try to make her marriage more rewarding, she needed help to conquer her guilt feelings over her past behavior. The following excerpt reflects her dilemma:

> "I had a nightmare last night. My husband said he heard me screaming: 'Jim, don't! Jim, don't! I woke up screaming. I was at a picnic. Sitting on this blanket, I wanted so badly to have Jim like me. He put ants down my back and I was screaming: 'Don't! Jim, don't!'"
>
> Her associations dealt with her inability to feel toward Jim as she once did and with a time shortly after marriage when they had gone on a picnic and both became sexually aroused and wandered off into the woods to have intercourse. When they returned to the group, they found ants on their food. She was given the interpretation that she felt very guilty about her recent behavior and was punishing herself in the dream by putting ants on her back — for cheating with her boss and for avoiding her husband's attentions. Unconsciously she retained guilt about that sexual experience with her husband at the picnic because she had "ants in her pants" for him.
>
> In an attempt to alleviate her guilt, past and present, she was told that mortals make mistakes and she need no longer punish herself. My knowledge of her deep religious faith allowed me to add that only saints are pure. For this woman, there were many associations and feelings which had to be worked through. Matters became more complicated as the replacement secretary was not found quickly and the boss fluctuated between avoiding her and making sexual passes at her.

Another sociocultural factor in infidelity is the current importance placed upon looking sexy (as stressed in mass media advertising and films). The covert message is for freer sexual behavior. This change in morality condones promiscuity. An increasing number of spouses no longer consider infidelity as a deviation from the norm. Willis concludes that " . . . unfortunately, in our acceptance of the average state as normal and therefore desirable, the idealized conception of stability and fidelity for monogamous pairs sounds not only 'square' and unrealistic, but also may come to seem a kind of deviation in itself."[48-50] Thus in some areas spouse swapping is common. For others, any extramarital behavior is accepted as long as it is done discretely.

Another sociocultural factor is the marked mobility of the population. This mobility removes the marital partners from the critical observations of their kinship networks. In addition to nuclear family mobility, there is the individual mobility of spouses, especially in upper-middle and upper classes, either for leisure or necessitated by occupational roles which afford opportunities and temptations for unfaithfulness. The following case excerpt involves a successful business executive whose out-of-town travel brought about a close relationship with a colleague at a branch office.

> Mr. B came for therapy because he was confused about what he should do about his marriage. "I have no specific complaints about my wife . . . She has been a good, loving, loyal wife and mother to our children . . . I respect and admire her . . . but I no longer feel the love I once had for her." As he continued, he mentioned his close friendship with a colleague at a branch office out-of-state. "Our relationship was strictly professional for the past five years. Then a year ago her husband suddenly died of a coronary. About six months ago I accidentally met her in a cocktail lounge. . . . I had always liked and respected her. She seemed lonely and told me how difficult it was to go home at night to an empty apartment. Gradually, I established a close relationship with her. Now I feel like my wife is my sister. I would like to change in the way I now feel toward my wife . . . but at the moment I haven't succeeded."
>
> Mr. B had a very understanding wife who was supportive and forgiving. Therapy gave them both a chance to strengthen their feelings toward each other and he altered his travel to that one branch office.

Another sociocultural force is the contraceptive pill and other improvements in contraception. Contraception has removed one real deterrent to infidelity, the possible unwanted pregnancy.

In evaluating the forces operating in the intrapersonal and interpersonal systems of the spouses involved in infidelity, I found it expedient to categorize them in degree of awareness. Thus motivating forces were found to be either conscious or unconscious, and present in different combinations.[51] The conscious forces present in terms of frequency were as follows:

1. Sexual frustration.
2. Curiosity.
3. Revenge.[52]
4. Ennui.
5. Recognition seeking.

The unconscious forces operating in infidelity could be classified in terms of frequency as follows:

1. Seeking "stroking" of the "inner child".
2. Rage at a partner or parent.
3. Proof of masculinity.

4. Expression of immature personality.
5. Partner acting out "unconscious homosexual defense" of spouse.
6. Severe personality disturbance.
7. Denial of unconscious homosexuality.
8. Figurative "penis envy."

In 1974 when a group of outstanding therapists[53] were asked what they viewed as the chief cause of marital infidelity, they replied:

Larry B. Feldman (psychiatrist): "failure to acquire *prior* to marriage a realistic set of expectations about the marital relationship."

David R. Mace (pioneer marital therapist and sociologist): "*libertine* (the person who desires or needs sexual variety), *bored, curious, disturbed* (people trying to compensate for persistent insecurity and inadequacy), and *sexually frustrated.*"

Leo I. Jacobs (psychiatrist): "unwillingness or inability to intimacy with one's spouse."

Leon Salzman (psychiatrist and psychoanalyst): "problems of commitment, adjustment problems, and personality problems."

Seward Hiltner (theologian): "infidelity may be more attitudinal than behavioral: communication, psychological immaturity, differences in values or life styles, peer group pressures, and 'backlash' of romanticism."

O. Spurgeon English (psychiatrist and psychoanalyst): "man's and woman's innate inclination for diversion, variety and change."

In my ongoing clinical experience, *sexual frustration* was the most common conscious factor I found in about two-thirds of my paircouplings. Two males to one female complained. In one young couple married ten years, the husband's major and only complaint was that his wife's sexual responsiveness was hardly observable! If she would not cooperate with his nightly requests (often two or three times per night), he would strike her. He could not accept her pleading fatigue, lack of interest, illness, etc. He questioned me about her honesty. How could she have fatigue for sex when she had energy for an evening party? His current solution was to seek affairs and he could not understand why she now wanted a divorce. For this man, sexual tensions and anxiety had to be relieved nightly and it did not matter who helped him to it. He did not feel that he was breaking his marital commitment as long as he offered her the "task" first. In evaluating this couple, I diagnosed the man as a severe obsessive-compulsive. Such excessive sexual desire can be a symptom of a psychiatric disorder and even organic brain disease and a careful approach to treatment is to gather as much data as possible.

Curiosity was the common factor present in over 50 percent of the spouses in the ration of three males to two females:

> Mrs. C began the initial conjoint session by complaining bitterly about her husband's infidelity, twice in the past six months. A blonde, well groomed, heavily made-up, married two times, dressed seductively. She was at a loss to understand his behavior. Their sexual relationship, before and during the marriage, has always been satisfactory. When they were engaged, she had suggested that they be true to each other and he readily agreed. She trusted him for the past ten years. If it hadn't been for a mysterious phone caller disclosing her husband's sex relations with his receptionist, she would never have known. "I followed him to a motel and saw this woman with him. She was nineteen, half his age. I threw him out, bag and baggage, but the next day I went over and brought him back. He promised that he would be faithful, but last weekend it happened again with another girl. This time I got a phone call from this girl's boyfriend, who was furious with her."
>
> Mr. C, somewhat embarrassed, defended his philandering by stating that it was only one of those things that really meant nothing serious. He loved his wife but had been curious. In the individual sessions, Mr. C said that he always had an occasional affair, even during their engagement. "I have always been very curious about women. I don't believe the saying 'if you turn them upside down they are all the same.' I love my wife but my curiosity always gets the upper hand."

In the above clinical illustration, Mr. C falsely entered into the marital contract, consciously knowing that he did not intend to abide contractually to the aspect of exclusiveness.

Revenge was the third most common factor, in about 40 percent of the spouses, in seeking extramarital affairs and was equally distributed between the sexes. An illustration follows:

> Mrs. D: "My husband is still seeing his secretary. Part of it is my fault. I have never had an orgasm with him. The first two years I was very much in love with him and enjoyed sex, although I was frigid. Then I began to resent having to read sex manuals he brought home and to be specific about sexual foreplay. It took all the fun and spontaneity away. He has never excited me. A year ago, the husband of my best friend said he would like to go to bed with me. Every time we were together he would say something sexy, squeeze my arm, and hold me tight when we danced. Each time I saw him I became more intrigued with the idea. Something happened to me emotionally when he kissed me on New Year's eve. Suddenly I did not have any sexual feelings for my husband. When we got home I rejected him.

He was upset. A month later my husband flipped his lid and went to bed with some secretary in his office. He certainly had reason to have an affair. I had been refusing him sex (frustration as a factor). I was mad! I was furious! I kept picturing this woman in his office. Finally, I woke up one day, was furious and seeking revenge. I said to myself, I've got to find out if I'm capable of orgasm and went to bed with my friend, after saying 'no' to him for a year. I haven't felt that womanly in ten years. I was relaxed, uninhibited, and enjoyed myself thoroughly, but to add dressing to the salad, I was also enjoying getting even with my husband. I have so many mixed feelings about it now. I would like to salvage our marriage because I am orgastic with my husband now. He thinks it is a reaction to his affair and that the other girl was a challenge to me. But the truth is, I know that I am a woman now."

Mrs. D illustrates how the unconscious, conscious and situational forces changed her sexual responsiveness. This is not an uncommon response in some women.

Ennui (monotonous, bored, humdrum, tedious, and "square" were some of the adjectives used by spouses to describe their current sexual relationships with their partners) was the fourth most common factor found and was equally distributed between the sexes. The following vignette is typical:

"My husband is very systematic and proper in his personality. Our conversations center around immediate family incidents and our mutual friends in our social club. Other than that it is usually a business type of conversation on what things have to be done around the house, including budgeting, repairs, and entertainments. Gradually I lost more and more interest in my family life and thus became negligent about duties around the house. I was getting so bored of the humdrum existence at home, I went back to teaching. My work was stimulating, and I felt in the swing of things. It all began when I began to stop for a drink at a nearby cocktail lounge. The conversation was stimulating the people congenial, the atmosphere exciting, and one thing led to another."

The fifth most common conscious factor producing infidelity and occurring in about one-fifth of the pair-couplings with equal frequency as to female or male was that of *seeking recognition*. As one woman said, "I am unable to talk or discuss things with my spouse. I seem to be on the defensive all the time . . . I feel lonely and neglected. He comes home when he feels like it; other peoples' problems come before mine! So, when I met Henry at a political meeting, his comments about my hairdo, my clothes, and the cute way I talk made me feel wanted, loved, important, and needed. I felt like someone special again."

The psychiatric conditions include personality disorders or psychiatric illnesses: hypomanic phase of a primary affective disorder (manic-depressive illness), paranoid state or psychosis (infidelity is delusional), depressive reaction (infidelity as an attempt to ward off overt manifestion of depression), and chronic alcoholism. The most common condition observed in my clinical material was the hypomanic behavior, characterized by pressure of speech, flight of ideas, and increased motor activity — one reaction of this activity being infidelity (for further details see Chapter XXVII). In a number of chronic alcoholics, the attempts at infidelity were made to overcome strong feelings of insecurity and lowered self-esteem due to either premature ejaculation or impotence.

In approximately 4 percent of my dyads complaining of one partner's infidelity, the partner was unjustly accused. For some innocent males falsely accused, an immediate reaction of violence occurred. These males did not realize that their partners were suffering from a paranoid condition. Therapy can help such pairs: Mr. E noted that once he was informed about his wife having a mental illness he was able to be patient with her false accusations. Mr E rapidly understood the concept of the mind functioning like a jukebox (see Chapter II) and that his wife's apparatus was repetitiously playing the wrong record.

Individuals with unconscious, destructive forces leading toward antisocial or dyssocial behavior often have an immature personality or character disorder. Approximately one-third of such people in my clinical practice indulged in sexual affairs. With such individuals, there is no recognition that their behavior is unacceptable to others; as a result, they feel no anxiety, remorse or guilt. It is the spouse that brings up the issue and demands change as their value systems conflict. In many instances, the person with the character disorder had appropriate educational training, religious training, and concerned parents; the environment was not, however, the determining factor. One male patient whose behavior demonstrates that of an immature personality had repeated episodes of getting drunk and chasing women. Prior to his marriage, his wife thought that she could help change him once they married. Because she did not go for premarital therapy, she was shocked when instead of marriage vows altering his behavior, he came to the wedding reception drunk and started fighting with some of the guests. During their marriage, he could never hold a job because of his manner of picking fights with his superiors. His drinking increased, and then he began to gamble and stay out more and more.

When the jukebox is adequate and internally operational, but the "records" being played are inappropriate for the developmental and chronological level of the individual, the individual's transactions with others will suffer. The following processes were most frequent when the complaint involved behaviors (learned in the past) not appropriate in the current situation. The most frequent process was unconsciously seeking "stroking" of the inner child. The next most frequent process was unconscious rage at a parent projected onto a spouse/partner (projective identification). Unconscious proof of masculinity, a partner acting out unconscious homosexual defense of the mate, denial of unconscious homosexual defense, and figurative penis envy are the other frequent processes (in descending order of frequency).

A normal attribute of all inner children is the need for warmth, tenderness, and loving care — I refer to this human desire as "stroking." It is both conscious and unconscious in origin. When a couple does not achieve a mutually satisfying way to stroke each other, their relationship drastically suffers. Some of these people then look to the excitement and affection people outside their relationship can provide.[54]

Mr. and Mrs. F, married for seven years, were in such a predicament. Mrs. F said, "I have the seven-year itch, when you wonder if you are still attractive. The complaints I have about our marriage are so general and difficult to label or call by a name. I'm not sure sexual dissatisfaction is the right word in our case. We both find it difficult to communicate our sexual needs to each other. Early in our marriage we performed sex very often, probably because we knew this was something married people were expected to do. Sex is also very mechanical with us and always has been. I start all the fights and he justs listens . . . I have been messing around with someone for two months. I should not have told him. After I told my husband, I packed my bags and started to leave, but stopped when he began to cry. This is my first affair and I am left wondering if I won't start another one soon should I stay married."

Mrs. F described a very unhappy childhood. She felt rejected by both parents. "My father advocated 'building a shell around oneself so no one can hurt you.' He smokes long cigars and talks gruffly, but obviously he didn't do too well with his shell. Mother was also a very cold, rejecting person. Father was always communing with nature and mother was never home."

A variety of forces were operative internally to Mrs. F and externally between herself and her husband. A prominent force (which the excerpt illustrates) is the projection of her original anger at her parents onto her spouse (projective identification — see Chapter XIX where a "record" of the past is projected onto a spouse). In addition, her husband's aloofness and coldness and inability to satisfy her inner child's needs made her projective identification all the more real to her.

An unconscious desire for proof of masculinity by a male is a common motivating factor in infidelity. The following clinical case beautifully illustrates this in the first dream one of my male patients related to me. "I was surfing at the ocean in the nude. I looked down and was surprised to see that my testicles were the size of coconuts and the board was a broad!" As he talked about his current situation, he felt unable to stop his affair with his receptionist. He did not understand why he could not calmly end it. During the following year, he underwent psychoanalysis and became very confident about his masculinity with "normal size" testes.

The two factors relating to the unconscious role of homosexual defense in infidelity (one partner acting out the unconscious homosexual defense of his mate) needs to be differentiated from the rather common phenomena of homosexual play in preadolescent boys and girls. The use of the term *unconscious homosexual defense* is a normal, maturational process in the psychosocial development of every individual. It is a reaction to the libidinal voice of the inner child of the person and varies from warmth and tenderness to sexuality. I view the unconscious homosexual defense as a reaction to the retaliatory anxiety resulting from the competitive hostility of the child toward the adult rival of the same sex.[55] For example, the little boy wants all of his mother's affection and attention. To get all the affection (rob the giant who owns the goose that lays the golden egg), he is placed in a competitive position where his opponent looms large and awesome. From the child's view his father looks like a giant. It matters not how one labels the anxiety (castration anxiety of Freud, non-being anxiety of existentialism, and so on) the little boy, because of his retaliatory anxiety, has to deny his hostile, competitive feelings by saying to Father: "I don't want to eliminate you (so can have all of Mother's affections and attention), I really love you." As soon as he reacts in this manner to someone of the same sex, he has established a homosexual defense — a secondary type of love for Father. Under normal circumstances, all boys have genuine positive feelings for Father from infancy on that are primary and noncompetitive. The little boy usually handles his unconscious homosexual defense by repression. It remains unconscious and can surface later in life when it is expressed in derogatory words, e.g. "fairies" or "fags." In some children, the anxiety presents itself in aesthetic, effeminate, and passive behavior. Or the anxiety can be reacted to with outbursts of rage. In a number of adolescents and men that I have treated in the past, their anxiety was so great that they became overt homosexuals. As if to say to Father: "Look Dad, I'm not interested in Mother, I'm only interested in men."

Another group of men handle their homosexual defense by overt Don Juan heterosexuality. They go from one affair to another, before and after marriage. In a number of situations involving infidelity, one spouse was acting out the homosexual defense of the partner. By projecting the homosexual defense onto the mate, the mate became the vehicle for the release of the anxiety. This was dramatically illustrated in one couple where the wife developed considerable guilt about her extramarital sexual acts. Her guilt about her cuckoldry changed to rage when she found out she was being used by her husband (unconsciously) to neutralize his homosexual anxiety. In one situation, the husband insisted his best friend stay with his wife and children while he was in Europe on a business trip.

The second question on #22b asks whether the partner is *aware* of infidelity.[56] I agree with Pinta's concepts that " . . . a spouse's tolerant behavior toward (the) partner's sexual involvement need not be regarded as pathologic . . ."[57] in all situations. The partner's acceptance of sexual affairs[58-60] may be due to the fear of losing the other, the fear of being alone (a phobia), the fear of loneliness (a nonphobic manifestation), the relief of guilt for one's own infidelity, the acceptance as permission to do the same, etc. While there are some who will forgive their partner's infidelity should the partner end the affairs, there are others that find this sufficient grounds for divorce. The majority of the couples react to infidelity as a crisis situation. For many men, they explore their sexual potency. If such a male is a premature ejaculator (40% of the men complaining of an adulterous partner consider themselves premature ejaculators) he is apt to develop self-blame and guilt over his poor sexual performance. He will blame himself as the main force in the wife's infidelity.

Another familiar reaction to infidelity in one's partner is the development of an obsession about the affair. If such an obsession develops, the "district attorney syndrome" may occur (see Chapter XII). In this syndrome, the persons asks incessant questions about the affairs and seeks all the details. The obsession is so great that even when a spouse reacts with violence, the district attorney partner does not stop the questions. Obsession with a partner's sexual affairs is a complicated issue. Commonly, it is ego-syntonic in protecting the partner

from conscious or unconscious homosexual feelings, wishes, or fantasies. In other dyads, it is used to enhance a poor self-image by depre-
cating the partner (a one-up gaming process). Occasionally, it
enhances the dyad's sexuality by vicariously heightening the partner
as a sexual object. There are other determinants as Landers points
out: "In the world of human relationships, there is hardly anything
that is truly casual. Interaction between two people cannot take place
without making some impact or leaving some mark on one or both.
This is a crucial truth about humans that must be understood in any
discussion of adultery. People may insist it is good for you or bad for
you, but no one can claim it does not make any difference."[61,62] While
monogamy is valued, adultery is often a fact of life — even in many
viable, loving dyadic relationships. Livsey suggests some "Do's" and
"Dont's" for happily married philanderers to prevent dyadic
disharmony and destruction of personal happiness.[63]

The third question of #22b inquires about partner swapping or
swinging and for details if any. In the past decade, I have treated more
couples who used to be or are swingers. In swapping groups, men
rarely relate to each other while the women might. Jealousy, possessiveness, and paranoid tendencies are present in many of these couples. Because of the unconscious forces present, the swapping
frequently leads to unforseen complications. Masters and Johnson
describe the experiences of five swinging couples. Four of them eventually had potency problems and/or divorce "apparently because they
liked to play around . . ." and one returned to exclusivity.[64] My clinical experience parellels theirs. I found that the cost of exploring new
life-styles often destroys any commitment of loyalty to one another.

Exclusivity seems an important core ingredient to durable and compatible relationships. On the other hand, the sociologists Libby and
Whitehurst have contributed numerous articles to emerging dyadic
life-styles and alternatives.[65] They and others view these alternative
styles as a beneficial expansion or "renovative" phenomenon for marriage.

A complication of experimentation with alternative life-styles is the
phenomenon of jealousy.[66,67] Pinta has discussed the meaning of jealousy and of tolerance. He points out two divergent viewpoints: the
more traditional concept regards jealousy as an instinctive reaction
indicating love and concern for the partner; the other viewpoint regards jealousy as a negative quality indicative of possessiveness, dependency, and inability to allow the partner's personal growth.[68]
Various attitudes on jealousy are present in different cultures and
subcultures in the same sociocultural setting. Pinta regards patholog-

ical tolerance as a symptom that occurs in a stable triadic relationship with certain characteristics including the sharing of a sexual partner.

Item #22c deals with sexual problems/satisfaction. This item has fourteen specific questions. Sexual dissatisfaction continues to be the fourth most frequent dyadic complaint — the same as a decade ago. The pioneering sexual studies by Masters and Johnson has fostered other research and clarification of this important area.[69-75] About 75 percent of the couples complained of sexual dissatisfaction with the ratio of three males to two females. Just as the two most common dyadic complaints were due to pathological communication, the next two most common complaints related to the inner child of each partner and dealt with unfulfilled emotional needs and sexual dissatisfaction. The sexual complaints of the *men* fell into four main categories: frequency, displeasure in the sexual act, performance of the partner, and the inability to perform adequately. The sexual complaints of the women fell into three main categories: displeasure with the sexual act, frequency of sex, and the husband's performance during intercourse or at other intimate times. An unexpected finding for me was that only one-third of the couples mutually complained about the performance of their spouse. Although some couples have unrewarding sexual experiences together, many remain committed to their relationship (durable incompatible relationships).[76]

GENERAL COMMENTS ON SEXUALITY

Interest in sexual functioning is no longer considered too private to discuss or too deviant to recognize and acknowledge. The sexual drive is an instinctual one, closely interlocked with the individual's intrapersonal,[77-81] interpersonal,[82-88] and environmental systems.[88-91] All three systems are intertwined,[92-94] but vary in importance with the chronological age of the individual and the cycle of the relationship.

In the past decade, Masters and Johnson described the stages of the sexual response — excitement, plateau, orgasm, and resolution — and recently a preliminary stage has also been recognized — *sexual desire* in the nature of a bell-shaped curve. Complicating the degree of sexual desire are the inputs from the other two systems, i.e. anger at partner (interpersonal system) or the fatigue of excessive work demands (environmental system). What I referred to in the past decade as the nonpassionate lover, is now diagnosed as *"inhibited sexual desire."* In retrospective evaluation of my clinical data, I found that a substantial proportion would now fit into the category of the *new syndrome* of "inhibited sexual desire." Inhibition can occur at all stages of the sexual response as described by Lief[95] (and others[96]).

1. "Inhibited sexual *desire*" syndrome.
2. Normal desire but inhibition of excitement:
   a. Men — impotence
   b. Women — general sexual dysfunctional (frigidity)
3. Normal desire but inhibition of plateau:
   a. Men — premature ejaculation (shortened time between maximum arousal and orgasm)
   b. Women — as yet no specific name
4. Normal desire, but inhibition of orgasm:
   a. Men — ejaculata retarda
   b. Women — orgastically dysfunctional

The syndrome of "inhibited sexual desire" is diagnosed by a lack of desire rather than performance anxiety. Martin has discussed the "happy sexless marriage" or relationship where both partners are not complaining since both would have similar inhibited sexual desire. However, I have observed couples where on their BRQs neither circled sexual complaint, but in later evaluative sessions the dissatisfaction would be mentioned. Often the statement would be that the mate was "distant" or "rejecting" or "disinterested unless I initiate intercourse". In the "nonpassionate lover" category, the patient often gave a long history of sexual disinterest dating back to adolescence. In the majority of my couples, this syndrome was secondary to factors in the interpersonal or environmental systems. The sexual feelings (intrapersonal) and behavior of a person are a reaction to the parental attitudes (interpersonal). These attitudes handed down by parents to children, and so on, were largely molded by broad cultural viewpoints specific to the family's social class (environmental forces). As a result of the interlocking of these three systems, distortions and misconceptions have become part of "doing what comes natural." Or as Stoller states: "Sexual excitement depends on a scenario the person to be aroused has been writing since childhood."[97]

A clarification of the phenomenological concept of the sexual (libidinal)[98] voice of the "inner child" is indicated at this point. The persistence of this voice begins in infancy and continues throughout life in various degrees (physiological responses, thoughts, feelings and behavior.)[99-105] Sexual performance in the elderly is dependent upon *cultural attitudes*, availability and cooperation of the partner, and physical condition of the individual. On the other hand, the libidinal voice in an infant includes a wide spectrum of feelings and behavior.

The discussion of the interplay of sex, love,[106] and commitment may be helpful. Vincent, among others,[107, 108] discusses these three subjects within the context of historical trends and social changes. The early rural stage era stressed the durability of marriage as a social institution with lifelong commitment of the parents to insure the bearing and rearing of children. The next stage, the companionship basis for marriage exphasized *love* as the foundation for happiness and success. In the 60s' and early 70s' *sex* came out of the closet and was regarded by many as the single most important factor in marriage. Vincent makes this important comment "The earlier and necessary emphasis on the specialness of human sexuality inadvertently and temporarily may have impeded (1) the recognition that to be functional sexually is no more and no less important than to be functional occupationally, financially, socially, or maritally, (2) the awareness that to be sexually dysfunctional is no more and no less important than to be dysfunctional in any of the foregoing areas, and (3) the application of some well-established techniques, treatment methods, and learning theories from other areas of human behavior."[109]

We must distinguish between gender and sex[110, 111] as well as, between genitality and sexuality. Sex differentiation in infancy merely indicates male or female without any necessary implications of sexual capacity. A penile erection in an infant male, a very common observation any mother will observe, is a manifestation of the libidinal voice of the inner child; however, it is certainly not a sexual response, but simply a neurophysiological reflex act. Research on intersexuality, imprinting, and the establishing of the *gender role* emphasized an individual's behavior as a male or female and is strongly influenced by the cultural factors rather than by an awareness of the sexual significance of one's sex. In fact, regardless of the sex organs, it is difficult to encode new libidinal records after the age of three. For example, if a male child is dressed in female clothes and encouraged to play with dolls, use cosmetics and be passive, and discouraged in athletics and so forth, this encoding in his records results in continuing effeminate behavior, and he will be resistant to behavior change later, should he consciously desire to do so. The following clinical extract, which occurred in 1943, vividly comes to mind:

> During WW II, an officer referred to my neuropsychiatric service had been in combat for the past six months and decorated for bravery twice. While convalescing after a bout with pneumonia, he began to complain of inability to hear. Otologic examination was negative so he was referred for consultation to my service. A diagnosis of hysterical deafness was made. He was told that my examination was negative and unless his hearing returned I would do an

intravenous sodium pentothal (truth serum) examination.

The following day he related this story. An only child, his mother was disappointed that he was not born a girl. She dressed him as a girl, fixed his hair in curls and discouraged any masculine toys, etc. When he went to school he avoided playing with the boys and preferred the company of girls of boys younger than himself. He would write plays and always play the role of the girl, wearing dresses and makeup. His father, although displeased, said nothing and his mother thought it was "so cute."

In high school he was seduced by a male drama teacher and thus began his homosexual relationships. These continued until he graduated college. While working as a teacher he met his wife. Before they were married he told her about his "deviant" sexual behavior and a real relationship developed. He detailed the long, laborious effort of three years practicing walking and talking in a deep masculine manner. After a complete change in behavior, he got married and made a good adjustment with the help of his wife. He had no difficulty after he was drafted into the army since he was stationed a hundred miles from home. Whenever he felt any homosexual tension he could drive home. But, when he was sent overseas, he noticed increasing homosexual tension and no way to cope with these feelings. Afraid of acting out and disgracing his family he had seized the opportunity of this illness to feign deafness in the hope to be sent home.

This case material demonstrates how a mother imprinted a female role in a male child, and as an adult, this man was able to create new "records." Thus, learning and social experiences clearly influence sexual behavior.

In pair-couplings there are two people in reciprocal transactions. One cannot understand a sexual complaint without evaluating the sexual attitudes of each, and their interpersonal system. Since both are seated at opposite ends of a seesaw, both are equally responsible for sexual incompatibility. The myth of male primacy is no longer tenable. On a seesaw, what goes up must come down. For maximum sexual pleasure each partner must be passive and aggressive with equal cooperative participation.[112] Thus, the myth of female coital nonaggressiveness has made men and women feel guilty, inferior, inadequate, or even "homosexual" when their inclinations are somewhat different from prevailing prejudices concerning the role of each sex. The following illustrates how destroying the myth of female coital nonaggressiveness led to the development of a satisfactory marriage after ten years of disharmony:

Mr. and Mrs. B, both intelligent individuals had met in their senior year of college at a local church dance. Their courtship was smooth. After graduation, they married and went on a honeymoon. Both agreed that their wedding night was a complete disaster because of their sexual inexperience. Mr. B added: "I was unable to complete the act of intercourse, and this initial experience resulted in a great lack of confidence that has never left me. Since then I've hardly ever initiated sexual activity for fear that I would not be able to follow through. My wife has always been very passive and has never initiated any sexual overture. For the past three years we have not attempted intercourse."

Mrs. B, with controlled anger, replied that her family were among the early settlers and respected as leaders in the community. At no time in her childhood had she seen any overt expression of affection between her parents. When she was about four years old, she and the boy next door played doctor and nurse and were peeking under each others clothes when they were discovered by her mother. She never forgot the look of disgust and worry on her mother's face and was told that a "girl does not do that sort of a thing!" When she began menstruating, she also began to masturbate. Unfortunately, her mother caught her in this act and had the same look of disgust and worry and said that a "girl does not touch that area!" Since then she felt ashamed, guilty and embarrassed about any sexual feelings and thoughts. Mr. B commented that he was convinced that their marital problems were due to the fact that "we've never gotten to the basic problems surrounding our marriage. I've never been able to express my real feelings."

Mrs. B is a good example of a woman raised with the standards of Puritan morality handed down from generation to generation, i.e. a woman is submissive, expected to be patient and long-suffering, to be passive and nonaggressive, and accept the particular program of her husband's sexual activity.

Sherfey, in her classic paper (1966),[113] destroyed the myth of male embryological equality and discredited the Eve-out-of Adam theory by an interdisciplinary study showing all human embryos begin life as female! Then, if the sex chromosomes dictate the production of androgen (male hormone), which gradually increases in the seventh week, the embryo transforms into a male. Thus, female development is autonomous, whereas the male fetus must undergo differentiation necessary for masculine characteristics.

Masters and Johnsons' physiological studies[114] and Sherfey's researches,[115] among others, have increased the understanding of the physiology of the female sexual apparatus, its role in sexual intercourse and the mechanism of orgasm. As a result, four sexual myths have been demolished: vaginal orgasm, ideal coital position, simultaneous orgasm, and superiority of the large penis. The orgastic response of men and women during sexual intercourse is physiologically similar, as Masters' and Johnson's data emphasize similarities rather than differences in the response of the female and male to sexual stimulation. Their research resolved the theoretical difference between clitoral and vaginal orgasm emphasized by Freud. Freud's notion of separate clitoral and vaginal orgasms, with the vaginal as the mature and desirable and the clitoral orgasm as evidence of immaturity, resulted in much dyadic dissatisfaction, especially in middle-class educated women. Strong efforts and feelings or inadequacy on the part of women to achieve vaginal orgasms or of making the partner feel inadequate as a lover if they do not have vaginal orgasms increases dyadic discord. The female orgasm is a total body response with idiosyncratic variations in intensity and timing.

Ongoing research continues to emphasize the child's curiosity and other adaptive interests instead of the myth of the infant's sex drive. Sensuality and sexuality are two different entities. Sex is rarely a human need until adolescence and it is misleading to apply the adult label "sexual" to genital play, penile or clitoral, prior to gonadal maturation. The extraordinary capacity of libidinal activities to fulfill many needs of an individual aside from procreation makes the issue of sex important in therapy.

Men have the capacity to sexually "start up" and "stop" almost instantaneously. Further, such masculine capacity is atypical of female psychology and physiology.[116] Arousal may begin by a provocative glimpse, sensuous thought, or even a casual brush against the body. Almost instantly, an erection and ejaculation can take place. Following ejaculation most men experience very little sexual interest, however, this does not mean that they cannot respond to a female's postcoital desire. After ejaculation, the length of time before sexual response resumes, is dependent upon fatigue, age, sexual stimulation, etc.[117, 118] In contrast, the average female may have multiple orgasms at any age as long as there is sexual stimulation and no fatigue. Most females require foreplay for sexual arousal unless they are at the midpoint of the menstrual cycle when biochemically the female body is easily aroused for procreation. The female, in contrast to the male, experiences a gradual subsiding of emotional excitement after intercourse and enjoys closeness, tenderness, kissing, fondling, and any other indicator that restates her partner loves her as much as the sexual act.

In spite of a voluminous amount of literature on the female sexual responses, there are no valid norms. Lief presents the best concept, that orgasm in a woman can be viewed along a bell-shaped curve indicating a spectrum of erotic responses. "The clitoris is the primary organ of female eroticism; indeed, the clitoris is the one organ whose only purpose is to provide pleasure."[119] He estimates the spectrum of female orgasm as: "10 percent total orgasmic inhibition; 20 percent can reach orgasm with masturbation; 40 percent potentially orgasmic with partner clitoral stimulation; 20 percent coitally orgasmic (some need 'clitoral assistance'); and, 10 percent highly responsive (multiple orgasm during coitus)." Each person differs, what is preferred by one individual may not be by another. Copulation takes partners who *share* the responsibility[120,121] for their sexual gratification; usually it is necessary for greaternsexual pleasure fornone partner to *communicate* his preference directly, yet with sensitivity. It is important to remember that most communication is nonverbal, through the verbal statements can qualify what is pleasurable. Leiblum suggests at least eight male errors that are common in lovemaking: overconcern with female coital orgasm,[122] ignorance of female needs for postcoital stimulation (afterplay[123] is desired by most women to enhance dyadic bonds), failure to appreciate the partner's desires, reliance upon one sexual technique, overvigorous clitoral stimulation, lack of romantic preparation, the view that sex is work, the lack of patience, and believing that sleep must immediately follow ejaculation.[124]

Gadpaille and others[125-127] have outlined what women find most difficult to understand in male sexuality. I am in agreement with them that women, in general, feel sexual intimacy as the endpoint of a mutual caring relationship and are often puzzled by the apparent ease which males can be "turned on" by a woman's appearance alone. Fischer observes among many males what she calls absent or insufficient "psychological foreplay." Her term includes the following tendencies: males ready to engage in sex without exchange of tenderness or other developmental steps to create a romantic mood; men able to initiate sex immediately after an argument or while children are fighting in the next room or while neighbors are ringing the doorbell; male concern about performance and inability to recognize such pressure makes a woman more likely to fake orgasm instead of sharing as to how the male can aid her experience an orgasm (Butler[128] found 58% of the females sampled, to state that they pretend to have orgasm);[129] inability in males to accept real physical complaints by their partners instead of assuming such statements indicate rejection; and, men's insensitivity to the sexual needs and rhythms of women.[130] Moulton, in her medical experience, comments on female patients who fail to understand men's fears, performance anxieties, and self-doubts. Because male penile erection and ejaculation are so conspicuous, male incompetence is hard to hide and contributes to feelings spurring the need to prove himself. Moulton feels that many women are unaware of a male's need for warmth and affection and of the depth of men's fear over female power. Male fears develop early in infancy and childhood when the original helpless and dependent relationship with his mother is real. Later, Moulton postulates that males cover up their dependency needs by a male chauvinistic facade.[131] In spite of all research, the data is still too ambiguous and value-oriented to make valid norms.[132]

Item #22c asks: What do you consider your partner's most significant problem? How does this affect your sexual function? What do you consider your most significant problem? A frequent reply was: "I have lost interest in my partner."[133]

What exactly is "sexual interest"?[134] I prefer Davidson's[135] two categories: the basic discharge of energy or consummative category (a creative desire/force for challenge and novelty) or the "appetitive"/exploratory category. It is the interplay between sexual drive and sexual desire that determines the sustainment of sexual interest. However, all three systems of the GST are involved in this complaint. The areas include homesexual thoughts, feelings, fantasies and/or behavior, unexpressed hostility (suppressed consciously or repressed unconsciously), crisis situations — usually involving interpersonal relationships, avoidance due to inability to commit oneself to a full relationship,[136] fear of success, medical conditions (especially overt or masked depression and complications from drugs used in the treatment of these), poor sexual communicational patterns, and so on. Mace finds that the important issue in loss of sexual interest involves excessive anxiety and the focus of exploration should be the relationship.[137] My clinical experience coincides with Mace's!

The next question on item #22c asks: How have you as a couple tried to handle the sexual problems so far? Turner[138] makes the crucial point that talking does not necessarily mean communication has gone on. He outlines ten causes of dysfuntional communication as seen in sexual communication: unverbalized assumptions, overprotecting one partner from information or news, silent collusion, mind reading one's partner, habitual defensiveness, ignoring facial expressions and voice tone (words account for only 7% of total communication), tactile deprivation, nonverbal assignment of different idiosyncratic meanings and feelings to tactile touching, improper framing of questions, and the inability and lack of skill in clearly stating one's needs.

The next item on #22c questions the patient about his feelings after sex and if sexual satisfaction occurs.[139] The professional literature on this topic is sparse. Polatin[140,141] points out that since coitus is a universal phenomenon and normally associated with satisfaction, then postcoital sadness is a pathological reaction if it is "constant" and "consistent". He excludes PADs and other psychotic reactions. He finds the condition more common in women than in men. I found as he did that this condition is relatively uncommon. If the individual is raised in an environment in which sex is considered dirty, something to be endured with apprehension, a form of exploitation and degradation, then a person could react toward sex with sadness. Polatin calls these women with sadness reactions "melancholy sexual martyrs." In the male, he finds similar findings as I have that the feelings of sadness is related to sexual dysfunction (often erectile and/or ejaculatory dysfunction). An inability to help a mate achieve orgasm often influences the development of feelings of inadequacy, unconscious hostility, homosexuality, suspicion of a partner's infidelity, etc. Asking *specifically* about an individual's feelings after sex can help relieve anxiety and foster the process of individual growth.[142] Some of the responses after revealing the problem are degrees of happiness, relief, powerfulness as well as sadness, guilt, anger, and disappointment. Most men fall immediately into a deep sleep after sexual intercourse whereas women tend to remain awake. The period of time a woman reflects about her sensations is often longer than a man's and may be related to the female sexual response pattern; since coitus usually ends for the male with his ejaculation, the female's reaction may provide more time to think about her feelings.[143]

Another question under #22c asks about the frequency of affectionate expression and of sexual intercourse per week. Hollender's concern in this area begin in the late 1960s.[144-146] Holding and touching play an important role in sexual behavior which reflects infancy and childhood experiences. The inner child of each person naturally enjoys cuddling, snuggling, caresses, and being held.

There are divergent opinions about what is the normal frequency for coitus to occur.[147-150] Pearlman's study of 2800 patients finds that age made a significant influence upon the frequency of sexual intercourse, the younger the person the more active sexually. Pearlman found that those under age twenty had sexual intercourse at least once a week (88% of the patients). Roughly 80 percent of those in the age group thirty to thirty-nine and 68 percent of those between ages forty and forty-nine had sexual intercourse once a week. Only "50 percent in their fifties, 25 percent in their sixties, and 10 percent in their seventies had intercourse at least once a week."[151]

Reasons for the diminishing sexual urge may be related to male testosterone levels, which diminish with age, beginning at age forty and leveling off by age sixty. Lower testosterone levels produce less firm erections, less ejaculatory fluid, and more time for stimulation prior to ejaculation,[152] etc.

The frequency of sex is congruent with physiological, behavioral, and emotional realities of aging.[153] In some marriages, sex is avoided with varying degrees of mutual approval. The dovetailing of needs and expectations can create a sexless marriage without displeasure. Edwards and Booth found the cessation of marital coitus for intervals of eight weeks in one-third a group of 144 men, relatively young in age, who had a marriage of approximately eleven years.[154] Because such a development may not be mutually satisfying for the couple, the Well-Marriage Unit (see Chapter XX) can be very helpful in preventing marital discord in this area. In many of my clinical dyads, complaints about sexual intercourse include women stating their displeasure with the "act" while the men complain about the infrequency of their coitus. Mrs. B complains that her husband shortly after their marriage had "minimal interest. From my reading I determined that he was to do specific things to interest me, but he never did. I was always anxious to continue trying, but I guess he didn't find it too satisfactory and would rather not bother. Very soon . . . sex became one of rehabilitating the act and not enjoying it on its own merits. It became laborious and finally avoided." Another couple had a similar complaint for the female, but the male seemed content with everything but the frequency; he enjoyed having sex more than once a month and she would not cooperate. Although she would tell him how to make it more appealing for her, he could not follow her suggestions.[155]

The next three question upon #22c gather information about female orgasm. Reading instructive books[156] may help some readers overcome orgastic difficulties, but 10 percent to 15 percent of the female population cannot be orgastic. Women have a unique control system which permits them to stop an orgasm after it has begun. In the past decade the term frigidity has been differentiated from "nonorgastic" since a variety of factors may precipitate a female's orgastic problems,[157,158] and all or any of the GST systems can be involved. One definition of the sexually dysfunctional person is one who " . . . is erotically responsive and lubricates but has difficulty reaching orgasm (orgastic dysfunctional) . . . while the general sexual dysfunctional (frigidity) does not respond at all (to the partner's lovemaking) . . ."[159] Over the past ten years, 195 women (15%) of dyads with sexual dissatisfaction as their marital complaint had orgastic dysfunctions. I note this percentage as an improvement since the decade prior to the 1970s included 20 percent of the females in such dyads.

Paradoxically, cultural permission for women to enjoy sex, in contrast to the old Puritan attitude that only women of ill-repute can have pleasure, has produced new problems for women. Permission for sexual satisfaction has imposed a new pressure for both sexes. A women feels inadequate if she fails to achieve orgasm and a man feels inadequate if he cannot bring his partner to orgasm. Such circularity contributes to dyadic discord as self-worth diminishes, anxiety and tensions increase, etc.

Looking for *the* cause of sexual dysfunction can have negative repercussions while the GST systems approach contributes to constructive growth. Moulton comments that " . . . sometimes there are specific fears based on childhood traumata, but these only gather importance due to the reinforcement from pervasive attitudes of significant people, operating insidiously and covertly over long periods of time."[160] Such trauma include rape, incest, and seductive behavior (from an older person). One patient recalls being raised in a large family during the depression. "To make ends meet Mother took in boarders. My parents quarreled frequently, mostly about Mother refusing to have sexual relations with Father. When I was approximately three years old, I saw one of the boarders rape my oldest sister. This frightened me a great deal and when I told Mother she cautioned me not to tell Father. She repeatedly warned me to beware of men but at times would ask me for the details of what happened." Another patient recalls the brutality of her father. "When drunk he would beat me and try to have sex with me. To this day I am deathly afraid of sex. I never told Mother about Father's advances because he threatened to kill me."

When parents are cold, nonresponsive, and unable to give positive responses toward their children and these same parents advocate severe inhibition of sexual expression, the offspring have trouble developing healthy attitudes toward sex. For many, sexual orgastic dysfunctions are the result. One patient who described unfeeling and rejecting parents added that "when I wanted love the most, I never received it, so I rejected it any other time. Dating was a difficult process for me to adjust to and I am never sure if I am truly loved and wanted."

An important influence upon orgastic development in women is their relationship with their mothers (interpersonal system). Half of the mothers described by my female patients were seen as unable to give positive "strokes" to their daughters. 10 percent of my female patients expressed contempt for their mother's ineffectualness and submissiveness to a domineering husband. For some of these women, they took on furious rage at what they felt was unjustly done by their father toward their mother; for these women, their spouse would end up feeling the anger bottled within their wife whether it was appropriate to their transactions or not.

In two-third's of the nororgastic women there was an inability to relate to their fathers in a constructive manner. Father was described as rejecting, disapproving, or disinterested. One father openly told his daughter that she was ugly and should resign herself to spinsterhood. For women involved in intensive psychotherapy, an unrequited and deep attachment for their fathers was apparent during therapy. Vivid recall about a father's disapproval would be spoken during therapy which reflects the long lasting effects of the relationship between parent and offspring.

Premature ejaculation contributed to a woman's inability to reach orgasm in 10 percent of the dyads with sexual dissatisfaction. Clinically, I found that many nonorgastic women and premature male ejaculators seek each other out and establish a relationship.[161] Many women choose to dramatize sexual excitement to reassure their partner of his masculinity.[162,163] Another reason for a relationship to develop between two people is the desire for dependency needs to be fulfilled. If the partner does not adequately satisfy this dependency need, sexual dysfunction can result. Of my female patients, 25 percent indicated that they selected their spouses in an attempt to get the nurturant stroking these females missed from their parents.

The third most common reason given by wives for their lack of sexual responsiveness was their husbands' infidelity (10% of my patients had this complaint). Other complaints included husbands being too passive or too aggressive. The blame was often placed upon the spouse. A major problem for the person who laid blame on the other was the extreme fear over expressing emotions. In 50 percent of all the nonorgastic females in my practice, the fear of expressing emotions manifested itself in nonspecific sexual anxiety in addition to other areas in their lives. (One male patient described his cold wife as a mannequin, which made kissing her unappealing.) For some women who controlled their emotions, this overt behavior was a symptom of an obsessive-compulsive character. These females sought such control out of a fear that a release of their emotions would result in sexual and aggressive outbursts, would make them vulnerable to their partner, and would cause rejection by their partner and possible exploitation. In some of these females, orgasm was feared unconsciously in association with a loss of self-image and potential body disintegration. The conscious behaviors associated with these women included control over clothing, makeup, physical appearance, sexuality, etc. The label narcissistic "doll" referred to this type of character.[164] Nonorgastic women may have a variety of personality and psychiatric disorders ranging from narcissistic illnesses to psychoses, and the partners may also have a similar condition.

The frequency of coitus was the next most common sexual complaint listed by females on the BRQ. Each couple must work together to find a comfortable level to function with special consideration placed upon avoiding physical or mental distress.[165]

The third category in sexual complaints by women included the assessment of the partner's performance. Of the women, 20 percent stated a dislike of their partner's premature ejaculation, and 10 percent spoke of their partner's inhibitions. One woman stated that "our sexual relationship is very poor. I have the feeling that my husband does not enjoy making love to me and tries to avoid any contact. He admits he feels like a little boy at making love and does not have any confidence in himself in this area. He is afraid he will not be able to satisfy me; therefore, it is easier to just avoid sex. When I tell him that he makes me feel great, he cannot accept it and so our relationship is deteriorating."

The sexual complaints of the men fell into four categories: frequency, pleasure, their partner's performance, and their own sexual inadequacy. The main complaint for 50 percent of my male patients was lack of enough coitus. These men gave such reasons as wives disinterest, fear of impregnation by their partner, religious beliefs, and so on. One male complained that he wanted his partner to make some of the advances and resented her comment that it was the "man's" job. Some men wondered if they were oversexed because their mate's sexual desire was much less than theirs. Therapy can reassure such dyads and encourage ways to mutually satisfy these couples' needs.

Approximately 20 percent of my male patients complained about the lack of pleasure from coitus with their partner. For marital couples in my practice, 5 percent of the husbands had general displeasure during coitus. The following is a typical comment by one male: "It's not pleasurable because I have the feeling that it's a duty she is performing. At times she will even have an orgasm, but most of the time she lays there inert. She never takes the lead in sexual matters and has never made a sexual overture to me in our ten years of marriage." Sexual performance was the third major category men complained about with the blame upon their partner. Of these men, 10 percent felt their partner was too inhibited, and 5 percent complained that the mate was too aggressive. One patient said that "when I am having sex with her, I feel her violent pelvic movements as though she is trying to rip my penis off. When I remonstrate with her about this, she ignores my complaint and persists in her behavior. I try to avoid sex with her."[166]

A number of the inhibited women turned out to have orgastic sexual dysfunctions whose passive behavior, as interpreted by the man, was an expression of an overall personality problem. On the other hand, many of the inhibited women were orgastic, but very passive in their total behavior patterns, sexual as well as nonsexual. The following clinical extract is typical:

> Mr. and Mrs. H came for help, because they felt a lack of communication. In addition, they felt they were not fulfilling each others emotional needs. Both were dissatisfied with their sexual relations.
>
> Mr. H quietly said, "My wife seems to be very passive about sexual relations, mainly because she does not reach a climax very often. The times she has experienced satisfaction has always been after she has been drinking. Then she overcomes her passiveness and really gets sexually aroused and active. Usually, though, she just lays there as though her thoughts are elsewhere. I get irritated by such passive behavior and want to find out how to help her. I think our whole marriage would improve if she'd enjoy sex."
>
> Mrs. H is reluctant to speak. Embarrassed, she finally says that "in three years I have only reached a climax a dozen times, but I still love my husband and feel happy. I am not bothered by my lack of sexual interest and don't resent the great length of time it takes to get me aroused. I know it bothers Harry, though, and I do feel badly for his sake. Somehow, I always start thinking about my father. He was a strict Lutheran minister. He did not approve of playing cards, dancing, smoking, or displaying interest in the opposite sex."

The fourth category of the men's complaints involved their own inadequacy. The majority were premature ejaculators. Some were impotent. Only one-third of the men openly stated their problem which reflected the painfulness associated with such a handicap. For one-third of the couples complaining of sexual dissatisfaction, there was no avoidance of speaking about the husband's premature ejaculation as early as the diagnostic phase. Although such aspects of a couple's sexual relations were freely discussed, many men had performance anxiety that contributed to the total problem.[167]

The other questions in item #22c are directed to the male about erectile difficulties:[168] "is he aware of morning erections, are erections easier with certain partners and not with others, and describe in detail the *first* episode when an erectile problem occurred (was it after excessive alcohol intake, after experiencing anxiety and/or anger, after ingesting medication, etc.)."

Various definitions have been offered to describe premature ejaculation and ejaculator. Meyer's definition is most operational and states that any male who ejaculates *before* fifteen thrusts after intromission is a premature ejaculator.[169] Many men would find some relief if they could experience ejaculation within the vagina. Some of my male patients complained of ejaculation as they were about to insert their penis — *before* intromission.

The majority of men place high value on erectile and ejaculatory control. Frank et al. found that 36 percent of *happily* married men stated that they ejaculated too quickly.[170] This figure is about the same finding of 33 percent of *unhappily* married couples in my data. It is important to know what the patient is referring to since the sexual dysfunction of premature ejaculation needs to be distinguished from the commonly experienced lack of ejaculatory control.[171] The causes of premature ejaculation are multiple. Whereas it is often easy to gain ejaculatory control, maintaining control may be difficult, due frequently to the sex partner.[172] Psychologically defining ejaculatory control is the ability to remain in the physiological plateau phase until the decision to ejaculate. To do this he must control his increasing excitement and penile pleasure. By attaining both the excitement and pleasure he feels sexually competent, personal mastery and capable in giving his partner "absolutely heightened" pleasure.

Once a man labels himself a premature ejaculator, he develops performance anxiety and is preoccupied during intercourse with the mechanical act rather than with the emotional feelings. Levine presents a flow sheet of the dynamic elements observed in premature ejaculation.[173] He differentiates primary vis-à-vis secondary pathways ending in the final common pathway of self-labeling-premature ejaculation. He describes four primary pathways leading to failure to learn ejaculatory control: sexual inexperience, unexplained anxiety about intimacy, disregard for partner's sexual wishes because of hostility or ignorance, and, victimization by partner. The four secondary pathways that lead to the appearance of the symptom after a long period of ejaculatory control include the following: relationship deterioration, unresolved interpersonal conflicts, unconscious equation of one's partner with one's mother, and possible physical factors.

Karacan,[174] Fisher and colleagues,[175] Masters and Johnson,[176] Kaplan,[177] and Lief[178] all discuss the sexual dysfunction of impotence, which can be differentiated into primary (biogenic or organic), secondary (psychogenic), and a mixture of the two. Erectile failure can be determined in a sleep laboratory or with a simple penile manometer that the patient can use at home to measure sleep related penile tumescence (NPT). Erections occur during the rapid eye movement (REM) phase of sleep.[179] REM sleep episodes, which are associated with dreaming, occur rhythmically about every ninety minutes, and each episode lasts about twenty to twenty-five minutes. Nonpsychogenic erectile failure may be due to drugs, especially antihypertensive medication, alcohol, and organic diseases as diabetes, vascular diseases,[180] or depressive illnesses. In 90 percent of secondary impotence, the causes include performance anxiety, attitudinal causes due to rigid antisexual indoctrination, problems about sexuality in general ("widowers' impotency" on renewal of dyadic relationships may be triggered by guilt — unfaithfulness, conscious/unconscious death wishes and so on for the deceased spouse), overt homosexuality etc. If erection can occur during REM phase on the electroencephalogram, on awakening, masturbation, or on NPT, the diagnosis would exclude organic factors. As Burt correctly states: "One must bear in mind that primary impotence is extremely rare. No male is considered to have "primary" impotence if he ever has been successful in having an erection and having successful intromission (heterosexual or homosexual)."[181] Limited by this definition almost all impotence becomes secondary.

The last three inquiries on #22c are about kissing, foreplay, and "afterplay." There is no specific method that is correct or insures erotic responses.[182] Katchadourian and Linde discuss foreplay extensively.[183] Very often, what transpires between partners after sex ("afterplay") can be of value in assessing the couple's relationship.

Item #22d deals with the entire subject of masturbation[184] from earliest to current activities, including feelings, fantasies, frequency, and if partner is aware of this behavior. There are many myths regarding masturbation, many the result of medical misinformation in the past.[185] The *Bible* states that it is a sin for males to masturbate. The former priests who I have treated stated that the guilt because of masturbating was the main reason for leaving the church. The women that I have treated reacted with anger when they discovered their partner masturbating — they questioned their desirability as a sex object or their inability to please their partner. There are many reasons why men masturbate: as a sexual outlet when the partner's attitude is "let's get it over with", when the partner is temporarily unavailable, when sexually aroused but want to make a hostile attack at partner (indicating my hand is more desirable than you), and when they want to enjoy fantasies alone.

Women masturbate for many of the same reasons. The Hite Report found that clitoral stimulation resulted in the most intense orgasms for most women and that only 30 percent climaxed regularly from vaginal stimulation. Further studies showed that there was a high correlation between a history or *no* masturbation and inability to achieve orgasm.[186] Hollender, who (among others[187, 188]) has written about women's fantasies since the early sixties, states: " . . . there are striking similarities psychologically when the use of fantasy accompanies both acts (masturbations and coitus)." His studies also showed that fantasies during coitus had three motivations: avoidance of discomfort, seeking sexual gratification, and the forestalling or dampening of sexual gratification. The latter

> "paradoxical reaction is readily understood as an instance of depriving or hurting oneself to deprive or hurt someone else . . . (Also masturbation may occur) when adult reality does not coincide with the indelibly 'imprinted' childhood picture of what is sexually fulfilling. Occasionally the fantasy contains elements so unacceptable or frightening that modification (e.g., attenuated rape) is necessary so that withdrawal does not occur. Other struggles involving the use of fantasy are also encountered. When the impulse to use fantasy must be fended off, much as the impulse to masturbate might have to be inhibited, the result is uninvolvement and coldness which may place a strain on the marital relationship."[189]

Question #22e permits patients to mention sexual variations that may be a source of conflict in the dyad. Mutual respect and mutual pleasure is the key ingredient to happiness. Surveys since the Kinsey report still indicate that the "missionary" position (female on her back with the male above) is the most frequent.[190] Transcultural studies, however, show more variation in coital positions. Although improved and open verbal and nonverbal communication can occur from reading and viewing sexual materials, the most success comes from a couple's willingness to demonstrate *caring* and mutual involvement.

There are no extensive statistics on the frequency and exceptance of fellatio, but O'Connor's study reveals most men enjoy it while only some females do.[191] For additional reading see Comfort's book,[192] Saddocks'[193] and Greenson's[194] articles. Another type of intercourse, anal intercourse, has been researched to some degree. The incidence varies according to what article or study one reads (3% to 25%).[195, 196] I ask about a couple's experience with anal intercourse on the BRQ to provide space for any complaints. Out of ten recent couples who mentioned participating in this sexual activity, three females wrote a complaint; the couples were all heterosexual. Reasons couples enjoy anal intercourse vary. The most frequent I found involved an unconscious denial of homosexual desires by the male and that the man used his wife for a substitute male figure. With two other couples, it was a form of overt and covert anger — a depreciation or a sadistic attack on the partner. For another couple, anal intercourse was fantasized about and later tried and enjoyed. The BRQ does not try to encourage discord or upheaval and whatever information revealed is assessed in a nonjudgemental way.[197] Anal intercourse in our society is considered a "normal" sexual variation between consenting dyads.

Subquestion #22f permits more details in the areas that might otherwise be left unstated either from inhibition, embarassment, guilt about family secrets, etc. Currently, American males seek purely genital erotica while females seek more romantic materials.[198] In the past, females did not have cultural approval for any involvement with sexually related materials, but times are changing and magazines, book, and movies are produced for the female public. The fact that five couples came for therapy when the wife found pornographic materials in their house is an indicator that this subject is still upsetting to many individuals.

Venereal disease is widespread in America, especially gonorrhea. For those partners maintaining their original marital vows, the appearance of venereal disease, particularly if both become diseased, can participate a dyadic crisis.

Contraception is a common topic of argument between partners. It is extremely important that mutual agreement occur and that pregnancy be a mutually desired event. A couple should feel *equal responsiblity* in maintaining the type of control necessary for *mutual* pleasure. Fortunately, there are many books and materials available to explain the pros and cons of any specific method.[199,200] One advantage of males using condoms is the protection it gives *both* participants against veneral disease.

Rape usually has profound psychological impact upon the victim.[201-203] While the victim can ·avoid the guilt feeling of self-blame, since it is an occurrence out of one's physical control, it is a frightening and stressful injustice and a crime against the victim. Rape is an act of violence and not sensual sexuality. Under such conditions, it is an act of humiliation because the victim's inner and most private space is invaded while a total loss of autonomy occurs.[204,205] It is not uncommon for severe emotional reactions of uncontrollable crying, incoherence, and/or hysteria to manifest itself in the victim.[206]

Another reaction is the "stress syndrome,"[207] which includes a brief and acute reaction with physical and psychological symptoms evident, a denial phase where the patient may appear normal while actually involved in a "controlled state" of dissociation, and finally the remembering of the details of the rape and overtly reacting to these. Gundlach reports that all the female children who are molested by a relative or a close friend of their mother's are permanently left with feelings of hatred and rejection toward men to the degree that they avoid men and seek female sexual partners in adulthood.[208] For some adult victims, the trauma is not as great because the level of violence and abuse in their lives is so high that an incidence or rape just adds another crisis to the many already experienced. Such case histories are labelled "sex assault recidivism."[209] For those victims who add guilt to their trauma, a sadder injustice occurs. Hilberman and Chappell blame societal myths about rape for such an unnecessary and inhumane burden to be inflicted upon the rape victim. They justly point out that the victim did not provoke or solicit such violence and needs support at this moment of stress rather than blame and guilt.[210,211] In contrast, Sagarin questions the victim's role when the rapist is cohabiting with the vitim (LTA). Can rape involve only people who are victimized by a stranger?[212] Recently a wife went to court with charges of rape against her husband; the definition of rape was left for a judge to unravel. Rape is a crime punishable by law if it can be proven to the satisfaction of a judge and jury, whose definitions of rape can vary. When motivation is considered, a whole set of variables complicate the issue.

Rada feels that the rapist's motivations is for power control and dominance.[213] In dyadic relationships, it is hoped that transactions involving coitus will be openly negotiated, mutually agreed upon and mutually upheld. The therapist, as a neutral professional, can help facilitate such discussions and encourage equal expression by the partners while emphasizing mutual respect and pleasure. When one partner has experienced the trauma of rape, such discussion and satisfactory resolution of any conflicts may be more difficult. It may be necessary for some individual sessions with the former rape victim before conjoint sessions around the issue of sexual relations are resumed.

For individuals who have rape fantasies, they may want reassurance that such occurrences are normal and natural. It is more frequent in women who have been conditioned to think of sex as dirty, sinful, unnatural, perverted, or prohibited. Dreams need never become reality; a partner's request for acting out a rape dream with the safe and willing cooperation of the partner may prove mutually enjoyable if mutually desired.

The three questions inquiring into specific fears, guilts, and hang-ups may produce the first disclosure of a sexual dysfunction, guilt, or naivety, e.g. the large number of men who fear that their penises are not of adequate size.[214,215]

It is not uncommon for nonmarital as well as harmonious marital dyads to lack coitus consummation in their relationship.[216] Some couples are extremely naive about sexual anatomy and physiology. Others are listening to internal parental voices (records) that discourage, prohibit, and view sex as sinful and disgusting. Still others are virgins and unable to communicate openly their needs. Still others are active sexually, but never penile penetration of the vagina. In several of the couples I have treated, there exists an unspoken agreement to maintain an unconsummated relationship. One couple even adopted children when their anatomy was perfect for procreation. The medical literature reveals that nonconsummated relationships often are due to males with impotency, either primary or secondary, and females with vaginismus.[217-222] Friedman finds that how the patient presents the problem is important. It may come up as direct complaint or in response to an alert physician or gynecologist — the doctors most likely to diagnose the problem. The presenting complaint may be contraceptive misadvice, infertility, sexual dysfunction, and/or psychosomatic complaints. During the female examination, an *intact* hymen can be noted and corrective steps advised. The doctor may hear such females express feelings of shame, guilt, inadequacy, and/or anxiety (as an outpouring of either the conscious or unconscious) and should then refer such patients to therapy. In Friedman's series of 100 couples, one-third had no coitus for less than one year, and one-fourth had none for more than *five* years, the longest being seventeen years. The causes he found included the following:

1. An inhibited, sexually uninformed couple.
2. Immaturity and overdependence on their parents.
3. Fantasies of destruction associated with men.
4. Problems in sexual identification and elements of a power struggle between the dyad.[223]

Incest, another question on item #22f, is a more common occurence than most therapists believe.[224-235] In the course of intensive psychoanalytic therapy, Freud recognized incest as a behavioral universality of modern man. In addition to Freud's theories, ethologists found it occurred in nonhuman primates and most likely such experiences occurred in the precursors of Man. Fortunately, " . . . natural selection has tended to preserve those mechanisms which prevent in-breeding."[236] Hewes supports psychoanalytic speculation that " . . . it was . . . a shock when the Japanese primatologists, who had carefully observed wild Japanese monkey groups for a decade or more, found *no* instances of mother-son copulation."[237]

Incest leaves a permanent impression with those children who have such experiences; for most children it is a harmful occurrence.[238-240] The motivations for adults to seduce their offspring are complex and multidetermined from their GST sytems. It is rare, however, that the society encourages such behavior; American culture discourages such activity and laws are prevalent in all states making incest a puni-shable crime. Some intrapersonal and interpersonal motivations in-clude dependency needs, role reversals between parent and offspring, alcholism, couples where one partner sexually rejects the other, and where such a pattern is present in the family of origin of the parent. Sexual frustration is not valid as the reason for such acts because sexual gratification is too easily achieved outside of the home envir-onment.

As American society provides more protection for women who choose to speak out against battering and abuse, these women will also have more courage to speak out against incest involving their children. Fear, humiliation, and false family loyalty among other reasons have prompted the observing adult from taking public action. As changing patterns occur with places of refuge available for the victims and the nonaggressive parent, there may be more people seeking therapy and other methods of remedy, legal ones included.

The patterns of incest can occur between fathers and sons,[241] between fathers and daughters, between mothers and sons,[242,143] and rarely between mothers and daughters. The involvement of step-children may be a phenomenon increasing as divorce creates many families with nonbiological parents who are having contact with teenagers. It is more likely as well when one parent chooses a mate who is much younger and has much in common with the teenage adolescent residing in the home of this new union. Clinically, I have not observed any situations where associations with a homosexual parent has produced a homosexual orientation in the child.[244]

This question, #22f, also asks about specific sexual types of enjoy-ment to inform the therapist of sexual areas that would not be men-tioned in the initial interview. It is not uncommon to read statements about transvestism or cross-dressing and the wearing of specific types of clothing to enhance sexual desire or pleasure. A major complaint in the female of one couple was that her spouse insisted that she wear a raincoat and hat and high rubber boots during coitus. Some of the female patients complaint was that they were pressured into wearing sheer black negligees, black stockings, and black shoes with high heels if they wanted sex. The psychologic dynamics for the partners with this type of sexual enjoyment is the "madonna complex," a so-called "women-in-red," the symbolic prostitute. Krueger[245] and Person and Ovesey[246] have collected data that is most valuable for further information. Fleming and Feinbloom suggest that the key question is not *why*, but rather *when* cross-dressing began with female articles of apparel. *Anger* mixed with anxiety finds relief in cross-dressing for these people.[247]

Item #22f permits homosexual fears and/or episodes and the partner's feelings about these to be stated. Therapy is frequently sought when the homosexual experiences high levels of stress and anxiety over his behavior.[248] Some sources for increased anxiety levels come from actual or imagined confrontations with police, actual or fantasized blackmail by former lovers or pick-ups, a partner's rejection or unfaithfulness, etc. Current statistics indicate that 10 percent to 17 percent of the male homosexuals have been married[249] while the numbers of married men silent about their homosexual activities is unknown.[250,251] Another unsampled populace are those males who have "latent homosexual" tendencies.[252,253]

The psychodynamics of homosexuality are quite complex.[254-257] Bieber and colleagues base their conclusions on more than 1,000 homosexuals and seventy-five parents of these homosexuals. Bieber concludes that the etiology of homosexuality is due to a psychosocial adaptation patterned in a family with an observably disturbed parent-child relationship. "My observations and the material I have collected replicate our early evidence of the central, determining influence of parents, especially a hostile, rejecting father. I find in the background of homosexuals, a ubiquity of anxiety-ridden relations with males, starting with the father, then including brothers and male-peers. A continuity of disturbed relationships with males proceeds through childhood and preadolescence, relationships that become eroticized with particular partners as part of the reparative maneuvers intrinsic to a homosexual adaptation."[258]

Sexual gender refers to the anatomical differences determined by genes and hormones. Between birth and age 3, the child learns from parenting figures how to interpret his or her body's sexual identity/sexuality. If homosexuality occurs early in childhood, it represents an attempted solution to psychological or parental pressures originating in the first five years of life. Usually homosexual behavior does not occur until after puberty, because part of a child's curiosity involves sexual explorations with both sexes and is normal in the psychosexual development of a child. If homosexual tendencies are not dealt with by the individual, either consciously suppressed or unconsciously repressed, that person will be heterosexual or potentially bisexual. If, however, an act of homosexual seduction or homosexual approach occurs during an individual's life span, the crisis confrontation may create a resolution. One twenty-year-old male patient, for example, was walking in a state park and was approached by a male homosexual. My patient's reaction was so negative that he became a skilled and rugged outdoorsman and displayed his masculinity in overt and easily recognized terms. During therapy, he revealed that occasionally he still had homosexual fantasies, but he did not want to put them into his daily life.

In the past decade, one-fifth of the dyads with sexual disharmony included women married to homosexual or bisexual men[259, 260] None of these husbands were effeminate in appearance or overt behavior, but many enjoyed professions that permitted creativity and the knowledge obtained from the humanities. (Only one male refuted his wife's accusations about homosexuality.)

Media exposure is encouraging more individuals to acknowledge their life-style preference. Because there is no such thing as *the* homosexual,[261 265] it is difficult for homosexuals to "come out of the closet" in every sense of this concept. It is an interesting hypothesis that homosexuality may be a barometer of social stress.

In conclusion, the Francoeurs' comments on sexuality may forecast America's future: "In essence, our society is slowly painfully, forging a new social structure in which intimate networks will serve human needs as well as the extended blood kinship networks once did so well. In these new networks, the bonding force will indeed be the 'pleasure bond' . . . within the broader sexual bonding that comes from the acceptance of social or non-productive sex . . . In effect, the society of tomorrow will be evolving as an yet unarticulated aesthetics of sex to replace the withering ethics of reproduction and patriarchal property."[266]

REFERENCES

1. Bieber, Irving: Sexuality — 1956-1976. *J Am Acad Psychoanal 5:* 195-205, 1977.
2. Burchell, R. Clay: Instructing women in effective sexual techniques. *Med Aspects Hum Sexuality, 9:* 89-90, 1975.

3. Schiavi, Raul C. (Ed.): The assessment of sexual and marital function — a special issue of the *J Sex & Marital Therapy, 5:* 167-300, 1979.
4. Denber, Herman C. B.: Treatment of excessive sexual desire. *Med Aspects HUM Sexuality, 13:* 131-32, 1979.
5. McCary James L.: Human Sexuality — past, present and future. *J Marr & Family Counseling, 4:* 3-12, 1978.
6. McCary, James L.: *Human Sexuality.* New York, Van Nostrand, 1973.
7. Scharff, David E.: Sex is a family affair: sources of discord and harmony. *J Sex & Marital Therapy, 2:* 17-21, 1976.
8. Waggoner, Raymond W.: Dealing with sexual problems in the marital situation. *Panel On Sexual Problems and the Physician,* Chairperson, B. L. Greene, MD., Annual meeting of the American Medical Association, Chicago, 1975.
9. Greene, Bernard L. and Greene, Marsha: Divorce attributed to sex problems. *Med Aspects Hum Sexuality* (in Questions and Answers), *13:* 11, 1979.
10. Greene, Bernard L. et al.: Clinical observations of sex as a reverberation of the toal relationship. *J Sex & Marital Therapy, 2:* 284-88, 1976.
11. Moulton, Ruth: The fear of female power — a cause of sexual dysfunction. *J Am Acad Psychoanal, 5:* 499-519, 1977, p.516.
12. Masters, William H. and Johnson, Virginia E.: Homosexuality in Perspective. Boston: Little, Brown & Co., 1979.
13. Masters, William H. and Johnson, Virginia E.: *The Pleasure Bond:* in association with Robert Levin. A New Look at Sexuality and Commitment. Boston, Little, 1975.
14. Masters, William H. and Johnson, Virginia E.: *Human Sexual Inadequacy.* Boston, Mass, Little, 1970.
15. Masters, William H. and Johnson, Virginia E.: Human Sexual Response. Boston, Little, 1966.
16. Warren, Carol (Ed.): *Sexuality — Encounters, Identities, and Relationships.* Sage Contemporary Social Sciences #35, Los Angeles, CA, Sage, 1978.
17. Offit, Avodah K: Common causes of female orgasm responses. *Med Aspects Hum Sexuality, 11:* 40-48, 1977.
18. Greenbaum, Henry: The psychological impact of the sex revolution. In Adelson, Edward T. (Ed.): *Sexuality & Psychoanalysis.* New York, Brunner-Mazel, 1975, pp 292-305.
19. Vincent, Clark E.: Side effects on the family from liberalized sexual attitudes. *Med Aspects Hum Sexuality, 7:* 80-96, 1973.
20. Whitehurst, Robert N.: Loss of virginity in college women. *Med Aspects Hum Sexuality, 12:* 7-23, 1978.
21. Peplau, Letitia: Men, women said to share common stance on sex. *Psychiatric News, 19;* 32-33, 1977.
22. MacCorquodale, Patricia and DeLamater, John: Self-image and premarital sexuality. *J Marr & Family, 41:* 327-39, 1979.

23. Moulton, Ruth: In discussion of the article by *George L Ginsberg.*
24. Leslie, Gerald R.: *Sexual behavior of college men: today vs. 30 years ago. Med Aspects Hum Sexuality, 12:* 102-117, 1978.
25. Leiblum, Sandra R.: Common male errors in lovemaking. *Med Aspects Hum Sexuality, 12:* 80-91, 1978.
26. Blum Harold P. (Ed.). *Female Psychology: Contemporary Psychoanalytic Views.* New York, Int Univ Pr, 1977.
27. Gray, Mary J.: Women's preferences regarding clitoral stimulation. *Med Aspects Hum Sexuality, 12:* 32-42, 1978.
28. Hite, Shere: *The Hite Report: A Nationwide Study on Female Sexuality.* New York, Macmillan, 1976.
29. Fogarty, Thomas F.: Sexual estrangement in marriage. *Med Aspects Hum Sexuality, 11:* 127-35, 1977.
30. Greene, B. L. et al., Clinical observations of sex as a reverberation of the total relationship.
31. Wall, Susan and Kaltreider, Nancy: Changing social-sexual patterns in gynecologic practice. *JAMA, 237:* 565-568, 1977.
32. Scharff, David E.: The power of sex to sustain marriage. *Med Aspects Hum Sexuality, 12:* 8-25, 1978.
33. Shostak, Arthur B.: Abortion as a fatherhood lost — problems and reforms. *Family Coordinator, 28:* 569-74, 1979.
34. Broderick, Carlfred B.: Brief guide to office counseling — extramarital sexual involvement. *Med Aspects Hum Sexuality, 11:* 93-94, 1975.
35. Kaslow, Florence and Gingrich, Gerald: The clergyman and the psychologist as marriage counselors — differences in philosophy, referral patterns and treatment approaches to nonmarital relationships. *zj Marr & Family Counseling, 3:* 13-21, 1977.
36. O'Neill, N. and O'Neill, G.: *Open Marriage.* New York, Avon, 1972.
37. Palson, Charles and Rebecca: Swinging in wedlock, Reflections. *Merck Sharp and Dohme, 8:* 30-54, 1973.
38. Denfeld, Duane and Gordon, Michael: The sociology of mate swapping — of the family that swings together clings together. *J Sex Research, 6:* 85-100, 1970.
39. Denfeld, Duane: Dropouts from swinging. *Family Coordinator, 23:* 45-19, 1974.
40. Winick, Charles: Swinging mate-swappers. *Medical Opinion & Review, 7:* 47-51, 1971.
41. Flach, Frederic F.: Viewpoints — can a marriage really ever recover after a spouse has had a discovered affair? *Med Aspects Hum Sexuality, 13:* 12-24, 1979.
42. Bell, Robert R. and Peltz, Dorothyann: Extramarital sex among women. *Med Aspects Hum Sexuality, 8:* 10-43, 1974.
43. Greene, Bernard L.: Commentary on Bell & Peltz. *Med Aspects Hum Sexuality, 8:* 1974.
44. Johnson, Ralph E.: Some correlates of extramarital coitus. *J Marr &*

Family 32: 449-56, 1970.

45. Ryder, Robert G.: Husband-wife dyads versus married strangers. *Family Process, 7:* 233, 1968.

46. Bell, Robert R., Turner, Stanley, and Rosen, Lawrence: A multivariate analysis of female extramarital coitus. *J Marr & Family, 37:* 375-84, 1975.

47. Vincent, C. E., Side effects on the family from liberalized sexual attitudes.

48. Willis II, Stanley E: Sexual promiscuity as a symptom of personal and cultural anxiety, Med Aspects Hum Sexuality, 1: 16, 1967.

49. Wolf, Alexander: The problem of infidelity. In Rosenbaum, Salo and Alger, Ian (Eds.): *The Marriage Relationship.* New York, Basic Books, 1968, pp. 175-196.

50. Neubeck, Gerhard, Bellville, Carol, Johnson, Arthur, and Bellville, Titus P.: Roundtable: the significance of extramarital sex relations. *Med Aspects Hum Sexuality, 3:* 33, 1969.

51. Greene, Bernard L. et al: Conscious and unconscious factors in marital infidelity. *Med Aspects Hum Sexuality, 8:* 87-105, 1974.

52. Roth, Nathan: Sexual revenge. *Med Apects Hum Sexuality, 13:* 8-19, 1979.

53. Viewpoints: What is the chief cause of marital infidelity. *Med Aspects Hum Sexuality, 8:* 90-110, 1974.

54. Hollender, Marc H., Luborsky, Lester, and Scaramella, Thomas J.: Body contact and sexual excitement. *Arch Gen Psychiat, 20:* 188, 1969.

55. Gardner, Richard A.: Sexual fantasies in childhood. *Med Aspects Hum Sexuality, 3:* 121, 1969.

56. Salzman, Leon: What should a woman do on learning her husband is having an affair. *Med Aspects Hum Sexuality, 12:* 110-117, 1978.

57. Pinta, Emil R.: Husband's acceptance of wife's affairs. *Med Aspects Hum Sexuality, 12:* 51, 1978.

58. Goldberg, Martin: Extramarital sexual desires. *Med Aspects Hum Sexuality, 12:* 32-47, 1978.

59. Sexual survey #3: Current thinking on sexual fantasies on extramarital sex. *Med Aspects Hum Sexuality 11:* 25, 1977.

60. Pinta, Emil R.: Pathological tolerance. *Am J Psychiat, 135:* 698-701, 1978.

61. Landers, Ann: The Ann Landers Encyclopedia — A to Z, Part X, Adultery: marriage seasoning or marriage sell? *Chicago Sun-Times,* Nov. 1, p. 73, 1978.

62. Flach, Frederic F.: Viewpoints: Can a marriage really ever recover after a spouse has had a discovered affair. *Med Aspects Hum Sexuality, 13:* 12-24, 1979.

63. Livsey, Clara G.: Coping with adultery that threatens marriage. *Med Aspects Hum Sexuality, 13:* 8-18, 1979.

64. Masters, W. H. and Johnson, V. E., *The Pleasure Bond.*

65. Libby, Roger W. and Whitehurst, Robert N. (Eds.): *Marriage and*

Alternatives: Exploring Intimate Relationships. Glenview, Illinois, Scott, 1977.

66. Clanton, Gordon and Smith, L. G. (Eds.): *Jealousy.* Englewood Cliffs, N. J.: P-H, 1977.

67. Bernard, Jessie: Jealousy in marriage. *Med Aspects Hum Sexuality, 5:* 200-15, 1971.

68. Pinta, E. R., Pathological tolerance.

69. Kaplan, Eugene H.: Normal ebb and flow of marital sex relations. *Med Aspects Hum Sexuality, 13:* 87-109, 1979.

70. Auerback, Alfred: Role of sex in happiness (in Questions and Answers). *Med Aspects Hum Sexuality, 11:* 42 (May), 1977.

71. Sadock, Benjamin J., Kaplan, Helen I. and Freedman, A. M.: *The Sexual Experience.* Baltimore, Williams & Wilkins, 1976.

72. Kaplan, Helen S.: *The New Sex Therapy.* New York, Brunner-Mazel, 1974.

73. *Human Sexuality.* Chicago, The American Medical Association, 1972.

74. Katchadourian, Herant A. & Lunde, Donald T.: *Fundamentals of Human Sexuality.* (second ed.) New York, HR&W, 1975, pp. 285-94.

75. Comfort, Alex: *The Joy of Sex.* New York, Crown Pub., 1972.

76. Cavanagh, John R.: The durable incompatible marriage, psychological characteristics of the mates. *Southern Med J, 55:* 396, 1962.

77. Monti, Peter M., Brown, Walter A. and Corriveau, Donald P.: Testosterone and components of aggressive and sexual behavior in man. *Am J Psychiat, 134:* 692-94, 1977.

78. Fox, Cyril A.: Multiple climax — clarifying patients' concerns and misunderstandings. *Med Aspects Hum Sexuality, 10:* 19, 21, 1976.

79. Nadelson, Carol and Nadelson, Theodore: Developmental determinants of sexuality. *Psychiatric Opinion, 12:* 14-19, 1975.

80. Gadpaille, Warren J (edited by Lucy Freeman). *The Cycles of Sex.* New York, Scribners, 1975.

81. O'Conner, John F. and Stern, Lenore O.: Developmental factors in functional sexual disorders. *New York State J Med, 72:* 1838-43, 1972.

82. Derogatis, Leonard R., Meyer, Jon K and Gallant, Bridget W.: Distinctions between male and female invested partners in sexual disorders. *Am J Psychiat, 134:* 385-90, 1977.

83. Derogatis, L. R. and Meyer, J. K.: The invested partner, *Am J Psychiat, 136:* 1545-49, 1979.

84. Miller, Jean B.: *Toward a New Psychology of Women.* Boston, Beacon Press, 1976.

85. Greene, Bernard L. et al., Clinical observations of sex as a reverberation of the total relationship.

86. Auerback, Alfred: Altered sex drive over course of marriage, (in Questions and Answers). *Med Aspects Hum Sexuality, 9:* 24, 1975.

87. Adelson, E. T. (Ed.): *Sexuality and Psychoanalysis.* New York, Brunner-Mazel, 1975.

88. Abernethy, Virginia: Dominance and sexual behavior — a hypothesis. *Am J Psychiat, 131:* 813-17, 1974.

89. McCranie, E. James: How life crises affect the sexuality of middle-aged men. *Med Aspects Hum Sexuality, 13:* 61-75, 1979.
90. Visotsky, Harold M.: Commentary of Peter A. Martin's article, The Happy sexless marriage, *Med Aspects Hum Sexuality, 11:* 75-85, 1977.
91. Chilman, Catherine: Some psychosocial aspects of female sexuality. *Family Coordinator, 23:* 123-131, 1974.
92. Weitz, Shirley: *Sex Roles: Biological, Psychological & Social Foundations.* New York, Oxford Univ Press, 1977.
93. Shainess, Natalie: Sexual problems of women. *J Sex & Marital Therapy, 1:* 110-123, 1974.
94. Denber, Herman C. B.: The use of sexuality to externalize inner conflict. *Med Aspects Hum Sexuality, 7:* 44-58, 1973.
95. Lief, Harold I.: Inhibited sexual desire. *Med Aspects Hum Sexuality, 11:* 94-95, 1977.
96. Kaplan, Helen S.: Inhibited sexual desire. *Med Aspects Hum Sexuality, 13:* 26-47, 1979.
97. Stoller, Robert J.: Sexual excitement. *Arch Gen Psychiat, 33:* 899-909, 1976.
98. Oziel, L. Jerome and Munjack, Dennis J.: Libido vs potency (in Questions & Answers). *Med Aspects Hum Sexuality, 12:* 35, 1978.
99. Lief, Harold I: Sexual survey #23 — current thinking on age and intensity of sexual desire in men. *Med Aspects Hum Sexuality, 13:* 48-51, 1979.
100. Gadpaille, Warren J.: Adolescent sexuality — a challenge to psychiatrists. *J Am Acad Psychoanal, 3:* 163-177, 1977.
101. Comfort, Alex: Old men's need for increased stimulation (in Questions & Answers). *Med Aspects Hum Sexuality, 11:* 9, 1977.
102. Cleveland, Martha: Sex in marriage: at age 40 and beyond. *Family Coordinator, 25:* 233-40, 1976.
103. Trainer, Joseph B.: Sexual incompatibilities. *J Marr & Family, 1:* 123-34, 1975.
104. Goldman, Arlene: Sexual needs of aged are often ignored. *JAMA, 230:* 359-60, 1974.
105. Weinberg, Jack: Sexual expression in late life. *Am J Psychiat, 126:* 713, 1969.
106. Lasswell, Thomas E. and Lasswell, Marcia E.: I love you but I'm not in love with you. *J Marr & Family Counseling, 2:* 211-24, 1976.
107. Money, John: Sex, love, and commitment. *J Sex & Marital Therapy, 2:* 273-76, 1976.
108. Grunebaum, Henry: Thoughts on love, sex and commitment. *J Sex & Marital Therapy, 2:* 277-83, 1976.
109. Vincent, Clark E.: Historical and theoretical perspectives — sex, love, and commitment. *J Sex & Marital Therapy, 2:* 265-72, 1976.
110. Stoller, Robert J.: *Sex and Gender: On The Development of Masculinity and Femininity.* New York, Science House, 1968.
111. Ovesey, Lionel and Person, Ethel: Gender identity and sexual

psychopathology in men — a psychodynamic analysis of homosexuality, transsexualism, and transvestism. *J Am Acad Psychoanal, 1:* 53-72, 1973.

112. Auerback, Alfred: The battle of the sexes. *Med Aspects Hum Sexuality, 1:* 6, 1967.

113. Sherfey, Mary L.: The evolution and nature of female sexuality in relation to psychoanalytic theory. *J Am Psychoanal Assn, 14:* 28, 1966.

114. Masters, W. E. and Johnson, V. E., *Human Sexual Inadequacy.*

115. Sherfey, Mary L.: Some biology of sex. *J Sex & Marital Therapy, 1:* 97-109, 1974.

116. Gadpaille, Warren J., Fischer, Ilda V., Moulton, Ruth, Tyrer, Louise B., Warren, Frank Z., Bess, Barbara E., and Lewis, Selma: Viewpoints: What do women find most difficult to understand about men's sexuality? *Med Aspects Hum Sexuality, 13:* 69-91, 1979.

117. Jensen, Gordon D.: Men's unresponsive period after orgasm. *Med Aspects Hum Sexuality, 13:* 50-64, 1979.

118. Pearlman, Carl K.: Frequency of intercourse in males at different ages. *Med Aspects Hum Sexuality, 6:* 92-113, 1972.

119. Lief, Harold I.: What's new in research? Controversies over female orgasm. *Med Aspects Hum Sexuality, 11:* 136-38, 1977.

120. Kroop, Merle S.: When women initiate sexual relations. *Med Aspects Hum Sexuality, 12:* 16-29, 1978.

121. Smith, Elaine P. and Meyer, Jon K.: Attitudes and temperaments of nonorgastic women. *Med Aspects Hum Sexuality, 12:* 66-79, 1978.

122. Wabrek, Alan J. and Wabrek, Carolyn J.: How emphasis on orgasm can make sex sexless. *Med Aspects Hum Sexuality, 11:* 40-49, 1977.

123. Crain, Irving J.: Afterplay, *Med Aspects Hum Sexuality, 12:* 72-85, 1978.

124. Leiblum, S. R., Common male errors in lovemaking.

125. Gadpaille, Warren J., et al., What do women find most difficult to understand about men's sexuality?

126. Marcotte, David B., Carlson, Noel, and Weiss, Daniel S.: Women's misunderstandings about male sexuality. *Med Aspects Hum Sexuality, 10:* 76-81, 1976.

127. Pietropinto, Anthony and Simenauer, Jacquiline: *Beyond the Male Myth: What Women Want to Know About Men's Sexuality.* A Nationwide Survey. New York, Times Books, 1978.

128. Butler, Carol A.: New data about female sexual response. *J Sex & Marital Therapy, 2:* 40-46, 1976.

129. Rosenbaum, Salo: Pretended orgasm. *Med Aspects Hum Sexuality, 4:* 84-96, 1977.

130. Fischer, I. V., What do women find most difficult to understand about men's sexuality?

131. Moulton, R., What do women find most difficult to understand about men's sexuality?

132. Butler, C. A., New data about female sexual response.

133. Kroop, Merle S., Davidson, Leah, Ruben, Harvey L., Massler, Dennis J.,

Klenbanow, Sheila, Roback, Howard B. and Boutelle, William E.: Viewpoints — What usually underlies the statement: "I have lost sexual interest in my spouse?" *Med Aspects Hum Sexuality, 12:* 28-45, 1978.

134. Renshaw, Domeena C.: "I'm just not interested in sex, doctor." *Med Aspects Hum Sexuality, 12:* 32-40, 1978.

135. Davidson, Leah, Viewpoints.

136. Poze, Ronald S. and Poze, Philippa J.: Sexual avoidance. *Med Aspects Hum Sexuality, 12;* 130-42, 1978.

137. Mace, David: Revising sexual interest in wife (in Questions and Answers). *Med Aspects Hum Sexuality, 11:* 8, 1977.

138. Turner, Nathan W.: Overcoming poor sexual communication patterns. *Med Aspects Hum Sexuality, 11:* 99-100, 1977.

139. Bell, Robert R. and Bell, Phyllis L.: Sexual satisfaction among married women. *Med Aspects Hum Sexuality, 6:* 136-144, 1972.

140. Polatin, Phillip: Postcoital sadness. *Med Aspects Hum Sexuality, 7:* 12-32, 1973. (see *Gerald L. Klerman's* commentary p. 32.)

141. Klerman, Gerald L.: Commentary on Polatin's article. *Med Aspects Hum Sexuality, 7:* 32, 1973.

142. Weiler, Stephen and Cavenar, Jesso O.: Postcoital feelings in men and women. *Med Aspects Hum Sexuality, 11:* 69-79, 1977.

143. Rosenbaum, Maj-Britt: Commentary on Postcoital feelings in men and women. *Med Aspects Hum Sexuality, 11:* 79-81, 1977.

144. Hollender, Marc H. and Mercer, Alexander J.: Wish to be held and wish to hold in men and women. *Arch Gen Psychiat, 33:* 43-49, 1976.

145. Huang L. T., Phares R., and Hollender M. H.: The wish to be held: A transcultural study. *Arch Gen Psychiat, 33:* 41-43, 1976.

146. Hollender, Marc H.: The need or wish to be held. *Arch Gen Psychiat, 22:* 445-53, 1970.

147. Goldberg, Martin: Commentary on sexual survey #8 — current thinking on sexual norms in marriage. *Med Aspects Hum Sexuality, 12:* 122-27, 1978.

148. Cuber, John F.: The natural history of sex in marriage. *Med Aspects Hum Sexuality, 9:* 51-75, 1975.

149. Weissberg, Josef H. and Levay, Alexander N.: Sexual scorekeeping. *Med Aspects Hum Sexuality, 13:* 8-14, 1979.

150. Friedman, Morton: Commentary on Sexual scorekeeping. *Med Aspects Hum Sexuality, 13,* 1979.

151. Pearlman, C. K., Frequency of intercourse in males at different ages.

152. Kaplan, H. S., *The New Sex Therapy.*

153. Cleveland, M., Sex in marriage.

154. Edwards, John N. and Booth, Alan: The cessation of marital intercourse. *Am J Psychiat, 133:* 133-36, 1976.

155. Offit, Avodah K., Ryder, Robert, G., Gomez, Madelaine, Dormant, Paul and Farrer-Meschan, Rachel: Viewpoints — Does expression of anger help or hurt the marital-sexual relationship. *Med Aspects Hum Sexuality, 13:* 53-65, 1979.

156. Silverstein, Judith: *Sexual Enhancement for Women.* Arlington, Mass, Jay, 1978.
157. Oziel, L. Jerome: Inconsistency of coital orgasm in women. *Med Aspects Hum Sexuality, 12:* 16-28, 1978.
158. Offit, A. K., Common causes of female orgasm responses.
159. Kaplan, Helen Singer, *The New Sex Therapy.*
160. Moulton, Ruth: Multiple factors in frigidity. In Masserman, Jules (Ed.): *Sexuality of Women, Science and Psychoanalysis,* Vol. X. New York: Grune & Stratton, 1966, pp. 75-93.
161. Greene, B. L. and Solomon, A. P.: Marital disharmony. *Am J Psychotherapy, 17:* 443, 1963.
162. Mead, Beverley T.: "Showing off" sexually. *Med Aspects Hum Sexuality, 12:* 44-50, 1978.
163. Rosenbaum, Salo: The significance of the orgastic pretense. In Rosenbaum, Salo and Alger, Ian (Eds.): *The Marriage Relationship.* New York, Basic Books, 1968, pp. 157-174.
164. Schmiel, John L.: Narcissism as barrier to heterosexual relations. *Med Aspects Hum Sexuality, 11:* 38-52, 1977.
165. Salzman, Leon: The highly sexed man. *Med Aspects Hum Sexuality, 6:* 36-49, 1972.
166. Schmiel, J. L., Narcissism as a barrier to heterosexual relations.
167. Gould, Robert E.: Sexual survey #28: Current thinking on sources of sexual arousal. *Med Aspects Hum Sexuality, 13:* 48-50, 1979.
168. Schiavi, Raul C.: Sex therapy and psychophysiological research. *Am J Psychiat, 133:* 562-66, 1976.
169. Meyer, Jon K.: Sexual Problems in Office Practice. In Meyer, J. K. (Ed.): *Clinical Management of Sexual Disorders.* Baltimore, Williams & Wilkins, 1976, p. 11.
170. Frank, E. et al.: Frequency of sexual dysfunction in "normal" couples. *New England J Med, 299:* 111-16, 1978.
171. Levine, Stephen B.: Barriers to the attainment of ejaculatory control. *Med Aspects Hum Sexuality, 13:* 32-56, 1979.
172. Levine, Stephen B.: Premature ejaculation — some thoughts about its pathogenesis. *J Sex & Marital Therapy, 1:* 326-34, 1975.
173. Levine, Stephen B., Premature ejaculation.
174. Karacan, Ismet: Advances in the diagnosis of erectile impotence. *Med Aspects Hum Sexuality, 12:* 85-97, 1978.
175. Fisher, Charles, Schiavi, Raul C., Edwards, Adele, Davis, David M., Reitman, Mark and Fine, Jeffrey: Evaluation of nocturnal penile tumescence in the differential diagnosis of sexual impotence. *Arch Gen Psychiat, 36:* 431-37, 1979.
176. Masters, W. E. and Johnson, V. E., *Human Sexual Inadequacy.*
177. Kaplan, H. S., *The New Sex Therapy.*
178. Lief, Harold I.: What' s new in sex research — progress in diagnosing organic versus psychogenic impotence. *Med Aspects Hum Sexuality, 11:* 111-12, 1977.

179. McCarley, Robert: Erections during sleep (in the section Questions and Answers). *Med Aspects Hum Sexuality, 12:* 135, 1978.
180. Machleder, Herbert I.: Sexual dysfunction in aortic-iliac occlusive disease. *Med Aspects Hum Sexuality, 12:* 125-26, 1978.
181. Burt, Loren G.: Causes and treatment of primary impotence (in Questions and Answers). *Med Aspects Hum Sexuality, 11:* 65-67, 1977.
182. *Human Sexuality.* The committee on Human Sexuality, Am Med Assn., Chicago, Ill., 1972.
183. Katchadourian, Herant A. and Lunde, Donald T.: *Fundamentals of Human Sexuality* (2nd ed). New York. HR&W, 1975, pp. 295-308.
184. Lassen, Carol L.: Issues and dilemmas in sexual treatment. *J Sex & Marital Therapy, 2:* 35-37, 1976.
185. Jensen, Gordon J.: Masturbation by married men. *Med Aspects Hum Sexuality, 12:* 37, 1978.
186. Hite, S., *The Hite Report.*
187. Fisher, Seymour: *The Female Orgasm: Psychology, Physiology, Fantasy.* New York, Basic Books, 1973.
188. Barclay, Andrew M.: Sexual fantasies in men and women. *Med Aspects Hum Sexuality, 7:* 205-16, 1973.
189. Hollender, Marc H.: Women's use of fantasy during sexual intercourse (Chap 13). In Marcus, Irwin M. and Francis, John J. (Eds.): Masturbation from Infancy to Senescence. New York, Int Univ Press, 1975.
190. Croft, Harry A.: Most popular coital positions (in Questions & Answers). *Med Aspects Hum Sexuality, 12:* 26, 27, 1978.
191. O'Connor, John F.: Loss of erection during fellatio (in Questions & Answers). *Med Aspects hum Sexuality, 12:* 147, 1978.
192. Comfort, A., *The Joy of Sex.*
193. Saddock, Benjamin J. and Saddock, Virginia A.: Coital positions. *Med Aspects Hum Sexuality, 13:* 114-19, 1979.
194. Greenson, Ralph R.: What is the psychological significance of various coital positions. *Med Aspects Hum Sexuality, 5:* 8-16, 1971.
195. Hunt, Morton: *Sexual Behavior in the 1970s.* Chicago, Playboy Press, 1974.
196. Jensen, Gordon D.: Anal coitus by married couples (in Questions & Answers). *Med Aspects Hum Sexuality, 9:* 115, 1975.
197. Levay, Alexander N. and Kagle, Arlene: Motives for anal coitus (in Questions & Answers). *Med Aspects HUM Sexuality, 11:* 132, 1977.
198. Lief, H. I., What's new in research?
199. Hatcher, Robert A.: Reasons to recommend the condom. *Med Aspects Hum Sexuality 12:* 91-92, 1978.
200. Hatcher, Robert A. et al.: *Contraceptive Technology,* 1978-1979. New York, Irvington, 1978.
201. Hilberman, Elaine: *The Rape Victim.* New York, Basic Books, Inc., 1978.
202. Metzger, Deena: It is always the woman who is raped. *Am J Psychiat,*

133: 405-08, 1976.
203. Notman, Malkah T. and Nadelson, Carol C.: The rape victim — psychodynamic considerations. *Am J Psychiat, 133:* 408-13, 1976.
204. Lief, Harold I.: Rape — is it sexual or an aggressive act? *Med Aspects Hum Sexuality, 12:* 55-56, 1978.
205. Groth, Nicholas A, Burgess, Ann W., and Holstro, Lynda L.: Rape — power, anger, and sexuality. *Am J Psychiat, 134:* 1239-43, 1977.
206. Schuker, Eleanor: Psychodynamics and treatment of sexual assault victims. *J Am Acad Psychoanal, 7:* 553-73, 1979.
207. Chappell, Ann L.: "Stress syndrome" in rape victims (in Questions & Answers). *Med Aspects Hum Sexuality, 13:* 63-4, 1979.
208. Gundlach, Ralph H.: Sexual molestation and rape reported by homosexual and heterosexual women. *J Homosexuality, 2:* 367-75, 1977.
209. Miller, Jill, Moeller, Deborah et al: Recidivism among sex assault victims. *Am J Psychiat, 135:* 1103-4, 1978.
210. Hilberman, E., *The Rape Victim.*
211. Chappell, A. L., "Stress syndrome" in rape victim.
212. Sagarin, Edward: Rape of one's wife (in Questions & Answers). *Med Aspects Hum Sexuality, 12:* 153, 1978.
213. Rada, Richard T. (Ed.): *Clinical Aspects of the Rapist.* New York, Grune, 1978.
214. Rowan, Robert L.: Patients' concerns about variations in penile size and appearance. *Med Aspects Hum Sexuality, 13:* 84-93, 1979.
215. Toussieng, Povl W.: Men's fear of having too small a penis. *Med Aspects Hum Sexuality, 11:* 62-69, 1977.
216. Schmiel, John L.: Interview — do we overestimate sex? *Med Aspects Hum Sexuality, 12:* 8-18, 1978.
217. Friedman, Leonard J.: Unconsummated marriages. *Med Aspects Hum Sexuality, 4:* 16-29, 1970.
218. Friedman, Leonard J.: *Virgin Wives: A Study of Unconsummated Marriages.* London, Tavistock, 1962.
219. Masters W. E. and Johnson, V. E., *Human Sexual Inadequacy.*
220. Fertel, Normal S.: Vaginismus — A review. *J Sex Marital Therapy, 3:* 113-118, 1977.
221. O'Sullivan, Karl: Observations on vaginismus in Irish women. *Arch Gen Psychiat, 36:* 824-26, 1979.
222. Zussman, Leon and Zussman, Shirley: Dealing with the unconsummated marriage. *Med Aspects Hum Sexuality, 12:* 115-6, 1978.
223. Friedman, L. J., Unconsummated marriages.
224. Justice, Blair and Justice, Rita: *The Broken Taboo — Sex in the Family.* Human Sciences, Pub., 1979.
225. Bernstein, Gail A.: Physician Management of incest situations. *Med Aspects Hum Sexuality, 13:* 66-87, 1979.
226. Weaver, Beverly M.: Intrafamily sexual abuse of children. *Psychiatric News, 14:* 1, 6-7, and 27-28, 1979.

227. Esman, Aaron H.: More on a neglected problem (letters to the editor). *Am J Psychiat, 135:* 1438, 1978.

228. Finkelhor, David: Psychological, cultural and family factors in incest and family sexual abuse. *J Marr & Family Counseling, 4:* 41-49, 1978.

229. Meiselman, Karin C.: *Incest — A Psychological Study of Causes and Effects with Treatment Recommendations.* San Francisco, CA, Jossey-Bass Pub., 1978.

230. Boekelheide, Pricilla D: Psychopathology of incestuous mothers. *Med Aspects Hum Sexuality, 12:* 37, 1978.

231. Herjanic, B. and Wilbois, R.: Sexual abuse of children, detection and management. *JAMA, 239:* 331, 1978.

232. Rosenfeld, Alvin A.: Incidence of a history of incest among 18 female psychiatric patients. *Am J Psychiat, 136:* 491-95, 1979.

233. Browning, Diane H. and Boatman, Bonny: Incest: children at risk. *Am J Psychiat, 134:* 69-72, 1977.

234. Nakashima, I. and Zakus, G.: Incest: review and clinical experience. *Pediatrics, 60:* 696, 1977.

235. Masters, William H. and Johnson, Virginia E.: Incest: the ultimate sexual taboo. *Redbook, 54:* 1976.

236. Jonas, A. David and Jonas, Doris F.: A biological basis for the oedipus complex — an evolutionary and ethological approach. *Am J Psychiat, 132:* 602-06, 1975.

237. Hewes, Gordon W.: Communication of sexual interest — an anthropological view. *Med Aspects Hum Sexuality, 7:* 66-92, 1973.

238. Finch, Stuart M.: Adult seduction of the child — effects on the child. *Med Aspects Hum Sexuality, 7:* 170-87, 1973.

239. Tsai, Marvis: Women who were sexually molested as children. *Med Aspects Hum Sexuality, 13:* 55-56, 1979.

240. Dixon, Katherine, Arnold, L. Eugene, and Calestro, Kenneth: Father-son incest — underreported psychiatric problem? *Am J Psychiat, 135:* 835-8, 1978.

241. Dixon, K., Arnold, L. E. and Calestro, K., Father-son incest.

242. Margolis, M.: Preliminary report of a case of consummated mother-son incest. In *The Annual of Psychoanalysis,* Vol. V, edited by the Chicago Institute for Psychoanalysis. New York, N. Y., Internat Univ Press, 1977.

243. Boekelheide, P. D., Psychopathology of incestuous mothers.

244. Hunt, Samuel P.: Influence of a homosexual father (in Questions & Answers). *Med Aspects Hum Sexuality, 23:* 103-104, 1978.

245. Krueger, David W.: Difference between transvestism and homosexuality. *Med Aspects Hum Sexuality, 12:* 117-18, 1978.

246. Person, Ethel and Ovesey, Lionel: Transvestism — new perspectives. *J Acad Am Acad Psychoanal, 6:* 301-23, 1978.

247. Fleming, Michael and Feinbloom, Deborah: The Cross-dresser — therapeutic challenge. *Psychiatric News, 19:* 40-41, Nov. 4, 1977.

248. Pillard, Richard C.: The homosexual as patient. *Psychiatric Opinion,*

12: 23-26, 1975.

249. Ross, Michael W.: Heterosexual marriage of homosexual males — some associated factors. *J Sex & Marital Therapy, 5:* 142-51, 1979.

250. Dank, Barry M.: Why homosexuals marry women. *Med Aspects Hum Sexuality, 6:* 14-23, 1972.

251. Coleman, Eli: Married bisexuals still show same sex feelings. *Psychiatric News, 15:* 19-26, 1979.

252. Schmiel, John: The patient who thinks he is a "latent" homosexual. *Med Aspects Hum Sexuality, 9:* 125-26, 1975.

253. Bieber, Irving and Bieber, Toby: Heterosexuals who are preoccupied with homosexual thoughts. *Med Aspects Hum Sexuality, 9:* 152-168, 1975.

254. Levy, Norman J.: The middle-aged male homosexual. *J Am Acad Psychoanal, 7:* 405-18, 1979.

255. Hendin, Herbert: Homosexuality — the psychosocial dimension. *J Am Acad Psychoanal, 6:* 479-96, 1978.

256. Socarides, Charles W.: *Homosexuality.* New York: Jason Aaronson, 1978.

257. Altshuler, Kenneth Z.: Some notes and an exercise with regard to male homosexuality. *J Amer Acad Psychoanal, 4:* 237-48, 1976.

258. Bieber, I., Sexuality.

259. Hatterer, Myra S.: The problems of women married to homosexual men. *Am J Psychiat, 131:* 275-77, 1974.

260. Ross, MW: Heterosexual marriage of homosexual males.

261. Evans, Ray B.: Homosexuality and the role of the family physician. *Med Aspects Hum Sexuality, 13:* 10-31, 1979.

262. Bell, Alan P. and Weinberg, Martin S.: *Homosexualities: A Study of Diversity Among Men and Women.* New York, Simon & Schuster, 1978.

263. Bieber, Irving: Commentary on the new "Kinsey Report." *Med Aspects Hum Sexuality, 12:* 43-45, 1978.

264. Levine, Edward M. and Ross, Nathaniel: Sexual dysfunctions and psychoanalysis. *Am J Psychiat, 134:* 646-51, 1977.

265. Fink, Paul J.: Homosexuality — illness or life-style? *J Sex & Marital Therapy, 1:* 225-33, 1975.

266. Francoeur, Robert T. and Francoeur, Anna K.: The aesthetics of social sex — a revolution in values. *J Operational Psychiat, 6:* 152-61, 1975.

Chapter XVIII

ADDITIONAL COMMENTS ABOUT YOUR RELATIONSHIP

THE *last item,* #23 on the BRQ, is unstructured and asks each partner to make any additional comments about their relationship. Frequently, this question elicits several pages of important data about the dyadic transactions and additional confidential material; this question's ambiguous wording encourages each partner to "freely associate." Furthermore, the previous items of the BRQ may have mobilized anxieties and/or hostilities or raised issues in need of clarification. Occasionally, the real areas of conflict may be expressed under this heading.

"Free association," a controversial concept, can lead the individual into unconscious layers by using conscious and preconscious elements. Clinically, free association has provided unexpected insights into both the individual's fantasies and current situations. The following example illustrates an unconscious recall by a patient:

> The patient, while discussing his current difficulty with his superior at work, suddenly began to talk about his venerable ninety-three-year-old patriarchal grandfather. The grandfather was described as a learned, respected, and very religious scholar. He demanded strict obedience from his children.
>
> The patient related visiting his grandparents' home and being invited into the bedroom while he was just four years old. The patient recalled entering the bedroom and being blessed by his grandfather. In relating the incident, the patient raised his left hand spontaneously. Since he was right-handed, I commented on the use of his left hand which in turn caused him to pause and have a "aha" reaction (this type of reaction indicates that something meaningful is just recognized or that a new "insight" is occurring).
>
> The patient, after his pause, said: "I haven't thought of this in thirty-five years, but Grandfather was left-handed. To escape induction into the Russian army, he put his hand in a loaf of bread and courageously cut off his trigger finger. I've always admired him, and I wonder how often I do use my left hand?"

Free association works on the principle of psychic continuity and determinism. According to this concept, every psychic phenomenon (conscious or unconscious) is determined by preceding ones and be-

219

comes itself a determinant of the future. The associations of the determinants affect the psychic continuity. Often this continuity appears interrupted or ended. Such seeming discontinuities correspond to unconscious areas of psychic continuity. This continuity has limits, since it exists only within the person's mind and is based on the individual's own past history, i.e. its repertoire of records in its jukebox. You cannot recall a record unless it was previously encoded. Freud's important discovery of psychic determinism remains relatively unchanged and continues to be a basic construct of most psychiatrists.

Chapter XIX

THE CONJOINT DIAGNOSTIC AND DISPOSITION SESSION

$\mathbf{F}$OR couples with dyadic discord, the end point of the evaluative phase is the routine conjoint and diagnostic session (CDD). After the individual sessions with each partner, unless conjoint sessions occurred at the outset, the couple is seen together for both diagnostic and planning purposes.[1] At the end of the CDD (which often lasts two hours), a diagnosis is made with definite recommendations for the options available at the present time.

During the CDD, I repeat the concept that a *meaningful relationship* between them must be based on *mutual respect*, which is possible when each has *self-respect*.[2-5] Further, I make it clear that each partner must accept full responsibility for his behavior and contribution to their relationship. The CDD is a spontaneous unfolding of their current transactional patterns. Because their script has its inner logic along intrapersonal, interpersonal, and environmental systems' inputs, their drama can undergo rapid alteration when conscious and unconscious forces influence its course. Consequently, all members in the session cannot be sure of what will transpire as the additional environmental input of the therapist is a most new and unpredictable influence upon their world. The *triadic setting* creates a distinct and new dimensional level in the dyadic process of communication of the couple.

Each individual has three reactional options within the session: to be a silent *observer*, to *participate* verbally (including obvious non-verbal messages), and to be a *participant-observer* (or any combination of these).

The therapist who emphasizes the individual's strengths and the positive bonds in their relationship is better able to then gain their willingness to explore the areas of conflict and the various factors involved. The therapist may choose at this time to use an Adlerian approach to focus upon the earliest recollected childhood memories by each patient.[6] Frequently, current complaints are ones that were present in the early phases of the couple's relationship but were not openly discussed or resolved (from either conscious or unconscious reasons). Such recall can focus upon the *change* in each's *tolerance*

221

level for accepting annoying or irritating behavior instead of pointing an accusing finger at each person's flaws. In my experience, 60 percent of the couples who recalled early courtship patterns react with surprise in the CDD at how little each has changed since those early dating days.

There can be no adequate therapy without a diagnosis.[7-10] Because a significant percentage of patients (15% in my practice) have severe psychiatric disorders, a diagnosis is a prerequisite for appropriate therapy (see item #16 of the BRQ in Chapter XII). My diagnosis is based upon the medical model and incorporates medical terminology.[11] The most accurate diagnosis includes significant others whose influence may be complicating the dyadic relationship — perhaps as much as 25 percent additional information is achieved by the inclusion of such people.[12,13] Dyadic diagnosis continues to remain a postulate with no generally accepted classification. I continue to find Pollak's concepts of failure of need complementarity in the areas of interpersonal orientation, sexuality, finances, and ego strengthening helpful in evaluating the disharmony. The unfolding projective identifications and unconscious collusion displayed in the CDD is a great help in diagnosis.[14] If I diagnose complementary closure vis-à-vis mutual escalation, to illustrate clearly, I will ask the couple whether they have seen the play or movie, *Who's Afraid of Virginia Woolf?*[15] This play depicts, not only mutual escalation, but also the game of "Uproar." There are also many other games a couple may employ in their relationship.[16] I always discuss clinical observations when the game gets underway. The value of the CDD is obvious; the couple's doing, viewing, and reviewing can easily take place when *both* partners are present.

The therapist must constantly be on the alert as to the varied ways dyadic disharmony may express itself in vocational ineffectiveness, alcoholism, psychosomatic complaints, neurosis, and so on. Often a referral is based upon what would appear as an intrapersonal problem alone, whereas the experienced clinician will not exclude the dyadic relationship and use my BRQ to help present the fullest data to base a diagnosis. The behavior manifestations just presented are phenomena that relate either with the intrinsic needs and psychological motivations of the partners or with the demands made upon such individuals by their culture. As one describes a person's needs and motivations, the implication is often made that these patterns of behavior are pathological per se. Thus it is easy to talk of a man's need to be mothered or of his need to dominate or of his need to escape reality. None of these needs are necessarily pathological, and many are worthwhile and emotionally healthy. In evaluating a meaningful relationship, I observe the totality of the transactions between the couple and single out only transactions creating conflict. It is essential to recognize the feelings and biases that each individual has, including mine. In respect to my biases, I state plainly and openly my feelings whenever it is professionally indicated.

My diagnosis includes a review of the stages in the couple's dyadic development with regard to those transactional patterns providing for their mutual satisfaction. I believe that problems in a relationship frequently occur by failure of need complementarity between partners. My observations that the patients are utilizing projective identification and/or unconscious collusion is of great help in the diagnosis. Because this phenomena is prevalent in many problem couples, I will discuss it more fully.

PROJECTIVE IDENTIFICATION

Since this phenomenon of projective identification involves a couple so completely (when present in the CDD), the triadic setting is the best place to discuss its presence. The phenomena of projective identification in object relationships was first introduced by Melanie Klein.[17] She knew that Freud was aware of the process but that he was mainly interested in the process of identification by introjection. The valuable phenomena of projective identification in marriage (all pair-couplings) was highlighted by Dicks and his co-worker. They point out that such identifications are the basis for an unconscious collusive process in the marital transactions. Their statements on marital disharmony are equally applicable to courtship: " . . . in marital disharmony one or both partners often fail to confirm the other's personality or identity. Instead they require the other to conform to an inner role mode, and punish them if the expectation is disappointed." I agree with Dicks that much conflict stems from efforts to coerce or mold the partner by very rigid and stereotyped tactics to these inner models and " . . . although these techniques arouse resistance and frustration of the other spouse's ego, needs at a deeper level are part of a collusive process." I am in accord with these observations and with his comment that, where projective identifications have taken place, " . . . hate is felt both inside the self and towards object, and towards the self in the object from the outside."[18] Laing et al. succinctly describe the phenomena of projective identification as " . . . a mode of experiencing the other in which one experiences one's outer world in terms of one's inner world. Another way of putting this is that one experiences the perceptual world in terms of one's phantasy system, *without realizing that one is doing this* (italics added)."[19] As one patient said, after viewing himself from a new perspective, "The realization came to me that basically our problem is my doing. The things I have done to her and made her feel were barbaric. I made her feel inadequate. I did everything to annoy her. Basically I set her up as my mother and then destroyed her. Mother is not a warm, giving person. She is brilliant, dynamic, strong and substantial. She doesn't have maternal attributes. She is the opposite of my wife. What I have done is set my wife up as my mother, many times *I was unaware I was doing this*, and then destroyed her. I feel I put my wife in this position. The blocks she set against me — it's amazing they didn't come sooner."

At times it is necessary to describe these phenomena to the couple in the CDD. They are given the jukebox and record analogy. Their disharmony is seen as the result of one partner or both playing an inappropriate record (projective identification can be part of this incorrect selection of records to play). An example which reveals how the jukebox-record analogy can be the first step in the process of rebuilding a dyadic relationship occurs in the illustration below:

> Mrs. L: "I have become morose, insecure, and generally miserable. He is very distant. He shuts me out of his emotional life almost entirely. Any gesture I make seems to bear intrusion, and he admits to simply not being affectionate, enthusiastic, and loving."
>
> I asked: "Have you felt this way for a long time?"
>
> Mrs. L, "It seems to have started six months ago when I mentioned wanting to have a baby."
>
> Mr. L, "I agree. It did start about six months ago when I found my feelings toward her altered. I am not sure why, though. I feel that my wife and I have not been happy with each other. We have grown farther apart these last months, and today we barely speak to each other. I do not feel affection toward her and I do not believe that she feels any for me . . . although she professes to. A year and a half ago my wife was firmly against having children, and I felt the same way. Recently, she changed her mind, but I have not. This is a major problem in our marriage."
>
> Mrs. L, "I wonder if the conversation I had with Joe's mother might broaden your understanding of our problem, Doctor Greene . . . My mother-in-law told me that she resented Joe, her first baby, because she wanted a girl. She told me that she never expressed her feelings outwardly, but she was so happy when two years later Susan was born. I guess she told me all this because I cannot help complaining to her about Joe's unwillingness to have a baby . . . "

I explained that humans have a permanent library of records which they play throughout their life. The choice of which record to play at any given time, however, can influence how others react to our behavior and statements. Sometimes our choice of record is based upon what worked or seemed appropriate in a past, 'similar' situation; however, the current situation might be different enough to cause a problem in response to the record we play. Also, what we hear may not be exactly was was said or what was meant. I think that Joe may have unconscious anger toward his mother, because Joe's mother probably transferred some of her resentment at having a boy instead of a girl, even if she did not intend to show it. My statement is made from the knowledge that most infants and young children are keenly sensitive to nonverbal as well as verbal cues in regard to love. In addition, the birth of another child causes young siblings to feel "dethroned" and in competition for mother's attention and love. Now, if Joe was a normally reacting child, he would have felt some anger and pain which he would associate with his mother. Over the years, much of his anger has laid dormant, but when you spoke about having a baby, Joe reacted with a "record" learned in his childhood: babies-mother-anger.

Mr. L, "Oh, I couldn't think Mary is anything like my mother! . . . but, I just don't like the idea of having a baby . . . but I am not angry at Mary, really . . . "

As this couple understood the concept of projective identification, they began to re-establish their wholesome relationship. The issue of babies was dropped while their relationship was emphasized.

Communicational Clarification

Another dimension of information relates to pragmatic communication. As so often is observed in conjoint sessions, what one relates about a happening and what the partner says about the same incident and what really happened are often conflicting. Thus the conjoint session is valuable in the clarification of communications. An important observation is that dyads may play their "records" as though no one was watching or listening, which eliminates that so-called contamination of the transference that Freud was so concerned about. (Frequently, a pyrotechnical verbal CDD may intensify suppressed anger forcing the therapist to intervene.) This topic is fully presented in Chapter V.

DYADIC GAMES

I continue to find that couples have well-defined transactional patterns. Berne[20] cleverly outlined many of these games that couples play in laymen language, which I find most helpful in the CDD and in therapy. When I use the term *game* in the CDD, I specifically tell the couple that a game should not be taken to have any playful implication, but that it refers to sequences of behavior that are governed by rules. A game follows the various abstractions that define a system, e.g. time, openness, and feedback. A game involves a process between people that helps clarify their relationship and/or establish bonds. Relationship patterns exist independently from content, e.g. the game of "Uproar," where the content can vary from a new hat to a visit by a mother-in-law, but which ends with tempers growing. Games involving dyads can be seen as a "seesaw" with a person on each end. When one is up, the other is usually down, but, if one gets "off," then the game ends.

In 1966, I reviewed Berne's fourteen marital games for a panel with Berne as the chairperson. I found in my review[21] that the processes underlying the games can be readily understood by couples, and the language the therapist chooses to express these processes can vary greatly. (My use of the "jukebox-records" is equally effective and its purpose is the same as Berne's — to point out transactional patterns and for me, to help explain causation and effect.)

Games involve all three systems (intrapersonal, interpersonal, and environmental) in varying degrees. Games, as Berne points out, are both desirable and necessary if they are directed toward useful and constructive ends. In the following paragraphs, some of the most common dyadic games are presented.

The most frequent dyadic game is that of projection (it is also the most common defense mechanism humans use) or as Berne calls it — "If It Weren't For You." Projection may have started with mankind as one pastor mentioned at a seminar, "If it weren't for Eve, mankind would be in paradise . . . and as Eve would have said, 'If it weren't for the Serpent. . . . . '" Berne feels that the game of projection occurs as a counterphobic mechanism in many cases. Such responses are a way to avoid doing something that causes fear by blaming another as the one responsible for the avoidance. The couple Mr. and Mrs. M were caught up in this type of game.

> Mr. and Mrs. M were referred as a result of their son's psychiatrist making the suggestion. Mrs. M had no complaints about their marriage while Mr. M spoke right away. He said that his corporate position demanded that he entertain prospective customers and their wives, but his wife hindered his fulfilling this aspect of his job. She was afraid of social gathering which included even just a new couple on a business entertainment basis.

I asked Mr. M if his wife during their courtship had displayed any behavior similar to what he just described.

Mr. M described meeting his wife through his father. (She was the daughter of a mutual friend.) He remembered how impressed he felt after meeting Mrs. M as she was intelligent, good-looking, and preferred to spend a quiet evening at home rather than joining the activities of the jet set . . . He recalled, however, that her shyness seemed to increase after their marriage. She seemed afraid to be in closed places and it lead to fewer and fewer evenings spent with others. Now he felt like a recluse.

Based upon these facts, Mrs. M was seen to evaluate any phobic tendencies or symptoms. As Mrs. M began to improve and expressed a desire to entertain friends, Mr. M began to display increasing anxiety. For the first time in their marriage, he expressed phobias almost identical to those of his wife. He began to fear attending board meetings at work. He began to avoid the usual luncheons with his executives. At Mr. M's request, he began intensive therapy, too.

Mr. M did not have to show his phobic tendencies as long as his wife's behavior made it unnecessary. Mr. M did not have to acknowledge such fears and may not have been fully aware of this aspect of himself. The records playing on his wife's jukebox served to mute his records so that he was able to function occupationally; however, as these people sat on a seesaw the therapeutic improvement occurring with his wife changed their positions on the seesaw. Mr. M now felt the ground hitting his side of the seesaw and panicked. Seen another way, Mrs. M's phobic symptoms served to maintain Mr. M's self-image and self-respect. It became easier and easier for him to explain to his bosses that "If it weren't for her . . . " he would entertain clients and their wives.

"Indoor commando" is the label I attach to the process described by Berne as "Uproar." It occurred second in frequency in my practice. The purpose of this game, either consciously or unconsciously, is to avoid dyadic intimacy. It is often the terminal phase of another game, sexual dysfunction. Sexual dysfunction games include "frigid" women (general sexual dysfunctional) and erectile problems with men.[22] Occasionally, the game of "Indoor commando" occurs between a seductive/domineering father and his teenage daughter. The game has the same process whether the two are married, not married, or family members. A concise interchange illustrates this game:

Mr. and Mrs. N and their teenage daughter have adjoining bedrooms with a connecting door.

Mr. N: "Leave your door open, Sue. I feel better when I know I can hear every sound and protect you should there be an intruder in the house."

Sue: "Daddy! We live in an apartment on the thirteenth floor!"

Mr. N: "Do as I say!"

Sue: "Mother! This is ridiculous. I want my door closed!"

Mrs. N: No answer.

Sue: "I am going to close the door."

Mr. N: "I'm only thinking of what's best for *you.*"

Sue: "This is silly, you are acting like an old woman."

Both get angry at each other and the door is slammed by the daughter.

The dyadic relatonship was the core to the above family's problem. I told the parents that they were mutually responsible for their discord and its resolution. They needed to explore their intimate transactions instead of bringing the daughter into their avoidance of each other. The daughter was verbalizing what the wife should say to keep a healthy distance between a maturing teenager and an adult parent. The husband was missing an active sexual relationship with his wife, fearing the loss of his daughter whose presence gave him much pleasure, and many other factors appropriate to his age and development. As all the GST systems' inputs were felt, he translated his anger at his unresponsive wife into premature ejaculation; he made his daughter distance him through incurring scenes of anger; and he was left with few constructive lines of communication and physical outlet. The couple chose to work on developing constructive lines of communicating and behaving, which included developing greater sexual intimacy between them. Further work included renewing their feelings of self-respect, which lead to reestablishing mutual respect.

Anger can be expressed in many ways: *repressed* unconsciously, *expressed* consciously, *suppressed* consciously, and *denied* totally. The material below summarizes how one individual experienced four different levels of anger:

"I was thinking over our last therapy session, and I told John I couldn't get over the fact I had to practice new 'records,' reaching my goals, just as he did. I mentioned it was like when we learned how to dance, we had to count the dance steps until it became automatic. John turned up the radio as I was speaking. That was rude, to say the least, and it made me mad. I knew he didn't want to hear what I had to say so I shut up *(suppression)*. I claimed to myself that he took me up wrong. He didn't let me finish my thought. If I sounded like a broken record to him, why couldn't he put me in my place instead of being rude?

"He stopped the car, and we went into the restaurant. There was a line waiting to be seated. John placed himself at the end of the line and waited there too. I became perturbed because I should think John would know the score by now. In a situation of this sort, you seek out the attendant who is doing the seating, and you give him your name and number of people in your party. It seems to me John is extremely self-conscious and doesn't like to make a spectacle of himself, so he stays in the background. By walking to the front of the line and telling the hostess his name does not make a public show in my opinion . . . We waited too long, and we had a big argument going home *(expression)*. We didn't talk the rest of the evening."

John did not recall turning up the car radio or that he was particularly annoyed that evening *(denial)*, but he did recall a dream he had that night in which he had just dropped an atom bomb on some enemies *(repression)*.

THE USE OF DREAMS IN THE CDD

I encourage the recall of dreams in the CDD session. Dreams are helpful in understanding the psychodynamics of the couple, pinpointing their current relationship and attempts at solution of their conflict, and as a symbol of their current behavior, e.g. a dream of obstacles might indicate the dreamer was making things rough in wakeful hours as a form of self-punishment. The clinical use of dreams is a neglected tool by many therapists. Once some skill is developed in interpreting dreams, the therapist, like Freud,[23] can use dream information to understand psychodynamics and relationships involving the patient. Dreams continue to be the topic of numerous books and articles.[24-27] In the CDD session, dreams related by one partner, whether the other member makes any comments or not, can serve as a dynamic force in viewing the full scope of the dyad's transactions as well as revealing concealed feelings and attitudes within the dreamer, but which affect the dyad. It is a frequent clinical observation that a day's experiences may be included in that night's dreams. Thus the activities and thoughts of a partner prior to the CDD may be more revealing than verbal communications already shared. The following dream was very helpful to all participants in the CDD: "I dreamt last night that I was to appear before a bankruptcy hearing. I was telling the referee about my assets, but was concealing some information. I was smiling inwardly at putting one over him." This man was aware that he was only going through the gestures of the therapy process. Although he had stated he was willing to do anything to save the marriage, in reality he had decided on a divorce (bankruptcy). He was going through the marital evaluation and perhaps therapy to mollify his wife.

My mentor, Thomas M. French, was mainly responsible for my ongoing study of dreams since 1950.* In a book to be published, *The Illustrated Dream Book*,[28] I review 10,000 of my patients' dreams. I chose the 10,000 from over several hundred thousand, which I recorded with shorthand during therapeutic sessions. In analyzing the themes of these dreams, I noted twelve most frequent themes as well as some of their variations. The following list is in order of frequency:

1. Danger	7. Nudity
2. Pursuit	8. Money
3. Falling	9. Indecision
4. Water	10. Examination
5. Food	11. Moving
6. Fire	12. Helplessness

Danger, whether it is real danger in the external world and/or dangerous feelings or thoughts within the "inner world" of the individual, is dealt with symbolically. These feelings and thoughts relate to envy, jealousy, and/or competition. These feelings cause anxiety, anger, and fear of retribution. Possible rejection can be feared as deeply as a potential physical attack. Thus being *pursued* or *falling* are very common too. Themes that deal with anger often include the symbols of water, food, fire, nudity, money, and motion. The symbolic fire can represent being "consumed" by anger, being caught in the "heat of passion" or being ready to "erupt" with the violence of a volcano.

Falling dreams can have a number of meanings: fear of rejection, yielding to sexual temptation and becoming a "fallen women," fear of inability to control desires, e.g. to start drinking again — "falling off the wagon," fearing loss of control over one's anger, e.g. "I fell into a fit of rage", and so on.

Water dreams are frequent. A baby floats in a "bag of water" in its mother's uterus during pregnancy and images of water can reflect wanting to return to that isolated and insulated uteral environment. Many people associate "paradise" with the prenatal state where all needs are taken care of without personal effort. Just as water flows down the mountains in Spring (a form of rebirth), so water in a dream may represent the wish to make a fresh beginning, "make a

---

*Doctor French conducted a special dream seminar at the Chicago Institute of Psychoanalysis in 1949-50. There were eight of us in the seminar; Thomas Szasz and Heinz Kohut were in our group. *See* The Integration of Behavior, I, II. Chicago, Univ Chicago Press, 1952, 1953.

new start." In many dreams, water indicates *strong emotional currents* e.g. sexual desires, anger, anxiety — "I sure got myself into hot water" and so on. Thus, water may be calm or turbulent or even symbolize hostility (as the flow of urine would).

Food has at least five symbolic meanings: hunger (real or imagined), anger, immaturity, punishment, and deprivation. Thus instead of taking positive action during consciousness, one makes the desired attack during the relatively safe period of sleep, e.g. "biting comments" or "attacking food." The feelings of deprivation may relate to the need for tenderness, love or sex, companionship, etc., and the need for dependency which "mother" can supply best. To be fed is often associated with to be loved. Overeating with obesity as the outcome is the physical symbol for feeling unloved (for many people), and, for some, their shape can symbolize "a heavy load on their conscience." To distort ones figure by obesity can be a source of punishment and the obese child at school is the one frequently picked upon by school mates.

Fire usually has three main variations. The most common being the equation of "being consumed by sexual passion." Another variation is the use of fire for punishment, either for sexual or hostile feelings, e.g. going from the "Frying pan into the fire." The other variation deals with anger: "I could burn his house down."

Nudity was next in frequency with several variations: exhibitionism as symbolized by seductiveness or, in a male, the reassurance of masculinity.

The theme of *money* is seen more commonly in males. Two of the most common variations deal with financial problems or competition, or both. Money can be equated with anger: "lousy with money" or "he and his filthy lucre." Other meanings include having a hoard of money as an attempt to deny the threat of death. Frequently money can represent things of value, but wasted foolishly — time, energy, life, and so on.

Indecision can deal with relationships (objects) or with specific situations or events. A "fork in the road" dream gives two alternatives. Usually the correct decision is to turn right.

The *examination* dream was tenth in frequency. Several variations are familiar: an attempt to solve a current or past problem, guilt over some action — masturbation or some sexual act, inventory of oneself in time, etc.

Moving or flying may symbolize several variations: running away from a situation or feeling or driving a vehicle or a sports car de luxe may deal with feelings of inferiority or concern about one's masculinity, envy, and so on.

The last theme of *loss* or *helplessness,* e.g. "Handicapped" can have several meanings: fear of being helpless or growing old, losing a loved one, something happening to one's body, e.g. teeth falling out, penis missing, are a few.

DYADIC STATUS AND MENTAL DISORDER

Approximately 15 percent of my clinical cases had psychiatric problems that added to the interpersonal problems of the dyad. This incidence corresponds to the same percentage in the general population.[29,30] The three most common disorders in psychiatric emergency rooms are affective disorders, alcoholism, and antisocial personality.[31] Thus, in addition to the dyadic diagnosis, the *second* task of the CDD is to assess the individual personality of each partner: intellectually, perceptually, defensively, and so on. The personality is dependent upon the perceptual apparatus of each person, his retrieval of units of past information, his integrative capacity, his defensive maneuverings and, finally, his executive abilities.[32-35] The various types of personality and psychiatric disorders were discussed before in Chapter XII. A major improvement was made by a task force of American Psychiatric Association in the new Diagnostic and Statistical Manual (DSM-III) published in 1979 with fifth-digit axes of taxonomy, traits, organicity, stress, and disability.[36-38] Other clinicians have suggested more comprehensive clinical appraisals.[39-41]

An important dimension of the intrapersonal system is the assessment of the patient's ability or motivation to enter therapy.[42] The unmotivated patient is multidetermined and reflects a wide variety of conditions both conscious and unconscious. On a conscious level, the individual may be indifferent to continuing the relationship due to an outside sexual affair, fear of change, or the dislike of the therapist or even therapy. Most frequently unconscious resistance involves denial and/or projection — the partner is completely at fault. Nir and Cutler[43] have discussed the "unmotivated patient syndrome" which they found in five groups of patients: individuals from lower socioeconomic groups, delinquents, drug-addicted persons, alcoholics, and military psychiatric patients. Finally, the CDD evaluates the cohesion involving levels of conflict, communicational patterns,[44] ability to compromise, and level of dyadic satisfaction. At times psychological tests and surveys may be indicated.[45,47] *Clinical judgement* is the ultimate basis for pragmatic therapy.

After the diagnostic survey of both partners and their dyadic transtactions, the final step is to determine the tentative goals and to plan the operational approach of therapy.[48,49] There are four possible results of the CDD:

1. The couple is *accepted* for treatment.
2. The couple is *rejected* for treatment, since the malfunction may be a symptom of a severe dysfunction in the intrapersonal system of one partner, or the relationship is beyond repair.
3. One or both partners may *refuse* my suggestions.
4. The couple may be referred elsewhere (financial or individual reasons, e.g., lack of time, specific type of intervention needed — religious, psychoanalytic, etc.).

If referral is indicated, this can be done with the facts and tact. In order to formulate a treatment plan, it is necessary to contrast the evaluation of the disharmony with the ideal type of relationship for goal direction as well as the available treatment resources for goal limitation. The therapist tentatively decides on the best possible dyadic adjustment within the range of each partner's current situation, needs, present strengths of ego, and motivation. In the CDD, the various therapeutic techniques are briefly outlined, and the couple is told that my approach will vary as I individualize therapy according to their changing problems and needs.

The final point I make in the CDD when therapy is contracted is the setting of a *target date*. I usually give an arbitrary figure of three months and inform the couple that the rate of therapeutic progress may shorten this time allocation. However, if therapeutic progress has not attained a mutually accepted resolution at the target date, I reevaluate their situation. I will then recommend continuance of therapy if indicated, or I will recommend discharge and/or referral. Using the target date is from my Freudian background. Freud proposed a trial analysis as the only type of preliminary examination by which to determine suitability of the patient-analyst relationship.[50]

In this chapter some of the relevant dimensions of the CDD have been presented. First, I have pointed out that the opportunity to see both partners concurrently enables a shaping up of what has transpired in the individual conferences and how individual patterns are reflected in the relationship. Secondly, I have elaborated on how disharmony may be due to either transactional discord or may be a manifestation of an individual psychiatric problem. A psychiatric problem in a partner requires individual help prior to triadic therapy. I blend sociological and psychoanalytical concepts to characterize various forms of relationships; I note the projective identification and unconscious collusion when present; I clarify and identify communicational patterns whenever necessary; and, I explain any games the couple is playing.

REFERENCES

1. Wells, Carl F. and Rabiner, Edwin L.: The conjoint family diagnostic interview and the family index of tension. *Family Process, 12:* 127-44, 1973.
2. Rosenblatt, Paul C., Titus, Sandra L., and Cunningham, Michael R.: Disrespect, tension and togetherness — apartness in marriage. *J Marr & Family Therapy, 41:* 47-54, 1979.
3. Stapleton, J. and Bright, R.: *Equal Marriage.* Nashville, Abingdon, 1976.
4. Satir, Virginia: *Peoplemaking.* Palo Alto, CA., Behavior Science Pub., 1972, p. 2.
5. Satir, Virginia: Conjoint marital therapy. In Greene, B. L. (Ed.): *The Psychotherapies of Marital Disharmony.* New York, Free Press (Macmillan Co.,) 1965, pp. 121-34.
6. Crandall, John W.: The diagnostic uses of the early spouse memory in marriage counseling. *J Family Counseling, 1:* 18-27, 1973.
7. Grunebaum, Henry and Christ, Jacob (Eds.): *Contemporary Marriage: Structure, Dynamics and Therapy.* Boston, Mass, Little, 1976.
8. Balint, Enid: Marital conflicts and their treatment. *Compr Psychiat, 7:* 403, 1966.
9. Dicks, Henry V.: Mental hygiene of marital interaction. Proceedings of International Congress on Mental Health, Paris 1961, Group XVI, pp. 216-219.
10. Sollod, Robert N.: Behavioral and psychodynamic dimensions of the new sex therapy. *J Sex & Marital Therapy, 1:* 338, 1975.
11. Lebensohn, Zigmund: Private practice of psychiatry: future roles. *Am J Psychiat, 135:* 1359-63, 1978.
12. Schless, Arthur and Mendels, Joseph: The value of interviewing family and friends in assessing life stressors. *Arch Gen Psychiat, 35:* 565-67, 1978.
13. Andreasen, N. C., Endicott, J., Spitzer, R. L. and Winokur, G.: The family history method using diagnostic criteria. *Arch Gen Psychiat, 34:* 1229-35, 1977.
14. Dicks, Henry V.: Object relations theory and marital studies. *Brit J Med Psychol, 37:* 125, 1963.
15. Albee, Edward: *Who's Afraid of Virginia Woolf?* New York, Atheneum, 1962.
16. Berne, Eric: *Games People Play.* New York, Grove Press, 1966.
17. Klein, Melanie: On identification. In Klein, Melanie, Heiman, Paula, and Money-Kryle, Roger (Eds.): *New Directions in Psychoanalysis.* New York, Basic Books, 1954.
18. Dicks, H. V.: *Equal Marriage.*

19. Laing, Ronald D., Philipson, Herbert, and Lee, A. Russell: *Interpersonal Perception*, New York, Springer, 1966, pp. 16-17.
20. Berne, E., *Games People Play*.
21. Greene, Bernard L.: *Panel of Transactional Analysis in Marital Therapy*. Eric Berne, moderator, annual meeting, American Psychiatric Association, Atlantic City, New Jersey, May 10, 1966.
22. Kaplan, Helen S.: *The New Sex Therapy*. New York, Brunner-Mazel, 1974, p. 250.
23. Freud: *The Interpretation of Dreams*. New York, Basic Books, 1958.
24. Boss, Medard: *The Analysis of Dreams*. London, Rider, 1957.
25. Bonime, Walter: *The Clinical Use of Dreams*. New York, Basic Books, 1962.
26. Perls, Fritz: *Gestalt Therapy Verbatim*. New York, Bantam Books, 1969.
27. Kramer, Milton: Manifest dream content in normal and psychopathologic states. *Arch Gen Psychiat, 22:* 149, 1970.
28. Greene, Bernard L.: *The Illustrated Dream Book — The Meaning of Dreams*. (1977) to be published.
29. Pardes, Herbert: Future needs for psychiatrists and other mental health personnel. *Arch Gen Psychiat, 36:* 1401-08, 1979.
30. Bachrach, Leona L.: *National Institute of Mental Health, Marital Status and Mental Disorder: An Analytical Review*. DHEW Pub., No. (ADM) 75-217, Supt. of Documents, U. S. Govn Printing Office, Washington, D. C. 20402, 1975.
31. Robins, Eli, Gentry, Kathye A., Munoz, Rodrigo A., and Marten, Sue: A contrast of the three most common illnesses with the ten less common in a study and 18-month follow-up of 314 psychiatric emergency room patients. *Arch Gen Psychiat, 34:* 259-65, 1977.
32. Helzer, John E, Robins, Lee N, Taibleson, Mitchell, Woodruff Jr, Robert A, Reich, Theodore, and Wish, Eric D.: Reliability of psychiatric diagnosis: a methodological review. *Arch Gen Psychiat, 34:* 129-33, 1977.
33. Helzer, John E, Clayton, Paula J, Pambakian, Robert, Reich, Theodore, Woodruff Jr, Robert A., and Reveley, Michael A.: Reliability of psychiatric diagnosis: the test/retest reliability of diagnostic classification. *Arch Gen Psychiat, 34:* 136-41, 1977.
34. Reveley, Michael A. et al.: Evaluation of a screening interview for Briquet syndrome (hysteria) by the study of medically ill women. *Arch Gen Psychiat, 34:* 145-49, 1977.
35. Strauss, John S.: A comprehensive approach to psychiatric diagnosis. *Am J Psychiat, 132:* 1193-97, 1975.
36. Figley, Charles R, and Sprenkle, Douglas H.: Delayed stress response syndrome: family therapy indication. *J Marr & Family Counseling, 40:* 53-60, 1978.
37. Lief, Harold I.: DSM-III field trials. *Psychiatric News, 12:* Oct 21, 1977.
38. Spitzer, Robert L, Endicott, Jean, and Robins, Eli: Research diagnostic criteria: rationale and reliability. *Arch Gen Psychiat, 35:* 773-82, 1978.

39. Masserman, Jules: Response to the presidential address. *Am J Psychiat,* *135:* 902, 1978.
40. Weissman, Myrna M and Klerman, Gerald L: Epidemiology of mental disorders. *Arch Gen Psychiat, 35:* 705-12, 1978.
41. Mendelsohn, Frederick S, Egri, Gladys, and Dohrenwend, Bruce P.: Diagnosis of nonpatients in the general community. *Am J Psychiat,* *135;* 1163-67, 1978.
42. Kieren, Dianne and Tallman, Irving: Spousal adaptability — an assessment of marital competence. *J Marr & Family, 34:* 247-56, 1972.
43. Nir, Yehuda and Cutler, Rhoda: The unmotivated patient syndrome — survey of therapeutic interventions. *Am J Psychiat, 135:* 442-47, 1978.
44. Gurman, Alan S: Couples' facilitative communication skill as a dimension of marital therapy outcome. *J Marr & Family Counseling, 1:* 163-174, 1975.
45. Phillips, Clinton E.: Some useful tests for marriage counseling. *Family Coordinator, 22:* 43-53, 1973.
46. Spanier, Graham: Measuring dyadic adjustments — new scales for assessing the quality of marriage and similar dyads. *J Marr & Family, 38:* 15-28, 1976.
47. Allred, Hugh G. and Graff, Thomas T: The AIA, a mental map for communicators — a preliminary report. *J Marital & Family Therapy, 5:* 33-42, 1979.
48. Greene, Bernard L: (Discussion of paper by *Marc H. Hollender*) Marital problems: the selection of therapy. In *Current Trends in Psychiatry.* Des Plaines, The Forest Hosp. Foundation, 1968, pp. 41-44.
49. Hollender, Marc H. Selection of Therapy for Marital Problems In Massermann, Jules (Ed.) Current Psychiatric Therapies, Vol 11. New York, Grune, 1971, p 127.
50. Freud, Signmund: Further recommendations on the techniques of psychoanalysis. *Standard Edition, 12:* 157, London: Hogarth Press, 1958.

PART TWO
PREVENTION

Chapter XX

PREVENTION

*It is sad to face the
fact that so many
marriages begin in
heaven and end in hell.*

Rudolf Dreikurs

ALL behavioral scientists, many attorneys, and the body politic are concerned about the mounting evidence that family disruption due to divorce, desertion, and separation has increased.[1] The damaging consequences extend beyond the nuclear family to all levels of society. Kunzel's[2] European studies show how the socioeconomic structure of those countries influence the family with regard to the rate of marital disruption. He notes a correlation of the latter between increasing industrialization, earlier age marriages, smaller number of children per family unit, the growing absorption of women in the labor market, and the increase in life expectancy. Fifteen years ago I stressed the importance of prevention in premarital, marital (dyadic) situations and in divorce.[3,4] As a physician, prevention has always been primary in the medical model. Recently, behavioral scientists, religious institutions[5] (one Catholic diocese now requires *six months* of premarital counseling) and others now stress prevention.[6,7] The family is still the cornerstone of society,[8] which necessitates prevention as an important procedure.

I have been influenced by the early studies of Caplan[9] and his co-workers on preventive psychiatry. Bolman[10] recently has endeavoured "to connect theory, general programmatic approaches, and specific programs related to family-oriented programs in a systematic and meaningful way." He writes: "First, prevention is characterized as primary, secondary, or tertiary, depending upon the point in the course of disorder at which a given program is aimed. Primary prevention attempts to prevent a disorder from occuring, secondary prevention attempts to diagnose and treat at the earliest possible point so as to reduce the length or severity of the disorder, and tertiary prevention attempts to minimize the handicap or chronicity of the disorder."

Vincent,[11,12] the pioneer marital therapist, among others, has

239

written on preventive efforts.[13-15] Several authors discuss the effects of dyadic discord upon society with regard to *stress responses* from desertion, separation, and divorce,[16] from life events and traffic accidents,[17] and from its impact on industry with billions of dollars lost due to absenteeism and work efficiency.

General Comments

The foundation of a meaningful existence for the individual and the prevention of disorders either intrapersonally or interpersonally is contingent upon an appropriate philosophy of living. My pragmatic philosophy coincides with that of O. Spurgeon English who states:[18] "... an emotionally healthy person can entertain himself, entertain someone else, entertain a new idea, and work productively." In my therapeutic contacts with individuals, students, and all professionals, I stress this philosophy for personal growth and equanimity. This topic will be explored further in Chapter XXI.

All therapists, particularly the clergymen, because of their multiple and longitudinal contacts with their congregants, are in a unique position to expound the value of prevention. As Kirkendall over a decade ago stressed: "The church has an important and essential contribution to make to a comprehensive sex education program because it plays a vital role in the formulation of ideals and in the development of moral values. Instruction concerning ethical and moral standards must be approached positively and should include all aspects of life and all periods of the life cycle. The central problem is always the development of a *philosophy of life* (italics added), the creation of a set of socially meaningful and understandable values, and the enthronement of a wholesome personality for oneself and for others as a major goal of life."[19] Following the classification of Bolman,[20] I shall present my philosophy and approach to prevention as it influences the emotional functioning of individuals within the dyad, their relationship, and those people in contact with both or either member of the pair-coupling.

PRIMARY PREVENTION OF
PAIR-COUPLING RELATIONSHIPS

Primary prevention attempts to eradicate dyadic disharmony. There are three main areas of primary prevention in dyadic relationships:

1. Living together dyadic therapy

2. Premarital therapy
3. Remarital therapy.

In 1965, I stated that the focus in the Forest Hospital's Marital Department should be stressing *prevention*. In so doing, the first priority would be premarital therapy and, secondly, to develop a "Well-Marriage Unit"[21] (a term I coined to indicate a similar philosophy as the well-baby clinics in various cities).

This past decade has seen a marked increase in alternative life styles.[22][24] To quote Trost's statistics, among the twenty to twenty-four-year-olds who have developed an intimate cohabitative union, 70 percent to 80 percent cohabit without marriage: "Only 20-30 percent are married. In the most 'religious' county in Sweden fully 60 percent of couples in this age group cohabit without marriage. The same tendency is evident in older age groups. Thus, for those aged 25 to 29, the percentage of unmarried cohabitants range from 23 percent in the most religious county to 58 percent (in others)."[25] Behavioral scientists and many professionals in social and religious organizations are stressing not only premarital counseling, but similar counseling for those who are unmarried cohabitants (living-together-arrangement).

One would expect nonlegalized unions simply to "split" rather than seek therapy. Yet, each year the number of cohabitants that enter into therapy increases. Since the mid-sixties I have noticed a rise in statistics from 7 percent to 15 percent in my patient case load. I still discourage therapy for couples whose relationship is less than six months duration as I feel it takes at least that amount of time to develop a meaningful relationship.[26,27] Trost is studying the stableness factor between married dyads and unmarried dyads of a six month duration or longer, but, as yet, has no precise answer.[28] The stability of families and/or dyads who have been previously married is not fully known and the multicausational influences are complex since children and spouses (etc.) from former marriages may still effect and affect the partners and, in turn, their new relationship.

Premarital therapy, occurring after a verbal contract for therapy is agreed upon[29] (see Chapter XXI), involves a spectrum of interventions[30,31] with the couple contemplating marriage and, at times, with "significant others," e.g. parents, friends, etc.[32-36] Even with unmarried cohabitants I use the same procedures and point out a frequent myth: couples in love experience no ambivalence or conflict. Often, couples complain of disappointment in each other and/or their relationship that develops from unrealistic expectations and inability to anticipate future living problems, for which they lack judgement due to maturity level and family of origin values, attitudes, and learning experiences. Even remarital therapy may have to include a discussion of what is and what is not realistic with regard to the dynamics and experiences from intimate dyadic relationships.

Premarital and remarital therapy is more judgmental than other therapies since it involves making evaluations about intrapersonal, interpersonal, and environmental vectors. I always recommend the couple seek another professional view and evaluation if I feel that the marriage is too fragmented to help rebuild it. The value of another opinion rests upon the knowledge that a definition of a "normal" marriage is unavailable. Each therapist contributes conscious and unconscious prejudices and it is difficult to be anything but subjective:[37] however, the therapist uses his professional skills to be as objective as possible and evaluate each couple in the context of their individual personalities, their relationships with others, and the social field in which they live. A contraindication for one couple may not necessarily be so for the next couple!

Any therapist's decision about a dyad must include the exploration of the couple's current conflicts. In my current review of my clinical data, 60 percent of the conflicts were noticed by the couple during their courtship. Couples are more alert to transactions today then they were ten years ago; mass media and education has encouraged sensitivity to what is happening in the "here and now". The three procedures I use to focus upon current conflicts include the BRQ data, the data from individual preliminary sessions, and the CDD. A common issue is the extent each partner must reveal past experiences; I agree with Mace who feels that honesty and openness in marriage is essential, but the ethic of honesty must be subservient to the higher ethic of love.[38,39] I encourage patients to view the past as past and the current relationship as paramount unless the relationship is not an important and growing one.[40,41]

An important determinant in evaluating the potentiality of the dyadic relationship is the presence of severe personality traits or psychiatric disorders. This subject also is explored under BRQ #16 (Chapter XII). Obsessive-compulsive defenses from an adaptive point of view (along a spectrum of severity) can be most helpful in evaluating the dyadic relationship. Doubt is a characteristic trait of obsessive character types and frequently severe anxiety in such people results from paralyzing indecision about marriage. In a situation where paralyzing indecision is upsetting an obsessive person, I recommend suspension of a decision to get married at that time. Such a recommendation may be very hard for the other member of the dyad to accept as Sheri poignantly stated to me: "I'm at a loss to understand both my feelings and behavior. My common sense tells me to forget about John . . . I know he backed away from the wedding date after we sent out invitations all three times . . . but I can't stop loving him and wanting to marry him. Basically I think he doesn't love me. I don't think he possibly could because he criticizes me so much. I am very sensitive to rejection. . . . ." As John states briefly, "I don't want another girl. I want her. But on the other hand, I don't want to get married, yet I do. Yet I can't give her up. Several times we've discussed separating. She says if this will make you happy, I'll give you up and she really means it. I'm always the one who goes back to her. I don't know what to do." His statement is that of an obsessive-compulsive while Sheri's statement relfects a very poor self-image and confusion. The other dialogue with both, reveals Sheri as a passive-aggressive personality. I recommended the classical therapeutic approach and that marriage plans be postponed for the present. Individuals with this type of psychiatric disorder should not be encouraged to marry because the anxiety will only increase for the obsessive-compulsive and bring more pain to the partner.

Primary affective disorder (manic-depressive illness) and schizophrenic dysfunctions are personality disorders which often produce havoc for those closely involved with them. Schizophrenics in remission make poor marriage material because an acute crisis (such as the birth of the first child) could precipitate a recurrence of the psychotic symptoms. The manic-depressive illness in one partner often leads the other partner to feel anger. If the anger is withheld in outward expression, depression often occurs. Because primary affective disorder personalities have periods of exurberance, productivity, and excitement, to mention only a few behavior manifestations, the partners of such people are frequently confused and hide their anger when the highs in personality swing into the downs. Caution about marriage is advised when premarital therapy occurs.

Cyclothymic reactions present a difficult challenge to the therapist in predicting the outcome of a marriage. The cyclothymics outgoing life-of-the-party, hail-fellow-well-met personality frequently attract inhibited individuals who want to participate more in life rather than observe life. My recent research has encouraged my belief that these patients with a family history of recurrent severe mood disorders should be given advice not to marry[42] (see Chapter XXVII). The core reason for my firm stand is that such individuals contribute to the devastation of a spouse's and children's emotional environment. One case excerpt may help illustrate my viewpoint:

The Es came for help following a severe suicidal attempt by Mrs. E when she discovered her husband had a mistress. Married fifteen years with four children, Mrs. E was moderately depressed when she came in initially. An intelligent, attractive woman of forty, she described herself as always being outgoing and gregarious. In high school, she was a cheerleader and active in all school activities. Her first serious suicidal attempt was at the age of sixteen when her parents refused permission for her to get engaged. She made a complete recovery after being absent from school for two months. She was well until twenty, when she had another severe depression. For a month before this depression, she described a period of tremendous energy. During this time she got involved with a lifeguard. Again she wanted to get engaged, and again her parents objected. She spontaneously recovered in two months and returned to school. At this time, she met the man she later married. He was quiet, studious, and shy. Their courtship was uneventful. They were married just before college graduation. Her next severe depression occurred two years later following the birth of their first child. At that time she received electroconvulsive therapy.

Mr. E, a quiet, reserved, intelligent man described a most difficult marriage. "Until the first baby was born we got along fine. However, in the last ten years we have had a difficult time. When she is good, she is terrific. But when she is depressed or racing her motor, she becomes hard to live with. Her alternating moods upet the children. Two children are seeing psychiatrists. I did not want any more children after the first, but she insisted. Following the birth of the last child she has been chronically depressed and rejected everyone. She has been seeing a psychiatrist for the past three years. After awhile I turned to someone else to meet my emotional and sexual needs. I'm not sure anyone can help her or our marriage, but I'm willing to try."

This vignette illustrates how recurrent episodes of either hypomanic spiraling or severe depressive reactions with or without suicidal attempts can be devastating to the other spouse and frequently disturbing to the children.

The projective defense reactions, described in Chapter XII, under item #16, are frequently contraindications to pair-couplings, as well as personality disorders that consist of hard to treat antisocial and dyssocial behavior.

There are no absolute contraindications to marriage, but, if there seems to be too many real or potential areas of conflict, a marriage should be postponed until adequate exploration[43] can be carried out: all relationships usually follow an orderly *time* sequence, that enables the new dyad to develop transactional patterns, roles, functions, and systems. Providing an adequate time period becomes crucial. In this process, levels of uncertainty, anxiety, and ambivalence may become pronounced, environmental influences may precipitate the beginnings of conflictual areas, and kinship network influences may develop marked effects upon the couple.[44-46]

SECONDARY PREVENTION

Secondary prevention in dyadic disharmony attempts to recognize and treat dyadic crisis at the earliest possible time so as to reduce the length or severity of the problem. Since 1964 when the "Well-Marriage Unit" was introduced, my goals for such a prevention unit have undergone progressive change. This clinic functions now on primary and secondary preventive interventions will all types of pair-couplings. Its original goal was that of offering marital couples an opportunity to come in for periodic checkups. At first, no recommended time intervals were set, but clinical experience indicated that the couple return yearly,[47] thereafter three visits are scheduled, then every three years for the same amount of sessions, and, finally, every five years. The periodic checkup[48] offers the couple (with the therapist's help) the opportunity to explore the current condition of their relationship. If the couple spends time assessing their current situation, it should strengthen their bonds and encourage continued sensitivity by each for the others needs. Clinical experience indicates that intimate marital or nonmarital pair-couplings' transactions change over time and often in a negative manner;[49-52] however, many couples have an upswing in satisfaction as the later stages of their family cycle occur.[53] That is not to say that ongoing effort is no longer needed to maintain a mutually satisfying relationship.[54,55] What effort is put into the relationship is usually what determines the quality of that relationship; with such a philosophical premise in mind, David and Vera Mace guided the creation of the British Marriage Guidance Council in World War II and the creation of the Association of Couples for Marriage Enrichment in 1973. They have worked for more than a decade to strengthen the family as the basic unit of society.[56-62] There have been others involved in advancing family harmony and that includes church-related marriage encounter groups[63,64] and non-denomination groups.[65-74] Whenever the focus of therapy includes the individual's sense of fulfillment and reduction of stress, the marriage relationship benefits as well (another implication of the GST theory).[75] Recently, several articles have advised caution about the enrichment approach.[76-78]

Two other functions of the Well-Marriage (Nonmarital) Unit are in the field of secondary prevention: (1) where couples can come for therapy in the early phases of marital crises[79-81] and (2) a therapist can request consultation for a couple under his treatment. A crisis can occur in a dyadic relationship when a woman decides to return to school.[82] The following vignette is an example:

> Doctor and Mrs. F, former patients, called for an emergency appointment. The relationship had been fine until Mrs. F unilaterally chose to apply for admission to a medical school. Her husband was furious when she told him that she was accepted. He stated that he had not previously objected to her going to school, but as a physician he knew the demands on her time would be enormous and result in neglect of the children and his needs. She was adamant about attending school. The situation was explored with both in a double conjoint session. The pros and cons were explored in detail, personal growth vis-à-vis their relationship with the additional factor of the precipitating factors of their previous marital discord. At the conclusion of the session, the anger had been dissipated and the decision was left to them.

Within the past five years I have seen more divorces occurring when the wife, dissatisfied with the routine and mundane chores of family, returned to school in one of the behavioral sciences.

SECONDARY PREVENTION WITH RECONSTITUTED FAMILIES

In the past decade, an increasing number of *reconstituted* families (pair-couplings where one or both adults have been married before and a child(ren) is present in the new family),[83-89] have sought help for their problems. In the BRQ, under item #15 (Chapter IX) this area is covered in some detail with reference to all three systems of the GST. In dealing with problems centering around parents and relatives, the couple should be given the following pragmatic axiom: "His family is his problem, and your family is your problem. You can invite your partner to help, but, if the anwer is no, you should accept it without anger. When your relationship is harmonious, all conflictual content areas, including this one, can be resolved by communication, clarification, and compromise."

Any time a unilateral decision reverses an agreed upon contract, dyadic discord may arise. One familiar complaint is the desire by only one partner to have children. Another area of potential discord is the adjustment to new family roles and ties when children are not the biological offspring of the new marriage. It is not uncommon for the sudden arrival of the new husband's children and a unilateral decision to keep them is made. Also, stepchildren may resent a stepmother who is close to their age — is she a "friend", "parent" or an "adult"? Another pressure increasing the liklihood of conflict occurs when one member of a nonmarital cohabiting twosome demands marriage; an undercurrent of anger develops as no one likes to be pressured.

In our complex technical and mobile society, the individual often feels estranged from the community and its members. The illusion that living a single lifestyle is a pleasant alternative to the demands of a marriage is later found to be unrealistic. If the decision to marry is made because of loneliness without consideration of objective and rational inputs, the lack of mutual respect between the couple results in conflict.

The following clinical vignette underlines the value of secondary prevention:

> Mr. and Mrs. P had been previous patients of mine about seven years ago and had received marital therapy with good results. Shortly after the completion of their therapy, Mr. P was transferred to the main plant of his corporation on the East Coast. They had been very happy until two years ago when he was sent back to Chicago to straighten out a research project. Both had been unhappy about this, especially Mrs. P. Because of personnel problems, Mr. P had run into a series of disappointments and sabotage from his superiors. At first he reacted with anger and later with depression. To add insult to injury, Mrs. P had impulsively made some very expensive purchases without consulting her husband, and this at a time when he was seriously considering changing his employment.
>
> The Ps' were seen conjointly for one and one-half hours. Mr. P was moderately depressed as he explained his situation at work. He was given considerable reassurance ("Greene" stamps) about his superior intelligence and creativity and was told he would have no problem at all in getting a better position if he did not get the cooperation from his superiors.
>
> Mrs. P interrupted to state that perhaps she was at fault too and went into detail about her impulsive expenditures. She knew that, although her husband was silent about this, he was angry at her.
>
> When asked if these purchases were impulsive, she replied in the affirmative, and I then strongly suggested her husband handle all the finances. His suppressed rage was only deepening his depression and what he needed most of all at this time was TLC — tender, loving care. The interview ended with the suggestion they try to follow the many suggestions made and to call me again if they had not solved their problems.
>
> A week later I received the following letter from Mrs. P:

Dear Doctor Greene:

I want to thank you for your positive suggestions. Last week I was so angry at you, hurt, frustrated, because I couldn't verbalize my feelings, and depressed. I could have cheerfully strangled you. This morning I could hug you.

The proof of the pudding is in the eating. Last night for the first time in nearly two years, Jim and I had intercourse successfully (this complaint had not been raised in the interview with them). For the very first time in my life I had absolutely no sense of guilt about it. He warmed up like an eighteen-year-old. Most surprising of all, for weeks I had been extremely depressed. This morning every trace of that depression has vanished. Apparently, I needed this love-making as much as he. He was so happy and so was I. I wish you could see the difference.

Pursuant to your request, I immediately consigned all our money to Jim. We are each taking a weekly allowance which Jim determined for personal needs and I am following a weekly budget.

One of my reasons for always acting unilaterally is my inability to verbalize my wants, even with Jim. Rather than ask, I have taken. It's hardly the way to conduct a marriage. My fear of rejection is one of the prime reasons for my inability to say no to a salesman.

I am now working (another suggestion I had made in the session was that she go back to work).

For my part I will do everything I can to help Jim by applying liberal doses of TLC. I worked last night and ought to again. Thanks for helping out.

This couple's reaction is an example of secondary marital prevention. Since they were former patients of mine, not only did they come in with positive transference feelings toward me, but more important perhaps, was that I knew their components in their three systems and could be very active in my management of their problems.

TERTIARY PREVENTION

Tertiary prevention in dyadic disharmony attempts to minimize the reactions to the request for dissolution of the relationship[90] or consists of postcretal (divorce and/or separation) therapy per se.[91-98] Spanier and Anderson[99, 100] report on the dramatic increase in the number of divorces in this country over this past decade. Their article begins with the following paragraph: "Current projections of divorce trends estimate that more than one-third of first marriages among recently married Americans are likely to end in divorce (Glick and Norton, 1976). In addition, more than a third of those who obtain one divorce and remarry are likely to obtain a second divorce. By adding married couples who separate but never divorce to these statistics, it is likely that nearly half of all recent American marriages may be disrupted by divorce or separation."

In 1977, a new journal, *The Journal of Divorce*,[101] under the able editorship of Esther Oshiver Fisher, was started and its main objective is *prevention*. It deals with the entire spectrum of divorce, through physical and/or legal separation, to litigation and legal divorce, and finally to the many problems of adjustment presented by the postdivorce experience.[102,103]

Robbins clearly and briefly stated: "It is a common fallacy to believe that the obtaining of a judgement of a divorce, where there are minor children, is the last legal encounter the disunited spouses will have with each other; more likely it may be the beginning of a miasmic maze of legal entanglements. The parties may continue to snipe at each other for reasons best known to themselves or due to legitimate legal reasons."[104]

A single or combination of the following reactions usually occur in one or both members of the dyad: *mourning process*,[105] *narcissistic insult* with decreased self-esteem, and *varying degrees of anger* from verbal to physical violence. The latter may be due to rejection anger, disruption of accustomed life-style, separation from one's child(ren), and very often, to protracted legal problems and/or delays over the terms of separation involving visitation rights or financial disagreements. The majority of postdivorce problems are not due to the content of the complaint, but to the fact that there has not been a successful separation or divorce. It is very important during or after a divorce that the therapist offer to see the child(ren). Many of the children I have seen feel guilty and blame themselves for the breakup of the family. Since the child(ren) did not ask to come into the world, it is paramount that the parents submerge their grievances and *work together* for their children's best interests.[106-108]

The mourning process occurs in every separation as the loss of an object, of a relationship, of a lifestyle, etc. Reactions to the mourning process occurs along a spectrum following a bell-shaped curve. Where there has been an "emotional divorce" for many years, the grief reaction may be absent or minimal. However, in the vast majority of people I have treated, the mourning process lasted from several months to a year.[109,110] The mourning process may be unconscious and chronic; therefore, unless resolved, new relationships or new functional transactional patterns may not develop. Obviously, one cannot solve a mourning process if it is unconscious until it is brought into the individual's attention and constructive *action* initiated. Insight usually follows three phases if it is to be of value: intellectual insight, emotional insight, where one feels in their "gut," and action,[111] where constructive activities result in new patterns of behavior.

The literature on mourning is, at times, confusing because of semantics (mourning and grief are not synonymous), also, the inability to categorize the response to loss into a syndrome — the uniqueness of an individual and his culture results in as many unique reactions as there are people. Thus, the GST offers a framework to view the reactions since all three systems are involved. Also, the internalized mental representation of the object (introject in Freudian terminology) involves the intrapersonal system. The loss of the relations and "significant others" involves the interpersonal system. The loss of life-style, social network supports among others involves the environmental system. The transactional intertwining of all three systems in varying dgrees is an additional complicating factor.[112-117]

Within the whole loss process, the intrapersonal and interpersonal systems include the age factor and the length of the marriage; two significant implications in the object loss process is the older the individual and the longer the relationship, the more painful the response. Usually, the partner experiencing the greatest loss is the rejected one.

Pollak's concepts (see Chapter II) about the family life cycle is helpful to therapists working with patients experiencing pain from an object loss. Pollak's four phases with four areas of need complementarity can help structure a constructive set of goals for the individual facing loneliness, loss of companionship, unmet sexual needs, a lowered standard of living from the end of the relationship (a frequent circumstance),[118] and social network loss, i.e. a "single" often becomes a threat to former friends; the old situation "three's a crowd"; and kinship networks are usually altered after a loss; etc.

Mourning is a process[119] that undergoes phases dependent on the interplay of all three systems of the GST. Bowlby's studies (based on children separated from their parents and cared for in hospitals) record that children experience three phases: protest, despair, and detachment.[120] In adult clinical treatment, my experience parellels that of Parkes' who has outlined seven areas of mourning that may occur.[121]

Each individual must move from denial or avoidance to acceptance. The speed and progress made depend on many variables including psychosexual developmental stage, level of autonomy, separation, and individuation, level of guilt or regret, and so on. The mourning process varies from individual to individual, and can become chronic and interfere with other interpersonal relationships, e.g. by withdrawing from new or even old relationships. Usually this process can be lifted when the individual is made aware that his depression is due to mourning. The following vignette is illustrative:

The BRQ revealed that the courtship of Mr. and Mrs. M was uneventful and smooth and of two years duration. After threee years of marriage, Mrs. M accidentally became pregnant. She was a good mother. When the child was three, Mrs. M, according to her husband, complained of being tied down and wanted more excitement in their activities. It was at this time that he noticed a change in her attitude toward him. His childhood was pleasant. The oldest of three, he got along well with his parents, siblings, and peers and did well academically and socially. After college graduation, he became associated with his father's business. Currently, he felt depressed, disinterested in his work, and had trouble concentrating. He blamed his feelings of depression and inability to concentrate onto his marital situation.

Mr. M, consulted me at the suggestion of his family physician. A handsome male in his early thirties, he appeared moderately depressed as he stated: "I am in the process of getting a divorce. Three months ago we separated when she announced she no longer loved me and wanted a divorce. I was very upset. It had come out of the blue. But I should have suspected something was wrong. Our sex life was once very wonderful but for the last year, virtually nil. She was not interested. I was a little overbearing about it. She didn't feel it and didn't want it. 'Go get a mistress if you want it that badly.' She said she felt dead in the relationship emotionally and wanted out. At first we decided to separate physically in the house, so I moved into another bedroom. That arrangement did not work out, so I moved out at her suggestion."

In his sixth session he brought in to the discussion a dream in which he was in a funeral home but this was all he could remember. His associations centered about his favorite grandmother, who had singled him out as her favorite grandchild. She had died while he was in high school, and he mourned her loss. Following my interpretation that perhaps his current emotional state could be due to a mourning process, a normal reaction to the loss of a loved object, he began to show small but progressive improvement.

Two months later, at his tenth session, he reported he was back to his old self again, in good spirits and productive and creative at his work. "You've given me a lot of help, not only in relation to the divorce but in myself. When I first moved away from my home, child and wife I was very traumatized. Your exposure to the mourning process was very valid and helped me a great deal. I've rediscovered who I am. I think I can now carry on alone. But I should like to feel

I can call upon you if I need to."

He was told he could call upon me anytime, and therapy was discontinued.

Dealing with the mourning process can prevent serious emotional reactions.

Violent emotions during the transition period from a family system into a "singlehood" life-style frequently occur. Intense reactions may develop from a *narcissistic* insult, which triggers feelings of rejection: loss of self-worth, self-esteem and self-image. Rice discusses the recent developments in the psychology of narcissism that are applicable to either partner in a dyadic separation or divorce.[122] In my clinical experience, the decision to end a dyadic relationship is rarely a mutual one. Obviously, the rejected partner reacts with lower self-esteem, a narcissistic insult.

Kohut, and later his colleagues, expanded Freud's concepts of the role of narcissism in self development. Kohut's reformulations postulates two phases: a grandiose self (the earliest phase of valuing of self) and the idealized self (which is a reflection of the significant others whose influence helped determine the individual's self-image).[123] Rice uses Goldberg's therapeutic formulations[124] (Goldberg incorporates Kohut's observations) when Rice states that the narcissistic self-esteem injury is a frequent phenomenon.[125]

The recognition of an intense "narcissistic insult" reaction may have additional significance for therapists who are treating males suffering from this phenomenon. Until recently the problems, feelings and concerns of the separated or divorced MALE has not been focused upon.[126] These studies on the problems of the separated or divorced male have confirmed my data, especially with regard to the intensely emotional response during a narcissistic insult reaction by males who experience homosexual panic or severe castration anxiety. A rejected male with this type of reaction may become violent and attempt to disfigure or even threaten to murder his partner. Occasionally, the angered partner may turn the rage inward and threaten or even attempt suicide. Also, occasionally, the rejected partner may misinterpret the erotic fantasy level of transference of his mate and blame the therapist for the decision to separate or divorce. Thus, the therapist must be alert to becoming the victim of physical assault.

The following vignette is typical of rage that is outwardly directed:

The Ns, at the suggestion of their lawyers, came in for consultation. They both came for the initial interview. He appeared the athletic type and had a slight stammer. She was petite and had a very soft voice. He appeared relatively calm and poised throughout the session. His view of the problem reflected a unilateral opinion that it was all his wife's doing. She was the one who wanted a divorce. He felt he had gone as far as he could in tolerating some of her attitudes and behavior which was directed at him. He felt she was as inflexible as a brick wall. Also, she took advantage of him, especially at time of financial adversity. He resented her complaints about their lack of social life. He characterized himself as easygoing, although he later added he had a volatile but short-lived temper. He admitted working almost seven nights a week, but added that he sacrificed his nights in order to build up financial security for his family. He was shocked when his wife carried out her "occasional threat" to divorce him. This surprise, however, soon gave way to furious resentment and rage. At first he thought there must be another man and, at that point, threatened to kill her.

Mrs. N was distraught over her husband's violent reaction. She said her husband knew their marriage was ready for a break and had put it off because of their daughter. Her initial complaint was his neglect of her personal and social needs. He could only think of business. Feelings of rejection were the primary cause of her insensitivity and intolerance toward her husband. Things had escalated since the onset of her climacteric sexual phase, a recent occurrence. He was making accusations that she had a lover and had trailed her surreptitiously during the day. Worse yet, he threatened to kill her if she did not stop divorce proceedings.

The next sessions were set up to be dyadic with each and told that individual time was necessary before a marital assessment could be completed (concurrent approach).

In Mrs. N's individual sessions, she was adamant in getting divorced. I was able to convey the need for her husband to get "anchored" into therapy before she continue legal process. I predicted his violence would change from threat to action if she refused. She agreed to wait the few months needed to anchor him into a "working alliance," and I suggested another therapist for any problems she may later want to discuss.

It took four months of therapy before Mr. N was emotionally receptive to allow his wife to proceed with the divorce. Typical of his dreams during his second month of therapy was the following nightmare, which always seemed to wake him in a cold sweat: "I am on my way to the airport to board a plane. I am late. I glance down at my feet and see that I am wearing *women's high heel shoes*. I am embarrassed. I look around for a shoe store. All sorts of obstacles get in the way. Tremendous anxiety. . . . I must buy some shoes and still make the plane."

This dream illustrates why he had reacted to his wife's request for a divorce with such anxiety and rage. His reference to "women's shoes" illustrates the core of his anxiety and rage at his wife.

Without her he did not feel masculine. No wonder the rage at her and unconscious "castration anxiety." He was threatened with becoming a woman, his wife being his alter phallus.

As mentioned previously, the third reaction to the request for separation/divorce is *anger* toward the partner due to rejection, separation from child(ren), to loss of a lifestyle, to protracted legal maneuverings, etc. When the anger is turned inward, depressive reactions, most often in women, may develop. The following clinical extract illustrates this type of reaction:

> Mr. L called for an emergency appointment. When seen that evening he appeared quite depressed and stated that he had been furious at his wife since their divorce two months ago. At first all he could think about was his fury at his wife for separating him from his children. Visitation rights had been set for the weekends only. He felt his wife had been most unreasonable in her settlement demands, and, further, he was furious at her lawyers for their prolonged legal maneuverings. For the past two weeks he had been unable to concentrate at his office, he slept fitfully, and had lost ten pounds. Recently he had nightmares which had awakened him in a cold sweat. In some of his dreams he was strangling his wife, who would turn into a huge lizard. However, it was his last night's dream which prompted him to call: "I see a man behind me. Like Frankenstein. He put on a black mask and said, 'alms for the poor.'
>
> "I woke up. I was scared out of my mind. I was terrified. I have no financial problems. But this divorce has turned me into a monster. I don't miss Helen, but I do miss the children. We had a very close relationship. Before I kept thinking of all sorts of ways to kill her, so I could get the children. I almost turned into a Frankenstein."
>
> As Mr. L talked about his rage, his depression began to lift. Four months of therapy was necessary before emotional stability returned. It was at this point that he began to accept the repercussions of his divorce and worked out some realistic arrangements on his visitation rights.

Anger may be repressed into the unconscious, but conscious expressions frequently slip out: "I wish he would drop dead" or "How nice if the car or airplane crashed." At all times, I ask if the patient had these thoughts. Since "punishment is the currency of guilt" (a statement I use with my patients), such guilt precipitates many "masochistic" behavior patterns. Thus they need to reduce their "currency" of guilt to be able to stop their self-punishment. One cannot have a meaningful relationship without ambivalence. There are two sides to the coin — love and hate. If one could meet the other's needs *all the time*, there would be no frustration (and no anger as a result). What an experienced lawyer Frolich[127] noted about the anger in divorce proceedings was put to good use in his practice. He tried to get the negotiation process to work in his office in an effort to reduce conflicts before divorce proceedings began or finished. When lawyers do not facilitate negotiation, the couple's anger and conflicts often escalate and prove very painful.[128-131]

Another important area in tertiary prevention deals with the issue of religion.[132,133] The Barnharts encourage divorce therapists to "... help their disturbed Christian clients to appreciate Saint Paul's doctrine of divorce in historical perspective.[134]

An important phase of therapy is helping family members adjust to a new life style: separation and divorce. Parents often request advice and guidance in developing transactional patterns which ease the strife and turmoil in their children.[135] There are a number of parental behaviors that are helpful and a number that should be avoided. Helpful patterns include supportive measures: establishing quality time with offspring, not disparaging the other parent, sensitive listening to what the child is thinking about or what activities the child would like to participate in, arranging visitation time with the child's wishes foremost in mind, keeping the exchange of communication between the child and parent open and without intimidation, and establishing patterns based upon mutual respect, etc.

Specific parental behaviors to be avoided include: coalitions between one parent and the offspring against the other parent (many times such patterns develop from unconscious motivation, which is why therapy can be most valuable intrapersonally and interpersonally), consciously encouraging children to choose sides, disparaging the other parent while that partner is absent, using verbal abuse or violence as a means of communicating between spouses in the presence of children, using the child as a spy on the other parent, using the child's visitation period as a time to renew hostilities and disperse guilt and revenge, making promises to children that are never intended to be fulfilled, encouraging dependence and lack of generational ego boundaries, relying on the child to take over the missing parent's role or to make a role reversal with a child, creating guilt in the child that the divorce was his fault, creating guilt that financial straits are due to the children, suddenly overturning a child's way of life, having visitation periods that are not in the child's best interest, and trying to buy the offspring's affection through material possessions or outings, etc.[136]

When families experience divorce, three main areas of disagreement must be resolved: custody,[137-143] visitation,[144-148] and child support.[149]

If therapy is an option, but the marriage is proceeding toward divorce, then at least therapy can help create a more comfortable separation.[150] (Usually postcretal problems indicate an unresolved relationship between the former partners.)

If negative transactional patterns persist, children may react with self-blame, increased anxiety from guilt, a poor self-image with little self-esteem, and a feeling that they are "evil." As yet, there is no legal recourse for children whose parents are divorcing.[151] Children may act out their feelings and become involved with disciplinary administrators in school,[152,153] juvenile authorities in the community, and with peers who will often encourage drug/alcohol abuse and a spectrum of violent behavior. Other children will withdraw into themselves and inflict self-punishment in a more covert way than acting out behavior. These children may suddenly quit trying to do a good scholastic job at school. Unfortunately, school guidance counselors have too huge a student body case load to be able to help these youngsters, but some conselors do bring the problem to the attention of the parents.

For the child caught in the turmoil and dissolution of a family, the situation may help create a loss of self-respect as the child identifies with the demeaning of either or both parents caught in that transactional pattern, a fear of being "orphaned" because reality showed that one parent "deserted" the family and so perhaps the other parent will follow suit, and a fear of rejection from kinship and peer group networks. Divorce/separation breaks up whole sets of relatives as the in-law network crumbles and many people take "sides" in addition to the feeling of isolation from a set of in-laws once the legal bonds are destroyed. Also, peers who are unfamiliar with the phenomena of divorce may alienate themselves from someone who is now "different", etc. Shame and self-consciousness can arise if neighbors' attitudes and behavior suggests to the child(ren) that approval has been withdrawn, etc. For teenagers, in particular, the normal adolescent maturation of separation-individuation and sexual growth may come to a standstill or result in a variety of adverse reactions if adequate contact with *both* parents is absent. Williams suggests we take a closer look at some of the conclusions made about parents and children going through or having gone through the divorce process, because often shortsighted accusation and conclusions about these people has occurred.[154]

The statement to children that a divorce/separation is imminent can be less traumatic if parents are given the knowledge by their therapist as to feelings, attitudes toward separation, and probably reactions from peers, etc. so that the parents can present the situation in a sympathetic and empathetic manner. For some children, it is less traumatic if both parents are present and neutral, and, for others, one parent might present the problem and solution in a less upsetting way. It is best if neither parent shares the hostility with the child. Further, the child will react in ways contingent upon the child's three systems described in the GST model. These influences will include the age and developmental phase of the child, the level of cognition, preception, integration, and coping mechanism.[155-159] In addition, the feelings about ones parents, ones peer's reactions, and general self-esteem[160, 161] are other influences. In the past decade numerous articles and books have appeared in the literature[162-174] that can be a good reference source for anyone involved in family dissolution. (Chapter X and XI also have references under BRQ items #14 and #15.)

Two recent developments in this decade include the establishment of conciliation courts and postdivorce clinics. Elkin was instrumental in California to develop the conciliation branch of the judicial system as early as 1973 in hopes of resolving dyadic problems.[175] His work lead to the formation of an organization to continue his efforts. Court prevention procedures help many couples to work on a reconciliation without compromising their legal rights.[176]

Sheffner and Suaraz described their clinic, which evaluates court-referred families. These men work with lawyers, the court system, and the former spouses. The focus of their clinic is the resolution of pathological family dynamics rather than legal issues.[177] The state of Michigan responded with concern to the traumas within their borders by establishing its Child Custody Act of 1970. This act had the input from behavioral scientists who helped define the "best interests" of the child caught in the divorce process.[178-183] The court, in turn, could determine the child's needs based upon the Act's guidelines. California, in 1980, has given the courtroom judge the right to grant "joint custody" as long as it is in the child(ren)'s best interests.[184] Several other states have a similar arrangement, and it appears more states are likely to follow the example set by these states.[185,186]

Divorce laws and divorce rates are likely correlated; permissive laws appear, and higher divorce rates frequently occur. Further, reconciliation is more likely when the divorce process is detailed and time consuming: restrictive divorce policies have effectively prevented many couples from remarrying.[187, 188] An example where permissive laws and a high divorce rate is prevalent is in the state of California. That state has the no-fault divorce.[189, 190] where either partner may file a court petition claiming that there have been irreconcilable differences and an irretrievable breakdown of the marriage. It is a nonadversary system or legal doctrine, but the legal fights still occur *both* during the drawing up of the settlement and child related matters and after the divorce has been granted. (Monahan suggests creating a cabinet office in the United States government that would devise a uniform code for marriage and divorce with the purpose to protect and promote a stable family unit, the basic unit of a stable society.)[191]

Prevention involves the creative personal growth of each member of the fragmented family and includes postdivorce situations.[192,193] The postcretal phase parallels the adolescent's separation and individuation phases with regard to changing roles, especially as pertains to sex and sexuality in the former spouses,[194,195] maintaining a healthy self-image, avoiding distortion of one's sense of power, and dissipating feelings of isolation.[196-198] Uncoupling can be a maturing experience for the divorcing adults if they seek therapy that emphasized constructive behavior and attitudes. When children are involved, the adults should subjugate their bitterness, hostility and/or anger over their dyadic situation, and be guided by their children's long-range interests.

REFERENCES

1. Cantor, H. and Glick, P. C.: *Marriage and Divorce: A Social and Economic Study.* Cambridge, Mass, Harvard Univ Press, 1976.
2. Kunzel, Renate: The connection between the family cycle and divorce rates — an analysis based on European data. *J Marr & Family, 36:* 379-88, 1974.
3. Greene, Bernard L.: Training clergymen in marriage counseling. *Pastoral Counselor, 5:* 42, 1967.
4. Greene, B. L. The family in therapy. In *The American Family in Crisis.* DesPlaines, Ill., Forest Hospital Foundation, 1965, pp 35-46.
5. Holoubek, Alice B. and Holoubek, Joe E.: Pre-marriage counseling. *J Arkansas Med Society,* Oct 1973.
6. Shonick, Helen: Pre-marital counseling: three years experiences of a unique service. *Family Coordinator, 24:* 321-24, 1975.
7. Silverman, Hirsch L. (Ed.): *Marital Therapy: Moral, Sociological and Psychological Factors.* Springfield, Ill., Thomas, 1972.
8. Lewis, Jerry M., Beavers, W. Robert, Gossett, John T., and Phillips, Virginia A.: *No Single Thread: Psychological Health in Family Systems.* New York: Brunner-Mazel, 1976.
9. Caplan, Gerald: *Principles of Preventive Psychiatry.* New York, Basic Books, 1964.
10. Bolman, William M: Preventive psychiatry for the family: theory, approaches, and programs. *Am J Psychiat, 125:* 458, 1968.
11. Vincent, Clark E.: Barriers to the development of marital health as a

health field. *J Marr & Family Counseling, 3:* 3-11, 1977.

12. Vincent, Clark E.: *Sexual and Marital Health.* New York, McGraw-Hill, 1973.

13. Lesse, Stanley: The influence of socioeconomic and sociotechnologic systems on emotional illness. *Am J Psychother, 22:* 571, 1968.

14. Adler, David A, Levinson, Daniel J., and Astrachan, Boris M.: The concept of prevention in psychiatry. *Arch Gen Psychiat, 35:* 786-89, 1978.

15. Werner, Arnold: Sexual dysfunction in college men and women. *Am J Psychiat, 132:* 164-68, 1975.

16. Chiriboga, David A. and Cutler, Loraine: Stress responses among divorcing men and women. *J Divorce, 1:* 95-106, 1977.

17. Selzer, Melvin L. and Vinokur, Amiram: Life events, subjective stress, and traffic accidents. *Am J Psychiat, 131:* 903-6, 1974.

18. English, O. Spurgen: Changing techniques of psychotherapy. *Voices, 2:* 91, 1966.

19. Kirkendall, Lester A.: Sex education. *Med Aspects Human Sexuality, 2:* 40, 1968.

20. Bolman, Preventive psychiatry for the family.

21. Greene, B. L.: The Family in Therapy. In *The American Family in Crisis,* DesPlaines, Forest Hospital Found., 1965, pp. 35-46.

22. Newcomb, Paul R: Cohabitation in America. *J Marr & Family, 41:* 597-603, 1979.

23. Weitzman, Lenore J: To love, honer and obey? Traditional legal marriage and alternative family forms. *Family Coordinator, 24:* 531-48, 1975.

24. Olson, David H.: Marriage of the future — revolutionary or evolutionary change? *Family Coordinator, 21:* 383-93, 1972.

25. Trost, Jan: Dissolution of cohabitation and marriage in Sweden. *J Divorce, 2:* 415-21, 1979.

26. Gardner, Richard A: Social, legal, and therapeutic changes that should lessen the traumatic effects of divorce on children. *J Am Acad Psychoanal, 6:* 231-47, 1978.

27. Jackson, Don D.: Personal communication.

28. Trost, Dissolution of cohabitation and marriage in Sweden.

29. Wells, J. Gipson: A critical look at personal marriage contracts.*Family Coordinator, 25:* 33-37, 1976.

30. Schumm, Walter R. and Denton, Wallace: Trends in premarital counseling. *J Marital & Family Therapy, 5:* 23-32, 1979.

31. Croft, Harry A.: The sexual information examination. *J Sex & Marital Therapy, 1:* 319-25, 1975.

32. Trainor, Joseph B: Pre-marital counseling and examination. *J Marr & Family Therapy, 5:* 61-78, 1979.

33. Hyatt, I Ralph: *Before you Marry . . . Again.* New York, Random House, 1977.

34. Gangsei, Lyle B.: *Manual for Group Premarital Counseling.* New York, Association Press, 1971.

35. Fisher, Esther O.: *Help For Today's Troubled Marriages*. New York, Hawthorn, 1968, pp. 194-202.
36. Rutledge, Aaron: *Pre-Marital Counseling*. Cambridge, Mass, Shenkman, 1966.
37. Vincent, Barriers to the development of marital health as a health field.
38. Mace, David R. Viewpoints: should spouses know about each other's premarital sexual experiences? *Med Aspects Human Sexuality, 12:* 7-22, 1978.
39. Mace, David R. and Vera: *How to Have a Happy Marriage*. Nashville, TN, Abingdon Press, 1977.
40. Gilbert, Shirley J.: Self disclosure, intimacy and communication in families. *Family Coordinator, 25:* 221-31, 1976.
41. Seidenberg, Robert: Candor about premarital experiences (in questions and answers). *Med Aspects Hum Sexuality, 11:* 28, 1977.
42. Greene, B. L. et al.: Marital therapy when one spouse has a primary affective disorder. *Am J Psychiat, 133:* 827-30, 1976.
43. Freeman, David S.: Phases of family treatment. *Family Coordinator, 25:* 265-70, 1976.
44. Anspach, Donald F.: Kinship and divorce. *J Marriage & Family, 38:* 323-30, 1976.
45. Rose, Vicke L. and Price-Bonham, Sharon: Divorce adjustment: A woman's problem? *Family Coordinator, 22:* 291-97, 1973.
46. Bohannon, Paul. Divorce chains, households or remarriage and multiple divorcers. In Bohannan, Paul (Ed.): *Divorce and After*. New York: Doubleday & Co., 1971, pp. 127-139.
47. Lasswell, Marcia E. and Lasswell, Thomas E.: *Love, Marriage, Family: A Developmental Approach*. Glenview, Ill: Scott, Foresman & Co, 1973.
48. Raush, Harold L., Barry, William A. Hertel, R. K., and Swain, Mary Ann: *Communication Conflict and Marriage*. San Francisco, CA, Jossey-Bass Pub, 1974.
49. Vines, Neville R.: Adult unfolding and marital conflict. *J Marital and Family Therapy, 5:* 5-14, 1979.
50. Hunt, Richard A. and Rydman, Edward J.: *Creative Marriage*. Boston, Holbrook Press, 1976.
51. Feldman, Harold and Feldman, Margaret: The family life cycle: some suggestions for recycling. *J Marr & Family, 37:* 277-84, 1975.
52. Spanier, Graham B., Lewis, Robert A., and Cole, Charles L.: Marital adjustment over the family life cycle: the issue of curvilinearity. *J Marr & Family, 37:* 263-75, 1975.
53. Gilford, Rosalie and Bengston, Vern: Measuring marital satisfaction in three generations — positive and negative dimensions. *J Marr & Family, 41:* 387-98, 1979.
54. Fogarty, Thomas F.: Sexual estrangement in marriage. *Med Aspects Hum Sexuality, 11:* 135, 1977.
55. Rogers, Carl R.: *Becoming Partners: Marriage and Its Alternatives*. New

York: Delacorte Press, 1972.

56. Mace, David: Marriage and family enrichment — a new field? *Family Coordinator, 28:* 409-19, 1979.

57. Mace, David: Preventive training for creative family relationships — some experimental programs in North America. Personal communication, May 1978.

58. Mace, David and Mace, Vera: Measure your marriage potential — a simple test that tells couples where they are. *Family Coordinator, 27:* 63-67, 1978.

59. Mace, David and Mace, Vera: *How to Have a Happy Marriage.* Nashville, TN, Abingdon Press, 1977.

60. Mace, David and Mace, Vera: The selection, training, and certification of facilitators for marriage enrichment programs. *Family Coordinator, 25:* 117-125, 1976.

61. Mace, David and Mace, Vera: Marriage enrichment — wave of the future? *Family Coordinator, 24:* 131-35, 1975.

62. Mace, David: Marriage enrichment concepts for research. *Family Coordinator, 24:* 171-73, 1975.

63. Bosco, Antoinette: *Marriage Encounter: The Rediscovery of Love.* ST. Meinrad, Ind., Abbey Press, 1972.

64. Regula, Ronald R.: Marriage encounter— what makes it work? *Family Coordinator, 24:* 153-59, 1975.

65. Otto, Herbert A.: Marriage and family enrichment programs in North America — report and analysis. *Family Coordinator, 24:* 138, 1975.

66. Otto, Herbert A.: Marriage and Family Enrichment: New Perspectives and Programs. Nashville: Abingdon Press, 1976.

67. L'Abate, Luciano: *Enrichment: Structured Interventions with Couples, Families, and Groups.* Washington, D. C.: University Press of America, 1977.

68. L'Abate, Luciano, Wildman II, R. W., O'Callaghan, J. B. et al.: *J Marr & Family Counseling, 1:* 351-57, 1975.

69. McCary, James L.: *Freedom and Growth in Marriage.* Santa Barbara, CA, Hamilton Pub. Co., 1975.

70. Guerney, Bernard G., Jr.: *Relationship Enhancement.* San Francisco, Jossey-Bass, 1977.

71. Kelly, L. J.: *Sex Through Affection.* Philadelphia, Dorrance and Co., 1976.

72. Travis, Robert P. and Travis, Patricia Y.: The pairing enrichment program — actualizing the marriage. *Family Coordinator, 24:* 161-65, 1975.

73. Stein, Edward V: MARDILAB — and an experiment in marriage enrichment. *Family Coordinator, 24:* 167-70, 1975.

74. Sauber, S. Richard: Primary prevention and the marital enrichment group. *J Family Counseling, 2:* 39-44, 1974.

75. Kerckhoff, Richard K.: Marriage and middle age. *Family Coordinator, 25:* 5-11, 1976.

76. DeYoung, Alan J: Marriage encounter — a critical examination. *J Marital & Family Therapy, 5:* 27-34, 1979.
77. Doherty, William C., McCabe, Patricia, and Ryder, Robert G.: Marriage encounter — a critical appraisal. *J Marr & Family Counseling, 4:* 99-107, 1978.
78. Gurman, Alan S. and Kniskern, David P.: Enriching research on marital enrichment programs. *J Marr & Family Counseling, 3:* 2-11, 1977.
79. Boss, Pauline G and Whitaker, Carl: Dialogue on separation — clinicians as educators. *Family Coordinator, 28:* 391-98, 1979.
80. Bloom, Bernard L. and Hodges, William F.: Marital separation — a community survey. *J Divorce, 1:* 7-19, 1977.
81. Meyer, Jon K., Schmidt, Chester W., and Lucas, Mary J.: Short-term treatment of sexual problems — interim report. *Am J Psychiat, 132:* 173, 1975.
82. Mott, Frank L. and Moore, Sylvia F.: The causes of marital disruption among young American women — an interdisciplinary perspective. *J Marr & Family, 41:* 355-65, 1979.
83. Albrecht, Stan L.: Correlates of marital happiness among the remarried. *J Marr & Family, 41:* 857-67, 1979.
84. Visher, Emily B. and Visher, John S.: *Reconstituted Families.* New York, Brunner-Mazel, 1979.
85. Visher, Emily B. and Visher, John S.: Common problems of stepparents and their spouses. *Am J Orthopsychiat, 48:* 252-62, 1978.
86. Visher, Emily B. and Visher, John S.: *Step-families — A Guide to Working With Stepparents and Stepchildren.* New York, Brunner-Mazel, 1978.
87. Nichols, William C., Jr.: Divorce and remarriage education. *J Divorce, 1:* 153-61, 1977.
88. Glick, Paul C. and Norton, A.J.: Marrying, divorcing and living together today. *Population Bulletin 32 (5),* Washington, D C: Population Bureau, 1977.
89. Bernard, Jessie: *Remarriage: A Study of Marriage,* (2nd ed), New York, Russell & Russel, 1971.
90. Coogler, O. J., Weber, Ruth E., and McKenry, Patrick: Divorce mediation — a means of facilitating divorce and adjustment. *Family Coordinator, 28:* 255-59, 1979.
91. Colletta, Nancy D.: Support systems after divorce — incidence and impact. *J Marr & Family, 41:* 837-46, 1979.
92. Levinger, George and Moles, Oliver (Eds.): *Divorce and Separation: Conditions, Causes, and Consequences.* San Francisco, CA, Jossey-Bass, Pub, 1978.
93. Hunt, Morton and Hunt, Bernice: *The Divorce Experience.* New York, McGraw-Hill, 1977.
94. Kaplan, S. L.: Structural family therapy for children of divorce — case reports. *Family Process, 16:* 75-83, 1977.
95. Dell, P. F. and Applebaum, A. S.: Trigenerational enmeshment —

unresolved ties of single-parents to family of origin. *Am J Orthopsychiat, 47:* 52-59, 1977.

96. Kessler, Sheila: *The American Way of Divorce: Prescriptions for Change.* Chicago, Nelson Hall, 1975.

97. Lieb, Judith: Divorce therapy (moderator workshop 11), resource participants — *Meyer Elkin, Bernard L. Greene, Kitty La Perriere and Alfred P. Solomon.* Emphasis on identification of clinical issues in divorce therapy and ways of dealing with them. 51st annual meeting, Amer. Orthopsychiatric Assn, San Francisco, CA, April 11, 1974.

98. Colletta, Nancy D.: The impact of divorce — father absence or poverty. *J Divorce, 3:* 27-35, 1979.

99. Spanier, Graham B. and Anderson, Elaine A.: The impact of the legal system on adjustment to marital separation. *J Marr & Family, 41:* 605-13, 1979.

100. Spanier, Graham B. and Castro, Robert F. Adjustment to separation and divorce. *J Divorce, 2:* 241-53, 1979.

101. Fisher, Esther Oshiver: *Journal of Divorce, 1:* 5, 6, 1977.

102. Fisher, Esther Oshiver: *Divorce: The New Freedom.* New York, Harper & Row, 1974.

103. Fisher, Esther Oshiver: A guide to divorce counseling. *Family Coordinator, 22:* 55-61, 1973.

104. Robbins, Norman N: There ought to be a law! End of divorce — beginning of legal problems. *Family Coordinator, 23:* 185-95, 1974.

105. Weiss, Robert: *Marital Separation.* New York, Basic Books, 1975.

106. Kurdek, Lawrence A. and Siesky, Albert E., Jr.: An interview study of parents' perceptions of their children's reactions and adjustment to divorce. *J Divorce, 3:* 5-17, 1979.

107. Arnold, L. Eugene (Ed.): *Helping Parents Help Their Children.* New York, Brunner-Mazel, 1978.

108. Rose, Rhona: Some crucial issues concerning children of divorce. *J Divorce, 3:* 19-25, 1979.

109. Clayton, Paula J.: The effect of living alone on bereavement symptoms. *Am J Psychiat, 132:* 133-37, 1975.

110. Clayton, Paula J.: The sequalae and nonsequelae of conjugal bereavement. *Am J Psychiat, 136:* 1530-34, 1979.

111 Raschke, Helen J: The role of social participation in postseparation and postdivorce adjustment. *J Divorce, 1:* 129-40, 1977.

112. Greenblatt, Milton: The grieving spouse *Am J Psychiat, 135:* 43-47, 1978.

113. Weiss, *Marital Separation.*

114. Herman, Sonya J.: Women, divorce, and suicide. *J Divorce 1:* 107-17, 1977.

115. Wiseman, Reva S.: Crisis theory and the process of divorce.*Social Casework, 56:* 205-12, 1975.

116. Siegal, Barry and Short, Jan: Post-parting depression. *Marriage & Divorce, 1:* 77-83, 1974.

117. Volkan, Vamik D.: The linking objects of pathological mourners. *Arch*

Gen Psychiat, 27: 215-221, 1972.

118. Espenshade, Thomas J.: The economic consequences of divorce. *J Marr & Family, 41:* 615-25, 1979.

119. Rosenthal, Perihan A.: Sudden disappearance of one parent with separation and divorce — the grief and treatment of preschool children. *J Divorce, 3:* 43-54, 1979.

120. Bowlby, John: Pathological mourning and childhood mourning. *J Am Psychoanal Assoc, 11:* 500-41, 1973.

121. Parkes, C. M.: *Bereavement — Studies in Adult Life.* New York, Int Univ Press, 1972.

122. Rice, David G.: Psychotherapeutic treatment of narcissistic injury in marital separation and divorce. *J Divorce, 1:* 119-28, 1977.

123. Kohut, Heinz: *The Analysis of Self.* New York, Int Univ Press, 1971.

124. Goldberg, Arnold: Psychotherapy of narcissistic injuries. *Arch Gen Psychiat, 28:* 722-26, 1973.

125. Rice, Psychotherapeutic treatment of narcissistic injury in marital separation and divorce.

126. Hetherington, E. M., Cox, M., and Cox, R.: The aftermath of divorce. In Steven, J. H., Jr, and Matthews, M. (Eds.): *Mother-Child, Father-Child Relations.* Washington, D. C., NAEYC, 1978.

127. Frolich, Newton: *Making the Best of It.* New York, Harper & Row, 1971.

128. Elkin, Meyer: Postdivorce counseling in a conciliation court. *J Divorce, 1:* 55-65, 1977.

129. Goldman, J. and Coane, J.: Family therapy after the divorce — developing a strategy. *Family Process, 16:* 357-62, 1977.

130. Houck, John H.: Marital disruption and divorce. *Psychiatric Annals* reprint, July, 1975.

131. Hardy, Richard E. and Cull, John G. (Eds.): Techniques and Approaches in Marital and Family Counseling. Springfield Ill., Thomas, 1974.

132. Keane, Philip S.: *Sexual Morality: A Catholic Perspective.* New York: Paulist Press, 1977.

133. Silverman, Hirsch L.: *Marital Therapy: Moral, Sociological and Psychological Factors.* Springfield, Ill, Thomas, 1972.

134. Barnhart, Joe E. and Barnhart, Mary Ann: Saint Paul and divorcee — divorce counseling. *J Divorce, 1:* 141-51, 1977.

135. Tessman, Lora Heims: *Children of Parting Parents.* New York, Jason Aronson, 1978.

136. Pollack, Jack H: When parents separate. *Today's Health,* June 1967. Pp. 17, 60, 66.

137. Kargman, Marie W.: A court appointed child advocate (Guardian ad litem) reports on her role in contested child custody cases and looks to the future. *J Divorce, 3:* 77-90, 1979.

138. Warner, Nancy S. and Elliott, Carla J.: Problems of the interpretive phase of divorce — custody evaluations. *J Divorce, 2:* 371-82, 1979.

139. Woody, R. H.: Behavioral science criteria in child custody

determination. *J Marr & Family Counseling, 3:* 11-18, 1977.

140. Stack, C. B.: Who owns the child? Divorce and child custody decisions in middle-class families. *Social Problems, 23:* 505-15, 1976.

141. Derdeyn, Andre P.: Child custody contests in historical perspective. *Am J Psychiat, 133:*1369-76, 1976.

142. Saxe, O. B.: Some relfections on the interface of law and psychiatry in child custody cases. *J Am Acad Psychoanal, 3:* 501-14, 1975.

143. Kestenberg, Judith H. S. Determining child custody (in questions and answers). *Med Aspects Hum Sexuality, 11:* 87, 1978.

144. Nichols, Robert C. & Troester, James D: Custody evaluations — an alternative? *Family Coordinator, 28:* 399-407, 1979.

145. Jenkins, Richard L: Maxims in child custody cases. *Family Coordinator, 26:* 385-89, 1977.

146. Bohannan, Paul: The six stations of divorce. In Bohannan, Paul (Ed.): *Divorce and After.* New York, Doubleday, 1970.

147. Pais, Jeanne and White, Priscilla: Family redefinition — a review of the literature toward a model of divorce adjustment. *J Divorce, 2:* 271-81, 1979.

148. Musetto, Andrew: Evaluating families with custody or visitation problems. *J Marr & Family Counseling, 4:* 59-65, 1978.

149. Combs, E. Raedene: The human capital concept as a basis for property settlement at divorce — theory and implementation. *J Divorce, 2:* 329-56, 1979.

150. Schlesinger, Benjamin: Children and divorce in Canada — The law reform commission's recommendations. *J Divorce, 1:* 175-82, 1977.

151. Sheffner, David J. and Suarez, John M.: The divorce clinic. *Am J Psychiat, 132:* 442-44, 1975.

152. Drake, Ellen A.: Helping the school cope with children of divorce. *J Divorce, 3:* 69-75, 1979.

153. Cantor, Dorothy: School-based groups for children of divorce. *J Divorce, 1:* 183-87, 1978.

154. Williams, Frank S.: Children of divorce . . . detectives, diplomats or despots. *Marriage & Divorce, 1:* 24-28, 1974.

155. Kelly, J. B. and Wallerstein, J. S.: Brief interventions with children of divorcing families. *Am J Orthopsychiat, 47:* 23-26, 1977.

156. Kelly, J. B. and Wallerstein, J. S.: The effects of parental divorce — experiences of the child in early latency. *Am J Orthopsychiat, 46:* 20-36, 1976.

157. Wallerstein, J. S. and Kelly, J. B.: The effects of parental divorce — experiences of the child in later latency. *Am J Orthopsychiat, 46:* 256-268, 1976.

158. Wallerstein, J. S. and Kelly, J. B.: The effects of parental divorce — experiences of the preschool child. *J Am Acad Child Psychiat, 14:* 600-16, 1975.

159. Wallerstein, J. S. and Kelly, J. B.: The effects of parental divorce: The adolescent experience. In E. J. Anthony and C. Koupernik (Eds.): *The*

Child In His Family, Vol 3. New York, Wiley, 1974.

160. Gardner, Richard A.: Brief guide to office counseling — children's reactions to divorced parents new sexual companions. *Med Aspects Hum Sexuality, 12:* 65-66, 1978.

161. Katz, Sanford N.: *The Law's Response to Family Breakdown.* Boston, Mass, Beacon Press, 1971.

162. Cantor, Dorothy W.: Divorce — a view from the children. *J Divorce, 2:* 357-61, 1979.

163. Noshpitz, Joseph D. (Ed.): *The Basic Handbook of Child Psychiatry.* Vol IV, Prevention and Current Issues (with introduction by Leon Eisenberg). New York: Basic Books, 1979.

164. Magrab, Phyllis R.: For the sake of the children — a review of the psychological effects of divorce. *J Divorce, 1:* 233-45, 1978.

165. Hunt, Morton and Hunt, Bernice: *The Divorce Experience.* New York, McGraw-Hill, 1977.

166. Kalter, Neil: Children of divorce in an outpatient psychiatric population. *Am J Orthopsychiat, 47:* 40-51, 1977.

167. Sorosky, A. D.: The psychological effects of divorce on adolescents. *Adolescence, 12:* 123-36, 1977.

168. Lamb, M. E.: The effects of divorce on children's personality development. *J Divorce, 1:* 163-74, 1977.

169. Hozman, Thomas L. and Froiland, Donald J.: Families in divorce: a proposed model for counseling the children. *Family Coordinator, 25:* 271-76, 1976.

170. Morrison, James R.: Parental divorce as a factor in childhood psychiatric illness. *Comprehensive Psychiat, 15:* 95-102, 1974.

171. Toomin, M. K.: The child of divorce, in Hardy, R. E. and Cull, J. G. (Eds.): *Therapeutic Needs of the Family.* Springfield, IL, Thomas, 1974.

172. Martin, Gilbert I.: Helping the child of divorcing parents. *Consultant, 13:* 44-45, 1973.

173. Westman, Jack C.: Effect of divorce on a child's personality development. *Med Aspects Human Sexuality, 6:* 38-55, 1972.

174. McDermott, John F.: Divorce and its psychiatric sequelae in children. *Arch Gen Psychiat, 23:* 421-27, 1970.

175. Elkin, Meyer: Conciliation courts: the reintegration of disintegrating families. *Family Coordinator, 22:* 63-71, 1973.

176. Sonne, John C: There ought to be a law! On the question of compulsory marriage counseling as a part of divorce proceedings. Family Coordinator, 23: 303-5, 1974.

177. Sheffner & Suarez, The divorce clinic.

178. Lamb, Michael: The effects of divorce on children's personality development. *J Divorce, 1:* 163-74, 1977.

179. Derdeyn, Andre P.: A consideration of legal issues in child custody contests — implications for change. *Arch Gen Psychiat, 33:* 165-71, 1976.

180. Goldstein, Joseph, Freud Anna, and Solnit, Albert J.: *Beyond the Best*

Interests of the Child. New York, The Free Press, 1973.

181. Benedek, Elissa P.: Child custody laws — their psychiatric implications. *Am J Psychiat, 129:* 326-28, 1972.

182. Westman, Jack C.: The psychiatrist and child custody contests. *Am J Psychiat, 127:* 168-88, 1971.

183. Bernstein, Barton E: Lawyer and counselor as an interdisciplinary team — preparing the father for custody. *J Marr & Family Counseling, 3:* 29-40, 1977.

184. Shucart, Martin E: Personal communication (12-20-79)

185. Benedek, Elissa P. and Benedek, Richard S.: Joint custody — solution of illusion? *Am J Psychiat, 136:* 1540-44, 1979.

186. Galper, Miriam: *Co-Parenting: Sharing Your Child Equally, A Source Book for the Separated or Divorced Family.* Philadelphia, Running Press, 1978.

187. Stetson, Dorothy M. and Wright, Gerald C., Jr,: The effects of laws on divorce in American states. *J Marr & Family, 37:* 537-46, 1975.

188. Rheinstein, Max: *Marriage Stability, Divorce, and the Law.* Chicago, Univ Chicago Press, 1972.

189. Wheeler, Michael: *No-Fault Divorce.* Boston, Mass, Beacon Press, 1974.

190. "No-fault" divorces — they're catching on. *U. S. News and World Report,* June, 1973, pp. 41-42.

191. Monahan, Thomas P.: National divorce legislation — the problem and some suggestions. *Family Coordinator, 22:* 363-57, 1973.

192. Singer, Laura J: Divorce and the single life — divorce as development. *J Sex & Marital Therapy, 1:* 254-70, 1975.

193. Krantzler, Mel: *Creative Divorce. A New Opportunity for Personal Growth.* New York, M. Evans, 1973.

194. Granvold, Donald K, Pedler, Leigh M. and Schiellie, Susan G.: A study of sex role expectancy and female postdivorce adjustment. *J Divorce, 2:* 383-93, 1979.

195. Cleveland, Martha: Divorce in the middle years — the sexual dimension. *J Divorce, 2:* 255-62, 1979.

196. Dreyfus, Edward A: Counseling the divorced father. *J Marital & Family Therapy, 5:* 79-85, 1979.

197. Rice, Joy K.: Divorce and a return to school. *J Divorce, 1:* 247-57, 1978.

198. Granvold, Donald K. and Welch, Gary J.: Intervention for postdivorce problems: The treatment seminar. *J Divorce, 1:* 81-92, 1977.

PART THREE
TREATMENT

Chapter XXI

GENERAL THERAPEUTIC PRINCIPLES

THIS chapter will present general therapeutic principles used with couples and family dysfunctions. Despite recent progress made in the behavioral sciences, psychotherapy is still mostly an art dependent on the therapeutic goal, "working alliance,"[1] and therapeutic alliance. The therapist evaluates the couple or family using the diagnostic process outlined in Chapter XX and decides intuitively (art) which technique is applicable at this point of *time*. Thus, the therapy is tailored to the couple's individual and mutual needs. Therapy should parallel the patient's motivational state and his ego strength.[2] In 1963, we differentiated five foci of transference phenomena.[3] The first focus of transaction involves the relationship to the therapist as a *real person* and, subsequently, *as a new object* as well. The second focus of transaction pertains to those situations where the therapist is experienced as a *symbolic figure* endowed with qualities of existing fantasies, as those involved in projections and displacements. The regressive phenomena manifested in the dyadic, one-to-one, *transference neurosis** comprise the third focus of transaction. These three foci of transactions between patient and therapist are fundamental in all therapeutic relationships. In triadic therapy, because the transference reactions of both partners are directed toward the same therapist, as well as toward each other, two other foci of transaction related to the triangular transactions are introduced. The first of these is the *triangular transference neurosis,* such as the reproduction of the oedipal constellation. The second, the *triangular transference transactions,* concern the production of adaptive feedbacks, not only toward the therapist but also to the other partner, who, in turn, feeds back to his partner, to the therapist, or to both. If the first focus develops, there is a "working alliance" established because the patient's ego strength fosters nonneurotic, rational, and realistic attitudes toward the therapist.[4,5] The "working alliance" is a result of factors in all three GST systems which establishes the other transference phenomena as well.[6]

---

*The transference neurosis is a Freudian psychoanalytic term to describe a symbolic reaction to the therapist, in which the feelings and reactions of the patient toward important people of childhood are currently projected onto the therapist.

Human beings do not find full satisfaction in their biological functions only, they need the guidance of a conceptual system[7] which determines the meaning of all behavior. The simple philosophy of the four circles (see figure 10) has helped many find tranquility.[8]

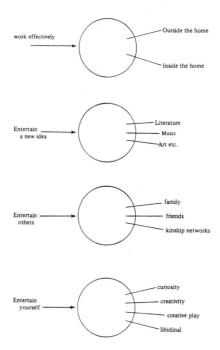

Figure 10. A philosophy for living and equanimity. Marcus Aurelius said, "Tranquility is nothing else than good ordering of the mind . . . constantly then give to thyself this retreat, and renew thyself."

Each individual is unique in his existence and possesses untapped potential. Developing this potential is an ongoing process. Now, to develop this process, I draw and describe each circle. The first circle involves the utopian goal of doing whatever task or role, assigned or accepted, to the best of one's ability. Goethe wisely stated that work is nature's physician and essential to human happiness. The second circle, entertaining new ideas, involves the creative process inherent in every "inner child" and is an ongoing process that explores the world around us and requires nurturing.[9] The third circle, entertaining others, is developing relationships with others[10] (no man is an island unto himself) and includes meaningful relationships with members of one's nuclear family, with kinship networks, and with friends. The fourth circle, entertaining yourself, explores the innate attributes of the inner child: the need for warmth, closeness, fondling and all the subtleties of love, creativity, curiosity,[11] and play — *not* competition, which is part of the first circle and is dependent on genuine effort.

When a patient says "When I play a better game I get more enjoyment" perhaps what he is actually saying is equivalent to the "spectatoring" phenomenon of observing one's own sexual performance. "We say 'I am going to play tennis,' but we really work on our strokes, concentration, and footwork. We have learned to work at playing. When we carry this distortion into our sexual behaviors, lack of enjoyment and dysfunctions are created and perpetuated, since 'success' is determined by the answer to the question 'How am I doing?' This answer is obtained only by spectatoring."[12] The interplay of the four circles involves open transactions, but has been presented for didactic purposes.[13] Orthner[14] has stressed the importance of leisure in family living.

One of the goals in therapy is to help the couple recognize and tolerate the uniqueness of each other. Leon Saul, among others,[15] has described the creative process " . . . a quantitative combination of elements and motivations, including imagination (with sources chiefly in the unconscious); knowledge of the medium; mastery of the techniques of the medium; sublimated, usually ego-syntonic exhibitionism; and, for great productions, almost single-minded ceaseless application and hard work."[16] Carkhuff and Berenson discuss four different dimensions of commitment, discipline, skills, and strategies in therapy.[17]

PRINCIPLES OF TREATMENT

Mutual Responsibility

Except for an undiagnosed severe mental illness, both members of a dyad are mutually responsible for problems in their relationship, as I have previously emphasized in the CDD. The concept of "historical necessity" is explained as important in the therapeutic process.[18] Historical necessity means that people, including significant others, are unique in their existence as the result of inputs from all three systems of the GST. When an individual can accept the historical necessity, particularly of their parents' behavior ("I have never picked up a bad baby in a nursery"), the therapy proceeds more constructively.[19]

Unless the partners accept responsibility for their singular and interpersonal behavior, therapy does not proceed rapidly. It is essential to relationships forming a "seesaw" (my metaphor, see Chapter II) that equal responsibility be shared alike. When the couple is anchored in therapy and that premise is established we can discuss the couple seated on the seesaw of their design (their unique transactional pattern), the ride they are having is acceptable, since, at any given point in time, either one can get off. If conflict continues, the couple is no longer in a playground, but on a battlefield. My approach is, and I am emphatic about this, that my office is not a place for adversaries, but for partners attempting to understand each other and work out a mutual satisfying relationship.

Dyadic Contract

Dyad disharmony, as Peter Martin points out, " . . . is a manifestation of disease in a relationship that results from the absence of one or more solid, constant, mutually gratified expectations capable of overcoming the ungratified expectations in either mate or both. Where important and sufficient expectations are mutually gratified, marital (dyad) harmony results. This principle leads directly to the subject of the marriage (dyad) contract."[20] The contract, either explicit or implicit, involves expectations, conscious and often unconscious, of what each expects from the other. Weiss, Birchler, and Vincent point out that mutual gain and reciprocity are central to dyad relationships and contracts. In their study, they found that the *quid pro quo*[21,22] category provided greatest contingency control, but that implicit exchange or "good faith" contractual format "seemed to fit more easily into the overall goal of marital (dyad) therapy."[23] Dyadic contracts are not new, but are an essential feature of many cultures. I continue to find contracts helpful in solving dyadic disorders.[24] I repeat my moral (bias) and therapeutic contract with the couple. In the past decade, I have routinely written the contract in the presence of both partners. The written contract is referred to when either partner does not adhere to the agreement. Writing prevents future arguments since a basic principle in communication is, that *what is said and what each hears* are often subject to different interpretations, but, what is written is concretely in black and white and subject to *visual* perception. Sager's[25] book on marriage contracts is useful in all dyadic relationship therapy. A contract is workable only when both partners are willing to negotiate and compromise. Fundamental to my contracts are the principles of reciprocity and social exchange.[26]

The contract I present stresses two areas: (1) sexual, a meaningful relationship that includes the display of warmth, tender loving care, positive feelings and behavior and (2) nonsexual, a collaborative relationship that is voluntary, permanent, exclusive, and goal oriented. I specifically emphasize that past behavior is a "historical necessity" while each partner will be responsible for current behavior. The contract I present is a biased one, and, after the relationship is reequilibrated, it is the couple's prerogative to change the contract as long as it is mutually acceptable. In many couples where infidelity was a major source of conflict, the stress on exclusiveness in the relationship often alleviates anxiety and hastens the therapeutic process. In effect, I am *actively setting limits*. Clinical experience indicates that a therapist cannot avoid communicating his values, even if he tries to avoid giving directives. By his verbal and nonverbal cues and metacommunications, he directly or indirectly persuades, suggests, and controls the behavior of his patients. I point out that setting limits to behavior produces anxiety and/or anger, but helps in uncovering the motivations behind the behavior. Abroms[27] has written an excellent article on setting limits; he outlines five types of behavior that may call for explicit limit setting by a therapist: destructive behavior, disorganized behavior, deviant behavior, withdrawn behavior, and dependent behavior.

The concept of anxiety (a major hurdle in beginning therapy)[28] has many definitions depending on the theoretical orientation of the therapist. Perhaps it is best described in terms of a diffuse, physiological feeling. It is related to threatened life-styles in which structure and function go together, i.e. closely related to one's personality and modes of behavior. It is *anger*, however, that is the core of dyadic discord.[29-33]

Target Date

The target date is twelve sessions of therapy — usually a therapeutic trial of three months. The couple is told that at the twelfth session, the progress of the therapy will be assessed. The continuance, termination, or referral will be determined at that time. The couple should feel that they can interrupt the therapy before the three month target date if they choose to work out their own problems. This will be satisfactory to the therapist.

Nuclear Model

The nuclear dynamic model[34, 35] is presented to the couple as a visualization of the internal and external forces that influence their transactional relationship. This nuclear model can be visualized as a circle containing an enclosed smaller circle and thus having an internal and external boundary (see fig. 11).

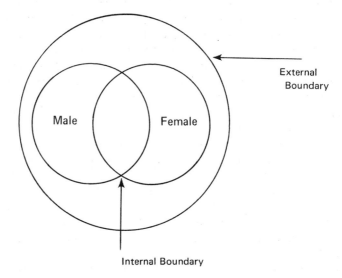

Figure 11. Nuclear dynamic model of the family.

The external environmental factors are outside the external boundary and consists of sociocultural forces. The internal forces are within the external boundary and include dyadic transactions and if children are present, those are additional influences.

Five Progressive Stages in Dyadic Dissolution

Stage One: Durable Incompatible Relationship. This has both internal and external boundaries intact (see fig. 11). The conflicting partners constantly take advantage of one another, playing the dyadic games previously described (see Chapter XIX).

Stage Two: Intermittent Incompatible Relationship. This phenomena occurs in a special type of pair-coupling[36] A striking group of individuals emerge whose behavior is depressed or hyperactive and sometimes hostile and/or destructive, but the relationship rarely ends in separation or divorce. During the diagnostic phase, it becomes evident that one of the partners has a primary affective disorder (manic-depressive illness). This topic will be discussed in detail in Chapter XXVII. These relationships are stable most of the time, but are subject to periods of change when the partner with the primary affective disorder becomes depressed or displays hypomanic-manic behavior with periods of "uproar." In this type of pair-coupling, the couple's external boundary remains intact but the internal boundary is subject to intermittent fragmentation (see fig. 12).

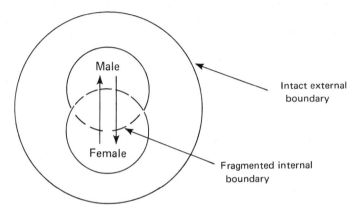

Figure 12. Nuclear dynamic model in intermittent incompatibility.

Stage Three: Emotional Divorce. This has the external boundary intact, while the internal boundary is disrupted (see fig. 13). Each partner goes his separate way but maintains the facade of his relationship. The partners make neither psychological nor physiological demands upon one another and preserve their relationship only for

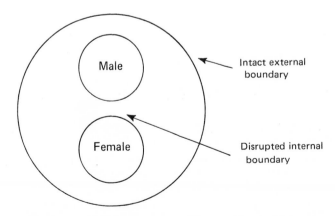

Figure 13. Nuclear dynamic model in emotional divorce.

economic, religious, or social reasons, e.g. homosexuality or "for the sake of the children." The following clinical extract is typical:

> Mr. J describes his early years on the farm as the oldest of two children, emotionally abandoned by a cold, disinterested farmer father to the tyrannical control of a suspicious, religious, moralistic and socially self-isolating mother. He believes his parents' marriage was entered into because of mutual loneliness and mutual convenience: "Mother did not love my father, only respected him. Before I entered grammar school, there were constant protracted arguments between them. After I started school, the arguments ceased as Father tolerated Mother with resignation for the sake of us children. As the years passed, they settled into a condition of cold coexistence. There ceased to be any affection of any kind between them: they went their separate ways and slept in separate bedrooms."

Stage Four: Separation. Separation disrupts the internal boundary and fragments the external boundary. While the couple live in separate households, they maintain the relationship for economic, social, societal, or legal purposes (see fig. 14).

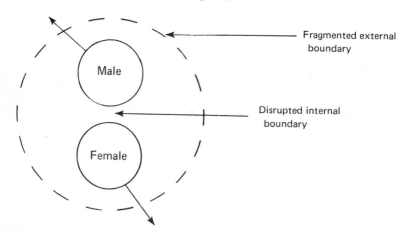

Figure 14. Nuclear dynamic model of family in separation.

Stage Five: Total Disruption. A total disruption occurs when both external and internal boundaries dissolve. The couple return to their single status, and, if there was a marriage, divorce is sought.

Diary

An important principle I have used for many years is instructing the dyad to keep a daily written record or diary[37] of any situation or behavior by the partner that causes anxiety and/or anger. These are later brought into either the single or conjoint sessions — preferably the latter. Patients are instructed to date entries and to keep their thoughts or feelings confidential until the next therapy session. My purpose for confidentiality is to prevent the indoor game of "Uproar"; couples find it startling how differently each viewed and recalled the same event. At the therapeutic session, the anger for the entry may have dissipated to the degree necessary for rational and objective views to be expressed. Frequently, the entry is related with the same degree of emotion, but the presence of the therapist is helpful. Many times I have the couple or family record — audiotape — examples of their behavior at home. I first used this technique for didactic purposes and did not realize the value of this type of confrontation technique until Alger and Hogan first presented their technique a decade and a half ago.[38-40] Kaslow has written another version of confrontation utilizing family photos and/or movies. This technique is useful in helping partners reexperience the past together and is helpful in appreciating one another's current feelings and behavior.[41] I have found this intervention useful in mobilizing conflicts and helpful in therapeutic impasses.

Transient Structured Distance (TSD)

This therapeutic contractual intervention has been used in my therapy for many years.[42-46] Its value is recognized by other psychotherapists.[47-49]

I continue to value its contribution in diagnosis and intervention. TSD has three parts that form a sociopsychological maneuver in a couple's relationship in terms of environmental structuring. First, it *distances* the couple by minimizing transactions that are conflictual in nature. This is accomplished by having the couple use journals or diaries to record conflict instead of continuing to act upon the conflict at that time. It is further implimented by *structuring* the type of rules and roles each will follow. The last part of the procedure is its *transiency;* the maneuver is of short duration during which time the healthier and satisfying elements of the dyad's relationship will have time to flourish or appear. It is the love and intimate bonds that form the essence of a meaningful relationship based upon mutual respect and self-respect. The purpose for TSD is to permit the couple to feel and notice the positive side of their union and to permit their distancing from conflictual areas so the unpleasant transactions can be viewed from a more rational, objective, and concerned viewpoint.

The evolution of the TSD is an example of serendipity. Approximately twenty years ago I witnessed a distancing process between a patient and her husband.

> Mrs. A sought psychoanalysis for her obesity. During her therapy she related that her husband packed and left after a virulent argument. (Their marital disharmony was typical of Martin and Bird's "the love-sick wife and the cold-sick husband).[50] Due to her severe emotional reaction, I suggested having him come to her next session. He agreed and both were started on marital therapy. At first things improved, but a therapeutic impasse occurred. When I suggested she move out of the home, Mr. A became upset and suggested a "border" status to calm things down. The arrangement was, separate bedrooms and no sexual demands on Mr. A unless he initiates sex. Thus, the *"Star Boarder Arrangement"* came into effect. (Of interest, that night they had sex — a good example of paradoxical intention).[51]

Experimenting with other couples, when distancing with the "boarder" arrangement failed, the next step was the *"outside dwelling,"* either in a hotel, apartment, or condominium setting. This intervention was necessary for escalating arguments with the potential of physical abuse. This arrangement is not infrequent when one partner has a primary affective disorder. In 1965, I coined the term: Transient Structured Distance in treating marital (dyadic) crises.[52]

The rules and roles of the TSD include all or some of the following:

1. Intercourse can be initiated only by the spouse who complains of a too demanding partner; the latter has the choice of accepting or rejecting the advance.
2. Either partner may ask the other to participate in a social function, and the partner need not acquiesce.
3. Specified roles are assigned and carefully spelled out in a conjoint session to avoid later arguments.
4. Separate bedrooms or dwellings are at times indicated for each spouse.
5. Partners can go their own way without accounting to each other. However, this is not intended to imply that either has the right to break existing secular or sacred laws governing the marriage.
6. A courting arrangement is made. The couple is asked to date each other once a week with a tabu on arguing. Commencing with the wife, each spouse takes turns in deciding what the date will be. Any experience of anxiety of hostility is to be recorded and brought to the next conjoint session for discussion. This

practice leads either to a new closeness or further distancing.

TSD is a cooling off arrangement and is useful as a *diagnostic tool* to uncover the basic elements of the dyadic disharmony quickly. A concern of using the "outside dwelling" arrangement is the possibility of a sexual affair starting, developing, or maintained by either partner. Another adverse aspect is the viability of the relationship as it is brought into focus and the dyadic discord is visible to offspring, relatives, neighbors and friends. Not only is the physical distance in terms of coitus established, but a dramatic physical distance occurs as clothes, meals, and time spend in separate abodes develop. This latter distancing quickly brings into focus the viability of the pair-coupling since the partners either move closer or further apart.

Nontherapeutically, many individuals in dyadic relationships have, consciously or unconsciously, used extended business trips, financial pressure to insist upon long working hours or several jobs, the need for relaxation to seek activities that are time consuming and fatiguing, etc., to establish a distancing pattern that reduces dyadic conflict. Medically, on a less formal basis, doctors have used hospitalization as a form of TSD. In a five year study (unpublished),[53] at least one-third of hospitalizations in a private psychiatric hospital fell into this category.

In using TSD, the therapist accepts the responsibility that this radical and stressful intervention can aggravate an acute panic reaction or precipitate a suicidal threat. In a panel on TSD chaired by the author, the risks in the use of the TSD were identified as " . . . existing in the intrapsychic state of the marital partners. Careful evaluation of spouses' capacity to tolerate distancing and isolation is essential, as in many marital relationships hostile interaction between spouses serves to maintain internal equilibrium of one or both partners. There may be unequal acceptance of TSD by both spouses, or one may choose divorce, leaving the other alone or in a precarious state. There was consideration but no conclusion of the possible effects of this technique on children in a conflicted marriage."[54] If the couple is receiving legal advise, they must clear the TSD procedure with their lawyers.

The TSD is used for *diagnostic purposes* in any of the following four situations:

1. A pair-coupling may admit they have problems but are in conflict as to resolution. In this situation, the TSD can determine the depth of the relationship. Clarification of the dyadic relationship occurred in one-third of the couples.
2. To determine readiness for separation or divorce. This occurred

in one-sixth of the couples. Usually one of the partners has begun divorce or separation proceedings. The therapist must determine the purpose of the consultations:
   a. To get the partner to do something, e.g. to get therapy.
   b. Is the partner who started the legal process really ambivalent about the decision?
   c. Is the partner determined to separate but wants the other to be helped to accept the decision?
   d. Are both testing their ability to accept living without the other. Not infrequently is to differentiate *phobic fear* of being alone from the capability for loneliness.
 3. To test motivation for therapy. This occurred in 5 percent of the couples. Both have mutually agreed upon the separation/divorce but want changes made to improve their relationship.
 4. Therapeutic impasse, which occurred in 10 percent of the couples.

The TSD is useful for the several categories of *therapy:*
 1. Where the couple does not want to separate, this procedure enables them to live together — the *intermittent incompatible* dyadic relationships found in relationships where one partner has a primary affective disorder. This situation was present in 15 percent of the couples.
 2. In severe personality dysfunctioning other than PAD. Martin[55] refers to this type of relationship as characterized by "obnoxiousness." Our figures are parallel — 15 percent of the couples.
 3. In the dyadic game of "Uproar," which occurred in 10 percent of the couples. Temporary distancing was used for management purposes.[56] This maneuver permits exploration of the dyadic dynamics. Another purpose is to permit the therapist to focus on sensitive conflicts early in the treatment process.

Ongoing experience with the TSD has helped in understanding some of its parameters.[57] Since our last study[58] of 100 couples, I now use this technique in one out of five pair-couplings. The mean age of the seventy-three males was 40.30 years with a standard deviation of 7.00, while the mean age of the females was 36.80 years with a standard deviation of 7.60. The mean length of the relationships was 14.30 years (standard deviation 7.00). The data suggests that the TSD could be useful in crises of couples who are in their mid-thirties to the late-forties. The TSD was used for evaluation of the dyadic relationship in 60 percent of the couples and for treatment purposes in the remaining couples.

In a five year follow-up of 80 percent of the couples who had received the TSD, 40 percent has separated permanently. In 25 percent there was no improvement in the relationship and, although there was no separations, the dyad continued in a condition of durable incompatibility. In another 25 percent there was marked improvement, many of the "intermittent incompatibility" type I described in 1976. However, in 10 percent, there was an ongoing re-equilibration of the relationship. Thus, about one-third of the dyads profited from this intervention.

To summarize, TSD is valuable for evaluative or management purposes where there is acute or chronic marital disharmony. Ignoring the transference relationship and subsequent insight to enable behavioral change, the TSD breaks old interactional patterns and forces spouses to move further apart or closer together. In sanctioning the distancing process, the therapist enables spouses to cope with any fears that distance will destroy their marriage or put the other spouse at a legal advantage. Even so, the TSD is not without risks. Besides the production of an anxiety attack or homosexual panic, a TSD can endanger someone who is physically ill. However, these risks are minimized when the TSD is skillfully applied. The risks are also justified by excellent results with couples where other alternatives include years of conflict, misery, and bad health.

GST Principles

Two therapeutic principles in keeping with the GST should be kept in mind:

1. It is impossible to alter significantly one element in any of the three systems (intrapersonal, interpersonal, or environmental) without producing changes in the entire system.
2. It is futile to select one element for attention and action while ignoring and disregarding the others.

Confidentiality

Confidentiality is stressed to the couple in terms of our therapeutic relationship. Under no circumstances will I give legal deposition or appear in court should a couple encounter legal problems at any time, unless *both* agree to my testimony. I have my patients sign a contract that *protects them* (see Chapter XXVIII). A recent judicial opinion may have far reaching consequences for therapists when a judge in Virginia denied the privilege of confidentiality in conjoint marital therapy: ". . . when a husband and wife are in a counseling session with a psychiatrist which is between the husband and wife, there is no confidentiality because the statements were made not in private to a doctor, but in the presence of the spouse."[59]

This topic on confidentiality will be discussed further in Chapter XXVIII.

Behavior Modification

Franz Alexander's[60] prediction that "learning theories" would become part of psychoanalysis is closer to actualization,[61,62] especially in phobias and sex therapies. Many behaviorists now admit that the analytic concepts of resistance and transference play a critical issue in behavior therapy.[53-65] In fact, behavior desensitization and reenforcement, in dilute doses, are part of analytic therapy.[66] If therapists could acquire a sound technical knowledge or relaxation training, hierarchy formation, and pairing hierarchial images with relaxation, patients would certainly find such techniques beneficial. Ferguson et al.[67] suggest that although many prerecorded texts are commercially available: "patients usually prefer hearing their own therapists voice on a relaxation tape." Phobias respond many times to this approach where time is of essence. The following vignette is illustrative:

> Mr C, a concert virtuoso, consulted me because he had developed a sudden fear of performing in public. Because he had to leave for his European tour in four weeks, I suggested the approach of Doctor Wolpe.[68] Doctor Wolpe did not have available therapeutic time, but recommended a former student. In three weeks Mr. C was able to resume his career.

Brady defines learning as the: "process by which changes occur in an individual's behavior as a consequence of his reacting to encountered situations, excluding of course, those changes directly attributable to maturational processes and physical causes (toxins, drugs, injuries, etc.)."[69] He describes clearly and briefly four clinical levels of insight: (1) the patient's awareness that he is ill to degree that he recognizes his feelings, thoughts, and/or behavior are abnormal. (2) the patient's recognition of the nature of his disorder — in particular, the consequences it has for his own satisfactions and adjustments and its effect on others (*what I include in the interpersonal system,*) (3)

---

*Many behavior therapists have made excessive claims for superiority stating that their techniques are based upon theories derived from laboratory evidence. Their methodology is not substantiated by controlled clinical proof. But this approach has a definite place in selected situations.

self-awareness of dynamic factors which give rise to various symptoms and now operate to maintain them, (4) self-awareness into the unconscious roots of the *original* conflict, that is, the inadequately resolved. Brady next points out what every experienced therapist has observed, that the old differentiation between intellectual versus emotional insight is no longer warranted.

The level of insight obtained by the spouses, irrespective of the therapist's conceptual framework, is not as important as the relationship between the therapist and the patients. It is this relationship that consciously or unconsciously persuades individuals to accept the model of "mature" or constructuve behavior. Thus the therapist encourages, not only intellectual and emotional insight but *repetitive, constructive activity.* In other words, behavior therapy may be "new wine in old bottles." But there is no doubt as to its efficacy with certain individuals and in certain types of maladaptive behavior patterns.

Projective Identification

This important principle in therapy was previously presented in detail in Chapter XIX.[70-72]

Clinical Use of Dreams in Therapy

Although dreams were discussed in Chapter XIX, I will elaborate further because of its great value in treatment. The therapeutic use of dreams is dependent on the therapist's training and attitude on its importance.[72-77] I discuss several uses of dream material in my dream book,[78] e.g. options for solving current problems. It is important for the therapist to select the appropriate dream level for discussion. Since there are many levels in every dream, the area selected is determined by both the current therapeutic focus and the therapist's experience. Disguised dream material which could be counter-productive is avoided, but may be used at a future time. The manifest dream content level provides symbolic[79] metaphors for the therapeutic dialogue. Concentrating on constructive dream elements increase empathy between patient and therapist. The specific symbols used by the patient become reference points for verbal understandings. Interpretations can be correlated with the manifest content of past dreams to point out progress in therapy. A unique type of communication from dream interpretation develops between patient and therapist.

Throughout history, dreams have been recorded.[80] Dreams have intrigued people as an omen of things to come,[81] as a source of divine revelation, as a means to gain insight into the soul of the dreamer,[82] as a special phenomena noted, used by novelists (Henry Fielding 1742),[83] and so on. While dreams do occur in many animal species, only man can relate his dreams. Ullman defined dreams as: " . . . creative and aesthetic experiences that depict in the form of visual metaphors the present state of our connections and disconnnections with the world about us."[84]

Freud stimulated the interest in dreams as a modern psychological phenomenon and as the royal road to the unconscious.[85] He viewed dreams as a creative force giving rise to knowledge inaccessible to the rational waking mind and built his concepts on his neurobiological model of the brain.[86] He used his dreams (disguised in his book, *The Interpretation of Dreams*, 1900) to analyze himself and he developed the groundwork for our knowledge about the inner world of dreams. Jung and his followers[87,88] added another dimension in dream interpretation.

Just over two decades ago, scientists found that they could record *physical data*, providing that people dream while asleep. They recorded rapid eye movements in individuals while they slept. These eye movements reflected the visual images created by the dreamer. Just like an electrocardiogram (EKG) records changes in the heart beat, so eye movements correlate with the changes in the electrical currents produced in the brain. Recent neurophysiological research suggests the possible structural (pontine physiological processes) and functional substrates of formal aspects of the dream process with " . . . a more direct route to their acquisition than anamnesis via free association, since dream origins are in basic physiological processes . . . less complex to their interpretation than conversion from manifest to latent content."[89,93]

Dreams have several important purposes. One is to allow the dreamer to feel refreshed on awakening — a reactive process designed to protect consciousness from the disruptive effect of disturbing unconscious wishes and affects; another function of dreams offer possible realistic solutions or options to current problems, personal or otherwise.[94] The structure of the dream reflects the individual's adjustment to his various levels of thought and feeling, e.g. a dream full of obstacles likely is indicative of creating problems of his everyday existence. The meaning of the dream can be compared to the orderly, unplanned events that reflect the changes in the dreamer's day to day life.[95]

The content of each dream is enriched when verbalized or contemplated by the dreamer, and, if decoded, can aid in problem solving.[96, 97] Dreams can offer *options*. The brain is the world's finest computer — its memory bank of stored information records all happenings from early infancy throughout the life-cycle. Thereby, in a problem to be solved, the individual can draw upon his accumulated experience (inputs). The possible options (output) are reproduced in visual images (print-outs) either in metaphors or symbols.[98]

The following vignettes from my dream book are examples of problem solving in dreams:

> A production engineer was baffled by a difficulty that had stopped an assembly line for two days. He had a dream that outlined the solution to the problem. He woke up and wrote the dream on a pad of paper and returned to sleep. When he woke up several hours later, he had no recollection of anything. Fortunately, he saw the scribbled note on his night table. As he read the note, he realized he had solved his production line problem in his dream.

Another patient's dream:

> A twenty-three year-old WW II hero described a dream that gave clues in understanding the cause of his panic over his forthcoming marriage. This dream occurred about two weeks after his first session. He was walking along a beach on an island in the Pacific when he found a beautiful white pearl. On examining it he found that the half that was buried in the sand was rough and imperfect.
>
> On reporting the dream he was puzzled and could not find any meaning to it. After a long pause he did recall some pearl earrings he purchased for his fiancee during his army days. However, these earrings had no special meaning. When I asked him what an imperfect pearl could mean to him, he thought about it for a long time. Then he blurted out a deep *forgotten secret:* when he was four years old his mother, who was Caucasian, divorced his father who was Oriental.

The dream of the "imperfect pearl" helped my patient focus on a very important current concern of his. In his sleeping hours, his mind was exploring his present conflict, the forthcoming marriage. He was worried that their first child may show some Oriental characteristics: What a potential shock for his bride who had no knowledge of his background. We worked on this problem and it was happily resolved.

Most people have trouble recalling and recounting their dreams. The following simple method may be helpful: keep a pad of paper and pencil at your bedside. Some people find it easier and quicker to use a tape-recorder. As an adjunct for awakening at your usual hour, set an alarm clock with a loud bell, if possible, as your dreams are fresh in your mind, the loud jarring of the alarm may help in remembering. Discourage anyone from talking to you for about 15 minutes and see whether you can recall your dream(s). Should you be awakened during the night by a dream or nightmare, immediately record it. Should your partner hear you mumbling, or if you are tossing or turning restlessly, he/she should awaken you to ask what you have been dreaming about. Since the dreamer usually will not remember awakening nor being awakened, he is surprised at hearing his dream.

In summary, dreams are a valuable diagnostic and therapeutic tool. The brain's complexity and computer-like processes encode every feeling, thought, and experience into a detailed memory bank system.

REFERENCES

1. Greenson, Ralph R.: *Explorations in Psychoanalysis.* New York, Int Univ Press, 1978.
2. Kernberg, Otto: Psychotherapy and psychoanalysis — final report of Meninger foundation's psychotherapy research project. *Bull Meninger Clin, 36:* 1-275, 1972.
3. Greene, Bernard L. and Solomon, Alfred P.: Marital disharmony — concurrent psychoanalytic therapy of husband and wife by the same psychiatrist — the triangular transference transactions. *Am J Psychotherapy, 17:* 443, 1963.
4. Greenson, *Explorations in Psychoanalysis.*
5. Schmiel, John L: Two alliances in the treatment of adolescents — towards a working alliance with parents and a therapeutic alliance with the adolescent. *J Am Acad Psychoanal, 2:* 243-53, 1973.
6. Riggs, Benjamin C.: Selective responsiveness and the ontogeny of the therapeutic alliance. *Am J Psychoanal, 32:* 74-84, 1972.
7. Miller, Jean B.: *Toward a New Psychology of Women.* Boston, Mass, Beacon Press, 1976.
8. Aring, Charles D.: Gentility and professionalism. *JAMA, 227:* 512, 1974.
9. Aring, Charles D.: Commentary — creativity requires nuture. *JAMA, 237:* 1205, 1977.
10. Farnsworth, Dana L.: Preparing for retirement. *Psychiatric Annals, 2:* 14-25, 1972.
11. Despert, J. Louise: *The Inner Voices of Children.* New York, Brunner-Mazel, 1975.
12. Jackman, Lawrence S.: Viewpoints — what are the best ways to overcome "spectatoring" during sexual relations. *Med Aspects Hum Sexuality, 11:* 34-40, 1977.
13. Travis, R. P. and Travis, P. Y.: Self-actualization in marital enrichment. *2:* 73-80, 1976.
14. Orthner, Dennis K.: Familia ludens: reinforcing the leisure component in family life. *Family Coordinator, 24:* 175-83, 1975.
15. Anshin, Roman: Creativity, mid-life crisis, and Herman Hesse. *J Am*

Acad Psychoanal, 4: 215-26, 1976.

16. Saul, Leon J.: A note on tension, creativity, and therapy. *J Am Acad Psychoanal, 3:* 277-91, 1975.

17. Carkhuff, Robert R. and Berenson, Bernard G.: *Beyond Counseling and Therapy,* 2nd ed. New York. Holt, Rinehart & Winston, 1977.

18. Erikson, Erik H.: *Intentity* (Youth and Crisis). New York, Norton, 1968, p. 74.

19. Framo, James L.: Family of origin as a therapeutic resource for adults in marital and family therapy — you can and should go home again. *Family Process, 15:* 193-210, 1976.

20. Martin, Peter: *A Marital Therapy Manual.* New York, Brunner-Mazel 1976, pp. 50-64.

21. Dixon, David N. and Sciara, Anthony D.: Effectiveness of group reciprocity counseling with married couples. *J Marr & Family Counseling, 3:* 77-83, 1977.

22. Watzlawick, P., Weakland, J., and Fisch, R. Change: *Principles of Problem Resolution.* New York, Norton, 1974, p. 73.

23. Weiss, R. L., Birchler, G. R., and Vincent, J. P.: Contractural models for negotiation training in marital dyads. *J Marr & Family, 36:* 321-30, 1974.

24. Salita, Matthew L.: Personal communication. Excerpts for court request for "Stipulation for Reconciliation". Complete copy may be obtained by writing to Attorney Matthew L. Salita, 69 W. Washington St., Chicago, Ill, 60602.

25. Sager, Clifford J.: *Marriage Contracts and Couple Therapy.* New York, Brunner-Mazel, 1976.

26. Bagarorozzi, Dennis A. and Wodarski, John S.: A social exchange typology of conjugal relationships and conflict development. *J Marr & Family Counseling, 3:* 53-60, 1977.

27. Abroms, Gene N.: Settings limits. *Arch Gen Psychiat, 19:* 113, 1968.

28. Napier, Augustus Y.: Beginning struggles with families. *J Marr & Family Counseling, 2:* 3-11, 1976.

29. Frey, Joseph, III, Holley, Judy, and L'Abate, Luciano: Intimacy is sharing hurt feelings — a comparison of three conflict resolution models. *J Marr & Family Therapy, 5:* 35-41, 1979.

30. Mace, David R.: Marital intimacy and the deadly love-anger cycle. *J Marr & Family Counseling, 2:* 131-37, 1976.

31. Saul, Leon J.: *Psychodynamically Based Psychotherapy.* New York, Jason Aronson, 1973.

32. Saul, Leon J. with Wrubel, Barbara: *The Psychodynamics of Hostility.* New York, Jason Aronson, 1976.

33. Charny, Israel: *Marital Love and Hate.* New York, Macmillan, 1972.

34. Greene, B. L.: Sequential marriage. In Rosenbaum, Salo and Alger, Ian (Eds.): *The Marriage Relationship.* New York, Basic Books, 1968.

35. Aldous, Joan: Intergenerational visiting patterns — variation in boundary maintenance as an explanation. *Family Process, 6:* 235, 1967.

36. Greene, Bernard L., Lee, Ronald R. et al.: Treatment of marital disharmony when one spouse has a primary affective disorder (manic-depressive illness) I. General overview — 100 couples, *J Marr & Family Counseling, 1:* 39-50, 1975.

37. Gene, R. and Boren, John J.: Specifiying criteria for completion of psychiatric treatment. *Arch Gen Psychiat, 24:* 446, 1971.

38. Alger, Ian and Hogan, Peter: The use of videotape recordings in conjoint marital therapy in private practice. Paper presented at the annual meeting of the AM Psychiat Assn, Atlantic City, May 1966.

39. Patterson, Gerald R, Hops, Hyman, and Weiss, Robert L.: Interpersonal skills training for couples in early stages of conflict. *J Marr & Family, 37:* 295-301, 1975.

40. Daitzman, Reid J.: Methods of self-confrontation in family therapy. *J Marr & Family Counseling, 3:* 3-9, 1977.

41. Kaslow, Florence: What personal photos reveal about marital sex and conflicts. *J Sex & Marital Therapy, 5:* 134-41, 1979.

42. Greene, B. L. et al.: Transient structured distance as a therapeutic activity in marital crises. Paper presented Aug 31, 1965, at the Seventh Western Divisional meeting, Amer Psychiatric Assn, Honolulu, Hawaii.

43. Greene, B. L.: Chairperson, panel on transient structured distance in management of marital disharmony, Newsletter — *Am Ortho-psychiatric Assn, 15:* 51-52, 1971.

44. Greene, B. L. et al.: Transient structured distance as a maneuver in marital therapy. *Family Coordinator, 22:* 15-22, 1973.

45. Greene, B. L. et al: Marital therapy when spouse has a primary affective disorder. *Am J Psychiat, 133:* 827-30, 1976.

46. Federation American Scientists, Public Interest Report. The role of GRIT. *30:* 4, 1977.

47. Martin, *A Marital Therapy Manual.*

48. Hight, Evelvn S.: A contractual, working separation — a step between resumption and or divorce. *J Divorce, 1:* 21-30, 1977.

49. Barcai, Avner and Rabkin, Leslie Y.: Excommunication as a family technique. *Arch Gen Psychiat, 27:* 804-8, 1872.

50. Martin, Peter A. and Bird, H. Waldo: The "love-sick" wife and the "cold-sick" husband. *Psychiatry, 22:* 246, 1959.

51. Soper, P. H. and L'Abate, L.: Paradox as a therapeutic technique — a review, *Int J Family Counseling, 5:* 10-21, 1977.

52. Greene et al., Transient structured distance as a therapeutic activity in marital crises.

53. Greene, B. L.: Five-year study conducted in 1965 at the Forest Hospital, a private psychiatric hospital, Des Plaines, Ill.

54. Greene, Transient structured distance in management of marital disharmony.

55. Martin, Peter A.: Obnoxiousness in psychiatric patients and others. *Psychiatric Digest,* August, 9-16, 1971.

56. Weissman, Myrna N, Klerman Gerald, and Paykel E. S.: Clinical

evaluation of hostility in depression. *Am J Psychiat, 128:* 261-66, 1971.

57. Greene et al., Transient structured distance as a maneuver in marital therapy.
58. Greene, et al., Marital therapy when spouse has a primary affective disorder.
59. Herrington, B. S.: Privilege denied in joint therapy. *Psychiatric News, 14:* 1, 9, 1979.
60. Alexander, Franz: The dynamics of psychotherapy in light of learning theory. *Am J Psychiat, 120:* 440, 1963.
61. Birk, Lee, Brinkley-Birk, Ann W.: Psychoanalysis and behavior therapy. *Am J Psychiat, 131:* 499-510, 1974.
62. Liberman, Robert P., Wheeler, Eugenie G., de Visser, Louis A. J. M., Kuehnel, Julie, and Kuehnel, Timothy: *Handbook of Marital Therapy* — a positive approach to helping troubled relationships. New York: Plenum Pub Corp., 1979.
63. Marmor, Judd and Woods, Sherwyn M. (Eds.): *The Interface between Psychodynamic and Behavioral Therapies.* New York, Plenum, 1979.
64. Braff, D. L., Raskin, M., and Geisinger, D.: Management of interpersonal issues in systematic desentization. *Am J Psychiat, 133:* 791-94, 1977.
65. Marks, Isaac M.: The current status of behavioral psychotherapy — theory and practice. *Am J Psychiat, 133:* 253-61, 1976.
66. Shapiro, Arthur K.: The behavior therapies: therapeutic breakthrough or latest fad? *Am J Psychiat, 133:* 1554-59, 1976.
67. Ferguson, J. M., Marquis, J. N., and Taylor, C. B.: A script for deep muscle relaxation. *Dis Nerv System, 38:* 703-8, 1977.
68. Wolpe, J. and Lazarus, A. A.: *Behavior Therapy Techniques.* London, Pergamon Press, 1966.
69. Brady, John P.: Psychotherapy, learning theory, and insight. *Arch Gen Psychiat, 16:* 304, 1967.
70. Stewart, Ralph H., Peters, Tom C., Marsh, Stephen, and Peters, Melinda J.: An object-relations approach to psychotherapy with marital couples, families, and children. *Family Process 14:* 161-78, 1975.
71. Greenspan, Stanley I. and Mannino, Fortune V.: A model for brief intervention with couples based on projective identification. *Am J Psychiat, 131:*1103-06, 1974.
72. Meissner, W. W.: Correlative aspects of introjective and projective mechanisms. *Am J Psychiat, 131:* 176-80, 1974.
73. Boss, Medard: *"I Dreamt Last Night . . . "* New York, Wiley, 1977.
74. Hall, James A.: *Clinical Uses of Dreams: Jungian Interpretations and Enactments.* New York, Grune, 1977.
75. Mattoon, Mary Ann: *Applied Dream Analysis,* New York: Wiley, 1978.
76. Mendel, Werner M.: Open end therapy with planned interruption. *J Operational Psychiat, 6:* 127, 1975.
77. Foulkes, David: *A Grammar of Dreams.* New York, Basic Books, 1979.
78. Greene, Bernard L.: *The Illustrative Dream Book: The Meaning of Dreams* (1977), to be published.

79. Fliess, R.: *Symbol, Dream, and Psychosis.* New York, Int Univ Press, 1973.
80. Kurland, Morton J.: Oneiromancy — an historic review of dream interpretation. *Am J Psychotherapy, 26:* 408-16, 1972.
81. Freud, Sigmund: Analysis terminable and interminable. In *Collected Papers,* London, Hogarth Press, 1950, Vol 5 pp. 322-23.
82. Marmor, Judd: Psychoanalytic therapy as an educational process. In Masserman. Jules (Ed.): *Science and Psychoanalysis.* New York, Grune, 1962, vol 4, pp. 286-99.
83. Fielding, Henry: *The Opposition. A Vision.* London, 1742, pp. 1-2.
84. Ullman, Montague: The transformation process in dreams. *Am Acad Psychoanal, 19:* 8-10, 1975.
85. Alexander, Franz: *The Western Mind in Transition.* New York, Random house, Inc., 1960, p 209.
86. McCarley, Robert W. and Hobson, J. Allan: The neurobiological origins of psychoanalytic dream theory. *Am J Psychiat, 134:* 1211-21, 1977.
87. Boss, *"I Dreamt Last Night. . . . "*
88. Hall, *Clinical Uses of Dreams.*
89. Hobson, J. Allan and McCarley, Robert W.: The brain as a dream state generator — an activation-synthesis hypothesis of the dream process. *Am J Psychiat, 134:* 1335-48, 1977.
90. Stone, Michael H: Dreams, free association, and the non-dominant hemisphere: an integration of psychoanalytical, neurophysiological, and historical data. *J Am Acad Psychoanal, 5:* 255-84, 1977.
91. Vogel, Gerald W.: An alternative view of the neurobiology of dreaming. *Am J Psychiat, 135:* 1531-35, 1978.
92. Labruzza, Anthony L.: Hypothesis of dreams — a theoretical note. *Am J Psychiat, 135:* 1536-38, 1978.
93. Ey, Henri, et al.: *Psychophysiologie du Sommeil et Psychiatrie.* Paris, France, Masson & Cie, 1975.
94. Palombo, Stanley R.: *Dreaming and Memory: A New Information-Processing Model.* New York, Basic Books, 1978.
95. Kramer, M., Hlasny, R., Jacobs, G. and Roth, T.: Do dreams have meaning? an empirical inquiry. *Am J Psychiat, 133:* 778-81, 1976.
96. Altman, Leon L.: *The Dream in Psychoanalysis.* revised ed., New York, Int Univ Press, 1975.
97. Masserman, Jules (Ed.): *Dream Dynamics,* Vol XIX. New York, Grune, 1971.
98. Greene, *Illustrative Dream Book.*

Chapter XXII

CRISIS THERAPY
A CUSTOM-TAILORED APPROACH

CRISIS therapy differs from other techniques in that the *current problem* of the individual or social unit is the focus of effective short-term treatment. Schneidman succinctly defines crisis therapy as a technique that is: ". . . oriented toward a limited goal, that of restoring the crisis bearer to his previous level of coping."[1] Currently, the focus is not on the stress, but how the individual copes with the psychosocial stressors, e.g. disturbed family members or dyadic problems, loss of an object or situation — death, divorce, separation, child (ren) and life style as a result in divorce.[2] In depressive symptomology, there is a complex interrelation between stress and coping resources.[3]

As a psychiatrist, psychoanalyst, and behavioral scientist, I still find psychoanalytic concepts[4] most helpful when combined with the figure-field configuration as the unit of focal treatment stressing the adaptive processes of coping with a crisis. Stress[5,6] creates effective motivation for change. Since all therapists see many couples in a crisis problem, a review of the pertinent literature may be of value. Erik Erikson,[7] using Freudian concepts, developed a theory of psychosocial development based on the gradual unfolding of the personality through phase-specific crises; precipitated by both environmental and societal pressures and the person's readiness and capacity to deal with these forces. Otto Pollak[8] extended the theories of Freud, Erikson, Hartmann, and others[9] and presented a valuable framework in dealing with the family. Neo-Freudians, especially Sandor Rado,[10] have differentiated between the adaptive process of *coping* with a crisis and *defensive* Freudian *mechansims* as crystallized by Anna Freud[11] in her classic monograph.

The psychic activities of the adaptive process has been defined as coping behavior and consist of all the strategies utilized by a person to deal with a current threat to his psychosocial stability. Thus coping is a universal and more inclusive name than defense and not associated with the negative implications of the term defense. The important differentiation between coping and defense is that there are adaptive phenomena which serve no defensive purpose. On the other hand, the psychoanalytic usage of the term defense generally connotes two func-

293

tions: (1) restraining and containing the instinctual drives of the id and (2) serving adaptation to the environment. Freud would certainly have been interested in and perhaps incorporated into his writings recent information from ethology, e.g. imprinting, which pointed out the interrelationships between learning and instinct.

The adaptive process of coping behavior is a reaction to a crisis and consists of intrapersonal defensive responses, which protect the person from disruptive levels of anxiety, as objectively evaluated from the degree of comfort shown by the individual and defensive responses directed either toward the interpersonal or environmental systems and judged for effectiveness in social terms. The relationship between the intrapersonal defensive aspects of coping and the total coping process is a very intimate mixture. Thus, if the relationship is a constructive one, the individual can freely focus on the current crisis. On the other hand, if the intrapersonal defensive responses are inadequate, the individual will be overwhelmed with anxiety. Another destructive relationship occurs when the adaptive coping defenses become so distracting to the individual that he is unable to concentrate effectively on his external problem. Thus, coping maneuvers can be scaled on a continuum with an indeterminate range of defensive strength in the center that permits optimum coping, whereas deviations at either end of this continuum would have unfavorable effects.

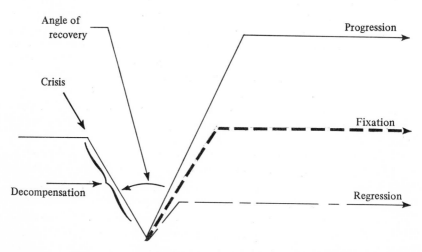

Figure 15. Adjustment to a crisis (after Ruben Hill).

I have found Reuben Hill's[12] truncated form of a roller coaster very useful in explaining the adjustment to a crisis; each crisis results in disintegration with the usual phases of recovery and reintegration. I have modified his profile to include three levels of reorganization: regression, fixation, or progression. The angle of recovery model has been very useful clinically when patients complain of impatience (see fig. 15). The concept of crisis resolution, as formulated by Gerald Caplan[13] and presented by Lydia Rapoport,[14] involves "correct cognitive perception" of the problem, and "management of affect" through awareness of feelings and their discharge, and development of patterns of seeking and using help" that is action oriented. Erikson's[15] theory of psychosocial development describes the relationship of the individual to the interpersonal and environmental systems and the functions of the ego in the intrapersonal system with respect to the individual's adaptive processes. He examines so-called growth crises through phase-specific stages in the individual's development of interpersonal relationships. Erikson, influenced by his psychoanalytic background, correlates the psychosocial crises of various ages with the particular psychosexual problems of the stages of instinctual development. He states that each individual solves the problem of adaptation in his own unique way. For example, in infancy, the psychosexual adaptive problems center on the oral zone and the incorporative function; its resolution confronts the infant with the dilemma of trust versus mistrust in relation to the mother. The problem of trust versus mistrust, in Erikson's theory of psychosocial development, represents a universal adaptive crisis. According to Erikson, each individual develops through an unique innate maturational design. He has extended the study of the adaptive processes beyond the early and adolescent stages of development to encompass the entire human life cycle.

While psychoanalysis clarifies the limits of the individual's adaptive potential at different phases of psychosexual development, the theories of adaptation help to comprehend the impact of the interpersonal and environmental systems on the developing psyche. Erikson suggested a mutuality and "cogwheeling" between generations, e.g. the sense of mutuality that develops between mother and child. The mother and child each exercise adaptive functions in relation to one another, specific to the needs of each at his phase-specific crisis in his respective life cycle. Thus the generations are cogwheeled together because of their mutual needs. The concept of autonomous ego functions elaborated by Hartmann and his co-workers[16] is related to Erikson's thesis of particular modes of functioning. He describes how a characteristic function of a specific body zone becomes separated from that zone and then functions autonomously. For example, the process of incorporation is originally oral, but the infant gradually, as a result of interpersonal and environmental influences, soon "takes in" in other symbolic manners. This change in the function in incorporation and response to multiple external influences results in variation in cultural patterns and resultant diversity in dyadic relationships.

Maturational crises are experienced by all individuals as part of the life cycle. These crises are characterized by expectable behavioral, cognitive, and affectional reactions. For example, the normal hostile, competitive reactions of the child to the parent of the same sex, the complex biopsychosocial reactions at puberty, the "stormy decade of adolescence," and "getting married phase," and so on, all represent maturational crises that must be mastered before the individual can proceed for further development. On the other hand, the differentiation between maturational and situational crises at times is difficult. Thus the mourning process following death, desertion, or divorce represent situational crises, and puberty constitutes a maturational crisis; but the birth of the first child has both maturational and situational elements. The combined impact of a situational crisis superimposed on a maturational crisis can often result in a major crisis: for example, where the birth of the first child was the beginning of alcoholism in the father. I have found the studies of Rhona Rapoport[17] on the "critical transition points in the *normal, expectable* development of the family life cycle" of great value.

Finally, in understanding the maturational and situational crises in dyadic relationships, the hypotheses of Otto Pollak (see Chapter II) are valuable in dealing with pair-coupling discord. His characterization gives equal attention to the perceptual principle of figure (intrapersonal system) and to the patient's background (interpersonal and environmental systems). Thus, he is fully aware of the psychodynamics of intrapsychic conflict, unconscious motivation and ambivalence as well as interpersonal and environmental influences of transactional patterns, group processes, and social roles involved in social change. Each dyadic relationship goes through various phases in its life cycle with differences in "life tasks" (crises) at each phase, e.g. the first phase reflects the effort of the pair-coupling to form a new system distinct from their background families. Each phase is separated from another by a *crisis* of transition in which the function of the partners is that of mutual assistance. Failing to assist one another leads to disharmony:[18-20] however, coping with the crisis can lead to personal growth, which Gerald Caplan recognizes as the strategic meaning of the crisis during developmental phases.[21] The earlier the individual, couple, or family are seen, the more likely therapy can be brief and constructive.[22]

Indications for dyadic crisis therapy include the following: minimal disharmony readily treated by supportive psychotherapy; inability of the couple to use any form of therapy due to intellectual or cultural factors; a relationship so chaotic that active environmental interventions are the only therapeutic alternative; and where intensive therapy could precipitate a severe psychiatric disorder in one of the partners.

The *contraindications* for crisis therapy include the following: a *durable incompatible* relationship (see Chapter XXI) where an attempt to change the equilibrium could precipitate a psychosis in either or both partners; an *intermittent incompatibility* in the relationship due to primary affective disorder in one of the individuals rather than a reaction to the relationship (see Chapter XXI); a relationship where one of the partners is agreeing to therapy to rationalize a wish for separation and/or divorce — in this case the therapy is a form of rationalization to falsely establish an inability to be helped therapeutically; a partner describing acting-out behavior which requires other therapeutic approaches; and, escalating hostility and/or individual objectives which the therapist interprets as an indication for referral to another therapist.

This chapter's data reflects 375 couples who had crisis therapy as an approach (see Table I). The changing picture of the nuclear and extended family in our culture demands an even greater *personally tailored approach* to pair-couplings, since many couples are now living together, but are not married. Another recent professional change is the use of *therapy* instead of *counseling*. Until recently, most individuals have been frightened by the stigma of professional therapy; it had been easier to go to a "counselor."

The transition of therapeutic orientation has included many professional contributors. A pioneer in marital interventions is Emily Mudd who established the Marriage Council of Philadelphia* four decades ago. This organization became a model for the rest of the country. In 1965, she prophesized that "... the methods and techniques of Marriage Counseling ... are being challenged by new knowledge from

---

*A nonprofit community organization affiliated with the University of Pennsylvania, School of Medicine, Department of Psychiatry, Division of Family Study, whose chairman is now Doctor Harold I. Lief.

the social sciences, from biology, and from dynamic psychology."[23] Clinical experience over the past ten years has, in fact, produced change in therapeutic approaches.[24] In the early 1970s, the pioneer pastoral counselor Rev. Carroll A. Wise† dropped the title *counselor* and referred to himself and his co-workers as therapists. On the other hand, Ard (1975) wrote what he and some counselors believed, that ". . . a fine-line distinction between counseling and psychotherapy is admittedly difficult if not impossible to draw."[25] In 1979, the members of the American Association of Marriage and Family Counselors officially changed their name to the American Association for Marriage and Family Therapy to express more accurately the *professional* function they perform. *Counselors* should label only those sales-oriented nonprofessionals who give advice in the process of mutual exchange of ideas and opinions.

Crisis therapy is for therapists and includes all the basic elements that Mudd and Goodwin[26] described fifteen years ago plus new ones derived from other disciples. They state: "It is an (ongoing) art, in which a *professionally* (italics added) trained person has acquired basic knowledge, attitudes, and skills, which he (she) has integrated in a disciplined capacity to apply himself *therapeutically* (italics added) within the immediate experience of the interview." The goal of crisis therapy is to help the individual(s) or families cope with the acute crisis, whether the "identified patient" is the individual, couple, or family. In treatment, all elements of the three systems of the GST are taken into consideration. A recent innovation is the creation of crisis interventions in the emergency rooms of general hospitals of a medico-psychosocial team.[27, 28] Therapy is limited to helping the patient and significant others[29] cope with the crisis alone so that once the crisis is resolved, therapy is terminated. If the individual(s) want more intensive therapy, obviously this should be forthcoming, but the technique is no longer that of crisis intervention. A number of articles and books are of value in doing this approach.[30-37] The following vignette is illustrative of crisis therapy:

> Ms. A, a thirty-year-old Caucasian, was seen in an acute crisis characterized by moderate depression which suicidal thoughts. She was seen twice weekly in double sessions. Therapy lasted one month. A college graduate with a degree in business administration, she was employed shortly after getting her degree and was already advanced to an executive position. Previous to this crisis, she felt herself well adjusted, active in sports, politics, and had many friends. On a recent

---

†Wise, Carroll A.: The founder of the American Assn of Pastoral Counselors. In his latest book, he preferred the term therapist instead of counselor for pastors providing such services.

trip, she had met a man, quite older, very athletic, a professional in the medical field, and not only handsome, but a perfect gentleman. They soon became close friends and since he worked near her place of employment, what started out meeting for lunch, soon led to consistent dating.

Ms. A. spoke nervously about how she had pursued this relationship clandestinely, since her friend was Korean.

She assumed her family and his would object to their decision to marry. After they deliberated for some time, they told their respective families. It was shortly afterward she became depressed. Since both families had reconciled themselves to the marriage, she was at a loss to understand her depression.

As an only child, she had always been the favorite of both her family and relatives. Her evaluative sessions were relatively normal and typical for one of her background. A "working alliance" was quickly established and she was told to keep a diary of her dreams.

By the sixth clinical session, her depression had lifted and she brought in her first dream:

My Mother and I are at a restaurant in France. A very nice Korean man and his girlfriend approach us. He suddenly kisses me upon the cheek and tugs at my arm to have me join his table. His girlfriend laughs nervously. I am aware it's very nice of him, but somehow I feel it is not right."

My patient laughs nervously and after a long pause stated that she felt uncomfortable in her dream. It has bothered her, too, after she had awakened that morning, especially by the look of disapproval on her mother's face in that dream. Even the people at a nearby table had looked haughtily at her. I asked her if she could be *both* girls in that dream: is she feeling any nervousness like the other girl in the dream? As she continued to associate feelings and thoughts about the dream, she finally mentioned some ambivalence about her forthcoming marriage. Here she was in a quandry to know why . . . she had readily adopted her parents' liberal political and racial attitudes from childhood, so why she occasionally felt this funny pit in her stomach while discussing the marriage arrangements (she was at a loss to comprehend this physical response). She did add, as an after thought, that she had no acquaintances who had ever dated and then entered into an interracial marriage.

At the next therapy session, she was still in an anxious mental state and related her dream from the previous night:

She is on a Carribean cruise with many other women. All the women are happily planning the day's excursions: looking at advertisements, maps, etc. She is alone, however, and feeling very 'left out and empty.'

Ms. A freely associated about this dream and spoke of the recent feelings of rejection she had since none of her relatives or friends have called for any social gatherings; she showed signs of depression as she told how horrid it would be if none of these people ever called her again.

At the following week's session, she described another dream. In this one she was *hiding* in a decrepit apartment with her fiancé. She felt confused in this dream and wondered why people looked at them so haughtily as she and her future husband made their way through the crowd and into the Opera House. I pointed out that she was concerned that her future involved living furtively and clandestinely while "always *hiding* their marriage." She left this session pondering the ramifications of her upcoming marriage.

During this time of therapeutic treatment, the patient's depression gradually lifted and two weeks before termination of therapy she brought in a dream that had shocked her and which she had been reluctant to relate. It was a nightmare and she woke up screaming.

"I was in a hospital about to deliver my baby. The delivery began and was most painful and difficult. The doctors and nurses were efficient, but impersonal. I finally deliver my baby and when I finally see it, I am shocked — it is oriental looking!"

Ms. A added, "I was terribly frightened and shocked. Just before I came to see you I had many thoughts about what would our first child be: white or oriental. I have not been able to tell you about this before, doctor. I am really concerned about the possibility of an oriental baby! I would be a shocker for me and my family and friends. I can fight the world for what I believe in — that all people are created equal — but bringing a child into my prejudiced peer group and current society just isn't fair. I would despair if my child would be avoided or made the brunt of hostile comments, and I could never think of marriage without having children. Perhaps this is the cause of all my current problems. I cannot even hurt a fly, let alone see a child belittled. I know how *mean and nasty* classmates can be — I was part of a small religious minority in my youth and picked upon at school . . . it was horrible. I suppose I see no alternative but to call off the marriage. I know he will be very hurt — he is such a wonderful person. You name it — an important asset to his community, highly respected, handsome. In reality, our relationship is out of step with society's views. I do not live in a utopia, but acknowledge that my world is filled with bigoted and hedonistic people. I *know* now the reason for my depression: I am furious at the injustice of it all. I realize, doctor, that you talked of my 'anger' but I denied it existence. It now makes sense, as you were trying to point out, that my anger was real and instead of my acknowledging it and voicing it outwardly, I turned it inwardly and my dreams punished me and yet finally offered solutions too. . . ."

The patient had several more sessions, but no symptoms of depression reoccurred. She reached a decision to terminate therapy and informed me that she had ended her engagement.

In conclusion, emergency care, crisis therapy, and short-term psychodynamic therapy represent different points on a spectrum of brief therapies. Thus, emergency care involves *immediate* relief to an individual who has decompensated because of internal or external stresses with maladaptive coping behaviors. Crisis custom-tailored therapy is directed to the individual(s) who is in *danger of decompensating* and is coping inadequately. In short-term dynamic therapy, the goal is primarily on coping abilities and only secondarily on alleviating stress.

REFERENCES

1. Schneidman, E.: Crisis intervention — some thoughts and perspectives. In Specter, G. A. and Clairborn, W. L. (Eds.): *Crisis Intervention*, Vol II. New York, D C Heath, 1973.
2. Puryear, Douglas A.: *Helping People in Crisis*. San Francisco, CA, Jossey-Bass, 1979.
3. Warheit, George J.: Life events, coping, stress, and depressive symptomology. *Am J Psychiat, 136:* 502-07, 1979.
4. Jahoda, Marie: *Freud and the Dilemmas of Psychology*. New York, Basic Books, 1977.
5. Kansas, Nick, Kaltreider, Nancy, and Horowitz, Mardi: Repsonse to catastrophe: a case study. *Dis Nerv System, 38:* 625-27, 1977.
6. Selig, Andrew L.: Crisis and family growth. *Family Coordinator, 25:* 291-95, 1976.
7. Erikson, Erik H.: Identity and the life cycle. *Pscholo Issues, 1:* 1, 1959.
8. Pollak, Otto: Sociological and psychoanalytic concepts in family diagnosis. In Greene, B. L., (Ed.): *Psychotherapies of Marital Disharmony*. New York, MacMillan, 1965, pp. 15-26.
9. Hartman, Heinz and Kris, Ernest: The genetic approach in psychoanalysis. *Psychoanal Study Child, 1:* 11, 1945.
10. Heath, Robert G.: Applications of Sandor Rado's adaptational psychodynamic formulations to brain physiology. *J Am Acad Psychoanal, 2:* 19-25, 1974.
11. Freud, Anna: *The Ego and the Mechanisms of Defense*. London, Hogarth Press, 1937.
12. Hill, Reuben: Generic features of families under stress. In Parad, Howard J. (Ed.): *Intervention: Selected Readings*. New York Family Service Association of America, 1965, pp. 32-52.
13. Caplan, Gerald: Patterns of parental response to the crisis of premature birth. *Psychiatry, 23:* 365, 1960.
14. Rapoport, Lydia: The state of crisis: Some Theoretical Considerations. In Parad, Howard J. (Ed.): *Crisis Intervention: Selected Readings*. New York, Family Service Association of America, 1965, pp. 22-31.
15. Erikson, Identity and the life cycle.
16. Hartman and Kris, The genetic approach in psychoanalysis.

17. Rapoport, Rhona: Normal crises, family structure, and mental health. *Family Process, 2:* 68, 1963.

18. Manderscheid, Ronald W., Silbergeld, Sam and Dager, Edward Z.: Alienation — a response to stress. *J Cybernetics, 5:* 91-105, 1975.

19. Lipman-Blumen, Jean: A crisis framework applied to macro-sociological family changes: marriage, divorce, and occupational trends associated with World War II, *J Marr & Family, 37:* 889-902, 1975.

20. Hirschowitz, Ralph G.: Crisis theory: a formulation. *Psychiatric Annals, 3:* 36-47, 1973.

21. Caplan, Gerald, *An Approach to Community Mental Health.* New York: Grune, 1961, pp. 18-20

22. Silverman, D. C.: Sharing the crisis of rape — counseling the mates and families of victims. *Am J Orthopsychiat, 48;* 166-73, 1978.

23. Mudd, Emily H. and Goodwin, Hilda M.: Counseling couples in conflicted marriages. In Greene, B. L. (Ed.): *The Psychotherapies of Marital Disharmony.* New York, MacMillan, 1965.

24. Langsley, Donald G. and Kaplan, D. M.: *The Treatment of Families in Crises.* New York, Grune & Stratton, 1968.

25. Ard, Ben N. Jr.,: *Counseling and Psychotherapy. Classic on Therories and Issues,* revised edition. Palo Alto, CA, 1975.

26. Mudd, and Goodwin, Counseling couples in conflicted marriages.

27. Gerson, Samuel and Bassuk, Ellen: Psychiatric emergies — an overview. *Am J Psychiat, 137:* 1-11, 1980.

28. Bartolucci, Giampiero and Drayer, Calvin S.: An overview of crisis intervention in the emergency rooms of general hospitals. *Am J Psychiat, 130:* 953-60, 1973.

29. Holmstrom, Lynda L. and Burgess, Wolbert: Rape — the husband's and boyfriend initial reactions. *Family Coordinator, 28:* 321-30, 1979.

30. Marmor, Judd: Short-term dynamic psychotherapy, *Am J Psychiat, 136:* 149-155, 1979.

31. Lieberman, Morton A., Borman, Leonard D., and Associates. *Self-help Groups for Coping with Crisis* San Francisco, CA, Jossey-Bass, 1979.

32. Ewing, Charles P.: *Crisis Intervention as Psychotherapy.* New York, Oxford Univ Press, 1978.

33. Flegenheimer, Walter V.: The patient-therapist relationship in crisis intervention. *J Clin Psychiat, 39:* 348-50, 1978.

34. Silbergeld, Sam, Manderscheid, Ronald W. and Koenig, Gail R.: Evaluation of brief intervention models by the Hill interaction matrix. *Small Group Behavior, 8:* 281-302, 1977.

35. Enelow, Allen J.: *Elements of Psychotherapy.* New York, Oxford Univ Press, 1977.

36. Bellak, Leopold and Small, Leonard: *Emergency Psychotherapy and Brief Psychotherapy,* 2nd ed., New York, Grune, 1977.

37. McCombie, Sharon L., Bassuk, Ellen, and Savitz, Roberta: Development of a medical center rape crisis intervention, *Am J Psychiat, 133:* 418-21, 1976.

Chapter XXIII

THE CLASSIC TECHNIQUE IN DYADIC DISHARMONY

THE classic approach in dyadic discord consists of a dyadic one-to-one therapeutic relationship between the patient and therapist. In this type of treatment, the therapists of each partner *do not communicate.* Thus, confidentiality of all transactions between therapists and patient is crucial. In the past, some analysts, including Giovacchini,[1] expressed considerable concern abouat the "complications" of multiple-oriented therapy vis-à-vis individual psychonanalytic psychotherapy, but this criticism has not stood the test of time.[2-5] My clinical experience reveals that when one partner is seen, the other partner, although not present, "shadows" the therapy, just as the therapist shadows[6] the couple-relationship. It is a myth to think that confidentiality of the classic one-to-one is *sine qua non* for therapeutic depth,[7] because the nontreated partner indirectly knows what is being dealt with in therapy and usually chooses consciously to suppress the knowledge or unconsciously to repress it. However, for pragmatic purposes, confidentiality is insisted upon. I used the classic approach in 10 percent of the couples (135) and in 15 percent of the crisis therapy patients. This approach is applicable to only a small proportion of dyadic disharmony.

The insights provided by a thorough grasp of psychodynamic concepts are an essential ingredient for a therapist.[8] Basic psychoanalytic principles include the role of the unconscious, transference phenomena, repression, and the unconscious adaptive-coping mechanisms of defense used in dealing with anxiety, conflict, and unacceptable feelings. As a student of Franz Alexander and Thomas French,[9] and many other neo-Freudian analysts,[10-13] I see no conceptual criteria for differentiating between psychoanalysis and psychoanalytic psychotherapy, even though some analysts still do.[14] I treat some patients in the classic couch position, three to four sessions per week, using free association and a regressive transference neurosis, which is resolved through interpretation. I agree with Guntrip, who suggests a nondeterministic, nonpositivistic, teleological theory of understanding of the psychodynamic phenomena of individuals as these persons function in relationships.[15] I use interpretations oriented to understanding

303

current conflicts from which extrapolation to the past may or may not be possible. Marmor,[16] in a scholarly article (1979), traces the historical background of short-term psychodynamic psychotherapies and presents a synthesis of contemporary views.

In the classic approach, confidentiality of all information is explicitly stated at the outset of treatment with three exceptions: written permission from the patient to release information, self-destructive thoughts or behavior that necessitates the involvement of "significant others" in dealing with this life threatening situation, and potential homicidal thoughts or behavior towards others. A tactful way to manage a request about a patient is to reply: "I will be willing to, but I will have to get permission from my patient first. I suggest that you discuss this with my patient first." This usually stops further attempts, but, if the patient agrees, then my position is to obtain written permission first. To avoid any misunderstandings later, I have a session with the patient and the individual who requested the information. Where a patient has potential suicidal thoughts or has made a suicide attempt, the involvment of "significant others(s)" does not require the permission of the patient as this has been stated in the original therapeutic contract. The question of potential homocide, because of the recent "Tarasoff" decision by the California State Supreme court, makes it mandatory, where indicated, that the threatened individual(s) be notified and/or proper legal authorities (see Chapter XXVIII).

The question is often raised as to what criteria exists for selecting individual or multiperson approaches. In the classic approach, therapy is focused on the problems of the individual within himself or in his relationship to the world outside himself. The focus is on individual psychodynamics with the relationship as the backdrop. How patterns of behavior develop receives selective focus over how partners react to these patterns. The indications for the classic approach include the following:

1. Therapist's knowledge of acting-out behavior by one partner, but the other partner is unaware, e.g. continuous infidelity or homosexuality. If the unsuspecting partner confronts the therapist with the "secret," premature discussion of the "secret" could disrupt the partnership.
2. Personal preference of one or both partners.
3. An emotional immaturity exists in one partner that precludes sharing the therapist.
4. One partner feels that he has to work out the problem his own way irrespective of the consequences of his partner.

5. Where it is evident that the couple have widely differing goals in terms of their problem.
6. Failure of previous techniques to reequilibrate the dyadic disharmony.
7. When the disharmony is due primarily to severe nonpsychotic psychopathology in one partner, e.g. phobias, obsessions, or complusions which require Wolpian systematic desensitization.[17, 18] (The Birks'[19] have integrated psychoanalytic psychotherapy with behavior therapy to form a complementary system.)

The contraindication to the classic approach in dyadic disharmony is when one partner has a moderate to severe paranoid reaction of being "told on" or being influenced by the other partner. This suspicious behavior leads to repeated questioning as to what went on in the individual's session and frequent distortion. This type of situation is handled best in the triadic clinical setting.

The following clinical vignettes illustrate indications for the classic approach in dyadic disharmony:

1. *Where the male is bisexual and his partner is unaware of his behavior:*

> Mr. and Mrs. F were referred for therapy by Mrs. F's parents who were former patients of mine. Mrs. F stated that for the past six months their marriage had been deteriorating, and, unless something was done, she wanted a divorce. Her husband had insisted on one night a week out with no questions asked. She suspected another woman was involved, although this was only a vague possibility since they were very compatible sexually.
>
> Mr. F when seen in an individual session, stated that he loved his wife and children but that she did not understand him. Also, during his freshman year at college he had a homosexual relationship. After he met his wife, he was able to discontinue this behavior. Their courtship was smooth and wonderful and with excellent premarital sex. About a year ago, following an important promotion, he became extremely anxious. He found relief by seeking out transient homosexual partners. Then he met Bob and a different type of relationship began. Bob opened up a new world of music, art, ballet, and so on. On the other hand, he realized that he was not cut out for the "gay world" and wanted to discontinue the relationship with Bob, but he could not, although the relationship was no longer sexual but intellectual. His wife knew nothing about his behavior. He loved his wife and wanted to save his marriage.
>
> Mr. F, was started on intensive therapy, receiving a total of 450 hours over the next three years — a classic analysis with therapy three times per week on the couch. A good marriage followed.

I prefer to treat both partners where there is no "family secret" that the partners know of either the homosexuality or bisexuality.

2. *Where one or both partners express preference for separate therapists:*

> The Bs came for therapy at the request of their minister. In the first individual diagnostic session, Mr. B stated: "My basis complaint is that Alice is selfish and self-centered to the point of excluding everyone. Her basic orientation is "me first" without any regard for the needs or feelings of me or anyone else. Our marriage has been marked by five years of Alice's inability to be concerned over anyone or anything but herself. During these first two years, when I began my practice, she suffered and was forced to do a good deal for me because of the demands on my time and no money. Even then it was forced and strained, and this too took its toll. In the past two years, since she started psychotherapy, she has been more bitchy and nasty. Her self-centered attitude manifests itself in many different ways, especially as she is always a little bit sick, and so, spends 90 percent of her time in bed reading or watching TV or eating. Her 'migraine headache' is common as long as there is nothing Alice wants to do. Finally, I am very angry about our infrequent sex."
>
> Mrs. B was cooperative during her interviews, but appeared bored and annoyed. Her main complaints centered on her sexual dissatisfaction with her husband. Also, that he did not meet her emotional needs. "There is no meeting of the minds. There used to be. Now there is a lack of communication and no sharing of interests. Things we had in common before marriage, no longer exists. Sexually, I am dissatisfied. I have structured things so that there is no pleasure on my part in the act. At times I am close to being repelled by him and, at times, completely frigid. There has always been a sexual problem in our marriage.
>
> The CDD was so stormy that I suggest a "star boarder arrangement" (TSD) to lower the level of hostility between the couple. I also suggested a three-month trial of conjoint therapy.
>
> Mr. B appeared alone at the next session. He stated: "After you made the suggestion of "star boarder" routine, Alice's reaction was marked when we got home. What a game of "Uproar." She got more depressed and disabled. She spent the next four days in bed and finally phoned her former therapist and returned to him. She felt that you wouldn't be objective and would side with me. She laced into you as being a 'cold fish.' She asked me to tell you that she prefers her own therapist."

3. *Where an emotional immaturity in a partner precludes sharing the therapist:*

> The Cs' were referred by a friend. Mrs. C, a petite blonde, had met

her husband at work where he was a junior executive. She was in her early twenties, he was ten years her senior, also the boss' son. In her individual diagnostic session she gave the following information. "I can't come during intercourse. Nothing is wrong with me physically. I get to a cerain point, and it stops. I've been refusing my husband sexually. We've talked about it often. In all other areas we get along fabulously, but I dread going to bed. We've been married nine months. Last night I dreamt that our minister was telling me to go ahead and have intercourse. Our minister is like a second father to me. I woke my husband and we tried so hard, but it was frustrating." She also said, that she is an only child. Her parents are happily married. Her father is "very wonderful and I am very dependent on him. I am very close to him. He was against my marriage. I guess he just didn't want to lose a daughter." She described her mother as "warm and affectionate, but I never thought she understood me. She never explained the facts of life to me. Both parents are very religious. Sex is taboo in my house. You don't talk about your menstrual period in the home. She never wanted me to shave my legs or use deodorant.

When I was twenty-one I went to work. I noticed this tall man. I was told he was the boss' son. He was handsome, well built and I fell for him from the beginning. I've always liked older men, but not that old. Imagine my surprise when he asked for a date. Our parents knew each other. We dated a lot and he was always a gentleman. He danced like a dream. After some time we decided we were in love and decided to marry. We had much in common, good music and the same kind of music, and even the same kind of food."

Mr. C, at his first interview presented the same picture that his wife described. He was a serious male, very much in love with his wife, and completely at a loss to understand his wife's reaction to sex: "She has a certain tenseness and fear, the anticipation of the climax; what to expect. She reaches a certain point and automatically wants to stop. We have only had one good sexual experience since our marriage. She feels that she can't function as a woman, and that she is really not a woman unless she reaches and has a climax. Her father is a rather domineering man, but very personable. I cannot get close to either of her parents. Aloof. I never felt they approved of our relationship, which they didn't. We were seriously considering eloping. I had asked his permission to marry his daughter, and he felt I was too old for her. Some time shortly after that she and they had a big discussion. It ended that she hadn't communicated about what she wanted. Everyone cried and it was accepted. We get along pretty well now."

In the CDD it was obvious that Mr. C was very protective toward his wife. She acted like a little girl throughout the session. At one point she attempted to set up a coalition with the therapist and tried to exclude her husband. Mr. C appeared fairly well adjusted. I suggested treatment for Mrs. C only, and said I would call Mr. C later if the need arises.

Mrs. C began her second session by commenting: "I don't really understand it. Before we were married I really wanted sex, but on our wedding night I said: 'Let's go at it slowly.' We have had sex once since our visit with you three weeks ago. I had a little more reaction. When I had my premarital examination, the doctor was unable to put the speculum in because I was so tensed up.

"I wonder how my father would feel if he were to find that I am going for psychotherapy because I was so tied to his apron strings. I feel guilty that I am taking the 'pill.' Mother told me 'Don't try to prevent pregnancy.' I've kept a lot of things from them, my smoking. Father was always worried about who I would marry. I would always be too young to marry if Father had his way. I've always enjoyed dancing with Father, he is a fabulous dancer."

In the next session, Mrs. C continued to talk about her close relationship with her parents: "Father and Mother have called me a great deal recently because of the weather. He would never let me drive when there was snow. Mother doesn't drive. She really gives me to my father or my father to me. I really don't know how to state it."

I comment: "Perhaps his closeness to you has encouraged you not to give him up?"

"I dont't want to give him up. Does that sound terrible. Mother will still say to me after we visit them that it is so hard to see you go away with Jack and not coming home. We have a very close family. In some ways I'm quite a child and soon to be twenty-three. I have to cut out seeing them as often, like three times a week."

In the following six sessions, her dreams and associations dealt with feelings about her father plus a new theme — her fear of losing control of her feelings, e.g. in a dream everyone in the neighborhood went psychotic. She was the only one who was calm.

When asked, what psychotic could symbolize, she replied: "Letting go completely, not in control. I really remain quite calm during the whole sexual act. I hold back in every area."

In her twelfth session, she reported having sex for the first time in a month: We had sex last night. I was pleased with myself that I did it, for Jack's sake. It hurt something fierce, but I told him to continue. I feel suddenly I am taking my marriage seriously."

In her fourteenth session, three months after starting therapy, Mrs. C related the following dream: "Jack and a friend organizing some kind of a dance. We invited all kinds of couples and they came. Jack and a friend were to teach the dance. The couples formed a circle. Then I am on a real high stool, but I was scared because I couldn't figure how to get down. Then some giant came along and helped me down. I woke up scared. I couldn't figure how I would get down from the stool. This giant helped me.

"I could remember the sensation going down. You and my husband are organizing my life. The dance represents something a couple do, that two people do, sex? When I sat on the real high stool, I thought of a dunce's stool."

When I asked her how a little girl views her father, she replied: "Like a giant. I felt a sensation of an elevator coming down too fast. Like butterflies in the stomach. The feeling was real. I remembered the feeling when I awoke."

When asked what problem she was trying to solve in the dream, she replied: "Being a woman and trying to join the circle of couples. I don't want to see my husband as a father. For if I do, I will never grow up and will keep sitting on the dunce's stool."

In the next two months Mrs. C reported increasing sexual tension, more frequent sex with her husband that she would occasionally initiate, and awareness of some pleasure in the act itself. Concomitant with her increased sexual behavior were dreams expressing fears of becoming promiscuous and erotic transference phenomena toward me, disguised in her dreams as reacting to her gynecologist. Upon a return from a vacation, she stated: "Jack is very pleased with the change in me. Once we had intercourse twice in one night. Once I woke him up. I get on top of him now. I get more sensation that way. Sex is no longer painful but I still haven't reached an orgasm." In her twenty-fifth session, she related how all her girl friends had one or two babies now, but that she wasn't interested in having one. She concluded her session by commenting: "My parents said I was a pleasure as a child, no problem. They could take me anyplace, lay me down and I would immediately fall asleep. I had so many relatives taking care of me and making such a fuss over me. Perhaps I don't want a baby because that would make me a mother, and I would have to relinquish my position as baby!"

In her next session she reported: "We had sex last night. It didn't hurt. But nothing special. I was a little more relaxed and for the first time I wasn't depressed; usually I cry afterwards."

The four following sessions revealed the slow development of the negative transference: her dreams showed me as a depreciated person, displaced anger onto her mother-in-law (therapist) with open arguments and for the first time forgot to pay for her therapy.

"We've been getting along fine. I'm reacting better sexually. Intercourse four times in the past two weeks. Once two nights in a row that shocked both of us. I wonder if I'm hypersexed."

In her thirty-fourth session Mrs. C reported that she was doing better in many areas of her behavior. She commented: "It is ten months since I first started seeing you. We had intercourse once this week. For the first time I felt sensation inside my vagina. Before I only enjoyed the clitoral stimulation."

In her thirty-ninth session she stated she was feeling so much better and asked whether she could come every other week. She reported: "Our marriage seems much better. My mother-in-law aggravates me less. Jack keeps commenting on how I have improved."

In her next session she commented that she felt better, even though her last session was two weeks ago: "I had a dream: I'm walking with my gynecologist. We had to separate. We were walking very close. We separate. I took it in stride.

I felt OK, that you were the gynecologist and I was accepting the fact of coming every other week. Jack and I have been getting along fine. We had sex three times since I was here, more excitement and much better."

In her forty-first session (one year after the onset of therapy) she reported being very aggravated with her husband over little things. On the other hand, they have been having sex twice a week.

In her forty-third session she reported a dream in which she was getting married again but felt sad at leaving her home. Her material indicated an awareness of her improvement and her depression at the approaching end of her treatment.

In her forth-fifth session (her final one and fourteen months after the onset of therapy) she reported everything was fine and that twice in the past week she had reached an orgasm. "I had a dream last night: 'I'm on an airplane. Lots of people. In the back the people are decrepit. But I am seated in the first-class compartment.' "

In her associations she stated: "I wasn't part of the decrepit group. I was separated from the sick people. I felt secure and sure of myself."

I comment: "This dream is a far cry from your dream in which you are seated on a tall high stool with a dunce cap on."

She replied that it was and that in the past week she had been thinking about stopping her therapy. I don't feel I have that many things to say either. Sexually I'm OK.

I suggested that I still keep her next appointment four weeks hence but that she could cancel at the last moment if things were going satisfactorily. Three weeks later she called to state that everything was fine and that she and her husband felt satisfied. Thirteen months later I received a brief note announcing the birth of her first child.

4. *When one partner feels he has to figure out his own way irrespective of the consequences:*

The Ds' were referred for therapy by Mrs. D's parents. Both were in their early thirties. Married ten years, they have three children, the youngest is two years old.

Mrs. D, attractive and well groomed, tearfully stated her complaints: "He does not desire me sexually anymore. He goes out by himself all the time. He doesn't enjoy being with the family. We were getting along fine until three months prior to the birth of our last child. Since his birth, we have had sex about six times. We separated about a year ago. He returned after being gone three months. During that time, he had an affair and now he carries guilt feelings. He told me that he had promised to marry the girl after she got a divorce. She did get a divorce and that is when he decided to come home. I don't understand what has happened but I do want to make a go of our marriage."

Mr. D appeared nervous and tense at his first individual diagnostic session. "I don't love her anymore. I resent her. She seems to be pushing. She is the type who is always wondering what will the neighbors think. I find her repulsive. I respect and love her in some ways. She is faithful, a good mother and housewife. But it's always, "What will the neighbors think?"

She is just like her mother who knows everything. I told my wife many times to shut her mouth. A few months ago we were visiting a couple and the discussion centered on a Japanese family that had moved near them. They said they tried to make them comfortable. I raised the issue of real estate values. Not against the Japs, not prejudice, but an economic fact. Right away she became very upset. That I was sounding like a bigot, making an ass of myself, or shaming her. All I tried was to point out the economic facts to this couple. She said these things in front of our friends!

"Just before our boy was born, two years ago, I did something I wanted to do all my life. Buy a foreign sports car and join a sports car club. I bought an Austin-Healy. I loved it, and it became an addiction. Soon I was leaving her alone quite often on the weekends. She resented this. Things got farther and farther apart. I felt no love for her. Occasionally I would put my arm around her. I feel lonesome without her. Yet when I'm with her, I feel nothing.

"We had a big fight about her mother a year ago, and I left home for three months. But I kept thinking about the children. They kept pulling at me, not my feelings about my wife. I was ready to go out of my mind. For a period of time I thought if I had the guts, I would kill myself. Between my three children and ten years of marriage and Mabel, my girl friend, on the other side. I still haven't been able to make a decision. I don't want to lose Mabel. I love her. She is the other woman that my wife thinks I have given up. She got a divorce to marry me.

"I had a most unhappy childhood. My parents quarreled continuously. Father left home repeatedly for short periods, just like I'm doing. Much of the arguing was blamed on my bad behavior. Father was intolerant and impatient. Mother was nagging and both were headstrong. Mother, at times, went into rages and struck me with anything available. There were many times when I came so close to striking her. Once I did strike her, moved out, and shortly after, I got married. When my wife nags me she sounds like my mother (projective identification).

"I need a psychiatrist and know it. I'm confused about Mabel. I've got to come to terms with myself regardless of how it affects my wife. Will you please treat me!"

I agreed to treat him and would refer his wife to another therapist. I did see Mrs. D once again and she gave the following information: "My husband seemed better after he talked to you. I've been thinking of his lack of sexual desire for me. For the past seven years he has not been adequate sexually. He refused to do anything about it. He went his way and I went my way. One day he said he was fed up, and he left. While separated he met another woman. He said: 'With this woman I feel like a man. If you could only treat me like this woman treats me. She doesn't nag, is kind and considerate.' I can be that way with others, but not with him. I was always interested in the opposite sex, so hungry for affection. I have a good idea why he feels this way about me. I'm a very giving person to every one except him. I did not realize that until he pointed it out. He took up the hobby of sports cars and I showed no interest. I refused to go on the races they had. He met this girl at one of the meets. She showed him consideration, kindness, and just being a nice person. Two weeks before he came back I started to change my ways. But I wonder if we should remain married. He has no respect for my parents. He is selfish. He calls me very filthy names when we argue."

I suggested the classic approach for him and referred her to another therapist.

5. *Where the couple have widely differing goals in terms of their discord:*

From the very onset, both Mr. and Mrs. E approached the matter in a very intellectualized, cold, and highly unemotional manner. Mr. E's opening comment was that their problem is that they are both angry at each other and neither one knows wholly why it is this way. He said his wife insisted on coming with him for his first interview as she did not think he would accept therapy and keep his appointment.

"Materially, we have everything we need, yet, we are both unhappy people, within ourselves not necessarily with the marriage. I don't think I am essentially a happy person. I'm restless but with a lot of drive for what I want. I'm not a joyful person. I have difficulty relating to people, but not because I'm not verbal. Basically I have difficulty relating to females. All these things lead to difficulties with my wife. At times our relationship is excellent. We have three wonderful children, whom I enjoy greatly, plus the mechanical things, a place to hang your hat and sleep. I expect to go to the closet and find my suits clean and my shoes heeled. She objects to taking care of these things. I don't take particular pride in dressing or apparel, but like to be neat and clean. I have a poor self-image of myself."

Mrs. E stated her complaint that he would not talk, that he dismisses any subject that she brings up because she supposedly can't understand and resents how he totally categorizes anything she states by, "I never," or "I always."

She stated, what he wants and expects in marriage just does not exist. As a result, we have had explosive arguments in all areas, and recently they have become more vehement and frequent. I don't know why I am afraid of him, but when I do get frightened, I just shut up.

"I take my marriage on a day-to-day basis. We have our children. Jim is exceedingly involved in his business and proud of its success. He has very little else. Next he is most interested in his reading. His business is a great challenge to Jim. He says, 'My family is more important to me than my business,' but he doesn't live it. Our marriage is based on a 'potential.' We live in hopes of what Jim could be. But that isn't reality.

Usually he is lazy around the house, but when he does the things that need to be done, he goes at it hammer and tong. If he could be less serious. The other day our oldest child, ten years old, wouldn't listen and he called it insubordinate, like when I don't obey him or they don't obey him. He is very unrealistic in regards to sex; Jim feels I am frigid, and this is not so. I do enjoy sex with him when he is tender and we have not argued earlier over something trivial." Mrs. Louisa delivered the above comments in an academic manner that sounded like a dull lecture.

Mr. E replied that he would cooperate in any manner that would help the marriage. "I love my wife and children. She says she loves me too. Marriage is a sacred thing, and it is very unfair to place the children in a home with only one parent. We have created the children, and we have a parental responsibility to provide a family for them. Besides I have a certain type of ego that can never admit failure. I belong with the family and the children. Neither one of us wants a divorce."

At the end of the evaluation and the CDD, it was suggested that each have his individual therapist. This suggestion was offered, since both had deprived childhoods and each needed the intense dyadic relationship with his own therapist to clarify his expectations of marriage and explore his inner world of thoughts, fantasies, and feelings.

The sixth and seventh indications for the classical approach are so typical that illustrative vignettes are not given.

In conclusion, I continue to use the classical approach whenever it is indicated, in about one out of ten pair-couplings. Occasionally, the use of neurotropic medication for patients with moderate to severe anxiety has hastened the analytic process.[20]

REFERENCES

1. Giovacchini, Peter L., Treatment of marital disharmonies: the classical approach. In Greene, B. L. (Ed.): The Psychotherapies of Marital Disharmony, New York, MacMillan 1965, pp. 39-82.
2. Crowley, Ralph M.: Opinion — the gap between psychoanalytic theory and practice (The Academy Forum). *Am Acad Psychoanal, 23:* 1, 16, 1979.
3. Martin, Peter A.: *A Marital Therapy Manual.* New York, Brunner-Mazel, 1976, p. 114.
4. Sager, Clifford L.: *Marriage Contracts and Couple Therapy.* New York, Brunner-Mazel, 1976.
5. Balint, Enid: Marital conflicts and their therapy. *Comprehensive Psychiat, 7:* 403-7, 1966.
6. Neubeck, Gerhard: Toward a theory of marriage counseling. *Family Coordinator, 22:* 117-22, 1973.
7. Boszormenyi-Nagy, Ivan: Loyalty implications of the transference model in psychotherapy. *Arch Gen Psychiat, 27:* 374, 1972.
8. Loewald, Hans W.: *Psychoanalysis and the History of the Individual.* New Haven, Conn, Yale Univ Press, 1977.
9. Alexander, Franz and French, Thomas M.: *Psychoanalytic Therapy,* New York, Ronald Press, 1946.
10. Malan, David H.: *Individual Psychotherapy and the Science of Psychodynamics.* Boston, Mass, Butterworths, 1979.
11. Saul, Leon J.: *Psychodynamically Based Psychotherapy.* New York, Science House, 1975.
12. Redlich, Fritz: Psychoanalysis and the medical model. *J Am Acad Psychoanal, 2:* 147-57, 1974.
13. Marmor, Judd: The future of psychoanalytic therapy. *Am J Psychiat, 130:* 1197-1202, 1973.
14. Dewald, Paul A.: The process of change in psychoanalytic psychotherapy. *Arch Gen Psychiat, 35:* 542, 1978.
15. Guntrip, H.: Science, psychodynamic reality and autistic thinking. *J Am Acad Psychoanal, 1:* 3-22, 1973.
16. Marmor, Judd: Short-term dynamic psychotherapy, *Am J Psychiat, 136:* 149-55, 1979.
17. Liberman, Robert P., Wheeler, Eugenie G., deVisser, Louis A. J. M., Kuehnel, Julie, and Kuehnel, Timothy: *Handbook of Marital Therapy.* New York, Plenum, 1979.
18. Wolpe, Joseph, Brady, John P., Serber, Michael, Agras, W. Stewart, and Liberman, Robert P.: The current status of systematic desenitization, *Am J Psychiat, 130:* 961-65, 1973.
19. Birk, Lee and Brinkley-Birk, Ann W.: Psychoanalysis and behavior therapy. *Am J Psychiat, 131:* 499-510, 1974.

20. *Pharmacotherapy and Psychotherapy: Paradoxes, Problems and Progress.* Formulated by the committee on research. New York: Group for the Advancement of Psychiatry. Vol. IX, report #93, 1975.

Chapter XXIV

THE COLLABORATIVE TECHNIQUE
IN DYADIC DISHARMONY

IN the collaborative approach in dyadic dishar-
mony, both partners are treated individually but synchronously by
separate therapists who communicate with the knowledge and permission of each partner. This approach is a dyadic one-to-one therapeutic relationship and was used in 8 percent of the couples receiving
crisis therapy, and in about 6 percent of couples where one or both
spouses received intensive psychotherapy. The collaborative approach
enables the therapist-in-training to enhance his knowledge about
dyadic transactions as he gradually acquires the experience of treating
two or more individuals in the same clinical setting. Martin and Bird[1]
were pioneers in 1948 in the development of collaborative approach
in marital disharmony. In 1952, they reported this technique, which
they called the "stereoscopic technique."[2]

About the same time Dicks, in England, began to experiment with
new techniques in marital problems, including the collaborative approach: "For therapy, we took on a small proportion of cases, each of
us treating the partner we had interviewed on our familiar lines, with
periodic (italics added) conferencing to coordinate findings and
policy."[3]

Initially, Martin and Bird met only occasionally about their patients, but soon they developed their occasional meetings into a regularly scheduled program. I used this approach for the first time in
1955 and also found that collaborative therapy requires *regular* scheduled meetings between the therapists — not by telephone or during
lunch or dinner. Many more therapists are now using this technique.[4]

In his recent textbook, Martin[5] succinctly discusses the advantages
and disadvantages of collaborative approach as it pertains to both the
patient and therapist. The advantages of this approach are as follows:
a broader perspective of the patient and his problems due to other
inputs of information, decrease in distortions of reality and projective
identifications of the couple, the knowledge of the couple that two
therapists are involved tends to reduce anxiety and destructive behavior, the interlocking unconscious reaction of one patient to the
unconscious actions of his partner may be more readily observed,

316

one/both therapists can help in preventing transference-counter-transference deadlocks in therapy, and, by removing isolation, both therapists' are aided in their personal growth. The disadvantages include regular planned conferences between the therapists with loss of time and additional cost to the couple, and each therapist is confronted with the need at times with coping with narcissistic reactions of the other. Tact is required between the therapists, who may be of different disciplines, as each works out his relationship with his colleague. This relationship can be as sensitive as those between the therapists and their patients.

The following are indications for the collaborative approach:

1. Opposition of one partner to being treated by the same therapist.
2. Initial hostility of one partner toward the referring therapist.
3. Referral from another therapist because of his personal reasons, e.g. uncomfortable in the triadic situation, inexperience with the triadic approach, and/or nonacceptance of the frame of reference of triadic techniques.
4. Where a couple have differing goals in terms of their relationship and need individual rather than a triadic therapeutic approach. In this situation, should divorce/separation ensue, this may require two therapists to give emotional support to each partner, and if children are present, to help with postcretal problems, e.g. child custody, visitation, financial, etc.
5. Referral from another therapist because one partner has created therapeutic complications. This approach is ususally a *sine qua non* where one partner has a moderate to severe primary affective disorder (manic-depressive illness) (see Chapter XXVII).

The contraindications for collaborative technique are the same as for the classic dyadic one-to-one approach as outlined in Chapter XXIII.

The following is Martin's chapter,[6] slightly condensed and edited, as it is still the best description and presentation of a clinical case of the collaborative approach in the literature.

"These clinical data have been extracted from the concurrent therapies of a middle-aged husband and wife, both of whom suffered from severe psychiatric disorders. Work with this couple began after the family physician recognized that it would become necessary to hospitalize the wife if psychotherapy were not promptly undertaken. As he was unable to persuade her to seek help, he advised her husband to consult a psychiatrist first, in the hope that she would later follow suit. This device was successful, and the wife usurped her husband's fourth appointment. During her third hour, she insisted that she remain in treatment with the first psychiatrist and that her husband be referred to the colleague.

During the early phase of the wife's treatment, she did little more than criticize her spouse. She complained that he did not love her, that he treated her as his social inferior, and that he wanted to be free of her. She accused him of using alcohol to excess, of neglecting his business, and of failing to discharge his responsibilities as a father. Finally, she condemned him because he had had an affair with his secretary and because he was impotent with her. In this connection, she reported that her husband had once encouraged her to have intercourse with a mutual friend in their own home. She placed little emphasis on her own emotional problems, which she summarized as a tendency to be "inadequate" when forced by the husband's defections to assume unwarranted responsibilities.

The husband made no protest at being referred to a second psychiatrist. He quietly accepted the blame that the wife heaped upon him, admitting that he had neglected his family and business, that he drank excessively, and that he was impotent with her. He denied, however, her charges that he did not love her, that he wanted to be free of her, and that he had urged her to have an extramarital affair. He said that he wanted to co-operate fully with the therapist and to find out what in his childhood had caused his present difficulties. The opening hours of his treatment were filled with fantasies about an idyllic love relationship with his wife, free of strife and also of physical contact.

In one of the initial conferences between the two psychiatrists, the wife's therapist presented his reconstructed version of the incident in which she had had intercourse with a close friend, allegedly at her husband's instigation. This occurrence was offered as evidence of his rejecting attitude toward her and his inability to act the role of a man. The husband's psychiatrist reacted with skepticism and with sympathy of his patient. He expressed the opinion that the husband had been cuckolded, in view of the fact that the husband had become enraged when he first heard about the incident and had retaliated by revealing to his wife for the first time the earlier affair with his secretary. On this occasion, the stereoscopic technique not only demonstrated its usefulness in detecting a distortion of reality — the falseness of the wife's accusation — but also brought to light what was later recognized as positive countertransference reactions to their respective patients on the part of both psychiatrists. In attempting to understand this distortion and others of equal importance contained in the productions of both marital partners, the therapists became aware of the necessity to investigate further with each patient defense mechanisms and underlying instinctual impulses involved.

During the next phase of the wife's treatment, the complaint that her husband did not love her recurred constantly. She made only passing references to her own drinking bouts and outbursts of rage and to her inadequacy in domestic and social situations. As memories of her childhood emerged, it became evident that her early life experiences had been characterized by intense fear of being alone and by an exaggerated need to depend on the adults in her home. As a terrified little girl, she had insisted on sleeping on a cot in the dining room, where she would listen intently to family conversations in the adjoining parlor. When finally she was unable to tolerate her loneliness any longer, she would cry out and thus bring her father to her side. She then customarily demanded that he carry her tenderly upstairs. It was as the result of a long series of demands, similarly expressed and met, that she came to be known in her family as the "pink goddess."

An incident of fascinating interest and significance took place during this phase of the wife's therapy. Late one afternoon, the husband urgently summoned her psychiatrist to their home, where the wife was found to be completely inebriated, disheveled, and furious with her husband, who fled the scene as soon as he had admitted the physician to the house. The wife thereupon delivered an hour-long tirade against her spouse, berating him again and again for the affair with his secretary some ten years earlier. The patient's attitude was so violent that the physician too became frightened. Note should be made of the fact that the wife was in the midst of making preparations for her daughter's forthcoming marriage at that time.

During this phase of the husband's therapy, he continued to take full blame for his wife's problems and to protest that the loved her. Psychodynamically relevant material brought into focus a poignant picture of his childhood. As a boy, he had been saddled with the responsibility for the care of a mentally defective younger brother. Their mother had refused to act on recommendations that his boy be institutionalized. The patient was both terrified and humiliated by his brother's violent outbursts and frequent episodes of soiling. One day he forgot to bring his brother home from school for lunch. When he returned for him, he found the school locked but managed to break in to reach his brother. For this action, he was severely reprimanded by both his parents and the school authorities.

In the stereoscopic meetings dealing with the foregoing material, the wife's psychiatrist presented his reconstructed version of the episode of rage that he had witnessed in the patient's home. He concluded that her anger represented intense jealousy of her daughter, who, in the first place, was now the center of the family's attention and whose marriage, in addition, promised to provide her daughter with the love that the patient felt unrealistically she was not receiving from her husband. The colleague's version was somewhat different. He postulated that such rages were not uncommon and that they recurred as often as several times a week. He also concluded that the wife was not acknowledging her spouse's constant protection and his acceptance of her uncontrollable outbursts.

Work with the couple had by that time reached the point at which it was possible to identify each patient's defense system. It was clear that the husband's defense against his own intense hostility toward his brother and mother was a reaction formation in which he became a "good boy" whose ideal was the virtuous, long-suffering tragic saint. This facade also protected him against fear of castration by his mother and provided satisfaction of his great need to be loved. The defense had, however, began to crack in recent years, as indicated by the *passive expressions of hostility manifested in his impotence* (italics added), his alcoholism, and his periods of absence from home and from his work. The wife defended herself against hostile impulses and the dependent strivings of a clinging, controlling nature by maintaining her infantile wish to be omnipotent, expressed as a demand that she be treated as a "goddess." This defense mechanism was first threatened by the birth of her oldest child. She was described as having been transiently "psychotic" by the family physician who cared for her at the time. In the intervening seventeen years, the onslaughts of these underlying instinctual impulses had impaired the functioning of her ego to the point where she had become ineffective and inadequate as a wife and mother.

The insights provided by the stereoscopic approach were utilized by the psychiatrists in identifying the pattern of this marriage. The husband's neurosis contained a repetition compulsion in which he recreated with his wife his martyrdom in caring for the uncontrolled idiot brother. His wife's inadequacy, inability to control her violnt feelings, and great need for attention certainly strengthened his unconscious identification of her with his brother. The wife was similarly driven by a repetition compulsion, specifically to maintain her infantile wish to be the "pink goddess" who would be loved unconditionally and on demand by her husband, as she had been by her father. Fascinatingly enough, the wife, in her dreams, showed that she had identified herself with the husband's brother. For both partners, the pink goddess and the idiot brother had thus become fused in a single image. As a consequence, an unconscious vicious circle was set in motion, in which the wife's identification with the frightening and demanding idiot forced the husband to adopt the role of an overpassive, martyred "good boy."

We now have come to the point at which we can fully define our approach: the stereoscopic technique, as used in collaborative psychotherapy of marriage partners, consists of planned, regular reviews of two psychiatrists' reconstructed versions of important events in the lives of the partners for the therapeutic purpose of recognizing distortions of reality in the productions of their patients. The therapeutic possibilities of the stereoscopic technique are not limited to this recognition of reality distortions. We found that such recognition led more quickly to recognition of the ego defenses of the patient. Once this important recognition was accomplished, a third important recognition followed: it became possible to recognize the instinctual impulses that were being expressed or warded off.

Even more important, as we became more sophisticated in the use of our technique, a further recognition became possible. We could understand the complementary neuroses that existed between the partners, that both drew them together and pushed them apart. In our example, the wife's representation was that of a baby or idiot child. The husband's neurosis involved self-identification martyred, saintly older brother.

We believe that the recognition and exposure of such transference neuroses in the treatment situation are necessary for permanent therapeutic endeavors.

Our approach is in keeping with that of Grotjahn,[7] who states that he mother-child symbiosis is the prototype of the later family, that it is the basis of the child's conscious and unconscious, and that only later will he include the image or ideal of father, brother, sister, grandparents, or whomever he meets. Grotjahn argues, "All through our later life we transfer our inner childhood family onto the realistic family and each of us maintains a complicated circular relationship between his parental family, the inner family of his conscious and unconscious, and the projection of these images upon his own family, established when he becomes an adult." He defines the marriage neurosis as the transfer and projection of unresolved, unconscious conflicts from the past of both partners into the present, that is, from childhood families into the marriage situation. (This is the phenomenon of projective-identification.)

The study of current experiences between the spouses reproduced and made possible for us the reconstruction of even the earliest autistic, symbiotic, or separation phases of infant-mother relationships. Our therapeutic approach is therefore basically psychoanalytically conventional.

One of the greatest advantages of the stereoscopic technique is its offer of a possibility for ending transference-countertransference duels between diffferent therapists working with members of the same family. This point can be illustrated by the following clinical material on the recognition and reduction of negative countertransference reactions.

As the husband's treatment proceeded, he began to describe the lurid details of his wife's violent bouts of alcoholism. He related how she criticized him endlessly and how she often kept him awake all night long, with the result that he was unable to go to work in the morning. It also became apparent that, on other occasions, she refused to allow him to arise, insisting that he remain in bed to cradle her in his arms. There was, by this time, no doubt in the psychiatrists' minds that the husband's accounts were authentic and realistic. Yet he maintained that he and he alone was "at fault," and he accepted as valid even obviously unfair accusations by his wife.

In relating this material at the regular meetings of the psychiatrists, the husband's therapist at first expressed sympathy for a man who was so burdened by a near-psychotic partner. But, as time wore on and the husband continued to present the same material in the same manner, his psychiatrist's reports carried a different tone. These later comments implied that it was difficult and unrewarding to work with such a passive male, a man who continued to be sexually impotent, who rarely went to work on time, and who drank as much as he ever had. The physician went on to emphasize that the patient strove mainly to play the role of "good little boy" in the treatment hours, while running away from masculine responsibilities in his daily life. Because the patient sometimes clowned in the company of his friends, who then bought him drinks, the psychiatrist derisively likened him to Little Tommy Tucker, who "sang for his supper." In further observations, the psychiatrist stressed the difficulty of inducing the patient to face the perfectly obvious fact that his activities resulted from fear of and anger toward his wife. The psychiatrist finally insisted that the prognosis was very poor.

As the wife's psychiatrist listened to his colleague's reports in one of their meetings, it occurred to him to remind his associate that he himself had been frightened by the wife during the visit to the couple's home. After the reality of the wife's violent nature had been re-emphasized in this manner, the question was then raised as to why the husband's therapist had lost sight of this reality. It became apparent almost immediately that his vision had been obscured by strong negative countertransference feelings. When he was thus confronted with his own reaction, he did a bit of self-analysis that forced him to become aware of his own derisive feelings toward a passive male who allowed a woman to run him ragged and who, in this specific instance, was not dealing with the problem of his castration anxiety as the psychiatrist himself had done earlier in his own personal analysis. Once this understanding had been reached by the husband's therapist, a change in the therapeutic *milieu* ensued. It became easier for the psychiatrist to sit patiently through the succeeding hours and to bend his efforts to help the husband with his problem. In the course of time, the patient was able to express openly his repressed hostility toward his wife, and he made progress in working out the castration anxiety excited by her violence. For the purpose of this paper, it suffices to say that the patient thereafter became more openly aggressive and that he regained his potency with his wife.

During this phase of the husband's therapy, the wife's material and behavior continued to be much like that described earlier. As the husband began to assume masculine responsibilities, however, her projections and distortions stood out in bold relief against his more mature activities. For example, the wife reported that her husband, at a birthday party he had arranged in her honor, had attempted to "embarrass" her by being attentive to another woman. The stereoscopic technique revealed that the husband had not favored another woman but that the patient had become so intoxicated as to become a source of embarrassment to all the guests. On another occasion, the patient referred to her husband as being unduly dependent upon her because he had lost his way on a recent motor trip and could not correct his mistake until she had given him explicit directions. The facts were quite different. The husband, an experienced traveler, had made a wrong turn at the insistence of his wife, who had become confused in reading the road map. On still another occasion, immediately following their first successful intercourse in years, she announced her decision to leave her husband. She gave as her reason, "If I were gone, he would not have to be so stubborn and go against my wishes." When the therapist pointed out that it was she who embarrassed her husband, that it was she who was overly dependent, and that it was she who sought to avoid sexual relationships, she retorted that she was being "falsely accused." Almost invariably such denials were followed by overt attempts to gain approval and affection from the doctor. She would protest that she was a pleasant, kind, well-meaning person who did nice things for her family and friends. She recalled, for example, helping a friend's husband select a fur coat for his wife and mowing the lawn in place of her son, who wanted to keep a social engagement.

In the course of the stereoscopic meetings dealing with this material, the wife's psychiatrist at first expressed positive feelings for his patient and stressed her need for understanding and affection. Somewhat later, however, he confided to his colleague that she had proved to be a frustrating patient and that it had become a chore to work with her. In general, his comments took on a note of angry desperation, and he concluded on one occasion by saying that he would go on with the patient because "there just isn't anything else I can do." He reminded the other psychiatrist that the referring physician had called the patient a "pathological liar" and remarked that the term was most appropriate for one who so blithely continued to project and to distort reality. He reported that he had inexplicably cut one of her hours short by ten minutes and had subsequently felt guilty at having deprived a person who so needed love and consideration.

After the husband's therapist had repeatedly heard his colleague place what seemed to be disproportionate emphasis on the wife's "need to be loved," he made two discerning observations. He commented that the wife's psychiatrist not only had "fallen for the pink goddess line" but also was overlooking the fact that the wife needed to become more adequate. This confrontation placed the responsibility squarely on the wife's therapist to investigate and eliminate the blind spots he had developed. His subsequent self-analysis disclosed a negative countertransference attitude toward the wife, which he had until then denied. In reality, the psychiatrist feared and disliked her, a destructive woman, but he had defended himself against these feelings through the device of overevaluating and overprotecting her. As a consequence, he had been led into establishing the same kind of relationship with her as had existed between her and her father, the first person to be controlled by the "pink goddess." It was then evident that, as long as she could maintain her omnipotent defense against the recognition of her inadequacy, hostility, and dependence, no progress could be made.

Once her therapist had dealt with his negative countertransference, his need to support her powerful defense no longer existed. With the lifting of this defense, work with the underlying impulses proceeded. As a result, the wife took some forward steps. She enlarged the scope of her activities and the circle of her friends, came to demand less of her husband, and eventually agreed to dispose of their pretentious and financially burdensome house.

The following vignettes from my clinical practice illustrate the various indications for the collaborative approach in dyadic disharmony:

1. *Where there is opposition of one partner to being treated by the same therapist:*

Mr. and Mrs. A were referred by their physician for marital therapy. Mr. A was seen first and stated: "This blowup has been building up for several years. Ann has a great drive for excitement. I am the quiet sort of person, and she is just the opposite. She has a great amount of personal drive and is extremely vocal and social. Many of these things I have not. I realized this after the first years of our marriage, that I would have to change a lot to please her. She has always leaned to extremes. I have been the conservative one. I had hoped that when she went back to work, it would have helped her. She reads rapidly and a great deal. I have been trying to read more. She is so adamant about being free of me. She is very affectionate to our son. At times a little more self-centered than other mothers I have seen. But she is very interested in the boy and his welfare. I will do anything to save this marriage.

Mrs. A, an attractive, vivacious woman, appeared much younger than her stated age of twenty-seven. She stated that they married while they were in college because she wanted to settle down. She was not in love with him when they married, but she felt quiet with him and content.

"There is no communication and no challenge to my growth. He doesn't perceive my needs or reactions. He is a marvelous father. But I want out — a divorce. I want to live, to see and be with people. I'm in no great rush to remarry. Six months ago I told him I couldn't make love to him any more. First, I got pregnant, but it ended in a miscarriage. Secondly, I went back to work. Being at work only increased my unhappiness. I told him I wanted a divorce. He agreed on the condition that I see a psychiatrist for six months.

"John reacted very positively to his session with you. But I am not going to see you again. I feel you will try to brainwash me into staying married to him. I want you to send me to another therapist. He will be my therapist, and you two can cooperate."

When I next saw Mr. A he agreed to collaborative therapy. When seen a week later, he angrily stated: "I am very irritated at my wife. She wants to sell the house and move into an apartment with our child. I do not feel it is fair to uproot the boy." I told him that I would get together with her therapist to discuss the situation.

(Comment: At our first collaborative session it was decided that Mrs. A could move out as she wished, and her husband remain in the home, and that I would attempt to help him improve his self-image. In the interim, an attempt would be made to understand the psychodynamics of Mrs. A. Two months later Mrs. A moved back into their home having reestablished a meaningful relationship with her husband. Since there had been a strong therapeutic alliance between Mrs. A and her therapist, I suggest that the As' both continue with him conjointly. Six months later he reported they were doing well and he had discontinued their treatment.)

2. *Initial hostility of one partner toward the therapist:*

Mr. B, a tall, thin male in his late thirties stated he was at his wit's end in coping with his wife's extravagant spending. When he would remonstrate with her, she would get furiously angry at him and throw things. Finally, in desperation he moved out of their apartment into a nearby motel. A week later she had reached him at work and agreed to psychiatric help, provided he also went.

Mrs. B was an exotic-looking woman, who came for her first interview wearing black, tight toreador pants with a gray sweater. She looked older than her stated age of twenty-nine and wore heavy makeup and thick false eyelashes. She spoke in a very precise fashion. Her main complaint was about her husband being so penurious: "He has turned out to be like my father. My parents were always arguing about money. Father was always ranting and raving in the home about Mother's spending and that we would all end up in the poorhouse."

At one point in the interview she became annoyed with me when I inquired about how she met her husband. Her answer was evasive, and she quickly changed the subject.

When Mr. B came for his next interview, he stated that his wife felt that I did not like her and was not going to return but that she would see someone else, preferably a woman doctor who understands women.

3. *Referral from another therapist because of his personal reasons, e.g. inexperience with the triadic approach:*

Mr. C was referred by the psychiatrist who was treating his wife for a reactive depression. Doctor K felt Mrs. Cs' emotional state was due principally to marital disharmony. He had referred Mr. C, since he was inexperienced in treating couples. The Cs were in their late twenties and worked at the same factory where she was a nurse and he, a skilled maintenance worker.

Mr. C. began his first session by commenting: "We are not getting along. Worse since our honeymoon two years ago. She acts neurotic with a lot of anxiety. We met at a party four years ago. I was going to night school, taking electronics. I noticed her but didn't call her until a month later. She responded to things I said. She is very intelligent.

"We are both very athletic and enjoy skiing. She reads a lot and is interested in accomplishing things. We first ran into problems during our courtship. I couldn't find the right kind of job. She would get very upset when I wouldn't look for two days. I got a job I liked but the placed burned down in a month. I looked around again. She would give me ultimatums: If you don't get a job in two weeks, I'm calling off the engagement. We had arguments. I tried to pacify her. One night she said let's break it off. I was undecided but said maybe it's a good idea. I told her I wasn't ready to settle down. She got emotional and blew up. I figured I would forget the deal.

Prior to this I had received a call from a former Army buddy. He wanted me to go into business with him in California. I had told her about his call. The next day she called and suggested that we get married. I told her I wasn't sure. I was thinking about California. I was undecided, and she was superpositive. She told me she was really in love with me. I felt I was getting involved sooner than I wanted. I quit my job. I felt I met her too early, I was only twenty-seven, that I wasn't mature enough for marriage. Also, I wanted to get California out of my system. She didn't like this at all. I took a plane and asked her if she would wait. She said, Yes. I wrote her factual letters, but that I missed her. I didn't like California and knew I would be happier in Chicago. I called Jane and told her I was coming home. She was happy.

It seemed like I was a bad employment risk. I started working at this place as a mechanic but didn't like my boss, so quit. When I told Jane this, it was like an atom bomb. I told my father and he said: Don't feel so bad, start thinking positively, get married. So I went out and bought a ring. I asked her to marry me. I didn't tell her that I wasn't working. Later I began to feel guilty and decided to tell her. She gave the ring back to me and told me not to bother her anymore, but the next night she called me and said she thought it over and would marry me. But we kept having arguments. We would be in a movie, and she would say something to me. I wouldn't hear her and she would storm out. She was continually mad over nothing. Finally the arguments stopped and we got married.

Our honeymoon was a fizzle. The first night she was a little nervous. We were both tired from the wedding, so when we got into bed, she said she was tired and maybe it would be a good thing to get some sleep. I felt I didn't have a good erection so it didn't bother me. The next day we left for Niagara Falls. We drove 150 miles. I felt I wanted to sweep her off her feet. I had never had intercourse before. I had read quite a bit about it. I had trouble finding the entrance. But before I got that far, I had an ejaculation. The same thing happened the next night. She started getting emotional and didn't like it.

We has sexual problems for a year. During this time she was getting disgusted with me and sleeping in another bed. Finally she began to feel extremely nervous and went to see a psychiatrist. He suggested I see you, that my sex drive is not as it should be — that I need some help. So here I am."

At the first collaborative session, Doctor K reported that Mrs. C was very happy that her husband was receiving help, and that she would like her marriage to be successful but had her doubts. If she could control her emotions and accepts things the way they were, there would be no problems to consider. She made many demands on Jim and he, very few. All he wanted was that she be calm and good natured. She didn't feel useful, needed or married. There was little communication with her husband, and his procrastination in all areas was most frustrating.

Doctor K also stated that Mrs. C complained that her husband was very inhibited sexually, and that some of her sexual aggressive behavior had shocked him and embarrassed him to passivity. He quoted her social and intellectual activity, planning together, acting on problems, and above all, his procrastination has had its effect. It's what Jim does not do. I imagine his complaints concern what I do.

Jim was seen twice weekly for six months with considerable improvement in his total behavior at work and in his sexual performance. He had regained his sexual adequacy but discovered his wife to be frigid. Weekly collaborative sessions with Doctor K confirmed my clinical impression of Jane as a very controlling obsessive-compulsive personality. Six months after the onset of therapy, with Jane's continually questioning her husband as to everything discussed in his sessions, I suggested to Doctor K that he try conjoint therapy with the couple, and I would supervise him in this technique.

4. *Referral from another therapist because the patient is complicating the therapy of his patient:*

Mr. D, a handsome, intelligent executive, was referred by his wife's therapist. She had gone for marital therapy, but her husband refused to cooperate until threatened by the possibility of divorce. Mrs. D's therapist was pessimistic about the marriage and wanted the collaborative technique, both as a last attempt to salvage the marriage and to help structure the various family arrangements should the couple separate.

At the first collaborative session, Doctor M stated that he had been treating Mrs. D for the past six months with considerable improvement in her depressed moods. However, Mrs. D had been increasingly angry at her husband for not wanting to work on the marriage. Her main complaint was unfulfilled emotional needs. He quoted her as saying: "I feel that I would like to know, to understand, to be totally intimate with the person who is going to share my life. He does not possess the same needs for a relationship in depth. We do not communicate. We have a superficially compatible pattern of dealing with each other, and frankly I'm tired of my role."

Doctor M described Mrs. D as very intelligent, very attractive, and an extrovert.

In his first session, Mr. D stated that he was at a loss to understand what has happened to his marriage: "Everything had been fine until a year ago when Ann began to complain that I was insensitive to her needs as a woman: I make too few gestures of love, am not spontaneous enough, and show little in the way of tokens of affection. Under different circumstances my ego would be hurt. However, three years after we were married, Ann and I got this irritation out into the open, and I discovered that her needs are excessive. Not that I could not fulfill her needs, but I resent her incessant reminding me about her emotional needs and my not fulfilling them. Somehow, when my wife reminded me to bring home something cute or funny or just surprise her, I would balk. I can't be creative by manifesto. Then we got along fine, until a year ago when the same bit started up again. The friction and continuous reminding me was most irritating, and I began to withdraw from her. We now virtually have separate lives, which I can live but do not like.

"I would like my marriage to last. Both Doctor M and my wife have pushed me to see you. I don't feel I have been remiss and have really worked hard to be better in the marriage situation. I've tried to meet the excessive needs of my wife.."

In the next six sessions, Mr. D expressed rage at his wife's demands and recalled how his parents continually stressed performance in everything he did, e.g. if he got 95 on an exam, why didn't he get 100.

It was pointed out to him that perhaps he was overreacting to his wife's demands with the anger he could not express toward his parents, who kept making increasing demands on him. That he was reacting, not only with anger to his wife, but also projecting on her an old performance record in his jukebox — an angry one from his inner child voice to the perfectionistic demands on the parental voices (an excellent example of projective identification).

In the next collaborative session with Doctor M, the role of projective identification in the marital disharmony of the Ds' was discussed, and it was suggested that Ann keep her demands and criticism to a minimum and how her husband was overreacting to them.

In his next session, Mr. D commented: "You have helped me to see myself differently. I'm easier with people now. Now I see myself acting more strongly as a man. For years I've tried not to react to other women. But now I could. That's something I'm concerned about. Ann doesn't feel the same way about moral behavior as I do. I have been very faithful since I got married. I know many men who step out on their wives. Ann says, if you step out on a convention, it's OK — unless you fall in love. My parents told me otherwise. It bothers me that Ann doesn't think that way. The one thing I have been hanging onto morally is weakening. We had sex last night, the first in over two months.

"Ann has had extreme lows and extreme highs this week. I see things now that I don't like, that I didn't see before. She was screaming at the kid and me. I called her aside in the bedroom and said, 'Don't talk to me that way again.' I never was that firm with her before. She was surprised.

"I keep not delivering. Her theory is that if everything is swell in bed, you can manage anything. But sex is something you lead up to. I can't turn on that easy. When we had sex the other night, she was not too responsive. She feels she is not capable of responding to me. She feels I am losing my desire for her. She is right. She doesn't make me feel virile lately."

At the next collaborative session, Doctor M stated that Mrs. D was frustrated with her husband, especially sexually. She likes to be freewheeling and allow her inner child to play. He puts a damper on it. Most of the time she has had to initiate sex. At times she rebuffs him. Sex is not satisfactory for her. She has noticed an improvement in her husband in terms of communication. I raised the issue of whether Ann was insatiable in her needs and demands. Also, whether we were dealing with a cyclothymic personality because of her marked mood swings.

Mr. D reported that things had been going very nicely for the past three weeks. "It's scary. She is trying. I think she is enjoying making a meal for me now. She did a lot of nice things for me."

At the next collaborative session, Doctor M reported that Ann was again angry at her husband. She had gone out of her way to do all the things he likes, e.g. gourmet meals. All she got was a lot of nice compliments but no display of affection. Doctor M related these incidents with considerable annoyance at Mr. D, but was unaware of his countertransference. When this was pointed out, at first he was annoyed at me then laughingly pointed out how protective I was about Mr. D. We both discussed our respective feelings and cleared the atmosphere.

In his fifth month of therapy, Mr. D was depressed: "The knowledge that whatever I do won't pay off. I think she is turned off, intellectually and sexually. I don't have anyone to talk to. She does not inquire about my work, but is absolutely scintillating when we get out of our environment. I am preparing myself for separation from Ann. Something originally I could not have been prepared to do six months ago. The other night we had a slight argument and she said: 'This stalemate — when the hell is it all going to end.' She has tuned me out because of my noninvolvement with her. Yet, you tell me that we could make a go of our marriage if I could be emotionally involved with her again. When she tries, I move away, and when I try, she doesn't respond. We are caught in a vicious cycle."

In the collaborative session, both therapists agreed that, although their respective patients were developing in their personal behavior, the marriage was coming apart. Paradoxically, as Mr. D showed increased aggressivity at home and at work, where he had just received a promotion, Mrs. D was becoming depressed and not so sure she wanted a separation now. She knew she was rejecting her husband but couldn't react to him in a positive manner. We decided to tell each spouse that if there was no improvement within two months, we would discontinue collaborative sessions.

Mr. D reported that Ann had reacted to the two-month target date with another attempt at trying to make the marriage work: "She was seductive and sat on my lap. I said, 'Let's to to bed.' She said, 'Do you remember how?' but not in a sarcastic manner. I said, 'It is you who has been avoiding it.' We had a good sexual experience. First time in several months. I've changed since coming here. Ann is no longer the physical pursuer as she has been for years. I am going to have to initiate it. I've never been emotionally built like that. I didn't know she was going to run out of steam. I've never seen my parents embrace. Mother is an absolutely frigid person. Ann came into my life with this open display of affection."

At the next collaborative session, Doctor M stated that Mrs. D noticed no change in her husband's sexual patterns. He quoted her as follows: "Dick has been nice enough to me lately. I can tell he is trying, but he's so inhibited in his ability to show love that I can only feel sorry for him. I am an affectionate, romantic, feminine person. He turned me into someone who sought professional help because I began to think I was frigid. I have since experienced profoundly beautiful sexual love and I no longer have any reason to assume any guilt of an unsuccessful sexual relationship. Love for him, especially sexual love, if it exists at all, and strangely I think he does love me, is not comprehensible to me in my terms of expression. In such an environment, my love has died. At this point in the marriage, I don't inspire him, I don't nag him and the wall grows." Doctor M had taken down her comments verbatim. It was decided that the marriage was no longer meaningful, that we should stop our sessions, and that we would tell our patients and focus on them ·instead of the marriage.

Mr. D at his next appointment commented: "I never realized how distant Ann is. I was out of town for a week at our New York branch. I missed Ann and the boy. But when I returned, such blankness. She is a master at turning me off. We are in bed. She said, 'Rub my back.' I was rubbing her back when she said, 'What was the weather like in New York?' It turned off my sexual desire. I felt certain that we are mismated. I laid back in misbelief. A week later I told her that the only level of communication was in terms of our child, that she was distant, and that physically she turned me off when I came back from New York. She didn't say anything. I said I want to make a go of our marriage. I said I hope it's only a phase. She said, 'It's just two people finding out how different they are.' It turned off my hope. I said it's been a bad six months. She said it's been two years. She keeps pushing me farther and farther away."

I told Mr. D that Doctor M and I had discontinued our collaborative sessions. I suggested he and his wife separate, but start dating each other again to see if they could play the old records of their courtship. Also I set a target date of three months, and if there is no change in their relationship, to consider a divorce.

He replied: "Three months ago I could not have accepted this. Now I can. She isn't interested in being with me anymore. She is just a social vehicle, not an intimate companion."

Mr. D began his ninth month of therapy and his forty-fifth session by looking very unhappy and concerned. For the past two weeks he and his wife had gone their separate ways and slept in separate bedrooms. They were friendly with each other but treated each other as strangers (emotional divorce).

"My unhappiness is getting oppressive. Two weeks ago Ann and I had a talk. No arguments. But we are not making it. Socially, each going separate ways. Ann is right, we are not communicating. I told her my thinking about moving out of our house. Then she began to cry. "I am now absolutely and totally turned off toward her. The saddest thing I feel is about our child. I'm not in love with her. She can't motivate me to anything. We have had this emotional divorce you have been talking about for the past year or two."

I suggested that perhaps he should move out. That sometimes distance is necessary to clarify a marital relationship and frequently the meaning of the partner. Either they draw farther apart or move closer to each other.

He replied: "Everyone I know is having other outlets. I never had. Maybe if I did, the marriage would be better. She said maybe I should have an affair. Maybe I need to get my ego or organs reinforced. It might give me more tolerance with Ann's needs and demands. I think Ann thinks it is all right. That is the most palatable solution to my marriage. To have two women in my life: my wife to run the house, take care of our child, and to go out with socially, and another woman to turn me on sexually. There is nothing in her behavior to send me or to indicate that I send her. Something I used to do with other women — five or six times in an evening."

In his next session, he continued to be depressed: I've been looking around for an apartment. We are not on the same wavelength. If Ann was sitting here she would say, 'All I have allowed you the past ten years is to indulge your needs.' I've been brought up differently.

Wait and see things a bit longer. It was her idea to see Doctor M. She is more expressive. She then got me to go. She made an honest attempt. In doing this she accelerated the breakdown, the inequities in our marriage."

It took Mr. D five weeks before he could move out: "I had the most traumatic week. I moved out a week ago. It was a terrible week. Moving out of my house and from my child. Being uprooted was a terrible, upsetting thing to me. I can hardly sleep. I am closer to my son now. At one o'clock we are seeing the lawyers. I saw this girl last night. A total explosion of chemistry. She felt the same way about me. I've regained my self-respect."

An amiable settlement was worked out between the couple without any problems. Two months later, during which Mr. D received divorce therapy, he asked to discontinue treatment. He was advised to take at least two years before he remarried and to call for remarital therapy. Through referrals over the past few years from both Ds' I heard that they are both doing well in their separate ways.

5. *This indication for collaborative therapy, where one partner has primary affective disorder (manic-depressive illness) will be discussed in a special section in Chapter XXVII.*

In the collaborative approach, both partners are treated concurrently by different therapists who communicate at regular, scheduled intervals. The collaboration of the therapists permits the partners to gain some understanding of their partner's psychodynamics as it influences the dyadic transaction, thus enabling some containment of excessive anxiety and/or hostility. Experience has shown difficulties of communication between therapists with this technique. Mutual trust and confidence does not prevent cross-transference difficulties between the therapists. Each therapist identifies with the viewpoint of his patient and gets a biased picture of the real situation at home. Most important in this technique is the loss of the strategical center for integrating all relevant observations of the marriage, when the events and perceptions are parceled out between two therapists.

REFERENCES

1. Martin, Peter A.: Treatment of marital disharmony by collaborative therapy. In Greene, B. L. (Ed.): *The Psychotherapies of Marital Disharmony.* New York, Free Press, 1965, pp. 83-101.
2. Martin, Peter A. and Bird, H. Waldo: An approach to the psychotherapy of marriage partners — the stereoscopic technique, *Psychiatry, 16:* 123, 1953.
3. Dicks, Henry V.: *Marital Tensions.* New York, Basic Books, 1967, pp. 53-54.

4. Jameson, Jean D.: The theory of Sandor Rado of adaptational psychodynamics. *J Am Acad Psychoanal, 2:* 3-10, 1974.
5. Martin, Peter A.: *A Marital Therapy Manual.* New York: Brunner-Mazel, 1976.
6. Martin, Treatment of marital disharmony by collaborative therapy.
7. Grotjohn, Martin. *Psychoanalysis and the Family Neurosis.* New York, Norton & Co., 1960, pp. 91-2.

Chapter XXV

THE CONCURRENT APPROACH IN DYADIC DISHARMONY

$\mathbf{M}$ORE than forty years ago, the famous analyst Clarence Oberndorf (1938) wrote about the psychoanalysis of married couples. He did not, however, see this approach as concurrent but as *consecutive*. Treatment of the patient must be complete before help is offered to the patient's partner. Bela Mittlemann was the first to report his analytic experiences with concurrent therapy just a decade later (1948).[1] This technique began the first *triadic* setting in dyadic disharmony and was valuable when therapy included intrapsychic (intrapersonal), interpersonal, and/or environmental system inputs. As a technique, it offered additional dimensions for the mobilization of unconscious material, for the timing of mutative interpretations, for the production of emotional and intellectual insights, and finally for the constructive adaptive patterns of behavior — that is *action*.

My first use of this approach dates back to 1955 when two female patients in my practice (classical couch analysis) were divorced from their respective husbands. Since eight children from these two couples were involved, I began to do both marital therapy and psychoanalysis in an attempt to bring in the husband in order to reduce misunderstanding, anxiety, and all emotional upheavals the therapy of one spouse might influence. Some colleagues at that time did not see the value of including the marital system, but Conn,[2] among others, later did. In the past twenty-five years, I have used the marital approach and, in 1960[3] and 1963[4,5] I published papers that described my concurrent approach.

The indications for the concurrent approach in dyadic discord include the following:

1. Where the power structure of one partner has overwhelmed his partner.
2. Where insight into their behavior patterns as they affect each partner is needed to produce changes in behavior.
3. A test of previous procedures has indicated that one or both spouses could profit from a deeper understanding of the components of their three systems (intrapersonal, interpersonal, and

environmental).
4. Therapeutic impasse with other approaches.
5. Couples who experience difficulties both inside and outside their relationship.

The contraindictions for concurrent therapy exist in some dyads with the follow:

1. Severe psychoses or severe character disorders.
2. Paranoid reactions, until a therapeutic alliance is established.
3. Suspicious attitudes toward the communications of the partner.
4. Excessive sibling-rivalry attitudes that preclude sharing the therapist.
5. "Family secrets" revealed in individual evaluative sessions.
6. Very rigid defenses that, if broken, might produce a severe psychosomatic crisis or a psychosis.
7. Severe character disorders.

The selection of concurrent psychoanalytic therapy as the form of treatment is determined by the couple's clinical need for a therapy in depth, their capacities for self-observation, their tolerance of the tensions of an uncovering therapy, their possibilities for change in ego resources. absence of contraindications, and the availability of a therapist with psychoanalytic orientation and technical ability to apply this knowledge in a flexible manner.

THERAPEUTIC ELEMENTS AND THERAPEUTIC ACTION

Concurrent therapy contains specific therapeutic elements and a therapeutic action inherent in its design. A couple that is under considerable stress reacts to concurrent therapy with feelings of emotional support and with relief of their anxiety. We are reminded here of Alexander's[6] comment that the supportive effects of the psychoanalytic process (as well as other therapeutic processes) have not been sufficiently recognized as one of the main factors favoring both insight and recognize as one of the main factors favoring both insight and emergence of new behavioral patterns. There is another important therapeutic gain in a technical procedure that extends the integrative force of hope for the restoration .of equilibrim in a marital relationship.

Another therapeutic element in concurrent therapy is the multidimensional view of the dyadic transactions gained by the therapist from the communications, often contradictory and constantly changing, of the partners. Through this triadic communication system, knowledge is gained in minimal time of both the nuclear and kinship transactions and of the immediate and peripheral environmental situations and influences (environmental system). The therapist hears both sides of long-standing controversies, and each partner is aware that the therapist is hearing two sides of a complaint. As the concurrent therapy proceeds, partners frequently discuss between themselves ideas gained through insights. Particularly in the later phases of the therapy, this type of communication may become an extension of the learning process. On the other hand, these incidents often reveal to the therapist additional information about his patients resistances or about the significance of the resentments, frustrations, or projections produced by these interpartner communications. The communications of unconscious sibling-rivalry attitudes or oedipal feelings, as highlighted in the triangular representation of the original family constellation, is a further therapeutic element.

I direct the spouses to report their dreams. I find that dream material enables me to grasp important preoccupations behind the behavioral facades as well as the current conflicts and possible options for solutions. This knowledge aids me in planning therapeutic maneuvers. Further, dreams furnish many important clues about the partners' coping maneuvers and brings freely into focus the precise nature of their projective identifications and their feedbacks. Frequently when one partner reports his dream in his session and both partners become involved in the interpretation, anxiety and/or hostility between the couple may be eased.

Another distinctive therapeutic element in concurrent therapy is the triangular transference transactions. We have differentiated five foci of transactions in the transference relationships.[7] The first focus of transaction involves the relationship to the therapist as a *real person*, and subsequently, as a *new object*. The second focus of transaction pertains to those situations where the therapist is experienced as a *symbolic figure* endowed with qualities of existing fantasies, as those involved in projections and displacements. The *regressive phenomena* manifested in the dyadic, one-to-one transference neurosis comprise the third focus of transaction. These three foci of transaction between patient and therapist are fundamental in all therapeutic relationships. In concurrent therapy, because the transference reactions of both partners are directed toward the same therapist as well as toward each other, two other foci of transaction related to the triangular transactions are introduced. The first of these is the *triangular transference neurosis*, such as the reproduction of the oedipal constellation. The second, the *triangular transference transaction,* concerns the production of adaptive feedbacks, not only toward the therapist, but toward the other partner (who in turn feeds back to his partner, the therapist, or both). Interpretations of the transference phenomena in concurrent therapy are made from the frame of reference of both the dyadic and triangular aspects of the transference. The additional foci of transaction favor the increased production of emotional and intellectual insights, which is conducive to the learning process. Franz Alexander described the nature of the therapeutic learning process as when the patient unlearns ". . . the old patterns and learns new ones. . . . This process . . . contains cognitive elements as well as learning from interpersonal experiences which occur in therapeutic interaction." He compared emotional insight to any intellectual grasp ". . . motivated by some kind of urge for mastery and is accompanied by tension resolution as its reward. In psychotherapy, the reward consists in less conflictual, more harmonious interpersonal relations, which the patient achieves first by adequately relating to his therapist, then to his environment, and eventually to his own ego ideal."[8] A clinical vignette follows to illustrate the concurrent approach.

> The Cs' both in their late twenties, were extremely intelligent and made a handsome couple. After six years of marriage, they were divorced for the past three months. They both came for their first interview and stated they were unhappy at their separation. Their two main complaints of their marriage were lack of communication and periodic arguments.
>
> Mr. C stated that after an argument he would crawl into his shell because he felt that she should apologize.
>
> Mrs. C commented that she had a great deal of personal pride, and that each waited for the other to do the apologizing. "After an argument I would be wishing I were dead. I would be lonely and crying and he would not speak to me for several days."
>
> Mr. C interrupted: "After we divorced I felt so miserable I couldn't concentrate and neglected my work, but I couldn't pick up the phone and tell her how much I missed her. I felt it was her place to call me."
>
> After the usual diagnostic workup, I suggested the concurrent approach. Both readily agreed. The therapy lasted three months, each seen once a week. On Mrs. C's birthday they remarried: three years later they reported getting along very well. The following illustrates the course of their therapy.
>
> Mr. C began his first individual session by stating: "After our session with you I gave considerable thought about why we argued, and I find myself laughing about how foolish the arguments were. We would argue about the things she would say to her parents or

family. Then, many of the times I would feel that Jill was just looking for an argument for the sake of trying to see how far she can go without my reacting. After an argument I would be hurt and unwilling to make up, but Jill was ready just after a few minutes.

Our courtship was wonderful. Doing things together, going to the theatre, shows, meeting our relatives, and just getting to know each other. Our honeymoon was a new experience for both of us. I felt we were adjusting to each other emotionally and physically without much hesitation. Everything fell into place and was so natural."

He described himself as very competitive and determined to be successful. Thus he was captain of the basketball team in college and rapidly promoted at work. His father was a quiet man, an accountant, but a strict disciplinarian. He was fair, but unforgiving and would hold a grudge for years: "I am like him. Once one of my aunts slapped me over a small argument. I didn't talk to her for three years" (an excellent example of parental voice projection in his records").

He further comments: "If I did something wrong, my father would not speak to me for days." His parents were very religious Mormons.

The precipitating reason for their separation was a minor incident, but neither would make the first overture of apologizing. Thus the chasm between the two widened and finally led to divorce: "Sometimes I get angry, but by the time I get over it, I don't know what it was about. We were in bed and Jill lightly pinched me. For some reason this irritated me and I retaliated by pinching her severely. She cried but I couldn't apologize for some reason. She didn't talk the next day, so I didn't talk to her. Later we talked but had no sex relations at all for two months. Things got worse, and she left like I did twice before. Although I missed her, I made no effort to talk to her. I felt a man does not do that sort of thing, since she was the one who left. Both of us are very proud and so we divorced."

He related his first dream as the hour ended: "I am back in Salt Lake City, Jill is with me. We are at a night club. A man comes up to me and hands me a note written by Jill: 'Don't wait for me. I will come home with this man.' I leave alone. I am driving ninety miles an hour when I realized I was speeding and woke up."

His interview ended before he could associate to the dream. But the dream reveals a wish to be back with his wife. But time is fast running out and he is afraid his wife will become interested in another man.

Mrs. C began her first individual session by stating: "I'm a little confused about my emotions. Your idea that we start dating again as though we had just met was wonderful. I missed him so and am happier since I have been seeing him. I think we have both profited from our separation. We have had some sexual dissatisfaction. He gets aroused too soon. He said everything had to be sexually the way

I want. He doesn't realize that women are slower to be aroused than men. For him, the act itself was it. He didn't realize that sex was closeness, kissing, tenderness. To him, I'm selfish.

"Living with Tom can be compared to living with a keg of dynamite. You never know when or what may set him off. Insignificant comments or actions done on my part seem to be significant enough to cause him to explode when I least expect it, for instance, teasing or an affectionate gesture. Sometimes reference to my family or upbringing is interpreted on his part as bragging in comparison to his background. We are of different family and economic backgrounds. I come from an old well-established New England family. I would not have married him if I didn't respect his values, morals, and character more than his economic position. These are often causes of our arguments. Then I become extremely unsatisfied emotionally for I am forced to endure long periods of silence and lack of affection for periods as long as three and four weeks. Communication is impossible unless you are able to beg for it day after day. It is as if he hates me so much he receives pleasure from my loneliness and tears. I did not ever want a divorce. I am very much in love with my husband, and I know he loves me. However, twice before he got angry and left, 'calling it quits.' Because I knew we were both miserable I eventually called him, and we reconciled. The last time I left after we quarreled. I had to go through with his request for divorce for fear I would spend the rest of my life in long, lonely silences and separations. I want more than anything for him to receive help in communicating his feelings instead of harboring them and running away. In spite of all the misery I often underwent, and so did he, I was happy in our marriage and I still want to be his wife, but only if you can help me deal with our problems more maturely. This time he called me!"

In his second session we discussed the clash of cultural values that was playing a factor in the arguments between them. It was pointed out that he was demanding of his wife's "inner child" what he demanded of his "inner child," that a meaningful marriage was based on mutual respect.

He next reported a dream of the previous night: "I am in a cocktail lounge with Jill. Some man walks in and tries to butt into our conversation. I was going to object and hit him. Then I decided it's not worth it. So we go about our business. The scene changes. I'm on top of a hill. Below is a big valley. Large mountains surrounding the valley. The Viet Cong are taking over the valley and digging in. Then suddenly see the Green Berets chop them to pieces."

In his associations he stated that someone is trying to help him but that he began by rejecting the help, but then decided to accept this man.

When I asked him who the man could be, he answered, "probably you." I replied, this was a normal reaction to the invasion of his privacy and that he was quite angry about it — "You chop me to pieces."

He commented: "I'm strongly dug in and someone really shattered it — things I need to hold on, my very conservative values and ideas about marriage, just like my father. My wife could perhaps represent the Green Berets chopping those values to pieces." (This is a good example of the triangular transference neurosis, both oedipal and sibling rivalry, a common reaction to triadic therapy — two is company and three is a crowd).

In her second session, Mrs. C stated things were going well between them. But she was still concerned whether he would get angry at her and stop talking.

This had first happened shortly after their engagement. They were playing golf, and when he paid the caddy, she had asked him if he tipped him sufficiently. He didn't answer but had both a hurt and angry look. Just silence on his part. This occurred later — these periods of silence.

It was pointed out to her that when she acts in a manner to question his masculinity, he counterattacks by withdrawing into silence. Actually she was playing a record in which her parental voice was loud and clear, telling him his inner child was stupid.

In his third session, Mr. C stated: "We are getting along better. The things you have pointed out to me have been most helpful. Before I wanted things my way, instead of seeing her side of the picture. I am honestly trying to solve this problem. I'm very grateful to you."

With the positive dyadic transference to me as a real object as well as the dyadic transference neurosis — the ominpotent and omniscient powers of father — I asked him about his sexual relationship with his wife.

"We had sex for the first time, twice over the week-end. In many ways I am confused about it. That it is not right. We are no longer married. I was brought up to wait until you were married. I always had such a strong guilt complex when I was single and had intercourse. She could be someone's sister. But sex was very enjoyable this past weekend. Much more than previously. The last time was one of the best and longest I ever had. In the past there were times I would come very fast. A feeling to get it over with as rapidly as possible. At times she is aggressive verbally, she would make a few hints; I felt it was a man's job to do all the advances. This made me angry at times."

He was praised at his improvement and given some of the basic facts about sexuality, e.g. that both partners are on the seesaw and both can be agressive in the sexual act. Secondly, his parental voice comes on too strongly when he is having sex, making him feel guilty and thus to get sex over as quickly as possible (there was no need to raise the issue of other psychodynamic forces).

In her third session, Mrs. C stated that for the first time she and Tom were able to sit down and communicate about how they managed their finances in the past, and how they would handle their money if they remarried. "I'm apt to be more impulsive than he is, but he is much too conservative. He doesn't want to buy things on credit. Although it ended in a slight argument, we really talked."

In his fourth session, Mr. C commented: "She is trying to counsel me as to the way I should spend my earnings. She said, if we go back we should each give a little — I should be less conservative and she, more restraining. It got a little heated toward the end. I started to retaliate by becoming silent, then realized this was an old record and said, let's talk about it further at another time."

Mrs. C opened her fourth session by commenting: "We had a very nice week. No longer any of the silent treatment when we argue. You are helping both of us. He looks forward to his sessions with you."

When I saw Mr. C at his fifth session a few days later, I told him Jill said everything was coming along fine. Mr. C seemed very pleased and stated: "I've been seeing her every day. We've been getting along fine. We went to a dance, and for the first time I didn't react when she was doing a Charleston step. I know what she is afraid of — that I'll revert back to my previous behavior. I have no intention of doing that."

Mrs. C began her fifth session by relating the following dream: "I came to your home for an appointment. I was greeted by a bevy of fine and lovely daughters. You were friendly. One of your daughters and I are sneaking cake off the table.

"The dream was full of fun and happiness. I had a nice, warm feeling toward you, as though I was one of your family. Tom and I are getting along fine. I have a sense of pride in voicing every thought I have up here. I have never disciplined myself. You mentioned why fight over little things. The cake was a special cake we used to have on special occasions in the sorority house."

(Comment: Instead of dealing with the dyadic transference level — she has become one of my daughters — I focused on her current marital situation by asking: "In your marriage you would like to have your cake and eat it too?"

Mrs. C replied: "Yes, on two levels. I would like it to be "we," but Tom is such a strong personality. I was competing with him. I was afraid he would take complete control of me and turn me into a passive submissive nonentity."

In her sixth and seventh sessions, Mrs. C reported increasing harmony and love in her relationship to Tom. "We are getting along fine. My birthday is in three weeks, and we would like to get remarried on that day. He was elated, but said he would like to get your opinion."

In his sixth and last session, Mr. C said: "We are getting along fine. Sexually it has been great. I had a dream: I'm with this person I work with. We are at Harvard — the school of business administration. He passes and I failed. We are co-workers. He is only interested in one phase of the operation, bonds, whereas I am interested in all types of securities."

I asked him why he thought his marriage had failed. He replied that he had not really understood himself, his wife, and what marriage entailed. I commented: "You focused on one area in your marriage and missed the total picture, like your co-worker who is only interested in one phase. I see no reason why you and Jill cannot remarry. If a major problem arises, call for an appointment."

In her eighth and final session, Mrs. C stated: "We are getting along fine. We are getting married on my birthday. I think I have grown up and so has he. Like he enjoys me more as I am, not as he wants me to be. I have no complaints in my relationship to him now. If we have any future problems, this will be the first place we will come to. Tom planned to come in with me today but had an emergency meeting. He said to thank you for everything."

In conclusion, the concurrent triadic technique offers distinctive advantages. It makes possible an analysis of the dyadic, one-to-one transference neurosis and an analysis of the resistance of a patient who knows that another member of his family is being treated synchronously by the same psychiatrist. It brings under focus a more comprehensive view of family transactions in both the dyadic and triadic transference relationships. The analyst is thus able to achieve a multidimensional view of dyadic transactions and disharmony; and, with this view, a better comprehensive basis for diagnosis and treatment is established. This technique finds selective use for couples who require understanding of intrapsychic processes as they are reflected in and become part of the dyadic transactions. Indications and contraindictions for selecting this therapy have been given. Furthermore, my working with this technique has significantly expanded my understanding of individual, dyadic, and family dynamics.

REFERENCES

1. Mittlemann, Bela: The concurrent analysis of married couples, *Psychoanal Quart, 17:* 182, 1948.
2. Conn, Jacob H.: Letters to the editor, *Am J Psychiat, 136:* 992, 1979.
3. Greene, Bernard L.: Marital disharmony: concurrent analysis of husband and wife. I. Preliminary report, *Dis Nerv System, 21:* 1-6, 1960.
4. Solomon, A. P., Greene, B. L.: Marital disharmony: concurrent analysis of

husband and wife by the same psychiatrist — an analysis of the therapeutic elements. *Dis Nerv System, 24:* 105-13, 1963.

5. Greene, B. L., Solomon, A. P.: Marital disharmony: concurrent psychoanalutic therapy of husband and wife — the triangular transference transactions. *Am J Psychotherapy. 17:* 443-56, 1963.

6. Alexander, Franz: Psychoanalysis and psychotherapy. In Masserman, Jules (Ed.): *Psychoanalysis, III. Psychoanalysis and Human Values,* New York, Grune, 1960, pp. 250-259.

7. Greene and Solomon, Marital disharmony.

8. Alexander, Franz: The dyanamics of psychotherapy in light of learning theory, *Am J Psychiatry 120:* 440-8, 1963.

Chapter XXVI

THE CONJOINT APPROACH IN
DYADIC DISHARMONY

Since 1930, the literature written by social workers frequently had references to joint interviewing with couples having marital problems. In 1959, Don D. Jackson[1] introduced the term *conjoint therapy* in marital disharmony in psychiatric circles. Not long afterward, Watson,[2] Satir,[3] and I participated at the American Orthopsychiatric Association meeting in Los Angeles. Over breakfast, prior to our presentations, they challenged me to try conjoint therapy. When I returned to Chicago after the meeting, I tried this approach with three couples and found it very useful. From then on, I made it part of my spectrum of techniques. From 1962 through 1979, I used this technique with 45 percent of dyads needing crisis therapy and with 15 percent needing intensive therapy (see Table I).

In the conjoint dyadic approach, both partners are seen together, by the same therapist, in the same session. This technique is the most often used of dyadic therapies by most therapists.[4-9]

I have previously described the indications for conjoint therapy in dyadic disharmony.[10] I have enlarged its application over the years. The following list is my current one:

1. Therapeutic impasse with the concurrent approach.
2. Paranoid or suspicious behavior of one partner who reacts with anxiety and distortion of the comments which either the therapist or the partner are reputed to have stated in the individual session.
3. Economic — the cost of the treatment is less. (There is ample evidence that the decision as to which spouse gets therapy depends to a large extent on economic considerations.)
4. Explosiveness of the dyadic situation demands speed in bringing order to the family environment.
5. Couples in which the problems in the relationship are largely of an acting-out nature.
6. Need to foster communication between the partners.
7. Couples who perceive relationships between events and their own responses only when confronted with them acutely. These

345

couples lack capacity to traverse time and space, which is necessary for gaining appreciation and conviction about such experiences and their meaning.[11]

8. To point out not merely the differences, but the possibility of complementation in the transactions between the couple.
9. Agoraphobias in relation to dyadic disharmony.[12]
10. Sexual dysfunction.[13,14]
11. Obsessive-compulsive neurosis with dyadic disharmony.[15]

Contraindications to conjoint therapy include the following:

1. Folie à deux — separation of the couple results in gradual subsiding of the psychotic disorder in the partner.[16]
2. Where one partner has a psychotic disorder requiring hospitalization.
3. In some couples where one partner has a *hysterical psychotic disorder* in which transient structured distance, either separation or hospitalization, enables the person to regroup his coping defenses with reequilibration of personality resulting.
4. Excessive narcissistic attitudes of one partner, e.g. sibling rivalry attitudes, which precludes sharing the therapist.
5. A family secret in one partner, e.g. infidelity or homosexuality where premature disclosure would disrupt the relationship. Actually, if the partner *knows of the homosexuality,* this therapeutic modality is very helpful. My experience parallels that of Bieber.[17]
6. Where one partner prefers a different therapeutic approach.
7. Either partner's nonambivalent desire to terminate the relationship.

There are many advantages in the conjoint dyadic approach. For some couples, this technique provides more access to the dynamics of their relationship. For these couples, conjoint sessions may disclose that, although on a conscious level the partners are distrusting each other and frequently using physical abuse, unconsciously, they have mutual strivings and interdependent needs. If partners identify with the therapist's interpretations, they may on occasion act as an auxiliary therapist in the home environment and often during the session.

The learning therapeutic process includes developing new coping maneuvers to deal with the core anger behind the complaints — the other side of ambivalence is love. Frequently in the conjoint sessions, not only does the phenomenon of projective identification come into focus but it can be pointed out to the couple as part of their disharmony.

Having the couple in a conjoint session affords the therapist the advantage of heightened perception of their conscious and unconscious thoughts, feelings, and behavior of the unfolding transactions. The therapist has a better objective evaluation of the couples' behavior and decreases the necessity to evaluate distortion from indirect data. Witnessing the dyadic relationship in action permits observation of nonverbal transactions, both positive and negative. For example, one partner may complain about the other's lack of love, although his partner has his arm around her, or vice versa; the therapist can point out the demonstrative behavior occurring at that moment. Moreover, in the conjoint session, the therapist can observe the positive strivings and values of the relationship, which is difficult to infer from individual sessions.

A distinct advantage of the conjoint approach is the facilitation of reality testing by the couple. In fact, this technique places mounting pressure on the dyad to reexamine reality testing. Frequently, a couple will present a common front of harmony during the session but resume quarreling as soon as they reach their car. I suggest to all dyads, that each keep a daily diary of any situation that causes anxiety and/or hostility and not to discuss this until their next session. This procedure frequently decreases hostile transactions at home. Frequently, in the conjoint sessions, reality problems causing dyadic dysfunction can be clarified and negotiated in the neutrality of the session. In essence, what the therapist is doing is child and/or adolescent therapy of *setting limits*. Obviously, therapy aids each individual in the relationship to change their coping processes, which is reflected in new ways of communication and personal growth. The interpretations, by the therapist, enables each partner to work through the neurotic distortions of their interlocking adaptive coping and communication systems. I prefer interpretating all five foci and transference described in the preceeding chapter, utilizing psychodynamic constructs and valid concepts of other behavioral disciplines as indicated. The conjoint session are "living-learning situation(s),"[18] which are important in any triadic therapy. The therapist confronts the couple with interpretations of their behavior as displayed in the session which parallels their behavior in the current interpersonal relationship. Thus, each partner is in a "face to face" confrontation of the thoughts and feelings of the other. leading to a better "gestalt" or holistic view of their current communication and behavior. As Freud would say it, what was previously unconscious is brought to conscious awareness. In the same vein, Saul L. Brown states: ". . . conjoint sessions represent an effort to reduce the 'field resistance' to therapeutic progress. The conjoint session then would reflect the recognition that the patient's inability to change constructively is a function of the psychological field of the patient and his spouse."[19]

Another advantage of the conjoint technique is the leverage it places on the couple to reexamine their reality testing. When an interpretation of feelings or behavior, frequently in terms of content and relationships in their transactions, is made to one partner, the other also hears it and may further discuss it outside the sessions. Not only does this improve communication between the couple, but, in effect, each partner indirectly provides the therapist with a "co-therapist" who may reinforce the interpretations made during the session. As Watson[20] notes: "While there is a possibility and even a probability that interpretations will be used for nontherapeutic purposes, the general summation-effect is reinforcement of, and mounting pressure toward, reality testing by both spouses. . . . The speed with which conjoint therapy improves reality testing is a distinct advantage" (a clinical observation I have repeatedly observed).

The disadvantages of the conjoint approach include the more complex transference phenomena (described in the previous chapter) and the countertransference reaction of the therapist(s). It is necessary for the therapist to promptly comprehend all areas of pragmatic communication in concrete psychodynamic terms. The flow of material is so fast that there is little time to pause and reflect before dealing with interpretations. The emotional significant events may not appear again for some time. This timing problem is always present, although there is much reiteration of all communicative material. Some couples present a particular form of resistance to giving up maladaptive coping defenses in relation to their partner; then the partner suddenly reacts differently than he has in the past. If the first partner fails after trying different approaches, he may project his anger onto the therapist or the efficacy of the treatment. Occasionally, when high levels of anxiety occur, one partner may join in the attack upon the therapist or the progress made in treatment in an effort to placate the mate. This unconscious coalition has been referred to as forming a "triangle." For some patients, the expression is to discontinue therapy or to demand a different therapeutic approach. Resistance is expected during therapy when change occurs, because there is increasing anxiety that may be conscious and/or unconsciously recognized. I include a discussion with my patients stating that the normal reaction to change is one of increased anxiety: Unless there are definite indications that such a discussion would not be beneficial, I interpret the unconscious factors influencing the resistance and encourage the continuation of working through the problem.

Conjoint sessions often cause a patient to speak directly to the therapist and not to the partner which means that the therapist has to be alert at all times. Some patients try to use the therapist as a vehicle to attack the partner (it is like the old "saw" where the patient talks about the uncle but means the aunt). Sometimes one partner may resist talking about a subject for fear it will upset the other. I point out, for such individuals, that their relationship is like a seesaw, which means that both people are on the same board and equally responsible for the conflicts and resolutions between each other. When there is a display of hostile feelings that exceeds the intensity of those at previous sessions, the therapist often can feel trapped into identifying with one partner against the mate and expressing it. Triangles can prevent the progress in therapy and conjoint sessions can lead into such pitfalls. Sager,[21] as well as others,[22-24] have discussed this area in detail.

Virginia Satir's approach offers much for the therapist. She has been influenced by psychoanalytic concepts and the GST model. The main emphasis of her work on conjoint dyadic therapy has broadened the understanding of communicational skills. Her therapeutic interventions are directed at the adaptive-coping processes of each individual, which alters the system of transactions of both partners so that new ways of communication can develop. She encourages individuality, self-worth, and relatedness. Satir's concepts form a phenomenological base of interpersonal behavior in which reality is validated by literal interactional negotiation in which any behavior that occurs between two people is the product of both of them. The focus of her approach is authenticity and spontaneity regardless of the danger of uninhibited reporting of feelings, thoughts, and perceptions. Thus, everything can be understood once programatic communications are made explicit and clear, and the meaning of all behavior can be given, received, and checked out without risk to oneself or the partner. Although now out of print, Satir's classic chapter on conjoint marital therapy[25] is valid for those using this approach. The following pages present many of the ideas, concepts, and therapeutic approaches she wrote in the book, *The Psychotherapies of Marital Disharmony.*

"The concepts that underlie my treatment approach to marital therapy add up to phenomenological theory of interpersonal behavior in which reality is validated by literal interactional negotiation. This theory means that any behavior that occurs between any two people is the product of both of them. The focus is on how to be personally authentic and spontaneous, which means how to encourage each person to commit himself to risk complete and uninhibited reporting of all that he feels and thinks, sees, and hears about himself and any other person. I aim to demonstrate that everything can be understood once the premises from which any behavior is derived are made explicit and clear. I teach a method by which meaning can be given, received, and checked out without destroying oneself or another.

I believe that action is a separate negotiation, which follows after understanding is achieved. It is not an automatic follow-up of understanding. The manifestation of any thought or feeling therefore conveys nothing definitive about what will be done about it. That is another negotiation. For example, A's report in B's presence that he is angry says nothing definite about what he will do as a follow-up. It also says nothing definite about what B will do about A's report.

I expect to make three kinds of changes in each member of the marital pair: a change in his perception of himself and of others, which has both cognitive and affective parts; a change in his way of manifesting thoughts and feelings; and a change in his way of reacting to the stimulus and feedback of others. Briefly, these three parts form the patterns of interaction that compose the couple's 'system.' The couple's behavior both creates the system initially and, as experience accumulates, becomes the product of the system. Each system then becomes predictable through repetition. A set of behavioral rules inevitably develops, which may or may not be apparent to the members of the system. In any event, these rules become powerful shapers of each individual's behavior. I think that symptoms develop when the rules for operating do not fit needs for survival, growth, getting close to others, and productivity on the part of each member of the system.

My therapeutic efforts are designed to change the rules, which means changing the system. This aim requires that I be active and have an explicit and clear structure that will bring about change. I shall try to describe the structure, the premises underlying it, and the ways in which I use it.

Conjoint marital therapy is, by my definition, a therapeutic method in which both marital partners are seen together by the same therapist or by cotherapists, one male and one female, and in which the signaling symptom or condition is viewed by the therapist as a comment on the dysfunction of their interactional system.

I am talking about a marital pair *that has no children* and a pair that fits one or both of the following descriptions:

   A. One member has a psychiatric diagnosis of schizophrenia, delinquency, neurosis, or psychosomatic disorder.

B. One or both members have a social diagnosis of alcoholism, gambling, extra-marital affairs, or inability to provide financially.

If the couple has children and the above conditions exist, I use the family therapeutic approach. I do so because, as a therapist, I believe I have an educational and preventive function, as well as a treatment function, for all the members of the family in which there is an identified patient or condition.

Returning to the marital pair, my treatment *process* is the same, regardless of whether the diagnosis is a psychiatric or a social one, because I believe the two are merely different ways of labeling dysfunctional processes. The dysfunctional condition is the result of dysfunctional communication processes, and it is the evidence of pain experienced by both members of the marital pair in their unsuccessful efforts to achieve joint outcomes.

In analyzing any outcome — a symptom is one kind of outcome — I use three major tools: a communication analysis, a model analysis, and a label or role-function analysis.

The therapist takes his diagnostic cues from his or her observation of the ways the couple has of communicating with each other. That is, he observes the ways in which the partners give and receive meaning and the ways in which each checks out meaning with the other. I call this observation *communication analysis*.

Briefly, *communication analysis* is made up of four parts. The first part involves who speaks, who speaks for whom, and who attributes blame and credit for his actions to someone else. The second part involves the "how" of getting messages across, which I call *congruency*. This congruency encompasses the matching of meaning in terms of the verbal symbols (language), voice tone and pace, facial expression, body position, and tonus. The third part involves what I call *delineation*. The term refers to how obvious, clear, and specific the verbal symbol is, the voice tone and pace, the facial expression, or the body position and tonus: How easily and clearly is the person heard and seen? The fourth part has to do with the *sequence* of four interchanges, that is, A's manifestation, B's response, A's response to B's response, and B's response to A's response to B.

By using these four aspects of communication analysis, I can see the method by which A and B attempt to give, receive, and check out meaning with each other. To the degree that meaning is not given or received clearly, specifically, and directly, validation of self and other (in terms of predictability, trust, and lovability) is potentially in question. One of the therapist's goals, then, is to make it possible for the couple to give, receive, and check out meaning, clearly, specifically, and directly. To go from being unclear, unspecific, and indirect to being clear, specific, and direct requires changes in one's ways of extending and maintaining self-esteem, one's use of feedback, and one's use of words.

From his observations of communication between the husband and wife, the therapist can make analytic and diagnostic inferences about the self-esteem and self-image of each. He can also observe the ways in which each person uses the other to increase his own low self-esteem and to complete his own self-image. From these inferences, further inferences can be drawn about individual processes for maintaining survival, continuing growth, and managing closeness to others.

I believe that all human beings are geared toward survival, growth, and getting close to others. Behavior that appears otherwise I believe is the result of what the person has concluded about his *chances* for survival, growth, and getting close to others. He has derived these conclusions over time from his perception of past experience. People who cannot openly manifest their wishes and abilities to survive, grow, and get close to others usually have a combined sense of littleness, powerlessness, incompetence, and absence of sexual delineation. All such people have difficulties with authority, autonomy, and sexuality, which are clearly revealed in their ways of communicating.

In an adult, feelings of low self-esteem are at variance with the common expectation that an adult will be big, powerful, competent, and sexually delineated (self-image). Each person is faced with closing the gap between his low self-esteem and how he would like to see himself. People in a dysfunctional situation usually have a wide gap. The dysfunctional person tries to close this gap through the other person, using overt or covert demands managed through guilt, anger, or helplessness.

In a dysfunctional pair, the husband uses the wife, and the wife uses the husband. The result is that neither receives gratification, and each feels himself being slowly strangled. Ensuing efforts to survive lead to symptomatic behavior and bring the couple to the therapist's office.

The goal of therapy is first to make explicit the means by which each uses the other to increase his own self-esteem, which I label the *parasitic operation,* and then to enable each to change those means so that he takes charge of maintaining it himself, rather than expecting it of his spouse. The goal is not to maintain the relationship nor to separate the pair but to help each to take charge of himself. Then people can manage their own outcomes: They decide for themselves whether to stay together or to separate.

(I have found) . . . that mates in dysfunctional marital pairs see their spouses as they expect them to be, rather than as they are, and treat them accordingly. Because they cannot comment directly on the resulting situations, they rarely discover these expectations. The inevitable consequence is that each partner continually finds disappointment, which he experiences as betrayal or rejection. This process is manifest in accusation, attack, withdrawal, or acting out outside the marriage. The marriage becomes a war, with a victor and a vanquished, a victim and a victimizer. The question is continually raised, overtly or covertly, of who is right, loved, sick, bad, stupid, or crazy. This continual questioning becomes self-perpetuating and acts as a predictable assault on both individual's wavering self-esteem. When self-esteem is under assault, each individual's survival mechanisms are naturally activated.

Mate selection has long been recognized as fairly closely related to the male and female images that each spouse has developed in his growing-up years in his experience with his parents. That is, the basis for selecting a marital partner is linked to perceptions of the satisfactory or unsatisfactory outcomes of the interaction between parents, as well as perceptions of mother and father as separate and different entities. The image underlying the husband's expectation of how his wife should treat him and how he should treat his wife (and the wife's expectations of how her husband should treat her and how she should treat her husband) is derived initially from the interaction of his own parents as marital partners. It is also derived from the image of each parent in his role as parent to the child. I call the analysis of these images *model integration analysis*.

Model integration analysis involves the ways in which each child made room for the differentness of his parents and how he selected from them, as models, those things that would be useful and appropriate in his own development. As no human being is born with a set of instructions how to grow and develop, each child must take his cues and clues from those who are labeled his 'teachers' for growing up, that is, his parents.

A child cannot discard recommendations from the adults around him as unfitting unless he is openly encouraged to experiment for 'fit,' with no penalty attached. Most adults do not realize that they serve as continuous models for their children. How they talk and act toward a child and toward others in his presence becomes material for the child's blueprint for his own behavior. Many adults are naive enough to think that a child takes from an adult only what the adult consciously directs toward the child. It is often a shattering experience for an adult to be confronted with a child's performance that matches what he considers an intolerable part of his own behavior.

We have found an amazing parallel between the interactions of the spouses in the families of origin and the interaction between the present marital pair. This parallel has led me to the conclusion that, in dysfunctional marital pairs, there is a continuing effort by marital partners to accomplish, through their relationship with each other, what was not accomplished in their families of origin.

This hypothesis may account for another observation: that the marital pair, although labeled husband and wife, are functioning in some form of parent-child or sibling-sibling relationship. For example, the husband-wife relationship resembles that between father and daughter, mother and son, or brother and sister. In the marriage, label and function are thus discrepant. I call this discrepancy the *role-function discrepancy*. It should not be hard to see that this situation leads to the presence of incongruence. There is an expectation of behavior that accommodates the perception of the label, and because of the way of operating there will also be behavior that fits the way the role is lived. These types of behavior do not match, and only confused behavioral messages can result.

In all dysfunctional marital pairs, neither partner has achieved the kind of change in his relationship with his own parents that would enable him to live as a colleague in the world of adults. As a result, dysfunctional marital pairs frequently live and function as children, with one or both sets of parents still in charge of their lives.

Through the use of the tools or instruments I have referred to as *communication analysis, model integration analysis,* and *role-function discrepancy analysis,* I am in a position to find clues that lead me in turn to an assessment of each individual's self-esteem and self-image. I work for the development of high self-esteem and a complete self-image, which show themselves in clear, specific, and direct communication between the partners.

I have isolated five processes that seem to me to furnish a universal and comprehensive base from which to design treatment plans:

Manifesting Self

"Manifesting self" means the ways in which one comments in the presence of another person about what he feels and thinks, sees and hears about himself and others. These ways may be described in three dimensions: congruence, delineation, and completeness. Congruence is the relationship among different ways of manifesting feeling: language, voice tone and pace, facial expression, body position, and tonus. *Delineation* refers to how obviously and clearly one speaks, looks and acts. *Completeness* refers to the wholeness and specificity of the message.

The observer or the receiver of the manifestations of any person (the sender) evolve meaning from these three dimensions. The more congruent, obvious, and specific the manifestation is, the more it is possible for the receiver to grasp the explicit meaning intended by the sender. In my therapy with couples, I 'check out' the receiver's conclusion about the intention of the sender, which makes it possible for me to help each toward clarity in giving and receiving meanings and in "checking them out" in their turn.

So often partners seem so sure of each other's reactions that they do not hear or see reactions that do not fit their expectations. Little change can come about such a situation until each is able to see and hear the other. A gross rule of thumb for separating functional from dysfunctional couples is to find their respective ways of matching current experience and previous expectation. The dysfunctional way is to tailor the current experience to fit the previous expectation, which obviously allows for no growth. The functional way is to reshape the expectation to fit current experience. A person with low self-esteem almost automatically acts dysfunctionally — I suspect because of anxiety engendered by venturing into something new. Although painful, the old is nevertheless familiar.

Separating Self from Other

This phrase refers to the ways in which each person recognizes the presence of the other's 'skin boundaries' and the degree to which he acts on recognition that the other has a separate operating mechanism that runs on its own time. Indeed, it is sheer accident when the timing of one coincides with another in all situations.

My observation of the dysfunctional marital pair is that each member behaves as though the other should at all times match his own timing. Each behaves as if he expects the other to be hungry, to be thirsty, or to desire sex, recreation, or sleep at the identical times that he does himself. That their wishes are not identical raises questions of worth and lovability. Such questions seem related to perceptions that the condition of loving presupposes exact similarity of the loved one to the lover. Differentness, which is inevitable because of the uniqueness of every individual, is viewed as an assault on one's own lovability and worth. To fulfill an expectation of similarity then, uniqueness must be obliterated — but to obliterate the uniqueness of any individual is to risk his psychological death.

I take every opportunity to translate the concept of differentness, which is often used as a prelude to war, into a concept of uniqueness, which can be used as a stimulus to growth. This process essentially shows the gaps in the partners' perceptions of subject-object relationship.

Making Room for Self and Other

This process involves decision-making and is related to a universal human dilemma. A marital pair commits itself to the execution of joint outcomes like going to the movies together or having intercourse. Although the partners may agree on such an outcome the question inevitably arises, Which movie and when? The dilemma is how can two people achieve a single outcome and still make room for the uniqueness of each? If each wants to see a different movie, who decides what both will do? What is the process of negotiation that makes it possible for them to be together in the same movie on the same evening?

There are several possibilities. One person can be decision-maker and the other capitulator. That is, the wife can go along with the husband (domineering husband and passive wife), or the husband can go along with the wife (domineering wife and passive, ineffectual husband). In these two cases, the uniqueness of one person may be bypassed. Alternatively, the two can fight openly until one wins by brute force (literal assault or, in its milder form, competition). In all these ways, the two can arrive at the same movie — but only at some cost to their self-esteem, their individual uniqueness, or their physical health. Another way to cope with this situation is to agree to go to separate movies. This solution may result in individual gratification, but it will be achieved at the expense of the hoped-for joint outcome — companionship — which was the original goal *vis-à-vis* isolation and distance. They can, of course, give up the idea of going to the movies at all and stay home. Then a different joint outcome is achieved but perhaps at the expense of mutual joy, learning, or productivity.

Decision-making requires a tailoring process in which the shaving of one individual's autonomy does not result in feelings of attack on his self-esteem, in bodily injury, in feelings of isolation, or in personal deprivation. Instead, the process should enhance self-esteem, prevent bodily injury, create closeness, produce a feeling that the other is giving to him, and demonstrate productivity. These results come if the shaving of autonomy takes place within a context of *what fits* rather than of *who is right or boss*. In dysfunctional pairs, decision-making is usually done in terms of authority (who is right) rather than in terms of reality (what fits).

Ways in Which Differentness Is Acknowledged

If each member of a marital pair can comment openly on what he feels, thinks, sees, and hears about himself and the other, if each can treat the other as a separate being in search of real matching of 'life needs,' and if joint outcomes can be achieved through negotiating for what fits, then the acknowledgment of and reaction to the presence of any differences is that of search and exploration. Functional and fitting outcomes are assured.

If members cannot comment openly, however, if each expects to be a duplicate of the other, and if each in turn arrives at joint outcomes through power tactics, then the acknowledgment of differences must be avoided. To acknowledge difference is to raise the question of worth. Joint outcomes will consequently be chaotic, unpredictable, inappropriate, ungratifying, and unrealistic.

The Ways Joint Outcomes Are Achieved

These ways offer opportunities to assess the processes connected with self-esteem and self-images. Inappropriate or incomplete outcomes can be used as clues to the ways in which each person tries to raise his self-esteem and to complete his self-image.

In this discussion, I have defined by implication my treatment goals. My therapeutic interventions are aimed at changing the processes of coping for each individual, which in turn alters the system for both individuals and is reflected in their new ways of communicating and in their increased productivity.

To make these changes possible, the therapist must make fuller use of self than is usually the case. I divide the utility of the therapist into three major parts. The first is that of *a device* that reports fully what it sees and hears and how it interprets what it sees and hears. Often therapists report their interpretations, which are their conclusions from what they see and hear. They do not, however, provide the evidence from which these conclusions have been drawn. This omission contributes to the patient's vulnerability to harm, for what any one person sees and hears is, to a great degree, idiosyncratic. In my opinion, the failure of some therapists to report fully what they see and hear is responsible for much of what they describe as resistance by patients. To reduce further the patient's puzzlement about what the therapist means, the therapist should report clearly, directly, specifically, and completely as possible.

In the process of reporting, the therapist, acts as a *model of communication*. In this role, I can ask and tell, that is, I can demonstrate how to ask questions and to negotiate for meaning. In this process, I enable any other two to ask, tell, and check out.

This experience can serve as an ego-enhancing corrective and eventually reflects itself in clearer, more specific, and more direct communication between husband and wife. By commenting on anything and everything that seems obvious, I encourage patients to give up fears of dangerous information. Anything that comes up in the way of content can be viewed in terms of the processes of communication; integrating models; delineating roles; sorting out past, present, and future implications of present events; developing self-esteem and self-images; and achieving outcomes. And these elements are all in the interest of survival, growth, getting close to others, and being productive.

As a *resource person*, finally, I have special knowledge that, if my treatment is successful, my marital pair can share and use.

I enter the therapeutic situation with the expectation that change is possible and with a clear, delineated structure for encouraging change. This structure embraces concepts of communication, interpersonal and intrapersonal constructs, self-esteem, and self-image. It is a structure in which the therapist actively intervenes, completely reports, asks for complete reports, acts as a model of communication, and gives freely of his or her own resources. By doing so, the therapist enables the marital pair to identify and use its own resources."

Obviously, each therapist, being unique in his existence will develop his own personal variations of conjoint therapy. Regardless of how nonjudgemental we all should strive for, our value system is part of us and does influence what is viewed as healthy or nonhealthy in a relationship. What the therapist strives to do is to help each partner in the relationship to shape behavior and solutions in response to conflicts, to personal growth, and hopefully toward constructing a mutually rewarding relationship.

When couples participate in the conjoint sessions and choose separation or divorce, the rapport with the therapist can continue to be very helpful in arriving at a reasonable settlement of custody arrangements, property, and visitation of the children. If the couple cannot achieve a successful relationship, at least they may have less tramatized and less bitter separation or divorce by knowing that both have tried their best under professional guidance.

The following couple is illustrative of my conjoint approach:

Mr. and Mrs. B have been married ten years. At the insistence of Mrs. B, they both came for their initial interview. The Bs' concurred in their respective beliefs that there is virtually no communication in their marriage. Neither one tells the other what they are doing, and Agnes states that this condition produced extreme tension between them and has spilled over onto the children. She says that she wants to feel that when she suggests something, that she has Jim's wholehearted approval. She feels that while he is making some attempt at supporting her is this direction, that these efforts at best are superficial.

Jim concurred with his wife's complaint and stated: "We see things quite differently. There is no mutual understanding between us, and this void has been present right from the start of our marriage. It has always been very hard for me to express what I feel."

He is convinced that the marital problem arises from the fact that they have never gotten to the basic problems surrounding the marriage. The decision for seeking help was mutually decided upon. Jim comments that he has his own successful business that he himself started just before his marriage. He has a good relationship with his employees and customers. The Bs' agreed that there is "no warmth" in the home, with either themselves or between them and the children. Their social life has been maintained somewhat. Agnes states that she really felt she loved Jim until three years ago. For the past three years there has been total avoidance of any sexual relationship between them. Both spouses indicate that there hasn't been any real personal gratification in sexual relations. They both agreed that their wedding night was a "complete disaster." Jim had been unable to complete the act, and this initial experience resulted in a great lack of self-confidence which has never really left him. Since then, he has hardly ever initated sexual activity for fear always that he would not be able to follow through in the completion of the act.

Agnes stated that she had sensed Jim's inability to obtain or give sexual gratification at the beginning of their marriage and on the wedding night. (It was obvious during the interview that she was really challenging his manliness.) She hoped that whatever his problem was in this regard, it would be resolved. This was communicated with real anger and disgust.

Jim added that he had had a classical psychoanalysis for four years with four visits weekly. It was terminated after they had "reached an impasse." Although the decision to terminate was mutual, for the past two years he has had sporadic visits with his analyst. In assessing his period of analysis, Jim stated that for as long as he could remember he has been "role playing." He indicated that he has always had difficulty in being able to judge people's reactions and that because of this he has found it difficult to judge how he should act in relation to them. He said the reason for undergoing analysis was fear that he would act out his homosexual fantasies. Agnes interrupted that she hated his analyst, since he would never talk to her, and she resented this!

I outlined my procedure: two individual diagnostic sessions and a conjoint diagnostic and disposition session at which time I would tell them both my impressions and recommendations.

In her diagnostic sessions, Agnes indicated that she suspected infidelity. Jim has a sustained pattern of being away from home Friday and Saturday evenings, ostensibly to go to the movies, but that movies don't let out at two or three in the morning. I have never asked what he does because perhaps I am a coward. So many things have been going wrong that I guess I didn't want to add to the already existing complications.

We also have financial disagreements. Jim's idea of success is having a nice home, a maid, and extensive vacations. I feel he needs material things to bolster his ego because he is not big enough inside to fulfill his role as husband and father adequately.

During their two-year courtship, Agnes stated that they saw each other practically every day. She described their courtship as having been a very happy period in their lives. There had not been any premarital sex. Both were very moral and religious, and both their respective fathers were ministers. However, Jim had appeared pretty aggressive, and there had been extensive petting. They enjoyed each other's company and had the same cultural interests. During their courtship there had been no evidence of Jim's inability to adequately fulfill her emotional needs and gratifications.

An only child for the first six years, she had been overindulged not only by her parents but by all the relatives. All this attention was shattered by the arrival of her twin brothers. At first she was angry and jealous, but after a few years she got over this feeling. Conspicuous in both sessions was the theme of anger at Jim's former analyst, not only the effect he had on Jim, but also his excluding her from any discussion about the lack of progress in their marriage.

In his individual sessions, Jim was much more verbal in his concerns regarding his marriage than he had been in the initial conjoint. He reported that Agnes did not fulfill his emotional needs. He had sought and needed warmth and affection for a very long period in his life which he had never received. Though he did not think so at the time, he felt now that his marriage to Agnes was basically not born out of love but because it was the thing to do. He stated that Agnes had never really actively shown any degree of warmth or affection to him after their marriage as she did during their court-ship. When she did now, he shied away from response because of his concern and inability to know how to react.

With regard to a complaint made by his wife about "financial disagreement" that he was preoccupied with material things, he stated he guessed she was right, since this was an easier way to demonstrate manliness — father and provider. Likewise, in regard to his wife's concern over possible infidelity, he stated that this was certainly not true. His excursions from home on Friday or Saturday nights were to go to the movies as a form of running away, though he did indicate later that these occasions also were in pursuit of homosexual fantasies which were never carried out.

His childhood centered about a strong, seductive but rejecting mother and a nonexistent father who was always buried in his study. He described his social life in high school as having been virtually nil. His relationships were basically centered among five school-mates — all identified as being top academically but all of whom were having "dating problems." His few female dates were "adolescent disasters." His first homosexual fantasy began in his senior year when he was elected class president.

At the CDD, the Bs' appeared extremely receptive to treatment. I felt the prognosis, ego strength, and motivation to change were good. Since there was no family secret, I suggested a trial period of conjoint sessions with a target date of three months.

The Bs' received forty conjoint sessions, once weekly, over a period of eighteen months, with marked improvement in their marriage in all areas.

In the first conjoint session, Mrs. B reported one dream: "I was climbing a very steep cliff. Found it very difficult. People watching me struggle and no one offering assistance. Finally, a man gives me his hand and assists me."

In her associations she identified the man as her family physician, the personification of a solid, compassionate, helpful man, a solid person. "The opposite of my husband" (note the needle!).

When Jim was asked what he saw in his wife's dream, he replied: "The steep hill is the therapy and it is going to be difficult." (Jim has had four years of psychoanalysis and is more sophisticated psychologically.)

I agree, but also comment that she is very angry at her husband and needles him, he withdraws, then she complains that he rejects her. In the dream she sees a man who offers her a helping hand. I wonder out loud why she makes things so difficult for herself, climbing a steep hill.

Jim was next asked whether he had had any dreams.

He replied all week he had recurring dreams which were full of hostility and anger. All evidenced an underlying struggle, a battle of some kind and there was both, danger and great anger.

I posed a question to Agnes: "Are you aware of the tremendous rage in your husband?

To this she replied: "Not always because I don't think it shows, he has rarely shouted at me in our ten years of marriage."

I comment that Jim is afraid of the tremendous emotions within himself. When he curbs it in one area, it's curbed in other areas as well. I suggest that in my approach I encourage the couple to reach out to the limit of their anxieties. On this note, I ask when was the last time they had a date.

Mrs. B replied that not for several months. I ask her, what she would like to do? She replied: "Go out for dinner and then to a play." Since this was acceptable to Jim, it was agreed upon.

He closed the session by adding: "I've always been aware of my anger. When I was a kid, I hit my brother on the neck with a stick after an argument. When he died ten years later from cancer. I vividly recall his mentioning this incident to me prior to his death. I've had an awful long history of controlling not only my emotions but anger as well, and this has included embarrassment, a propensity to cry, and feelings of love."

In the second conjoint session, both reported a good week and their date had been a lot of fun. The following three sessions dealt with two themes, hostility on the part of Mrs. B toward her mother in relation to the twins and guilt about these hostile impulses, and anxiety dreams on the part of Jim in which he is seeking something and unable to find it.

In the sixth session, Mrs. B reported that the past week Jim had been cold and rejecting and preoccupied. I had a dream last night: "I am engaged to Ted Kennedy. I am at their mansion. We were always together, but he always moved away. His whole family disapproved of me. A relative arrives. He makes some remarks — heckling me. Saying that I wasn't good enough for him.

"I woke up feeling very sad. I've never felt accepted by my friends or relatives. Yet I know they all liked me. Jim was the first person I really dated. I always expected him to stop seeing me. People have always told me I was very attractive, yet I don't feel that way."

I ask why she expects to be rejected.

Jim commented that he always felt he had married a very attractive wife, but somehow he couldn't express his feelings to her. "I've been dreaming every night, the same theme. It's not easy to tell you the dream: I am attending a convention. Some conversation that one of the men, prominent in the field, was a homosexual. Most of the dream was spent in trying to find out if he really was. I had sympathy for him. Also some desires on my part toward him."

In his associations he talked about how he was trying to overcome his problem but finding it difficult.

(Comment: I told him the problem is not love for men but a defense against his hostile, competitive feelings with them — the prominent man was perhaps the therapist and a deeper level his father. As a little boy he wanted to displace his father and have all of mothers love and affection. But to a little boy, father is a giant and the little boy fears severe retaliation — so he runs away, just as in Jack and the Bean Stalk, where Jack wants to steal the hen that lays the golden egg (mother) and runs away from the frightening giant. "I don't hate you father, I love you." Thus homosexuality is nothing more than a defense against hostile competitive feelings. Every child has to solve this problem in one way or another. (A good example of the triangular transference neurosis — his wife has previously equated me with Ted Kennedy and mobilized his competitive feelings toward me.) I actively suggest that since it is now six months since the onset of our therapy, they begin to attempt sex. For him to make an attempt to reach her to the level of his anxiety. No matter how little the reaching out to her, she was not to react with anger but encourage him.

In the next session, Jim proudly reported that they had sexual relations, the first in three years.

Mrs. B, smiling happily, concurred that their sex was most enjoyble. "We have had a better week. Jim has not been as cross. More freedom in talking. Not so critical toward the children. The entire atmosphere in the home has changed. The children are happy now. I had a dream: You and another man here. Your office is dimly lit. Before I could sit down I had to move a bunch of papers off your couch. I felt warmly toward you. In the dream I was disgusted that I had to move all the things before I could sit down. Perhaps I am rearranging my thoughts and feelings."

Mr. B added: "I've been thinking about what you said at the last session. Finally I gathered up courage and approached Agnes, and we had sex. That night I had a highly charged dream: I am visiting you at your home office. I was told to take notes, since you were moving out. You asked me to check to see if all your things had been moved. This bothered me, since I didn't want to let you down. I walk down to the pool. A fish pool. The water is low and slimy."

In his associations he commented: "The dream had strong sexual connotations. I had a strong erection and discharge during the dream. I was surprised when I woke up, since we had had sex that night. That night we had sex again. Excellent sex."

I ask Mrs. B how she felt during the act.

She replied "The best sex we ever had."

He interrupted and commented: "The first night especially. I was so surprised to want sex two nights in a row."

I ask about the pool in the dream.

Jim: "My soul. Basically I am pretty rotten inside. But perhaps not altogether. It was the accumulation of all past sins and inadequacies. I am going to Bermuda and am taking Agnes along. It's both business and pleasure. I have never invited her to come along before."

Upon their return, after two weeks in Bermuda, both commented on the wonderful time they had, like a second honeymoon. Unfortunately, Jim's reaction a week later was progressive anxiety and sexual withdrawal from his wife. Mrs. B became depressed, and her dreams revealed increasing sexual frustration and, finally, fantasies of promiscuity. Repeated interpretations were made of her reacting to his withdrawal as rejection instead of seeing his behavior resulting from severe anxiety due to remobilization of his hostile competitive feelings (with the therapist) and fear of retaliation. Gradually his anxiety decreased and sexual relations resumed. Six months later both reported a good relationship, not only between themselves, but also in the general atmosphere of the family.

Bieber,[26] a psychiatrist and psychoanalyst with extensive experience treating male homosexuals, recommends encouraging wives to enter therapy parallel with their husbands when there is no family secret.

REFERENCES

1. Jackson, Don D. and Satir, Virginia M.: A review of psychiatric developments in family diagnosis and family therapy. In Ackerman, Nathan W., Beatman, Frances L., and Sherman, Sanford N. (Eds.): *Exploring the Base for Family Therapy.* New York, Family Service Association of America, 1961, pp. 29-51.

2. Watson, Andrew S.: The conjoint psychotherapy of marriage partners. *Am J Orthopsychiat, 33:* 912, 1963.

3. Satir, Virginia M.: Conjoint marital therapy. Greene, B. L. (Ed.): *The Psychotherapies of Marital Disharmony.* New York, Free Press, 1965, pp. 121-134.

4. Segraves, Robert T.: Conjoint marital therapy. *Arch Gen Psychiat, 35:* 450-55, 1978.

5. Nadelson, Carol, Bassuk, Ellen L., Hopps, Christopher R. and Boutelle, Jr. William E.: Conjoint marital psychotherapy: treatment techniques. *Dis Nerv System, 38:* 898-903, 1977.

6. Goldberg, Martin: Conjoint therapy of male physicians and their wives. *Psychiatric Opinion, 12:* 19-23, 1975.

7. Fitzgerald, R. V.: *Conjoint Marital Psychotherapy.* New York, Jason Aronson, 1973.

8. Silk, Sheldon: The use of videotape in brief marital therapy. *Am J Psychotherapy, 26:* 417-24, 1972.

9. Alger, Ian and Hogan, Peter: Enduring effects of videotape playback experience on family and marital relationships. *Am J Orthopsychiat, 39:* 86, 1969.

10. Greene, Bernard L.: Multi-operational Psychotherapies of Marital Disharmony. Paper presented at the annual meeting of the American

Psychiatric Association, May 7, 1964, in Los Angeles, California.

11. Frankel, S: An indication for conjoint treatment — an application based on an assessment of individual psychopathology. *Pscyhiatric Quarterly, 49:* 97-109, 1977.

12. Milton, Frank and Hafner, Julian: The outcome of behavior therapy for agoraphobia in relation to marital adjustment. *Arch Gen Psychiat, 36:* 807-11, 1979.

13. Greene, Bernard L.: Clinical observations of sex as a reverberation of the total relationship. *J Sex and Marital Therapy, 2:* 284-288, 1977.

14. Cole, Collier M., Blakeney, Patricia E., Chan, Frances A., Chesney, Alan P., and Creson, Daniel L.: The myth of symptomatic versus asymtomatic partners in the conjoint treatment of sexual dysfunction. *J Sex & Marital Therapy, 5:* 79-88, 1979.

15. Stern, R. S. and Marks, I. M.: Contract therapy in obsessive-compulsive neurosis with marital discord. *Brit J Psychiat, 123:* 681-4, 1973.

16. Martin, Peter A.: *A Marital Therapy Manual.* New York: Brunner-Mazel, 1976, p.122.

17. Bieber, Irving: The married male homosexual, *Med Aspects Hum Sexuality, 3:* 76, 1969.

18. Jones, Maxwell: Therapeutic community practice. *Am J Psychiat, 122:* 1275, 1966.

19. Brown, Saul L.: Personal communication.

20. Watson, The conjoint psychotherapy of marriage partners.

21. Sager, Clifford: The treatment of married couples. In Arieti, Silvano (Ed.): *The Am Handbook of Psychiatry,* Vol III, Chap 15. New York, Basic Books, 1966, pp. 217, 218.

22. Gurman, Alan S.: Dimensions of marital therapy — a comparative analysis, *J Marital & Family Therapy, 5:* 5-16, 1979.

23. Bell, John E.: Contrasting approaches in marital counseling. *Family Process, 6:* 16, 1967.

24. Ravich, Robert A.: Short-term, intensive treatment of marital discord, *Voices, 2:* 42, 1966.

25. Satir, Virginia M.: Conjoint Marital Therapy. In Greene, B. L. (Ed.): *The Psychotherapies of Marital Disharmony.* New York, Macmillan, 1965, pp. 121-133.

26. Bieber, The married male homosexual.

Chapter XXVII

THE COMBINED TECHNIQUES IN DYADIC DISHARMONY

THE combined techniques in dyadic and family disharmony consists of five principle approaches utilizing a variety of clinical sittings:

1. *Simple*—a pragmatic combination of individual, concurrent and conjoint sessions in various purposeful combinations.
2. *Conjoint family therapy*—includes one or more children where indicated, and it views the way the family functions as an interdependent unit. This approach is used for as short a period as possible and then shifted to dyadic/triadic therapy.
3. *Combined-collaborative therapy*—each partner has a separate therapist in addition to regular joint sessions where all four participate. This is a new approach which I presented, for the first time a decade ago.
4. *Group therapies*—of various combinations, e.g. couples group therapy, combined group therapy with ongoing members seen individually. The leader can opt to lead alone or with a cotherapist.
5. *Special therapies*—
   a. Sexual dysfunctions
   b. Where one partner has a primary affective disorder (manic-depressive illness).

SIMPLE COMBINED APPROACH

I have used the combined techniques with 200 couples and/or families since 1962.[1] It was appropriate in 18 percent of those couples receiving intensive therapy, and in 15 percent in crisis therapy (see Chapter I, table I). I have found this approach valuable because of the unpredictable therapeutic course and changing life events. Marc Hollender[2] has expressed some concern about the use of this approach, that this may cause confusion to some couples if a plan of therapy is not made explicit or if the rules are changed. This has not been my experience.

The treatment process in the combined techniques is based on a plan of active support, including environmental manipulation, complementary goals, clarification of role expectations and enactments, redirection of intrapersonal energies, and evocation of "healthier" communication.

An increasing number of therapists are beginning to devote more attention to multipersonal approaches to the treatment of dyadic disharmony. The work of some group therapists has much to offer the student of the "combined approach." As more and more therapists use multiperson interviews, one notices the gradual development of new therapeutic techniques shared by all of them. Should this process continue, a broader range of treatment possibilities and greater acceptance of multipersonal approaches may ensue. This possibility does not mean that the dyadic one-to-one therapy is to be replaced in dyadic disharmony, but it does promise greater latitude for therapists in the choice of treatment methods.

The combined approach differs in many ways than the other approaches. When the dyadic and triadic and other clinical groupings are combined, the clinical material takes on additional meanings for the participants. The form of the "combined" approach represents various aspects of functioning in the individual, in his interpersonal and other relationships. As previously described in the GST (see Chapter II), a human being may be regarded as incorporating three separate systems: an intrapersonal system, an interpersonal system involving transactions with significant others, and an environmental system responding to an interplay of forces between the individual and society. The three systems are reflected in the combined approach through the use of dyadic, triadic, family and/or group sessions, which alternately focuses on the individual, his partner, their relationship, and others involved. The process of treatment demonstrates the therapist's dual concern with understanding the origin of feelings in the past and their reenactment in current dyadic and other relationships.

The combined techniques increase the perception of all participants — the couple and others as well as the therapists(s). In triadic interviews, the aim is to eliminate incongruity and distortions from communication so that covert and overt meanings and messages become identical. The opportunity to experience different environments points up the contrast between individual and multipersonal relationships and brings out different sides of the personality that could well be lost in dyadic treatment. There is a tendency for therapists to make the mistake of assuming that a person will behave in the same way in all situations. The opportunity for feedback through the use of dyadic, triadic, and group sessions furnishes a corrective for the therapist for misperceptions and misinterpretations. As Martin[3] points out, it allows the therapist(s) and even the group, a strategic point of observation of the varying reactions of individuals to different environments.

The indications for the simple combined approach in dyadic disharmony include:

1. Initial evaluation indicates triadic sessions to manage the dyadic relationship in order to achieve harmony and dyadic sessions for entrenched personal conflicts.
2. Therapeutic impasse with other techniques.
3. Acting out by one or both spouses that cannot be dealt with by the other techniques.
4. A patient's obsessive-compulsive personality pattern that makes it necessary to enlist the cooperation of the partner.
5. A spouse's relationship with a single parent introjected to the degree that he is threatened by a dyadic setting (sexual, hostile, or oral dependent needs).
6. An impass in concurrent therapy because of transference difficulties: either too intense (libidinal or agressive) or involving insufficient emotional involvement of the patient.
7. A therapeutic impasse occurs in dyadic interviews because the dyadic transference neurosis can be activated and interpreted only in the triadic sessions.
8. When there is an expressed desire to change sexual orientation, e.g. homosexuality. My experience as well as that of others[4,5] has shown that the partner can be of considerable help to the therapist by understanding the possible reasons for the homosexuality, for offering support — patience etc. Five percent of my last 100 referrals were for this type of dyadic relationship.
9. In depression due to situational or reactive factors. In constrast to others using conjoint dyadic therapy,[6,7] I found the simple combined approach, with drugs as needed, more successful than the conjoint dyadic approach.[8]

The contraindications for the combined approach are similar to those listed under conjoint therapy (see Chapter XXVI).

The following vignette is an example of the simple combined approach:

> The As' received a total of sixteen sessions, Mrs. A had three individual sessions, Dr. A had five individual sessions, and both had eight conjoint sessions. The As' were in their late twenties, married five years. Dr. A is a physician and Mrs. A is a schoolteacher.

In his first individual session, Dr. A stated: "I love my wife very much, but recently we have been arguing constantly. These center primarily about my wish for children, and her desire for a career. She wants to become principal. I feel if we don't have children now, we never will. As a physician I know the risks involved in having children after she reaches thirty. This incessant drive toward a career has had our marriage on the rocks many times; besides, my friends and colleagues rib me about "shooting blanks," as if I am not virile enough. Another point of dissatisfaction is our sexual problem. She has a difficult time reaching a climax. I want her to reach a climax when I do. I will work fifteen or more minutes until she does. Further, she complains about my overdominance.

Mrs. A, a beautiful and extremely intelligent woman, was dressed seductively and acted so in her first session. She began the interview stating: "I will not even try to become a mother while my husband and I cannot communicate. I am unable to express my feelings or thoughts because he gets hurt and pouts. I keep things inside, and my only outlet has been my career.

When we got married, Jack felt strongly that a woman's place is in the home — cooking, cleaning, and children. It has been a constant struggle for me to complete my B.A. degree, and he finally gave me his permission. The past two years of our marriage has been stormy because he has tried to dominate my behavior and to control my thoughts and actions.

Jack is not a lover. While we are making love, he will ask if I have reached my climax. This turns me off. He is very offended when I don't respond. Sometimes we would have intercourse for what seems hours before I reach an orgasm. It's not love, but performance that seems to be important to him. I resent his attitude."

Dr. A began his second session by commenting that he and his wife had a bitter quarrel the previous night. He felt badly when she accused him of treating her like an object instead of a woman. A year ago, after a similar quarrel about his desire for children, he had decided he was through with the marriage and was walking out when she blurted out in tears that she was afraid of having a baby—that perhaps she would not make a good mother, and that she was afraid of childbirth. So he had remained.

Since the argument had been over his demand for sex, I suggested to him not to approach her, and to wait until she made the initial overtures. That I would explore this complaint with his wife.

In her second session, Mrs. A was deeply disturbed about her ambivalence toward her marriage and marriage therapy. "I feel very screwed up. I come from a very close family. I want a family but I don't want it with Jack. All he talks about are his patients. I need mental stimulation. Jack thinks that having a baby is the panacea. Otherwise we should split."

I suggest that perhaps we should change the classic approach where the individual's needs are primary and the marriage secondary. To think it over and let me know — and I would send her to another therapist whose primary focus would be her welfare. The next night she called to state that she had decided upon working on her marriage.

Dr. A seemed very happy as he began his third session. "It was quite a session you had with Ann last Friday. She was on the verge of tears when she came home. She was very quiet and moody. Later in the evening she broke down, not completely, and presented herself to me very passionately. Lovemaking ensued. Then she broke down and said, you inferred she see another therapist. Separate therapists, who would concentrate on the individual with the marriage secondary. I said, if there is a divorce, I would do whatever was the gentlemanly thing to do for her.

"I've never seen her so completely spent after her session with you. I have a different attitude since talking to you. I was emotionally confused. At the hospital I make many important decisions each day and stick with it. I would like to save our marriage. But if it's to be a divorce, perhaps it is best now while there are no children involved. Later she said she called you to save the marriage. I was floored. The next night we had nothing planned. So we stayed home, watched a play on TV — a very enjoyable evening on both our parts. That night she asked for sex. Two nights in a row! I could not believe my ears. She reached a climax on her own and exclaimed happily, 'I feel like a woman.'

"When I came home that evening, she kissed me and said: 'Guess what? I love you!' I don't know what to make of it. We are now able to talk. I do have a different attitude. I feel now that we both have indulged in some soul searching."

I commented that in our last session one of her main complaints about the marriage was that he was too controlling of her behavior.

"When we first started out I was. But not now, I want to wear the pants in the family. I know she feels I control her, but it is not so. She had such a dominating home. Her parents are very dominating. Any slight suggestion on my part later set her off. This is where the root of the problem comes from."

(Excellent example of projective identification — this was pointed out to him, how his wife overreacts to his suggestions not only by hearing old records from her parents but also projecting these records onto him and doubly reacting as though her records were coming from him. That he was to consider his words before he addressed them to her.)

Dr. A commented: "It makes sense to me, and I will try not to be critical of her behavior. I think another problem is her fear of pregnancy. Her mother and her aunt had difficult labors."

In his fourth individual session Dr. A came in upset that his wife had reverted back to her old patterns: "No change. When am I going to be treated like her husband. My ulcer pain returned. No tenderness, no concern, no asking 'Can I get you something?' I think she needs help in finding out whether she wants marriage or a career. If she wants a career then it is no marriage, not with me."

Mrs. A opened her third session as follows: "We have really been working together, trying very hard and enjoying each other."

I ask about the last few days which were very tense according to her husband.

"It was very tense. He has been nagging at me. He is too possessive. He makes lists of things each morning for me to do. I really resent this. He is like a child about illness — and he is a doctor. I had a dream: My mother, sister and I are all going up a tall ladder. They fell off. I don't know what the dream means."

I inquire about her hostile feelings toward her mother and sister? "They do fall off!"

"I knew you were going to ask me about this. They are always telling me how much they love Jack, and want the marriage to work. Her wonderful son-in-law — just because he gives them free medical advice and samples. My mother and sister are very close. Mother keeps telling me that I should have children before it is too late."

In his fifth and last individual session, Dr. A reported things were going well again at home. I suggest that we now have conjoint sessions to further open the channels of communication between them. His wife had cued me in to his recent extensive quizzing her about her individual sessions with me. He readily agreed to conjoint therapy.

In the first conjoint session, Dr. A opened the session with a dream in which the focus was on an event in which he performs in an outstanding manner.

He was asked if performance was so important. He replied: "I don't think so."

Ann interrupted to comment: "Performance is very important to him. He wants his friends to know how much he does at the hospital — the way he handles emergencies. We have many arguments about using his standards. I had worked all day. I didn't have time to have his car greased. He tore into me and embarrassed me in front of my girl friend who was visiting me."

Jack replied: "I'm not interested in performance. I'm only efficient. It is easier to do things the right way. She is always procrastinating."

It was pointed out that a big source of argument was his demand of her inner child to act on the same level of performance that he demanded of his inner child. When he did this, she rebelled by a "sit-down strike."

After two good weeks, both the second and third sessions dealt with the preceding theme of performance, the As' left for a three-week vacation. Dr. A began the fourth conjoint session as follows: Just before we left, she said she has been thinking of separation frequently. We slept in separate beds. Now everything is going smoothly. I can't understand why one week is fine and the next week horrible.

"He makes me feel inadequate, that I don't show enough affection toward him. I feel very badly and guilty about it. Yet once we arrived in Hawaii, we had a wonderful time. He was sweet, romantic, entertaining. I could not have asked for a better husband. What really gets me mad is when he says publicly, 'things will be different with my second wife.' Nothing I do seems to satisfy him."

In the fifth session both reported a good two weeks. Mrs. A stated: "We are starting to verbally express ourselves instead of holding back and sulking. I have been very happy these two past weeks."

He replied: "What little disagreements we had later seemed non-sensical. She wants to cut down our visits here to every other week. I think we should explore the area of children first."

In the sixth session, Mrs. A opened: "We had a wonderful first week then, a week later, Jack said he wanted a divorce. I was shocked! The next morning we had sexual intercourse. That night we made love again. The next night we had a little quarrel, and he said he wanted a separation. I said, what do you want? (crying) I'll give up my teaching, if this will make you happy. I don't know what he wants. When he says these things I get colder and colder inside of me."

Dr. A: "I've accidentally discovered what is wrong with our marriage. I've hit on one word. Need. You don't need me. I want to be needed."

Two nights later the As' called for an emergency appointment, that they had had a breakthrough in their marriage. When seen that evening they came in looking very happy.

"I saw things in my wife I didn't see before — compassion, tears, never seen before in here. A deep feeling for me. She looked up and said she loved me and doesn't want to live without me. I love her, too, I told her."

Mrs. A replied that it was her idea for this appointment. That, perhaps, this could be their last session. I suggested, they keep their next appointment, two weeks hence, and if everything was going satisfactorily, we would stop therapy.

In their eighth and final session, Mrs. A began by stating: "We have been getting along beautifully. No complaints. Not a single one, except, I'm dreaming like crazy. Jack and I are developing a very good relationship. For the first time we are communicating. I'm trying very hard. We are starting to work out our problems. He was the one who threw me for a loop, asking for a divorce. I have tremendous guilt feelings about what my role is, career versus motherhood. We really are getting along fine now. Yes, we are. No arguments. No fights. Really trying to please each other."

He commented: "What she has said is also what I feel. We are getting along beautifully. How do you feel about discontinuing and our trying to work out our problems alone?

She added: "There have been no periods before where we have been able to talk things out without explosion. You have opened the avenues of communication."

I suggested that I schedule an appointment one month later but, to cancel if things were working out satisfactorily. Three weeks later she called to say that the marriage was fine and cancelled the appointment. At that time I explained my philosophy of the well-marriage theory of prevention and suggested they come in yearly for the next three years. At the second years's preventive check-up, they had two children and were getting along fine. Shortly afterwards, I received a thank you letter stating they were moving out of the state.

An important advantage of the combined approach is its flexibility; it lends itself to both the styles of various therapists and the marked variability of dyadic patterns. The triadic sessions are fairly standardized, but great variations are possible in the dyadic sessions. One partner may receive supportive psychotherapy while the other is analyzed, both may be analyzed synchronously, both may receive psychotherapy, one may receive psychotherapy while the other participates only in the triadic sessions, or one may be in analysis, while the other participates only in the triadic sessions.

In the triadic sessions, the partners sit upright facing the therapist, who usually sits equidistant between them at the apex of a triangle, a design which makes for easier observation. In the dyadic interviews, either the upright or the couch position is used, depending on the clinical material. I use dreams extensively in both the dyadic and triadic sessions. Dreams afford valuable insights, not only into each partner's personality and behavior, but also into the dyadic transactions. Dreams reported in the triadic sessions provide verification and clarity of understanding of the dyadic transactions and also of the various levels of transference phenomena. In the triadic interviews I observe how the ideas of one partner elicit reactions in the partner. Although one partner may continue to discuss his partner's concepts, soon his own unconscious feelings and thoughts gain the upper hand and reveal his true attitudes and bring to light areas of conflict. This type of communication makes possible a new dimension in understanding the couple. At the end of the session, I usually summarize and add a more comprehensive interpretation. In the triadic setting, dreams offer a point of departure for communication.

Combined therapy is a useful therapeutic tool when both triadic and dyadic transactions are necessary, either for the successful treatment of the dyadic disharmony or of one of the partners. The form and character of the treatment processes using these different treatment settings are determined by the training and goals of the therapist.

CONJOINT FAMILY THERAPY

In my experience, contrary to the observations of other family therapists, only occasionally do I find it necessary to include the children in the therapeutic setting, when the presenting complaints of the parents are those of dyadic disharmony.[9, 10] Usually, when the relationship improves, the behavior of the children changes in a positive direction. On the other hand, when the child causes a therapeutic impasse in the parents' therapy, then the child is invited to participate in the therapy or, in some cases, sent to another therapist for individual help. DeWitt,[11] in a recent review of outcome research on the effectiveness of conjoint family therapy, *vis-à-vis* nonconjoint techniques, stated that both methods are equally effective. Perhaps part of the statistics reflect the *charismatic factor of the therapist* as one of the most important ingredients in therapeutic success.[12]

Family therapy is now well into its third decade as a therapeutic innovation, although I did not use this approach until 1960. The first two-hour family session I treated was taped for didactic purposes. Recently, Kaslow[13] devoted an entire issue of a journal to the state of family therapy, at the end of the 70s. The twenty contributors included first, second, and third generation family therapists, and no two papers were similar. This was true of those contributing in Ackerman's book (1970),[14] *no two papers were alike.*[15-19] What is interesting to note is that more of the family therapists are slanted toward the marital dyad than to the larger system of the family now then a decade ago. The broad field of family therapy includes a number of specific techniques: psychodynamic,[20-26] general system theory and family systems,[27-32] communications,[33-36] pragmatic-strategic,[37-41] structural,[42,43] expressive techniques,[44-47] and miscellaneous approaches.[48,49] It is important to keep in mind that many of the approaches utilize additional concepts.

The indications[50] for conjoint family therapy include the following:

1. A child contributing to dyadic discord by acting out parental unconscious impulses or being used as a pawn in the struggle with another family member.
2. When the child is being used as a scapegoat[51] in the dyadic conflicts, and this is producing increasing friction between the couple. The scapegoated child is used as a homeostatic function for the family.
3. Where a dysfunctional couple unable to solve its conflicts may attempt distancing by using a child as a pawn between them or to establish protective alliances.
4. Dyadic problems in the reconstituted family ("step-family").[52,53] Complicating the problem is the absence of established norms and societal expectations for the step-parent's role.

The contraindications for conjoint family therapy has not, as yet, been clearly defined. Perhaps this is due to the differing clinical settings and populations as well as to the diversity of those calling the approach family therapy. Guttman has been impressed by a number of patients where this approach was "harmful in treating extremely anxious young patients who are on the verge of decompensating into or have scarcely recompensated from an acute psychotic breakdown."[54]

In 1965, Nathan Ackerman wrote a chapter on "The Family Approach to Marital Problems" in the *Psychotherapies of Marital Disharmony*.[55] His comments are worthy of the reproduction that follows:

"It is common knowledge today that the social institution of marriage is not working as we should like it to. To be sure, *the institution of marriage is here to say, but it is not the same any more.** It is rickety: its joints creak. It threatens to crack wide open. Although marriage may be ordained in heaven, it is surely falling apart on earth, at least in our part of the world. Three generations survey the record with dismay. The older married folks look down with silent reproach on the younger ones. The younger married folks look at themselves in shock and perplexity and wonder how on earth they got this way. The children look at their parents, not with reverent respect, but with bitter accusation. They indict their parents: "You are wrecking our family. What are you doing to yourselves and to us? You are failing miserably. Why?"

In the present-day community, anxiety about the instability of mar-

---

*All the italics from now on are my own.

riage and family is widespread. The sources of worry are the *"side-wise"*† *marriage*, the teen-age marriage, infidelity, desertion, divorce, multiple marriages, the loosening of sex standards, the war between the sexes, "momism," the weakness of fathers, the reduction of parental authority, the broken home, emotionally injured children, the anarchy of youth, and the trend toward delinquency. With all these problems comes a growing disillusionment with the tradition and sentiment of marriage and family.

If today the marriage bond is unstable, it is because the entire constellation of the contemporary family is itself unstable. As our way of life at all levels — family, community, and culture — is in a state of flux, the style of marriage must also echo the profound currents of change and instability.

Healing forces do emerge, but the healing itself is often warped. It is analogous to what surgeons call "the pathological healing" of a wound. For a multiplicity of reasons, we are challenged to take a new look at this old problem and, if possible, to discover a fresh approach to the marital disorders of our time.

For me, a psychiatric clinician, the marital problem poses a tantalizing challenge, comparable to that of a complicated jigsaw puzzle. We find one part that fits; instantly we hope and expect that all the others will fall quickly into place and reveal the hidden design; but it is not so easy.

Marriage is more than sex; it is a whole way of life. It is a joining together in the work, joys, and sadnesses of life. Disorders of the marital relationship cannot be understood in a social vacuum. The fit or lack of fit of the partners can be properly appraised only within the framework of the family viewed as an integrated behavior system with dominant values and a definable organizational pattern. The marital adaptation must be seen within that larger network of relationships that reflects the identity connections of each partner with his family of origin and with the larger community. Relevant beyond sexual union are the basic functions of family that have to do with security, child-rearing, social training, and the *development of the marriage partners both as a couple and as individuals.*

To illustrate: A social worker of twenty-four years, married six months, was considering divorce. In the initial psychiatric interview, try as I might, I could not find the slightest hint of her motive. Why divorce? Finally, in desperation, I asked, "Is it your sex life? What in the world is wrong."

"Oh, no," she said "my husband is an expert lover. Believe me,

---

†Currently called the living-together-arrangement.

sexual intercourse is just great. The only trouble is that there is *no verbal intercourse at all."* Diagnosis: physical relations, good; emotional interchange, none. The complaint of "silent treatment" in married life is a frequent one these days.‡

Interviewing another couple, a kewpie doll of a wife and a big, burly police captain of a husband, I had a different experience. This couple had been married ten years and had three children. The wife threatened divorce. She was cute, childlike, but she breathed fire. She let loose a barrage of bitter accusations. For the better part of an hour her husband sat mute; he could not get a word in edgewise. What was her complaint? Her husband had cheated her out of her rights as a woman. When they married, she had been naive and innocent. For ten years, her husband had not given her the remotest hint that a woman is supposed to enjoy sex. Only recently, at the New School of Social Research, had she learned for the first time that a woman may have an orgasm. Through gnashing jaws, she spat out a furious ultimatum. it was her husband's duty to see to it that she had an orgasm or else!

An interesting phenomenon is the group of couples who *swap partners for weekends.* Many of these marriage deteriorate rapidly. In a few cases, however, there is a *paradoxical response.* The *adventure of infidelity seems to have a remarkable healing effect on the marriage.* It is a disturbing invasion of the lives of both partners, but strangely enough, if they pass through this crisis, each may emerge a stronger person. They experience mutual learning, and their companionship grows closer, their love life richer. They both grow as people. In one such case, the wife reacted to the shocking discovery of her husband's romance with an attractive Negro actress with the prompt disappearance of her sexual frigidity. This change delighted her husband and impelled him to characterize his Negro *amour* as the best psychotherapist he and his wife could have had.

This case is but one small example of the attitudes of the *sex-seekers of our time.* One way or another, they engage in a *frantic search for new sexual kicks that they expect to be magic cure-alls.*

In another case, a wife reacted with *pathological jealousy.* She was "bugged" on her husband's imagined sexual antics with other playmates; she plagued him incessantly.* She was depressed, agitated, unable to sleep — nor did she let her husband sleep. She knew that her husband had erotic interests in women wrestlers and weight-lifters. When her husband asked her to lift him or hold him in her lap she refused. "It might break my back." She entered the role of detec-

---

‡The number one complain since my first study fifteen years ago.
*What I refer to as the "District Attorney syndrome."

tive in order "to get the goods" on her husband. She discovered in his desk a batch of pictures of female weight-lifters in scanty attire. Finding a stain on her husband's underclothing, she sent a piece of it to the chemical laboratory. The report came back: "positive; many spermatozoa were found together with large numbers of squamous epithelial cells. The finding of many squamous epithelial cells is indicative of the presence of vaginal secretion along with the spermatozoa." This evidence clinched the wife's case. She crucified her husband with this "proof." She demanded that he confess the truth. What new sexual tricks had he learned from "these other broads"?

Both partners had been previously married, so that in this household there were three sets of children, the wife's children by her former marriage, the *husband's children* by his former marriage, and *a new baby.* From the word "go" the partners failed completely to build a true marital union. The courtship phase was intense. Both parties moved fast to dissolve their previous marriages to make way for this one. But they were hardly married before the husband began to withdraw interest. When his wife became pregant, he stopped making sexual advances altogether. Sensing his sexual rejection, she then began to develop jealous delusions.

In this case, husband and wife came from very different cultural and religious backgrounds, but they had in common the special experience of a philandering, unfaithful father. Each, however, reacted in a different way. The husband sided with his father. He felt convinced that his father had in fact been killed by his mother. Through her persisent nagging and accusations of infidelity, he believed she had caused his father's final heart collapse. The wife, on the other hand, entered in empathic alliance with her mother, in an attempt to protect the wounded pride of the females of the family against what she felt was her father's cold, ruthless, and indiscriminate indulgence in sexual escapades.

In therapy, the wife related *four dreams* in succession. In each, she depicted a threesome involved in a horrible tangle, reflecting the profound emotional connections between conflict in her marriage and older sources of conflict in her family of origin.†

To illustrate, in one such dream, she found herself in an automobile, a convertible accompanied by her husband and his secretary, who was the object of her paranoid sexual jealousy. The three drove to the home of the patient's former husband, where she found other people. First, she spotted her father hiding in the bedroom, as if

---

†The Bowenian triangle!

he were up to some mischief. Although he offered a plausible excuse for his presence, she knew that it was a complete lie. Then she became aware of the presence of other people — children, her husband's parents, his office secretary's parents, and so forth.

In this dream, we see three networks of family relationships, the husband's family, the wife's family, and the family of the secretary. We see the patient in the roles of both child and wife. At the very least, this dream reflects the complexity of the origins of marital jealousy in a way that embraces an extensive web of conflicted family relationships stretching across three generations. Marital disorders are clearly anything but simple. They are one aspect, a focal one to be sure, but nonetheless one aspect of an ongoing family phenomenon.

In our studies at The Family Mental Health Clinic in New York City, we have been oriented mainly toward these problems in the wider context of the family. We have preferred, at least in the first phase, to interview distressed marital partners together with their children and sometimes with their parents. The procedure is *first to conduct a series of exploratory interviews with the whole family* and then *at the appropriate time to shift to specialization on the marital part* of the broader family problem.

We learn to diagnose marital disorders by treating them. The marital relationship neither exists nor evolves in isolation. It has family in back of it; it has family ahead of it. Where there is marital conflict, it often involves prior conflicts between the respective partners and their families of origin. Marital conflict is often displaced and reprojected, in modified form, into the relations of each partner with the offspring. The original problems of each partner with the family of origin are thus projected across time into husband-wife and parent-child relations.‡ The *marital relationship does not and cannot stand still*. It moves forward or backward. It grows, or it withers. *It must be nourished,* it must make way for change, it must respond to new experience — otherwise it dies. As the marital balance shifts from one stage of the family cycle to the next, the diagnostic judgment must change accordingly. The diagnosis of marital disorders is complicated. It is influenced by the ways in which the disorder is viewed from different places by different people with different interests and purposes: by the marital partners themselves; by other parts of the nuclear and extended families and community; by the professional worker. The range and diversity of marital disorders in our culture enormous. Our interest is not only how the relationship works but

---

‡The phenomenon of projective identification.

also to what ends. *Diagnosis can be approached at three levels: descriptive, genetic, and functional.*

At the descriptive level, we can classify disorders of the marital partnership in terms of symptom clusters reflecting deviant patterns of interaction — for example, in sexual failure, economic or social failure, persistent quarreling, misunderstanding, alienation, and disturbances of communication, sharing, and identification.

At the dynamic level, diagnosis means the definition of the core conflicts, the *ways of coping*, the *patterns of complementarity and failure of complementarity*, the distortion and imbalance of the multiple functions of the marital interaction, and finally, the realism, maturity, stability, and growth potential of the relationship. From an estimate of these characteristics, *we can delineate what is inappropriate* and warped *alongside what is appropriate* and healthy in the quality of the marital adaptation.

At the genetic level, we trace the dynamic evolution of the relationship *through the phases of courtship, early marriage, the arrival of the first child, and finally the expansion of the family with more children.*

Diagnosis of marital interaction may be subdivided according to current performance, level of achievement, origin and development, and deviation measured against an ideal of a healthy marital relationship.

1. *Current Performance*
   a. capacity for love
   b. mutual adaptation, adaptation of external change, and adaptation of growth
   c. levels of benign conflict and destructive conflict; patterns of coping; interplay of shared defenses of the continuity of the marriage relationship with individual defenses against conflict and anxiety; and finally the characteristic patterns of complementarity. (In clinical terms, two features of defense are of special importance: first, the use of the relationship and adaptation to the marital roles of compensate for anxiety in one or the other partner, to offer support against emotional breakdown, and second, the use of external relationships to mitigate failure in the marital relationship and to provide compensatory satisfactions of the individual needs.)
   d. the quality of each partner's integration into his marital role and the fit of marital with other family roles
2. *Level of Achievement*
   a. the strivings, expectations, values, and needs of the relationship and of each partner
   b. the maturity, realism, and stability of the relationship

    c. the trends toward fixation, regression, disintegration, and so forth

    d. the discrepancy between actual performance and an ideal

3. *Origin and Development of the Relationship: From Courtship to the Time of Referral*

    a. influence of the evolving patterns of motivation, of the ideals and images of future marriage and family on the development of the marital partnership

    b. influence of the same factors (including children on the development of the parental partnership

    c. areas of satisfaction, dissatisfaction, harmony and conflict, and healthy and unhealthy functioning

    d. past achievement in relation to values, expectations, and strivings

4. *Discrepancy Between the Actual Performance and an Ideal Model of Healthy Marital Functioning*

Disorders of the marital relationship are clinically expressed in two ways: as conflict over differences and failure of complementarity.

Conflict over differences becomes organized in a special way. Neither of the marital partners fights the battle alone. Each tends to form a protective alliance with other family members, children, grandparents, collateral relatives. In this way, the family splits into opposing factions. *One partner engages in prejudicial scapegoating of the other.* Each warring partner puts on blinders and attaches a menacing meaning to the difference. The inevitable result is a war of prejudice revolving around subjectively distorted representations of difference, rather than around actual ones. The war rests on the false belief that striving for one way of life automatically excludes another. Each faction then tries to impose its preferred set of aims and values on the relationship. The manifestations of this conflict appear as disturbances of empathy, union, and identification; as *chronic destructive quarreling*,* often about wrong or trivial matters; as defects of communication: as the failure of devices for restoration of balance following upset; and finally in progressive alienation of the partners.

The outcome of such conflict depends less on the nature of the conflict than on the ways of coping with it. Coping with marital conflict is a shared function. It is carried on at both *interpersonal* and *intrapersonal levels*. In this connection, it is essential to trace the interplay between specific patterns for group defense of the continuity of the marriage relationship and individual defenses against the destructive effects of conflict and anxiety. At the relationship level, we

---

*"Durable incompatible" marriage by Cavanagh.

may specify these patterns of defense; enhancement of the bond of love, sharing, co-operation, and identification; shifts in the complementarity of marital role adaptation brought about by a shared quest for the solution of conflicts, improved mutual need satisfaction, mutual support of self-esteem, support for the needed defenses against anxiety, and support of the growth of the relationship and of each partner as an individual; rigidification or loosening of the marital roles; reduction of conflict intensity by means of manipulation, coercion, bribery, compromise, compensation, denial, or escape; shifting alignments and splits within the family and prejudicial scapegoating of one part of the family by another, repeopling of the group, that is, the elimination of one member or the addition of another or a significant change in *environment*.†

Failure in these patterns of coping produces, in turn, progressive failure of the quality of complementarity. The manifestations of such failure can be identified as particular units of interaction that become rigidified, automatized, inappropriate, and useless for the shared tasks of marital living.

The marital partnership may be oriented mainly to different goals as in these examples:

1. A marital relationship in which each partner egocentrically preserves his premarital individuality largely untouched by the requirements of the marital bond.
2. A relationship in which the individuality of each partner is subordinated to the requirements of his marital role.
3. A relationship in which the individuality of each partner is subordinated to the requirements of his parental role.
4. A relationship in which the individuality of each partner is subordinated to conformity with the demands of the surrounding community.

Genetic or developmental failures include

1. The accidental or unintended marriage like, for example, a marriage necessitated by pregnancy.
2. The abortive or temporary marriage, begun as a kind of adventure, a *trial marriage*, or a conversion of a sexual affair and not basically intended to endure or to evolve into a family group.
3. The marriage used as a means to escape from conflict to rebel against the family of origin or to rebound from a prior disappointment in love.
4. The arranged marriage, which is a matter of security, of expe-

---

†Ackerman was thus pointing out the interplay of three systems of the GST, but he never characterized them in this manner to my knowledge.

diency, or of joining two larger families.

From the functional point of view, there are

1. The *immature* or protective marriage, motivated mainly by the need of one partner to relate, in the role of child, to the other in the role of parent.
2. The *competitive* marriage based on concealed envy, jealousy, and competitive admiration.
3. The marriage of neurotic *complementarity*, in which the special neurotic needs of one partner are complemented by those of the other, in which one partner serves as the healer of the conflicts and anxieties of the other. (The stronger partner in this arrangement is intended to serve as a provider of immunity against emotional breakdown in the more vulnerable partner.)
4. The marriage of *complementary acting out*, in which the two partners share an unconscious complicity in patterns of acting out conflicted urges.
5. The marriage *of mutual emotional detachment*,‡ in which a tolerable balance is struck between the partners on the basis of a degree of emotional distance and isolation.
6. The *master-slave marriage*, a role partnership in which one partner seeks omnipotent control of the other. (Neither partner is a complete being. The master needs the slave; the slave needs the master. The one is aggrandized as the other is demeaned. The natural goals of love, sharing, and identification are perverted to the *goal of power* to dominate, degrade, and ultimately destroy the partner. In essence, this bond is a symbiotic one, in which one partner expands at the expense of the other. A pathological balance of this type can be maintained only by means of cocercion and intimidation.)
7. The *regressive marriage* dominated by a negative orientation to life. (There are shared fear of and prejudice against life and growth, shared expectation of imminent catastrophe. Implicit in the emotional content of such a partnership is the theme of total sacrifice. One partner must surrender the right to live and breathe in order to ensure the continued life of the other. In emotional orientation, the persons involved move backward in life, rather than forward. This type of marital couple is the most likely to produce psychotic offspring.)
8. The *healthy marriage*. (In this theoretical model or "pure" type, the partners have a *good "fit"* in the marital roles. They are able to share realistic goals and compatible values. When conflict arises, there may be transitory upset, yet, in the main, they are able to co-operate in the search for solution or appropriate compromise. A temporary disturbance does not involve excessive or

---

‡"Emotional divorce."

persistent accusation, guilt feelings, and scapegoating. *Each partner* has a *genuine respect* for the *acceptance of the other as a person*, a tolerance of differences, and, *more than* that, a willingness to use them for the *creative growth of the relationship.)*

To a large extent, *diagnosis rests on the therapist's special interest* — on what he is trying to do about the marital condition. In this context, *diagnosis is no mere label but an integral aspect of a plan of action, a strategy for inducing change.* Through the implementation of the principles and criteria described here, we seek a more precise definition of the functional pattern of the marital partnership, not only how it works but also to what ends. We want to know what it stands for, its goals and aspirations, what keeps the couple together, what pulls the partners apart. *In essence, we seek to learn what is separate and what is shared in the relationship.*

We turn now to the challenge of treatment. In keeping with the concepts we have outlined, the *psychotherapy of marital disorders is viewed as the focused treatment of a component of family disorder.* It is a phase of family therapy, adapted to and specialized for the specific features of a marital problem. Because family begins with marriage, the *disorder of marital interaction is a focal point in family dynamics and development.*

As I have discussed elsewhere my views of the method of family psychotherapy, I shall merely highlight here those special considerations pertaining to problems of marital interaction.

Professional contact begins with exploration of the salient problems, a function of any therapeutically oriented interview. In fact, we initiate the treatment process before we know what the problem is all about. Only as we become engaged in the adventure of therapy, do we achieve, step by step, a *systematic diagnosis.**

How is the marital trouble viewed? How do the partners see the problem, the family, and the community? What is the same and what is different in these several views? What alternatives loom up? What has the couple tried? What has it not tried? Or what has it tried in the wrong way? Do the partners feel discouraged, beaten down? Have they surrendered hope and given in to feelings of despair? Do they console themselves with mutual punishment? *In any case, what do the partners now want?* What does the family want of them? What does the community expect? What does each partner need of the other, of the family, and of the community? In turn, what is each partner

---

*Ackerman was strongly influenced by his psychoanalytic orientation. This was one area where we originally disagreed. He intuitively made a rapid diagnosis. I have the BRQ filled out ahead of the first interview, whenever possible, so that every session makes maximum use of my professional skills.

willing to do for the other, for the family, and for the community? Finally, what is the orientation of the therapist? What does he, in his turn, propose to do?

These are the pertinent questions that confront the *therapist at the outset.* To make effective progress in clarifying the issues and exploring the alternatives, he must *cultivate an optimal quality of contact, rapport, and communication between the marital partners and between them and himself.*† He uses this rapport to catalyze the main kinds of conflict and coping. He claries the real content of conflict by dissolving barriers, defensive disguises, confusions, and misunderstandings. By stages, he moves toward more accurate mutual understanding with the marital partners of what is wrong. By stimulating empathy and communication, he seeks to arouse and enhance a live, honest, and meaningful emotional interchange. Figuratively speaking, he strives to make the contact a touching experience, a spontaneous and deeply genuine kind of communion. *As the partners feel in touch with the therapist, they come into better touch with each other.*‡ Through the therapist's use of himself, his open, earnest sharing of his own emotions, he sets an example of the desired quality of interaction between the marital partners.

In the therapy of marital disorders, the therapist must know what he stands for, what he is trying to do. He must also know what he can and cannot do. He must have explicit awareness of his own ideology of marriage and family life. He must clearly define, in his own mind, whatever discrepancy prevails between his personal family values and those of the marital couples.

So often a central feature of marital conflict is competitiveness. *Both partners are dedicated to the game*§ of one-upmanship. Each seeks to get the best of the other. It is as if the business ethic of profit and loss invades the inner life of the married couple. Neither can be convinced of a gain unless he imposes a loss upon the partner, a semblance of sacrifice. The game of one-upmanship is the pursuit of a delusion. It is misleading, for it can end only in futility. The essence of the delusion is that the well-being of the one partner comes only with a measure of sacrifice and surrender from the other. In the marital relationship it cannot be that what is good for one is bad for the other. In the long view, what is good or bad for one must also be good or bad for the other. The *very survival, continuity,* and *growth of marriage and family hinge on the acceptance of the principles of love, sharing, and co-operation. Without such acceptance, marriage and*

---

†Another semantic way of defining "working alliance."
‡The "therapeutic alliance" has begun.
§This antedates Berne's popularization of "games."

family have no meaning.||

The *goals of therapy* for marital disorders are to *alleviate emotional distress and disability and to promote the levels of well-being of both together and of each partner as an individual.* In a general way, the therapist moves toward these goals by strengthening the shared resources for problem solving; encouraging the substitution of more adequate controls and defenses for pathogenic ones; enhancing immunity against the disintegrative effects of emotional upset; enhancing the complementarity of the relationship; and *promoting the growth of the relationship and of each partner as an individual.*

The *therapist is a participant-observer.* To achieve the goals of marital therapy, the *clinician must integrate his trained knowledge and his use of himself in the therapeutic role in a unique way. He must be active, open, flexible,* forthright, at times even blunt. He must make the most free and undefensive use of himself. He moves alternately in and out of the pool of marital conflict. He moves in to energize and influence the interactional process; he moves out to distance himself, to survey and assess significant events, to objectify his experience, and then he moves in again. The marital partners engage in a selective process of joining with and separating from specific elements of the therapist's identity. The marital partners absorb, interact with, and use the therapist's influence in a variety of ways. The partial emotional joinings and separations reflect elements of transference and realism. The therapist must be adroit and constantly alert to shift his influence from one aspect of the marital relationship to another, following the shifting core of the most destructive conflict. He engages the partners in a progressive process of working through these conflicts. In the process, he fulfills multiple functions. He is catalyst, supporter, regulator, interpreter, and resynthesizer. These functions cannot be conceived in isolation but rather as a harmony of influences expressed through the unity of the therapist's use of himself.

He undercuts the tendency of the marital partners to console themselves by engaging in mutual blame and punishment. He stirs hope* of a new and better relationship. He pierces misunderstandings, confusions, and distortions to reach a consensus with the partners about what is really wrong. In working through the conflicts over differences, the frustrations, defeats, and failure of complementarity, he shakes up the old deviant patterns of alignment and makes way for new avenues of interaction. He weighs and balances the healthy and

---

||A nonhedonistic society. Predates the current focus on nonhedonism.
*The key ingredient of therapy as Thomas M. French stressed.

sick emotional forces in the relationship. He supports the tendencies toward health and counteracts those toward sickness by shifting his function in accordance with need at changing stages of the treatment.

To sum up in more specific terms, once having established the needed quality of rapport, empathy, and communication and having reached a consensus about what is wrong, he moves ahead, implementing the following special techniques:

the counteraction of inappropriate denials, displacements, and rationalizations of conflict;

the transformation of dormant and concealed interpersonal conflict into open, interactional expression;

the lifting of hidden intrapersonal conflict to the level of interpersonal interaction;

the neutralization of patterns of prejudicial scapegoating that fortify the position of one marital partner while victimizing the other;

the penetration of resistances and the reduction of shared currents of conflict, guilt, and fear through the use of confrontation and interpretation;

the use of the therapist's self in the role of a real parent as a controller of interpersonal danger, a source of emotional support and satisfaction, a provider of emotional elements the marital couple needs but lacks (The last function is a kind of substitutive therapy in which the therapist feeds into the emotional life of the parties certain more appropriate attitudes, emotions, and images of marital and family relationships, which the couple has not previously had. By these means, the therapist improves the level of complementarity of the relationship.);†

the therapist's use of himself as the instrument of reality testing;

the therapist's use of himself as educator and as personifier of useful models of health in marital interaction.

Using these various techniques, he proceeds, together with the marital couple, to test a series of alternative solutions to the marital distress."

Another important chapter in the *Psychotherapies of Marital Therapy* was that by Martin Grotjahn "Clinical Illustrations from Psychoanalytic Therapy."[56] His chapter is as valid today as its impact fifteen years ago. I introduced his article as follows: "Dr. Grotjahn is well known as a provocative teacher, a deeply intuitive clinician, and a sophisticated experimentalist. He carries the torch of experimentation in psychotherapy that Franz Alexander carried before him, yet he works at all times within the psychoanalytic system. His book *Psychoanalysis and the Family Neurosis* ia another 'must' for those interested in marital problems. His opinions are based on clinical analytic

---

†Franz Alexander has described this as the "corrective emotional experience."

experience and 'are stated with indifference to both *conformity* and *controversy.*' " (italics added).

His latest book, *The Art and Technique of Analytic Group Therapy* (1977)[57] continues to be *highly controversial.* He now defines his approach as analytic group therapy of the "slow-open type" consisting of small groups of patients that are not homogeneous and meet two hours a week. His focus is on communication of feelings, personal growth, learning, and courage to express the uniqueness of one's existence. In his words the aim of therapy: " . . . is to help the individual to become a conscious, direct, frank, honestly communicating person who begins to understand himself, his unconscious and that of others and who responds to others spontaneously and without anxiety and fear about his need for intimacy or aggression."[58]

Grotjahn's chapter continues to be a classic and should be read in its entirety to be fully appreciated. The following paragraphs give the reader a flavor of its contents (italics added):

"In all the years of my practical work as a psychiatrist, psychoanalyst, and psychotherapist, I have been guided by *therapeutic skepticism,* which is almost traditional for a German psychiatric background. I consider *psychoanalysis an essential part of training for almost any member of the healing profession.* . . . The *use of psychoanalysis* as an instrument of treatment *is not a sacrosanct* ritual, and *we should feel free to change it as our analytic insights into the dynamics of the therapeutic process deepen.* More *and more of the same is not enough*: If an analysis of *300 hours* has not shown the desired results, it is not certain that an analysis ten times as long will finally yield success. . . . The future of psychoanalysis does not seem to lie in unaltered technique. Combinations of all kinds of action and interaction with pharmacology and group approaches will have to be tried, and Sigmund Freud himself would approve of this experimentation — for he predicted and hoped for many changes in this science of which he laid the foundations in his pioneering work. . . . Freud knew the dynamics of the family neurosis, which he described for the first time in his paper, 'The Family Romance.' He was also aware of unconscious communication ("The Unconscious," 1915): 'It is remarkable that the unconscious of one human being can react upon that of another without the conscious being implicated at all . . .' (he describes the phenomenon of projective identification and so-called "family secrets" development).

This clinical essay is not the place to go into the details and theories of unconscious communication. . . . The man who came to me for help was a lawyer who was being persecuted by a former client of his, who had some reason to feel injured, as the lawyer had had a brief affair with the client's wife. There was some evidence that the client — unconsciously — had arranged the seduction of his wife by the lawyer, who then reacted with great guilt and fear. . . . (A spouse who helps set up the seduction which was just described may be expressing unconscious homosexuality.)

Diagnostic Family Interviews . . . may reveal family dynamics in ways that are more dramatic and convincing than those of any other conceivable method of teaching psychodynamic reasoning. Much can be learned from a well conducted interview with an individual patient, from his productions, his free-associative anamnesis, perhaps from a few dreams. And we can gain additional clues and hints from his motoric behavior in the interview situation and his relationship with the therapist. But our interpretation is to a large extent a matter of applied experience, of preconceived concepts and well confirmed conclusions, which make the patient and his unconscious understandable. During a family interview, the unconscious dynamics of such a group of people become evident before our eyes — we must only be able to see it. . . . " (italics added). (The rest of the chapter continues in this vein).

In one conjoint family therapy session, I observed the interchange between adolescent son and mother. The two were vituperatively attacking each other while the father watched. While the family was interacting on one observable level, I also noticed that another level of communication was occurring — the son and mother had their shoes off and were rubbing each others toes. Such unconscious communication (which the father could not observe from his seating position) represented *collusion* in this family system. After watching the family system operate, I changed the therapeutic approach from conjoint to concurrent.

The following couple, Dr. and Mrs. C, came for marital therapy. The therapeutic approach began as conjoint *marital* therapy but soon became apparent that conjoint *family* therapy was indicated. The therapist's alertness to family systems is crucial to successful therapy and flexibility in approach is a point I stress. A brief summary of Dr. and Mrs. C's therapy will illustrate the need to shift approach in order to be most helpful to the couple.

> Dr. and Mrs. C, married twenty years, had an only son, aged seventeen, who was completing his last year of high school. The couple complained of increasing aruguments which centered about Dr. C's total enmeshment in his career.

Mrs. C began her inital interview as follows: "Actually most of our other problems seem to derive from lack of communciation. I feel our arguments are chiefly initated by me, and I often wonder if it's because I would rather have *any* kind of communication than none. Bob has always acted unilaterally about everything without consulting me: the house, neighborhood, furniture, you name it. My husband is devoted to his practice and his son. I feel there is little energy and devotion left for me. We have had very little vacation time alone. He always insists on taking our son along. My husband does not really understand why I feel a need for this."

Dr. C, when seen alone, stated: "I love my wife very much. If not for that, our marriage would have collapsed. Part of her unhappiness stems from the fact that my practice requires a considerable portion of my time. She has many insecurities. It has been a difficult problem for me to provide her with reassurance. I an a taciturn person who doesn't easily engage in light talk. At times she feels I am unattentive. I come from a typical old New England family who is quiet. A recurring theme is that she thinks I devote too much time to my work. This has been explosive. At times I have felt I was precluded from doing what I would like to do. I have normal obligations to patients that I feel I should do. What really upsets me is that she thinks I am too involved with our son. Disagreements have developed over the proper handling of discipline. For my part, I have been distressed at the harshness expressed by my wife to my son at times. I have feared the effect of the pressures so produced on the boy.

The Cs were started on conjoint marital therapy in an effort to open up avenues of communication between them. Dr. C, beneath his cold and intellectualized facade, was very anxious and frightened. Mrs. C fluctuated between periods of anger and moderate periods of depression. Early in the sessions, Mrs. C complained about her husband being overly concerned about their son, his friends and dates.

Dr. C replied: My son and I have been close. Closer than the relationship between my wife and son. This has been a source of tension. I was insensitive to this until after the situation developed. My wife has told me in recent years that she felt excluded. It is true. My wife has, in various degrees of intensity, resented this, and it led her to be very harsh to him. When I protest, she interprets this as a preference for my son. She has said that I've given him attention that I should have given her.

An attempt was made to structure the marriage so that the son was permitted to begin his individuation from his father. The boy reacted to this attempt to stop his parentification by his father by joining a group of hippies at his school. When his mother discovered some marihuana cigarettes secreted in his room, I suggested that they invite him to join therapy, and conjoint family therapy was started. The C family was seen weekly in one and one-half hour sessions for about one year.

As early as 1931, I was interested in the family unit. I was later influenced by Ackerman and enjoyed the friendship which developed between us. Over the years I became more convinced that the dyadic relationship was primary even where family therapy was indicated. The children were important for the therapist to consider, but that children were not the focal point of therapy, rather an element of a subsystem of the nuclear family. There was no dichotomy between marital and nonmarital therapy and the family approach.[59-62] I used conjoint family therapy in 1960 and have never discontinued this technique in the spectrum of my approaches.

THE COMBINED-COLLABORATIVE APPROACH IN DYADIC DISHARMONY

The third type of combined therapy is that of the combined collaborative approach in dyadic discord. The technique consists of the partners in each dyadic relationship having their separate therapist and once a week the dyad and the therapists have a session which includes all parties.[63-67] The indications for this technique are the same as for the simple combined approach:

1. Previous treatment has indicated the possible separation or dissolution of a relationship which is destructive for one or both partners.
2. One or both partners will need ongoing personal therapy after separation or divorce.
3. Further therapy for immaturity, for working through the mourning process, for narcissistic injury, and for anxiety and/or rage reactions on part of either partner. My usual comment at the beginning of therapy is: "if you cannot reach a successful relationship, hopefully, you can have a successful separation without prolonged and painful legal procedures."

Martin[68] lists the contraindications for this approach, in addition to the ones I listed under the simple combined approach, as the following: inability of the two therapists to work constructively with each other and, where one of the partners cannot cope with the presence of a person of the same or opposite sex in the therapeutic session.

The advantages of the combined-collaborative techniques include those listed under the simple combined and the conjoint dyadic technique. In addition, when there are cotherapists, the dynamics of the larger group frequently brings into focus more information and data. The behavior of the cotherapists toward one another can model for the couple a relationship built upon mutual respect, positive communication, and goals. Also observable for the couple are the ways the cotherapists cooperate, compromise, and problem solve. The disadvantages for this approach are the same as for conjoint dyadic and simple combined approaches. The following vignette demonstrates combined-collaborative therapy:

> Mr. and Mrs. C were treated for a period of nineteen months, for a total of 120 sessions: two months concurrent, five months of the combined approach — single and conjoint sessions — then eight months of weekly combined-collaborative sessions, and finally, the classic approach with Mr. C for four months, after which his therapy was terminated while Mrs. C continued with her therapist.
>
> Mrs. C was an attractive, thin young woman, smartly dressed and neatly groomed. Initially tense and apprehensive, she stated that she was willing to seek marriage therapy so that she could be shown how to change her behavior to prevent a divorce. Mrs. C assumed a fair share of blame for their marital difficulties, especially berating herself for her immature ideas. She described herself as basically a happy person who had a troubled marriage. She felt selfish, demanding, and too interested in material things. She added that she and her husband had been separated for the past two months and had come for treatment at the advice of her lawyer, who had recommended marital therapy before proceeding with the divorce.
>
> Mr. C, a tall, well-built, extremely intelligent man, ten years older than his wife, was pessimistic about the value of marital therapy in their marriage. He described his marriage as having been a continual setting of tension with no surcease. Whenever he spoke of his wife, a vehement flavor crept into his voice. He took responsibility for walking out of the house, since he felt he was growing even more bitter and did not want to subject his two children to more conflict than has already been extant. Although he denied it when directly asked, it seemed that he was merely going through the motions of seeking marriage therapy and had already emotionally divorced his wife once and for all. He stated he was curious to become a better person with his wife or the next. At no time during the initial interview did he convey any feelings other than controlled anger and passive compliance with the demands of the situation.
>
> At the conjoint diagnostic and disposition session I suggested that we try the concurrent approach, that they remain separated, and recommended each to be seen twice weekly.
>
> In Mrs. C's next session she complained that she was very unhappy. "I didn't realize how much a demand marriage was. I am basically immature. I thought marriage had to do with love and sex.

I found out that marriage is work. We are two different people. We have had no sex since our second child was born. No sex for two years. I am afraid of taking the pill, and he doesn't want any more children. Sex has never been too important to my husband, only on Sunday morning because he has to get up early during the week. I have never had an orgasm."

In his next session, Mr. C stated: "I was always very critical of Joan. The way she walked and talked. I always felt she was immature and flighty but felt I could mold her into becoming a woman. My parents were glad that I was getting married because they were concerned that I was enjoying bachelorhood. I knew my wife was naive but I was always hoping that marriage and responsibility would straighten things out. But it only made things worse. Our two children were not planned. Each time she said she had her diaphragm in but later told me she forgot. So no sex for the last two years."

Mrs. C began her second month of therapy by stating: "I've done a lot of thinking in the past month, a lot of self-analysis. He hasn't called nor invited me out. I was surprised when he was with us on Thanksgiving day. We were very congenial and friendly. I've been letter perfect as to money. I've been very lonely the past months. I miss the George I want. Not the one swearing at me. Not the constant bickering. Until I got married, my mother did everything for me."

At his next session Mr. C commented: "I am unable to get along with Joan. This melodramatic nonsense on her part. I find my wife to be a harassment with the children when I visit. 'Why aren't you playing more with them. Why aren't you rolling on the floor with them.' If she wants a TV husband, she isn't going to get one. I don't have the patience to be with the children for a long time. I suppose I never really was a child, always on guard."

In the next three weeks Mrs. C described her idyllic state when she was single, her doting parents, and how ill prepared she was for marriage. I suggested that she and her husband were ready for their first date and to begin courting again. Either they would start moving closer to each other or away. I felt her husband wanted to move back home, and I would suggest the courting process to him.

At her next session she stated: "About last night. I tried to make it like a first date. Like you told me to do. It was very pleasant! We had a very nice evening."

At his next session Mr. C commented that their first date was very nice: "If only she could be that way most of the time, instead of her incessant demands. Ninety-nine percent (99%) of what she does infuriates me. From the beginning I sat down with her, after a month of marriage, and tried to explain there are certain duties to perform even though you don't like it. You have to carry your weight. She didn't see it that way. I would go into a blind rage when I paid the bills. She would wring her hands and say it wouldn't happen again. I was pulling my weight and she wasn't pulling hers. I would always be angry at her. There was never any adult response on her part. Her parents would talk to her, but she was complaining morning, noon and night. You have no idea. Still, I would like to move back home if you think it is the thing to do."

A week later at a conjoint session the question was raised about Mr. C moving back home, and both agreed.

At his next session Mr. C stated: "I've moved back home. It's been fine. I was happy to get home. I missed the children and the surroundings. I hope it works out, but I am afraid Joan can't change. She is too much of a child. She makes promises but can't keep them."

Everything went along fine for two weeks, and then Mrs. C reported: "I feel a great deal of the arguing this weekend was my fault. I want to be a good patient. Why can't I grow up. I know better, yet I spend money foolishly and he gets furious." Two weeks after his moving home she stated: "We went out last night. I worked out fine. He was very witty It was fun to be with him. Besides, I had been on my best behavior that week. Very enjoyable. We had sex. The first time in about two years."

Two weeks later Mr. C came in furious at his wife. "She says, 'What do you want of me?' I said 'I want harmony.' I don't want to be confronted by her problems — ten thousand bits of trivia. She is extremely immature. I went over the bills. I went completely mad. Hundreds and hundreds of dollars spent on unnecessary clothes. We had decided on two hundred dollars a week for food, yet I found eight checks for fifty dollars made out to Jewel Food Store. She said, 'just figures.' I said, 'We are spending twice as much as I make.' Her answer was, 'So get a bank loan.' I hit the ceiling."

At her next appointment, I suggested to Mrs. C that we try the combined-collaborative approach. Perhaps she felt I was prejudiced against her and that her own therapist might be more helpful. She was very resistant and reluctant to the idea, and I suggested we have a conjoint session in three days to discuss my suggestion further. In my own mind this was a desperate last effort to save the marriage as Mr. C was reaching the limit of his tolerance. Also, I felt Mrs. C would need her own therapist to help her over a divorce should the combined-collaborative approach. Perhaps she felt I was prejudiced recommended the new approach, a three-month target date and to terminate therapy if no improvement.

Mrs. C began her first combined-collaborative session (CCS) by stating she liked her new therapist. They had worked out a budget which was agreeable with her husband, and she was going to adhere to it. (I had previously suggested this in an effort to decrease the variables in their marital discord so that we could get to the basis of their relationship.) "I had a frightening dream last night: My mother was there. She said, 'I am unhappy with your marriage. You have to get along better with your husband.' The scene changes. I am in our house. Very dark. See someone else. See a rat. I start screaming with fear. Someone said it is not a rat, only a mouse.

My mother was always very protective of me. Even when I was away at college, she would write and tell me what to do. I was very frightened in the dream." Mrs. C commented that she liked her new therapist even though she was young.

(Comment: Mrs. C approaches the CCS with great fear and attempts to reassure herself that it is not as threatening as it appears— not a rat, only a mouse.) Ten days later in his individual session, Mr. C reported: "My wife has been much better. One incident last night. I blew my cool over nothing." Three days later before the fifth CCS he stated: "A good week. Joan is trying very hard. Last night a very slight disagreement. She started to regress a bit. The material things her friends had. I did as you had suggested. I didn't escalate but left the room. Later in bed I said 'Joan this is the first time you caused me to leave the room since our four-way sessions. Why do you do it?' She said she was sorry. I'm much happier with what's going on. I think she likes her therapist very much. I really would like the marriage to work, but I doubt it. She will soon revert to her infantile behavior. I hope not."

In the sixth CCS, the main issue was her husband's complaint that although he had told her they were overdrawn at the bank and had suggested she only make necessary purchases, that evening she had purchased an expensive purse: "It was such a bargain she couldn't resist. It had been marked down 50 percent." This had resulted in a furious argument. Mrs. C's only retort was that all her friends had these things and why couldn't she.

In the tenth CCS, Mrs. C was unable to come in as her children were ill. Mr. C came in alone and with controlled anger stated: "Tuesday, believe it or not, she talked about needing a new dishwasher like her best friend just got. And here I'm trying to get caught up financially. Sure, I can borrow more money, but I'm getting deeper in debt. I make a very good salary and think we should live within our means. I don't mind drawing on our reserves for this treatment. She is just a vicious bitch. The tirade I got over the telephone at work because the cleaning woman was ill and couldn't come. And here I am busy with my salesmen. I don't think she has made any change. She is so immature! I had a dream I don't understand: Joan and I at her folks house. A real battle ensued. They were attacking Joan for her incessant demands upon me. I grabbed Joan and left. I was furious at them. I resented them being unpleasant to Joan."

It was pointed out that he was furious at the two therapists for the lack of change in his wife.

Dr. L, the cotherapist, suggested that he be patient and take her out once a week as a regular date, since his wife complained they didn't do anything.

At the eleventh CCS, the issue of Joan wanting a new dishwasher was raised. Although she admitted it was not wise since the old one was functioning well but, it was the old-fashioned kind, not the pull out type; and she complained all her friends had everything they needed, although their husbands made less money than her husband. Mr. C retorted that their parents bought these for them, and he felt they should live within their means. At this Joan began to cry.

At his next session, Mr. C said his wife wanted a divorce. After three days of noncommunicating he had told her that he was going to leave. "I don't love you. I don't think I can love you After this everything was fine."

At their twelfth CCS, the Cs reported a good week and sex for the first time in many, many months.

At his next individual session, Mr. C was very depressed and said that he and his wife had been quarreling for three days. I suggested that perhaps we try the classic approach, no communication between therapists, with the goal being what was best for each individual and with the marriage secondary. That I would suggest a structured relationship at the next CCS that would attempt to avoid arguing (TSD). They would either move closer or further apart.

At the next CCS, Dr. L opened the session by commenting that Joan, at her individual session, was quite upset and concerned about their financial situation, and that she was very sorry she was acting the way she had been.

Mrs. C stated: "We have both improved. Mr. C commented: After I left your office the other day I was very upset about the whole thing. I decided it was unfair to have it sprung on her today at our four-way session. So for two hours last night we talked. The first time since our marriage."

I suggested the classic approach with a six-month target date. They should live together, but on a landlord-boarder arrangement. The financial aspect was to be structured realistically as if they were divorced.

At the next CCS, both reported a good week, and that both were trying very hard to meet each other's needs. Mr. C observed: "I'm not as pessimistic as before. I feel either we will have a good marriage or separate."

A month later at the eighteenth CCS the discord had returned. Mr. C began the session as follows: "It's been a miserable two weeks. Her behavior has been as though we never have been here. She blows like the wind. This morning she was screaming like a fishwife over nothing. All the grief is self-inflicted. She created an incident over nothing: I have forgotten to bring home some egg rolls with the chop suey. I see it as a pattern of behavior that can't change. Either she needs to be changed or needs a new husband who is equally as goofy."

With no improvement in the following month, the CCS were discontinued, eight months after the original CCS. All participants mutually agreed on the classic approach. Mrs. C's closing comment was: "I am wholly in favor of the individual approach."

Five months later, Mr. C decided to stop coming; he was going to see his lawyer about a divorce. "The marriage is no better. She is a very, very bitter girl. She has a good relationship with her therapist but is as immature as always."

This couple illustrates the failure of the combined-collaborative approach to reequilibrate this conflicted couple. However, the wife was anchored in therapy with her therapist and needed two more years of therapy, although stormy, to weather the divorce trauma without falling apart. To date the combined-collaborative approach has been successful with one-half the couples.

GROUP THERAPIES IN DYADIC DISHARMONY

Group therapies, the fourth technique of the combined approaches, consists of various combinations of clinical settings and theoretical orientations. My clinical experience includes couples' groups with four dyads and homogeneous groups, i.e. a combined approach with group and dyadic sessions with individual members. During my medical career in World War II, I began groups of fifty patients to work out battle anxieties, psychosomatic symptoms and other war related problems. The effectiveness of this approach impressed me so that after the war ended I used it at the Veteran's Rehabilitation Center in Chicago (in the form of analytic groups[69]) and later at Forest Hospital (I organized a marital unit with group therapy one option).

Recently Framo,[70] among others,[71-75] found couples' group to be the treatment of choice for marital problems based on his experience with over 200 couples. My reservations about this technique involves group resistance, e.g. the group suddenly shifts focus away from a couple's open expression of hostile feelings to less threatening areas. Another disadvantage that I observed is the tendency to assign parental roles to one couple who are then attacked by the group to avoid exploration of the other couples' problems. Also, frequently, there was the maneuver to get either the therapist(s) or one couple to play the Bernean game of "Courtroom." Another disadvantage that I observed was where one couple feels that the therapist shows preference to the others. Occasionally, where one couple was obviously destructive against his partner and separation was indicated, the other couples responded with fear and/or confusion over the value to maintain their relationship, regardless of the emotional price. I can foresee other possible disadvantages, e.g. acting out by one individual or a pair coupling, and the group is overwhelmed and enmeshed.

My indications for couples' group therapy include the following:

1. Therapeutic impasse with other techniques.
2. Economic — less costly per dyad.
3. Relatively inhibited, noncommunicative couples where the dyads offer support and model for openness.
4. The couple labelled "sadomasochistic" whose behavior patterns are mutually provocative may profit from the group by helping to understand the interrelationship of the reaction to each other.

Martin[76] lists the contraindications as follows:

1. The presence of a "family secret".
2. Failure of one partner to work productively with the group.
3. When one partner is psychotic or unable to control their verbal destructiveness.

I would add another contraindication:

4. Where one partner has a primary affective disorder (manic-depressive illness).[77] On the other hand, Davenport and colleagues[78] found this approach extremely useful in a *homogeneous group.*

Over the past decade, my association with group analytic psychotherapy of dyadic disharmony has been limited to that of supervising other therapists, and occasionally that of cotherapists. In all these experiences, the approach has been of the *combined type,* groups with individual sessions for the patients as indicated. The demands of my time precluded participation, since these approaches were held in the evenings and/or weekends.

The emergence of group psychotherapies constitutes a significant development in the field of therapy. Jerome Frank[79] delivered a recent Award Lecture, the theme was the theory and practice on the eve of the '80s. The world is in a flux, he feels, and the challenge for psychotherapists is to prepare patients to cope with the potential world chaos. Also, that group approaches are "particularly promising" for this purpose, especially those that strengthen support systems such as "family and marital therapies.". Of interest is a recent report from the Tavistock Clinic, London, of a long-term follow-up study of psychoanalytic group therapy by Malan and his colleagues.[80] They raise questions about the appropriateness of this technique: "Comparison of psychodynamic changes in patients who stayed less than six months with those in patients who stayed more than two years gave a null result. The majority of patients were highly dissatisfied with their group experiences. However, there was a very strong positive correlation between favorable outcome and previous individual psychotherapy." The literature on group psychotherapy continues to be extensive.[81-89] I firmly agree with Kaplan and Saddock[90] who state so aptly:

> To be of help, the group therapist must have detailed knowledge of each individual patient's intrapsychic and interpersonal disturbances, and he must be aware of the patient's psychological strengths and assets. In addition, the therapist must understand how and why the patient's problems developed . . . Finally, the therapist must try to identify the various causes of the patient's illness — the stresses, adverse social and cultural influences, and somatic factors. With all this information in hand, the therapist can proceed with his formal *diagnosis* and begin treatment. . . . Clearly, then, the therapist must see each prospective candidate for group psychotherapy individually before he is admitted to the group. (italics added)

The last sentence of this quote is most important and not done as frequently as it should!

In conclusion, what Rome[91] said almost a decade ago is still valid: "The entire field of group psychotherapy awaits . . . a more rigorous scientific methodology." Having observed a number of group therapists including Moreno in the thirties and Ackerman and Bowen in the fifties (to name only a few), the one common denominator in all was their charismatic nature and strongly held beliefs in their techniques. Indicating the increasing importance of group therapy is the fact that 80 percent of approved psychiatric residency programs offer training in this approach.[92]

SEX DYSFUNCTIONAL THERAPY

At the beginning of the '70s, Masters and Johnson reported the successful treatment of sexual dysfunctions. Their current approach[93] was presented in 1976. The pioneering work by these two clinical researchers became the foundation and seminal for most current sex therapies.[94-102] Unfortunately, their success resulted in a mushrooming of many so-called sex therapists. In fact, recently, Masters and Johnson,[103] among others,[104-106] became quite concerned at the commercialization and preponderance of poorly trained sex therapists and sponsored a conference on ethical issues in sex therapy and research held in January, 1976.

A thoughtful article by Lassen[107] touched on five issues and dilemmas in sexual treatment: therapeutic values and conflict in values for the therapist; desperation of the impotent male and its relationship to coping techniques and cultural expectations; masturbation; the self-concept of the nonorgastic woman; and specific value conflict for the female therapist. In addition, the literature now is reporting on failures of those so-called cured.[108-111] This is nothing new as any experienced clinician has observed. First, the new approach or drug is heralded as a panacea. This is followed by a swing of failures, and over a period of *time*, a middle ground is found for its efficacy.

All competent sexual therapists and researchers stress the importance of improving the total relationship for the couple and/or personal growth of the individual.[112,113] My conclusion, after years of dealing with dyadic relationships, is that any complaint (content) depends upon its resolution by improving the dyadic *relationship*.[114,115] Over the past decade, sexual complaints continues to be fourth in frequency, it follows unfulfilled emotional needs. Sager,[116] an experienced therapist, notes that *how* a couple relate sexually may or may not be indicative of their total relationship. My pragmatic theoretical framework of the GST encompasses all possible factors influencing sexual dysfunctional problems.[117,118] An accurate diagnosis exploring all possible areas: intrapersonal, interpersonal, and environmental has been found very helpful. The transactional approach enables the therapist to select whatever area needs investigation to alleviate the sexual complaint. Flexibility of therapy permits refocusing technique to accomplish lessening of sexual conflicts in the most efficient, yet humane manner. As with all complaints involving another individual it is the reverberating quality of the systems in the relationship that is fundamental to change regardless of specificity of complaint.

A knowledge of the psychodynamic roots to a sexual problem and interpreting this with appropriate timing often alleviates the conflict. Bieber[119] presents the current psychoanalytic treatment of sexual disorder that most experienced analysts use in addition to other concepts. In addition to the intrapersonal system, the sexual aspect of the dyad's relationship has an equally important input into the ongoing changes of erotic interchange. Obviously, the ongoing changes in the couple's sociocultural matrix play a similar role (environmental system). It is this reverberating quality of all systems in the GST that suggests that the therapeutic input into the interpersonal system may, at times, be an effective factor in sexual dysfunctions.

Therefore, an adequate diagnostic evaluation of all three systems is mandatory before starting treatment. The biographical relationship questionnaire (sixth revision) which now contains a detailed sexual history is what I use as an aid. It is currently being used at the Marital and Family department of the Behavioral Sciences at Loma Linda University, California. A routine medical examination is mandatory, with the necessary laboratory tests.

The following vignettes are illustrative of the flexibility in therapeutic approaches and the impact of life events on sexual dysfunctions:

Mr. A, aged twenty-five, sexually impotent for the past five years, was referred for classical analysis by his wife's analyst. The impotence started on the honeymoon. Mrs. A was "insatiable" in her sexual demands. Mr. A felt that "she was gyrating her hips like she was trying to tear my penis off."

He had met his wife through a relative, after returning to the United States as a combat hero. A smooth, nonpassionate, nonsexual courtship of six months followed. He said he was attracted to his wife because she was the opposite to him — "beautiful, dynamic, and vivacious." He calmly stated that they both wanted the marriage, separate careers, and no children. His only complaint was the *overt* flaunting of her extramarital infidelity and caustic comments about his impotence. He felt extremely guilty about his impotence. He had never been sexually aggressive and had always suffered from premature ejaculation since his first experience of sexual intercourse at seventeen years of age. His past history was uneventful, except for witnessing at the age of five the murder of his father during a robbery. Mr. A felt that he had been an underachiever for many years. Three years of analysis, three times a week, was unsuccessful as far as his impotence but in all other areas he was very successful.

At this point, Mrs. A terminated her analysis. Since both wanted further treatment, I suggested the concurrent approach. After three months, this was changed to the simple combined technique. After a long period of time this therapy was unrewarding. I suggested three options: stop therapy, separation, or referral to another therapist. They chose the latter.

The core dynamics in the husband was related to his oedipal complex (especially his guilt over his father's death) whereas his wife's rage and guilt, both openly and covertly, related to an incestuous ongoing relationship in childhood, which led her to seek revenge and neutralize her guilt through pain. She exploited and discarded men frequently. The sadomasochistic bind seemed nonresponsive to solution. Three years more of treatment again proved unsuccessful and the couple requested referral to the Masters and Johnson Clinic, but they were not accepted. Mrs. A was killed in an automobile accident when a driver of the other automobile went through a red light.

Mr. A consulted me at this point because of a reactive depression. He was started on psychoanalytic psychotherapy on a once a week basis with antidepressant medication. The dyanamics of his depression was a reversal of his ongoing rage at his dead spouse, conscious guilt about her death, but the unconscious guilt about his death wishes toward her that was revealed in his dream material. At the appropriate time, I insisted that he dispose of everything that reminded him of his wife. This took Mr. A three months to dispose of all her objects, and when this was completed he began dating a woman regularly who was a divorcee and comfortable with sex. They fell deeply in love and she made little of his sex problem: "this sex thing is no big deal. I love you and we will work it out." Her behavior was the exact opposite of his former wife — considerate, stroking, supportive, and confident. After a six month relationship, Mr. A completely regained his potency. Remarital therapy for three months showed no contraindication to marriage, and they were married. My usual yearly dyadic check-up for the next three years showed a good remarriage.

Mr. and Mrs. B came for therapy after Mr. B discovered that his wife was unfaithful. "Accidentally," Mrs. B left a love letter from her lover on the nightstand.

Mr. B, in his early thirties, felt considerable guilt over his inability to satisfy his wife sexually, because of premature ejaculation, which started in adolescence. Mrs. B wanted help in terminating her first and only "affair". Mr. B was started on classical analysis and Mrs. B on supportive psychotherapy. The concurrent approach was used. The core of Mr. B's problem was oedipal and fear of success, which manifested itself in many areas. Underlying was a tremendous rage at a rejecting, but seductive mother, who he projected onto other women.

The breakthrough in therapy came when the wife mentioned that whenever she had pain during intercourse, because of inadequate foreplay, he could maintain his erection for a long period of time. As soon as she showed pleasure, he would immediately ejaculate. A suggestion to Mrs. B, that she fake signs of pain, worked on three consecutive sexual episodes. When Mr. B was told of the experiment, he was confronted with the interpretation that "you do not fornicate — you urinate during intercourse. Your premature ejaculation, at times even before entering, is a manifestation of your hostility toward your seductive, rejecting mother." His condition improved rapidly.

Unfortunately, although the couple no longer had a sexual problem, Mrs. B was unable to give up her lover so they agreed on an amicable divorce.

Some years later Mr. B phoned for an appointment with his fiancee for remarital therapy. He had no further problems sexually, since his divorce. The evaluative phase revealed no conflictual areas and they married. Yearly check-ups revealed a harmonious marriage.

Mr. and Mrs. C, referred for treatment because of his premature ejaculations and her anorgasmia. The Cs' had two years of concurrent analyis and one year of conjoint sessions, which improved their relationship considerably, but only mildly helped his premature ejaculation. Mrs. C was no orgastic and no longer a frightened, immature person. At this point, I changed the therapy to that of sex treatment. I had them purchase a copy of the booklet "You Can Last Longer"[120] and after three months more of therapy, Mrs. C was no longer hostile and uncooperative. Their sexual dysfunction disappeared.

Mr. and Mrs. D were referred for treatment because of Mr. D's ejaculatory problem. A thorough evaluation of their relationship revealed no underlying psychological problems warranting intervention. They stated they had been happily married for ten years and wanted to improve their sexual relationship after attending a lecture on that topic. I referred them to a competent local sexual dysfunction clinic where they did improve their sexual relationship.

In my experience, the Ds' had a very unusual sexual dysfunction. I agree with Nadelson in her questioning of "healthy" sexual dysfunctions: "Increasingly over the past five years the presence of a sexual complaint has been presented as the ticket of entry into therapy. Very often the symptom is the clue to more complex problems which may not be explicitly recognized. At times sexual symptoms may serve a protective function: to keep a manageable distance between partners or to prevent further stress or conflict from emerging. For some couples a problem-free sexual relationship would be inconsistent with the evident marital disharmony and disturbance."[121]

In conclusion, my ongoing clinical experience with couples with sexual dysfunction as one of the dyadic complaints, indicates that the *majority* respond to therapy utilizing all three inputs from the GST. This conceptualization enables the therapist to explore and utilize all modalities in the treatment of the sexual complaint. Also, although the great majority of sex therapy is done by cotherapists, it does not have to be.[122,123]

TREATMENT WHEN ONE PARTNER HAS A PRIMARY AFFECTIVE DISORDER (PAD)

It is a whirling, a motion, a spinning, a teasing of air —
like a voice.
The energy there finds in itself a closing, to spin, to whirl

and grow.
What energy! (J. W. C.)

The last type of special therapies that I have used in dyadic disharmonies deals with a psychiatric condition — Primary Affective Disorders (manic-depressive illness).[124] As of January 1, 1980, I have treated 129 couples and supervised seventy-five couples where one partner had a PAD. Akiskal et al., a pioneer in understanding this illness, in 1979, stated: " . . . the confidence with which the diagnosis could be made in the presence of any of these variables (early occurrence of 'pharmacological-hypomania,' family history of bipolar illness and family history in two or three consecutive generations) ranged from 88 percent to 100 percent."[125] A PAD involves alterations of mood where there is increasing empirical evidence that its etiology has both genetic and complex biochemical reactions in the nervous system.[126-138]

The PAD syndrome is *frequently overlooked by therapists* treating couples or families, also by some physicians unless they have a high level of suspicion about this disorder. Various therapeutic combinations are used according to the severity of the disease in the PAD individual, the specific needs of the family at different stages in the life cycle; and any particular crisis in the life situation. The approach that is used frequently is *collaborative.* However, *conjoint family therapy* is indicated when the child(ren) do not understand that the parent has an *illness* responsible for the disruptive or bizarre behavior.

My interest in this clinical entity begain in 1972 with the serendipitous discovery[139] of two clinical features: a *stubborn reluctance* on the part of partners of these dyadic relationships to *separate/divorce* (10%)[140] and an *intermittent incompatibility* in the relationship when compared with the durable incompatible relationships, so often seen by marital or family therapists. An ongoing research project, especially with one colleague, Ronald R. Lee, has resulted in four papers to date.[141-144] The first material was presented at the joint meeting of the NCFR and AAMFT, Oct 25, 1974, in St. Louis, Mo. The last paper on genetic factors was presented at the International Congress on Adolescence, in July, 1976, Jerusalem, Israel. The latest revision of the American Psychiatric Association coding — DSM-III (1979) — does not use the term "PAD" they use "Affective Psychoses" and lists six main categories:

1. Manic-depressive psychosis, manic type
2. Manic-depressive psychosis, depressed type
3. Manic-depressive psychosis, circular type but currently manic

4. Manic-depressive psychosis, circular type, mixed
5. Manic-depressive psychosis, circular type, current condition not specified
6. Manic-depressive psychosis, other and unspecified

My Sample

The sample used consists of 125 dyadic relationships, 13 percent of my total couples. The couples primarily came from white, upper, and upper-middle socio-economic classes (Hollingshead). The mean age of the males was 41.1 years (standard deviation 7.95) while the mean age of the females was 36.8 years (standard deviation 8.20). The mean age of the PAD male patient was 43.13 (standard deviation 9.75) and the female PAD patients was 34.62 (stand deviation 5.92).

Table III shows the diagnostic breakdown by sex of the 125 PAD patients seen between 1948 and 1979.

TABLE III

DIAGNOSTIC BREAKDOWN BY SEX

	Males	Females	Total
Unipolar Depression	8	44	52
Unipolar Manic...............	17	6	23
Bipolar......................	10	40	50
Total.................	35	90	125

$x^2 = 22.79$ p   .01

Of the fifty-two unipolar depressives, eight were males and forty-four were females. Of the twenty-three unipolar manics, seventeen were males and six were females. For the bipolar PADs, ten were males and forty females. The chi square ratio shows that the difference between males and females based on diagnosis is significant. This means that a far greater proportion of males are unipolar manics and a far greater proportion of females are unipolar depressives or bipolar then would be expected by chance.

This sample showed that in two-thirds of the PADs there was evidence of suicidal ideation and in 40 percent evidence or prior serious suicidal attempts. My data illustrates the potential seriousness of dyads or families involving a PAD partner. The data also shows that no one symptom can be used to diagnose a PAD. The instance of suicidal thoughts was not gender related from my statistics, nor was the chi square ratio significant. However, the chi square ratio of 6.12 was significant for suicidal attempts with a p<0.045 indicating a possible gender component to the diagnosing a PAD.

One of the unique advantages of this sample was the long range of therapy which occurred. There were 105 cases observed and treated. The mean length of treatment 3.35 years (standard deviation 5.85) and the range of observation had a mean of 4.90 years (standard deviation of 6.23). Our review of the lieterature revealed only one study based on a five year clinical follow-up by the same clinician.[145] The remainder of case studies were based on much shorter longitudinal data, if any. In this study, while the mean length of observation is five years, five of the cases have been observed over ten years, while another five have been observed for over twenty years. Some of my patients currently are offspring of my former patients.

It is this longitudinal relationship with families which has enabled me to observe features of PADs that may not have been as readily osberved in other studies. For example, in several cases, even with a thorough history taking process, the PAD did not mention any family history material that pointed to first degree relatives also being PADs. However, because it is my custom to routinely interview the partner, through this information I often get evidence for PAD diagnoses, and later confirmed from information from the PAD patient. I agree with Mendlewicz: " . . . more generally, one member of a married couple is an accurate reporter about the other. . . . *but a direct interview is necessary* (italics added) if one wants to estimate, in addition, personality characteristics and marital (dyadic) dynamics."[146]

I have found that our routine procedure of evaluating both partners in individual sessions before having a conjoint diagnostic and disposition session has made us particularly sensitive to diagnosing PADs and to the genetic component involved. Also, I have found in some PAD cases that the degree of the denial of PAD conditions in first degree relatives suggests that at some level, possibly unconscious, the PAD may be defending against the idea of a genetic basis to the disease. Not all genotypes express themselves as phenotypes, an appropriate environment is required for genetic expression.[147] Table IV indicates the amount of generational evidence in our latest study. It can be quite readily observed that there is generational support for a PAD diagnosis.

TABLE IV

GENERATIONAL DATA FOR 125 PADS

PAD diagnosis for 4 generations 2%
PAD diagnosis for 3 generations 23%
PAD diagnosis for 2 generations (forwards) 15%
PAD diagnosis for 2 generations (backwards).............................. 48%
PAD diagnosis for patient only 37%

    Total...100%

The mean years of dyadic relationships (marital as well as nonmarital) were 13.65 (standard deviation 7.55). In three-quarters of the couples who married, it was the first marriage for both spouses, in 10 percent it was the first marriage for one spouse.

The personality makeup of these pair-couplings was as one would expect psychodynamically — a complementarity of personality characteristics.[148] The PAD partner seeking unconsciously a partner who would help control the mood swings, and the non-PAD wishing a freer expression of emotions. To facilitate this hypothesis, we used two dimensions similar to those used by Eysenck. One dimension was extroversion- intraversion, the other control-noncontrol dimension. All 250 patients were diagnosed as belonging to one of the four end points of the dimension, 127 were extroverts, four were introverts, eighty-eight were controlling and thirty-one noncontrolling. As shown in Figure 16, when these personality dimensions were arranged according to their dyadic structure, the overwhelming proportion of pair-couplings, that is 65 percent, show an extrovert partner relating to a controlling person. In this dyad, a check of those who were PADs showed that all but eight were extroverts.

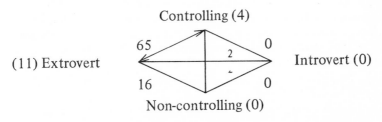

Figure 16. Personality dyads of 125 PADs and their spouses.

Our research on diagnoses and treatment in dyadic disharmony when one partner has a PAD necessitated further knowledge of the genetic literature in this area. Studies by Slater and Cowie (1971),[149] Harvald and Hauge (1975),[150] and Kringlen (1967)[151] have consistently shown that monozygotic twins have a higher concordance rate for the disease than dizygotic twins. Other studies show that relatives of PADs are more likely to suffer from the disease than individuals in the population at large. Whereas previously there were compelling arguments for the heredity component of this disease coming from genetic markers (color blindness and Xg blood) of the eighty-six traits indentified as being carried on the X chromosome,[152-154] some recent evidence questions these two markers.[155, 156]

As shown earlier in this section, 63 percent of the dyads showed evidence of a PAD in at least two generations of first degree relatives. In 23 percent of the couples, three generations were involved, while in three dyads there were four generations: Grandparent, parent, patient, and child. In sixty couples, where there were two generational data, fifteen patients gave evidence in their history of one child being a PAD. At first, we were inclined to be rather cautious about the diagnosis of a PAD for children, but our growing interest in prevention and reports in the literature (Kuhn, 1963[157]) of children and especially in adolescents, ecouraged us to diagnosis PAD as soon as possible.[158-69] The advantage of this is that, in a family where a spouse has disrupted the marital state for years, it is possible to give genetic counseling to the offspring without too much resistance.

The following vignette is illustrative:

> Mr. A, referred by his pediatrician because he was in an acute panic condition. He came for the initial visit with his fiancee. The marriage date was set for the very next day, all arrangements were made, etc.
>
> In his mid-twenties, nice appearing, Mr. A's past medical history showed two similar episodes: one three years ago, the other six years ago. Obviously, he was *very depressed*. I explained his condition to his fiancee and suggested postponing the wedding. I was amazed to hear that her father was a patient of mine fifteen years previously, for a similar condition. When she phoned to tell her father who they had seen, and to postpone the wedding, his reply was : "Anything Dr. Greene tells you, you follow his advice." The marriage was postponed immediately.

The specific nature of the genetic transmission is still very controversial.[170] Winokur et al.,[171] resurrecting a thesis proposed by Rosanoff in 1935,[172] stress the X linked basis to PAD. Not only does he point to color blindness and Xg blood factors as marker evidence, but he also reports studies in which there was an absence of a father-son incidence of the disease. As Winokur and Pitts explain: "the normal complement of sex chromosones is XY in the male and XX in the female. Because a son must receive X from his mother and Y from his father the distinguishing feature of X linked inheritance, both dominant and recessive, is the absence of father to son transmission."[173] In coming to his 1969 conclusion of an X linked genetic transmission, Winokur[174] discounted the evidence of Slater[175] who in his sample reported fourteen father-son pairs. Perhaps more important is that he later reversed himself on his own findings of 1965 where he reported that of 366 white PADs there were thirty-five clear cases where the father was PAD but the mother was not. Of these, twenty-one probands were female and *fourteen were male*. Logically he concluded in 1965: "in view of the fact that affected fathers have passed the illness on to sons, it does not seem that an X born dominant kind of transmission is feasible."[176] By 1969, the logic had not changed, but the sample had. In a study of fifty-nine manics he reports that fourteen ill fathers had only one ill son and, he concludes, that any transmission occurred by a sex-link single or double dominant gene. To reinforce his conclusion, he reports in another study that of sixty-one manic probands there were no father-son relationships.

It needs to be stressed that Winokur's 1969 samples were reported as manic probands, whereas, the 1965 sample contained a mixture of unipolar and bipolar PADs. Winokur himself admits that mixed samples of PADs do produce father-son combinations, but stresses that "when one studies manic probands and their families that father-son transmission is absent." *Our data does not agree with Winokur's position!* Of the seventeen unipolar manic male probands, there were six manifest father-son transmissions. Further, two of the six male transmissions are across three generations: grandfather, father (proband), and son in each case. The following vignettes are illustrative:

> Mr. B was referred by his lawyer. The patient was forty-four years of age, hypertalkative, and hyperactive with characteristic "flight of ideas" — flitting from on topic to another. Married for twenty years, he had three sons, aged eighteen, fifteen, and thirteen, and one daughter, ten years old. He was very personable and a successful business man. His opening comment was as follows: "I want a divorce and my wife won't agree." He stated the need for a divorce started three months ago while convalescing in Acapulco from a heart attack. He began to feel a progressive increase in energy as he convalesced and was able to add two more companies to his corporation. In spite of opposition from his board, he had gone ahead, and both were successful.
>
> He said he was like his father who had died from a heart attack at

the age of 65. "My father was dominant, domineering, and very successful in the operation of the present corporation I now operate. He had been married four times and I am from my father's first marriage. He was once hospitalized for a period of three months for a nervous breakdown. Afterward, he talked too much, had insomnia and made sudden "irrational" business ventures, but these turned out successful. We never got along, while he had no trouble with other people; he was president of his golf club, the life of the party, and well liked by everyone.

My eldest son is just like me. Always on the go during his high school years — outstanding scholastically, captain of the baseball team, class president etc. He is the same in his freshman year at college. He gets sudden blue moods for no reason and then there is no stopping him. I used to be like that too when I was in school."

Mrs. B was an attractive, well dressed, well groomed woman of forty-three, appeared very stable and had been his executive secretary for the past eighteen years. "This is the fourth time he comes back with the old divorce routine. We had sexual relationships before we married and I knew of his numerous affairs. He nows wants to marry his twenty-year-old secretary." Upon questioning, she described her *eldest son* as *"an exact duplicate of his father in looks and personality."*

In another clinical case of father-son genetic transmission was that of the following:

Mr. C was referred by the psychiatrist of Mr. C's father. The father had twenty years of psychiatric treatment for recurrent manic attacks. Mr. C was a thirty-four-year-old successful professional who had not gone into his father's business because of frequent clashes over the years about his behavior. Mr. C was an engaging, attractive male who established an immediate rapport with me. He loved his wife, whom he had married against his father's wishes, but now she was completely accepted by his family. "I would not be here except, stupidly, I left a motel slip in my suit that my wife found when she was sending my clothes to the cleaners. I had told her I had to be out of town on a convention. Unfortunately, the girl works in the same building and my wife found out she was the one. I have had affairs since I was thirty; for some reason, I have tremendous sexual needs which I could satisfy at home but each affair just occurred on the spur of the moment. This is the first affair my wife learned about and she is so furious at me, she wants a divorce."

Mrs. C was an attractive thirty-year-old with a minor degree in psychology. They had met at college and they had "immediate chemistry. In fact on our first date we ended up in bed. He is irresistible . . . " She stated that they were always happily married, but during the last two years her husband had two emotional episodes lasting two months each that were what she described as 'hypomanic episodes.' For the past month, he has begun to act the same way, bringing home "joints" that he insisted they smoke together. I don't understand his behavior now. I am furious at him. We have three lovely children: two daughters, eleven and eight, who idealize their father and our young son of six who is exactly his father in looks and behavior. For some reason recently he has periods of two to three days when he becomes moody, keeps to his room, then is hyperactive for a week or so, and then is perfectly normal. His grandfather thinks the sun rises and sets on little Johnny who is also a spitting image of him. I know 'Dad' has been treated for many years for manic-depressive illness."

At the end of the diagnostic conjoint session, I suggested concurrent therapy. I also started Mr. C on lithium and explained to Mrs. C in her individual sessions that her husband as well as her father-in-law and perhaps even her son had the same inherited condition. She had to realize that her husband was at the mercy of his emotions and so in less control of his behavior. I further recommended that if the son continued to be subject to mood swings that she have her son see a specialist who could work specifically with him.

Mr. C responded to the lithium maintenance therapy so that he was able to discontinue therapy after three months. The couple agreed to return to therapy if the mood swings return and were a problem. Within three years, the couple returned with the original complaint. I was informed that their son had continued to receive therapy during the preceeding three years, too.

It was apparent that this family had a recurring problem and that, as in the other cases mentioned (three generational PAD symptoms), the transmission from a recessive gene in the mothers was highly unlikely.[177] Rather, I agree with Loranger[178] who states that " . . . in the present state of knowledge it would be arbitrary if not circular reasoning to conclude that most cases of apparent father to son transmission were due to undetected illness in the maternal line. . . . "

The question arises as to what is valid evidence of father-son transmission among bipolar manic-depressives. Loranger's study[179] includes 100 male and 100 female bipolar patients. He found eleven father-son illness patterns. From a small sample of bipolars, von Grieff[180] gave an important index case of a son whose father suffered from bipolar illness which caused severe enough symptoms to make psychiatric treatment necessary. This father married three times and in each marriage the wife bore him a son who developed a bipolar disorder. In our data, of the ten bipolar male probands, seven had a PAD parent: of these parents, six were fathers. In other words, among the bipolars, we have six examples of father-son transmission, but like the data on father-son transmissions for manics, many of these cases (3) had male transmission across three generations: grandfather, father (proband), and son. Combining our data on manics and bipolars it can be said we have fourteen cases of father-son transmission of which seven have the male transmission across three generations. To round out the total picture of our father-son transmission in our sample, out of eight male unipolar depressives, two had father-son transmission, making a total of fifteen out of a possible thirty-five male probands.

While we have given these figures in their subcategories for comparison with other studies, we prefer to think of our sample as representing PAD in a unified way, yet there are doubts about the clearness of the distinctions between the three subcategories that are currently in use. This is because, when the course of the disease is followed for many years, it can shift from unipolar to bipolar. Of the 125 probands in our study, ten experienced a shift from a unipolar to a bipolar illness. The following vignettes reveal such personalities.

> Mrs. D sought therapy for obsessive-compulsive symptoms. During the course of treatment, she revealed that none of her immediate family had any manifest PAD symptoms. Her maternal grandmother, however, was severely obsessive-compulsive and was periodically depressed. During her analytic treatment, she gained considerable control over her compulsive symptoms and chose to discontinue treatment. Within a year, she returned for therapy in a very depressed state. The only effective method able to alter her depression was antidepressant medication. Once her depression lifted, the medication was stopped. Relief was temporary, however, and at the age of thirty-six she experienced her first manic high, which would respond only to lithium therapy. During the next twelve years, she remained bipolar though her euthymic periods got briefer. Mrs. D was hospitalized twice during the twelve years.

> Mr. and Mrs. E came for marital therapy because Mrs. E had stated to her husband that they either seek therapy or see a divorce lawyer! Mr. E was fifty-three-years-old and displayed a hypomanic condition.[181] He had recently argued with his sixteen-year-old son so severely that Mr. E fled away by car for a distance of 100 miles before calming down. When Mr. E related this episode, he began to cry and admit that he needed help. During the session, he related other hypomanic episodes, but did not relate periods of depression. Treatment consisted of the simple combined approach with conjoint family therapy periodically.

Although some probands are diagnosed as unipolar manics, I agree with those therapists who note that mania comes with some form of depression. I agree with Fieve[182] who thinks that bipolar and unipolar illnesses are genetically related and express the same gene type. I am not convinced by the data collected so far that PAD transmission occurs only with the X chromosome (see Winokur's work), but my research and experience does show a trend in family patterns. Such family characteristics can come from inheritance and other intrapersonal processes. I advocate *polygenetic* transmission.[183,184] I also note other interpersonal and environmental factors have a significant influence on the individual.

I presented a lengthy exposition on the family history because it substantiates the heuristic value for a polygenetic basis in the diagnosis of a PAD.

DIAGNOSIS

In the past decade a substantial increase in knowledge occurred in the understanding of the etiology, diagnosis and treatment of PADs.[185-210] These insights have led to improved diagnosis and treatment. Although, large numbers of PADs still go undiagnosed and are a challenge to all mental health professionals. Therefore, all clincans must be aware of the ways in which masked depression[211] or hypomanic states manifest themselves. A high level of suspicion is necessary in the prevention and treatment of dyadic and family problems as a result of one member having a PAD condition. In addition, there are the large number of undiagnosed PADs in *children and adolescents*. I have used most of the criteria of Winokur[212] and the other members of the St. Louis group (Feighner et al.) in our selection sample; however, in my experience, episodes of PAD may fluctuate for *days* to *weeks* and even *months*. I place great emphasis of exploring the possibility of PAD conditions in relatives.

In the diagnosis of the depressive phase of a PAD patient, the following symptoms are useful:

I. *Physiological* including
   1. Loss of appetite or weight.
   2. Disturbances of sleep (usually insomnia).
   3. Psychaesthenia.
   4. Impaired concentration.
   5. Agitation or retardation.
II. *Psychological* including
   1. Depression — overt or masked (usually a reactive depressive is anxious whereas a PAD is *hostile*).
   2. Irritability.
   3. Morbid ideation of having committed a sin.
   4. Suicidal thoughts or attempts.
   5. Lowered self-esteem, feelings of shame and/or guilt.

In the PADs, the above symptoms are found in various combinations, degrees of intensity, usually following a bell-shaped curve.

Helpful in the diagnosis of hypomanic behavior (the most common in frequency) and in mania are the following symptoms:

I. *Physiological* including
   1. Hyperactivity of the motoric type, e.g. excessive talking, marked restlessness etc.[213]
   2. Increased sexuality.
   3. Elevation of mood leading to euphoria.
   4. Overly gregarious — the "life of the party" type.
   5. Flight of ideas — easily flit from one topic to another.
   6. Easily distractible.

The bipolar type of PAD is characterized by cycles of either depression followed by hypomanic or manic behavior or vice versa — what Bunney and his colleagues[214] have described as the "switch process."

The sexual problems present in PAD dyads deserve further description.[215] Just as Murphy[216] stated: "marked variability of this disease seems to be one of its most striking features," also the various aspects of sexual behavior parallel this same variability. A breakdown of the various manifestations of sexual activities showed that these were dependent on the mood of the PAD. In one third of the PADs there were extramarital sexual affairs in the hypomanic or manic phase. This is illustrated by the following vignettes:

> Mr. E, aged forty-seven, married twenty-three years, became hypomanic. He was sexually very demanding of his wife — that was no problem to her. He had trouble sleeping and was drinking more than usual. After two weeks of this behavior, he suddenly withdrew $3,000 from their joint bank account and disappeared. In St. Louis, he had picked up an eighteen-year-old hitchhiker in his luxury car and married her a week later. A week later because of his manic behavior she left him. He repeated the same behavior a week later in Las Vegas and drove to Los Angeles. There, because of his behavior and lack of money — he ran up a large bill in the hotel — he was arrested and put in jail. Three weeks later she heard from the police in Los Angeles. At that time he phoned his wife, who picked him up, and they returned home. A successful business man, his wife related a similar episode ten years previously. He was started on lithium medication and concurrent dyadic therapy.

> Mrs. F (a bipolar PAD, married five years with numerous sex affairs) stated: "It is a release for me. I am a different person with these men. These people know very little about me. I enjoy listening to their problems. A series of men, each has a different quality. I know I can't stop this behavior — *that's why I want a divorce*. I can't understand why his lawyer can't convince him of this. When I feel

'high,' I need the release or go into a booby hatch, or be an extremely unhappy person all the time. I can feel myself getting depressed and an affair snaps me out of this mood."

Interestingly, in 7 percent of the PADs, extramarital activities was an attempt to ward off a depression. In 4 percent of the PADs, extramarital affairs was either a reaction to the controlling attitudes of the non-PAD partner or revenge because the non-PAD partner had an affair. Other justifications given for extramarital activities by the PADs are, in order of frequency: sexual frustration, ennui, and the complaint that the relationship is no longer meaningful.

Differential Diagnosis

The PAD syndrome is differentiated from depressions, which are a reaction to specific crises (situational or reactive).[217-222] The situational or reactive depressions are usually not severe, but, at times, the crisis can result in a psychotic reaction. I no longer use the diagnosis of involutional psychosis. Other psychiatric conditions to be ruled out in making the correct diagnosis are schizophrenia, the so-called schizoaffectives, which later often prove to be a variant of the PAD; organic brain diseases or those due to alcoholism, drugs, etc. The most helpful indicator in my ongoing studies has been a family history of PAD among probands.

GENERAL SYSTEM THEORY

The GST model described in Chapter II, offers the best approach in understanding, diagnosing, and treating the PAD dyadic and family relationships. The concept of all three systems having *open boundaries*, containing components in constant transactions of varying intensities, is most relevant. The other GST principle of "equifinality" is illustrated in the PAD syndrome by its multiple precipitating factors, the changing manifestations within one individual, e.g. the "switch process" of sequential behavioral changes. The characteristic of the individual with a PAD is his hypersensitivity and hyperactivity.[223] The psychological precipitant, whether real or symbolic, may be so slight as to be overlooked or the reaction so strong that the therapist cannot observe the cause, and finally, the impact of psychotropic drugs on the PAD and its repercussions on both the interpersonal system and the sociocultural matrix. Jacobson stated (1943)[224] that patients with depression are "psychologically identical," but changed her theoretical position almost four decades later and noted that they are not a homogeneous group as to their psychology and psychogenesis.[225]

Most research is now being directed to the neurophysiological mechanisms — the so-called biogenic amine model of polarity first proposed by Schildkraut[226] fifteen years ago. The biogenic amines are considered to be basic to the transmission of impulses from one nerve cell to another. When there is an increase or decrease in the quantity of these amines, there is a supposed corresponding elevation or lowering of the person's mood. A critical assessment of catecholamines and PAD has been recently published by Shopsin,[227] his colleagues, and others.[228-230] However, this hypothesis will continue to be useful until replaced by a more acceptable one, such as dysfunction of hypothalamic neuroendocrine processes.[231-234]

I use the interpersonal system in this section to refer to the relationship between the pair-couplings, their children, and their extended families. The preponderance of the controlling-extravert dyad supports the notion of a deep symbiotic attachment that takes place where a PAD spouse is involved and suggests a reason for the low incidence of divorce in this type of marriage. Jacobson[235] succinctly describes the way PADs and their spouses "cling" to each other.[236,237] Another important psychological factor in the tenacity of these marriages is the shame-guilt bind.[238,239] A frequent observation in the conscious and even unconscious material (dreams) is the non-PAD wish for the spouse to "drop dead." Another psychological variable relates to negative self-concepts. Thus, this deep symbiosis is a major characteristic of the PAD dyadic relationship and why they play "Uproar" and do not separate, but leads to a pair-coupling characterized by "intermittent incompatibility" and a low incidence of divorce.

The relevance of GST for a theoretical framework with the PAD is due to the open nature of the boundaries between the GST systems so that we see processes taking place effecting human behavior. As Judge Bazelon wisely warned: "My concern is that psychiatrists (all therapists) not forget — or worse, ignore the social determinants of human behavior."[240] One of the special features of a PAD is that his boundaries are even more open than usual during a hypomanic or manic episode. One way to conceive of this is to see the PAD as biochemically primed and supersensitive to family transactions and environmental influences. During such biochemically primed periods, the slightest external pressure seems to set off intense internal impulse bombardment. It is such a biochemical basis to the PAD illness which makes current crisis intervention theory especially useful in handling the problems associated with PADs. Whether the environment acts as a triggering device or not, once a PAD's illness starts to manifest itself, very destructive behavior in the environment can result. This may lead to all kinds of episodes involving community agencies. A patient can get into trouble with the police, with an employer, or with employees. The therapist must at times act as an "ombudsman." Thus, in the following subsection, all the concepts just presented must be incorporated into the treatment of a PAD relationship, because the marked variability of this illness is its most striking feature, a most ubiquitous disease.

TREATMENT

These couples with a PAD partner are stable most of the time, but are subjected to periods of "Uproar" when the PAD displays gradual to sudden, radical changes in mood, thoughts and/or behavior. Treatment is designed to bring stability back to the relationship as soon as possible. This is frequently accomplished by psychotherapy[241, 242] and/or somatotherapies of the PAD spouse[243-245] and by psychotherapy with the non-PAD spouse.

In about one-third of the *intermittently incompatible* dyads (65%), the couples were taught to manage a PAD crisis without the need of the therapist. Another one-half were taught to manage most of the PAD mood swings, but, at times, needed the help of the therapist ("open door" policy — available whenever needed) if the depression or mania was particularly severe. The remaining one-sixth needed ongoing regularly scheduled sessions spaced from several weeks to several months apart. This evolves when a particular couple does not have enough resources to cope with the behavior of the PAD partner. Of the relationships, 10 percent were able to reach stabilization for at least five years. Another 15 percent of the dyads followed the pattern of durable incompatibility. Of the couples, 10 percent either divorced or separated.

Before any treatment is undertaken, the therapist should be prepared for suicidal emergencies,[246-251] (see also Chapter VII). As stated in the beginning of this section, in two-thirds of the PADs there was evidence of suicidal thoughts and in 40 percent evidence of prior serious suicidal attempts. My experience is aligned with Fawcett's: "The most reliable and useful method of investigating the possibility of a potential for suicide is to directly ask the patient."[252] Thus, early in the biographical relationship questionnaire I now include the item which asks each patient: "Have you or your partner ever attempted suicide. If so, give date and details."[253] If a therapist treats dyads and one partner is a PAD, he should anticipate some harrowing experiences. For this reason we always take a medical history, including the name, address, and telephone number of the family physician. We strongly recommend all nonmedical therapists, when dealing with an individual who has made a suicidal attempt or expresses suicidal thoughts, to work closely with a psychiatric colleague or the family physician.

The more experience we have had with treating dyads when one has a PAD, the more we came to emphasize prevention. Our current advice in pre- or remarital therapy is against marriage where there is a history of a PAD in one of the individuals. However, it has been my experience that only 60 percent of the couples follow this suggestion because of the desirable qualities of the PAD individual. The As', previously presented at the beginning of this section, married after their original consultation. Mr. A, shortly after the birth of their first child was hospitalized after a *serious suicidal attempt*. Thus, a relationship with a PAD is hazardous because of the heredity component, the intermittent incompatibility, and the frequent chaos affecting the child(ren).

Group therapies, unless with homogeneous couples with one partner a PAD, is contraindicated. The PAD can disrupt the group by hypomanic behavior that is entertaining, but not productive. The hostile depressive[254] or hypomanic can involve others in his manipulation of the group including the therapist (and cotherapist).[255]

I started out as a classical psychoanalyst influenced by Frieda Fromm-Reichmann's[256] and Mabel Cohen and her colleagues' (1954) use of classical psychoanalysis of manic-depressives (PADs).[257] Being unsuccessful in treating PADs with this method led me to a combination of psychoanalytic psychotheray,[258] plus somatotherapies as indicated. As Freud predicted in 1930: "Our hope for the future lies. . . . in organic chemistry or in an approach to (psychosis) through endocrinology. Today this future is still far off, but we should study analytically every case of psychosis because the knowledge thus gained will one day direct chemical therapy."

A patient I psychoanalyzed for three years showed marked personal growth, but was still subject to periodic hypomanic episodes, during which the marriage became incompatible. Her husband, with my approval, took her to a famous psychiatric institution where classical five-year five times a week psychoanalysis was recommended. The patient refused and went to another psychiatrist who treated her with ECT. This brought some temporary benefit, but being bipolar, she continued to have recurrent episodes. Eventually she returned to therapy with me. I started her on antidepressants when she became depressed and used lithium with Thorazine® as required for her manic periods. Lithium maintenance therapy prevented future hospitalizations but with the patient's loss of personal vivacity and also resulting imbalance in her interpersonal relationships. Thus arose the need to evolve auxiliary strategies for the treatment of both partners when one is a PAD.

One of the first issues a therapist must decide is whether the PAD patient needs medication.[259-261] Many PADs with depression and even hypomania, tend to have a self-limiting course *without* medication. Because of the marked variability of symptoms in PAD patient, there is the need for knowledge of a variety of drugs.[262,263] During a depressive stage, tricyclics, whose shortcomings are marked in a slow onset and low level of potency,[264,265] or MAO inhibitors,[266,267] with the awareness of the potential serious side reactions, may be prescribed.

Recently, there has been an increase in publications[268,269] on the advantages of antidepressants given at bedtime in a single dose. We have found this of value, although occasionally the patient may need some medication during daytime. In a hypomanic or manic state the patient may be given lithium carbonate, haloperidol or phenothiazine derivatives.[270-273] Occasionally, the patient may need to be hospitalized. *Brief* electroconvulsive therapy may produce significant positive changes.[274] My experience as to prevention with lithium is equivocal. In most PADs there is only *attenuation* of mood and behavior. Frequently the non-PAD will express a desire that the partner stop medication because some of their partners "look and act like zombies," and because of their excessive weight gain.[275,276] Few clinicians have intensive contact with these dyads and do not have first hand knowledge or what living with a medicated partner is like. The blood level of the drug may be within normal limits, but we are still unable to determine the intracellular or perivascular level.[277] It needs to be emphasized that the PAD patient is encouraged to remain in individual treatment with the referring psychiatrist when the couple come for dyadic therapy. Experience shows that the relationship with another therapist does not interfere with dyadic therapy.

I have found it valuable to work with the non-PAD spouse in supportive and/or psychoanalytic psychotherapy. Our basic technique is to turn the non-PAD spouse into an *assistant therapist* and train him for the task of managing the relationship during the PAD crisis. We find that once the non-PAD accepts the fact that much of the partner's behavior arises out of a genetic and biochemical imbalance, there is greater willingness to cooperate. These sessions with the non-PAD spouse are worthwhile because they tend to break the shame-guilt cycles and enable him to mobilize more energy in dealing with the realities of the relationship. I do not hesitate to neutralize the pressures of the PAD spouse from the various subsystems of the environmental system. The following vignette is illustrative:

> Mr. H came into one of his sessions, hypomanic, angry, and paranoid at his employer who had threatened to discharge him because of his loquacity with his clients. I contacted the employer, with the patient's permission, explained the patient's treatment, and encouraged the employer to monitor the patient's mood with a view to increasing or decreasing the quantity of medication. This enabled the employee to give good service to his employer, enabled continuing financial support for the intrapersonal system, and gave both the employer and the employee more security because they felt a greater sense of control. While the illness was not completely curable, it was learned that, with a combined effort, it could be contained. The employer discovered that with minimal use of his time, he was able to retain one of his most valuable employees. In addition to any personal or humanitarian feelings, the employer found it economically worth his while to cooperate in the treatment.

CONCLUSIONS

Dyadic disharmony involving PAD partners can be difficult to treat, but such couples can be more successfully treated if the therapist is flexible and sets realistic goals. What Sachar wrote in 1967 on PAD is just as applicable today: "All of these interrelated dimensions, requiring an appreciation of the *kinetics* of mental illness, are more difficult to assess and require a more sophisticated level of clinical judgement . . . than the application of increasing sophisticated biochemical techniques. . . . "[278] I feel that once the diagnosis of PAD is made, the identified patient *and* the marriage should be viewed as deserving the same long-term commitment as with diabetes mellitus. Both diseases have many unsubstantiated etiologies, show a bell-shaped curve of intensity, and, affect all ages — from the young to the aged. Important to keep in mind is that there are the various degrees of heterogeneity in this PAD illness and thus there is the need to treat the relationship as well as the PAD illness. The best treatment is psychotherapy for the non-PAD partner and *both* psychotherapy and pharmacology for the PAD partner.[279] The current trend is to have PAD treatment centers that require the cooperation of all mental health professionals.

REFERENCES

1. Greene, Bernard L.: *A Clinical Approach to Marital Problems.* Springfield, Il., Thomas, 1970.
2. Hollender, Marc H.: Selection of therapy for marital problems. In Masserman, J. H. (Ed.): *Current Psychiatric Therapies.* New York, Grune, 1971.
3. Martin, Peter A.: *A Marital Therapy Manual.* New York, Brunner-Mazel, 1976, p. 126.
4. Rutledge, Aaron L.: Treatment of male homosexuality through marriage counseling — a case presentation. *J Marr & Family Counseling, 1:* 51-62, 1975.
5. Masters, William H. and Johnson, Virginia E.: *Homosexuality in Perspective.* Boston, Little, 1979.
6. Gurman, Alan S. and Kniskern, D. P.: Research on marital and family therapy: progress, perspective and prospect. In Garfield, S. L. and Bergin, A. E. (Eds.): *Handbook of Psychotherapy and Behavior Change: An Empirical Analysis,* 2nd ed., New York, John Wiley & Sons, 1979.
7. Friedman, A.: Interaction of drug therapy with marital therapy in depressed patients. *Arch Gen Psychiatry, 32:* 619-637, 1975.
8. Weissman, Myrna M.: The psychological treatment of depression — evidence for the efficacy of psychotherapy alone, in comparison with, and in combination with pharmacotherapy. *Arch Gen Psychiat, 36:* 1261-69, 1979.
9. Shapiro, Rodney J.: A family therapy approach in alcoholism. *J Marr & Family Counseling, 3:* 71-8, 1977.
10. Ferber, Andrew and Beels, Christian C.: Changing family behavior programs. In Ackerman, Nathan, Leib, Judith, and Pearce, J. (Eds.): *Family Therapy in Transition.* Boston, Mass, Little, 1970.
11. DeWitt, Kathryn N.: The effectiveness of family therapy — a review of outcome research. *Arch Gen Psychiat, 35:* 549-61, 1978.
12. Bowen, Murray: *Family Therapy in Clinical Practice.* New York: Jason Aronson, 1978.
13. Kaslow, Florence (Ed.): *J Marr & Family Counseling, 4:* 3-142, 1978.
14. Ackerman, Nathan W. (Ed.): *Family Therapy in Transition.* International Psychiatry Clinics, vol. 7, no. 4. Boston: Little, Brown & Co., 1970.
15. Fischer, Lawrence: On classification of families — a progress report. *Arch Gen Psychiat, 34:* 424-33, 1977.
16. Berg, Berthold and Rosenblum, Neil: Fathers in family therapy — a survey of family therapists. *J Marr & Family Counseling, 3:* 85-91, 1977.
17. Howells, John G.: *Principles of Family Psychiatry.* New York, Brunner-Mazel, 1976.
18. Robinson, Leon R.: Basic concepts in family therapy — a differential

comparison with individual treatment. *Am J Psychiat, 132:* 1047, 1975.

19. Foley, V.: *An Introduction to Family Therapy.* New York, Grune, 1974.
20. Stierlin, Helm: *Psychoanalysis and Family Therapy: Selected Papers.* New York, Jason Aronson, 1977.
21. Grotjahn, Martin: *The Art and Technique of Analytic Therapy.* New York, Jason Aronson, 1977.
22. Martin, *A Marital Therapy Manual.*
23. Boszormenyi-Nagy, I. and Spark, G.: *Invisible Loyalties.* New York, Harper and Row, 1973.
24. Kressel, Kenneth and Slipp, Samuel: Perceptions of marriage related to engagement in conjoint therapy. *J Marr & Family Counseling, 1:* 367-77, 1975.
25. Glick, Ira D. and Kessler, David R.: *Marital and Family Therapy.* New York, Grune, 1974.
26. Ackerman, Nathan W.: The growing edge of family therapy. In Sager, Clifford J. and Kaplan, Helen S. (Eds.): Progress in Group and Family Therapy. New York, Brunner-Mazel, 1972, pp. 440-456.
27. Epstein, Nathan B., Bishop, Duane S., and Levin, Sol: The McMaster model of family functioning. *J Marr & Family Counseling, 4:* 19-31, 1978.
28. Beavers, W. Robert: *Psychotherapy and Growth: A Family Systems Perspective.* New York, Brunner-Mazel, 1977.
29. Dell, Paul F., Sheeley, Margaret D., Pulliam, George P., and Goolishian, Harold A.: Family therapy process in a family therapy seminar. *J Marriage & Family Counseling, 3:* 43-48, 1977.
30. Skynner, A. C. Robin: *Systems of Family and Marital Psychotherapy.* New York, Brunner-Mazel, 1976.
31. Lewis, Jerry M., Beavers, Robert W., Gossett, John T., and Phillips, Virginia A.: *No Single Thread: Psychological health in family systems.* New York, Brunner-Mazel, 1975.
32. Pattison, E. Mansell, DeFrancisco, Donald, Wood, Paul, Frazier, Harold, and Crowder, John: A psychosocial kinship model for family therapy. *Am J Psychiat, 132:* 1246-51, 1975.
33. Zuk, Gerald H.: *Process and Practice in Family Therapy.* Haverford, PA, Psychiatry & Behavior Science Books, 1975.
34. Satir, Virginia, Stachowiak, J. and Taschman, T.: *Helping Families To Change.* Palo Alto, CA, Science and Behavior Books, 1975.
35. Watzlawick, P., Weakland, J., and Fish, R.: *Change: Principles of Problem Formation and Problem Solution.* New York, Norton, 1974.
36. Satir, Virginia: *Peoplemaking.* Palo Alto, CA Science & Behavior Books, 1972.
37. Fisher, Barbara L. and Sprenkle, Douglas H.: Assessment of healthy family functioning and its relation to goals of family therapy. Dept. of Child Development and Family Studies, Purdue University, Indiana. Preliminary report to be published.
38. Selvini-Palazolli, M., Cecchin, G., Prata, G., and Boscolo, L.: *Paradox*

and Counterparadox. New York, Jason Aronson, 1978.

39. Paul, Norman L. and Paul, Betty B.: The use of EST as adjunctive therapy to family-focused treatment. *J Marr & Family, 4:* 51-61, 1978.
40. Whitaker, Carl: The hindrance of theory in clinical work. In Guerin, P. J., Jr. (Ed.): *Family Therapy: Theory and Practice.* New York: Gardner Press (Halsted Press, John Wiley & Sons, 1976.
41. Haley, Jay: *Problem-Solving Therapy.* New York, Basic Books, 1976.
42. Rosenberg John B.: Two is better than one — use of behavioral techniques within a structural family therapy model. *J Marr & Family Counseling, 4:* 31-39, 1978.
43. Minuchin, Salvador: *Families and Family Therapy.* Cambridge, Mass, Harvard Univ Press, 1974.
44. Duhl, Frederick F., Kantor, D., and Duhl, B.: Learning space and action in family therapy — a primer of sculpture. In Block, D. (Ed.): *Techniques of Family Psychotherapy.* New York, Grune, 1973.
45. Anderson, C. and Malloy, E.: Family photographs — in treatment and training. *Family Process, 15:* 259-64, 1976.
46. Rubin, J. and Magnussen, M.: A family art evaluation. *Family Process, 13:* 185-200, 1974.
47. Hatcher, Chris: Intrapersonal and interpersonal models — blending Gestalt and family therapies. *J Marr & Family Counseling, 4:* 63-68, 1978.
48. Bell, John E.: Family context therapy — a model for family change. *J Marr & Family, 4:* 111-126, 1978.
49. Solomon, Michael A.: The staging of family treatment — an approach to developing the therapeutic alliance. *J Marr & Family Counseling, 3:* 59-86, 1977.
50. Rebner, Isaac: Conjoint family therapy. *Psychotherapy: Theory, Research & Practice, 9:* 62-66, 1972.
51. Ackerman, Nathan W.: *Treating the Troubled Family.* New York, Basic Books, 1966.
52. Visher, Emily B. and Visher, John S.: *Reconstituted Families.* New York, Brunner-Mazel, 1979.
53. Bezdek Patrick, Goldenberg, Irene, and Nadler, Jan: The adolescent and the step-parent. Meeting held at Cedars Sinai Thalians Community Health Center, Nov 6, 1978, Los Angeles, CA.
54. Guttman, Herta A.: A contraindication for family therapy, the prepsychotic or postpsychotic young adult and his parents. *Arch Gen Psychiatry, 29:* 352-355, 1973.
55. Ackerman, Nathan W.: The family approach to marital disorders. In Greene, B. L. (Ed.): *The Psychotherapies of Marital Disharmony.* New York, Macmillan, 1965, pp. 153-168.
56. Grotjahn, Martin: Clinical illustrations from psychoanalytic therapy. In Greene, B. L. (Ed.): *The Psychotherapies of Marital Disharmony.* New York, Macmillan, 1965, pp. 169-185.
57. Grotjahn, *The Art and Technique of Analytic Therapy.*

424   *A Clinical Approach to Marital Problems*

58. Grotjahn, Martin: *Psychoanalysis and the Family Neurosis.* New York, Norton, 1960.
59. Williamson, Donald S.: Board or Bored? Newsletter, *Am Assn Marriage & Family Therapy, 10:* 2, 7, 1979.
60. Ackerman, The growing edge of family therapy.
61. Framo, James L.: In Kaslow, Florence (Ed.): *J Marr & Family Counseling, 4:* 3-142, 1978.
62. Framo, James L.: Marriage therapy in a couples group. *Seminars in Psychiatry, 5:* 207-17, 1973.
63. Reding, Georges R. and Ennis, B.: Treatment of the couple by a couple. *Brit J Med Psychol, 37:* 325, 1964.
64. Courtney, Michael: *Sexual Discord in Marriage.* London, Tavistock, 1968, p. 46.
65. Gill, H. and Temperly, L.: Time-limited marital treatment in a foursome. *Brit J Med Psychology, 47:* 153-161, 1974.
66. Alger, Ian: Joint sessions — psychoanalytic variations, applications, and indications, in Rosenbaum, Salo, and Alger, Ian (Eds.): *The Marriage Relationship.* New York, Basic Books, 1968, pp. 259-262.
67. Bellville, Titus P., Raths, Otto N., and Bellville, Carol J.: Conjoint marriage therapy with a husband-and-wife team. *Am J Orthopsychiat, 39:* 473, 1969.
68. Martin, *A Marital Therapy Manual.*
69. Grunebaum, Henry and Kates, William: Whom to refer for group psychotherapy. *Am J Psychiat, 134:* 130-33, 1977.
70. Framo, James L.: Marriage therapy in a couples group. *Seminars in Psychiatry, 5:* 207-17, 1973.
71. Epstein, Norman, Jayne-Lazrus, Cynthia, and DeGiovanni, Ina Sue: Cotrainers as models of relationships — effects of the outcome of couples therapy. *J Marital & Family Therapy, 5:* 53-60, 1979.
72. Moulton, Ruth: Dr. Moulton Replies (in letters to editor). *Am J Psychiat,* 1977.
73. Kilgo, Reese D.: Counseling couples in groups — rationale and methodology. *Family Coordinator, 24:* 337-42, 1975.
74. Leichter, Elsa: Treatment of married couples groups. *Family Coordinator, 22:* 31-42, 1973.
75. Kaplan, Harold I. and Saddock, Benjamin J. (Eds.): *Group Treatment of Mental Illness,* vol 6. New York, Jason Aronson, Inc, 1972.
76. Martin, *A Marital Therapy Manual.*
77. Greene, Bernard L. et al.: Treatment of marital disharmony when one spouse has a primary affective disorder (manic-depressive illness). *Am J Psychiat, 133:* 827-30, 1976.
78. Davenport, Y. B., Ebert, M. H., Adland, M. L., and Goodwin, F. K.: Couples group therapy as an adjunct to Lithium maintenance of the manic patient. *Am J Orthopsychiat, 47:* 495-502, 1977.
79. McDonald, Margaret C.: Jerome Frank looks ahead. Blanche Ittleson Award Lecture, annual meeting. *Am Orthopsychiatric Assn,* 1979. *Psychiatric News, 19:* p. 1, 14, 15, 1979.

80. Malan, David H. et al.: Group psychotherapy — a long-term follow-up study. *Arch Gen Psychiat, 33:* 1303-15, 1976.

81. Greenbaum, Henry: Stages of development in group psychotherapy repeat the stages of historical development in the family, Chapter VIII. In Wolberg, L. R. and Aronson, (Eds.): New York: Stratton Intercontinenetal Med Book Corp, 1978, pp. 72-78.

82. Benningfield, Anna B.: Multiple family therapy systems. *J Marr & Family Counseling, 4:* 25-34, 1978.

83. Hare, Paul A.: *Handbook of Small Group Research*, 2nd ed. New York: Free Press (Macmillan Pub Co.), 1976.

84. Rabin, Herbert M. and Rosenbaum, Max: *How To Begin a Psychotherapy Group: Six Approaches.* New York, Gordon and Breach, 1976.

85. Yalom, Irvin D. et al.: The written summary as a group psychotherapy technique. *Arch Gen Psychiat, 32:* 605-13, 1975.

86. Weiner, Myron F. Group Therapy — when friends or patients ask about . . . *JAMA, 234:* 1181-2, 1975.

87. Horner, Althea J.: A characterological contraindication for group psychotherapy. *J Am Acad Psychoanal, 3:* 301-5, 1975.

88. Foulkes, S. H.: *Group-analytic Psychotherapy: Method and Principles.* New York, Gordon & Breach-Interface, 1975.

89. Rosenbaum, Max & Berger, Milton M.: *Group Psychotherapy and Group Function*, revised ed. New York, Basic Books, 1975.

90. Kaplan, Harold I. and Saddock, Benjamin J. (Eds.): *Comprehensive Group Psychotherapy.* Baltimore, Williams & Wilkins Co., 1971.

91. Rome, Howard P.: Group therapy: Part I, Introductory remarks. *Psychiatric Annals, 2:* 7, 1972.

92. Pinney, Jr., Edward L., Wells, Stephen H. and Fisher, Bernard: Group therapy training in psychiatric residency programs — a national survey. *Am J Psychiat, 135:* 1505-08, 1978.

93. Masters, William H. and Johnson, Virginia E.: Principles of the new sex therapy. *Am J Psychiat, 133:* 548-54, 1976.

94. LoPiccolo, Joseph and LoPiccolo, Leslie (Eds.): *Handbook of Sex Therapy.* New York, Plenum Press, 1978.

95. McCarthy, Barry W.: Strategies and techniques for the reduction of sexual anxiety. *J Sex & Marital Therapy, 3:* 243-48, 1977.

96. Mosher, Donald L.: The gestalt awareness-expression cycle as a model for sex therapy. *J Sex & Marital Therapy, 3:* 229-242, 1977.

97. McCarthy, Barry W., Ryan, M. and Johnson, F. A.: *Sexual Awareness: A Practical Approach.* San Francisco, Boyd and Fraser, 1975.

98. Laughren, T. P. and Kass, D. G.: Desensitization of sexual dysfunction — the present status. In Gurman, Alan S. and Rice, David G. (Eds.): *Couples in Conflict.* New York, Jason Aronson, 1975, pp. 292-99.

99. Kaplan, Helen S.: *The New Sex Therapy.* New York: Brunner-Mazel, 1974.

100. Annon, J. S.: *The Behavioral Treatment of Sexual Problems*, vol I. Honolulu, Kapiolani Health Services, 1974.

101. Barbach, Lonnie G.: Group treatment of preorgasmic women. *J Sex and Marital Therapy, 1:* 139-45, 1974.
102. Gurman, Alan S. and Rice, David G. (Eds.): *Couples in Conflict.* New York, Jason Aronson, 1975.
103. Masters, W. H., Johnson, V. E. and Kolodny, R. C., (Eds.): *Ethical Issues in Sex Therapy and Research.* Boston Mass., Little, Brown, 1977.
104. Meyer, Jon K.: Training and accreditation for the treatment of sexual disorders. *Am J Psychiat, 133:* 389-94, 1976.
105. Frank, Ellen, Anderson, Carol, and Kupfer, David J.: Profiles of couples seeking sex therapy and marital therapy. *Am J Psychiat, 133:* 559-62, 1976.
106. Saddock, Virginia A., Saddock, Benjamin J., and Kaplan, Harold I.: Comprehensive sex therapy training — a new approach. *Am J Psychiat, 132:* 858-60, 1975.
107. Lassen, Carol L.: Issues and dilemmas in sexual treatment. *J Sex & Marital Therapy, 2:* 32-39, 1976.
108. Levine, S. B. and Agle, David: The effectiveness of sex therapy of chronic secondary psychological impotence. *J Sex & Marital Therapy, 4:* 235, 1978.
109. Levay, Alexander N. and Kagle, Arlene: A study of treatment needs following sex therapy. *Am J Psychiat, 134:* 970-3, 1977.
110. Wright John, Perrault, Robert, and Mathieu, Mireille: The treatment of sexual dysfunction — a review. *Arch Gen Psychiat, 34:* 881-90, 1977.
111. Lansky, Melvin R. and Davenport, Adelaide E.: Difficulties in brief conjoint treatment of sexual dysfunction. *Am J Psychiat, 132:* 177-9, 1975.
112. Racy, John: How sexual relationships mirror the total relationship. *Med Aspects Hum Sexuality, 11:* 98-114, 1977.
113. Money, John: Time to end sexology taboo, give it department status. *JAMA, 235:* 2273-4, 1976.
114. Greene, Bernard L. et al.: Clinical observations of sex as a reverberation of the total relationship. *J Sex & Marital Therapy, 2:* 284-88, 1976.
115. Sager, Clifford J.: Editorial — a false dichotomy? *J Sex & Marital Therapy, 1:* 187-89, 1975.
116. Sager, Clifford J.: Sex as a reflection of the total relationship. *J Sex & Marital Therapy, 2:* 3-5, 1976.
117. Sager, Clifford J.: The role of sex therapy in marital therapy. *Am J Psychiat, 133:* 555-59, 1976.
118. Schiavi, Raul C.: Sex therapy and psychophsiological research. *Am J Psychiat, 133:* 562-66, 1976.
119. Bieber, Irving: The psychoanalytic treatment of sexual disorders. *J Sex & Marital Therapy, 1:* 5-15, 1974.
120. Vandervoort, H. E. and McIlvena, T.: *You Can Last Longer.* Multi Media Books, Box 439E, San Francisco, CA 94102.

121. Nadelson, Carol: "Healthy" sexual dysfunctions. *Med Aspects Hum Sexuality, 13:* 106-119, 1979.
122. Kaplan, *The New Sex Therapy.*
123. Fischer, Ilda and Linsenberg, Myrna: Problems confronting the female therapist doing couple therapy. *J Sex & Marital Therapy, 2:* 231-339, 1976.
124. Murphy, G. E., Woodruff, R. A, Jr., Herjanic, M., Fischer, J. R.: Validity of the diagnosis of primary affective disorder — a prospective study with a five-year follow up. *Arch Gen Psychiat, 31:* 751-756, 1974.
125. Akiskal, Hagop S. et al.: Differentiation of primary affective illness from situational, symptomatic, and secondary depressions. *Arch Gen Psychiat, 36:* 635-43, 1979.
126. Freedman, Daniel S.: Introduction. In Cole, Jonathan O., Schatzberg, Alan F. and Frazier, Shervet H. (Eds.): *Depression — Biology, Psychodynamics, and Treatment.* New York, Plenum Press, 1978.
127. Goodwin, Frederick K. and Potter, William Z.: The Biology of affective illness — amine neurotransmitters and drug response. In Cole, Jonathan O., Schatzberg, Alan F., and Frazier, Shervet (Eds.): *Depression — Biology, Psychodynamics, and Treatment.*New York, Plenum Press, 1978, pp. 41-73.
128. Fann, William E., Karacan, Ismet, Pokorny, Alex D., and Williams, R. L. (Eds.): *Phenomenology and Treatment of Depression.* New York, Spectrum Pub., 1977.
129. Klein D. F.: Endogenomorphic depression. *Arch Gen Psychiat, 31:* 447-454, 1974.
130. Schuyler, D.: *The Depressive Spectrum.* New York, Jason Aronson, 1974.
131. Cooper, J. R., and Bloom, F. E.: *The Biochemical Basis of Neuropharmacology.* London, Oxford University Press, 1974.
132. Beck, A. T.: *The Diagnosis and Management of Depression.* Philadelphia, University of Pennsylvania Press, 1973.
133. Mendels, J. (Ed.): *Biological Psychiatry.* New York, John Wiley & Sons, 1973.
134. Kaplan, H. I. and Saddock B. J.: An overview of the major affective disorders. *Psychiatric Annals, 4:* 13-52, 1973.
135. Angst, J.: Heredity seen as a major factor in depressive psychosis. *Roche: Frontiers of Psychiatry, 3:* 6, 1973.
136. Powell, A. et al.: Parent-child concordance with respect to sex and diagnosis in schizophrenia and manic-depressive psychosis. *Brit J Psychiat, 123:* 653-658, 1973.
137. Van der velde, C. D. and Gordon, M. W.: Biochemical and pharmacological variations in manic-depressive illness. *Am J Psychiat, 129:* 337-342, 1972.
138. Rosenthal, D.: Genetic studies of manic-depressive psychosis. In *Genetic Theory and Abnormal Behavior:.* New York, McGraw-Hill, pp. 201-221, 1970.
139. Jeste, Dilip V., Gillin, J. Christian, and Wyatt, Richard J.: Serendipity

in biological psychiatry — a myth? *Arch Gen Psychiat, 36:* 1173-78, 1979.

140. Briscoe, C. W. and Smith, J. B.: Psychiatric illness — marital units and divorce. *J Nerv Mental Dis, 158:* 440-445, 1974.

141. Greene, Bernard L. et al.: Treatment of marital disharmony when one spouse has a primary affective disorder (manic depressive illness) I. General overview — 100 couples. *J Marr & Family Counseling, 1:* 39-50, 1975.

142. Greene, B. L. et al.: II. *Sexual Problems.* Presented at the 7th Brief Psychotherapy conference on sexual and marital problems, Mar 21, 1975, Chicago, Il.

143. Greene, B. L. et al.: III. *Am J Psychiat, 133:* 827-30, 1976.

144. Greene, B. L. et al.: Marital therapy when one spouse has a primary affective disorder (Manic-depressive illness), IV: Clinical preventive applications pertaining to Adolescence. Paper presented at the International Forum on Adolescence, July 7, 1976, Jerusalem, Israel.

145. Murphy, G. E., Woodruff, R. A., Jr., Herjanic, M. and Super, G.: Variability of the clinical course of primary affective, disorder. *Arch Gen. Psychiat, 30:* 757-761, 1974.

146. Mendlewicz, J., Fleiss, J. L., Cataldo, M. and Rainer, J. D.: Accuracy of the family history method in affective illness. *Arch Gen Psychiat, 32:* 309-14, 1975.

147. Group for Advancement of Psychiatry. *Pharmacotherapy and Psychotherapy: Paradoxes, Problems & Progress.* New York, Group for the Advancement of Psychiatry, 1975.

148. Weissman, M. M. and Paykel, E. S.: *The Depressed Woman — A Study of Social Relationships.* Chicago, Univ Chicago Press, 1974.

149. Slater, E. and Cowie, V.: *The Genetics of Mental Disorders.* London, Oxford Univ Press, 1971.

150. Harvald, B. and Hauge, M.: Heredity factors elucidated by twin studies. In Neil, J. V., Shaw, M. W., and Schull, W. J. (Eds.): *Genetics and the Epidemiology of Chronic Diseases.* Public Health Service Publication 1163. U. S. Dept. of H. E. W., Washington, D. C., 1975.

151. Kringlen, E.: *Heredity and Environment in the Functional Psychoses.* An epideniological-clinical twin study. Oslo, Universitetsforlaget, 1967.

152. Fieve, R. R., Mendlewicz, J., Rainer, J. D., and Fliess, J. L.: A dominant X-linked factor in manic-depressive illness: Studies with color blindness. In Fieve, R. R., Rosenthal, D., and Brill, H. (Eds.): Genetic Research in Psychiatry. Baltimore, The John Hopkins Univ Press, 1975.

153. McKusick, V. A.: *Mandelian Inheritance in Man: Catalogs of Autosomal Dominant, Autosomal Recessive and X-lined Phenotypes,* 3rd ed. Baltimore, The John Hopkins Univ Press, 1971.

154. Mendlewicz, J., Linkowski, P., Guroff, J. J., and Van Praag, H. M.: Color blindness linkage to bipolar manic-depressive illness — new

evidence. *Arch Gen Psychiat, 36:* 1442-47, 1979.

155. Gershon, Elliot S., Targum, Steven D., Matthysse, Steven, and Bunney, Jr., William E.: Color blindness not closely linked to bipolar illness — report of a new pedigree series. *Arch Gen Psychiat, 36:* 1423-30, 1979.

156. Leckman, James F., Gershon, Elliot S., McGinniss, Mary H., Targum, Steven D., and Dibble, Eleanor, D.: New data do not suggest linkage between Xg blood group and bipolar illness. *Arch Gen Psychiat, 36:* 1435-41, 1979.

157. Kuhn, R.: The occurrence and the treatment of endogenous depression in children. *Schweiz Med Wochenschr, 93:* 86-90, 1963.

158. Davis, Richard E.: Manic-depressive variant syndrome of childhood — a premininary report. *Am J Psychiat, 136:* 702-6, 1979.

159. Philips, Irving: Childhood depression — interpersonal interactions and depressive phenomena. *Am J Psychiat, 136:* 511-15, 1979.

160. Anthony, E. James: Affective disorders in children and adolescents with special emphasis on depression. In Cole, J. D., Schatzberg, A. F., and Frazier, S. H. (Eds.): Depression, Psychodynamics and Treatment. New York, Plenum Press, 1978, p. 177.

161. Warneke, L.: A case of manic-depressive illness in childhood. *J Can Psychiat Assn, 20:* 164, 1975.

162. Ossofsky, H. J.: Endogenous depression in infancy and childhood. *Comprehensive Psychiat, 15:* 19-25, 1974.

163. Cytryn, L. and McKnew, D. H., Jr.: Factors influencing the changing clinical expression of the depressive process in children. *Am J Psychiat, 131:* 879-881, 1974.

164. Cytryn, L. and McKnew, D. H., Jr.: Biochemical correlates of affective disorders in children. *Arch Gen Psychiat, 31:* 659-661, 1974.

165. Cytryn, L. and McKnew, D. H., Jr.: Proposed classification of childhood depression. *Am J Psychiat, 129:* 149-155, 1972.

166. McKnew, D. H., Jr. and Cytryn, L.: Historical background in children with affective disorders. *Am J Psychiat, 130:* 1278-1279, 1973.

167. Feinstein, Sherman C. and Wolpert, E. A.: Juvenile manic-depressive illness. *J Am Acad Child Psychiat, 12:* 123-36, 1973.

168. Feinstein, Sherman C.: Diagnostic and therapeutic aspects of manic-depressive illness in early childhood. *Early Child Development, 3:* 1-12, 1973.

169. Gallemore, J. L., Jr. and Wilson, W. P.: Adolescent maladjustment or affective disorder? *Am J Psychiat, 129:* 608-612, 1972.

170. Goetzl, U., Green, R., Whybrow, P., and Jackson, R.: X linkage revisted. *Arch Gen Psychiat, 31:* 665-672, 1974.

171. Winokur, G., Clayton, P. J., and Reich, T.: *Manic-Depressive Illness.* St. Louis, CV Mosby, 1969.

172. Rosanoff, A. J., Handy, M., and Plesset, I. K.: The etiology of manic-depressive syndromes with special reference to their occurrence in twins. *Am J Psychiat, 91:* 725-6, 1935.

173. Winokur, G. and Pitts, F. W.: Affective disorder: VI. A family history

430   *A Clinical Approach to Marital Problems*

study of prevalences, sex differences and possible genetic factors. *J Psychiat Research, 3:* 113-23, 1965.
174. Winokur, G. et al.: *Manic Depressive Illness.*
175. Slater and Cowie: *The Genetics of Mental Disorders.*
176. Winokur, G. et al.: Affective disorder.
177. Mendlewicz, J., Fleiss, J. L., and Fieve, R. R.: Evidence for X-linkage in the transmission of manic-depressive illness. *JAMA, 222:* 1624-28, 1972.
178. Loranger, A. W.: X-linkage and manic-depressive illness. *Brit J Psychiat, 127:* 482-8, 1975.
179. Loranger: X-linkage and manic-depressive illness.
180. Von Grieff, H., McHugh, P. R., and Stokes, P. E.: The family history in 16 males with bipolar manic-depressive illness. In Fieve, R. R., Rosenthall, D., and Brill, H. (Eds.): *Genetic Research in Psychiatry,* Baltimore, John Hopkins Univ Press, 1975.
181. Lipkin, K. M., Dyrud, J., and Meyer, C. G.: The many faces of mania. *Arch Gen Psychiat, 22:* 262-267, 1970.
182. Fieve, R. R. et al.: A dominant X-linked factor in manic-depressive illness.
183. Bunney, W. E., Jr. et al.: The "switch process" in manic-depressive illness: I. a systematic study of sequential behavioral changes. II. relationship to CA, Rem sleep and drugs. III. theoretical implications. *Arch Gen Psychiat, 27:* 295-317, 1972.
184. Baker, M., Dorzab, J., Winokur, G., Cadoret, R.: Depressive disease — evidence favoring polygenic inheritance based on analysis of ancestral cases. *Arch Gen Psychiat, 27:* 679-686, 1972.
185. Winokur, George: Familial (genetic) subtypes of pure depressive disease. *Am J Psychiat, 136:* 911-13, 1979.
186. Goodwin, Frederick K. (Ed.): "The Lithium Ion" — impact on treatment and research. *Arch Gen Psychiat, 36(8):* 1979.
187. Buschsbaum, Monte S. and Rieder, Ronald O.: Biologic heterogeneity and psychiatric research — platelet MAO activity as a case study. *Arch Gen Psychiat, 36:* 1163-69, 1979.
188. Andreasen, Nancy A. and Winokur, George: Newer experimental methods for classifying depression. *Arch Gen Psychiat, 36:* 447-52, 1979.
189. Katz, Martin M., Secunda, Steven K., Hirschfeld, Robert M. A., and Koslow, Stephen H.: NIMH clinical research branch collaborative program on the psychobiology of depression. *Arch Gen Psychiat, 36:* 765-71, 1979.
190. Dunner, David L., Vijayalakshmy, Patrick, and Fieve, Ronald R.: Life events at onset of bipolar affective illness. *Am J Psychiat, 136:* 508-11, 1979.
191. Dunner, David L., Igel, Gerard J., and Fieve, Ronald R.: Social adjustment in primary affective disorder. *Am J Psychiat, 135:* 1412-13, 1978.
192. Rubinstein, David and Timmins, Joan F.: Depressive dyadic and triadic relationships. *J Marr & Family Counseling, 4:* 13-23, 1978.
193. Krauthammer, Charles and Klerman, Gerald: Secondary mania — manic

sydromes associated with antecedent physical illness or drugs. *Arch Gen Psychiat, 35:* 1333-39, 1978.

194. Loranger, Armand W. and Levine, Peter M.: Age at onset of bipolar affective illness. *Arch Gen Psychiat, 35:* 1345-48.

195. Weissman, Myrna M. and Myers, Jerome K.: Affective disorders in a U.S. urban community. *Arch Gen Psychiat, 35:* 1304-11, 1978.

196. Weissman, Myrna M. et al.: The efficacy of drugs and psychotherapy in the treatment of acute depressive episodes. *Am J Psychiat, 136:* 555-58, 1979.

197. Avery, David and Lubrano, Aldo: Depression treated with imipramine and ECT — The Decarolis study reconsidered. *Am J Psychiat, 136:* 559-62, 1979.

198. Ramsey, T. A., Frazer, A., Mendels, J. and Dyson, W. L.: The erthrocycte lithium-plasma lithium ration in patients with PAD. *Arch Gen Psychiat, 36:* 457-61, 1979.

199. James, Norman A.: Early- and late-onset bipolar affective disorder, *Arch Gen Psychiat, 34:* 715-17, 1977.

200. Baron, Miron: Linkage between an X-chromosome marker (deutan color blindness) and bipolar affective illness — occurrence in the family of a lithium carbonate-responsive schizo-affective proband. *Arch Gen Psychiat, 34:* 721-25, 1977.

201. Allen, Martin G.: Twin studies of affective illness. *Arch Gen Psychiat, 33:* 1476-78, 1976.

202. Gallant, Donald M. and Simpson, George M. (Eds.): *Depression: Behavioral, Biochemical, Diagnostic and Treatment Concepts.* New York, Spectrum Publications, 1976.

203. Akiskal, H. S. and McKinney, W. T.: Overview of recent research in depression — integration of ten conceptual models into a comprehensive frame. *Arch Gen Psychiat, 32:* 285-305, 1975.

204. Shopshin, B. et al.: Catecholamines and affective disorders revised a critical assessment. *J Nerv Ment Dis, 158:* 369-383, 1974.

205. Goodwin, F. K., Bunney, W. E., Jr.: A psychological approach to affective illness. *Psychiatric Annals, 3:* 19-53, 1973.

206. Fawcett, Jan: Seeing the skull beneath the skin. *Chicago Medicine, 76:* 919-21, 1973.

207. Feighner, J. P., Robins, E., Guze, S. B. et al.: Diagnostic criteria for use in psychiatric research. *Arch Gen Psychiat, 26:* 57-63, 1972.

208. Kotin, J., Goodwin, F. K.: Depression during mania: clinical observations and theoretical implications. *Am J Psychiat, 129:* 679-686, 1972.

209. Jacobson E.: *Depression: Comparative Studies of Normal, Neurotic and Psychotic Conditions.* New York, Int Univ Press, 1972.

210. Dorzab, J., Baker, M., Winokur, G., Cadoret, R. J.: Depressive disease: clinical course. *Dis Nerv System, 32:* 269-274, 1971.

211. Lesse, Stanley: Depression masked by acting-out behavior patterns. *Am J Psychotherapy, 28:* 352-361, 1974.

212. Andreasen and Winokur: Newer experimental methods for classifying depression.

213. Kupfer, D. J., Weiss, B. L., Foster, G., Detre, T. P., Delgado, J., McPartland, R.: Psychomotor activity in affective states. *Arch Gen Psychiat, 30:* 765-68, 1974.

214. Bunney, W. E., Jr. et al., The "switch process" in manic-depressive illness.

215. Greene, B. L., *Sexual Problems.*

216. Murphy, G. E. et al., Varibility of the clinical course of primary affective disorder.

217. Clayton, P. J. et al.: Mourning and depression: their simularities and differences. *Can Psychiat Assn J, 19:* 309-312, 1974.

218. Goodwin, F. K. and Bunney, W. E., Jr.: A psychological approach to affective illness. *Psychiatric Annals, 3:* 19-53, 1973.

219. Scott, J. P. and Senay, E. C. (Eds.): *Separation and Depression: Clinical and Research Aspects.* Washington, D. C., Amer Assn Advanc Science, 1973.

220. Baker, M. et al.: Depressive disease — classification and characteristics. *Comprehensive Psychiat, 12:* 354-360, 1971.

221. Davies, B., Carroll, B. J., Mowbray, R. M. (Eds.): *Depressive Illness: Some Research Studies.* Springfield, Thomas, 1972.

222. Zubin, J. and Freyhan, F. A. (Eds.): *Disorders of Mood.* Baltimore, John Hopkins Press, 1972.

223. Ludwig, A. M. and Ables, M. F.: Mania and marriage — the relationship between biological and behavioral variables. *Compr Psychiat, 15:* 411-421, 1974.

224. Jacobson, Edith: Depression — the oedipus complex in the development of depressive mechanisms. *Psychoanalytic Quarterly, 12:* chap 17, 1943.

225. Jacobson, Edith: *Depression: Comparative Studies of Normal, Neurotic and Psychotic Conditions.* New York, Internat Univ Press, 1972.

226. Schildkraut, J. J.: The catecholamine hypothesis of affective disorders — a review of supporting evidence. *Am J Psychiat, 122:* 509-522, 1965.

227. Shopshin, B. et al.: Catecholamines and affective disorders revised a critical assessment. *J Nerv Ment Dis, 158:* 369-383, 1974.

228. Wittenborn, J. R.: Deductive approaches to the catecholamine hypothesis of affective disorders. *J Nerv Mental Dis, 158:* 320-324, 1974.

229. Mendels, J. and Frazer, A.: Brain biogenic amine depletion and mood. *Arch Gen Psychiatry, 30:* 447-471, 1974.

230. Goodwin, F. K. and Sack, R. L.: The catecholamine hypothesis revisited. In Asdin, E. and Synder, S. (Eds.): *Frontiers in Catacholamine Research.* New York, Pergamon Press, pp. 1157-1164, 1973.

231. Chodoff, Paul and Goodwin, Frederick K.: Editorial: Depression — psychotherapy or pharmacology. *J Am Acad Psychoanal, 4:* 275-77, 1976.

232. Allen, J. P., Denny, D., Kendall, J. W. and Blachly, P. H.: Corticotropin release during ECT in man. *Am J Psychiatry, 131:* 1225-28, 1974.

233. Sachar, E. J., Hellman, L., Roffwarg, H. P., Halpern, F. S, Fukushima, D. K., and Gallagher, T. F.: Disrupted 24-hour patterns of cortisol

secretion in psychotic depression. *Arch Gen Psychiatry, 28:* 19-24, 1973.

234. Carpenter, W. T., Jr., Bunney, W. E., Jr.: Adrenal cortical activity in depressive illness. *Am J Psychiatry, 128:* 31-40, 1971.

235. Jacobson, *Depression.*

236. Gershon, E. S. et al.: Assortative mating in the affective disorders. *Biological Psychiat, 7:* 63-74, 1973.

237. Wadeson, H. S. and Fitzgerald, R. G.: Marital relationship in manic-depressive illness. *J Nerv Ment Dis, 153:* 180-196, 1971.

238. Stierlin, H.: Shame and guilt in family relations. *Arch Gen Psychiat, 30:* 381-389, 1974.

239. Harrow, M. and Amdur, M. J.: Guilt and depressive disorders. *Arch Gen Psychiat, 25:* 40-246, 1971.

240. Bazelon, Judge D. L.: The perils of wizardry. *Am J Psychiat, 131:* 1317-1322, 1974.

241. Levin, S.: Some suggestions for treating the depressed patient. *Psychoanalytic Quarterly, 34:* 37-65, 1965.

242. Goldberg, A.: Psychotherapy of narcissistic injuries. *Arch Gen Psychiatry, 28:* 722-726, 1973.

243. Lehrman, Samuel R.: Varieties of depression in one patient. *Psychiatric Quarterly, 48:* 1-12, 1974.

244. Beck, Aaron T.: *The Diagnosis and Management of Depression.* Philadelphia, Univerisity of Penn Press, 1973.

245. Fitzgerald, R. G.: Mania as a message — treatment with family therapy. *Arch Gen Psychiat, 26:* 547-554, 1972.

246. Paykel, E. S. et al.: Treatment of suicide attempters. *Arch Gen Psychiat, 31:* 487-491, 1974.

247. Zung, W. W. K. and Green, R. L.: Seasonal variation of suicide and depression. *Arch Gen Psychiat, 30:* 89-91, 1974.

248. Anderson, W. H. and Kuehle, J. C.: Strategies for the treatment of acute psychosis. *JAMA, 229:* 1884-1889, 1974.

249. Drye, R. C., Goulding, R. L. and Goulding, M. E.: No-suicide decisions: patient monitoring of suicidal risk. *Am J Psychiat, 130:* 171-174, 1973.

250. Minkoff, K., Bergman, E., Beck, A. T., and Beck, R.: Hopelessness, depression and attempted suicide. *Am J Psychiat, 130:* 455-459, 1973.

251. Mendel, W. M.: Depression and suicide — treatment and prevention. *Consultant, 12:* 115-116, 1972.

252. Fawcett, Jan: Recognition and management of the suicidal patient. *Chicago Medicine, 76:* 919-921, 1973.

253. Fawcett, Jan et al.: Suicide: clues from interpersonal communication. *Arch Gen Psychiat, 21:* 129-137, 1969.

254. Weissman, M. M., Klerman, G. L., and Paykel, E. S.: Clinical evaluation of hostility in depression. *Am J Psychiat, 128:* 261-266, 1971.

255. El-Yousef, M. K., Janowski, D. S., and Davis, J. M.: Manic patients show expertize in interpersonal demolition. *Roche Report: Frontiers in Psychiatry, 4:* 1, 1974.

256. Bullard, D. M. (Ed.): *Psychoanalysis and Psychotherapy: Selected Papers of Frieda Fromm-Reichmann.* Chicago, University of Chicago

Press, 1974.

257. Cohen, Mabel B. et al.: An intensive study of 12 cases of manic-depressive psychosis. *Psychiatry, 17:* 103-137, 1954.

258. Klerman, G., Dimascio, A., Weissman, M. M. et al.: Treatment of depression by drugs and psychotherapy. *Am J Psychiat, 131:* 186, 1974.

259. Raskin, A.: A guide for drug use in depressive disorders. *Arch Gen Psychiatry, Am J Psychiat, 131:* 181-185, 1974.

260. Kline, N. S.: Antidepressant medications — a more effective use by general practitioners, family physicians, internists, and others. *JAMA, 227:* 1158-1160, 1974.

261. Kotin, J., Post, R. M., and Goodwin, F. K.: Drug treatment of depressed patients referred for hospitalization. *Am J Psychiat, 130:* 1139-41, 1973.

262. Ayd, F. J., Jr. and Taylor, I. J.: Thirty-five years continuous treatment for recurrent depression: from ECT to drugs. *J Nat Assn Private Hosps, 6:* 32-35, 1974.

263. van Praag, H. M.: New developments in human psychopharmacology. *Compr Psychiat, 15:* 389-401, 1974.

264. Van der velde, C. D., Gordon, M. W.: Biochemical and pharmacological variations in manic-depressive illness. *Am J Psychiat, 129:* 337-342, 1972.

265. Morris, J. B., and Beck, A. T.: The efficacy of antidepressant drugs — a review of research (1958-1972). *Arch Gen Psychiat, 30:* 667-74, 1974.

266. Kupfer, T. P. et al.: Psychomotor activity in affective states. *Arch Gen Psychiat, 30:* 765-768, 1974.

267. Raskin, A. et al.: Depression subtypes and response to phenelzine, diazepam, and a placebo. *Arch Gen Psychiat, 30:* 66-75, 1974.

268. Ayd, F. J., Jr.: Editiorial — single daily dose of antidepressants. *JAMA, 230:* 263-264, 1974.

269. Hussain, M. Z. et al.: Single versus divided daily doses of imipramine in the treatment of depressive illness. *Am J Psychiat, 130:* 1142-1144, 1973.

270. Shopsin, B., Gershon, S., Thompson, H., and Collins, P.: Psychoactive drugs in mania — a controlled comparison of lithium carbonate, chlorpromazine, and haloperidol. *Arch Gen Psychiat, 32:* 34-42, 1975.

271. Carlson, G. A. and Goodwin, F. K.: The stages of mania. *Arch Gen Psychiat, 28:* 221-228, 1973.

272. Schildkraut, J. J.: The effects of lithium on norepinephrine turnover and metabolism — basic and clinical studies. *J Nerv Ment Dis, 158:* 348-360, 1974.

273. Stallone, F., Shelley, E., Mendlewicz, J., and Fieve, R. R.: The use of lithium in affective disorders, III: a double-blind study of prophylaxis in bipolar illness. *Am J Psychiat, 130:* 1006-10, 1973.

274. Ayd, Jr. and Taylor: Thirty-five years continuous treatment for recurrent depression.

275. Kraines, Samuel H.: Weight gain and other symptoms of the ascending depressive curve. *Psychosomatics, 13:* 1-11, 1972.

276. Demers, R. G. and Davis, L. S.: The influence of prophylactic lithium carbonate on the marital adjustment of manic depressives and their spouses. *Compr Psychiat, 12:* 348-353, 1971.

277. Heiser, J. F. and Wilbert, D. E.: Reversal of delirium induced by tricyclic antidepressant drugs with physostiamine. *Am J Psychiat, 131:* 1275-1277, 1974.

278. Sachar, E. J.: Corticosteroids in depressive illness. II: a longitudinal psychoendocrine study. *Arch Gen Psychiat, 17:* 554-567, 1967.

279. DiMascio, Alberto, Weissman, M. M., Prusoff, C., Zwilling, M., and Klerman, Gerald L.: Differential symptom reduction by drugs and psychotherapy in acute depression. *Arch Gen Psychiat, 36:* 1450-56, 1979 (December).

Chapter XXVIII

THE THERAPIST
Attributes and Pitfalls

$\mathbf{T}$HERE is not just one easy way to become a psychotherapist. There are many approaches to this goal, because the field of pair-coupling and family therapy is a heterogeneous one. Its therapists have a variety of professional backgrounds, theoretical frameworks, and techniques, and its patients present a broad sweep of conflicts and problems.[1-3]

Because of a great need for psychotherapists, it is my opinion that there should be, as currently, interdisciplinary but independent professional schools for this purpose.[4-6] Ideally, training would be in a university setting,[7] providing access to relevant courses needed for exposure of the different disciplines.[8] Kubie, the pioneer American psychoanalyst and theorist, over three decades ago, proposed an autonomous training program for psychotherapists. Holt[9] has shown how psychotherapy is becoming a profession in its own right. All therapists could benefit from the unique personal experience of exploration through intensive introspection, preferably, psychoanalytic.[10-15]

Ludwig[16] succinctly states: "This is the time for reappraisal and reconceptualization for psychiatrists (psychotherapists)." There is increasing criticisms from many areas in our society that mental illness is a myth and that special expertise is not necessary[17] for treating emotional disorders — it is primarily a social malady, etc. If this were factual, why the presence of mental illness in primitive societies where there has been no societal changes? Taylor[18] has written an excellent article on the myths of marriage counseling.

The term *counselor* should be restricted to those individuals who give guidance and advice, *vis-à-vis* the therapist who treats personal dyadic and family disharmonies covering the entire range of diagnostic psychiatric categories. Martin[19] states: " 'counseling' frequently has an unfortunate and misleading connotation of being neither an important nor depth-approached psychotherapy."

Being a therapist involves a life-long commitment to personal growth[20-24] and *ongoing supervision*, as indicated. Nichols, in his ever thoughtful way, suggests: "Training therapists in techniques without

436

reference to the substantive knowledge of the field in which they are practicing is a shortsighted way of preparing practitioners. Educating therapists so that they are not only acquainted with such materials in depth but also so that they are equipped to remain in touch with research and theory in the marriage and family field in their subsequent career is a major need."[25] Thus, professional growth permits flexibility in techniques and most important the capacity to know when and whom to refer. Every competent therapist must view each patient with a calm, cool *objectivity*. Furthermore, regardless of social class, all patients have similar needs, desires and expectancies for the best possible therapy.[26]

ATTRIBUTES OF A PSYCHOTHERAPIST

The hallmark of a successful therapist is an attitude of,

Compassion, caring,[27] creativity, competence, and commitment;[28]
Understanding:
Respect[29] which influences the rapport[30] and reputation of the therapist; and
Empathy.[31] All these elements hopefully lead to relief of pain (CURE).

In addition, Harold Lief's comments about sensitivity to everyone's feelings are worthy of repetition: "There are four aspects of dyadic transactions, all equally important: (1) sensitivity to one's own feelings; (2) sensitivity to the other person in the dyad; (3) sensitivity to one's own feelings in response to the behavior or words of the other person; (4) sensitivity to the impact of one's own words or behavior on the other person. Of these four (2) is termed empathy, and (3) 'recipathy,' a term used by Henry Murray, the famed Harvard psychologist. As far as I know, we have no shorthand term for (1), unless it might be 'self-awareness,' nor for (4), I would like to call the latter 'impact-awareness.' "[32]

Obviously, one cannot help all patients or correct all behavior problems, nor alter the ever-changing sociocultural condition. To be a therapist is to embark on the voyage of voyages in uncharted waters and unpredictable conditions. The voyager will be aided in his travels by the following books and articles written on the art and science involved in psychotherapy, and the important elements within the process of becoming a psychotherapist.[33-46]

Frank[47] suggests that every therapist should experiment with a variety of techniques[48] and try to master those techniques that suit his personal style. The greater the number of approaches mastered, the more patients the therapist will be able to help. The approach should be tailored to the patient's expectations and his preferrred ways of problem solving. Framo[49] also believes in having a full repertory of techniques — his exposure has been to at least twelve approaches — and exposes his trainees to all approaches so that they can develop a style which is most comfortable for them.

What Kerckhoff et al. said a decade ago about family life educators is applicable to therapists today: "One can do most effective work if one lives what he is teaching."[50] An important attribute is the calculated personal disclosure by the therapist with a specific purpose in mind.[51] Franz Alexander[52] indicated that the individual features of the therapist have an important influence upon the course of therapy. Obviously this requires experience since disclosure[53] is made to neutralize anxiety of the patient. For example, a patient will complain to the therapist, "You have no concept of the degree of pain involved in my feelings of anxiety." Because of my direct involvement in WW II, I have no difficulty relating an episode where my anxiety level was high!

In the clinical setting, there are three possible professional roles for the therapist: *observer, participant, and participant-observer.*[54] The therapist must integrate his training, knowledge, and the use of his personal interventions in a unique manner: the therapist must monitor activity, flexibility, openness, and the ability to move in and out of the presenting problems, thus permitting all participants present to engage in a selective way of joining and separating with specific elements of the therapist's identity. Marmor[55] emphasizes that the primacy of a good patient-therapist relationship provides emotional support and helps release tension. Basic to all attributes for therapists is the need for conceptual bases for *continuing self-education.*[56-61] Bertalanffy, in his GST, stressed the importance of man's use of symbolic thinking as the main feature differentiating homo sapiens from other species. Talking involves language, which is related to the brain and the society and culture the individuals come from.

An important attribute for therapists is their attitudes[63] in dealing with the sexual problems of their patients. Harold Lief,[96] among others, pioneered in alerting medical institutions to the restricted and inhibited sexual attitudes, not only of their students, but also of many faculty members. Sheppe wrote, about a decade ago, and is pertinent today: "If (the therapist) listens well, does not shock easily, and knows most of the answers, the (therapist) will be asked all the questions about sex his patients wanted to know but were afraid to ask."[64] In spite of the so-called sexual revolution too many therapists are still uncomfortable in the sexual area. Since sex is an important part of everyone's life, no evaluation of a patient is complete without a careful sexual history. The importance of this area can be noted by referring back to item #22 of the biographical relationship questionnaire (Chapter XVII).

In conclusion, the attributes necessary to become a successful therapist requires an ongoing personal and professional growth over a period of *time*.[65, 66] This involves actual practice of *various* techniques, competent supervision, and observation of experienced therapists. Then one can realize as did Luckey: "... that what I had finally learned to be was me! And it was by being me that I had become an effective therapist."[67]

TRANSFERENCE-COUNTERTRANSFERENCE PHENOMENA

When we view the constructs of transference and countertransference as reciprocal processes in the therapeutic relationship and introduce two persons into the therapeutic settings, we have conceptualized a new transactional model. The complexities of transference mount geometrically as we try to define its relation to reality, maturation, and social learning. In Chapter XXI, I discussed transference constructs. Countertransference can be an active, constructive element in the therapeutic relationship.[68, 69] Countertransference reactions are the *ambivalent* thoughts, feelings, and behavior of the therapist. Winnicott,[70] in 1947, wrote about countertransference with regard to hate. Malsberger and Buie[71] discussed countertransference hate in the treatment of suicidal patients, and Grinker, Jr.[72] presented his impressions of countertransference feelings of envy and anger by middle-class therapists toward the children (adolescents) of the super-rich. These antitherapeutic stances can be counter-productive for therapy. Countertransference constructively used enables the therapist to develop the use of his feelings, thoughts, and behavior as a *sensitive* instrument in understanding his patients.[73-75] On the other hand, countertransference distortions impede the therapist's effectiveness. Thus, the concepts of transference-countertransference are best viewed as reciprocal processes in the therapeutic relationship. Two recent papers by John P. Spiegel on the cultural aspects of transference-countertransference reflect his observations on stress during WW II and later studies with Florence Kluckholm and other colleagues at Harvard. These observations were later to occupy his concern about violence on the family, stress, and acculturation in general.[76-78]

The previous white minorities acculturation widely influenced all minority cultural values, but currently there is a surfacing of resentment against a broad, white, middle-class social system. Obviously this has had an impact on transference-countertransference relationships between therapist and patients. This is reflected in the literature, which is beginning to acknowledge the inability of many therapists to know and understand all possible cultural backgrounds of patients with some negative treatment outcomes. Cultural variations become important in selection of treatment goals in keeping with the patient's own cultural standards with parallel flexibility in therapeutic approaches. Therefore, a background in anthropology is relevant, especially if a dyad, under treatment is of racial or cultural mixture. If a therapist is from a different ethnic group than his patients, the transference-countertransference may require distinguishing between cultural misconceptions and personal misinterpretations. Ethnocentricity assumes added importance in treatment if the therapist or patient's believe their own race, nation, or culture is superior to all others.

The varying transference phenomena are demonstrated in the following vignette. This vignette is a composite of the clinical material of a series of couples seen concurrently in psychoanalysis. Each couple had several years of therapy with the women on the couch — frequently with marked annoyance at this position — and with the men, also, on the couch, offering no resistance to this position. The women were usually very attractive, aggressive, intelligent, and seductive in dress and behavior, but usually anorgastic sexually. These women were typical of Katharina in Shakespeare's *Taming of the Shrew*, shrewish, bad-tempered with a notorious disposition. On the other hand, the men were passive, well-dressed and well-groomed, gracious gentlemen, whose disposition outside of the relationship was like that of Bianca's, Katharina's sister, sweet and lovable. Outwardly, these men suppressed and repressed their hostility, but psychosomatically occasionally revealed this by essential hypertension (elevated blood pressure on a functional basis) or anginal (heart), pains, with or without premature ejaculation (urinating on their partners instead of fornicating — used here in the nonlegal sense). The relationships were characterized by frequent games of "Uproar," à la *Whose Afraid of Virginia Woolf*, in which the content of the arguments varied from finances to in-laws. In my experience, psychoanalytic psychotherapy has been moderately successful in both taming the shrew and emotionally maturing the man.

Mr. and Mrs. A came for therapy because of years of quarreling. Mr. A felt that he had been unduly criticized by his wife for his interest in his mother. Mrs. A felt that she could not stand her husband's close relationship to his mother because she rejected her as a daughter-in-law. Mr. A because he felt that his wife alone was the cause of their marital probelms, was angry and reluctant about therapy. His individual diagnostic interviews revealed his premature ejaculation, which he had never disclosed to anyone before. He went into great length about his feelings of inadequacy as a man and his wish to be cured.

Mr. A's "confession" of his premature ejaculation was his response to the therapist as a real object (focus one as described above under transference phenomena). Relating of his problem indicated that he saw me as a real person, that he accepted me as an individual and wanted help. On another transference level, the symbolic one, I represented the omnipotent, omniscient doctor who cures illnesses. His revealing his secret was both a plea for help and a fantasied wish for cure by the powerful physician.

In his next session, Mr. A brought in his first dream (the following are excerpts): "My wife is on a horse. Horse skids and falls. I think that now they will have to destroy the horse. My wife gets up and tearfully says she had lost the buckles off her shoes. I tell her angrily to forget the buckles, as long as she is all right. She suddenly has only a slip on and is exposed. Her cousin comes up. He has a stupid facial expression. I tell him about the horse incident. He looks unconcerned and bored."

His associations revealed great anger toward his aggressive wife, who he characterized as a "shrew" and who was always putting pressure on him to be more successful. He is also angry at the therapist, who he feels may hurt him ("destroy the horse." This anger is not expressed openly, but revealed in the dream as the "stupid cousin.") Moreover , he is angry at both his wife and his therapist for making him reveal himself as an inadequate male — a woman who has "only a slip on and is exposed." These are unconscious negative transference feelings toward the therapist.

Mrs. A who was being seen separately but synchronously with her husband, continued to be cooperative in her therapy. In her behavior, dreams, and associations, the emerging libidinal dyadic transference (to the therapist as a real object) became apparent as seen in a dream reported in the fifteenth week of therapy: "I am at a hotel in Acapulco. I am in bed with a short man with curly hair. He asked me to marry him." (I am of short stature and have curly hair.)

Mr. A's response to the interpretations of his anxiety about the nature of his repressed hostility led to excessive anxiety, which required the use of tranquilizers.

In his third month of therapy he reported the following dream: "My mother and I are in the the operating room. I am on the operating table. The doctor was putting on surgical gloves. He was going to perform a circumcision on me. I look down at my groin after the preparation and see that I have no testicles.

In his associations, the mother seemed to be the doctor's assistant. He related how his mother was both possessive and castrative. She was always belittling his father and him in front of the family. As a result he was an underachiever in school. Currently, he commented, his sexual performance at home was the poorest it had ever been, nocturnal emissions and even impotence now (sexless in the dream and castrated). This is a good example of the classical psychoanalytic transference neurosis (dyadic) in which feelings and fantasies from childhood in regard to the mother are transferred onto the therapist.

In his fifth month of therapy, Mr. A complained of being very irritable and having feelings of "boiling inside with rage.'" A dream at that time revealed hostility at a regressive level heretofore not manifested: "My wife, me and another man in a restaurant. Waiting for a table. Very crowded. Lots of tables available for two but not for three.[79] Go the the captain and get very angry at him. I shouted, and walked out. As I walked out my baby sister walked in."

This dream indicated anger at having to share the therapist with his wife — a frequent type of dream in triadic therapy. Further, the dream revealed reactivation of feelings experienced when his younger sister was born. In his associations, there was a wealth of memories about his hostile feelings toward both his mother and younger sister in his childhood. Mr. A had not, as yet, been able to express overt hostility toward his therapist. Unconscious repression was due to hostile components in the sibling rivalry transactions toward his wife in the triangular transference neurosis (the fourth focus of transference phenomena). On a deeper level the triangular transference involves the oedipal constellation.

The fifth focus of transference, triangular transference transactions producing adaptive feedbacks, became more manifest beginning with the tenth month of therapy when Mr. A reported a change in his wife, from a "shrill-sounding shrew to a soft-spoken and pleasant woman." Concomitant with Mrs. A's improved self-image was her increasing libidinal feelings toward the therapist, which were being directed toward her husband. The next two months of therapy were stormy for the couple.

However, Mr. A began to report progressively more agressive attitudes at home and at his office. He was in excellent mood when he reported the following dream: "Listening to a naval officer giving a speech. He tells about beginning as an enlisted man and going up the ranks to become an admiral. I ask where he went to school. He said, Annapolis."

His first association was that "Annapolis is similar to analysis." It was followed by a number of early close and positive memories about his father (focus one — the therapist as a real object). We see in this dream identification with the therapist with the encoding of new "records." He is the enlisted man who has become commander of his ship.

At this time A's left for a vacation, and upon return, Mr. A was in excellent spirits and proudly reported: "Don't ever remember having performed as well sexually in my life. We had a wonderful time. It was like a second honeymoon. It is one year since we first started coming to you." Mrs. A expressed similar thoughts about their vacation.

Therapy was continued for another year before the therapeutic changes were concretized.

THE PHENOMENA OF "ACTING OUT"

The psychological relationship between patient and therapist is of an affective nature. The relationship usually involves positive affects of the patient toward the therapist. Occasionally, the positive feelings on the part of the patient may become so strong that they may be openly stated. Not infrequently, the therapist may respond to his patients overt declaration of love — a situation to be avoided at all costs. At all times it is important to remember that the relationship is professional and not social. Although therapy moves forward in the climate of bilateral positive feelings, the therapist should control the level of these feelings. Thus the therapeutic setting should be structured, if possible, so that all sessions are in a professional setting. If the patient begins to display overt seductive behavior by act or dress, an excellent ploy is to shift the interviews from dyadic to triadic. Occassionally some private fantasies of libidinal nature will occur in the therapist. These fantasies will cause no trouble provided they remain private. The therapist should guard against double entendres, which reveal his covert feelings. This topic will be discussed in detail in the next section.

The usage of the term and the concept of "acting out" as a behavioral manifestation covers a wide spectrum of phenomena. All three systems of the GST are involved, but in varying degrees in acting out, and the behavioral manifestations vary in complexity. There is considerable variation in the degree acting out dominates the personality of any individual. Acting-out phenomena are best visualized as units of communication. Acting out as a circumscribed manifestation is best illustrated in the two following vignettes:

Ms. B had been in intensive therapy for the treatment of obesity. Laboriously and painfully she lost twenty-five pounds in the past six months. At this point I took my annual winter vacation of two weeks. When I returned I found she had regained her weight loss. Exploring the determining forces behind this act revealed the following: (1) conscious anger at me for going away and leaving her, (2), unconscious anger of her inner child at being rejected, (3), feeling frustrated and unloved. She fed herself, using the equation food equals love, i.e. her symbolic communication stating: "I have to feed myself, since you no longer love me by going away."

Mrs. C who was in treatment at the same time, reacted by becoming pregnant extramaritally. This created a "severe headache" for everyone concerned, especially her therapist. The unconscious motive was most dominant, that of revenge, which overlayed her strong rejection anger.

Acting out as a circumscribed manifestation also can occur as a hysterical conversion symptom. In the past three decades the incidence of hysteria is progressively decreasing. The following vignette is illustrative:

Mr. D was referred by his eye doctor because of "tubular or gun barrel" vision. He was unable to see anything except directly in front of his eyes and had no peripheral vision at all. The recent onset of his eye difficulty occured while attending his first out-of-town convention. A deeply religious and moral man, he was shocked at the behavior of some of his fellow conventioneers. His eye difficulty followed shortly after a suggestive comment by a model. The unconscious communication was not to wander from the straight and narrow and to focus on reaching his own room and not glance to the "happenings" in some of the surrounding rooms.

Another type of neurotic acting out can occur in individuals who make episodic suicidal attempts. All suicidal thoughts or attempts should be considered seriously, as the person may inadvertently commit suicide. For example, in a recent case the wife made several suicidal attempts, each structured so that the husband would rescue her at five o'clock when he returned from work. A flat tire on his automobile caused an hour's delay, and upon arrival home, his wife was dead. A suicidal threat may be an unconscious message for help.

In dealing with a psychotic spouse, the therapist should keep in mind the possibilities of that individual acting out, i.e. whether he will act upon his unrealistic perceptions and impulses, e. g. homicidal behavior. A physical attack may be the acting out of hallucinations or delusions. This assaultive behavior is unrealistic, but consistent with the delusional ideation or hallucinatory distortions. Not uncommonly, acting-out behavior can be observed in "normal" appearing individuals who tend to react to a stereotyped manner in certain situations. In these persons their stereotyped behavior is so ingrained in their style of living that they are clinically classified as having character disorders. Since their behavior patterns are part of their character, they are unaware of the inappropriateness of their reactions. Examples of this type of behavior are seen in seductive women who are being continually raped after leaving a tavern with a stranger who ostensibly is going to take them home; or by women who repeatedly permit themselves to be exploited by conniving men. It is as if these persons, when confronted with a set of stimuli, respond with inappropriate behavior as though programmed by a computer. These individuals do not profit from experience, since they do not connect their painful behavior with their unconscious motivations, but blame it on fate. Berne's[80] conceptualizations of games people play are valuable in understanding these individuals. In effect, these persons react to an unconscious script and do not realize the inappropriateness of their behavior.

ACTING OUT IN THE SEXUAL AREA

Seductive patients and sexual acts between the therapist and patients involve morals, ethics, and unfulfilled conscious and unconscious needs. It has only been in the past decade that professional journals began to publish editorials and articles on the subject of sex between patient and therapist.[81, 82] Barnhouse[83] believes this publicity is due to the feminist movement which has encouraged women to report incidents of sexual activity with their therapists. Women who have been sexually involved with male therapists turn to female therapists for help. Also, the prevailing climate of sexual openness and permissiveness has influenced outspoken statements on this topic.

The seductive patient has been the focus of research. Most current studies indicate that this behavior exists to a greater extent than has been previously believed. The importance of this area finally reached a point that the American Psychiatric Association, in 1976, at its annual May meeting, had a special session devoted to this topic which drew an over-flowing audience. Virginia Davidson,[84] Judd Marmor, Reed Brockbank, and Carol Nadelson presented articles, which were published in condensed form in four separate issues of the *Psychiatric News*.

Many patients behave in a seductive manner in the course of treatment. Some exhibit harmless flirtation with no desire of going beyond that, while others seek sexual intercouse. A female patient of mine, suddenly got off the couch, started to undress and said: "if we don't have sex I shall yell 'Rape!'" In a stern voice, I told her to dress, or else I would open my office door and call the receptionist. We then proceeded to discuss her feelings and behavior, and therapy continued. From that time on I had her sitting up and facing me. It is impossible to ignore an overt attempt at seduction, also, this behavior should be interpreted. If the patient thinks the message was not received, the reaction may be more effort to seduce, or worse, patient may feel rejected and angry. The dynamics of this behavior involves both, the conscious and unconscious factors. In 1973, Ishida, a gynecologist, classifed the seduction of male physicians (applicable to all therapists) into four categories: flirtation; "gray" area, i.e. subject to "subjective" interpretation by the physician; actual proposal making; and psychotic behavior. Doctor Ishida makes an excellent comment: ". . . that any attempt to grade the seductive patient is analogous to ordering steak in a restaurant. When one asks for 'medium rare,' he has no way of knowing if the chef's idea of 'medium rare' agrees with his own![85] Obviously, the more contact a physician (therapist) has with his patient, the greater the chance of seduction. Thus, psychotherapists who talk about sex with their patients or physicians, especially obstetricians or gynecologists, would be most apt to provoke fantasies and sexual impulses.

Harold Lief (1978)[86] revealed the following findings with the first 500 psychiatrists in a sexual survey:

1. Have you ever experienced attempted seduction by a patient? yes — 72%   no — 28%
2. Do you know of patients or physicians who have engaged in physician-patient sex relations? yes — 70%   no — 29%
3. Do you believe that patient-physician sexual relations are harmful to the patient and to the therapeutic relationship? yes (always) — 80%   yes (with exceptions) — 19%   no — 1%
4. Which is the best course to take with a seductive patient? ignore seductive efforts — 9%   counsel regarding inappropriateness — 79%   refer to another physician — 5%
5. Which age group of female patient is most likely to be seductive? 16-20 — 3%   20-30 — 36%   30-40 — 52%   40-50 — 8% 50+ — 0%
6. Which factor is most responsible for seductive attempts by patients? seeking parental figure — 24%   need to control physician — 23%   need to prove attractiveness — 31%

subtle encouragement by physician — 11%
7. Is seductiveness by patients more common now than in the past?
yes — 38%   no — 50%
8. Usual seductive ploy by patient? inappropriate undressing —
12%   dwelling on sexual aspects of personal history —
28%   explicit proposition or advance — 20%   unnecessary
visits or phone calls — 28%

Lief stated that replies to the first question confirms the assumption
that most physicians experience seductive behavior by their patients,
and what was *unexpected* was that about *one-third reported no* such
experience. I, and almost every therapist that I have supervised, have
experienced this behavior. Obviously, many factors enter into this
question, age of therapist and age of patient, attractiveness of the
parties, ethnic background, clinical setting, social class, etc. The data
on question #2 is as expected. Lief was curious about the 19 percent
exceptions in question #3 as the indications for sex between patient
and therapist. I have treated several physicians who had no guilt
about their behavior, their explanation was that they could not stand
the sexual deprivation of the patient. In fact, one reported that one
patient started seeing him when she was in her late thirties, and once
a month would come in for two injections — penile and estrogen. He
felt that without the first injection she might not be able to function
at her job. Plus, she was a most grateful patient. In #4, Lief gives the
figure as somewhere between 5 and 10 percent of physicians[87-92] report
having sex with their patients. Masters and Johnson report that about
25 percent of their patients claim such experiences with previous
physicians or therapists. Their patients are mostly wealthy class; there
are no reliable statistics as to social classes or ethnic groups because of
subgroupings in each class. It is a violation of the ethical code of
every professional society, that I know of, to condone such behavior.
As to question #5, the data is representative, and the procedure is
insight. There are two explanations that I give: an indication to the
improvements of self-image, and/or, that they are really talking about
dependent needs. These are perfectly normal at any age (the wish to
be taken care of by a parental figure, as when one was a child),
but now, as an adult, one is expressing the same feelings in
terms of intimacy. Do not make the mistake of saying: "under
different circumstances, if you were not my patient I would find
you desirable." I know of patients who have called their therapists after they were discharged and said, "now that I am no
longer your patient, how about meeting me at my apartment or
yours?"

On question #7 and #8, perhaps the hedonistic philosophy of our society plays a crucial factor. I agree with Lief's interpretation that the majority of seductiveness is indirect or covert. This may be due to transference feelings, fear of rejection, and so on. His concluding phrase is important: "exquisite tact is required of the physician (therapist)."[93]

The dynamics of the seductive patient may be both, conscious and unconscious.[94] Seductiveness may mask feelings of *hostility*, (what we label dynamically the "erotization of hostility" — it is easier to express love than anger (not an uncommon phenomena in dreams), fear, envy, depression, and loneliness. Consciously or even unconsciously, seductiveness may be an attempt to exert *power* and *control over the therapist*. The latter situation was beautifully illustrated in a patient's dream:

> Ms E was referred by her family physician for postdivorce therapy. She previously had seen three therapists of differing disciplines — the last one being a psychiatrist. Her main complaint was a phobic fear of being alone. During the evaluative phase she had casually stated she had seduced all three therapists. An attractive blonde in her mid-thirties, well groomed in the latest hair style, and dressed in a seductive designer's outfit, she displayed the characteristic features of the hysterical personality. She was most cooperative in therapy for three months. At the beginning of her third month of therapy, she was showing moderate improvement and became openly seductive. In spite of appropriate interpretations of her material, she persisted in her open invitations for sex. The following dream followed my statement that our relationship was a professional one and nothing else: "We are driving in my Mercedes Benz. We are together on this road going through the desert. There is not a person or car in sight. It is night time. I am driving without the lights on. You suggest I put them on. *I refuse* and pull over to the side shoulder. At that time, the dream is interrupted by the ringing of my alarm clock." Her feelings in the dream were of pleasure. I asked her why she refused to "put the lights on" and perhaps throw some "light on her situation"? After a long pause she replied that she could not understand my sexual rejection since the other three therapists had acquiesed. I told that she could not add another notch to her belt, because I would not acquiesce. I added that under such intimate demands I could not help her, and this was our last session. If she wanted to work on her problem she could call for another appointment. She walked out angrily, and I never heard from her again.

A seductive patient may feel inadequate as a person and that the only way to be accepted is as a love object — it is not uncommon behavior, bribing for acceptance at any price. As a character trait, it is observed most frequently in the hysterical personality. The provocative role of the seductive patient may provoke seductions in others, and then reflect a self view of being exploited. As mentioned before, seductiveness and/or sexuality may mask dependency needs as the erotic transference[95] toward the therapist who unconsciously is felt as the omnipotent parental figure who can satisfy all longings.

Countertransference feelings, thoughts, and behavior may produce stress and anxiety in therapists. Countertransference stress varies along a wide spectrum from distancing and unemotional reactions to seductiveness, anger, and even the mourning process in the therapist. The seductiveness and/or acting out of sexuality varies, depending on the length and degree of emotionality in the sessions. At times, the therapist may have sexual feelings toward a patient. Just as the patient sees the therapist as a real object, so does the therapist see the patient. This is perfectly natural — libidinal feelings and curiosity are two normal attributes of the "inner child." However, sexual thoughts and feelings are one thing, *acting out* is *unacceptable* for a professional. Many psychiatrists occasionally have observed severe neurotic or psychotic disorders occurring in a patient after an affair between patient and therapist.[96] Marmor succinctly comments: "As every experienced psychotherapist knows, erotized phantasies of transference-love often develop in female patients, but when the therapist lends reality to these phantasies by his overt behavior, he fosters a serious confusion between reality and phantasy in such patients."[97] [98]

A therapist may be frustrated sexually for any number of reasons:[99] loneliness, marital problems, boredom, etc. At times, the therapists' feelings and thoughts are unconscious-countertransference manifestations. This can be evidenced by feelings of hostility toward the patient, vague feelings that he can not account for, etc. On the other hand, Brockbank makes the interesting comment on countertransference love that: "The therapist has only himself as both doctor and patient. . . . (There) are responsibilities the therapist must deal with: his ethical and professional responsibilities to the patient, responsibilities to wife and family if married, his own libidinal impulses and defenses against them, and his awareness of the complications inherent in any attempt to deal with these problems by discussing them with either the wife or the patient."[100]

In the following clinical example, we see where transference and countertransference phenomena between a patient and her family physician almost resulted in disaster:

Mr. and Mrs. E were referred by their minister for therapy because of marital disharmony. Mrs. E became quite upset at her husband's interest in their neighbor's wife. Although this interest was purely platonic, she resented his doing little errands for her while her husband was out of town on business. His refusal to stop what he considered "being neighborly" had resulted in progressive arguments.

In her individual diagnostic sessions, Mrs. E stated: "For the past six months I had gotten to know our family physician pretty well through our PTA meetings. When things began to get difficult for me, I had thought of talking, to him about Jim (Mr. E). I also knew I was attracted to him several months ago. I accepted my feelings toward him as nice and normal. I didn't plan to do anything about it, but I felt I had to talk to somebody about our problems. I felt the only person I could trust was this doctor and his wife. One night I got so upset that I went to this doctor's house. He wasn't home, but his wife was. I told her about our marital problem. I felt better. Later that evening Edward (the physician) came to our house, and I told him what was going on, and that Jim was accusing me of having a dirty mind. Edward was very helpful. I felt he was helping me. He suggested that I tell Jim how upset I was becoming by his behavior.

"The next night I told Jim. He got very angry but said he would chop off the relationship with the neighbor if that is what I wanted. Our marriage was most important. The next day he was lying on our bed. He seemed woe begone and said, I've lost a friend, and started to cry. I've never seen him cry before. And this, a reaction to losing a neighbor. Something happened inside of me and I called Edward again. He suggested I come in to his office. He had done a lot of counseling. When I arrived I told him I hadn't eaten for a week and perhaps if we could talk over lunch, I could get some food down. We went to a nearby restaurant and I had coffee and a sandwich.

"He said: 'Shall I analyze this?' At this, bells started ringing in my ears. Shall we talk in your house, he asked. As Jim was at work and the children at school, I said, yes, and wondered why. We did go to my house and he started talking about his feelings for me and mine for him. In a sort of clinical way. Then he asked me if I trusted him and I said, Yes. He asked me to sit on his lap. I threw caution to the winds and did. I felt I belonged there. No feelings of guilt. I felt rather turned on. He was very nice. Not demanding. He just held me. He didn't take advantage of me. He told me that he had been attracted to me for some time since our PTA meetings. One light kiss and he left. I thought all about it the next day. Here I was involved. He knew I cared about him and he about me.

"The next day I called his office. He suggested I come for another appointment. I knew his nurse was there and asked him if he would make a house call. He did. I took a long time but I said: I love you. He held my hand for a moment trying to be the doctor. I could see he was struggling with himself. Suddenly he left.

"As he walked out I felt great. I had dumped my problems into his lap. The same lap I had sat on. I felt I could eat. I cleaned the house feeling great. The next morning the phone rang. It was Edward. It was the first time he said: 'I want to talk to you.' I felt it was important and said, 'Yes.' He came out. He told me he had been through a big struggle. He couldn't eat a thing yesterday. That yesterday he felt in control of the situation, but that today, no. He said: 'I feel so strongly about you. I want to express it physically. I feel stripped of all controls. I could go to bed with you right now. Would you? I said, 'no.' But I really meant yes! So we talked. He said he loved me. After a time he thanked me for saying, No! We both had our puritanical backgrounds. We sat there and kissed. I felt very loving and comfortable with him He left.

That evening he called again. Told he how grateful he was that I had said, no. That he loved his wife. That he couldn't see me again. In fact that he was going to stop being a psychiatrist and just be what he was trained to be — a general practitioner."

At this point Mrs. E began to cry bitterly. A near tragedy had been averted.

In conclusion, when the therapist is unable to cope with either the demands and/or hostility of the seductive patient's overtures in a professional manner, referral is indicated. Actually, no one knows what happens in those cases where the therapist does not consider this a problem.[101, 102] When a therapist leaves the professional role and reacts as a peer, the therapist has taken care of her or his problem, while the patient still has the original problems plus complications from the sexual encounter. From a psychodynamic viewpoint, the therapist is a parental surrogate who actually breaks the incest barrier that inevitably leads to damaging consequences for the patient. This issue leads to the next topic to be discussed, namely ethics.

ETHICS AND THE THERAPIST

Ethics refers to a set of principles, a set of rules of conduct, and a theory of principles and values.[103-106] Rollo May writes that: "Values are necessary and unavoidable in psychiatry and psychotherapy. Even if it were possible for a therapist to be value free, it would not be a desirable thing."[107] In the past decade, there has been a great interest in the ethics of all professionals;[108-110] this is partly due to egalitarian social changes demanding patients decide the type of treatment vis-a-vis professional experts.

Psychotherapists are in a unique position, since ethics are basically morals and fundamental to any society. The principal objective of all professionals is to render service to humanity with full respect for the dignity of everyone. Therapists' attitudes and morals[111] play an important factor in the selection of treatment and the importance of proper referral.[112,113]

Therapists today cannot rely on one approach, because, in the management of depression (or other serious psychiatric conditions), each patient's needs must be evaluated in the broadest perspective, which includes the options of pharmacology and, when necessary, hospitalization.[114]

In California, the first part of the Bar examination is devoted to an understanding of the code of ethics, and one cannot be licensed without passing that portion; however, there is no way to make colleagues act morally after licensing is granted.[115-118] Therapists' actions are equally difficult to monitor. Each individual must live with his own conscience. Complicating the picture are several thousand sex therapy centers, consortia of sex therapy programs, even a corporation arranging regional franchises.[119] Many of these "therapists" have questionable motivations and creditionals, especially where the universal problem is intimacy, both physical and psychological, between therapist and patient. Further, as Halleck states: "there is a new climate of concern over the power of psychiatrists (and other therapists) to shape behavior — a question made more critical by the increasing effectiveness of psychiatric treatment, including the use of drugs and the new behavior techniques."[120]

The inner child of every child and adult is born without any concept of right or wrong. Thus, our value system, which is important in our behavior, is the result of both conscious and unconscious forces. Obviously, the parenting figures, significant adults, and peers are an on going source of role molding. In spite of professional training and personal self-exploration, the therapist's value system will influence, overtly or covertly, their conduct toward patients and their treatment process.[121,122]

Ongoing social and political changes influence the totality of the experience in therapy; Brenneis and Laub[123] (current mental health trainees) describe the degree they engaged in the struggle for social change, their trend to attribute psychiatric illness to social ills, and to deal with their doubts about their therapeutic ability by action rather than reflection. This is likewise reflected in beginning therapists inconsistencies in attitudes and a divergence between attitudes and practice[124]

The intimate and dramatic influence each therapist has in regard to his or her patients makes many professionals duty bound to be "actively moral and virtuous in all decisions."[125] All our relationships with our patients are a reciprocal one of mutuality. Thus, instead of a therapeutic contract based on blind trust or finances, we should all be bound by informed consent, which the patient can understand in terms of his own background. If the patient is felt to be incompetent, then judicial channels are indicated. Finally, we should all be concerned about the ethics of *behavior control, intimacy* (especially as it pertains to sexual therapies), and the importance of *confidentiality* in our patients' interests. In the next section I will discuss the latter topic.

CONFIDENTIALITY

A unique characteristic of dyadic and family therapies is the intimate nature of the material of the patients. As a result, both the therapist and patients may worry about confidential material being revealed and its effect upon others and their current future welfare. Some of these "secrets" include suicidal and/or homicidal thoughts, homosexuality, fantasies or practices of "perversions," extramarital activities, and fear of any type of deed, thought and/or information that is felt could hurt others. The current sociopolitical scene contains threats to confidentiality from many sources. Teichner aptly states: "With the PSRO's and National Health Insurance, we must be sure ... that no local or national agency ... could possibly utilize (our) records by hooking up their computers to the computers storing medical records and 'raping' them."[126] The increasing amount of third party payments,[127] increase use of computers, data banks, and automated information systems increases the danger to confidentiality.[128] Dubey[129] proposes that communications and information of psychotherapy be excluded from public policy and that the therapist should not perform evaluative functions during litigation. This should be obtained from independent court-appointed professionals.

Plaut[130] distinguishes three different types of therapist-patient transaction — psychiatric, psychotherapeutic and psychoanalytic — that require different types of confidentiality. However, as Beigler states: "confidentiality is to psychotherapy as sepsis is to surgery."[131] The effectiveness of therapy is especially conditional if the patient is to deal with their most private thoughts, fantasies, feelings, and behavior. Any parameter that undercuts confidentiality impairs effective therapy. The therapist deals with the whole person and thus encompasses the patient's entire outside activities. Every psychotherapist becomes the repository of information that can be of value to third parties, e.g. legal, blackmail, etc. Unfortunately, as Beigler[132] points out, every therapist is confronted with two antithetical interests of society; each being valid. It is in society's interest to restore citizens who are dysfunctional to a contributing status. On the other hand, society also has a realistic interest in having access to the information disclosed in so open a treatment situation.

As Beigler[133] sees it, the most common problem has to do with health-insurance coverage. Many patients are fearful to use their benefits lest their immediate employment and/or future careers be harmed. Some civil service employees, executives, military personnel, teachers and even politicians have paid for my services privately even though they were covered by their insurance. One of my patients, a brilliant scientist, accepted a position from a multinational corporation that would cause a geographical change for him. I suggested he continue his analysis in the East, but the medical director of the new corporation told him to forget about that: "In our experience, those that finish their analysis, usually leave our employment." My patient chose to return to Chicago after a year's time and finished his analysis. He decided to pay for his therapy privately and avoided any further potential job discrimination.

I have used the following contract successfully for ths past decade. The focus includes protecting the patient(s) confidentiality and is in the *best interests of the couple:*

Date_____

Subject: Stipulation for Evaluation and/or
reconciliation of marital/relationship problem

IT IS HEREBY STIPULATED by and between the respective parties that they desire to attempt an evaluation and/or reconciliation of their marital/relationship problem. Further all information given by individuals involved should be kept *strictly confidential* by the therapist. Should the marriage or relationship problem involve *future* legal proceedings, the therapist *shall not* be involved unless *both* patients give their written permission for the therapist (psychiatrist) to do so.

_____

_____

This leads to the next topic facing every therapist — the dilemmas of his profession.

THE DILEMMAS OF BEING A THERAPIST

Consumer patient advocacy,[134,135] malpractice suits,[136] attacks for sexist practices,[137] and recent restrictive legal decisions, e.g. the Tarasoff decision in California,[138,139] are having profound effects on how all professionals will treat patients. The Tarasoff ruling stipulated that *therapists* must warn authorities specified by law as well as potential victims of possible dangerous actions of their patients. Another problem facing the therapist is setting patient fees — is the therapist influenced by the economic and social status of his prospective patient?

Other dilemmas confronting therapists include potential suicidal patients (previously discussed in detail in Chapter VII), and inpatient care decisions. For example, the problems faced with patients *involuntarily* hospitalized refusing accepted and standardized medications. Competent therapists thus need to be both clinically perceptive and legally astute (or have access to legal advice).[140-142] What each therapist defines as abnormal, healthy, or unhealthy reflects conscious or unconscious judgements based upon one's value systems or even rebellion against those values. Are we becoming purveyors of social control by the requirement of informed educated consent?[143,144] My analytic classmate, Szasz, has made 100 percent reversal and is so concerned about the infringement on patients' rights that he has promulgated the "myth of mental illness."

Another dilemma confronting therapists are the problems of staying abreast of the current literature and even recertification.[145] Lifelong learning is an accepted necessity for all professionals to aid personal and professional growth. Obviously, continuous growth is necessary, but are mandatory hours of continuing education the solution? Current criticism centers on commercialization, poor quality, bureaucratization, waste of time and money, and faulty requirements.[146]

Another problem, especially for pastoral therapists, are couples coming for help who are involved in an assortment of nonmarital sexual relationships.[147] With the pastoral therapists, I have maintained the same posture for the past decade. Granted they are confronted by a moral dilemma, but the individuals coming for help do not need the added burden of "sin." I stress, if at all possible, that they approach all patients with a *nonjudgemental* philosophy. If this is not possible, either because of personal values or, more frequently, the possibility of conflict with their superiors, then the safest course is to refer the individual(s) to another therapist. As Kaslow and Gingrich cogently state: "The identity of a counselor may make it easier for people to express religious values. It is not strange for clients to request that the clergy-counselor pray for them."[148]

Now with more women coming into the field, therapists' pregnancy presents a time-limited, but definite, dilemma with profound implications for the therapeutic relationships. Nadelson and her colleagues[149] have written an excellent article presenting the ramifications for all participants involved in this unique clinical setting. Obviously all participants know that pregnancy must lead to an interruption, or even a termination of therapy which may produce a wide variety of responses by each patient, e.g. anxiety and rejection anger to mention but a few. First, the therapist must deal with her changing identity complicated by changing roles of wife, mother, and therapist and the divided loyalties. Of primacy is the therapist's own physical and emotional vulnerability, which interferes with the therapeutic effectiveness. One cannot be pregnant without sex. Thus, an intimate aspect of the therapist — her sexuality — precipitates in patients' dormant dependency and other infantile needs, internal sexual conflicts and intensified maternal transferences, etc.

Another dilemma is that at one time or another all therapists have contact with a repulsive patient.[150] A simple axiom to keep in mind is to ask yourself, what is there about this patient that evokes this reaction in me? Will I be able to help the patient understand the underlying conscious and unconscious dynamics of his behavior. The simple solution is to refer the patient. Overtly or covertly, repulsive patients have one common trait, they are extremely demanding. Many of these patients are not aware of their needs incessant infantile demands, discontent, complaining and fault finding.

A frequent casualty of the psychotherapist is the destructiveness in their own intimate relationships, resulting in separation or even divorce. This is seen often in supervision where the supervisee dates his interpersonal problems to the beginning stages of therapeutic training. Although, at first encouraged by their partner, soon hostility ensues, since any serious involvement with the program necessitates less available time for relating. The rejection that follows produces hostility with increasing complaints. I have seen at least twelve couples where divorce was in the offing because of this situation. In one couple who were previously divorced because of obvious infidelity, marital therapy resulted in remarriage. Two years later I was consulted again when the wife was accepted by a prestigious university for professional training. Her husband did not want her to accept because he felt that their children and he would suffer because of school demands of time. This is a growing problem and can be noted in current articles in the professional literature.[151]

Another dilemma that all therapists have to face is the troubling fact at times they are ineffective.[152] Hadley and Strupp state that: "Practicing therapists, of course, have known for a long time that some patients fail to improve or actually seem to 'get worse' even in prolonged psychotherapy. Other patients experience a recrudescence of their original difficulties following the termination of psychotherapy and find it necessary to return to therapy at a later time. The term 'negative therapeutic reaction' has been used to describe patients who apparently fail to benefit from psychotherapy or get worse. . . . "[153]

The therapeutic impass has many adverse reactions on every therapist. The older one gets, the more one can accept the fact that our discipline is mainly an art and not a science. One cannot win them all, therefore, referral should be seen as an acceptable coping maneuver.

THE PITFALLS OF PSYCHOTHERAPY

Psychotherapists, because of their profession, are constantly going through personal and professional growth.[154] On the other hand, therapists should be aware of the potential negative impact of his professional services.[155, 156] Some negative manifestations include irritability, anxiety, suicidal ideation, fantasized sexual involvement with patient(s) or cotherapist (sometimes actual involvement), neglect of family by overcommitment to work, and interruptions at home due to frequent phone calls from patients at inappropriate times — can you tell a suicidal patient or their significant others that you will return the call after your dinner? An occupational hazard is the feeling of superiority that can result from the constant exercise of authority.[157, 158]

Another important pitfall is the therapists' anxiety. The early manifestations of increasing anxiety is irritability, restlessness, emotional outbursts, or even psychosomatic problems. Therefore, every therapist should continually be on the alert for any persistent mood changes in his attitude toward his patients and, also toward the significant others. Also, he should be aware of mood changes in his personal and social relationships. Very often it is the therapists partner who is the first to express concern or anger because of a mood change. Since every individual has his own threshold of tolerating stress, one must conserve one's energy. Whitaker recommends getting a "... professional cuddle group, a consultant for the second visit, a cotherapist, and a curbstone consult team. Anything to keep from carrying the stress home. Even the old poppa and mama store wasn't good enough to solve a full-time work load of stress."[159]

Just as patients are seen as workaholics, the same goes for the professional. Ottenberg[160] has coined the term *physician's disease* to describe success and work addiction. He observes that many physicians qualify as executives, and their secretaries have taken over the control of their time. Some therapists get on the treadmill-type of living with the early rationalization that it is *temporary* until a certain goal is reached; however, it often becomes a permanent way of life.

The most common condition among therapists, as well as the general population, is depression — *masked* or *overt*. A common symptom of this condition is a psychosomatic problem. Another symptom is withdrawal or detachment from loved ones. This frequently causes the healthy partner to react with feelings of rejection, and anger.

The following are some of the factors contributing to the stress of a therapist: responsibility for the care of his patients, increased awareness of one's intrapsychic conflicts, and a personal problem, to mention but a few. Suicide is not uncommon among psychiatrists and therapists.[161]

Another pitfall that the therapist should avoid is the Bernean game of "Courtroom"[162] or a variation that Haley[163] calls "the ever present triangle" in a dysfunctional couple, i.e. of forming coalitions with individual partners in the "court" of dyadic disharmony. Whereas Berne was well versed in psychoanalysis, Haley was not, so he avoided unconscious dynamics in dyadic discord. In a previous study of marital games that I did with 300 couples, "Courtroom" was seventh in frequency.

Another pitfall to be avoided is any social contacts with former patients. I can only report my own forty years of experience, which reveals that any individual or couple previously treated who has revealed personal and intimate fantasies, feelings, and behaviors will harbor some vague unconscious feelings of resentment. Especially when the patient(s) have been treated with intensive dynamic therapy. Although, theoretically, the relationship ends at the termination of therapy, the therapist is always an invisible member of the family — often-times in the bedroom. At times, it is impossible to avoid meeting in a social situation; therefore, I make it a part of the therapeutic contract to tell patients that if we should accidentally meet socially, I shall just nod my head and smile, but not acknowledge them directly. I do not want to complicate their living space. It is amazing how often patients try to develop a social realtionship during or after termination of therapy. In spite of the temptation with those patients whom I have developed a genuine desire to relate to socially, I acknowledge that once I have been a parental surrogate, I will always be one to that individual. One never knows when a request for help as a social friend could alter the ability to help objectively. Easson has a different stance than I have. He states that "The change of roles, the wider focus, and the difficult transitional stage in this growth to friendship give rise to many anxieties, but also allow much deeper understanding. Such a friendship relationship can enrich both the patient and the therapist and gives unique insights into the meaning and the effect of psychotherapy for both participants."[164]

A rare pitfall for psychiatrists and, potentially, other therapists is the deClerambault syndrome first reported in the forties in France. The patient, usually a female, has a delusional belief that a man, older and prominent is much in love with her. Raskin and Sullivan[165] reported two cases, in 1974, in which the delusion was the patient's psychiatrist, and Hollender and Callahan,[166] in 1975, reported four cases. These cases are usually diagnosed as paranoid state or paranoid schizophrenia. Although rare, this possibility should be thought of since these fantasies are not repressed unconsciously, but may be dramatized in real life with damaging repercussions to the innocent male, who may be the therapist, and who is cast in the role of the lover. Erotomania goes beyond the normal developmental schoolgirl's fantasies, which involves working through infatuation and finally to mutual heterosexual intimacy. "In erotomania, the focus is not on what the woman feels for her would-be-lover, but on the feelings she imputes to him; not on how she loves him but on how he loves her."[167] Hawkins has succinctly described the psychodynamics of erotic fantasies: "When the non-psychiatric physician (therapist) encounters someone who has clearly retreated into fantasy to avoid reality, he would do well to secure psychiatric consultation for him (her) . . . (the therapist) should be alert to the possibility of self-destruction or assault on others."[168]

Another pitfall among therapists is doing cotherapy ("therapeutic marriage") for colleagues in group therapy, dyadic and family therapy, and, lastly in sex therapy. These therapists come for treatment because of problems in their own marriage or in their "therapeutic marriage"[169] with nonrelated cotherapists. The following vignette is illustrative:

> Doctor and Mrs. A came for therapy when Mrs. A was told by her "best" friend that she saw her husband coming out of a motel with a woman. For the last several months Doctor A had been coming home later than usual from his evening group therapy sessions. His usual excuse was that this was a very disturbed group and several of the patients needed individual sessions following the group session. When confronted by his wife, after he had denied everything, he finally admitted being involved with his cotherapist, who also was married. He told his wife he wanted to save the marriage so they were started on the simple type of combined therapy — three weekly sessions for Doctor A and once a week in conjoint sessions. Part of the therapeutic contract stated that he would stop seeing his cotherapist after the group sessions. At the same time the cotherapist started individual therapy with her previous therapist.
>
> After three months of therapy Doctor A began seeing his cotherapist, which provoked his wife. Six months later they had a compatible divorce.
>
> Shortly thereafter, the cotherapist divorced her husband and married Doctor A.
>
> A year later Doctor and his *new* wife came for marital therapy because of a new sexual affair Doctor A was involved in.

Cotherapy first came to my attention by the article written by Reding and Ennis in 1964.[170] Cotherapy has been used for some time in couples' group therapy,[171] group psychotherapy, family therapy,[172] dyadic relationship therapy,[173, 174] also in the therapy of an individual to minimize transference reactions, plus avoidance of severe dependency and sexual reactions.[175] The Gomezs' (both psychiatrists) used this type of therapy with couples and couples' groups in Chicago in the past decade.[176, 177]

With the advent of sexual dysfunctional therapy, which was sparked by Masters' and Johnson's model of cotherapy.[178] many articles have appeared in the literature about the cotherapists' problems conducting this type of treatment. The clincial setting in sexual therapy is a highly charged one, for all the participants are dealing with erotic fantasies and/or sexual intercourse. At the American Academy of Psychoanalysis, in 1965, I was impressed by a characteristic I was later to observe in a number of cotherapists. Usually, the women radiate warmth, femininity, and spontaneity, while the men tend to be serious, scientific, and emotionally controlled. The Goldens'[179] state that differences in status, experience, and training combine with aspects of the personal relationship between cotherapists to make some aspects of cotherapy a substantial problem. Whether the cotherapists are married, otherwise involved in personal relationship, a physician and his nurse, or two independent therapists, the sexual content of their work inevitably raises issues that need to be resolved. These issues include erotic fantasies and power struggles between the therapist that can affect the outcome of treatment (and their relationship, as well as relationships with significant others, e.g. spouse, lover).

To avoid erotic involvement, which can be a two-way street, the cotherapeutic relationship should focus upon the patients' *needs* and problems. Thus, prior to starting cotherapy, there should be an open discussion as to whether the cotherapist is another professional or marital partner. When the cotherapist is the spouse of therapist, a sexual relationship already exists, in fact, in their intimate relationship, both have experienced the give and take of the negative and positive facets of sexuality. Furthermore, it is easier for self-disclosure, when indicated, to aid the dysfunctional couple as well as in modeling procedures. Dunn and Dickes[180] discuss other aspects of the erotic issues in sexual cotherapy: the nonrational but healthy sexual attraction between the therapists (a normal attribute of the curiosity of the inner child) that can influence the way the team functions; erotic fantasies of the others(s), the effects of the highly charged sexual material and voyeurism.

In conclusion, the recent article by the Russells[181] not only gives an overview of the advantages, disadvantages, pitfalls, and abuses of cotherapy over the past two decades, but also report their own cotherapy experiences.[182-184] The best antidote to the difficulties described is competent supervision.

SUPERVISION

It is only fitting that the final topic in this book should pertain to supervision. As a teacher and supervisor for many years, I have observed the great need for adequate supervision and also the need for ongoing supervision.[185-187] Supervision can be done either in a group or individual sessions. I have used group supervision in three clinical settings. It consists of a diaglogue between therapists and myself. The therapists learn to deal with the complex interrelationship between their therapeutic efforts and my supervision as related to their feelings and attitudes toward their patients (countertransference). Frequently, I use one of the supervisee's dreams, or a patient's to illustrate the current focus of their therapeutic setting.

The supervisory format provides an informational input[188] and a "learning alliance."[189] This helps neutralize the isolation that members of the mental health professions, by the nature of their techniques, are subjected to. Supervision is multidimensional, enabling the supervisee to develop a unique professional identity,[190] personal and professional growth, recognize and alter mistakes, and discovery of universalities.[191]

The observation of psychotherapy by a one-way secren[192] or video and audiotapes[193-195] is a valuable tool in supervision. Alger and Hogan[196] were early pioneers in the use of both audio and videotapes. Diagnosis is often descriptive, outcomes are measured in terms of subjective symptom relief, and most important is the difficulty in establishing cause-and-effect relationship because of the many psychosocial and other environmental unpredictables. Over the past decade, there has been an increase in books and articles on the supervisory process.[197-204] Of special value, is the recent book by Kaslow and her colleagues.[205]

Countertransference plays an important role in supervision.[206] The literature is equivocal as to whether supervision is teaching or therapy. My personal analytic supervisors, in my training years in Chicago, were teachers *and* therapists. Over the years as a supervisor, I developed a flexible position.

Since countertransference involves the unconscious, the supervisee is unaware of its presence, therefore it is an important area in supervision. At no time is the supervisee to feel he is being attacked or criticized. At all times the supervisor should be supportive, kind and empathic. The important focus is how the supervisee's feelings interfere with any therapeutic efforts. The learning effect is that the supervisee becomes aware of how the reactions and feelings toward the patient enhance conscious therapeutic interventions. Should the supervisee develop individual personal problems, I suggest that he temporarily put supervision aside and solve the personal problem first.

Appropriate supervision fosters cognitive development in the supervisee. To develop the learning process without delay, it is important that the supervisor keep in mind the level of anxiety of the individual in relation to the patient and/or supervisor.[207] The lower the level of anxiety, the higher the cognitive capacity. Neutralization of anxiety is hastened by enhancing the rapport beween the individuals involved. With tact, the supervisor lets the supervisee know that this is a typical reaction, that he, too, experienced a variety of painful experiences when he was a supervisee: lack of expertize, therapeutic inadequacy, and embarrassment among other feelings. On occasion, one may encounter a supervisee who reacts to supervision, more so if it is a requirement (for eligibility to a society) with competitiveness, hostility, or conscious and unconscious hostility to authoritative fig-ures.

In every relationship there is always ambivalence. De La Torre and Appelbaum[208] have pointed out the use of cliches as a defense against anxiety. The supervisory relationship should provide an opportunity for the supervisee to explore unconscious identification and dependence without inhibiting experimentation and creativity. With the changing role of women in our society, Alonso and Rutan suggest that the female supervisor may help the male supervisee "with the intrinsic limitations of empathy and with other problems, such as 'countertransference deafness' that may block his work with female patients."[209] Shershow and Savodnick[120] have identified six possible behavior patterns of supervisees that may respond to appropriate supervision: competition and identification, sexual feelings, and/or thoughts, aggression, depression and despair, dependency, and fusion with patients. My experience with supervisors and supervisees is that frequently they both avoid countertransference related to sexuality.

Tooley has found that home observations by supervisees are helpful to the supervisor as a "basis for reformulation of treatment goals of technical approaches."[211] On occasion, I, too, have found that a home visit is of value in understanding the transactions not only of the couple but of the child(ren) if present. There is no substitute for observations conducted on home territory when the individual(s) are "at home."

Another area of the supervisory process deals with the technical management of the financial aspects of the patient-supervisee relationship in regard to fees.[212-215] Usually, this occurs only with a beginner and is related to his doubts about one's value as a therapist, as well as other conscious and unconscious dynamics.

Financial issues should be fully understood in the overall context of the dynamic emotional conflicts of the supervisee. Unfortunately, because of changing sociocultural values, many patients are dishonest, manipulative in their fee considerations, and do not follow through on their verbal agreements as to payment. When the patient's first

first commitment is broken, it is important that this area be dealt with promptly. Flexibility on the part of the therapist is important: above all, a display of anger is counterproductive. Occasionally, when a patient refuses to pay his bill, it may not be because of finances but it may involve either a rebellion to the authoritative figure and/or a power struggle. Many complex emotional issues in both the patient and the supervisee are at issue, e.g. guilt, sociopathic trends.

From the start of my therapeutic efforts I have been influenced by my analyst, George Mohr, who maintained the inital financial contract. I have found this posture most rewarding. A patient usually reacts in a hostile manner, unconsciously, when the fee is raised. There is enough ambivalence in therapy without the need to complicate it further.

An important area of supervision is how to help the supervisee know when to terminate therapy with his patients.[216] Freud's famous dictum in his classic paper, *Analysis terminable or interminable,*[217] advised therapists to "let sleeping dogs alone." The decision to terminate therapy is influenced by many factors, e.g. problem-oriented goals, financial, personal. In intensive analytic psychotherapy I prefer the so-called resolution dream. Marmor[218] suggests another viewpoint in setting a termination date. The following two dreams illustrate the so-called resolution dream, the first one is my dream, in 1948, during my analytic training:

> I was back at the Elgin State Hospital on the Medical Staff. The chief psychiatric consultant (he looked like my analyst) was making rounds with me. (In 1936, we actually had consultants who came to the hospital from Chicago) I turned to the consultant and said to him that I think that I can handle future problems myself.
> On relating this dream to Doctor Mohr, I was lying on the couch, I suddenly sat up and we looked at each other and Doctor Mohr smiled. We both knew the meaning of this dream.

Another type of termination dream is by a patient who made excellent changes in most areas of his life.

> I am driving down the expressway from Chicago to Milwaukee (his place of birth) and there is a big truck in front of me driving slowly. I could easily pass him in the left lane but I don't.
> In his associations he said there was a feeling of sadness. Questioning him for the reason that he did not pass the truck since he had an important business meeting in Milwaukee. He did not know the meaning of this dream. My interpretation was that he was ready to terminate therapy but was ambivalent about stopping — the

usual reaction. I suggested that we decrease the sessions to once weekly, and from now on he is to sit up in a face-to-face manner, and in two months we would terminate therapy.

I have always believed in weaning my patients — affording them an opportunity to work through the unconscious rejection anger. All my patients are reassured that I will always be available should they need future therapy.

The termination of psychotherapy is a process that has a beginning, a middle, and an end-phase. Since all patients are unique in their existence due to variations in all three systems of the GST, no one patient ends therapy the same way. In my own analysis, these were telescoped rather acutely, while the example of the patient with the truck dream had a gradual terminal phase. My role was to get him to pass the "truck" so that he would tap all his potentialities with the added understanding from his total life experiences. Goldberg,[219] influenced by the recent work of Kohut on narcissistic personality disorders, has written an excellent paper on termination. He considers the readiness for termination from the perspective of narcissistic features. He describes the changes in the patient's self during the terminal phase of therapy as including the reexperiencing of narcissistic injury, a different response to interpretation, and a substantial alteration in the reaction to termination. In my experience, termination of therapy parallels the separation-individuation phases of Mahler, described earlier in this book.

The termination phase of therapy is a two-way street for the humanistic therapist. There is some degree of mourning process since there has been considerable emotional involvement in the loss of meaningful "objects;" however, there are also feelings of pride and the narcissistic one of accomplishment since the patient (a therapist's "child") is also a real person. The main difference is that there is no "empty nest syndrome" because there are other patients to be helped. In its absolute sense, psychotherapy is an ongoing *learning* experience for *all* participants — patients, therapists, and others involved.

CONCLUSION

Our field is in a crisis situation and all therapists must commit themselves to *ongoing learning* (personal and professional) and competent supervision when indicated. Nichols, Jr. succinctly states our aspirations: " . . . the actions of professional organizations in providing for continuous education, responsible practice, and public information and protection."[220]

Having recently participated in a paraprofessional two-year program, I feel that mental health professionals should assume a special responsibility to train laymen to help members of society adapt to the current and rapid sociocultural changes.[221-223]

Each professional has the ability to foster improvement in the primary areas of observation, formulation of a diagnosis, prevention, and treatment planning. Perhaps any new innovation in therapy should be labeled pilot protocol, which indicates the need to try out process in order to exhibit its difficulties and correct its weaknesses. Although difficult, therapists (like scientists) should attempt to separate the factual statements they make from any of their personal values.[224] Finally, the primary objective of every therapist should be to serve his patients competently with full respect for their dignity. The credo of the scholarly Max Black is one to which every therapist should subscribe:

> Without the skills of 'common sense' a scientist would be no better than an autistic child or a zombie . . . I mean such convictions as the following, which the ordinary person take for granted before exposure to philosophical skepticism: I exist, but so do vast number of other persons, each of whom can say the same. Besides myself and other persons, the world is full of things and events that are, no matter what I or anybody else would prefer be the case . . . are helpless to change. *Some things I know* (italics added) about this universe, but *I am ignorant of much more* (italics added), and sometimes *what I take to be knowledge* (italics added) *turns out to be only an illusion.*[555]

There is no substitute for an intelligent, conscientious, and well-educated psychotherapist.

In the final analysis, all therapists must develop a unique style that is flexible to meet the needs of each patient, pair-coupling, and family. Above all, we teachers should teach our students to be receptive to innovations, and not become disciples.

REFERENCES

1. Kaslow, Florence: Editorial, *J Marital & Family Therapy, 5:* 3, 1979.
2. Havens, Leston L.: *Approaches to the Mind.* Boston, Mass, Little, 1973.
3. Marmor, Judd: Change in psychoanalytic treatment. *J Am Acad Psychoanal, 7:* 345-57, 1979.
4. Brady, John P. and Brodie, H. Keith (Eds.): Controversy in Psychiatry. Philadelphia: W. B. Saunders Co, 1978.

5. Koran, Lorrin M.: Controversy in medicine and psychiatry. *Am J Psychiat, 132:* 1064-66, 1975.
6. Rogers, Carl R.: Remarks on the future of client-centered therapy, In Wexler, D. A. and Rice, L. N. (Eds.): *Innovations in Client-Centered Therapy.* New York, John Wiley & Sons, 1974, pp. 7-13.
7. West, Louis J: The future of psychiatric education. *Am J Psychiat, 130:* 521-28, 1973.
8. Pardes, Herbert, Papernik, Daniel S., and Winston, Arnold: Field differentiation in inpatient psychotherapy. *Arch Gen Psychiat, 31:* 311-15, 1974.
9. Holt, R. R.: *New Horizons for Psychotherapy.* New York, Int Press, 1971.
10. Brody, Eugene B.: Opinion. *Am Acad Psychoanal* (The Academy Forum), *22:* 2, 1978.
11. Chodoff, Paul: The question of lay analysis revisited. *J Am Acad Psychoanal, 5:* 431-45, 1977.
12. Crowley, Ralph M.: "What psychoanalysis means to me." *Amer Acad Psychoanalysis, 21:* 1, 1977.
13. Strupp, Hans H.: Psychoanalysis, "focal psychotherapy," and the nature of the therapeutic influence. *Arch Gen Psychiat, 32:* 127-35, 1975.
14. Baum, O. Eugene: Why a psychoanalytic core in psychiatric education? *Am J Psychiat, 132:* 1281-85, 1975.
15. Nichols, William C., Jr. (Ed.): *Marriage & Family Therapy — A Reader from NCFR Journals.* Minneapolis: Nat Council Family Relations, 1974.
16. Ludwig, Arnold M.: Commentary — The psychiatrist as physician. *JAMA, 234:* 603-4, 1975.
17. Gross, Martin L.: *The Psychological Society: A Critical Analysis of Psychiatry, Psychotherapy, Psychoanalysis and the Psychological Revolution.* New York, Random House, 1978.
18. Taylor, Alexander: Exploding the myths of marriage counseling. *Marriage & Divorce, 1:* 14-19, 1974.
19. Martin, Peter A.: *A Marital Therapy Manual.* New York, Brunner-Mazel, 1976, p. 1.
20. Wolberg, Lewis R.: *The Technique of Psychotherapy,* 3rd ed., Parts 1 & 2. New York, Grune (Harcourt Brace Jovanovich), 1977.
21. Martin, *A Marital Therapy Manual.*
22. Vriend, John and Dyer, Wayne W.: Creativity labeling behavior in individual and group counseling. *J Marr & Family Counseling, 2:* 31-36, 1976.
23. Luthman, Shirley G. and Kirschenbaum, Martin: *The Dynamic Family.* Palo Alto, Science and Behavior Books, 1974.
24. Leslie, Robert C. and Mudd, Emily H.: *Professional Growth for Clergymen Through Supervised Training in Marriage Counseling and Family Problems.* Nashville, Tenn, Abington, 1970.
25. Nichols, William C., Jr.: Education of marriage and family therapists — some trends and implications. *J Marital & Family Therapy, 5:* 19-28,

1979.

26. Frank, Arlene, Eisenthal, Sherman, and Lazare, Aaron: Are there social class differences in patients' treatment conceptions? — Myths and facts. *Arch Gen Psychiat, 35:* 61-9, 1978.

27. Floyd, Keith: Opinion on caring. (The Academy Forum). *Am Acad Psychoanal, 21:* 2, 1977.

28. Moore, Gordon L.: The adult psychiatrist in the medical environment. *Am J Psychiat, 135:* 413-18, 1978.

29. Lipp, Martin R.: *Respectful Treatment: The Human Side of Medical Care.* Hagerstown, Md., Harper & Row Med Dept, 1977.

30. Marmor, Change in   psychoanalytic treatment.

31. Kohut, Heinz: *The Restoration of the Self.* New York, Int Univ Press, 1977.

32. Lief, Harold I.: Editorial — sensitivity to feelings. *J Am Acad Psychoanal, 5:* 289-90, 1977.

33. Tuma, A. Hussain, May, Philip R. A. , Yale, Coralee, and Forsythe, Alan B.: Therapist characteristics and the outcome of treatment in schizophrenia. *Arch Gen Psychiat, 35:* 81-85, 1978.

34. Guldner, Claude A.: Family therapy for the trainee in family therapy. *J Marr & Family Counseling, 4:* 127-32, 1978.

35. Levinson, Peritz, McMurray Leith, Podell, Paul, and Weiner, Howard: Causes for the premature interruption of psychotherapy by private patients. *Am J Psychiat, 135:* 826-30, 1978.

36. Frank, Jerome, Hoehn-Saric, Rudolph, Imber, Stanley D., Liberman, Bernard L. and Stone, Anthony R.: *Effective Ingredients of Successful Psychotherapy.* New York, Brunner-Mazel, 1978.

37. Chodoff, Paul: Psychotherapy of the hysterical personality. *J Am Acad Psychoanal, 6:* 497-510, 1978.

38. Lewis, Jerry M.: *To Be a Therapist.* New York, Brunner-Mazel, 1977.

39. Beavers, W. Robert: *Psychotherapy and Growth: A Family Systems Perspective.* New York, Brunner-Mazel, 1977.

40. Allred, G. Hugh and Kersey, Fred L.: The AIAC, a design for systematically analyzing marriage and family counseling — a progress report. *J Marr & Family Counseling, 3:* 17-25, 1977.

41. Dimond, E. Grey: Courage beyond science. *JAMA, 236:* 2085-88, 1976.

42. Olson, D. H. and Dahl, N. S. (Eds.): *Inventory of Marriage and Family Literature.* Vol. 4. 1975-1976. Minnesota: Unversity of Minn. Social Science, 1977.

43. Lazare, Aaron, Eisenthal, Sherman, and Wasserman, Linda: The customer approach to patienthood. *Arch Gen Psychiat, 32:* 553-58, 1975.

44. Grinker, Sr., Roy R.: The futrue educational needs of psychiatrists. *Am J Psychiat, 132:* 259-262, 1975.

45. Kline, Frank, Adrian, Alfred, and Spevak, Michael: Patients evaluate therapists. *Arch Gen Psychiat, 31:* 113-16, 1974.

46. Anthony, E. James: The state of the art and science in child psychiatry. *Arch Gen Psychiat, 29:* 299-305, 1973.

47. Frank, Jerome: Psychotherapy — the restoration of morale. *Am J Psychiat, 131:* 271-74, 1974.

48. Pattison, E. Mansell: Residency training issues in community psychiatry. *Am J Psychiat, 128:* 1097-1102, 1972.

49. Framo, James L.: Personal reflections of a family therapist. *J Marr & Family Counseling, 1:* 15-28, 1975.

50. Kerckhoff, Richard et al.: The family life educator of the future. *Family Coordinator, 20:* 315-24, 1971.

51. Hawkins, James L.: Counselor involvement in marriage and family counseling. *J Marr & Family Counseling, 2:*37-47, 1976.

52. Alexander, Franz: *The Scope of Psychoanalysis: 1921-1961.* New York, Basic Books, 1961.

53. Weiner, Myron F.: *Therapist Disclosure: The Use of Self in Psychotherapy.* Woburn, Mass, Butterworths, Inc, 1978.

54. Chapman, A. H.: The Treatment Techniques of Harry Stack Sullivan. New York, Brunner-Mazel, 1978.

55. Marmor, Judd: Current trends in psychotherapy. Presented at the Second International Workshop on Short Term Dynamic Psychotherapy at Montreal, March 1976.

56. Steele, Thomas E.: Teaching behavioral sciences to medical students. *Arch Gen Psychiat, 35:* 27-34, 1978.

57. Knobloch, Ferdinand and Knobloch, Jirina: In search of a new paradigm of psychoanalysis. *J Am Acad Psychoanal, 7:* 499-524, 1979.

58. AAMFT committee: Continuing education — the AAMFT plan. *Am Assn Marr & Family Counselors (Therapists)* 8: 1, 1977.

59. Small, S. Mouchly: Recertification for psychiatrists — the time to act is now. *Am J Psychiat, 132:* 291-92, 1975.

60. McCarley, Tracey: The psychotherapist's search for self-renewal. *Am J Psychiat, 132:* 221-24, 1975.

61. Bruch, Hilde: *Learning Psychotherapy.* Cambridge, Mass: Harvard Univ Press, 1974.

62. Knapp, Jacquelyn J.: Some non-monogamous marriage styles and related attitudes and practices of marriage counselors. *Family Coordinators, 24:* 505-14, 1975.

63. Lief, Harold I.: Sexual attitudes and behavior of medical students — implications for medical practice. In Nash, E. M., Jessner, L., and Abse, D. W. (Eds.): *Marriage Counseling in Medical Practice.* Chapel Hill, University of North Carolina Press, 1964.

64. Sheppe, William M.: The family physician and human sexuality. *Med Aspects Hum Sexuality, 6:* 11-29, 1972.

65. Renshaw, Domeena C.: Physician sexuality training program — a unique elective. *Chicago Medicine, 77:* 868-70, 1974.

66. Waggoner, Raymond W. et al.: Training dual - sex teams for rapid treatment of sexual dysfunction—a pilot program. *Psychiatric Annals, 3:* 61-76, 1973.

67. Luckey, Eleanore B.: What I have learned about family life. *Family Coordinator, 23:* 310-311, 1974.

68. Alexander, Franz: Address before the annual meeting of the Academy of Psychoanalysis, May 7, 1961, Chicago, Illinois.
69. Hunt, Winslow: The transference-countertransference system. *J Am Acad Psychoanal, 6:* 433-61, 1978.
70. Winnicott, D. W.: Hate in the countertransference, originally published in 1947 and reprinted in *Voices, 1:* 102, 1965.
71. Maltsberger, John T. and Buie, Dan H.: Countertransference hate in the treatment of suicidal patients. *Arch Gen Psychiat, 30:* 625-33, 1974.
72. Grinker Jr., Roy R.: The poor rich — the children of the superrich. *Am J Psychiat, 135:* 913-16, 1978.
73. Spenseley, James and Blacker, K. H.: Countertransference and other feelings in the psychotherapist. *Dis Nerv System, 38:* 595-98, 1977.
74. Hunt, Winslow and Issacharoff, Amnon: Heinrich Racker and countertransference theory. *J Am Acad Psychoanal, 5:* 95-105, 1977.
75. Wolstein, Benjamin: Countertransference — the psychoanalyst's shared experience and inquiry with his patient. *J Am Acad Psychoanal, 3:* 77-89, 1975.
76. Spiegel, John P. Ethnic Factors, Presented at the Sixth International Forum of Psychoanalysis, West Berlin, Abstracted in *Psychiatric News, 13:* 42-43, 1978.
77. Spiegel, John P.: Cultural aspects of transference and countertransference revisited. *J Am Acad Psychoanal, 4:* 447-467, 1976.
78. Papajohn, J. and Spiegel, J. P.: *Transactions in Families.* San Francisco, CA., Jossey-Bass, 1975.
79. Bell, John E.: Contrasting approaches in marital counseling. *Family Process, 6:* 23, 1967.
80. Berne, Eric: *Games People Play.* New York, Grove Press, 1964.
81. Newman, Richard A.: MD-patient sex (in Questions and Answers). *Medical Aspects Human Sexuality, 13:* 104, 1979.
82. Kardener, Sheldon H.: Sex and physician-patient relaionship. *Am J Psychiat, 131:* 1134, 1974.
83. Barnhouse, Ruth T.: Sex between patient and therapist. *J Am Acad Psychoanal, 6:* 533-46, 1978.
84. Davidson, Virginia: Psychiatry's problem with no name — therapist-patient sex. *Psychiatric News, 9 (July 2):* 8, 1976.
85. Ishida, Yasuo: The seductive patient. *CMD, 40:* 321-326, 1973.
86. Lief, Harold I.: Commentary: sexual survey #7: current thinking on seductive patients. *Med Aspects Human Sexuality, 12:* 46-47, 1978.
87. Lief, Harold I.: What's new in sexual research? Sexual activity with patients. *Med Aspects Human Sexuality, 12:* 55-57, 1978.
88. Holroyd, J. C. and Brodsky, A. M.: Physical contact with patients. *Amer Psychol, 32:* 843, 1977.
89. Nadelson, Carol, Grunebaum, Henry, and Macht, Lee B.: Therapist-patient sex: survey findings speak. *Psychiatric News, 11 (Oct 1):* 28, 1976.
90. Perry, Judith A.: Physicians' erotic and nonerotic physical involvement.

Am J Psychiat, 133: 838-40, 1976.

91. Dahlberg, Charles C.: Sexual contact between patient and therapist. *Med Aspects Human Sexuality, 5:* 34-53, 1971.

92. Kardener, Sheldon H., Fuller, Marielle, and Mensh, Ivan N.: Characteristics of "erotic" practitioners. *Am J Psychiat, 133:* 1324-25, 1976.

93. Shochet, Bernard R., Levin, Leon, Lowen, Marc, and Lisansky, Ephraim T.: Roundtable: Dealing with the seductive patient. *Med Aspects Human Sexuality, 10:* 90-104, 1976.

94. Lief, What's new in sexual research.

95. Braude, Marjorie: Erotic transference. *Southern Calif Psychiat News, 27:* 5, 1979.

96. Kirstein, Larry: Sexual involvement with patients. *J Clin Psychiat, 39:* 366-68, 1978.

97. Marmor, Judd: Sexual acting-out in psychotherapy. *Am J Psychoanal, 22:* 3-8, 1972.

98. Voth, Harold M.: Love affair between doctor and patient. *Am J Psychotherapy, 26:* 394-400, 1972.

99. Lief, What's new in sexual research.

100. Brockbank, Reed: Observations on countertransference love. *Psychiatric News, 11 (Sept 3):* 20, 1976.

101. Lymberis, Maria: Ethics update — on sexual relations between doctor and patient. News: *Southern California Psychiatric Society, 25:* 6 & 9, 1978.

102. Freudenberger, Herbert J.: The male therapist as a returning patient. *Psychiatric News, 23:* 40-41, 1978.

103. Miller, Derek: The ethics of practice in adolescent psychiatry. *Am J Psychiat, 134:* 420-7, 1977.

104. Glasser, Lois N. and Glasser, Paul H.: Hedonism and the family — conflict in values? *J Marr & Family Counseling, 3:* 11-18, 1977.

105. Silverman, Hirsch L.: Value issues in marriage counseling — psychological and philosophical implications. *Family Coordinator, 22:* 103-10, 1973.

106. Silverman, Hirsch L. (Ed.): *Marital Therapy: Psychological, Sociological and Moral Factors.* Springfield, Il Thomas, 1972.

107. May, Rollo: Values, myths and symbols, *Am J Psychiat, 132:* 703-06, 1975.

108. Moore, Robert A.: Ethics in the practice of psychiatry — origins, functions, models, and enforcement. *Am J Psychiat, 135:* 157-163, 1978.

109. Friedmann, Claude T. H, Yamamoto, Joe and Wolkon, George: Videotape recroding of dynamic psychotherapy — supervisory tool or hindrance? *Am J Psychiat, 135:* 1388-91, 1978.

110. Redlich, Fritz and Mollica, R. F.: Ethical issues in psychiatry. *Am J Psychiat, 133:* 125-36, 1976.

111. Halleck, Seymour L.: Legal and ethical aspects of behavior control. *Am J Psychiat, 131:* 381-85, 1974.

112. Kaslow, Florence W. and Gingrich, Gerald: The clergyman and the psychologist as marriage counselors: differences in philosophy, referral patterns and treatment approaches to non-marital relationships. *J Marr & Family Counseling 3:* 13-21, 1977.

113. Hull, John: Psychiatric referrals in general practice. *Arch Gen Psychiat, 26:* 406-08, 1979.

114. Miller, Milton H.: *If the Patient is You (or Someone You Love). Psychiatry Inside-Out.* New York, Charles Scribner's Sons, 1977.

115. Elkin, Meyer: Licensing marriage and family counselors — a model act. *J Marr & Family Counselors, 1:* 237-49, 1975.

116. Rutledge, Aaron L.: State regulation of marriage counseling,. *Family Coordinator, 22:* 81-90, 1973.

117. McDaniel Jr, Clyde O.: Toward a professional definition of marriage counseling. *Family Coordinator, 20:* 30-37, 1971.

118. Towery, O. B. and Sharfstein, Steven S.: Fraud and abuse in psychiatric practice. *Am J Psychiat, 135:* 92-94, 1978.

119. Lowry, Thea S. and Lowry, Thomas P.: Ethical considedrations in sex therapy. *J Marr & Family Counseling, 1:* 229-36, 1975.

120. Halleck: Legal and ethical aspeacts of behavior control.

121. Middleton, John T.: The role of values in marriage counseling. *Family Coordinator, 19:* 335-42, 1970.

122. Abroms, Gene M.: The place of values in psychotherapy. *J Marr & Family Counseling, 4:* 3-17, 1978.

123. Brenneis, C. B. and Laub, Dori: Current strains for mental health trainees. *Am J Psychiat, 130:* 41-45, 1973.

124. Messner, Edward : Inspiration of psychotherapy by patients. *Am J Psychiat, 133:* 1462-63, 1976.

125. Redlich, Fritz and Mollica, Richard F.: Overview: ethical issues in contemporary psychiatry. *Am J Psychiat, 133:* 125-36, 1976.

126. Teichner, Victor J.: Psychoanalytic, ethical and legal aspects of confidentiality. *J Am Acad Psychoanal, 3:* 293-300, 1975.

127. Chodoff, Paul: Psychiatry and the fiscal third party. *Am J Psychiat, 135:* 1141-47, 1978.

128. Beigler, Jerome S.: The APA model law on confidentiality (Editorial). *Am J Psychiat, 136:* 71-73, 1979.

129. Dubey, Joseph: Confidentiality as a requirement of the therapist — technical necessities for absolute privilege in psychotherapy. *Am J Psychiat, 131:* 1093-96, 1974.

130. Plaut, Eric A.: A perspective on confidentiality. *Am J Psychiat, 131:* 1021-24, 1974.

131. Beigler, Jermone S.: Psychiatry and confidentiality — how great is a patient's right to confidentiality, and can it be protected? *Chicago Medicine, 81:* 461-63, 1978.

132. Beigler, Psychiatry and confidentiality.

133. Beigler, Psychiatry and confidentiality.

134. Strupp, Hans H., Hadley, Suzanne W. and Gomes-Schwartz, Beverly: *Psychotherapy for Better or Worse: The Problem of Negative Effects.*

New York, Jason Aronson, 1977.

135. Stone, Alan: The myth of advocacy. *Psychiatric News, 20:* 3, 8, 1979 (Oct. 19).

136. Slawson, Paul Fredric: Psychiatric malpractice — the California experience. *Am J Psychiat, 136:* 650-54, 1979.

137. Zeldow, Peter B.: Sex differences in psychiatric evaluation and treatment — an empirical review. *Arch Gen Psychiat, 35:* 89-93, 1978.

138. Gurevitz, Howard: Tarasoff: protective privilege versus public peril. *Am J Psychiat, 134:* 289-92, 1977.

139. Roth, Loren and Meisel, Alan: Confidentiality, and the duty to warn. *Am J Psychiat, 134:* 508-511, 1977.

140. Malmquist, Carl P.: Can the committed patient refuse chemotherapy.

141. Weitzel, William D.: Changing law and clinical dilemmas. *Am J Psychiat, 134:* 293-95, 1977.

142. Dawidoff, Donald J.: Some suggestions to psychiatrists for avoiding legal jeopardy. *Arch Gen Psychiat, 29:* 699-701, 1973.

143. Noll, John O.: The psychotherapist and informed consent. *Am J Psychiat, 133:* 1451-53, 1979.

144. Weigel, Charles L.: Medico-legal aspects of mental illness. *Chicago Medicine, 80:* 1101-05, 1977.

145. Aring, Charles D.: Recertification. *JAMA, 233:* 1063-64, 1975.

146. Talbott, John A.: Opposition to "coercive continuing medical education and mandatory recertification," *Am J Psychiat, 136:* 887-926, 1979.

147. Mazur, R.: *The New Intimacy: Open-ended Marriage and Alternative Lifestyles.* Boston, Beacon, 1974.

148. Kaslow and Gingrich, The clergyman and the psychologist as marriage counselors.

149. Nadelson, Grunebaum, and Macht, Therapist-patient sex.

150. Lieberman, Florence and Gottesfeld, Mary L.: The repulsive client. *Clinical Social Work J, 1:* 22-31, 1973.

151. Muchowski, Patrice M. and Valle, Stephen K.: Effects of assertive training on trainees and their spouses. *J Marr & Family Counseling, 3:* 57-62, 1977.

152. Keith, David V. and Whitaker, Carl A.: Struggling with the impotence impasse — absurdity and acting-in. *J Marr & Family Counseling, 4:* 169-77, 1978.

153. Hadley, Suzanne W. and Strupp, Hans H.: Contemporary views of negative effects in psychotherapy — an integrated account. *Arch Gen Psychiat, 33:* 1291-1302, 1976.

154. Norris, Jr., Charles R.: Residents' forum. *Psychiatric News, 13:* 37, 1978.

155. English, O. Spurgeon: The emotional stress of psychotherapeutic practice. *J Am Acad Psychoanal, 4:* 191-201, 1976.

156. Spenseley, James and Pepitone-Tockwell, Fran: Role strain of physicians. *Psychiatric Opinion, 12:* 6-9, 1975.

157. Marmor, Judd: The feeling of superiority — an occupational hazard in the practice of psychotherapy. *Am J Psythiat, 110:* 370-76, 1953.

158. Waring, E. M.: Psychiatric illness in physicians — a review. *Comprehensive Psychiat, 15:* 519-30 1974.
159. Whitaker, Carl A.: Burned out or burned up? Newsletter. *Am Assn Marr & Family Therapy, 10:* 1, 4, 1979.
160. Ottenberg, Perry: The "physicans's disease" — success and work addiction. *Psychiatric Opinion, 12:* 6-11, 1975.
161. Sargent, Douglas A., Jensen, Viggo W., Petty, Thomas A., and Raskin, Herbert: Preventing physician suicide — the role of family, colleagues, and organized medicine. *JAMA, 237:* 143-45, 1977.
162. Berne, Eric: *Games People Play.* New York, Grove Press, 1966.
163. Haley, Jay: *Problem Solving Therapy.* San Francisco, CA, Jossey-Brass, 1976.
164. Easson, William M.: Patient and therapist after termination of psychotherapy. *Am J Psychotherapy, 25:* 635-42, 1971.
165. Raskin, D. E. and Sullivan, K. E.: Erotomania. *Am J Psychiat, 131:* 1033-35, 1974.
166. Hollender Marc H. and Callahan III, Alfred S.: Erotomania or de Clérambault syndrome. *Arch Gen Psychiat, 32:* 1574-76, 1975.
167. Hollender and Callahan, Erotomania or de Clérambault syndrome.
168. Hawkins, David R.: Distrubing erotic fantasies. *Med Aspects Human sexuality, 8:* 177-178, 1974.
169. Lazarus, Lawrence W.: Family therapy by a husband-wife team. *J Marr & Family Counseling 2:* 225-33, 1976.
170. Reding Georges R. and Ennis, B.: Treatment of the couple by a couple. *Brit J Med Psychol, 37:* 325, 1964.
171. Low, P. and Low, M.: Treatment of married couples in a group run by a husband and wife. *Internat J Group Psychotherapy, 25:* 54-66, 1975.
172. Lazarus, Family therapy by a husband-wife team.
173. Gurman, Alan S.: The effectiveness of marital therapy — a review of the outcome research. *Family Process 12:* 162-70, 1973.
174. Rice, David G., Fey, W.F. and Kepecs, Joseph G.: Therapist experience and "style" as factors in co-therapy. *Family Process, 11:* 227-41, 1972.
175. Reckless, John B., Asnis, Stephen, Faunterloy, Alexandra and Allen, David: Cotherapist team manages sexual provocativeness. *Roche Report: Frontiers of Psychiatry, 3:* 5-8, 1973.
176. Gomez, E. and Gomez, M.: Co-therapy by a husband-wife psychiatrist team. Paper presented at the annual meeting of the Am Psychiatriac Assn, Dallas, TX, 1972.
177. Rice, David G., Razin, Andrew M. and Gurman, Alan S.: Spouses as co-therapists — variables and implications for patient-therapist matching. *J Marr & Family Counseling, 2:* 55-62, 1976.
178. Masters, William E. and Johnson, Virginia E.: *Human Sexual Inadequency.* Boston, Little, 1970.
179. Golden, Joshua S. and Golden, Margaret A.: You know her and what's her name — the woman's role in sex therapy. *J Sex & Marital Therapy, 2:* 6-16, 1976.
180. Dunn, Marian E. and Dickes, Robert: Erotic issues in cotherapy. *J Sex &*

Marital Therapy, 3: 205-11, 1977.

181. Russel, Axel and Russell, Lila: the uses and abuses of co-therapy. *J Marital & Family Therapy, 5:* 39-46, 1979.

182. Coleman, Sandra B.: A developmental stage hypothesis for non-marital dyadic relationships. *J Marr & Family Counseling, 3:* 71-76, 1977.

183. Luthman and Kirschenbaum, *The Dyanamic Family.*

184. Rice, David G. and Rice, Joy K.: Nonsexist "marital" therapy. *J Marr & Family Counseling, 32:* 3-10, 1977.

185. Rutledge, Aaron: The future of marriage counseling. *Merrill-Palmer Quarterly, 1:* 141-47, 1955.

186. Nichols, Jr., William C.: The field of marriage counseling — a brief overview. *Family Coordinator, 22:* 3-13, 1973.

187. Ard, Jr., Ben N.: Providing clinical supervision for the marriage counselors — a model for supervisor and supervisee. *Family Coordinator, 22:* 91-97, 1973.

188. Cohen, Raqueel E.: The functions of experimental participatory experiences in the learning-teaching process. *Am J Psychiat, 135:* 103-6, 1978.

189. Miller, Arthur A., Burstein, Alvin G. and Leider, Robert J.: Teaching and evaluation of diagnostic skills. *Arch Gen Psychiat, 24:* 255-59, 1971.

190. Drucker, John J., Klass, David B. and Strizich, Michael L.: Supervision and the professional development of the psychiatric resident. *Am J Psychiat, 135:* 1517-19, 1978.

191. Havens, Leston L.: The existential use of self. *Am J Psychiat, 131:* 1-10, 1974.

192. Stein, Stefan, Karasu, Toksoz B., Charles, Edward S. and Buckley, Peter J.: Supervision of the initial inteview — a study of two methods. *Arch Gen Psychiat, 32:* 265-68, 1975.

193. Mayadas, Nazeen S. and Duehn, Wayne D.: Stimulus-modeling (SM) videotape for marital counseling — method and application. *J Marr & Family Counseling, 3:* 35-42, 1977.

194. Birchler, Gary R.: Live supervision and instant feedback in marriage and family therapy. *J Marr & Family Counseling, 1:* 331-42, 1975.

195. Chodoff, Paul: Supervision of psychotherapy with videotape — pro and cons. *Am J Psychiat, 128:* 819-23, 1972.

196. Alger, Ian and Hogan, Peter: Enduring effects of videotape play-back experience on family and marital relationships. *Am J Orthopsychiat, 39:* 86, 1969.

197. Liddle, Howard A. and Halpin, Richard J.: Family therapy training and supervision literature — a comparative review. *J Marr & Family Counseling, 4:* 77-98, 1978.

198. Kurpius, Dewayne J., Baker, Ronald D., Thomas, Irene D.: Supervision of Applied Training — A Comparative Review. Westport Conn: Greenwood Press, 1977.

199. Rioch, Margaret J., Coulter, Winifred R., and Weinberger, David M.: *Dialogues for Therapists: Dynamics of Learning and Supervision.* San Francisco, CA, Jossey-Bass, 1976.

200. Havens, Leston L.: The choice of psychotherapeutic method. *J Am Acad Psychoanal, 6:* 463-78, 1978.
201. Ekstein, R. and Wallerstein, R. S.: *The Teaching and Learning of Psychotherapy.* New York, Internat Univ Press, 1972.
202. Miller, Paul R. and Tupin, Joe P.: Multimedia teaching of introductory psychiatry. *Am J Psychiat, 128:* 1219-23, 1972.
203. Schuster, Daniel B., Thaler, Otto, and Sandt, John J.: *Clinical Supervision of the Psychiatric Resident.* New York, Brunner-Mazel, 1972.
204. Mead, Eugene and Crane, D. Russell: An empirical approach to supervision and training of relationship therapists. *J Marr & Family Counseling, 4:* 67-75, 1978.
205. Kaslow, Florence W. and associates. *Supervision, Consultation, and Staff Training in the Helping Professions.* San Francisco, CA, Jossey-Bass, 1977.
206. Goin, Marcia K. and Kline, Frank: Countertransference: a neglected subject in supervision. *Am J Psychiat, 133:* 41-44, 1976.
207. Mueller, William J. and Kell, Bill L.: *Coping with Conflict: Supervising Counselors and Psychotherapists.* New York, Appleton-Century-Crofts, 1972.
208. de al Torre, Jorge and Appelbaum, Ann: Use and misuse of clichés in clinical supervision. *Arch Gen Psychiat, 31:* 302-06, 1974.
209. Alonso, Anne and Rutan, J. Scott: Cross-sex supervision for cross-sex therapy. *Am J Psychiat,* 928-31, 1978.
210. Shershow, John C. and Savodnik, Irwin: Regression in the service of residency education. *Arch Gen Psychiat, 33:* 1266-70, 1976.
211. Tolley, Kay: The diagnostic home visit: an aid in training and case consultation. *J Marr & Family Counseling, 1:* 317-22, 1975.
212. Pasternack, Stefan A.: The psychotherapy fee — an issue in residency training. *Dis Nerv System, 38:* 913-16, 1977.
213. Langs, Robert: *The Bipersonal Field.* New York, Jason Aronson, 1976.
214. Kilgore, James E.: Establishing and maintaining a private practice. *J Marr & Family Counseling, 1:* 145-48, 1975.
215. Buckley, Peter, Karasu, Tokaz B., and Charles, Edward: Common mistakes in psychotherapy. *Am J Psychiat, 136:* 1578-80, 1979.
216. Weddington, William W. and Cavenar, Jesse O.: Termination initated by the therapist — a countertransference storm. *Am J Psychiat, 136:* 1302-05, 1979.
217. Freud, Sigmund: Analysis terminable and interminable. *Int J Psychoanal, 46:* 373-405, 1937.
218. Marmor, Judd: Change in psychoanalytic treatment. *J Am Acad Psychoanal, 7:* 345-57, 1979.
219. Goldberg, Arnold: Narcissism and the readiness for psychotherapy termination. *Arch Gen Psychiat, 32:* 695-99, 1975.
220. Nichols, Education of marriage and family therapists.
221. Rogawski, Alexander S.: The new paraprofessional's role in mental

health. *Psychiatric Annals, 4:* 62-71, 1974.

222. Curtis, John H. and Miller, Michael E.: An argument for the use of para-professional counselors in premarital and marital counseling. *Family Coordinator, 25:* 47-50, 1976.

223. Heijn, C., Myerson P. G., and Schmitt, P.: An approach to the supervision of paraprofessionals working with the mentally ill. *Brit J Med Psychol, 48:* 281-87, 1975.

224. Romano, John: Romano calls for scholarship in psychiatry. *Psychiatric News, 14:* 18-19, 1979.

225. Black, Max: The objectivity of science. *Bulletin of the Atomic Scientists, 33:* 55, 1977.

APPENDIX

Phone 213 342 1300

Bernard L. Greene, M.D.
38676 Via Taffia
Murrieta, CA 92362

BIOGRAPHICAL RELATIONSHIP QUESTIONNAIRE

(First used at Loma Linda University, Division of Behavioral Sciences
Department of Marital & Family Therapy, Loma Linda, CA)

Date_____

Name_____Partner's _____

Address_____
                    street   city   zip code

Phone: Residence_____Phone: Work _____

1. Age_____Of Partner_____

2. Dyad   status: First   relationship   or   marriage?   yes   no

   How long_____

3. Is your religion the same as that of your partner? yes   no

   Of family? Yes   no

4. Occupation_____Of partner_____

5. Education_____Of partner _____

6. Children? Yes   No   Give names and ages_____

7. Who referred you: ?

   Name_____Phone _____

   Address _____
             street   city   zip code

481

a. Did you or your partner feel pressure from the other to come?_____

8. Why are you NOW seeking help?_____

_____

_____

_____

_____

_____

_____

_____

_____

9. What are your complaints and when did trouble first begin in your relationship? First circle and then describe:

a. Lack of communication

b. Constant arguments and/or physical abuse

c. Unfulfilled emotional needs

d. Sexual dissatisfaction   (describe more fully under item #22)

e. Financial disagreements

f. Conflicts about children

g. Infidelity

h. Problems with parents or in-laws

i. Alcoholism

j. Domineering partner

k. Suspicious partner

l. Other_____

_____
_____
_____
_____
_____
_____
_____
_____
_____
_____
_____

10. If you have ever received any help with respect to yourself, your marriage or relationship circle the following: psychiatrist, physician, psychologist, counselor, clergy, social worker, agency, or other.

Name of person and dates: _____

_____

Address:_____

                street   city   zip code

_____

                street   city   zip code

Give your opinion of the results: _____

_____

_____

_____

_____

_____

_____

_____

11. Have you or your partner ever attempted SUICIDE? yes   no
If so give dates and details. _____

_____

_____

_____

_____

_____

    a. Has anyone in yours or your partner's family or close relatives
ever attemped suicide? yes   no   If so give details. _____

_____

_____

_____

_____

12. The relationship phases:

    a. How did you meet your partner?_____

     _____

    b. Describe your courtship (relationship), giving duration and whether smooth, stormy, etc.: _____

     _____

     _____

     _____

     _____

     _____

     _____

     _____

     _____

    c. If married did you have a honeymoon? Yes No
     Describe your reactions, partner's behavior, etc.: _____

     _____

     _____

     _____

_____

_____

_____

_____

_____

_____

_____

_____

13. Any previous relationships or marriages?   Yes   No   If yes, did the relationships or marriages end by divorce, death or desertion? Give details:

_____

_____

_____

_____

_____

_____

_____

_____

_____

_____

_____

_____

_____

_____

_____

_____

_____

_____

_____

_____

_____

_____

14. Original family:

Retired? Yes No

a. Father: first name only_____Occupation _____

age at marriage and currently_____age at death _____

Cause _____

Retired? Yes   No

b. Mother: first name only_____Occupation _____

age at marriage and currently____age at death _____

Cause _____

c. Brothers and sisters: First name only   age   sex

_____

_____

_____

_____

_____

_____

_____

d. Describe your parents, what they were like as people, and how
they got along in their marriage. How did you get along with
them? Describe your family's circumstances as you were
growing up. Include anything else that would give a clearer
picture of your family experiences and relationships:

_____

_____

_____

_____

_____

_____

_____

_____

_____

_____

_____

_____

_____

15. Relationship with your children: Describe your children and your relationship with them. What are the problems and conflicts that arise and how do you deal with them? How do you feel about being a parent? Step-parent? Parental surrogate?

_____

_____

_____

_____

_____

_____

_____

_____

_____

_____

_____

_____

_____

---

16. Describe the kind of person you are: feelings of inferiority, sensibility, sensitivity, anxiety, etc.:

_____

_____

_____

_____

_____

_____

_____

17. School adjustment: How well did you do as far as grades were concerned? What extra-curricular activities did you participate in? What problems did you have in school?

_____

_____

_____

_____

_____

_____

_____

_____

_____

_____

_____

18. Medical History:

   a. Family physician: Name_____

      _____

           street   city   zip code   phone

   b. What is your present state of health?_____

      _____

   c. When did you have your last medical check-up? _____

   d. What serious medical illness have you, your partner or children have/had and when?

   e. Surgery: Yes No Partner: Yes No Children: Yes No

   f. Current medications: _____

   g. Habits:

      1. What drugs or "street drugs, e.g., coke, angel dust etc." are you presently taking: _____

      2. How much do you smoke?_____

      3. How much do you drink and how often? _____

      _____

      4. Do you think you or your partner drink too much? ____

19. Describe your participation in social and civic activities. What are your personal hobbies and interest? How much satisfaction do you get from these activities? What problems do you have in this area?

_____

_____

_____

_____

_____

_____

_____

_____

_____

20. Describe your job or occupation. Describe your feelings about your work. How do you get along with your co-workers and employer? Have you changed jobs frequently and if so give details:

_____

_____

_____

_____

_____

_____

_____

_____

21. Religion: What is your religious preference? What religious and other church sponsored activities do you participate in? How often is your participation? How have the teachings and values of your church and your faith influenced your marriage?

_____

_____

_____

_____

_____

_____

_____

_____

_____

_____

_____

22. Sexual history (With permission of Professor Domeena C. Renshaw, M. D. Director, Loyola University Hospital Sex Dysfunction Clinic, Stritch School of Medicine, Maywood, Illinois) (minor modifications).

   a. Miscarriages? Abortions(s)? Details: _____

   _____

   _____

   _____

   _____

   b. Extramarital or relationship activity?_____Does partner know?_____

Details:_____

_____

_____

_____

_____

_____

Does partner know?_____Details: _____

_____

_____

_____

_____

Partner swapping or swinging?_____ Details:_____

_____

_____

_____

_____

_____

c. Sexual problems/satisfaction: What do you consider your
   partner's most significant sexual problem? _____

_____

How does this affect your sexual function? _____

What do you consider your most significant sexual problem?

How does this affect your partner's sexual function?_____

How does he/she view your sexual problem? _____

How have you as a couple tried to handle the sexual problems so far? _____

What is your concept of optimum sexual function for a woman?_____

What is your concept of optimum function for a man?____

Own sexual satisfaction? Yes No What are your feelings after sex?

Comments:_____

Frequency of affectionate expression per week? _____

Frequency of intercourse per week? _____

Difficulties: Infrequent climax_____No Climax _____

    Female
        Infrequent climax_____No Climax _____

        Repulsion:_____Why? _____

        Pain:_____Where? _____

    Male

        Erection/ejaculation difficulty: Yes No_____

        Morning erections._____Frequency per week__

        With masturbation._____With specific partner__

        Describe in detail *first* episode of erection/
        ejaculation problem: e.g. . . . . . alcohol,
        anxiety and/or anger, following medication:

_____

_____

_____

_____

_____

_____

_____

_____

_____

_____

_____

_____

d. *Masturbation:*

Age first masturbated:_____Frequency pre-marriage:___
Frequency per week now:_____Does partner know? _____

Feelings:_____Masturbatory fantasies: _____
Ejaculation: premature:_____Delayed: _____
Kissing   yes/no_____Who   initiates?_____Preference_____
Aversion_____Conflict
Foreplay: yes/no_____Who   initiates?_____Preference_____
Aversion_____Conflict
Afterplay: Yes No
e. *Sexual Variations:*

Fellatio: yes/no____Who initiates?____Preference _____

Aversion_____Conflict

Cunnilingus: yes/no_____Who initiates?_____Preference_____
Aversion_____Conflict
Anal intercourse: yes/no____Who initiates?____Preference____
Aversion_____Conflict
Other variations: _____
f. *Additional sexual history/experience:*

Reading sexual material: yes/no_____Who initiates _____
Preference_____Aversion_____Conflict_____
Venereal disease: yes_____no_____Type: _____
Method of contraception:
    B. C. pill_____Duration_____Feelings_____
    brand_____Symptoms_____
    intrauterine device_____vaginal cap_____
    foam_____jelly_____rhythm_____condom _____
    Conflict in this area: _____

Rape (real):_____
Rape (fantasies): _____
Specific fears about sex: _____

Specific guilts about sex: _____

Specific hang-ups about sex:_____
Unconsummated sexual relationship: _____
Incest: (details - touch/full coitus. How much alcohol involved?)

Specific sexual enjoyment: (specific clothing, cross-dressing etc. ....)

Homosexual fears: _____

Homosexual episode/s: _____

Can you have sexual discussions with partner?_____

Any special comments (in detail): _____

23. Any additional comments you wish to make about your marriage:

AUTHOR INDEX

A

Abbott, Marcia A., 145
Abernethy, Virginia, 116, 210
Ables, M. F., 432
Abrams, Alan A., 147
Abroms, Gene M., 134, 275, 289, 472
Abse, D. Wilford, 144, 469
Ackerman, Brian L., 64
Ackerman, Nathan W., 12, 19, 364, 374, 375, 382, 384, 391, 399, 421, 422, 423, 424
Adams, Gerald R., 160
Adams, Paul L., 112
Adelson, Edward T., 207, 210
Adland, M. L., 424
Adler, Alfred, 221
Adler, David, 259
Adler, Herbert M., 110
Adrian, Alfred, 468
Agle, David, 426
Agras, W. Stewart, 314
Airing, Charles D., 288, 473
Akiskal, Hagop S., 132, 404, 427, 431
Albee, Edward, 234
Alberti, Robert E., 65
Albrecht, Stan L., 262
Aldous, Joan, 289
Alexander, Franz, xv, 5, 12, 68, 71, 89, 284, 291, 292, 303, 314, 338, 344, 387, 438, 469, 470, 475
Alger, Ian, 30, 65, 209, 214, 279, 290, 364, 424, 462, 469, 475
Allen, David, 474
Allen, J. P., 432
Allen, Martin G., 431
Allred, Hugh, 236, 468
Alonso, Anne, 463, 476
Altman, Harold, 148
Altman, Leon L., 292
Altschuler, Kenneth Z., 218
Altus, William D., 94, 110
Amdur, M. J., 433

Anderson, C., 423
Anderson, Carol, 426
Anderson, Elaine A., 248, 263
Anderson, Robert E., 111
Anderson, Scott M., 85
Anderson, W. H., 433
Andreason, Nancy, A., 234, 430, 431
Angst, J., 427
Annon, J. S., 425
Anshin, Roman, 288
Anspach, Donald F., 89, 260
Anthony, E. James, 34, 110, 125, 133, 265, 429, 468
Applebaum, Ann, 463, 476
Applebaum, A. S., 262
Araoz, Daniel L., 166
Ard Jr., Ben N., 298, 302, 475
Argras, Stewart, 134
Arieti, Silvano, 18, 30, 112, 133, 365, 595
Aring, Charles D., 33, 288
Arlow, Jacob A., 110
Arnold, L. Eugene, 217, 263
Arnott, Catherine C., 162
Asdin, E., 432
Asnis, Stephen, 474
Astrachan, Boris M., 259
Atkin, Samuel, 65
Auerbach, Alfred, 210, 212
Auerbach, Lynn S., 116, 118
Auerswald, Edgar H., 36
Aurelius, Marcus, 272
Avery, A. W., 116
Avery, David, 76, 431
Axelrad, Sidney, 34
Ayd Jr., F. J., 434

B

Babigian, H. M., 55
Bacal, Howard A., 11
Bachrack, Leona L., 235
Bagarorozzi, Dennis, 289

503

SUBJECT INDEX